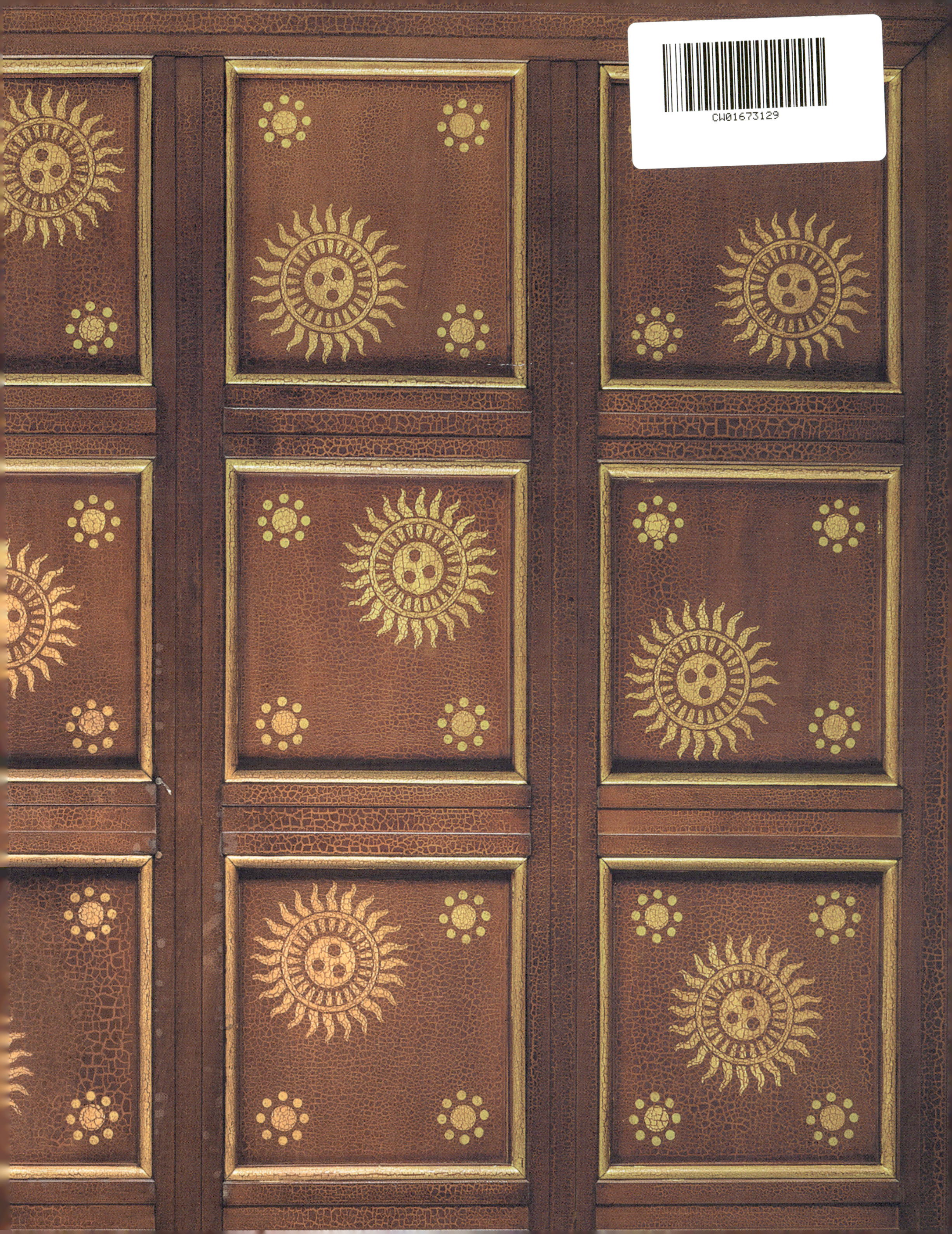

DANIEL COTTIER

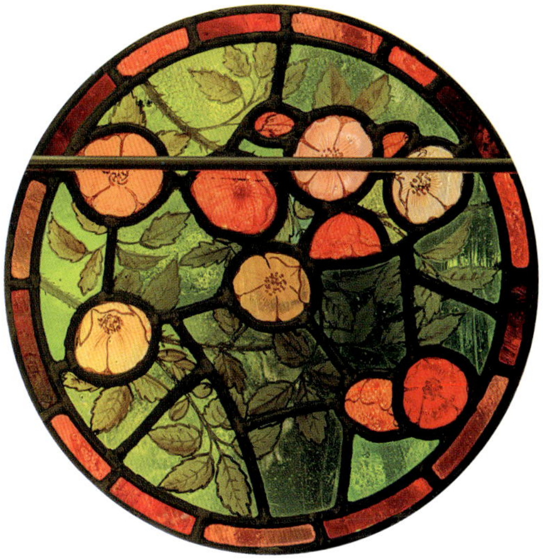

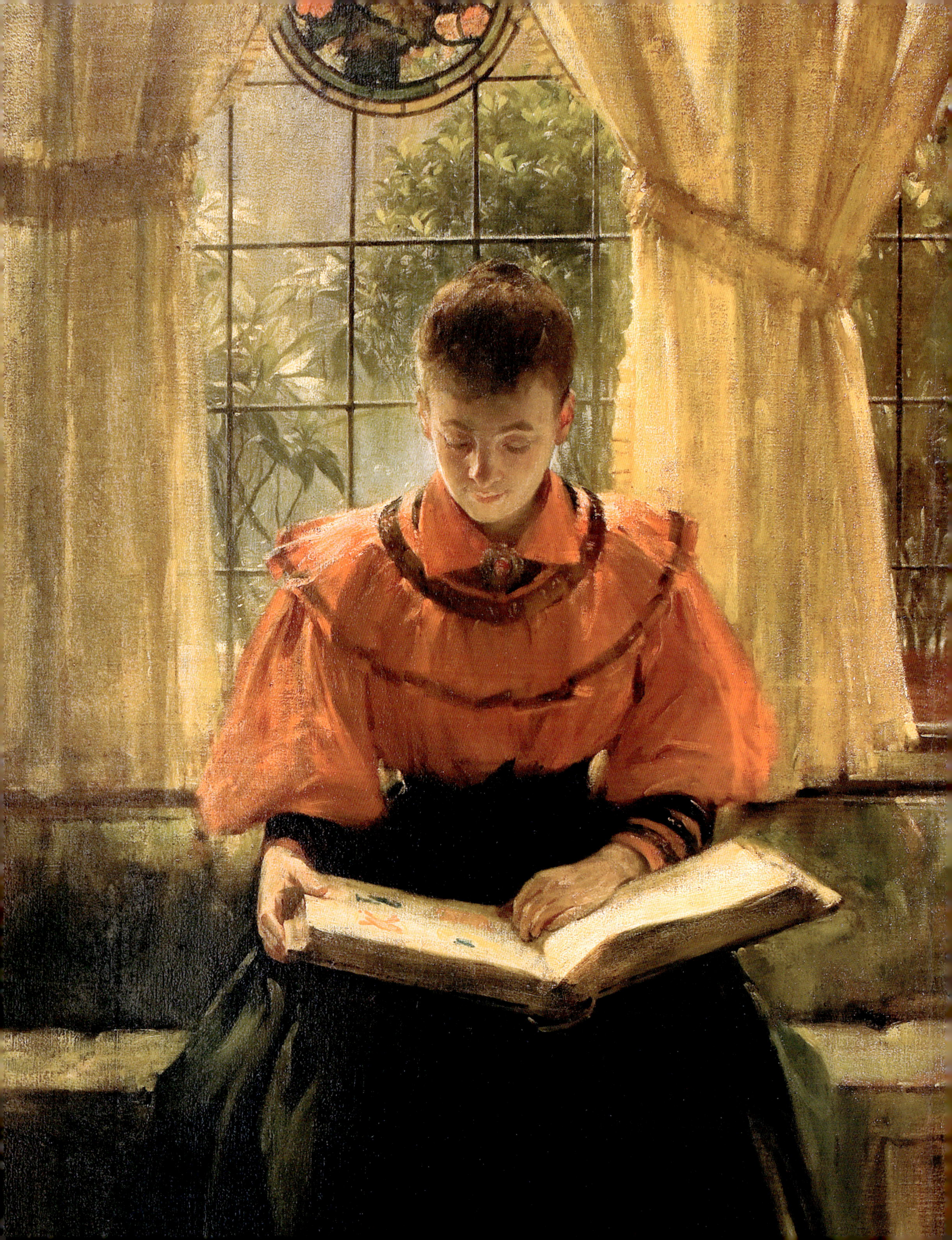

Petra ten-Doesschate Chu and Max Donnelly
with Andrew Montana and Suzanne Veldink

DANIEL COTTIER

DESIGNER ✺ DECORATOR ✺ DEALER

Paul Mellon Centre for Studies in British Art
Distributed by Yale University Press
New Haven and London

First published in 2021 by the Paul Mellon Centre for Studies in British Art
16 Bedford Square, London, WC1B 3JA
paul-mellon-centre.ac.uk

ISBN 978-1-913107-18-5 HB
Library of Congress Control Number: 2020950227

British Library Cataloguing-in-Publication Data
A catalogue record for this book is available from the British Library

Designed by Dalrymple
Origination by Evergreen Colour Management Ltd
Printed in China through World Print Ltd

MIX
Paper from responsible sources
FSC® C014688
www.fsc.org

Endpapers: Detail of the hallway ceiling, Cairndhu House, Helensburgh, Argyll and Bute, decorated by Cottier & Co., *c.*1873 (see fig. 43)

Image on p. i: Detail from the staircase window in Links House (now Links Hotel), Montrose, Angus, by Cottier & Co., London, *c.*1870–3 (see fig. 194)

Frontispiece: William Ewart Lockhart, *Miss Theodora Lockhart*, *c.*1895. Oil on canvas, 127.1 × 85.2 cm. Annan Museum, Dumfries and Galloway, given by Miss Theodora A. M. Lockhart

CONTENTS

ACKNOWLEDGEMENTS

The idea for this book originated in 2015 in the Morris Room of the Victoria and Albert Museum, London, where Petra Chu and Max Donnelly met to discuss their common interest in Daniel Cottier. Both had been working on Cottier for some time: in 1998 Donnelly wrote his masters thesis on Cottier & Co. for Sotheby's Institute, London, and in 2011 Chu was awarded a scholarship by the Getty Research Institute, Los Angeles, to embark on writing a book on Cottier. There she had come to the realisation (as had Donnelly earlier) that to attempt singlehandedly a monograph on the complex artistic personality of Cottier and his global decorating empire would be a huge enterprise requiring not only worldwide travel but also expertise in decorative and fine art as well as the art market. A Cottier book clearly called for a team approach.

Our team grew to four: Andrew Montana, based in Australia, had researched and published on Cottier there and was familiar with the work of Cottier's business partner John Lamb Lyon and the partnership of Lyon, Cottier & Co.; he and Max had valuable discussions about Cottier in the Morris Room, when Andrew was on study leave several times from the Centre of Art History and Art Theory at the Australian National University. The fourth member, Suzanne Veldink, had done much work on the taste, in Cottier's native Scotland, for Dutch paintings of the Hague School and on Cottier's role in creating that vogue and expanding it to England and North America.

Collaborating on a book with four authors located in three continents has had its challenges but these were far outweighed by the advantages. Collectively, we had physical access to most of the known works produced by Cottier and the companies that operated under his name, and the internet allowed us to communicate our findings easily and frequently. We have been fortunate that a partnership of four people – who, at the beginning of the project, barely knew each other – has grown into a bond of friendship.

The completion of this book has taken several years and we are particularly grateful for the sustained interest and support of Yale University Press in London (Mark Eastment and Gillian Malpass), and the Paul Mellon Centre for Studies in British Art, London, where Emily Lees never lost faith in the project and was patient in the face of setbacks and delays. Once the book was finished, the manuscript was submitted for anonymous peer review. The resulting insightful and detailed comments have substantially improved the content and narrative of our book. Likewise, we are indebted to Katharine Ridler for her painstaking copy-editing and editorial comments, to Jacquie Meredith for proofreading the text, and to Robert Dalrymple for his beautiful design of the book.

In the course of our research, we have received assistance from the staff members of numerous archives, libraries, museums and research institutes, who have helped with finding material, facilitating interlibrary loans, retrieving objects from storage for inspection and other related tasks. We thank them here collectively but that in no way diminishes our appreciation of their help. The same is true for all those who have aided us in obtaining images for the book. Given the Covid-related closure of museums and other institutions just at the time when the images were required, many of them went that extra mile. Nevertheless, each of the authors would like to extend their thanks to certain individuals and institutions who have helped them along the way.

Petra Chu is grateful to the Getty Research Institute, Los Angeles, for funding her scholarship in spring 2011 and to Seton Hall University for granting her a leave of absence. She also thanks the following persons, who have helped her in different ways: Dawn Reid Brean, James J. Callahan, Hsiao-Yun Chu, Alyssa Dreliszak, Gail Feigenbaum, Madeleine Fidell-Beaufort, Alice Cooney Frelinghuysen, Thomas Gaehtgens, Anne Helmreich, Chaz Jaquess, Juliet Kinchin, Aynne Kokas, Tom Miller, Andrea Selbig and Gabriel P. Weisberg.

Max Donnelly records his gratitude to the late Elsie Houston who first introduced him to Cottier, and to the late Catherine Hoover Voorsanger, who encouraged his early interest. He would also like to thank the following individuals for their considerable and generous help: Scott Abercrombie, Lucy Akehurst, Jane and Bill Church, Griffin Coe, Peter Cormack, Marc Fecker, Charlotte Gere, Cosmo Linzee Gordon, Oscar Graf, Flure Grossart, Iain Hopkins, Stephen Jackson, Allan James, Michael Jeffery, Paul Jeromack and the late Robert Tuggle, Martin P. Levy, Jenny Lister, John Mackie, Jamie Mackinnon, Anne Malone, Jennifer Melville, Geoffrey Munn, Paul Reeves, David Robertson, James Rylands, Paul Shutler, David A. Taylor, Clare Thompson, Emily Walsh, Clarissa Ward, Rosemary Watt, Michael Whiteway and Christopher Wilk. Finally, among the photographers who have contributed greatly to his chapters, he would like to thank Alastair Carew-Cox and Colin McLean, with whom it has been a pleasure and education to work.

Andrew Montana acknowledges the professional assistance of staff from the many cultural, educational and heritage institutions where he researched, and to the welcoming spirit of the church parishes and synagogues he visited throughout the project to study the interiors. He thanks the owners of private properties, who generously granted him access, and the conservation architects and artisans who have restored and protected Lyon, Cottier & Co. interior schemes. For their goodwill and practical assistance, he thanks Stephen Barlow, Michael Lech, John Lyon, Douglas MacKay, Shane Moran, the late John Schaeffer, Anne Sherry and Michael Hogan, Beverley Sherry, Felicity Strong and Graham Windridge. He extends thanks to the photographers Mandy Crook, Susan G. Hunt, Ross Schultz and Christopher Shain, and to Hin Lim and Noel Mclaughlin, respectively, for their inspired photographic artwork in his chapters.

Suzanne Veldink largely conducted her research during her internship at Glasgow Museums and doctorate years in Edinburgh and she thanks those involved: Frances Fowle, Vivien Hamilton and Robert Wenley, as well as Freek Heijbroek.

We are very grateful for the support of individuals who have contributed so generously towards the cost of the illustrations, which play such an important part in this book: Sir Angus Grossart, Margaret Baird and Clarissa Ward, as well as for a grant awarded by the Decorative Arts Society, Art & Design 1850 to the Present. We also thank the Paul Mellon Centre for its support towards the illustration costs.

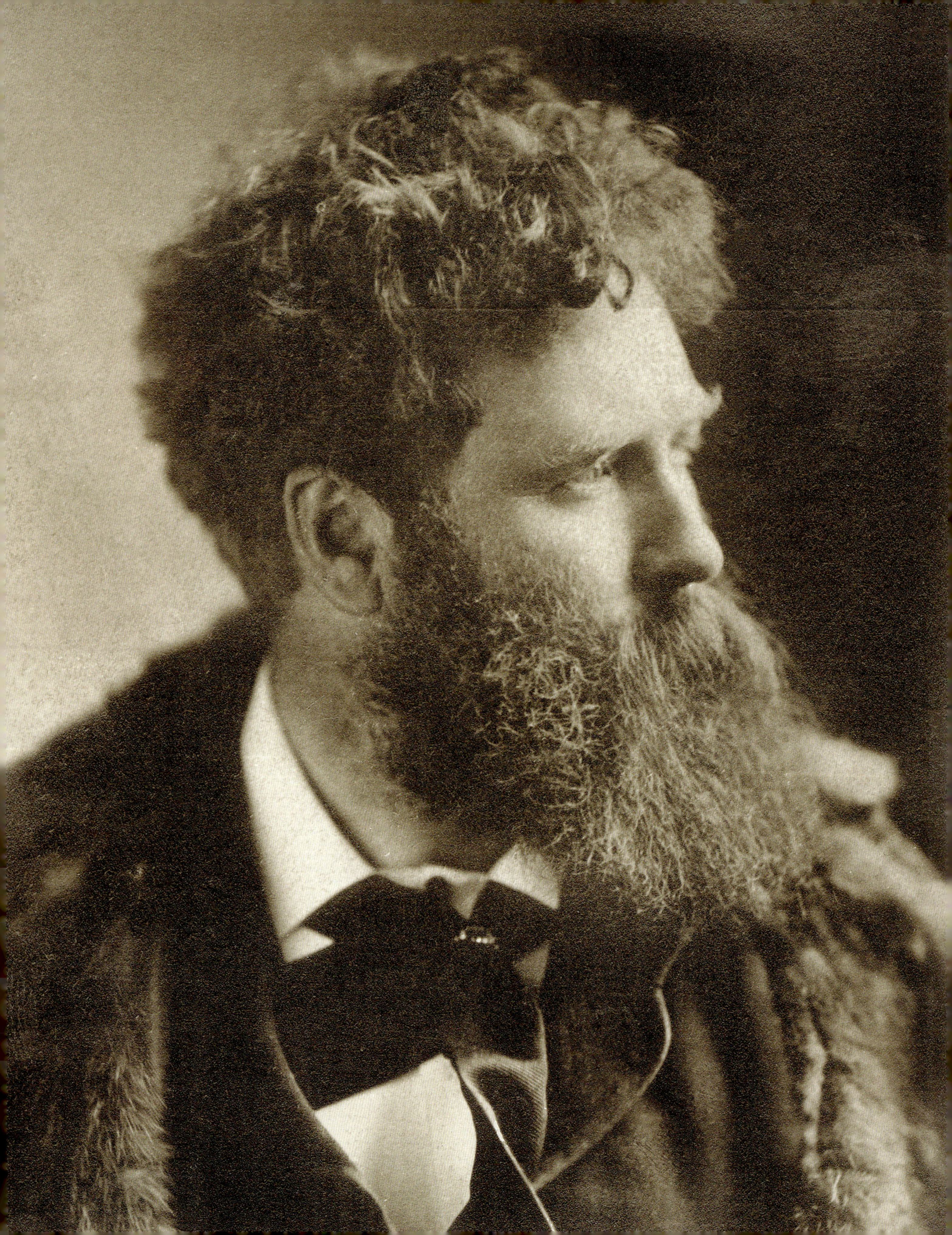

INTRODUCTION

He was, in every way, a singular and powerful personality, this son of a Manx sailor, who became one of the most potent factors in the advancement of the cause of art the world has ever known.
ANONYMOUS[1]

Mr. Cottier has been one of the most eloquent and unwearied persuaders to the love of art that we have had among us, and he has been as strong and earnest in his advocacy of whatever he has found good in our own art as of what he has found elsewhere. He is not only a man of convictions: he is a man with the finest perceptions, the most generous instincts, and he loves art too entirely and too unselfishly to allow of his being blinded by national prejudices.
CLARENCE COOK[2]

Cottier as a colourist has a range of performance beyond that of any other modern artist.
FORD MADOX BROWN[3]

His mind ... worked so vigorously and brilliantly that he could throw off designs enough in an hour ... to keep a factory going for weeks.
WILLIAM ERNEST HENLEY[4]

Cottier could tell a work of art a mile away.
C. E. S. WOOD[5]

1 Cottier in a photograph that he gave to his former assistant Andrew Wells in 1886, before Wells departed for Sydney to form the partnership of Lyon, Wells, Cottier & Co. Copy by T. & R. Annan & Sons, Glasgow, *c.*1914. Mitchell Library, Special Collections, Glasgow

Daniel Cottier (1838–1891), the subject of these accolades, was an artist, designer, decorator and art dealer, lauded in his day by artists and critics alike (fig. 1). As the quotations suggest, Cottier enjoyed an international, even intercontinental, reputation in the late nineteenth century and was admired on many accounts – as an artist for his original and daring use of colour; as a designer for his boundless creativity; as a picture dealer for his keen eye for quality and originality; and as a businessman for his instincts and entrepreneurship, as well as the true conviction he brought to his trade.

This book seeks to rehabilitate the reputation of a gifted designer and a brilliant art impresario industrialist, who keenly spotted and creatively exploited one of the key aspects of late nineteenth-century bourgeois culture – its focus on family, home and religion. Underpinned by economic prosperity, especially in the Anglo-Saxon world (Britain, North America and Australia), this emphasis led to a flurry of homes and places of worship being (re-)built and (re-)decorated. An aspiring stained-glass artist and decorative painter in the late 1850s, the young Cottier, born and raised in Glasgow, then one of the world's most prosperous cities, saw the artistic opportunities of the building and decorating boom and built an international business empire in response.

More broadly, this book intends to contribute to a fuller and more complete understanding of Aestheticism, an international trend in the history of culture, art and design from the mid-1860s to the late 1890s, in which Cottier played a crucial role. Within this period it also aims to present an in-depth view of the art business, broadly defined, to illuminate the way in which it at once fostered and distorted Aesthetic ideals. Aestheticism, according to the *Oxford Dictionary of Art*, 'was characterized by the cult of the beautiful and an emphasis on the sheer pleasure to be derived from it.'[6] This pleasure was primarily sensual (sight and touch in the case of visual arts and hearing in the case of music)[7] but also intellectual and emotional. 'True beauty', the British designer and theorist Owen Jones (1809–1874) wrote with reference to the visual arts, 'results from that repose which the mind feels when the eye, the intellect, and the affections, are satisfied from the absence of any want',[8] where the 'want', presumably, was for visual charm, intellectual stimulation and emotional fulfilment.

Walter Hamilton, in his 1882 book *The Aesthetic Movement*, defined Aestheticism as an artistic and literary movement, presumably with its own style (in the introduction to the third edition he writes that he would have preferred calling it *A Renaissance of Medieval Art and Culture*),[9] whereas the tendency today is to look at it, first and foremost, as an attitude – much as we look at Romanticism. This modern use of the term is exemplified in the titles and exhibitions that have been devoted to Aestheticism in the past decades, such as *In Pursuit of Beauty: Americans and the Aesthetic Movement* (Metropolitan Museum of Art, New York, 1986–7) or *The Cult of Beauty: The Aesthetic Movement, 1860–1900* (first shown at the Victoria and Albert Museum, London, 2011).[10] As is also the case with Romanticism, even when art historians do refer to Aestheticism as a movement, it is a movement without a fixed style.

This absence of a fixed style is especially true for the decorative arts, which flourished during the time when Aestheticism reigned. Aesthetic designers embraced a strategy that called for the selective use, contemporary adaptation and thoughtful combination of established Western and non-Western styles and motifs. This eclectic approach (often referred to as 'eclectic historicism') was the perfect stylistic strategy for Aesthetic designers as it allowed them to select among all historic styles, Western and non-Western, the elements to create the perfectly beautiful object. Theoretically, eclecticism was rooted in the philosophy of the French thinker Victor Cousin (1792–1867), who summarised what he called his 'eclectic' philosophy, as a process of 'select[ing] in all [systems] what appears to be true and good, and consequently everlasting'.[11]

Eclectic historicism was not restricted to the Aesthetic movement and may be seen as a broad artistic strategy in the nineteenth century, when international exhibitions, newly created museums, like the South Kensington Museum in London (1857), and illustrated design compendia, most famously

Owen Jones's *Grammar of Ornament* (1856), exposed artists, designers and the public at large to a broad array of both Western and non-Western styles of art and ornamentation. In Aestheticism, however, it was uniquely combined with the use of the best materials and superior artisanship. This emphasis on material and craft was something Aestheticism shared with the Arts and Crafts movement founded by the designer and social reformer William Morris (1834–1896), which flourished from the late 1880s. But, in common with the movement's spiritual founder, the writer and critic John Ruskin (1819–1900), Morris and his followers generally condemned the use of mechanised tools, which was more readily accepted in the Aesthetic context. Moreover, practitioners of the Arts and Crafts movement, though not *per se* averse to eclectic historicism, often favoured Gothic or medieval over all historic styles, in part because of the association of the Middle Ages with the manual production that the movement promoted.

Eclectic historicism may be seen in individual works of art and design but was most obviously present in the planning and design of entire interior spaces, especially (though by no means exclusively) in private homes, where Aestheticism reigned supreme.[12] Creating unity from the artistic diversity of the past was a hallmark of Aestheticism. In individual works of art such unity could be achieved by harmonious proportions and colours; in interior design, by a careful selection and juxtaposition of furniture and decorative objects against the backdrop of judiciously decorated walls (whether painted, stencilled or wallpapered), floors and ceilings. Colour was particularly important in creating a sense of harmony and unity and, as Cottier's contemporary, the designer and theorist Christopher Dresser (1834–1904), asserted, a conveyer of emotion.[13] One could argue that colour was 'reinvented' during the Aesthetic period, when artists increasingly turned to scientific colour treatises[14] to understand its physical and psychological properties in an effort to create 'agreeable' effects.[15]

With its emphasis on beauty – on individual works of art and created environments that could provide at once sensual, intellectual and emotional delight – Aestheticism was rarefied and even elitist. As such, it held an obvious appeal to late nineteenth-century upper-middle-class professionals and industrialists in Europe, North America and Australia who had both the education and wealth to indulge in this trend. Indeed, the affluent bourgeois interior became the main manifestation of Aestheticism and a favoured professional terrain for artists, decorators and art and antique dealers, who quickly realised its dual potential for artistic self-realisation and financial gain. Perhaps inevitably, commercialisation came to erode the principles of the movement, as the thoughtful placement of a few carefully chosen objects – a subtly coloured landscape picture, a Chinese vase, a Venetian glass – against the backdrop of tastefully decorated walls made way for the showing off of costly objects for the sake of gratifying, in the words of the well-known American cultural critic Thorstein Veblen (1857–1929), 'the possessor's sense of pecuniary superiority.'[16]

Cottier's artistic creations and activities reflect the tenets of Aestheticism and his career followed its evolutionary arc. He was born in Glasgow just when that city was becoming an economic powerhouse, expressing its growing confidence through innovative and experimental architecture and decoration. He was apprenticed in studios making stained glass in Glasgow and Edinburgh, taking classes at the Trustees' Academy in Edinburgh, where he was undoubtedly exposed to the colour theories of the Scottish decorative painter and theorist David Ramsay Hay (1798–1866). Hay's books, especially *The Laws of Harmonious Colouring, Adapted to Interior Decorations, Manufactures, and other Useful Purposes* (six editions, 1828 to 1847), were influential for decorators in the mid-nineteenth century. Having moved to London in the late 1850s, certainly by about 1858, Cottier took evening classes at the Working Men's College, attending lectures by Britain's leading art critic and champion of the Pre-Raphaelites, John Ruskin, and practising figure drawing in the class of the artist Ford Madox Brown (1821–1893). He was drawn to the monumental figural style of Brown, and his own designs for stained glass came to be characterised by large and boldly drawn figures. William Morris, whose furnishing and decorative arts firm Morris, Marshall, Faulkner & Co. opened in 1861 while Cottier was in London, was another important influence on the young Cottier. Morris's partnership provided him with a business model for his own company, Cottier & Co., established in London in 1869–70, followed by branches in New York and Sydney in 1873.

Cottier was not the only young designer to follow Morris's example. Aware of the growing available capital of the upper-middle class, many artists and craftspeople saw opportunities in the business of decorating the numerous newly built homes, churches, libraries, clubs and other buildings that this new wealth made possible. In London, firms like Collinson & Lock (established 1870), Watts & Co. (established 1874) and the decorating business of J. Aldam Heaton (1830–1897), who moved to London in 1876, all started their 'art' businesses around the same time as Cottier. Their founders came from different, mostly artisanal, backgrounds. Cottier was trained as a stained-glass artist, Collinson and Lock as furniture makers, while Aldam Heaton began as a textile designer and manufacturer and the founders of Watts & Co. were architects. What distinguished Cottier & Co. from rival firms was its scope, both commercial and geographic. While many other British firms had clients in the United States and Australia, Cottier's expansive vision prompted him to establish international branches in New York and Sydney, both cities with large Scottish immigrant populations, where he could easily make inroads. His vision also led him to create a business that was more comprehensive than all others in that it painted wall and ceiling decorations for houses; designed and manufactured furniture, stained glass and decorated ceramic tiles and chargers; supplied textiles, upholstery and carpets; dealt in antiques; and sold contemporary and Old Master paintings. Indeed, Cottier & Co. appears to have been the only decorating business of the period that included an art gallery, which became an integral part of its business model.

Like Christopher Dresser, Cottier believed that the interior decoration of a room should complement and not detract from paintings hanging on the walls,[17] but he did not simply sell pictures as decoration. Cottier was an important tastemaker, who built new clienteles in Britain and North America for the artists of the Dutch 'Hague School' as well as for the French painter Adolphe Monticelli, while at the same time creating a niche market for already established French artists, such as Camille Corot and Charles-François Daubigny. An artist and an art collector himself, Cottier genuinely admired the work of the artists he promoted and formed close friendships with many of them, including David Artz and Matthijs Maris in Holland, Monticelli in France and Albert Pinkham Ryder and J. Alden Weir in the United States.

While Cottier's expansion of the scope of interior decoration to fine art dealing may have been prompted by his keen business sense, it can also be understood as a logical conclusion of two key tenets of Aestheticism. The first was the notion of aesthetic harmony, already mentioned. By offering services as an interior decorator and selling everything that would go into the home, including the pictures on the wall, Cottier would be able to turn it into the kind of harmonious *Gesamtkunstwerk* that the Aesthetic movement fostered. The second was the equality of 'fine' and 'decorative' arts. Aestheticism played a pioneering role in erasing the boundaries between fine art and decoration, a trend that became increasingly dominant towards the end of the nineteenth century (Art Nouveau) and the beginning of the twentieth (early Modernism). Ruskin had made this equality between fine and decorative arts the subject of one of his lectures in the series 'The Two Paths', delivered in 1858 and 1859, around the time when Cottier first came to London.[18] In the third lecture, 'Modern Manufacture and Design', Ruskin said that

the only essential distinction between Decorative and other art is the being fitted for a fixed place; and in that place, related, either in subordination or in command, to the effect of other pieces of art. And all the greatest art which the world has produced is thus fitted for a place and subordinated to a purpose. There is no existing highest-order art but is decorative. The best sculpture yet produced has been the decoration of a temple front – the best painting the decoration of a room. Raphael's best doing is merely the wall-colouring of a suite of apartments in the Vatican, and his cartoons were made for tapestries. Correggio's best doing is the decoration of two small church cupolas at Parma; Michael Angelo's of a ceiling in the Pope's private chapel ... [19]

To young Cottier, trained as an artisan but an artist at heart, these ideas must have been exciting and his business model may have been a way to put them into practice.

Yet, as Cottier must have quickly realised, in practice both the ideal of the aesthetic interior as a harmonious whole and the equalisation of fine and decorative art were difficult to achieve as they depended on willing patrons, interested in the goals of Aestheticism, as well as tractable workers and flexible suppliers. As for patrons, few seem to have been willing to give Cottier & Co. completely free rein in an interior, whether domestic, ecclesiastic or public. With some notable exceptions – for example, John Forbes White (1831–1904) in Aberdeen and Dundee and Ichabod Williams (1824–1899) in New York – most clients followed their own ideas. They (or in many cases their architects or decorators) sourced elements such as furniture, stained glass, wallpaper and upholstery from different suppliers, patronising specialised art galleries to pick out works of art to hang on their walls. In public buildings and churches, Cottier & Co. may have been asked to paint the walls but other firms would provide the woodwork, tiles and ironwork. In churches, moreover, the windows, for the most part memorials, were commissioned by private donors from firms of their own liking.

As for the artists, designers and craftspeople who worked for him, in order to carry out the numerous commissions he received Cottier needed to employ a small army of specialists such as cabinetmakers, painters and upholsterers. It is assumed that, like most owners of interior design businesses, Cottier kept some control over the execution of important commissions by providing his workers with quick concept sketches for his designers and manufacturers to follow. The British critic William Ernest Henley (1849–1903) compared the effortless way in which Cottier produced such drawings with the improvisational skills of the Italian composer Gioachino Rossini at his piano. While busily talking, Cottier would apparently 'throw off designs enough in an hour ... to keep a factory going for weeks'. Henley also noted that Cottier 'had the faculty, common to all great artists, of picking his men, and therewith of so imposing himself upon them as to make them practically exponents and expressions of himself.'[20] This was true up to a point. Cottier's stained-glass designers, who included Frederick Vincent Hart (1843–1915), and for a time even the 'fine' artist Matthijs Maris (1839–1917), relied on their own creativity pushing the parameters of the Cottier 'house' style. The same may be said for some of the painters who decorated Cottier furniture, most notably the American artists Francis Lathrop (1849–1909) and Albert Pinkham Ryder (1847–1917). Both, like Maris, were trained as fine artists rather than craft decorators. Although he could not completely control the style of Cottier & Co., however, the fact that Cottier was able to maintain active relationships with a widely distributed network of artists and tradespeople across three continents during the late nineteenth century is evidence of his boundless energy and personal charisma.

Cottier & Co.'s house style itself changed over the years. In the 1860s, Cottier's stained glass was sometimes inspired by Ancient art – Assyrian, Egyptian and Graeco-Roman. The glass from the early 1870s additionally reflects the fashionable interest in Japanese art, especially in a new predilection for botanic motifs. The Cottier & Co. palette changed throughout the 1870s and 80s, becoming richer and darker and increasingly marked by the use of tertiary colours and the subtle colour combinations associated with Aestheticism. Cottier & Co.'s interior decoration and furniture drew on many of the same sources that informed his stained glass and built on the classicising eclecticism that Cottier had been practising in Glasgow with the encouragement of John James Stevenson (1831–1908), William Leiper (1839–1916) and Alexander Thomson (1817–1875) in the 1860s. In the 1870s the firm continued to employ

Greek, Roman and Egyptian forms and motifs in wall decoration, but some furniture produced during this decade was in the Anglo-Japanese style most often associated with Edward William Godwin (1833–1886). As fashions evolved around 1880, Cottier & Co.'s style moved away from Japan and embraced other historic periods. References to eighteenth-century design became more common in Cottier's furniture and domestic glass, reflecting the broader revival of early Georgian styles during that period. In ecclesiastical windows, especially in Australia, the early classicising Cottier style merged with Gothic Revival, following a more general trend described by Ayla Lepine of the overlapping and merger of Gothic Revival with Aestheticism.[21]

Despite these changes in style and the variations due to Cottier & Co.'s teamwork production, such was the firm's success in establishing a visual identity that by the 1880s a 'Cottier' home was recognised as evoking a certain type of décor different from what one would find in a 'Jones' or a 'Morris' house.[22] The opulent interior of Kepplestone, Aberdeenshire, may have featured the kind of painted scheme the author and critic Mary Eliza Haweis (1848–1898) was trying to evoke when she described Cottier interiors as spaces in which 'forms are studied and adapted from the finest examples in old Roman and Greek decoration, and their colors are all exquisite in themselves and exquisitely harmonized.'[23]

Cottier's own career path from admired artist, decorator and designer to intercontinental art entrepreneur parallels the Aesthetic movement's course from art for art's sake to conspicuous consumption. Was his expansionism motivated by the desire for financial gain, or by a missionary zeal to spread the ideas of the Aesthetic movement beyond the confines of Britain? Perhaps the answer lies in the middle. The American art critic Clarence Cook (1828–1900), who knew him well, saw Cottier as a man of convictions, tirelessly promoting the cause of Beauty with a capital B.[24] Vincent van Gogh complained about his shrewdness as a businessman who could spot good work but tried to pay as little as possible so as to maximise his profits.[25] The truth is that Cottier, as this book will show, was both an artist and a man living in the world – with a wife and three children to support and a chronic illness that, he knew, destined him to an early grave. Like most artists, he was forced to strike a compromise between idealism and reality. His business continued into the early twentieth century but Cottier's reputation followed the fate of many designers and decorators of the Victorian era: by that time, he had fallen into obscurity.

The challenges of drawing together Cottier's complex and geographically diverse business empire have delayed a full reassessment of his career longer than that of some of his contemporaries, particularly Morris in Britain or Louis Comfort Tiffany (1848–1933) in the United States. In part, this is due to a lack of documentation. Few Cottier & Co. designs and practically no business records have survived and none of the lectures he presented has been found in manuscript or print; we know about them only through secondary sources.[26]

In addition, the work produced by Cottier and his firm has been only partially preserved, making it difficult to get an accurate sense of the total production. This is especially true for his wall and ceiling paintings. Most of the decorative schemes the firm made for public buildings and private homes in Britain and North America have been destroyed or obliterated, whereas in Australia several of these painted decorations have survived and been restored. Stained-glass windows made by the firm in Britain, the United States and Australia have been easier to identify, especially those made for churches and public buildings, which are often signed and well documented and can be linked to specific clients. All these make it possible to create an accurate, even if not entirely complete, record of Cottier & Co.'s production in this area. The same is true for Cottier's ceramics, a significant corpus of his company's work, which are usually signed. In contrast, the furniture made by the company is rarely documented or marked and although a small body of work can now be confidently attributed, there are undoubtedly many pieces yet to come to light.

The scholarship undertaken, despite these challenges, on aspects of Cottier's life and career over the past fifty years has been invaluable in preparing this book. This includes the writings of the British authors Mark Girouard, Martin Harrison and Michael Donnelly,[27] as well as the American researcher Margaret H. Hobler, whose extensive unpublished thesis of 1987 was the first major attempt to revive Cottier's reputation.[28] Hobler's work was used by the organisers of the Metropolitan Museum of Art's groundbreaking exhibition *In Pursuit of Beauty: Americans and the Aesthetic Movement* (1986–7).[29] In this show, which gave a thorough overview of the international Aesthetic movement in America, Cottier was featured prominently and in its catalogue he was described as a 'harbinger of aestheticism in America and a profound influence on American decoration'.[30] More recently, in 2011, *Cottier's in Context*, a multi-authored in-depth study of Dowanhill Church in Glasgow, contained a number of important chapters specifically on Cottier by Juliet Kinchin, which threw new light on his early work in Scotland.[31]

Relying in part on the pioneering research just described, the authors of this volume have drawn together the available evidence to provide the first complete overview of Daniel Cottier and his tri-continental project of artistic entrepreneurship. The book brings to light a significant body of key works designed and executed by Cottier or under his direction, and charts his pioneering contribution to the international Aesthetic movement through the interiors, stained-glass windows, furniture and ceramics that his firm produced. It shows his importance as an art dealer, especially in Britain and North America, where he single-handedly created a market for the artists of the Hague School and for Adolphe Monticelli, while also playing a major role in building a market for the Barbizon School. It also shows how Cottier's tireless activities influenced and, in some cases, profoundly affected the lives and careers of artists, designers, craftspeople and dealers who worked for and with him, sometimes crossing oceans to do so. Cottier understood the Aesthetic era's desire for beauty and realised the possibility of commoditising beauty in the forms of opulent furniture, jewel-toned windows, richly painted walls and carefully selected artworks and *objets d'art*, inventively displayed. Beyond being the biography of a man and a global business empire, therefore, this book illuminates a significant event of late nineteenth-century cultural history – Aestheticism's 'cult of beauty' meeting with the bourgeoisie's financial ability to possess it.

Max Donnelly

CHAPTER ONE
SCOTLAND 1838–1869

Perhaps it was a portent that Daniel Cottier, whose arts empire spanned three continents, spent his early years living near the quays of Glasgow, in the heart of an area buzzing with international trade. The 1841 census records him, aged three, living on Carrick Street in the borough of Anderston, just south-west of Glasgow's city centre.[1] Anderston was then a thriving district of factories, warehouses and workshops (by coincidence Cottier ran a workshop on Carrick Street in the late 1860s). Today the street is truncated and surrounded by wasteland but its southern end still connects to the northern embankment of the River Clyde and the site of Glasgow's first quay, the Broomielaw.

Cottier's family background also led to the sea, shaping his character and influencing his career. His parents had seafaring connections. According to one source, the Cottiers were an established Manx family who had lived at Narradale in Lezayre, near Ramsey on the Isle of Man, since 1541.[2] His father, Daniel, was a seaman in the merchant navy;[3] his paternal grandfather, also Daniel, was from the same parish and had apparently been a mariner.[4] Cottier's maternal grandfather was a master mariner in Greenock (see fig. 32), a major port on the Firth of Clyde. It comes as no surprise to learn that Cottier chose an anchor, also a symbol of hope, as his company logo. An anchor appeared from the 1870s on his company letterhead and advertisements (see figs 24 and 70), as well as some of his stained-glass windows and on the reverse of ceramic chargers (see fig. 25).

YOUTH AND UPBRINGING

Cottier's mother, Margaret McLean (1807/8–1885) was in her mid-twenties when, in September 1834, she married his father, then possibly in his mid-seventies.[5] Had life at sea prevented him from marrying earlier? They were married in a chapel of ease in the Gorbals district of Glasgow and their three children were born in that city. The first, Isabella, arrived in March 1836, but died from 'water in head' ten months later on 19 January 1837. Daniel was born almost exactly a year later, on 12 January 1838 (the date on his memorial window, London; see fig. 57), followed by Mary Catherine in 1840. The 1841 census records the two children living with their mother at Carrick Street, together with Margaret's father and her younger sisters Mary and Euphemia.[6] Two years later, when Cottier was five years old, his father died.[7] Given that he was a seaman, an institution such as the Glasgow Seamen's Friend Society, founded in 1822, may have played a part in the young Daniel's formal education.[8] However, it has not been established how or where he was schooled and nothing else has come to light about his childhood.

Cottier must have been a pre-teen when, according to one obituarist, he worked as 'a message boy in connection with one of the boot and shoe shops of Messrs Paterson',[9] for by the time of the 1851 census he was aged thirteen and described as an 'apprentice coach painter'.[10] He evidently showed artistic promise, for some time later he was apprenticed to a glass painter.[11] During the second half of the nineteenth century, glass painting was a sought-after skill offering good prospects for employment, as stained glass was used increasingly in churches, public buildings and private homes. In Glasgow, as the self-proclaimed 'second city' of the British Empire developed into an industrial giant, an unprecedented building boom fuelled demand for stained glass. Cottier was probably an apprentice in one of the two main workshops producing stained glass, either that run by David Kier (1802–1864) or (perhaps more likely given Cottier's future reputation as a decorator) John Cairney & Co.,

2 *Miriam* in Dowanhill Church (now Cottiers Theatre), Glasgow, designed and made by Cottier, Edinburgh and Glasgow, 1867. Stained glass

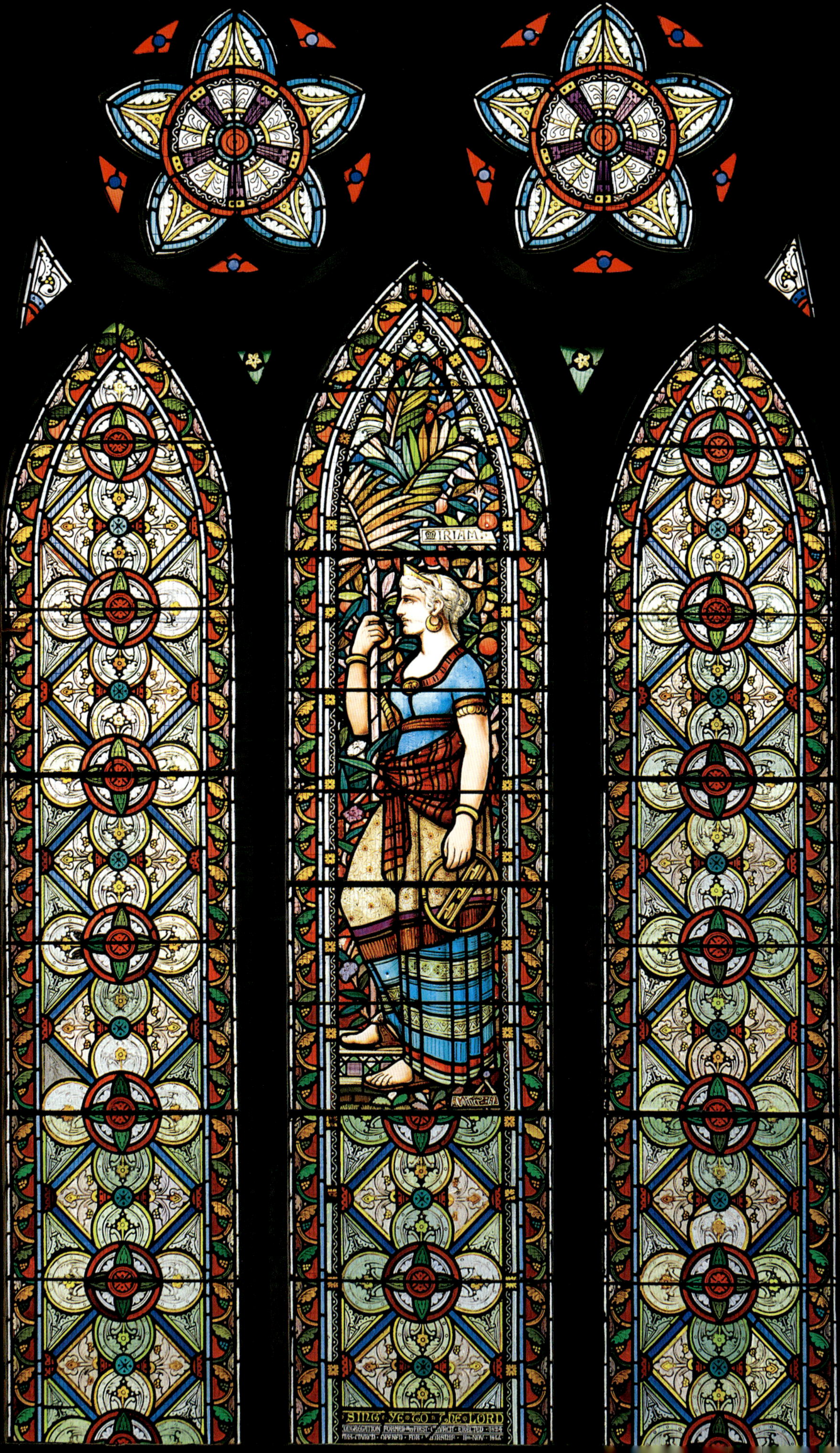
MIRIAM
SING YE TO THE LORD

3 Window, Pilrig St Paul's Church (formerly Pilrig Free Church), Leith, designed by Cottier for Field & Allan, Leith, 1862. Stained glass

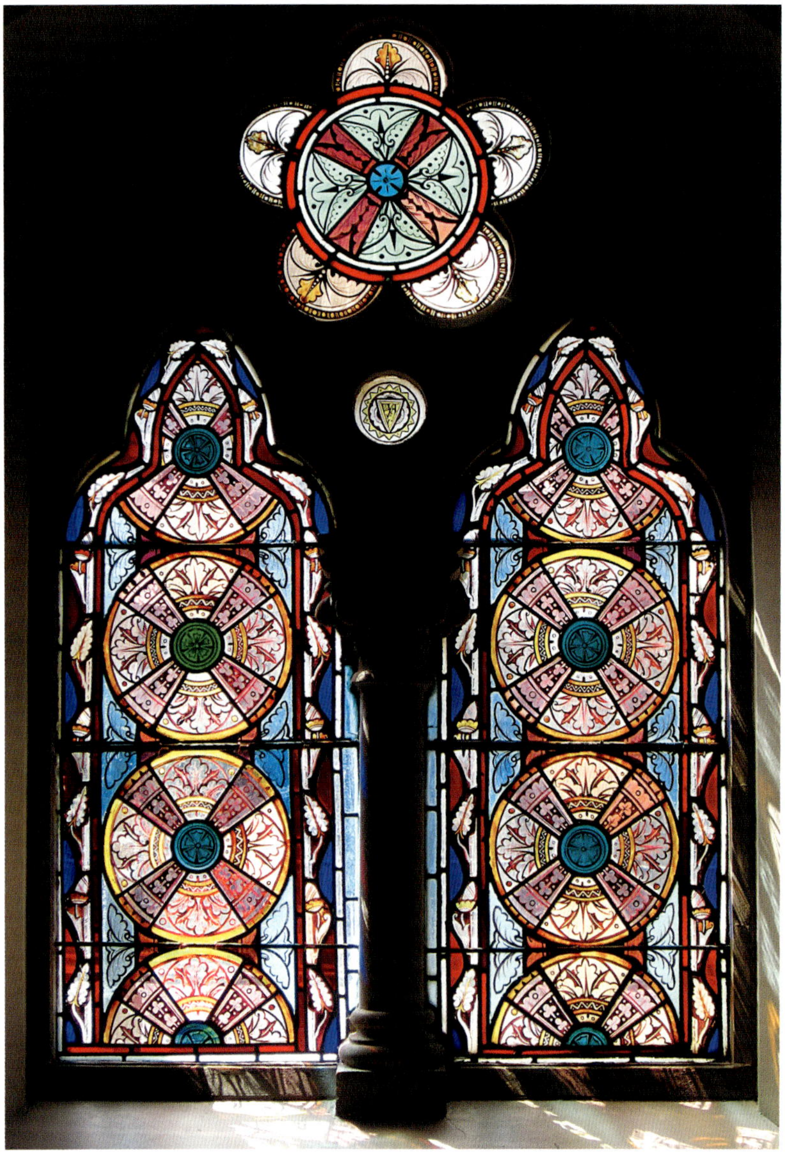

a firm that decorated interiors and made stained glass.[12] Assuming the latter, it is possible that during this time Cottier formed a friendship with the slightly older John Lamb Lyon (1836–1916), a fellow apprentice with whom he maintained a lifelong friendship and business association.[13]

In the mid-1850s Cottier moved to Edinburgh, where he had the opportunity to advance his career by apprenticing with a larger company. This may have been the leading stained-glass firm established by James Ballantine (1808–1877), which in the mid-1840s had made some of the windows designed by A. W. N. Pugin for the new Palace of Westminster in London.[14] Working in Edinburgh gave Cottier the opportunity to attend evening classes at the Trustees' Academy, for which Ballantine sponsored most apprentices.[15] By 1845 the curriculum of the School of Design included 'ornamental design, both in form and in colour, including architecture, geometry, perspective, modelling, fresco, and encaustic painting'.[16] His studies would have encompassed the colour harmony theories of the Edinburgh native David Ramsay Hay (1798–1866), such as *The Laws of Harmonious Colouring, Adapted to House Painting*, first published in 1828.[17] Hay inspired a new generation of decorators through his theories and work such as the painted interior of Sir Walter Scott's Abbotsford (1824),[18] near Melrose, Roxburghshire (open to the public after the writer's death in 1832 and described in the 1847 edition of *The Laws of Harmonious Colouring*) and his 'colourfully decorated' suite of rooms in the Palace of Holyroodhouse for Queen Victoria in 1850.[19] As a house painter, Hay played a part in the Scottish revival in decorative arts, which came from technological and artistic advances in house painting, glass staining and textile manufacture.

Cottier went on to develop his skills in London in the late 1850s. There is circumstantial evidence linking him to the firm of stained-glass makers Ward & Hughes in Soho, for his future business associate, Lyon, had joined that firm in about 1854.[20] Ward & Hughes made stained glass in the Gothic Revival style and in 1855 (under the firm's previous name, Ward & Nixon) had made one of the largest windows in England, the eight-light east window of Lincoln Cathedral.[21] During this period, Cottier is known to have taken evening classes at the Working Men's College in Great Ormond Street,[22] which had been founded in 1854 by Christian Socialists to provide a liberal education for skilled artisans. He was exposed to the latest theories of art and design, later describing himself as a 'pupil of Ruskin's'.[23] Cottier's claim is plausible, as Britain's foremost art critic, John Ruskin (1819–1900), taught regularly at the college until 1860.[24] Ruskin's lectures on art theory would have made an impression on the young Cottier, who remained in Ruskin's orbit through a circle of Aberdeen patrons who knew and corresponded with the critic from the late 1860s (see Chapter Two, p. 39). Another leading figure in the Victorian art world, the Pre-Raphaelite

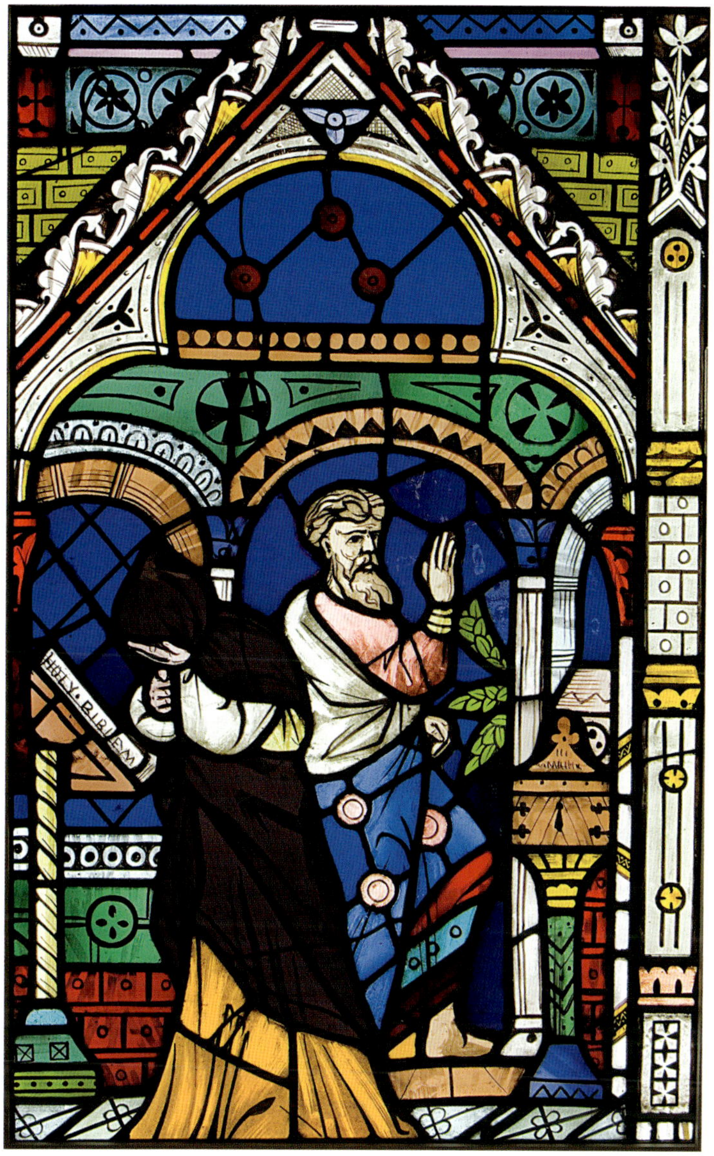

4 *The Parable of the Pharisee and the Publican*, made for Trinity United Presbyterian Church, Irvine, Ayrshire (removed), designed by Cottier for Field & Allan, Leith, *c.*1863. Stained glass, 119 × 79 cm. Stained Glass Museum, Ely, Cambridgeshire

artist Ford Madox Brown (1821–1893), succeeded Dante Gabriel Rossetti in teaching life classes at the Working Men's College from late 1858 until late 1860.[25] As recalled by Cottier's fellow student John Phillips Emslie (1839–1913), Brown 'took a great personal interest in his pupils'[26] and was assisted by Edward Burne-Jones (1833–1898), who 'was friendly in the extreme' to the students.[27] Brown invited students to his studio where they saw his painting *Work* in progress, and to his house, where they saw 'pictures not only by himself, but also by Rossetti, Holman Hunt, and others'.[28]

In April 1861 the stained-glass and decorating business Morris, Marshall, Faulkner & Co. was founded near the College at Red Lion Square, Bloomsbury; Brown and Rossetti, who were partners in the firm, and Burne-Jones became increasingly involved in designing stained glass. The glass painter George Campfield (1828–1910) met Morris at the Working Men's College and also joined the firm, and it has been suggested that Cottier, who was still living in London and was by then a 'Glass Designer',[29] did so too, albeit briefly.[30] Whether or not he did, judging from Cottier's later work (see figs 4, 13 and 14), his figural style was influenced by Brown as well as Rossetti, and other elements of the stained glass produced by Cottier from the mid-1860s show his awareness of that made by Morris's firm.

EARLY WORK AT FIELD & ALLAN

The earliest known examples of Cottier's stained glass date from the period after he returned from London to Scotland where, by early 1862, he was the manager of Field & Allan, based in Edinburgh and Leith.[31] The firm had begun as a slate business in 1793 but by the 1860s it also dealt in marble, decorated interiors and made stained glass. Cottier's windows, designed as part of a decorative scheme for Pilrig Free Church, Leith, in 1862 (fig. 3)[32] are in a richly ornamented Gothic Revival style – described at the time as 'mosaic glass' – which was typical of the time and unsurprising given that he had probably trained with Gothic Revivalists in Edinburgh and London. What is more significant is their range of subtle colours, which give an early indication of Cottier's study of chromatic harmony theory and of his talent as a colourist. Cottier also supplied figural designs for Field & Allan. Those for church commissions included windows for Trinity United Presbyterian Church, Irvine, Ayrshire, a Venetian Gothic church designed by Frederick Thomas Pilkington, opened in 1863. A panel originally positioned in the lower left light of the chancel window depicts the parable of the Pharisee and the Publican (fig. 4).[33] The dress and dramatic gestures of Cottier's figures, and the architectural settings they populate, are inspired by Gothic manuscript art with which Cottier would have been familiar through exhibitions and reproductions, and can be compared with some of the glass designed by Brown for Morris, Marshall, Faulkner & Co. in 1861.[34]

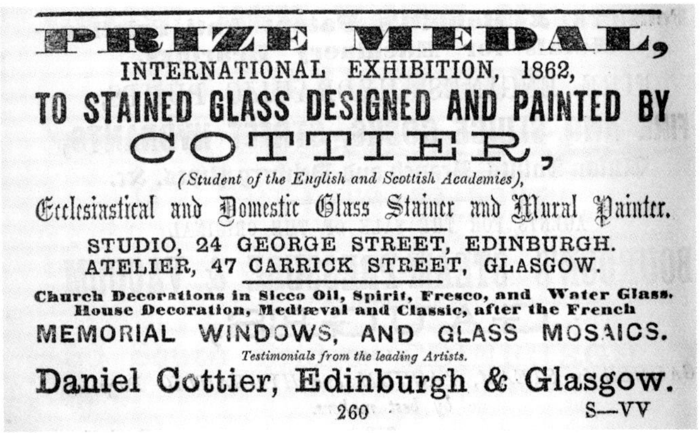

5 Advertisement for Daniel Cottier, Edinburgh and Glasgow, in *Slater's Royal National Commercial Directory and Topography of Scotland* (Manchester and London: Isaac Slater), 1867, p. 260. Mitchell Library, Special Collections, Glasgow

Field & Allan clearly valued Cottier from the moment they hired him for he was soon designing and painting a large armorial window for the London International Exhibition of 1862. Shortly before it was sent to London, in time for the Exhibition's opening on 1 May, it was displayed in Field & Allan's Edinburgh showroom.[35] Although the window has not been traced, a description of it in *The Scotsman* reveals that it was in the Renaissance Revival style that was becoming increasingly fashionable for public buildings and domestic glass, incorporating allegorical masks, figures and scrollwork.[36] Apparently 'intended for the hall of a mansion', it was effectively an advertisement for the firm, incorporating the heraldry of Leith as well as the company's monogram on a ground of 'rich ruby'. The report in *The Scotsman* concluded that 'the design displays artistic taste and freedom, the colours are rich and harmonious.'[37] In London, the window, nearly nine feet high, was displayed in the Central Division of the exhibition's South Court. It must have been accompanied by a smaller panel, because the glass designer Sebastian Evans (1830–1909) described a 'small window in the cinque cento style ... possibly the best English specimen of this kind in the Exhibition', before adding, rather crushingly, that 'this is owing more to the absence of competitors than to any great intrinsic merit'.[38] Notwithstanding this criticism, the jury awarded Field & Allan a medal for its stained-glass windows, singling out for praise its 'excellence of ornamental work in cinque cento style.'[39] Although the medal was awarded to Field & Allan, Cottier took ownership of the plaudit by later stating in advertisements and even on several stained-glass windows that he had received a medal in 1862 (see fig. 5).

In 1864 Cottier designed a panel (whereabouts unknown) for Field & Allan, to be shown at the Exhibition of Stained Glass and Mosaics held at the South Kensington Museum (from 1899, the Victoria and Albert Museum). Based on a pastoral play by the Scottish Enlightenment poet Allan Ramsay entitled 'The Gentle Shepherd', the principal figures in the window were the shepherd Patie and his sweetheart Peggy. A writer for the *Caledonian Mercury* thought the figures were 'drawn with much skill and truth. The picture is a fine specimen of the art, colours are admirably selected and skilfully put in, and the whole reflects high credit upon Mr Cottier, who has designed it.'[40] The panel was less warmly received in London. A writer for *The Ecclesiologist* thought it had 'some good parts about it' but that 'it is ruined by the coarseness of the drawing of the subject',[41] while in the opinion of another critic it served as 'an example to be avoided in every way, whether regarding subject, sentiment, or execution.'[42]

COTTIER: ECCLESIASTICAL GLASS STAINER AND MURAL PAINTER

With his work placed on the national and international stages, Cottier by 1864 felt sufficiently experienced and confident to set up his own business in Edinburgh's elegant New Town. An early advertisement taken out in *Slater's Directory* in 1867 (fig. 5) lists, among his services, 'Church Decorations in Sicco Oil, Spirit, Fresco, and Water Glass. House Decoration, Mediæval and Classic, after the French', in addition to memorial windows and 'glass mosaics'. The last was a reference to the type of glass he had designed for Pilrig Free Church (see fig. 3) and an early commission for this kind of 'rich mosaic glass' was for the north windows (since replaced) of Trinity Congregational Church in Glasgow, designed by John Honeyman (1831–1914) and inaugurated in April 1865.[43]

Joining Cottier's new enterprise were several young employees at the outset of their careers.

The glass artist Stephen Adam (1848–1910), a native of Edinburgh, had been apprenticed to Ballantine, and Charles Gow (1847–1893), the son of an Edinburgh glass stainer, followed in his father's footsteps, having been apprenticed to John Cairney & Co. in Glasgow. The decorator Andrew Wells (1845–1918), the son of a cleric, was raised in Edinburgh, initially serving an apprenticeship as a 'Japanner'[44] before working for Field & Allan, where he met Cottier in 1862.[45] As for Cottier, by the time he left Field & Allan he had become romantically involved with Marion Field (1838–1915), the daughter of William Field, whose family had founded the firm. Daniel and Marion married in Edinburgh on 19 June 1866, at 7 Union Street,[46] near his office at 24 George Street.

'A MASS OF GORGEOUS ORNAMENTATION': THREE GLASGOW CHURCHES

In 1866 and 1867 Cottier established his reputation as one of the most daring and innovative decorators of Scotland. During these years he worked on three important new churches in Glasgow, collaborating with progressive architects and other artist designers. Cottier's involvement with the first of these, Townhead Parish Church (largely demolished),[47] may be related to the fact that his studio was in the same building as the Edinburgh branch of the dynamic and prestigious architectural practice run by Campbell Douglas (1828–1910) and John James Stevenson (1831–1908). Douglas and Stevenson, whose main office was in Glasgow, specialised in ecclesiastical work. The church, designed in the fashionable fourteenth-century French Gothic Revival style, was largely the work of Stevenson, whose training had included a spell in the office of the leading London architect George Gilbert Scott (1811–1878).[48]

Townhead Parish Church presented Stevenson and Cottier with generous funding and a remit to be bold and experimental. The funds came from the legacy of Alexander Baird (1799–1862), an iron-master and member of the Church of Scotland, and the scale of the building and desire for rich decoration was an attempt by the congregation to mark a departure from normally plain Scottish Presbyterian churches in the face of a new rival, the United Presbyterian Church, established in 1847. It stood in a prominent position next to a proposed public park on Garngad Hill, to the east of the city centre, and Stevenson's massive spire was a landmark on the skyline near Glasgow Cathedral. Interestingly, given Cottier's exposure to artists in Morris's circle in London and his possible brief involvement with Morris, Marshall, Faulkner & Co., that firm was awarded the commission to glaze the east window, one of their earliest Scottish commissions.[49] Cottier's firm decorated the church and made geometric stained glass for the nave, clerestory and west windows.[50]

In February 1866, while decorating Townhead, Cottier presented a paper to the Glasgow Architectural Society entitled 'Colour the Handmaid of Architecture'. For many years no details of this paper, presented at a crucial point in Cottier's development, were known,[51] but an account of it has now been located in the *Building News* of March 1866. In his lecture, Cottier spoke at some length on painted decoration in ancient Egypt, including the tombs of Thebes where each ceiling, he said, 'reveals a fertility of fancy in pleasant contrast to our plain stamped repeats ... As architectural colourists the Egyptians were great. The happy warmth of their tones affords us food for reflection in our days of crude theories.'[52] He went on to discuss colour in Indian, Chinese, Greek, Roman, Pompeian, Saracenic and Gothic architecture, showing his awareness of the work of Owen Jones, whose seminal design book *The Grammar of Ornament* (1856) contained plates which included illustrations of Greek, Egyptian, Assyrian and Persian ornament, before discussing colour in medieval architecture. In his concluding remarks, Cottier compared Glasgow to Carthage 'in the magnitude of its commercial undertakings' and 'in its keen appreciation of works of genius in art'. He continued: 'The number of thriving artists which that famous city contained seemed something fabulous; even its sculptors could be counted by hundreds. Surely, then, there is in commerce nothing incompatible with art.' Cottier also emphasised the importance of the architect and artist working together:

6 Pulpit in Dowanhill Church (now Cottiers Theatre), Glasgow, designed by William Leiper with painted decoration by Cottier and assistants, 1866

To be a successful worker in colours, implies at the outset a correct eye for tone, form, and proportion, with the faculty to know when to leave off. All these advantages the artist cannot hope to acquire, unless by architectural training he is able to go hand in hand with the architect. Indeed, we wish the artist to be more the architect, and the architect more the artist. All the great works in colour linked to architecture bear on their front this truth, that they are part and parcel of the building, evidently if not painted by the architect, at least by an artist so far imbued with his mind, that the decorations, instead of detracting from the merits of the solid work, goes to produce a sight in true proportion, leading the mind, through the eye, to dwell with satisfaction on the whole as a work of art.[53]

Cottier's description suggests that at Townhead it was necessary for him, as 'an artist', to be fully aware of the architect's intentions in order to realise a decorative scheme in full harmony with a building. While Stevenson's role in the decorative programme of Townhead is not known, Cottier's description suggests that they worked closely together, each relying on the expertise of the other.

Andrew Wells, who assisted Cottier in making the designs for the decoration at Townhead, claimed that Cottier enjoyed shocking sedate church committees, shouting instructions to him in an assumed broad dialect very different from the language he had used in his lecture: '"Andra! Slabber on some broon [brown] there, just beside the wibble-wabble", his name for a wave ornament'.[54] Wells also asserted that Cottier 'laid himself out to be odd and remarkable ... on one occasion he wrote a tender for the painting of a church on the back of a soiled theatre bill.'[55] In the first half of 1866 Cottier and his men decorated the walls and ceilings of the galleried nave, and the organ, supplied by the London firm of Henry Willis, installed at the south end of the west gallery; this was 'lavishly decorated, the prevailing colour being imitation silver.'[56]

On the eve of the church's formal opening in June 1866, the *Glasgow Herald* described the interior and identified it as an example of civic progress and achievement:

The interior of the church is very magnificent. The walls and ceiling are a mass of coloured decoration. From the dark wood work of the pewing, the colouring is toned through bands of ornament up to the airy blue of the ceiling, ornamented with representations of palm leaves and sparkling with stars. This amount of decoration is new on this side of the Tweed, and rare even in England ... The general effect, however, of the decoration is rich, and at the same time solemn and church-like. The blending of the colours is harmonious, and the various patterns show great skill and fertility of invention on the part of the artist. From its splendour and the originality of its design this building is another proof that our own city can hold its own against its neighbours in art as well as mechanical skill.[57]

Reporting on the day, one writer observed that 'many persons were attracted by the report that the decorations of the interior were on a scale of magnificence to be equalled in very few edifices, sacred or secular, in the kingdom.' The writer continued: 'The walls and roof of the interior present a mass of gorgeous ornamentation ... From lining to roof an almost endless variety of design meets the eye, one set being engrafted into another with thorough artistic skill.'[58]

Cottier ran over estimate in Townhead but, as one of his obituarists wrote some twenty-five years later, the architects

befriended him, and in the late Mr Whitelaw and Mr James A. Campbell, who were interested in the church, he found men who were disposed to take a generous view of the case, and so he was enabled to set to work again with a light heart. He finally came out of the contract rather on the wrong side, but then he had decorated a church as it should be decorated.[59]

If this account is accurate, it shows the extent to which Cottier's early patrons had faith in a decorator then only twenty-eight years old and how highly they rated his work. Douglas and Stevenson sent a 'view', presumably a photograph (untraced) of the church interior to the Paris Exposition Universelle in 1867, although this was exhibited under their name, not Cottier's.[60]

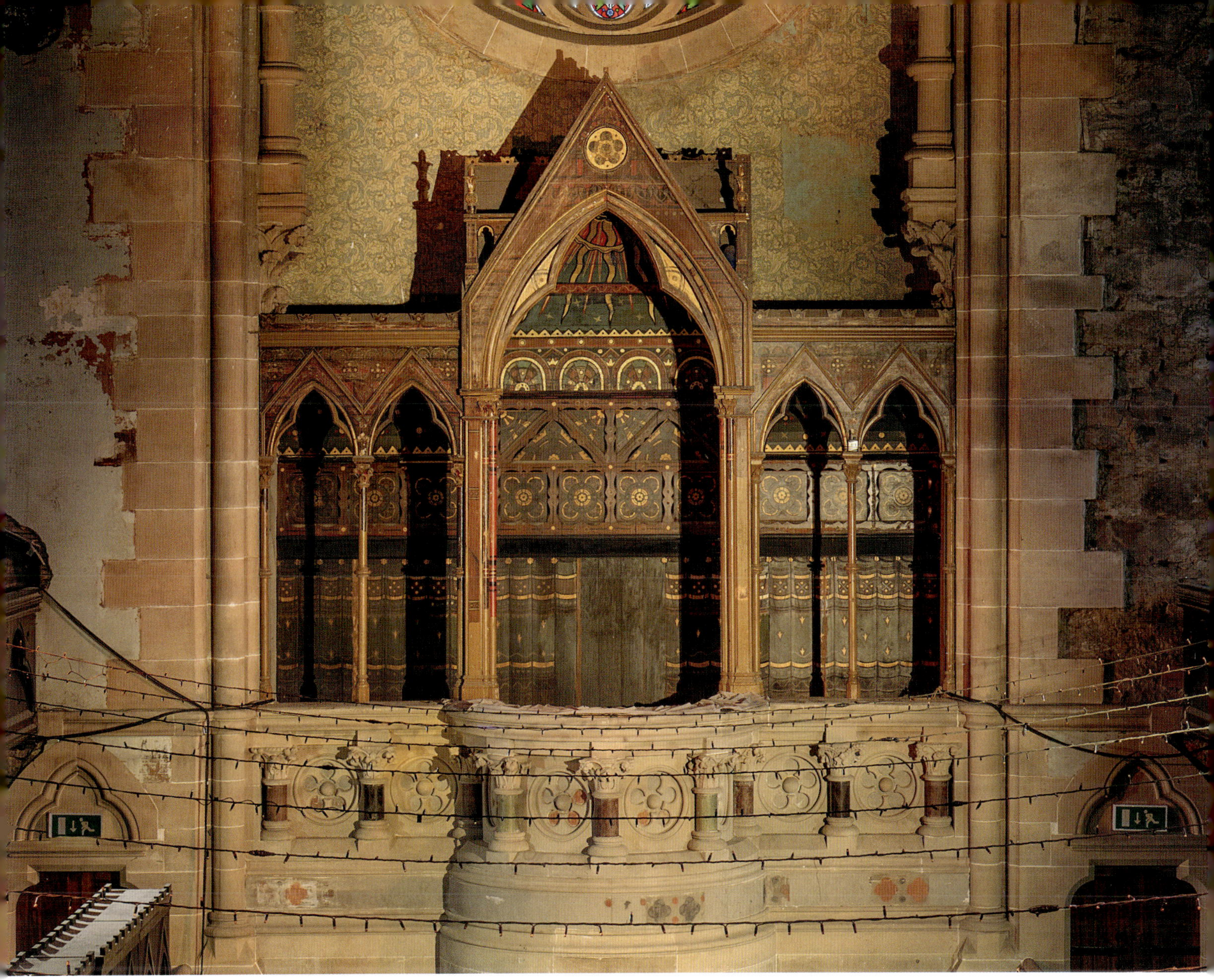

Townhead Parish Church marked a watershed in Cottier's career and two more important Glasgow church interiors followed swiftly. The first of these, at Dowanhill, in Glasgow's West End, survives and is now a theatre. Cottier's decoration and stained glass have undergone extensive restoration since the early 2000s. The church was designed for a United Presbyterian congregation by the young architect William Leiper (1839–1916), an almost exact contemporary of Cottier who was also born in Glasgow.[61] Leiper had trained in London at about the same time as Cottier, around 1861, as an assistant in the offices of the Gothic Revival architects William White and John Loughborough Pearson, then served as an assistant in the Glasgow office of Campbell Douglas & Stevenson while Townhead Parish Church was being designed.

Dowanhill, Leiper's earliest major commission, marked the first of many collaborations between the architect and Cottier over the next three decades.[62] The Gothic Revival decoration they devised, executed in 1866, shows the influence of two leading London-based architects, William Burges and E. W. Godwin, to whose work they had been exposed in London; indeed Leiper, who later studied painting in Paris, was what Burges would have described as an 'art-architect'.[63] The interior's focal point is the theatrical arcaded wooden pulpit canopy (fig. 6), which Cottier's painters embellished with simulated roof tiles. This decoration is comparable with the painted medieval-style furniture designed by Burges from the late 1850s, such as the 'Yatman' cabinet (1858; Victoria and Albert Museum, London), which Cottier and

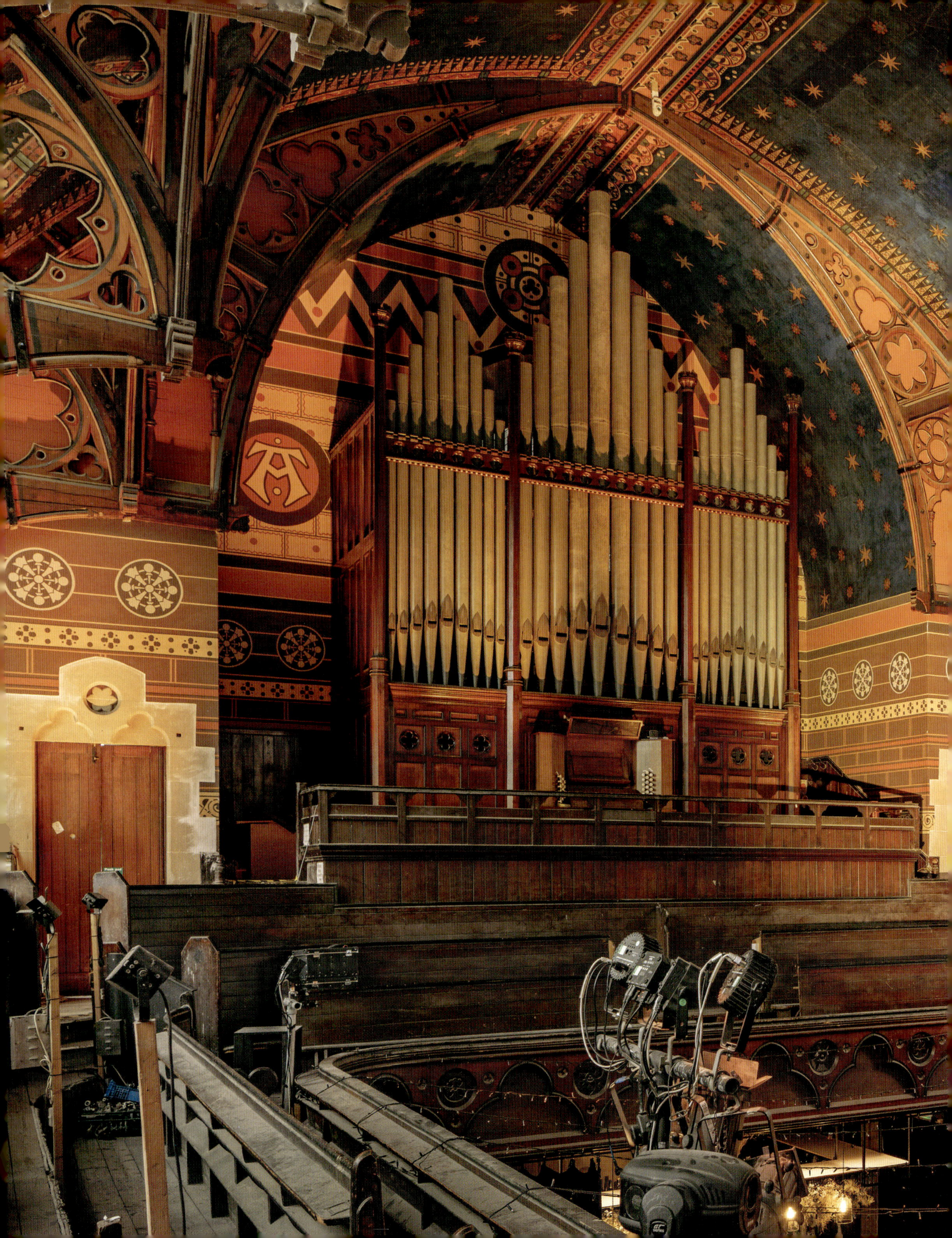

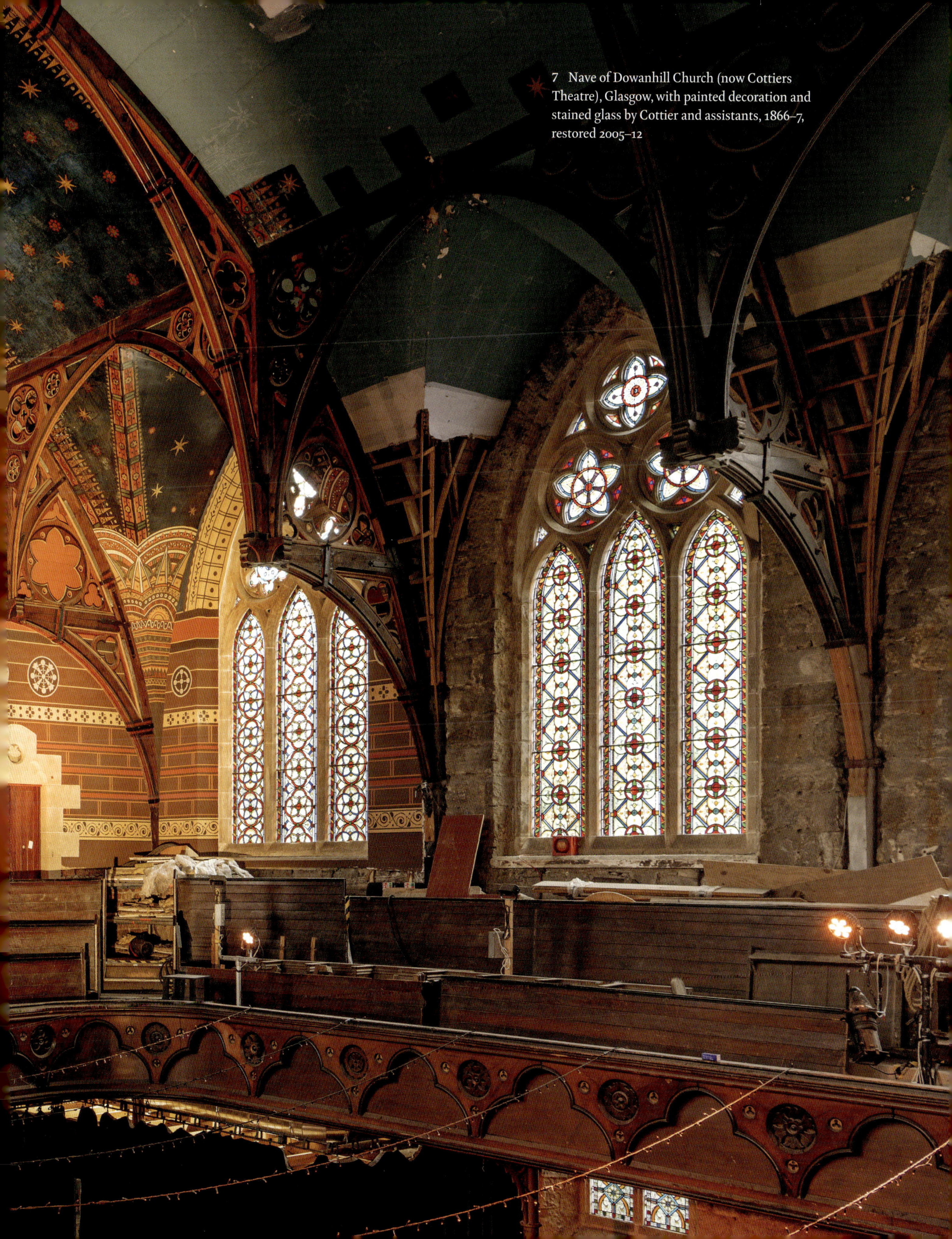

7 Nave of Dowanhill Church (now Cottiers Theatre), Glasgow, with painted decoration and stained glass by Cottier and assistants, 1866–7, restored 2005–12

Leiper may have seen in the Medieval Court of the London International Exhibition in 1862. Likewise, simulated drapes painted on the pulpit panels are strongly reminiscent of some of Godwin's designs for Dromore Castle, Ireland.[64] Cottier also devised vigorous geometric painted decorations for some of the church furniture, which was designed, probably by Leiper, in a muscular Gothic style. These included a painted minister's chair designed for the pulpit, the upholstered back decorated with a 'beautiful piece of crewel work' by Cottier's sister Mary,[65] as well as two collecting dish stands (fig. 8).[66]

Cottier and his assistants decorated the interior walls with simulated stone courses and painted the ceiling deep blue with gold stars (fig. 7). He experimented with different colours and effects while he was working, for, as he had stated in his 1866 lecture when referring to the ancient Egyptians, 'No theory fettered their minds nor stiffened their hands; but as artists they worked till the pleasure and rest they sought for the mind were gained to the eye'.[67] It is no surprise, therefore, that according to a later account: 'One day [the congregation] saw one design and scheme of colour: next day they would find it all washed out. The process of rubbing in and washing out went on for weeks, till some ... began to think ... he was "not all there"'.[68] The ceiling spandrels were filled with boldly coloured and gilded geometric bands and the woodwork was varnished and decorated with black and red stripes.[69] Cottier was paid £397 10s for this work,[70] and a congregation member, the businessman Alexander Kay, contributed a further £300. This paid for the 'mosaic' stained glass in the main body of the church, also made by Cottier, which was executed in a Gothic Revival palette of saturated blues and reds together with vibrant yellow. On the opening of the church, on 11 November 1866, the *Glasgow Herald* praised Cottier's decoration and stained glass:

The whole church is painted throughout after the mediæval manner, and, with the exception of the Townhead Parish Church, is perhaps the only Presbyterian church in Scotland in which painted windows and mural decorations have been carried out as in the old times. The decorations and painted windows have been admirably executed by Mr Cottier, to whom praise is due for the manner in which he has carried out the views of the architect. The aim of the latter has been to build a Presbyterian church which might have some claim to be reckoned artistic.[71]

These church interiors were considered so revolutionary in Scotland that they continued to draw comment for many years. In about 1875 the economist

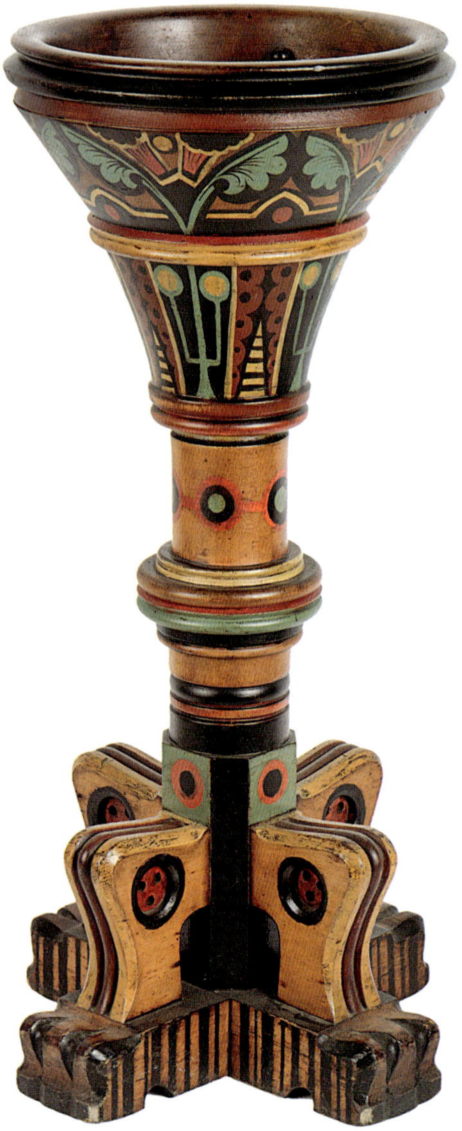

8 Collecting dish stand made for Dowanhill Church, Glasgow, designed by William Leiper with painted decoration by Cottier and assistants, 1866–7. Painted deal, 82.3 × 40.5 cm. Glasgow Museums

James Mavor (1854–1925), then a University of Glasgow undergraduate, 'heard a rumour of the startling character of the decoration' of a Cottier church interior in the city, which he went to see for himself, later recalling:

*Undoubtedly the decoration was startling enough. Great masses of positive colour – red and blue, with figures of dense black – the motive [*sic*] was Egyptian and the design might have found a fitting place in a great hall of one of the Pharaohs. In an ecclesiastical building it was inappropriate; in any building in Western Europe the effect would have been bizarre; the design was out of scale and wanting in the repose indispensable in church architecture and adornment. Nevertheless, the decoration was bold and in its way original. I felt at once here at least is the work of a designer of brains and courage.*[72]

Cottier's third major Glasgow commission was for another United Presbyterian Church, this one at Queen's Park in the south of Glasgow. It was designed by Alexander 'Greek' Thomson (1817–1875) and built in 1867–9 but destroyed by an air raid in 1943. Thomson was one of Scotland's most original and adventurous architect designers whose admirers, besides Cottier and Leiper, included the Glasgow-born designer John Moyr Smith (1839–1912) as well as Bruce Talbert (discussed shortly). Cottier may have known Thomson's work since his teens, for he had probably been apprenticed to Cairney, who worked for Thomson.[73] Thomson was a founding member of the Glasgow Architectural Society, instituted in 1858, which admitted associates who were 'members of all trades and professions connected with building operations'.[74] Cottier became a member at the Annual General Meeting in October 1865 and three years later was elected a councillor.[75] He and Thomson increasingly came into contact through the Society. At a meeting in May 1866 Thomson spoke about Glasgow's new university building, questioning the suitability of its Gothic Revival style and the choice of a non-Glaswegian architect (the English architect George Gilbert Scott). Cottier – together with Leiper, Campbell Douglas and Honeyman – participated in the 'animated discussion' that followed.[76]

As his sobriquet suggests, Thomson believed that a modern architecture could be based on the style of the ancient Greeks, although he also drew inspiration from Egyptian, Hindu and Assyrian design, as at Holmwood House (1857–9; fig. 10), the picturesque Neo-Greek villa designed for a paper manufacturer, James Couper, in Cathcart, Glasgow. Thomson drew on these influences in the design of his most remarkable church, Queen's Park, a temple-like structure crowned by an elongated dome. In an address to the Architectural Section of the Glasgow Philosophical Society in 1888, Thomson's friend the architect Thomas Gildard described the church's 'polychromatic decoration':

This decoration is rich and brilliant – it decorates surfaces, but in nowise disturbs an architecture that is independent of it. When it is said that it is from the pencil of Thomson himself, the severity, the delicacy, the power, the grace – in a word, the beauty and the appropriateness of the lines may be readily conjectured. In the colours, or rather in the harmonising of some of the tones, he had the assistance, frankly acknowledged, of the contractor, Mr. Cottier, now of London. The scheme of this decoration is as unique, as original, as is what is purely the architecture. Throughout the church there is not even one cubic inch of plaster, and the natural colour of the wood – yellow pine – contributes its tone towards the general harmony.[77]

Monochrome photographs (fig. 11) give some indication of the motifs 'from the pencil of Thomson himself', according to Gildard. A surviving watercolour of Queen's Park Church (fig. 9) reveals 'the harmonising of some of the tones' for which Cottier was responsible.

Ford Madox Brown visited Queen's Park Church in 1883. In a lecture delivered at Victoria Hall at the invitation of the Glasgow Sunday Society, Brown, who 'with a feeling of pride, claimed Mr Cottier ... as a pupil',[78] described the decoration at the church in glowing terms: 'Cottier as a colourist has a range of performance beyond that of any other modern artist. Here line and colouring are suggestive of paradise itself. I now know what has all along been wrong with my ceilings. Well done, Glasgow! I put ... this Thomson-Cottier church above everything I have seen

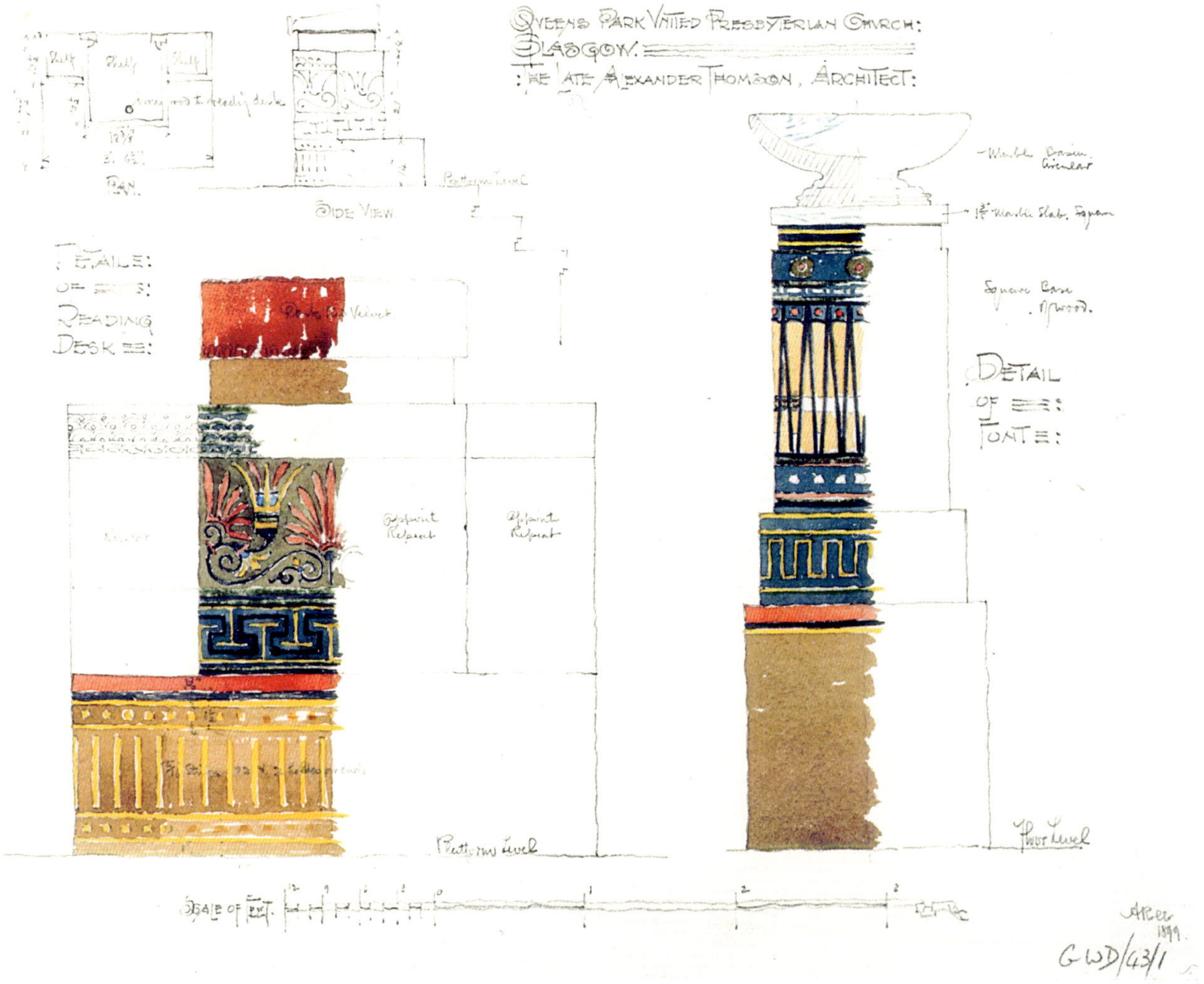
QUEENS PARK UNITED PRESBYTERIAN CHURCH:
GLASGOW:
:THE LATE ALEXANDER THOMSON, ARCHITECT:
PLAN.
SIDE VIEW
DETAILE: OF: READING DESK:
DETAIL OF: FONTE:
Marble Basin. Circular
Marble Slab. Square
Square Base
Platform Level
Floor Level
SCALE OF FEET.
GWD/43/1

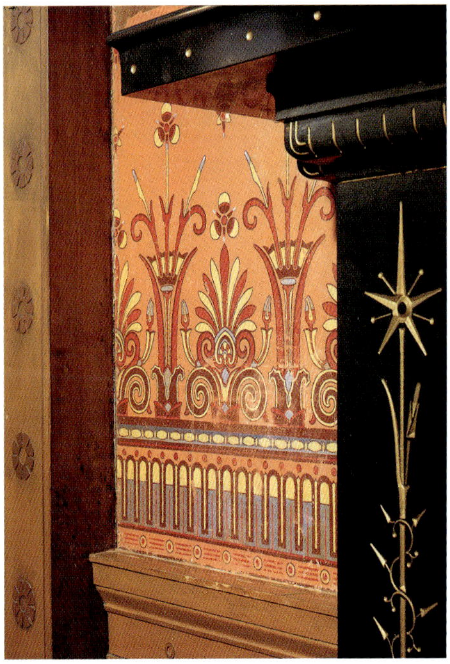

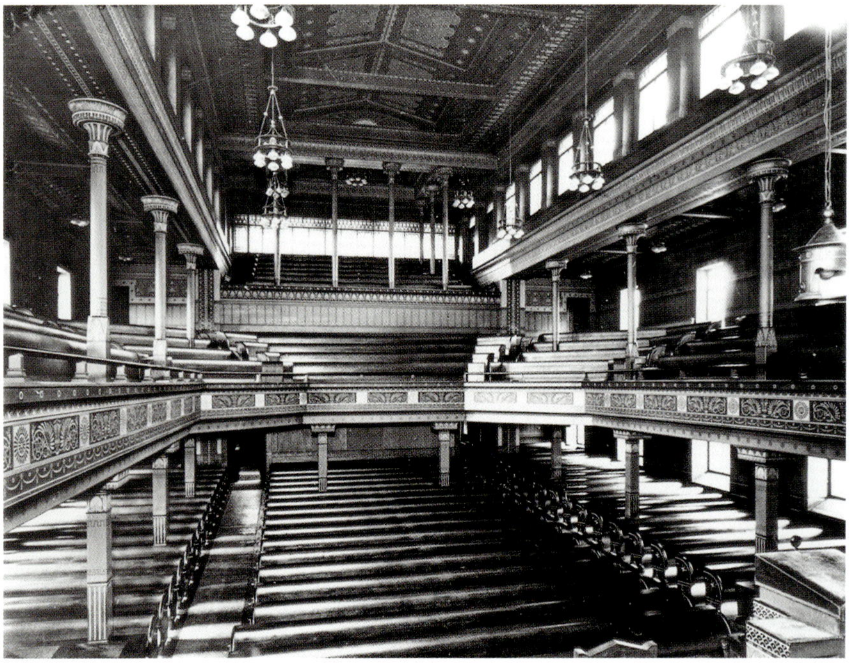

9 Andrew Rollo, *Reading Desk and Font*, 1899, for Queen's Park Church, Glasgow. Pencil and watercolour on paper, 24 × 33 cm. Historic Environment Scotland

10 Wall decoration in the dining room of Holmwood House, Cathcart, Glasgow, designed by Alexander Thomson, 1857–9. Painted plaster

11 Interior of Queen's Park Church, Glasgow (destroyed 1943), decorated by Cottier and assistants, 1867–9. Photograph *c.*1900. Historic Environment Scotland

12 *Deborah*, window made for Glasgow Cathedral (removed), designed by Franz Fries and made by the Royal Stained Glass Manufactory, Munich, 1861. Stained glass, 161.5 × 69.5 cm. Historic Environment Scotland

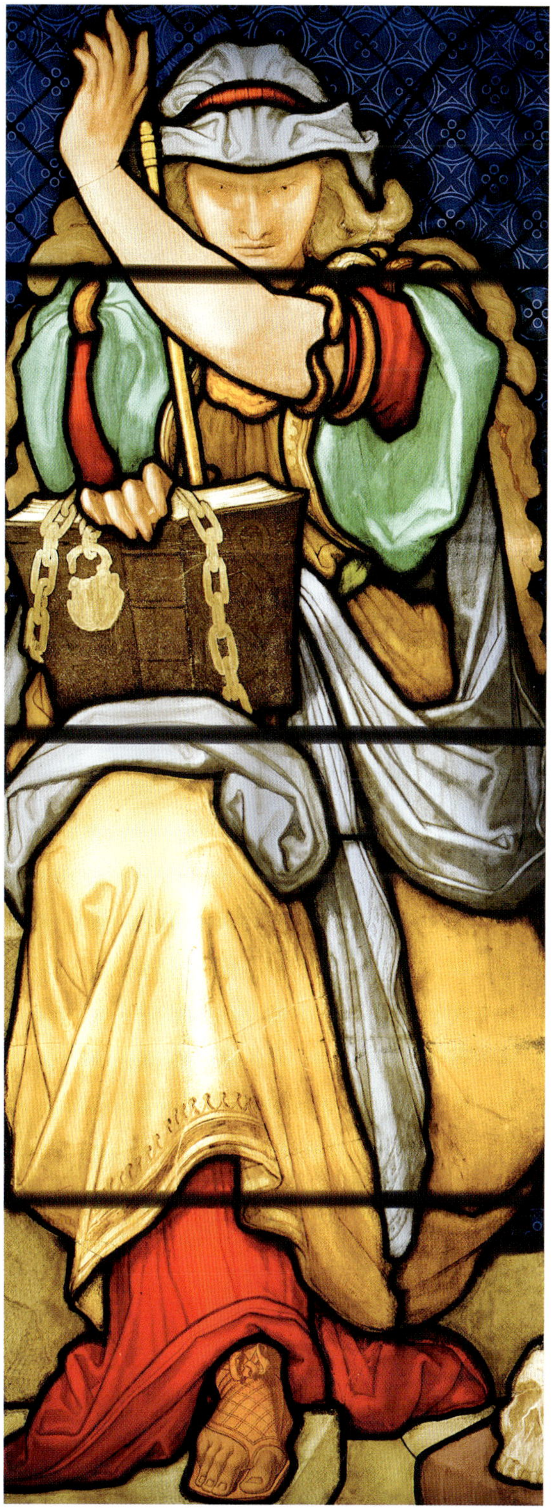

in modern Europe.'[79] Although surviving evidence of the decoration at Queen's Park is scarce, if Gildard's description of the relationship between Thomson and Cottier is reliable, it suggests that their collaboration was mutually beneficial. Thomson was able to draw on Cottier's sophisticated understanding of colour, while Cottier could study at first hand Thomson's ornamental language. It was this visual language which Cottier developed in his own domestic interior decoration and furniture from the late 1860s.

DEVELOPMENT OF COTTIER'S STAINED GLASS

By 1866 Cottier's many commissions in and around Glasgow led to his establishing 'works' at 47 Carrick Street, the street where Cottier had lived as an infant.[80] Daniel and Marion set up home in Glasgow and began a family there although he retained his Edinburgh 'studio'. During this period, he continued to formulate his ideas about stained glass with the goal of developing his own style. In March 1867, he set out his agenda in a paper, 'The Painted Windows of Glasgow Cathedral', delivered at a general meeting of the Society of Arts held at the Architectural Institute of Scotland in George Street, near his Edinburgh studio. Known only second-hand through newspapers and journals, Cottier's lecture included a description of the history of stained glass in different countries, outlining 'the modes adapted by artists both in Britain and on the Continent';[81] however, its main purpose was to denounce the stained glass made for Glasgow Cathedral. Controversially, this large and prestigious commission had been awarded to the Bavarian Königliche Glasmalereianstalt (Royal Stained Glass Manufactory) in Munich (fig. 12), much to the chagrin of British stained-glass makers. The pictorial treatment of the subjects was widely criticised but it was the palette of the windows that chiefly offended Cottier, as one Scottish newspaper correspondent reported:

Mr Cottier criticised in very unfavourable terms the specimens of German glass painting in the Cathedral in Glasgow, remarking that the sacred walls of the Cathedral resembled more a dyer's bleaching green than a sacred

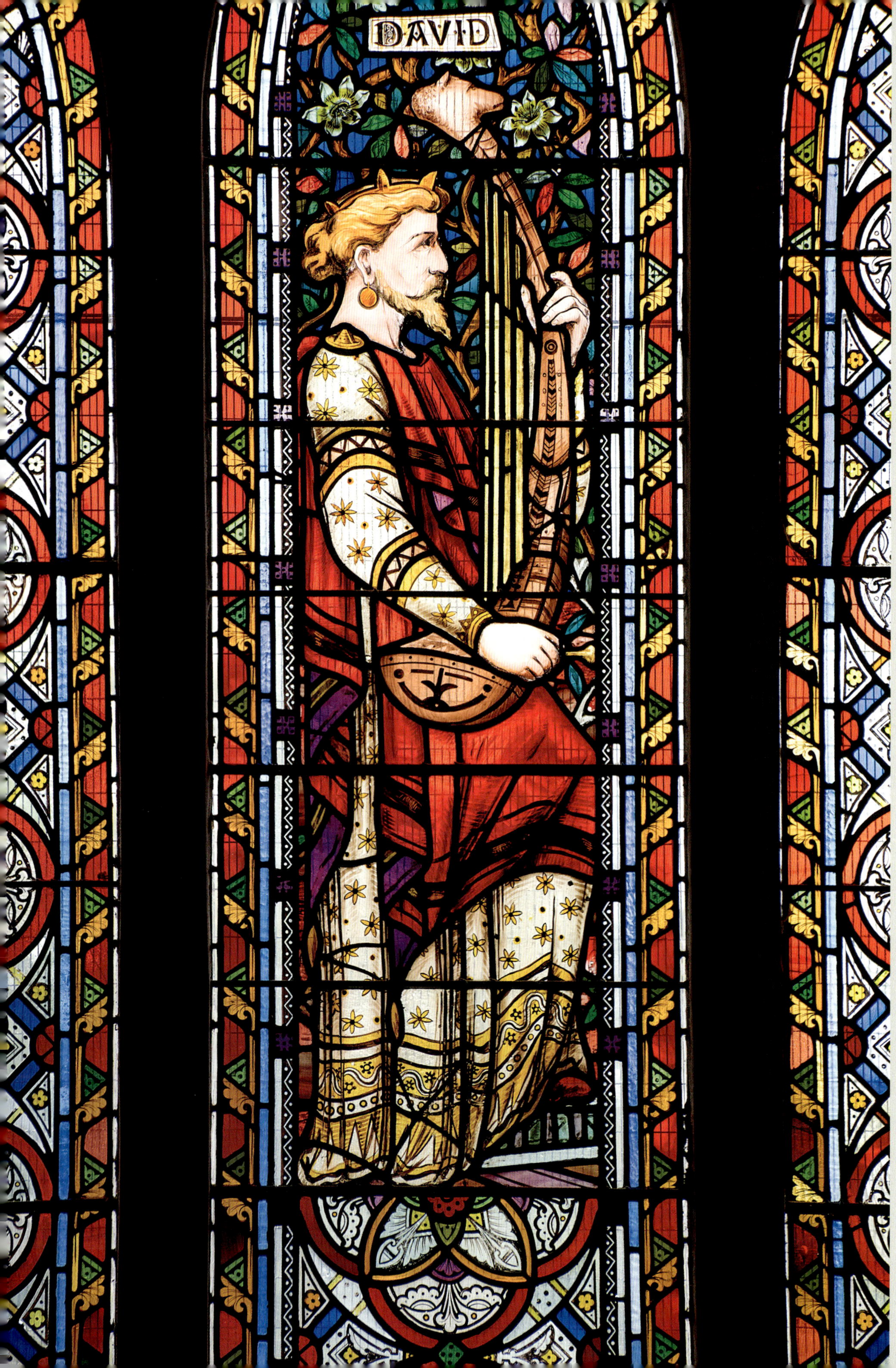
DAVID

13 *David* in Dowanhill Church (now Cottiers Theatre), Glasgow, designed and made by Cottier, Edinburgh and Glasgow, 1867. Stained glass

14 *Miriam* in Dowanhill Church (now Cottiers Theatre), Glasgow, designed and made by Cottier, Edinburgh and Glasgow, 1867. Stained glass

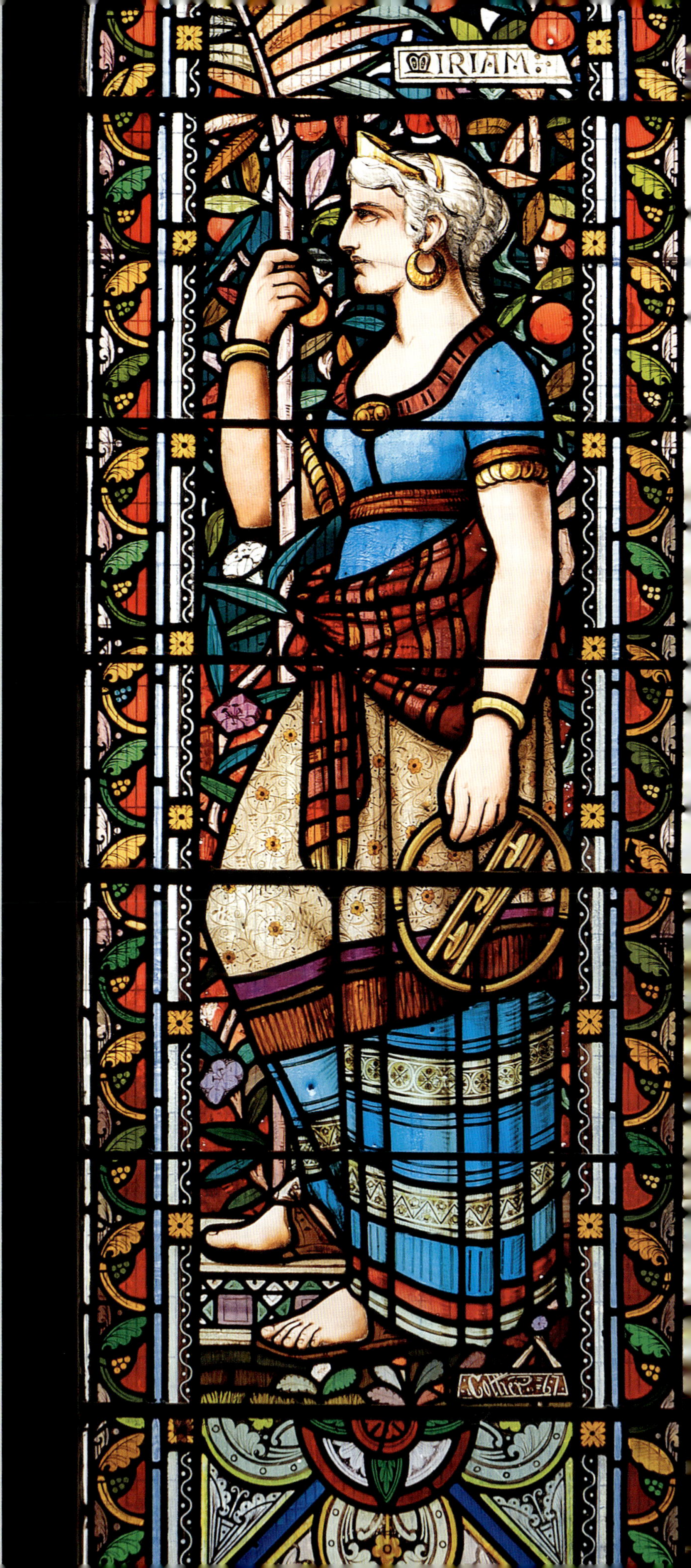

15 *Rembrandt*, made for the dining room of Seaton Cottage, Bridge of Don (removed) by Cottier, Edinburgh and Glasgow, *c.*1867. Stained glass, 27.3 × 25.7 cm. Private collection

16 *Emily*, made for the drawing room of Seaton Cottage, Bridge of Don (removed) by Cottier, Edinburgh and Glasgow, *c.*1867. Stained glass, 27.5 × 25.8 cm. Private collection

edifice ... The colouring of the windows, he maintained, was too bright and glaring, and the interior effect was harsh and crude. While they were thus faulty in colouring, they were also devoid of sentiment and even without any design and except in the large windows, on which the prophets were represented, there was a lack of feeling in them all. He admitted that they were the best windows that had come out of Germany; and, in concluding his paper, he gave it as his opinion that England would yet have a school of glass painting immensely superior to that in Germany.[82]

While some present thought that Cottier 'had been rather too severe in his criticisms of the German windows ... everyone agrees they were not in harmony with the Cathedral.'[83] Not everyone did agree, however, for 'A Scottish Artist' who read an account of the lecture in *The Scotsman* wrote to the paper describing Cottier's comments as 'grossly disrespectful' to the designers of the windows, who were 'members of some of the most distinguished European Academies'.[84] A report of the lecture also appeared in the *Building News*,[85] causing it to create further ripples as far as Berlin, where extracts were published in April 1867. There, the commentator asserted that just as the German military might make the French jealous, 'so does our superiority in the area of art now appear to be perceived as uncomfortable in England'. Cottier's 'unjustifiable attacks on Munich artworks' made him 'a harsh critic of the well-known beautifully painted windows in the Cathedral of Glasgow'.[86] Most of the windows were replaced in the mid-twentieth century.

Cottier's lecture came at a time when his stained-glass studio was expanding its purview, apace with the latest developments in British glass. The influence of Morris and his circle can be seen in the figural panels Cottier was commissioned to make for Dowanhill Church, to replace some of the patterned glass he had originally installed. In the rose window above the pulpit he inserted the heads of six male Old Testament prophets, in the panels at the top of the windows under the galleries he placed six female biblical heads, clearly inspired by depictions of women by artists of the Pre-Raphaelite circle, particularly Rossetti.

The most ambitious panels, originally located in two south gallery windows, were commissioned by 'the Elders, Managers and Trustees' of the church for about £40 and depict life-size figures of *David* and *Miriam* (figs 13 and 14),[87] early examples of Cottier's predilection for statuesque figures.[88] Like Thomson, with whom he was working at Queen's Park, Cottier was drawn to the severe archaism of Assyrian art. *David* and *Miriam* embody Cottier's attempt to create a new archaising style appropriate to a United Presbyterian setting, by depicting details such as musical instruments, jewellery and dress in accordance with current ideas in fine art. The depiction of biblical figures and scenes in a historically accurate way became a preoccupation with many mid-nineteenth-century artists, particularly Brown, who encouraged taking details of Assyrian and Egyptian sources when portraying biblical subjects.[89] Cottier would have been familiar with Assyrian and Egyptian artefacts in the British Museum and from published sources, such as Sir John Gardner Wilkinson's *Manners and Customs of the Ancient Egyptians* (1837), a publication to which Thomson referred, as well as publications on Assyrian art by (Sir) Austen Henry Layard.[90] *David* and *Miriam* also show the development of Cottier's stained-glass palette, with the saturated reds, blues and greens associated with the Gothic Revival being offset with deep reds, violets and other tertiary colours. These colours combine in the backgrounds of the figures, which consist of densely arranged leaves and fruits that create a lively and visually stimulating setting for the figures and appear to push them further out towards the spectator. The windows recall some of the contemporary work of the London firms of Heaton, Butler & Bayne and Lavers & Barraud, with whose work Cottier was probably familiar.[91]

While Cottier was designing ecclesiastical windows, he was also exploring the market for secular glass. His first international exhibit as an independent designer, at the Paris Exposition Universelle in 1867,[92] was an armorial window in Renaissance Revival style (whereabouts unknown), meant to show off the kind of designs he could produce for public or domestic buildings. The British glass painter Francis Kirchhoff praised what

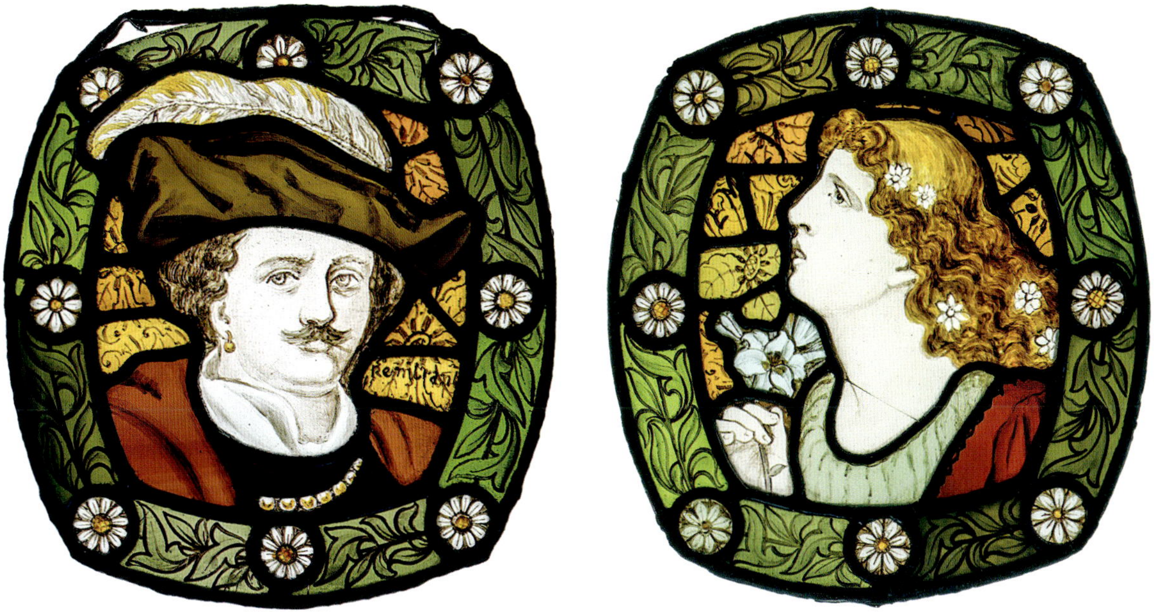

he described as 'a magnificent ornamental window, in the renaissance style: in the centre, arms on a fanciful shield; splendid design; ornament free and graceful; well-proportioned columns, with a richly-decorated pediment at top, surrounded with cupids; superb harmony of colours. This window, in my estimation, is the finest ornamental window in the Exhibition.'[93] The *Glasgow Evening Post* reported: 'We are glad to learn that Mr Cottier, a fellow-townsman, who is favourably known in connection with the decoration of some of our recently built and finest churches, has received an award from the French capital for the excellence of his stained glass windows in the great Paris Exhibition.'[94] The publicity generated by Cottier's church decoration and stained glass, and his award at an international exhibition, must have helped him obtain new commissions.

The businessman and collector John Forbes White (1831–1904) apparently first became interested in art shortly after his marriage in 1859, when he stayed at a friend's house which Cottier had recently decorated.[95] White became one of Cottier's early patrons and helped to shape his career. His income derived from the Aberdeen flour milling business established by his father and in the late 1860s he commissioned Cottier to design and execute painted decoration and stained glass for Seaton Cottage (now called Glenseaton Lodge), just north of Aberdeen's old town. Although little remains of Cottier's scheme, some has survived or is known from descriptions and photographs.[96]

Cottier glazed the front door of Seaton Cottage with quarries – small square panes of glass popularised by Morris – containing the initials of John White and his wife Williamina (Ina), some of which survive and have been reinstated.[97] The quarries were painted with a silver compound known as 'silver stain' before being fired, which created a range of colours varying from pale yellow to deep orange. In the drawing room, a space often given a more feminine character, the windows of the bay were filled with quarries, with inset roundels containing the heads of eight female literary characters, including Helen of Troy and Emily (fig. 16).[98] In the adjoining dining room, by convention a more masculine space, the bay window was filled with amber- and yellow-painted quarries with borders of green glass decorated with stylised flowers. In the upper sections of these windows were panels containing portraits of painters including Raphael and Leonardo da Vinci, the glass painter Dirk Crabeth and the ceramicists Luca della Robbia and Bernard Palissy; a side window contained panels depicting Zeuxis, Benvenuto Cellini and Rembrandt (fig. 15).[99] Cottier's domestic stained-glass style was influenced by that of Morris & Co., which, as noted earlier, he may have seen at two exhibitions in London, in 1862 and 1864. The friendship between Cottier and White also influenced the development of the decorative scheme of Seaton Cottage. Its iconographic programme in the stained-glass roundels, for example, was probably informed by White's artistic and classical education and became a staple of Cottier's repertoire. White also commissioned Cottier to make furniture for him.[100]

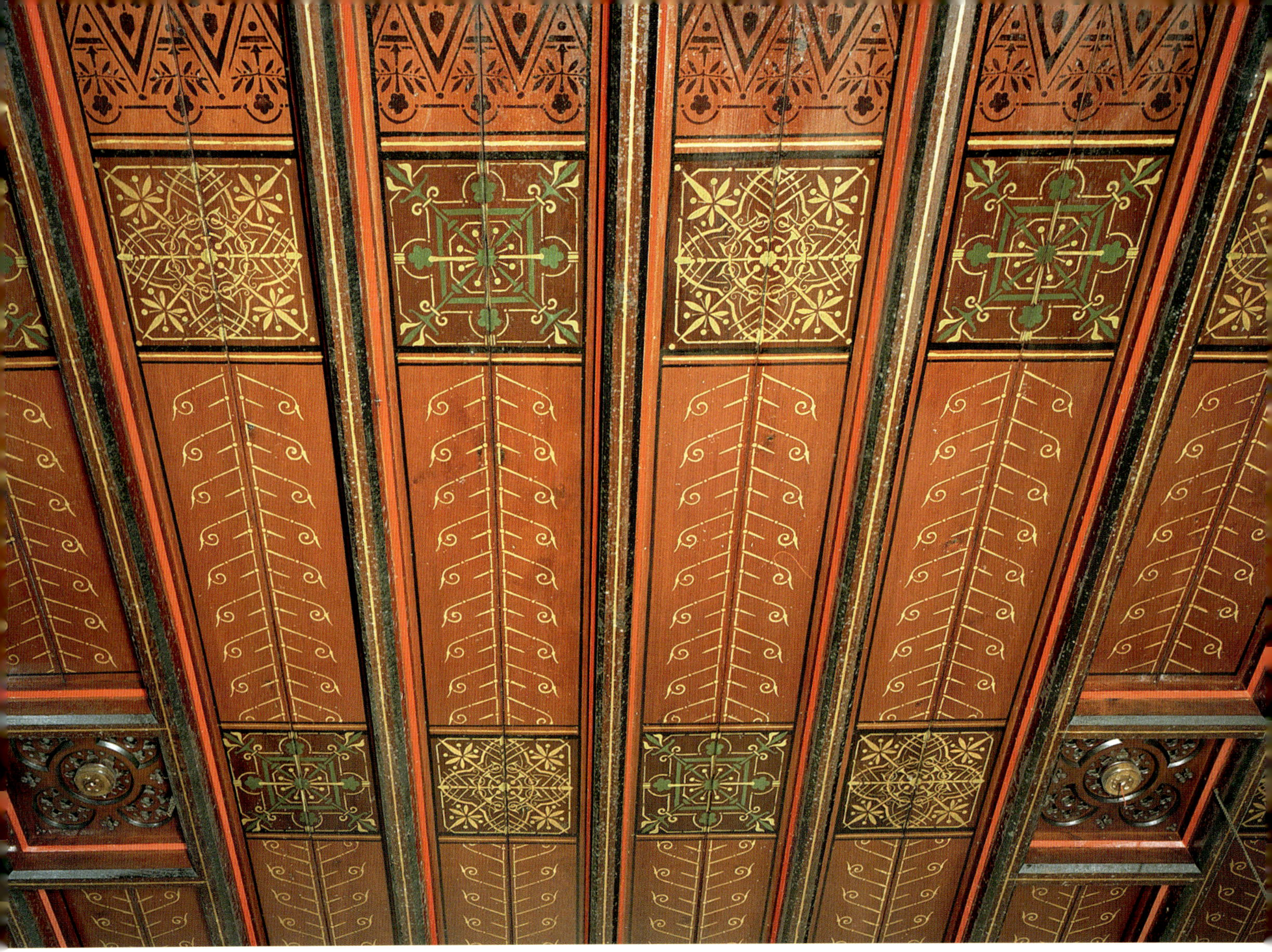

INTERIOR DECORATION

White allowed Cottier a degree of freedom to experiment, holding his tongue when, as he admitted years later, 'seeing Cottier, with a pot of paint and a stencil, putting the colours on the wall, and thinking how terrible they were'.[101] Some of Cottier's painted decoration in the drawing room has been uncovered – bands of olive green and stencilled patterning; the shallow plaster barrel-vaulted ceiling of the room, which has been replaced, was originally decorated with gold stars on a pale blue background.[102] The wooden dining-room ceiling bears the carved and gilded date 1867, the year that Cottier also began painting the timber ceiling of the south aisle of nearby St Machar's Cathedral with medieval-style decoration (which survives).[103] Cottier was also working with Thomson at Queen's Park Church in 1867, and at Seaton Cottage surviving painted decorations on window frames and a door show a blend of classical motifs executed in rich colours, hinting at what the painted woodwork at Queen's Park would have looked like. The painted motifs at Seaton Cottage are comparable with illustrations published by a protégé of Owen Jones, the industrial designer Christopher Dresser (1834–1904). Like Cottier, Dresser was born in Glasgow but spent most of his career in London.

The surviving decoration at Seaton Cottage also shows that Thomson was a formative influence on Cottier's early domestic interior decoration. While Cottier was decorating Seaton Cottage, he was not only working with Thomson on Queen's Park but may also have been employed to refresh some of the decoration designed by Thomson for Holmwood.[104] Likewise, in the late 1860s Cottier was involved in decorating some of the houses of Great Western Terrace in Glasgow, designed by Thomson.[105] This possibly included supplying enamelled brass hardware for the doors (some remaining *in situ*). The metalwork,

17 Stencilled ceiling decoration in the drawing room of the Elms, Arbroath, Angus, designed by Cottier, *c.*1868

18 Stencilled wall decoration in the drawing room of the Elms, Arbroath, Angus, designed by Cottier, *c.*1868

which Cottier may have designed, has marked similarities with the work of another designer, Bruce James Talbert (1838–1881). Born in Dundee, Talbert trained as an architect, joining Campbell Douglas and Stevenson by 1860, although he had left Scotland by 1863. Talbert's later career in London as a leading designer, particularly of 'Art' furniture but also wallpaper and textiles, in many ways overlapped with that of Cottier.[106]

The house decorating side of Cottier's business encompassed all the fashionable styles, from medieval to French classical (see fig. 5), and many commissions for decoration and stained glass in the late 1860s came via the architects for whom he had decorated churches in Glasgow, particularly William Leiper.[107]

Leiper continued to commission glass and decoration for houses and churches from Cottier throughout the 1870s and 80s (discussed in Chapter Two). Among these commissions was the Elms, Arbroath, for David Corsar, the owner of a local textile mill. In 1868 Cottier decorated the interior walls and ceilings with stencils (figs 17 and 18), which relate to several designs published by Dresser in his *Art of Decorative Design* (1862). Cottier also made stained glass for the house, including monogrammed panels, portraits, birds and genre scenes (fig. 20) including one depicting a group in Georgian dress with a lady playing an organ (fig. 19).[108] The last is unsurprising given Cottier's increasing friendship with J. J. Stevenson, who was about to pioneer the Queen Anne style in London.

Stevenson's father had founded a chemical works on the banks of the Tyne at Jarrow and he had many relations and contacts in the north-east of England. Cottier's professional relationship with Stevenson proved fruitful, playing a large part in his inroads into northern England.[109] Cottier made windows for Westoe Hall, County Durham, an idiosyncratic red-brick Gothic Revival house which J. J. Stevenson had designed in 1864 for his brother, James Cochran Stevenson MP; Cottier used glass quarries supplied by the London firm of James Powell & Sons of Whitefriars in 1867.[110] The following year Matthew Liddell, a Roman Catholic colliery owner, commissioned Cottier to supply stained glass for his house, Prudhoe Hall, in Northumberland.[111] Cottier also decorated the Mechanic's Institution of South Shields (from 1876, South Shields Museum), which was opened on 2 April 1869 with a lavish ball thrown by the mayor and mayoress and attended by Stevenson's brother James and his wife and several other relatives. The *Newcastle Courant* reported that 'The decorations had been got up regardless of expense. For some time past, at the Mayor's own expense, Mr Cottier, painter, of Glasgow, and a number of his men, have been engaged painting almost every room in the building, in order that everything in connection with the decorations might harmonize.' The *Shields Daily Gazette* described how the ceiling was 'painted in sky-blue, and spangled all over with gold and silver stars; the

19 Window with a group in eighteenth-century dress, made for the Elms, Arbroath, Angus (removed), by Cottier, Edinburgh and Glasgow, *c.*1868. Stained glass. Whereabouts unknown

20 Window with a medieval scene, made for the Elms, Arbroath, Angus (removed) by Cottier, Edinburgh and Glasgow, 1868. Stained glass. Whereabouts unknown

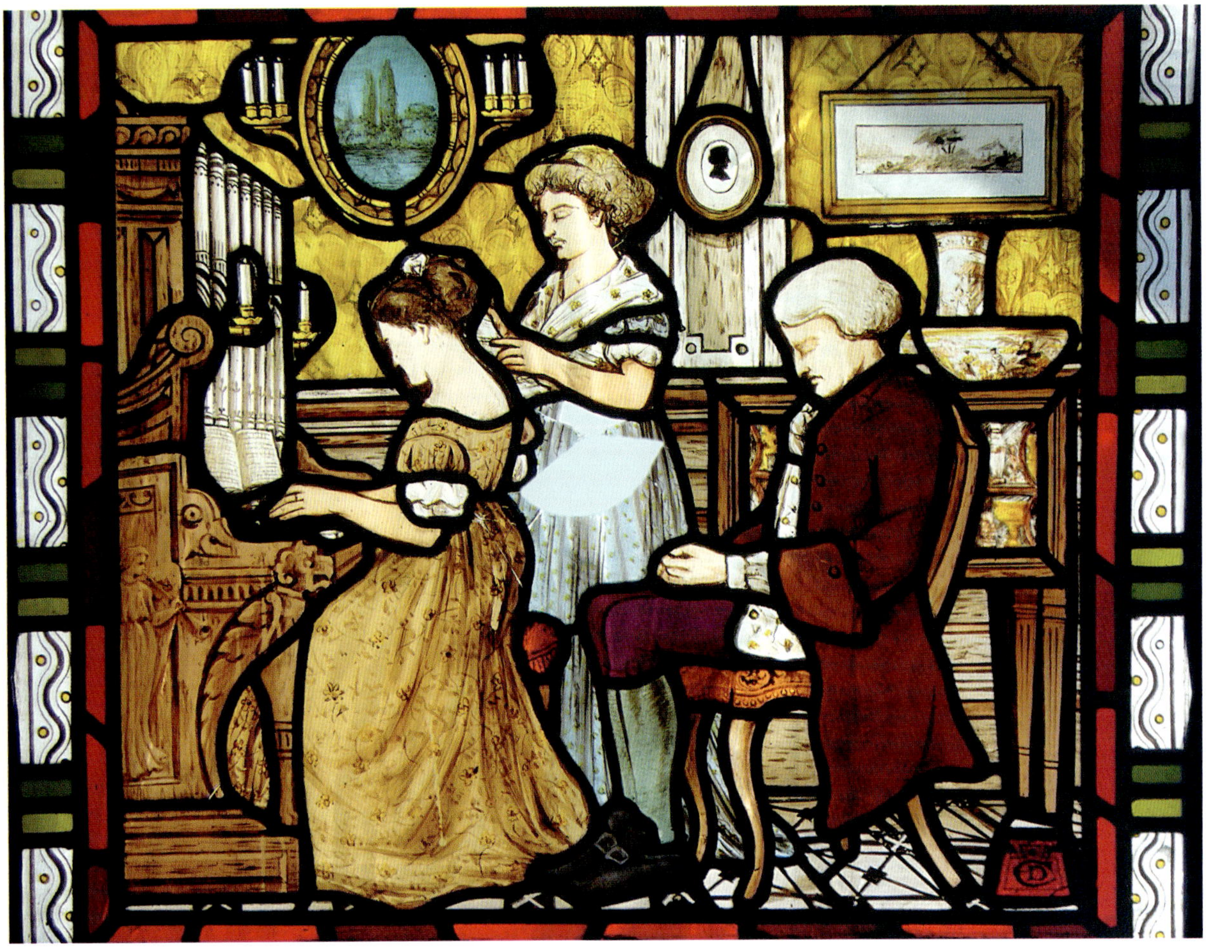

walls had been tastefully coloured, and figured, giving the room an effective appearance, and, indeed, last night, when all was brilliantly lighted up with the hundreds of additional burners, which had been fitted up for the occasion, the hall looked beautiful, especially from the gallery.'[112]

Cottier undertook some more unusual decorating commissions in Scotland in the 1860s. Shortly after the inauguration of Dowanhill Church, in 1866, the *Glasgow Herald* announced the opening of a remarkable, if ephemeral, interior in Glasgow. This was in the City Hall, where a bazaar was being held in aid of the Convalescent Fever Home and Sick Children's Hospital: 'The hall has been fitted up for the occasion in accordance

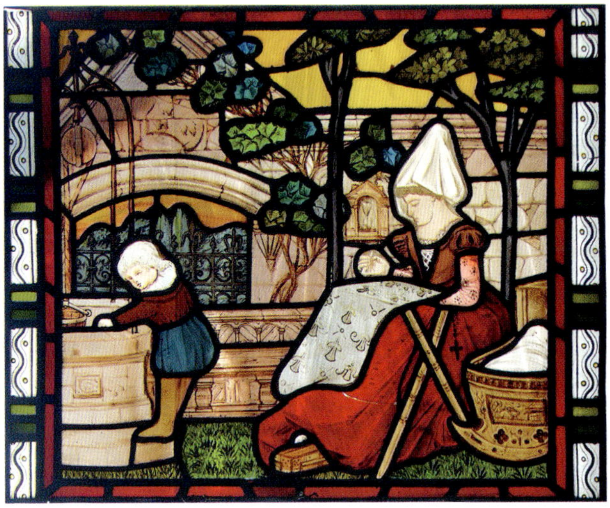

21 Coats Fountain, Fountain Gardens, Paisley, Renfrewshire, made by George Smith & Co., Glasgow, painted by Cottier and assistants, 1868, restored 2013–14

with a design prepared by Mr Cottier. The style of decoration is Byzantine, and, judging by what we saw yesterday, while the arrangements were yet incomplete, visitors have in store for them a spectacle of Oriental magnificence.'[113] Another project, near Glasgow, was the painted and gilded decoration of a new fountain erected in Paisley (fig. 21). Described as 'Franco-Italian', the cast-iron structure, twenty-eight feet high, was designed and made at the Glasgow foundry of George Smith & Co., an astonishing concoction of putti, dolphins, herons, walruses and aquatic plants, which a local paper described, accurately, as 'unequalled in this country, and probably in the world.'[114] The fountain formed the centrepiece of Fountain Gardens, which were opened in 1868 with great fanfare, on a special public holiday. In his speech the donor of the gardens, the thread manufacturer Thomas Coats (1809–1883), expressed his indebtedness to contractors including 'Mr Cottier, who decorated the fountain'.[115]

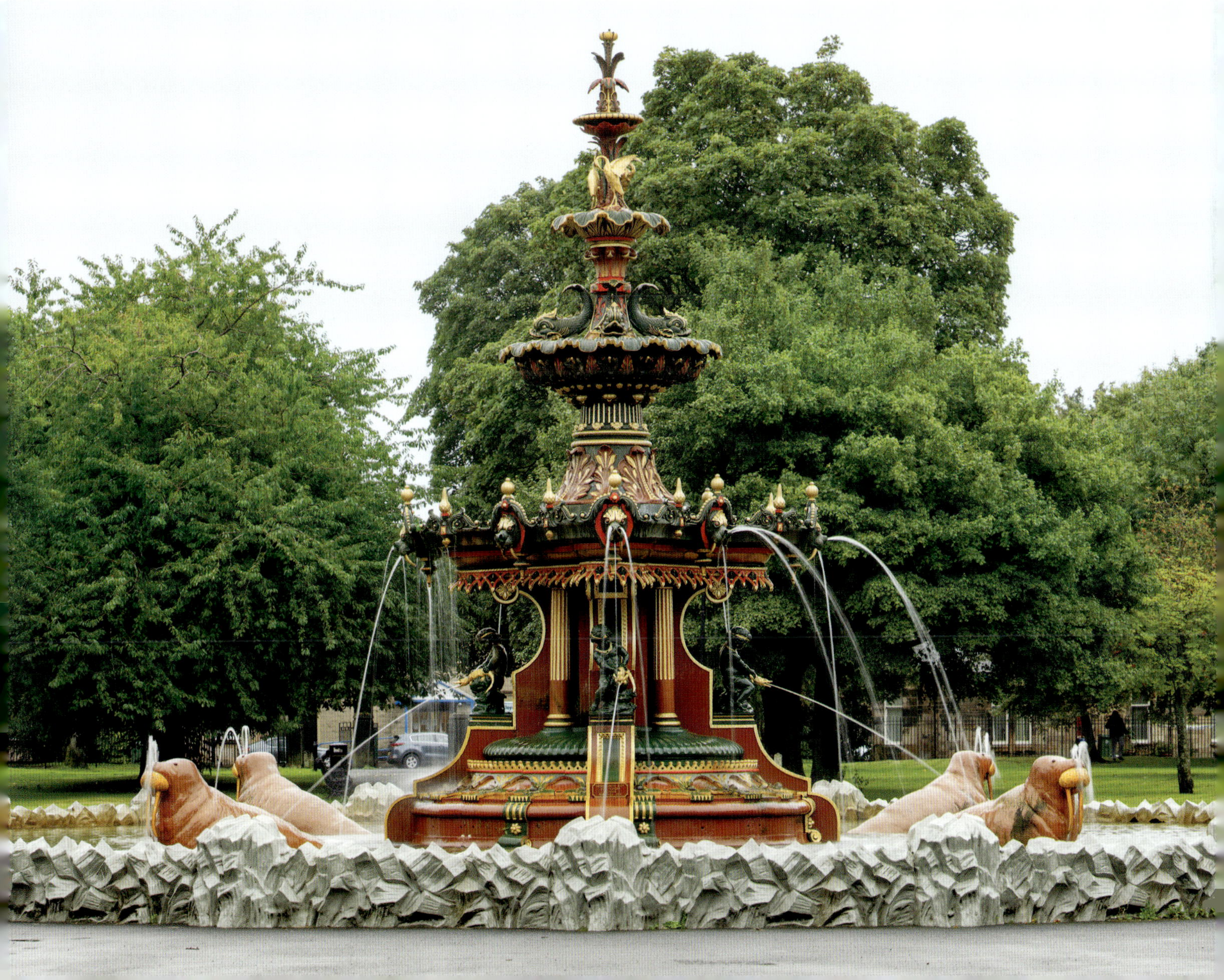

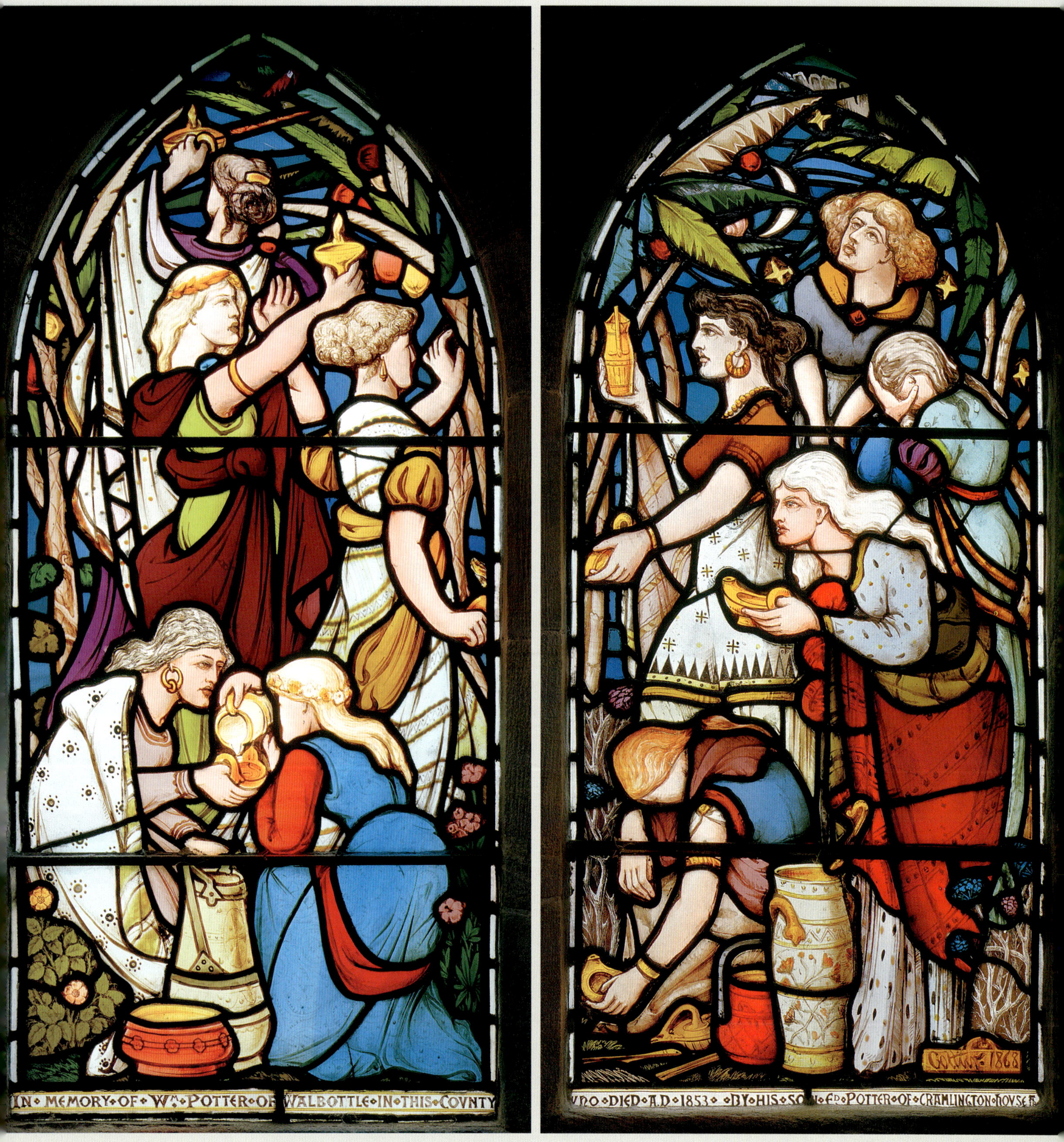

22 *The Wise and Foolish Virgins*, designed by Cottier, 1868. Church of St Nicholas, Cramlington, Northumberland. Stained glass

STAINED GLASS AND DECORATION FOR CHURCHES IN THE LATE 1860S

Following the publicity that his Glasgow churches attracted, Cottier received a number of commissions, many as the result of his friendships with White and Stevenson in Aberdeenshire and the north-east of England. In that part of England, Cottier was considered 'an artist whose decorative works are well and deservedly known', and in 1868 he was chosen to decorate the walls of St Andrew's, Bishop Auckland 'with some simple ornamentation, which might embrace the introduction of texts and inscriptions'.[116] In the same year, Cottier designed two striking lancets for the south aisle of the Church of St Nicholas, Cramlington, representing the parable of the Wise and Foolish Virgins (fig. 22).[117] Proudly signed and dated, these remarkable windows are in Cottier's trademark style, indebted to Rossetti,[118] while at the same time showing the archaism of the *David* and *Miriam* figures at Dowanhill – one of the figures in the right-hand window, in profile, is similar to Miriam. The colours, including vivid ruby and turquoise, are also similar to the Dowanhill windows. It is not surprising that the Cramlington windows were met with enthusiasm. A journalist writing for the *Newcastle Courant* thought that they 'appear to the greatest advantage, both in colour and drawing. They represent the parable of the wise and foolish virgins, and the story is well told, without any more of pictorial character than can properly be attempted in stained glass', and that they 'cannot fail to arrest the attention of the observer ... For artistic design and finished execution this window is perhaps the finest in the church.'[119] This was a significant claim, because other glass in the church was by the established workshops of William Wailes and Clayton & Bell. In addition to the nave window, the correspondent noted that Cottier presented a clerestory window, depicting the Prophet Jeremiah.

In Aberdeenshire, Cottier often worked in collaboration with the local architect James Matthews (1819–1898), the designer of the West Free Church in Aberdeen, which opened in January 1869. The building was later deconsecrated and became a casino and restaurant but Cottier's stained glass and ceiling decoration are well preserved. The nave ceiling is stained timber; when the church opened it was described as having 'gold and coloured ornaments studded over the surface, and the ribs ornamented with colour'.[120] The stained glass in the aisles consists of quarries with narrow borders of brown and green glass. Above the place where the pulpit once stood is a large and impressive rose window, made of 'Powell's patent glass' and described as 'particularly rich and beautiful, both in design and colour'.[121] The palette is similar to that of the *David* and *Miriam* windows at Dowanhill.

MOVE TO LONDON

Cottier's decision to relocate to London in the late 1860s is understandable in the context of his unfolding career, although it came at a busy and difficult period in his personal life. He and Marion had started a family while living in Glasgow; Isabella ('Ella') Field was born in April 1867, Archibald McLean in March 1868 and William Field in March 1869.[122] Although Cottier had been until this point 'a man of singular agility and strength', he contracted rheumatic fever.[123] By December 1869 he was so ill that the building committee at Dowanhill Church advanced him £20 for stained glass he was preparing, perhaps intended for his young family if he did not survive.[124] That same month, Archibald died of a respiratory infection, casting a further shadow; years later Cottier admitted that, for him and Marion, Archibald was 'far from forgotten yet ... sorrow wells up in our hearts at his loss.'[125] Despite his illness, Cottier was preparing to move to London, where artistic and commercial opportunities beckoned; at this moment it also provided a change of scene following his bereavement. He had already experienced life in the British capital, where many of his friends and associates, including Stevenson, had moved: the next chapter of his life and career unfolded there.

Max Donnelly

CHAPTER TWO
LONDON 1870–1908

Cottier moved to London in 1869,[1] possibly towards the end of the year, when fewer decorating projects were under way over winter. He was still plagued by illness; in May 1870 his friend the artist George Reid (1841–1913) wrote to John Forbes White in Aberdeen: 'Poor Cottier is always allowing himself to get into some complication or another – but he would get all right much sooner if his health was better. He is not nearly so careful of himself as he ought to be.'[2] There are many other references to Cottier's ill health in the 1870s.[3] Nevertheless, by June 1870 Cottier and his family were living at 3 St James's Terrace, a stucco-fronted townhouse (since demolished) on Albert Road (now Prince Albert Road), which runs along the northern edge of Regent's Park, where his youngest child Margaret ('Peggy') was born in October.[4] According to Reid it was 'a very nice house indeed' and, despite Cottier having 'exceedingly too much to look after', he was 'hopeful and happy – and that's good.'[5]

The area around St James's Terrace was rapidly developing as an artistic enclave. It was home to the artists of the 'St John's Wood Clique', co-founded by Henry Stacy Marks (1829–1898) in 1862. Also living nearby were Ernest Gambart (1814–1902), a leading figure in the picture trade, whose large house stood on Avenue Road; the Dutch-born artist Lawrence Alma-Tadema (1836–1912), who moved to Titchfield Terrace in 1871; and the French-born artist James Tissot (1836–1902) who settled at Grove End Road in 1873. In 1870 Cottier was elected to the Arts Club in Hanover Square,[6] which had been established in 1864, his election possibly ensured by some of the club's founding members, who included like-minded architect designers, among them Owen Jones, Edward William Godwin and William Burges, as well as the decorator John Dibblee Crace (1838–1919), elected in 1864. Cottier's membership of the Arts Club until 1875 introduced him to a wide circle of artists, collectors and dealers across London, including many of his new neighbours.[7]

St James's Terrace served as the Cottier family home for the next forty years, not without incident. In the early hours of 2 October 1874 a military barge, the *Tilbury*, caught fire nearby on Regent's Canal, igniting five tons of gunpowder which exploded as the vessel passed under a bridge.[8] The Cottiers' home was damaged, the Alma-Tademas' even more so.[9]

'THE LONDON BRETHREN'

Cottier's business initially involved a circle of ex-patriate Scots, a group described by Alexander Thomson as 'the London brethren'.[10] The lynchpin of this group was another architect who had worked with Cottier in Glasgow, John James Stevenson (as described in Chapter One). Stevenson subsequently moved to London and in 1870–1 built himself Red House (since demolished), a brown-brick house with red-brick dressings in Bayswater Hill.[11] It became a landmark of an eclectic new architectural style known as Queen Anne because its practitioners drew inspiration from eighteenth-century sources, setting a precedent for the many houses that he and others designed for artists and artistic clients in the 1870s. In her seminal book *Beautiful Houses* (1882), the writer and critic Mary Eliza Haweis (1848–1898), the author of articles and several instruction manuals on decoration and dress, devoted a chapter to Red House, describing its richly decorated interior filled with Persian tiles, Chinese enamels, antiques and paintings by artists including Rossetti.[12]

Cottier and Haweis must have met soon after his move to London, for in February 1872 she was already

23 Cabinet by Cottier & Co., London, *c.*1870–5. Ebonised, painted and gilded mahogany, 216 × 148 × 60 cm. Private collection

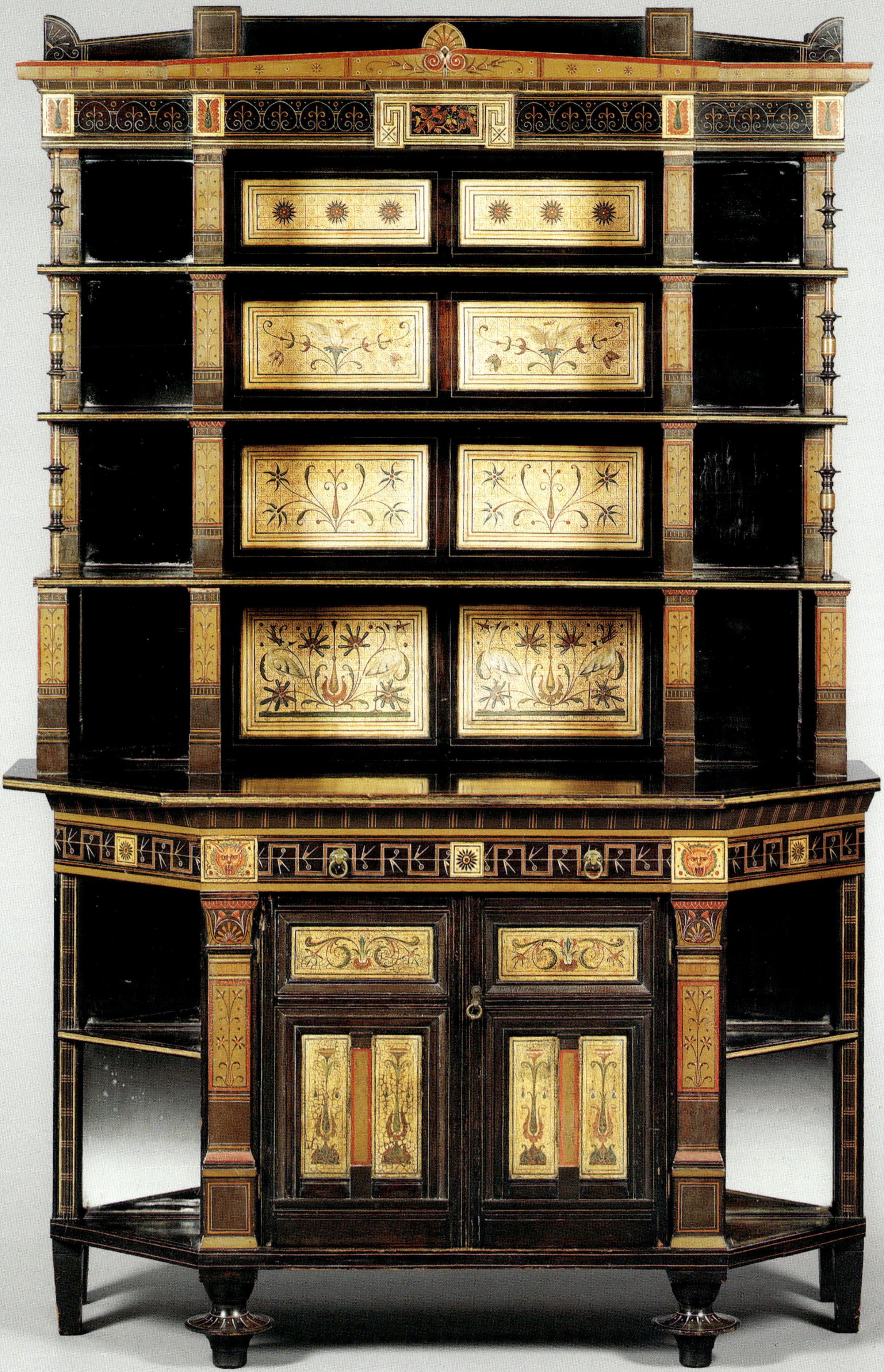

praising Cottier's work in *Saint Pauls Magazine*.[13] Realising her potential as what today would be termed an 'influencer', Cottier wooed the young writer, sending her what she described as 'a nice Xmas box' in 1875. It contained, she explained in a letter to her mother,

a painted glass window from Mr Cottier to fit over the front door. I made the design, myself, a year ago and he has worked on it and presented it to me. But do you suppose he sent it to me for love? No. I shall have to write an article somewhere to puff his manufactory. People don't do things for love in this world.[14]

Cottier & Co. itself was initially a partnership of Cottier with three other members of 'the London brethren', the architects John McKean Brydon (1840–1901) – 'a very nice sort of fellow', according to Reid[15] – William Wallace (1845–1926) and one John Bennet, who may have been a decorator and cabinet-maker.[16] Cottier probably knew Brydon and Wallace from Glasgow, where they had worked in the office of Campbell Douglas and Stevenson.[17] At the end of 1871 the partnership was dissolved[18] and, although Cottier and Wallace re-formed a partnership, they had dissolved that too by April 1874.[19] Wallace was hailed by Haweis as a 'rising architect' in 1882,[20] when she described the interior of a 'Bijou House' he designed in *Beautiful Houses*, praising it more warmly than Stevenson's Red House in her preceding chapter.[21]

Cottier maintained contact with Brydon and probably introduced him to Tissot, for whom Brydon designed a studio and adjoining conservatory in 1873.[22] Prior to joining Cottier, Brydon had trained alongside the Edinburgh-born James Smith Inglis (1845–1907). Although Inglis was not a partner in Cottier & Co. in London, he travelled with Cottier to New York in September 1873 to establish and then manage a branch of the business (see Chapter Four).[23] It was possibly through Brydon that Cottier knew Bruce James Talbert, as they had trained together in Campbell Douglas and Stevenson's Glasgow office. A fellow member of 'the London brethren', Talbert became a highly successful commercial designer of Gothic Revival and 'Jacobean' furniture, textiles, wallpapers and stained glass, well-known in Britain and the United States through his publications. In the early 1870s his studio was close to Cottier's, and for a time Talbert shared premises with the stained-glass maker George Edward Cook (1844–1914), as did Brydon.[24]

BEAUTIFUL HOUSES

In March 1870 George Gilbert Scott junior, soon to become one of Cottier & Co.'s competitors, noted in a letter to J. J. Stevenson:

I saw 'Cottier & Co.' on the door today in Langham Place. I hope he will do good work. There is a danger of giving in too much to the tone & general moral effect of a modern house even when improving the details, Effeminacy – called commonly comfort – and desire of display never produced good art and never can. A certain masculine character and a feeling of reality and a self-respect which does not heed the assistance of puffery, are essential to good domestic work. Otherwise we are but pandering to rich snobs.[25]

Cottier & Co. was one of a new generation of 'art' firms that decorated interiors, designed and made everything from stained glass to furniture and ceramics, and retailed textiles. The conditions which allowed this new breed of business to develop were created by an emerging middle-class market for 'Beautiful Houses' (the title of Haweis's 1882 book) with tasteful interiors and furnishings. This demand was fuelled by what became known as Aestheticism and by the 'Queen Anne' movement, which flourished in Britain from the 1860s to the end of the century, and from there spread to North America, Australia and, to a lesser extent, the European continent.

By 1870 the Gothic Revival and what later became known as Aestheticism had begun to converge. While Morris & Co. remained the pre-eminent artistic house and church furnishers during this period, Cottier & Co. was one of a number of new firms providing a range of comparable services. Cox & Sons, although founded as clerical tailors in 1838, broadened its offer and by 1872 was publishing an *Illustrated catalogue of gothic and other artistic domestic furniture, fittings,*

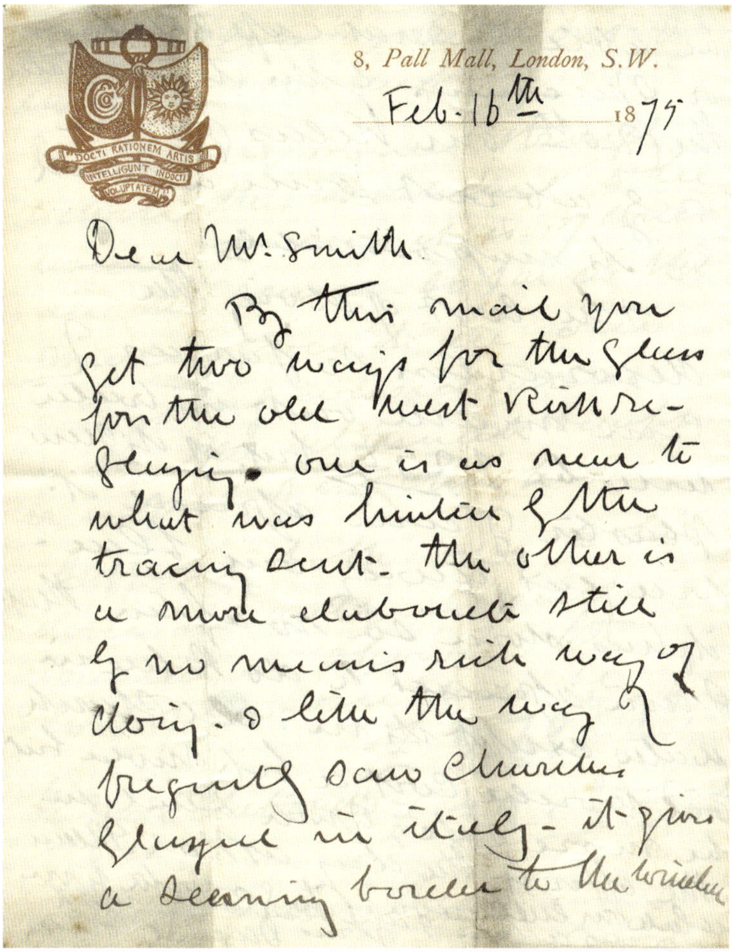

8, Pall Mall, London, S.W.

Feb. 16th 1875

DOCTI RATIONEM ARTIS INTELLIGUNT INDOCTI VOLUPTATEM

Dear Mr Smith.

By this mail you get two ways for the glass for the old west Kirk re-glazing. one is as near to what was hinted of the tracing sent. the other is a more elaborate still of no means rich way of doing. I like the way I frequently saw churches glazed in italy – it gives a dearning border to the window

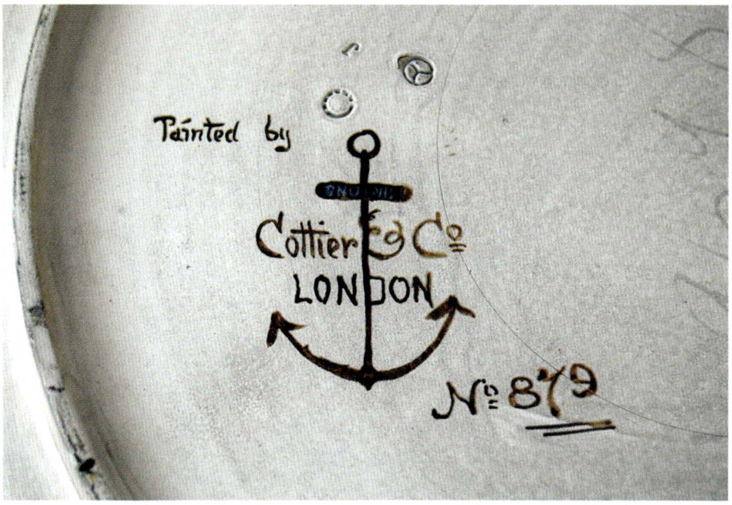

24 Cottier & Co. logo. Letter from Daniel Cottier to William Smith, Aberdeen City Architect, 16 February 1875. Aberdeen City Libraries

25 Signature on the reverse of a charger decorated by Cottier & Co., *c.*1883. Underglaze colour on earthenware plaque manufactured by Minton & Co., Stoke-on-Trent, Staffordshire. Four Acres Charitable Trust

decorations, upholstery and metal work.[26] Watts & Co., established in 1874 by the architects George Frederick Bodley, Thomas Garner and Gilbert Scott junior, made embroidery, textiles, wallpapers, carpets, jewellery and church plate and designed stained glass, the last manufactured by Burlison & Grylls.[27] In 1876 John Aldam Heaton (1830–1897), who had decorated a number of churches, moved to London where he supplied his business partner Richard Norman Shaw with domestic furniture, furnishings and wallpapers.[28] Another new business was Collinson & Lock,[29] founded in 1870 as cabinetmakers and by 1882 advertising as 'upholsterers, decorators, paperhangers, manufacturers of artistic furniture and constructive woodwork for interiors and paper hangings of special design and colour'.[30] Like Cox & Sons, Collinson & Lock was one of several British exhibitors who sent displays to the Philadelphia Centennial Exhibition in 1876, a few years after Cottier & Co. opened a branch in New York.

Cottier & Co. was probably unique among all its rivals for, besides 'Memorial Windows, and Stained Glass for the Church and the Home', 'Furniture of Special Design, in best Workmanship, and at Moderate Cost', and 'Decorated' walls and ceilings (as advertised in 1874),[31] it also decorated ceramic tiles and plaques and dealt in fine art. By 1875 the company logo (fig. 24), used by the London and New York branches, featured an anchor, a device also found on Cottier & Co. stained glass and ceramics (fig. 25). The anchor referred to Cottier's maritime ancestry, of which he was evidently proud, and fits Henley's recollection that 'in gait, and figure, and address' Cottier 'was far more like an ideal coasting skipper than an artist.'[32] The firm's motto, a quotation from Quintilian, *Docti rationem artis intelligunt, indocti voluptatem* ('the learned understand the principles of art, the unlearned feel its pleasure'), pinned his colours to the mast, associating his company's mission with a core tenet of Aestheticism: the appreciation of art's sensory pleasures.

ESTABLISHING THE NEW BUSINESS

Cottier & Co.'s showroom or gallery was located in a succession of premises in or close to Regent Street in the West End, initially at 2 Langham Place, by March 1870. The building no longer exists but it must have been spacious as, presumably, it housed both a showroom as well as the workshop where furniture was decorated. Stained-glass windows were probably designed and glass and ceramics may have been painted there, although it has not been established if these premises had a kiln for firing glass and ceramic tiles and plaques; in the case of glass, firing was required before windows could be leaded up in the workshop; otherwise a kiln must have been nearby.

A visitor to Langham Place would have been surprised to find two women working in Cottier's studio, the pioneering cousins Rhoda Garrett (1841–1882) and Agnes Garrett (1845–1935).[33] In about 1871 Cottier 'allowed them to occupy a room at his offices, where they might pick up what knowledge they could in the art of glass-painting, and here they awaited farther opportunity', according to an account published in 1882.[34] However, in 1925 the Garretts' former trainee Millicent Vince claimed that Cottier 'took them as his pupils, accepted their fees – and taught them nothing. They left him, after a rather hectic time'.[35] When Brydon established his own practice in 1872, the Garretts moved with him, going on to become Britain's first professional female interior decorators. Nevertheless, they maintained contact with Cottier and may have developed some of the ideas they were exposed to in his studio in their own work.[36] Agnes's sister, Elizabeth Garrett Anderson, is known to have owned a sofa made by Cottier & Co.[37] In 1874 Cottier's furniture, glass and selected artworks began to be promoted in the Glasgow showroom of the art dealer William Craibe Angus (1830–1899), Cottier's Scottish agent (on whom more later in this chapter and Chapter Three).

On 12 January 1875 – Cottier's thirty-seventh birthday – Cottier & Co.'s new 'Art Rooms', rented for £500 per annum, opened at 8 Pall Mall, operating there until 1881 (see fig. 70).[38] It was in a Regency building (since rebuilt) on the corner of Waterloo Place and Pall Mall, at the south end of Regent Street. The Pall Mall entrance of the Royal Opera Arcade, slightly further east, survives to this day; neighbours included a printseller, Henry Graves & Co., at number 6. These 'Art Rooms' were commercial premises to which 'Collectors, Amateurs, and those interested in Art generally are invited to call.'[39] The opening of an art gallery was not a whim. Cottier's interest in contemporary Dutch and French paintings had been sparked by White in Aberdeen and in 1874 Cottier asked the Dutch art dealer Elbert Jan van Wisselingh (1848–1912) to move to London to manage the picture dealing part of the business (see Chapter Three, p. 74). The relocation to Pall Mall, which had more pedestrian traffic than Langham Place, may have been made with this in mind although, despite the proximity of the National Gallery, there were few other commercial galleries in the area. However, nearby were several gentlemen's clubs of which many of Cottier's clientele were doubtless members.

When Vincent van Gogh visited his friend van Wisselingh at the Cottier gallery in October 1876 he saw, besides paintings, designs for memorial windows (discussed later). Stained glass, furniture, ceramics and textiles may have been displayed in a separate part of the premises, as was the case in New York. The launch of Cottier's Pall Mall gallery coincided with the opening of Liberty & Co. in nearby Regent Street (1875) and later of the Morris & Co. showroom on Oxford Street in 1877 and the establishment of the Art Furnishers' Alliance showroom under the direction of Christopher Dresser on New Bond Street in 1881. It marked the high tide of Cottier & Co.'s physical presence in London, for by July 1881 the gallery had moved to a slightly less prominent location, 32 Argyll Place, which runs off Regent Street,[40] soon relocating to 5 Argyll Place, in 1883, where it remained until 1895. From 1896 to 1900 the business appears to have operated from 4 St James's Terrace, the house next to Cottier's residence, which he had owned since at least 1886.[41] From 1901 to 1908 Cottier & Co. is listed at 15A Grafton Street, Mayfair, but the business is not mentioned in London directories after this date, suggesting that it closed soon after Inglis's death in 1907.

In 1875 Cottier wrote that the London kilns were fired about once a week and he described business as 'exceedingly busy in all things just now – making some fine things in glass'.[42] By 1878 the workshop where stained glass, ceramics and furniture are likely to have been made was at 33 Nicholas Lane off Lombard Street in the City; after 1885, it was on Crawford Street, Marylebone. In 1897 it was announced that Cottier & Co. was 'relinquishing manufacturing' and the contents of the workshops at 43 Crawford Street, including furniture, panelling, 'a large quantity of antique glass in ruby, white and colours', 'a quantity of painted tiles' and 'the entire fittings of glass kiln', were auctioned off.[43] It is not known where the windows supplied by Cottier & Co. for later British and American commissions were made.[44]

RUNNING THE BUSINESS

In 1872 Reid wrote to White expressing his concern that Cottier was abandoning his calling as a stained-glass artist for material gain: 'I think Cottier has just got a little infected with the universal go-a-head-ism of the age'.[45] From 1873 the business of running branches in London and New York, as well as the travel this entailed, not to mention periods convalescing, must have consumed an increasing amount of Cottier's time. Writing shortly after his death, W. E. Henley claimed that 'he could throw off designs enough in an hour ... to keep a factory going for weeks', adding: 'It is not insinuated here that these were all the work of his own hand.'[46] The implication was that Cottier produced sketches which were worked up by other designers, so that even when the design of a stained-glass window or piece of furniture was described as being by Cottier, it was largely the work of another hand. Fortunately, Cottier was an adept talent-spotter. Henley thought that he 'had the faculty, common to all great artists, of picking his men, and therewith of so imposing himself upon them as to make them practically exponents and expressions of himself.'[47]

A core part of Cottier & Co.'s business in London was the design and manufacture of stained-glass windows for churches, public buildings and private homes throughout Britain, and from 1873 the United States and Australia. The English artist Frederick Vincent Hart (1843–1915) designed stained glass and possibly furniture for Cottier & Co., probably initially on a freelance basis in the 1870s, firstly in London and then in New York. He trained in London as an architect and studied painting under the artist Albert Moore (1841–1893) and by 1871 was designing stained glass for George Edward Cook (1844–1914).[48] Hart's figural style was influenced by Moore and the Pre-Raphaelite circle and his first wife, Augusta Jones, was an actress and artists' model who sat to Pre-Raphaelite artists including Burne-Jones, Rossetti, Whistler and Frederick Sandys (1829–1904).[49] Many of the most refined Cottier & Co. windows are attributed to Hart (figs 28, 30–32 and see figs 35, 36 and 194). Hart continued to design stained glass and undertook other work for the firm throughout the 1890s.[50] In 1902, following Augusta's death, he emigrated to the United States where in 1904 he remarried and worked for Cottier & Co.'s New York branch, painting watercolours and decorating furniture (discussed in Chapter Four).

In the early 1870s Richard Rivington Holmes (1835–1911; see fig. 27) designed a window for Cottier, although the circumstances (discussed later) were exceptional. The Dutch painter Matthijs Maris (1839–1917) moved to London in 1877 and designed stained glass for Cottier & Co., although his attempts at actually painting glass apparently met with limited success (see Chapter Three, p. 86). It is unlikely that Cottier himself was involved in painting glass or ceramics after the opening of the London branch. Indeed, Maris later claimed that:

> *one of his finest workmen who has known him since he was an apprentice in a glass-painter's shop told Henry, he always found a way to get others to do it. I've to go somewhere, he would say, you just touch up a bitty for me and when he returned, that is very beautiful! You understand the man was pleased to hear this and didn't mind the next time.*[51]

The English artist William James Nelson (1850–1918) painted and possibly also designed glass and ceramics in the 1870s and 80s, signing his name on a staircase landing window at Cairndhu House, Helensburgh, of about 1873 (see fig. 35). Nelson must have been regarded as one of Cottier & Co.'s most talented artists as he occasionally signed or monogrammed ceramics,[52] and by the time of Cottier's death in 1891 was one of the firm's two foremen in London, the other being Charles Henry Gillard (1844–1908), a fretwork glazier who leaded up glass and installed windows.[53] Several Scottish stained-glass artists worked for Cottier in London, including Norman McLeod MacDougall (1851–1937).[54] Charles Gow (1847–1893) worked in the London studio before leaving for Australia in 1873 to work for Lyon, Cottier & Co. in Sydney (see Chapter Six, pp. 149–50).[55] However, Stephen Adam remained in Glasgow, establishing his own business in partnership with David Small and producing windows much indebted to Cottier's style.[56]

Cottier is known to have sourced some of his glass from the leading London firm of James Powell & Sons, which supplied many eminent leading stained-glass studios including that of Morris & Co. Different grades of glass were available to studios, depending on the desired effect and budget: 'Cathedral' glass was machine-rolled, while more expensive 'Antique' glass was mouth-blown, giving it the irregularity of medieval glass. In 1875 Cottier explained the difference, writing to the architect William Smith (1817–1891), with whom he was working on the glazing of the West Kirk of St Nicholas in Aberdeen:

as to glass there is two ways – 1st mulling all the glass what is called rough rolled Cathedral of several tints – this is very Cheap & Strong Glass, but its uncomfortable icy looking glass & bears in the interior having no clearness by which clouds trees &c &c make changes on the interiors – wholesome good antique glass altho more than twice its Cost is much better to look & helps out an interior wonderfully well.[57]

Details about the decorative painters who worked for Cottier are scant. As was the case with the stained-glass artists, some probably followed Cottier from Scotland. Andrew Wells apparently worked with Cottier in London, although his time with Cottier & Co. must have been brief for around 1870 he set up his own business in Glasgow, where he occasionally collaborated with Stephen Adam. Nevertheless, Wells and Cottier kept in touch and it was probably with Cottier's help that in the early 1870s Wells decorated the dining rooms of the London residences of two Scottish-born Royal Academicians, John Pettie and John McWhirter.[58] Wells's association with Cottier continued and was formalised when in 1886 he went to Australia and became a partner in Lyon, Wells, Cottier & Co. in Sydney from 1887 to 1895 (see Chapter Seven).

In the absence of business records, one newspaper report of 1873 gives a rare and fascinating glimpse into one of Cottier & Co.'s decorating commissions. This was for the decoration of Rushpool Hall, a magnificent mansion built for a colliery owner, John Bell, on the North Yorkshire coast (gutted by fire in 1904 but extant).[59] Cottier's employees in London 'received a telegram from their brother workmen employed by the same firm to the effect that they had struck work for a half-penny an hour advance. The men, about 17 in number, all Scotchmen, immediately turned out on strike. The matter was resolved two hours later when their demands were met.'[60] Bell, who was residing in his Algiers house while the decoration was taking place, would have been oblivious to the incident at the time. Materials and wages apparently increased in the early 1870s for, as Cottier told the architect Smith while working on the stained glass at the West Kirk in 1875, 'it would be impossible to do them so cheap this time as mens wages and also glass has gone up a deal since then.'[61]

STAINED-GLASS MEMORIAL WINDOWS

While many Cottier & Co. windows can be found in the south of England, even after Cottier & Co. was established in London the majority of commissions for memorial windows appear to have come from Scotland, for churches or cathedrals of the Church of Scotland. Cottier's network of Scottish contacts included White and his circle in Aberdeen in the 1870s. Other commissions came through architects, particularly William Leiper, who commissioned Cottier &

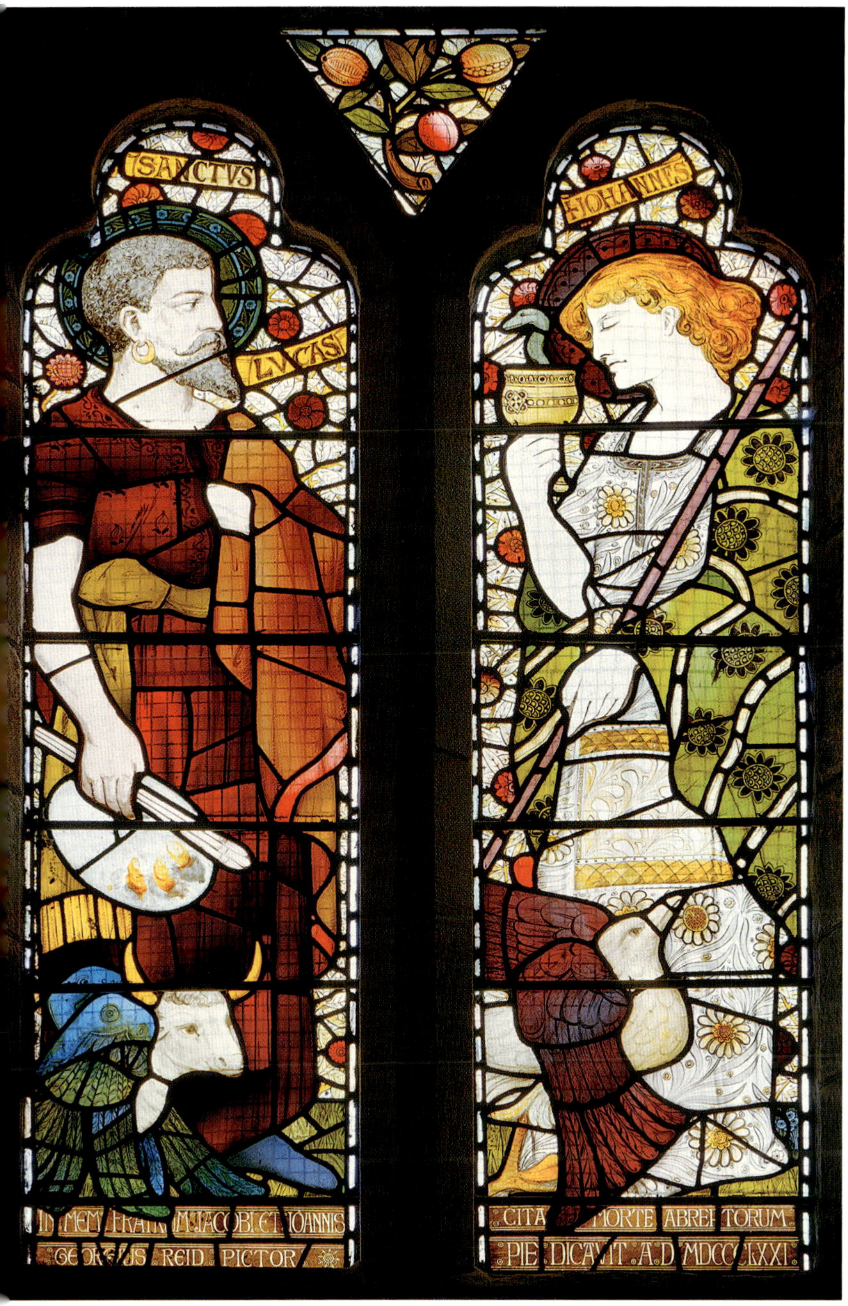

26 *St Luke* and *St John*, Cathedral Church of St Machar, Aberdeen, by Cottier & Co., London, 1871. Stained glass

Co. to supply windows for many of the churches and houses he built or extended until the 1890s.[62] Cottier also continued to gain a steady stream of commissions, some through J. J. Stevenson for Anglican (and occasionally Catholic) churches in the north-east of England.

The development of Cottier's memorial windows in the early 1870s can be traced in the two-light window unveiled at St Machar's Cathedral, Aberdeen, in July 1871. Commissioned by Cottier's friend George Reid in memory of his two older brothers, it depicts Saints Luke and John (fig. 26).[63] Like Cottier, who had severely criticised stained glass made by the Bavarian Königliche Glasmalereianstalt (Royal Stained Glass Manufactory) in Munich in 1867 (see Chapter One, pp. 21 and 24), Reid was critical of Munich glass, corresponding with John Ruskin on the subject in 1869.[64] In 1871 Ruskin wrote, apparently to White:

The German glass is very delicately executed, and as it consists of pretty sentimental pictures rendered striking by transparent lights, it always pleases the public, partly as a magic lantern does children, and partly because there is really much merit in the drawing and finish of the work, and sometimes considerable dramatic interest in the German revival of Catholic traditions. But the school is essentially a barbarism, and modern vanity in vulgar mechanism has not often erred more grossly than in the costly efforts it has made to paint pictures on windows.[65]

Ruskin enclosed a copy of an appendix from volume 2 of *The Stones of Venice* (1853) in which he had written: 'The true perfection of a painted window is to be serene, intense, brilliant, like flaming jewellery; full of easily legible and quaint subjects, and exquisitely subtle, yet simple, in its harmonies.'[66] Ruskin pointed the way to qualities of colour and composition that White and Reid desired in a window, aspirations they shared with Cottier, who had attended Ruskin's lectures in London. The windows for Reid, probably designed by Cottier himself, show his developing talent for conveying emotion through the rich, expressive colouring of the draperies worn by the large figures, which fill the window frames. The prominent inclusion of a bull and eagle at the feet of Saints Luke and John, and the serpent rising from John's goblet, are redolent of the iconography found in Ford Madox Brown's stained-glass designs for Morris & Co.

In the early 1870s, shortly before Cottier began exporting stained glass to the United States, his studio supplied two windows to Holy Trinity Church, the Anglican church in Nice in the South of France, where a community of wealthy Scots resided. They were presumably among the friends of the late British Consul Adolphe Ludovic Lacroix who after his death in 1871 donated a richly coloured three-light window depicting Aaron, Moses and Joshua. As Martin

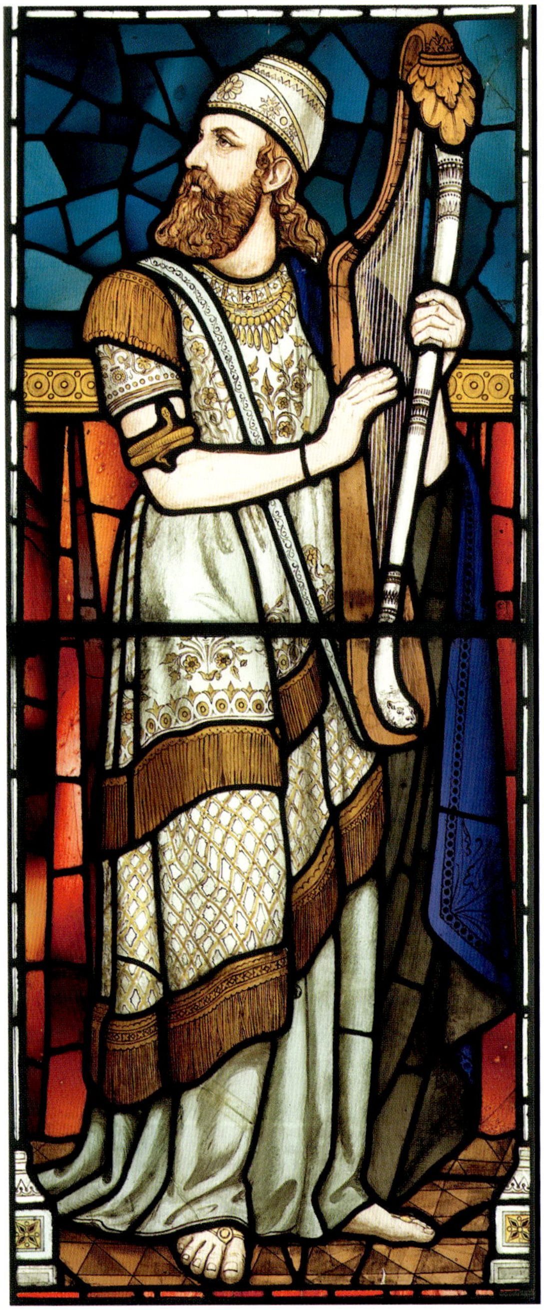

27 *King David*, detail of a two-light window made for Crathie Parish Church, Aberdeenshire (removed), designed by Richard Rivington Holmes for Cottier & Co., London, 1873. Stained glass, 78.5 × 64 cm. Glasgow Museums

Harrison noted, another example of the way in which Cottier's windows had developed rapidly since the late 1860s can be found at the Church of St Nicholas in Cramlington, Northumberland, in comparing the two-light window depicting the Wise and Foolish Virgins of 1868 (see fig. 22) with the three-light window installed by Cottier in the same church a few years later.[67] The Richardson memorial window installed at Paisley Abbey in 1873, depicting parables and Virtues, is even more ambitious, although criticised by a writer in the *Paisley Herald*, who thought that the lack of flesh tint on the faces and hands of the figures made them look like 'thin disembodied ghosts'.[68]

Cottier's stained glass clearly did not always meet with unqualified approval. In 1872 the company was commissioned to produce a two-light memorial window to the clergyman Norman Macleod junior (1812–1872), a commission led by another expatriate Scot, Alexander Strahan (1833–1918). Strahan, 'a power to be reckoned with in the publishing world of the 'sixties and 'seventies',[69] had appointed Macleod as editor of *Good Words*, the popular magazine founded by Strahan in 1859. Macleod served as Queen Victoria's chaplain in Scotland and the memorial was destined for Crathie Church, Aberdeenshire, where the queen, whose estate at Balmoral was nearby, had often heard him preach. One light was to depict the preacher St Paul, dedicated to Macleod, the other King David, dedicated to the late Prince Consort.

On its completion the two-light window in May 1873 was delivered to St George's Hall at Windsor Castle for inspection by the queen. However, although Strahan had presumably approved the design before the window was made, Queen Victoria apparently had not, for she wrote in her diary, 'It is very ugly & will never do there'.[70] Despite this, the window (similar to that in St Andrew's Church, Rose Bay, Sydney; see fig. 152) was installed at Crathie a few weeks later with much publicity. The *Manchester Guardian* described King David 'clad in blood-red garments relieved by a cloud of lace'[71] and the *Building News* noted that St Paul was 'clad in rich blue, soft green studded with stars, and greenish yellow, and stands out against a white-bordered background of ruby on blue.'[72] When the queen saw the windows *in situ* her consternation grew: 'Already, when I saw them at Windsor, I did not like them. They are 2 colossal figures of King David & St. Paul, to my mind, quite out of drawing, & the colouring bad.'[73] She discussed the matter with the minister of the church, Dr Malcolm Campbell Taylor, and her private secretary and confidante, Sir Henry Ponsonby, whose position as a former equerry to Prince Albert made his opinion on artistic matters especially important, and 'finally decided that the

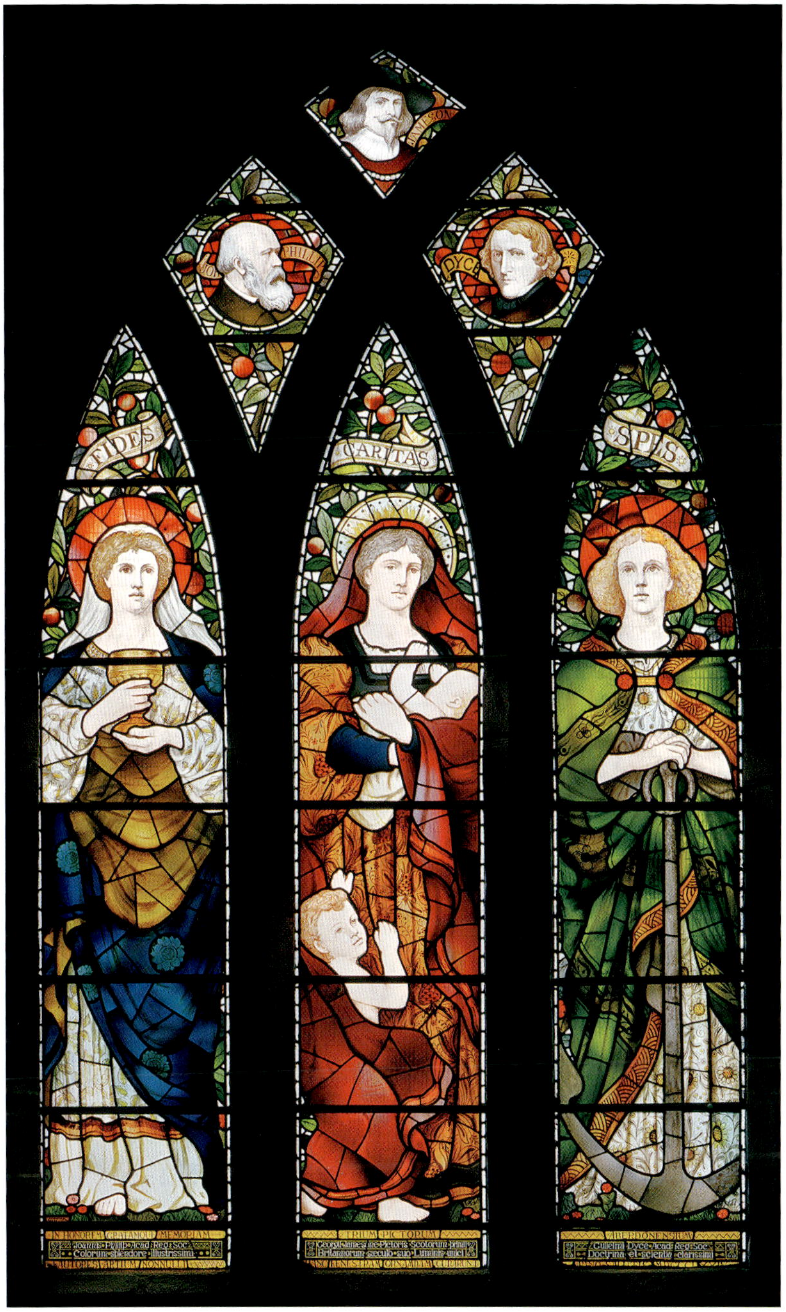

28 *The Painters' Window*, Cathedral Church of St Machar, Aberdeen, by Cottier & Co., London, 1874–5. Stained glass

windows could not remain up, & that I would give some appropriate ones instead.'[74] The upshot of this highly awkward situation was that Cottier & Co. remade the windows (fig. 27)[75] to designs approved by the queen, made by (later Sir) Richard Rivington Holmes, the librarian of Windsor Castle, who was also an artist and occasional stained-glass designer.[76] The queen was keen to see the replacements, visiting the church with Princess Beatrice as soon as they were installed in November 1873 and concluding that 'They certainly are a great improvement to the last'.[77] The windows were later removed and are now in the Glasgow Museums collection but the fate of the original versions is not known.[78]

Although the maligned designs for the original Crathie windows were reused by the Cottier studio on at least two occasions (see Chapter Six, pp. 163 and 165), it is possible that their perceived weaknesses encouraged the studio's shift away from monumental figures in awkward poses. *The Painters' Window*, designed in 1874[79] and installed at St Machar's Cathedral the following year (fig. 28), shows this tendency. Commissioned by a group of subscribers led by White, Reid, the wine and spirit merchant Alexander Walker (1825–1903)[80] and the granite merchant and art collector Alexander Macdonald (1837–1884), the window was designed to commemorate three Aberdeen artists. These were George Jameson, William Dyce and John Phillip, whose portraits were incorporated above full-length figures representing the Virtues Faith, Charity and Hope (in that order). In 1875 Cottier published a photograph of the design, describing it as being 'from the Cartoons of D. Cottier'.[81] It was common practice for Victorian stained-glass studios to subsume the identities of designers under the company name and, as noted earlier, it is more likely that the figures were sketched by Cottier and worked up and refined by a designer. The result was that the statuesque Archaic style Cottier had promoted in the late 1860s showed a distinct softening for, while the scale of the figures remains large, they have an elegance and poise which Queen Victoria had thought lacking in Cottier's window for Crathie Church. Combined with the rich and glowing palette, Cottier's mature style immediately found praise. The *Aberdeen Journal* waxed lyrical, describing how Hope's 'blonde hair in full folds, like those of the beauties of Palma Vecchio, is surrounded by a ruby nimbus of glowing and various dyes',[82] while the *British Architect* thought that 'the *tout ensemble* of the work is remarkably artistic'.[83]

Besides Morris & Co., the stained glass emanating from Cottier's studio can be compared with that of other stained-glass artists associated with Aestheticism. Harry Ellis Wooldridge (1845–1917) was a studio assistant to Burne-Jones and his bold figural

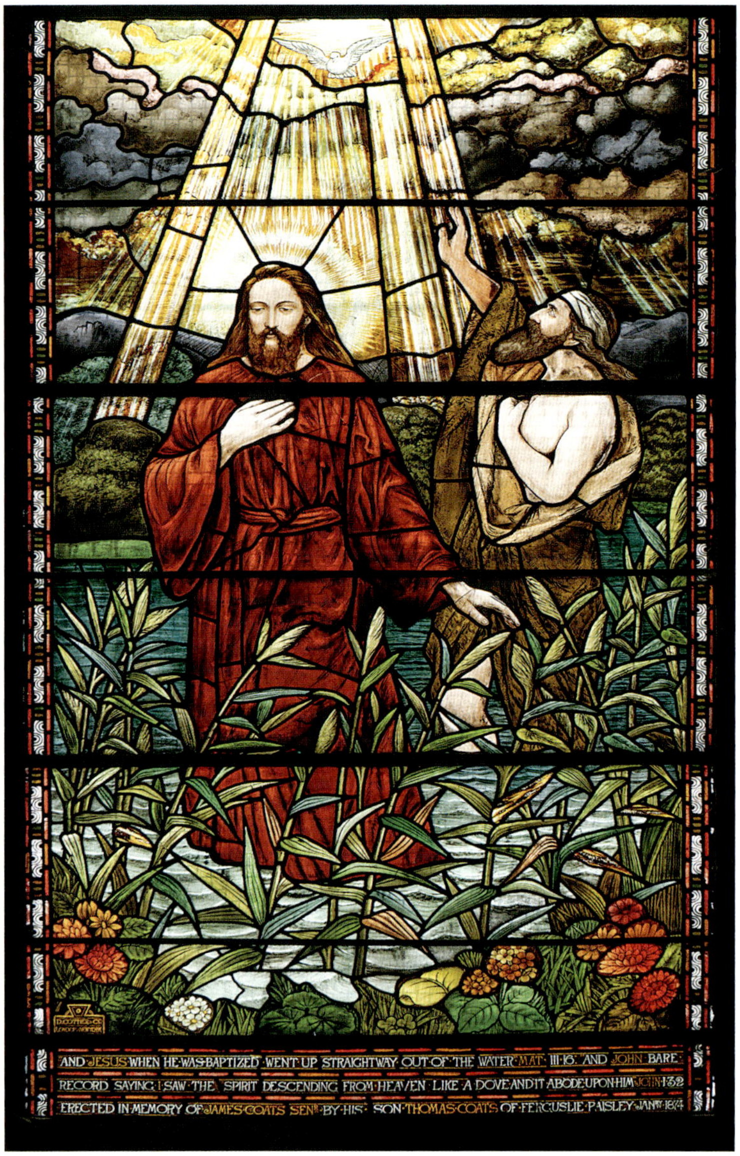

29 *Baptism of Christ*, lower section of the James Coats memorial window in Paisley Abbey, Renfrewshire, by Cottier & Co., London, 1874. Stained glass

style has some similarities with Cottier's oeuvre.[84] Another stained-glass artist whose work is similar to Cottier's was Henry Holiday (1839–1927), who worked with Wooldridge for some time.[85] Like Cottier, Holiday was drawn to the work of the Pre-Raphaelites in the 1850s and his early drawings were praised by Cottier's tutor Ford Madox Brown. But while many of Holiday's windows share the rich and sensuous colouring employed by Cottier, his figures tended to be less muscular and increasingly showed the influence of his lifelong friend Burne-Jones. Like Cottier and Morris, Holiday designed and made many windows for American clients.[86]

In the *Painters' Window* the Virtues stand before dense foliage and fruit inspired by the backgrounds to figures found in many Morris & Co. windows.[87] Cottier's window was praised at the time for 'The feeling for nature' conveyed by details such as 'the flower-sprinkled meadow on which the Virtues stand.'[88] His stained-glass windows often incorporated naturalistic flowers and plants, sometimes chosen for their symbolic associations but also used as decorative devices and vehicles for colour and conveying atmosphere. Another example occurs in the window depicting the Baptism of Christ made in memory of James Coats senior (of the thread-making dynasty) at Paisley Abbey in 1874, based on a painting by Robert Dowling (fig. 29).[89] It shows Christ clad in ruby red in bold frontal view being baptised by a partially nude John the Baptist in strict profile view, the figures set behind a screen of wetland plants bending in the breeze. This natural setting for a biblical scene seems to reflect the interests of Ruskin and the Pre-Raphaelites; the plants, which bear a resemblance to bamboo, may also reflect an interest in Japanese art, one of the sources of inspiration of Aestheticism.

Rich colouring, large and statuesque figures and natural details are combined in several unusual memorial windows made in the 1870s. One is dedicated to Mabel Fanny Hunt, commissioned by her widowed mother Augusta at St John the Evangelist, Birtley, Tyne and Wear, *c.*1873 (fig. 30). Mabel, who died aged eighteen, is shown being lifted from earth by the angel of death, accompanied by a quotation from the last two lines of Henry Longfellow's poem 'The Reaper and the Flowers' (see Chapter Four, p. 119 and fig. 109). Equally striking are the memorial windows installed in the chancel of St Andrew's Church, Owslebury, Hampshire (fig. 31), which were commissioned by the eighth Earl of Northesk and portray his wife and daughter.[90] When Vincent van Gogh visited Cottier's Pall Mall showroom in October 1876, he saw preparatory sketches which he described in a letter to

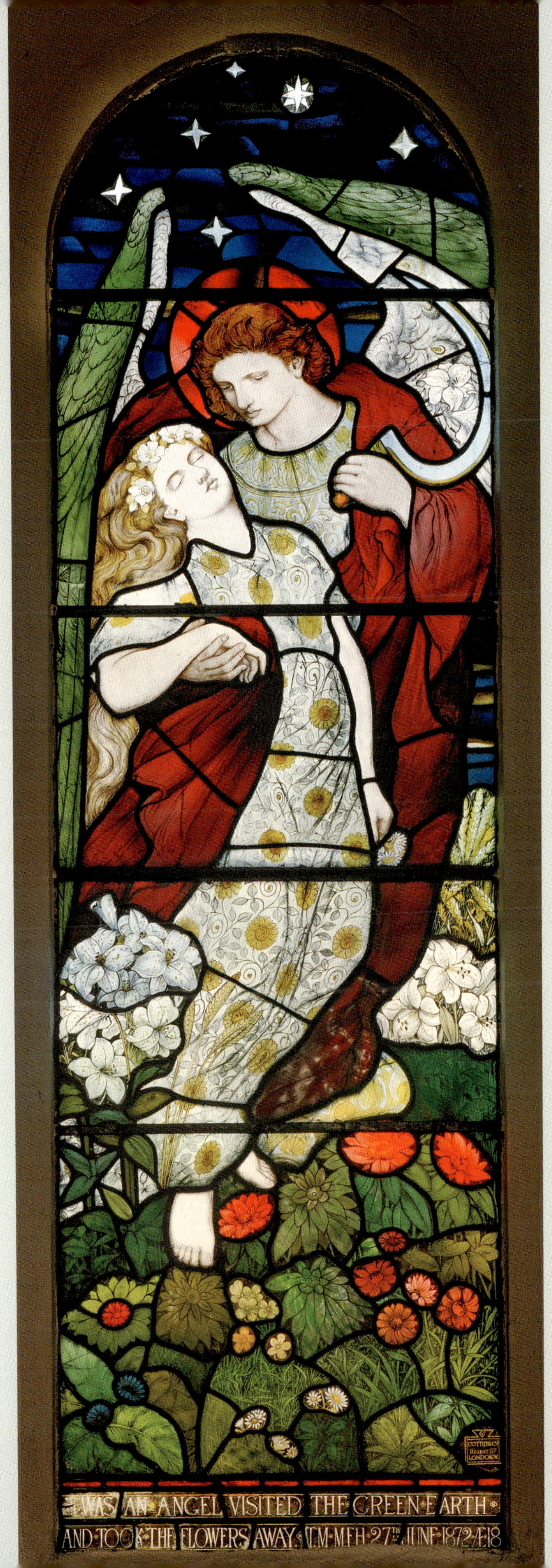

30 *The Reaper and the Flowers*, Church of St John the Evangelist, Birtley, Tyne and Wear, by Cottier & Co., London, *c.*1873. Stained glass

31 *Lady Margaret Carnegie* and *Georgina, Countess of Northesk*, St Andrew's Church, Owslebury, Hampshire, by Cottier & Co., London, 1876–7. Stained glass

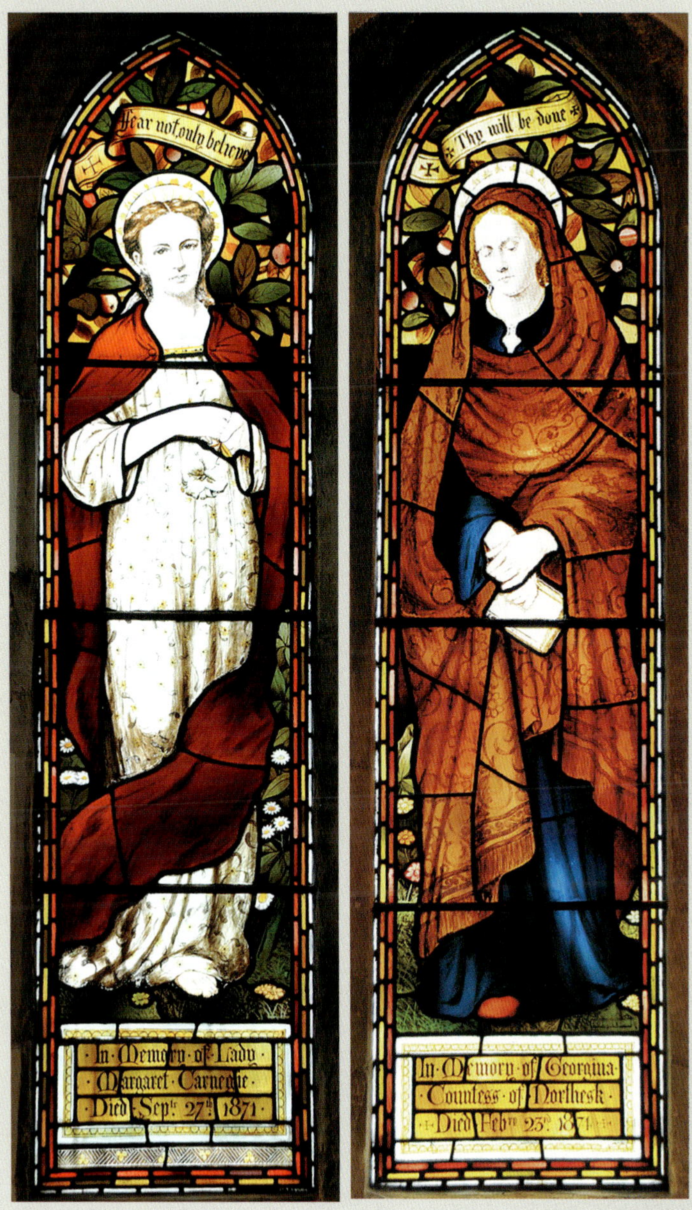

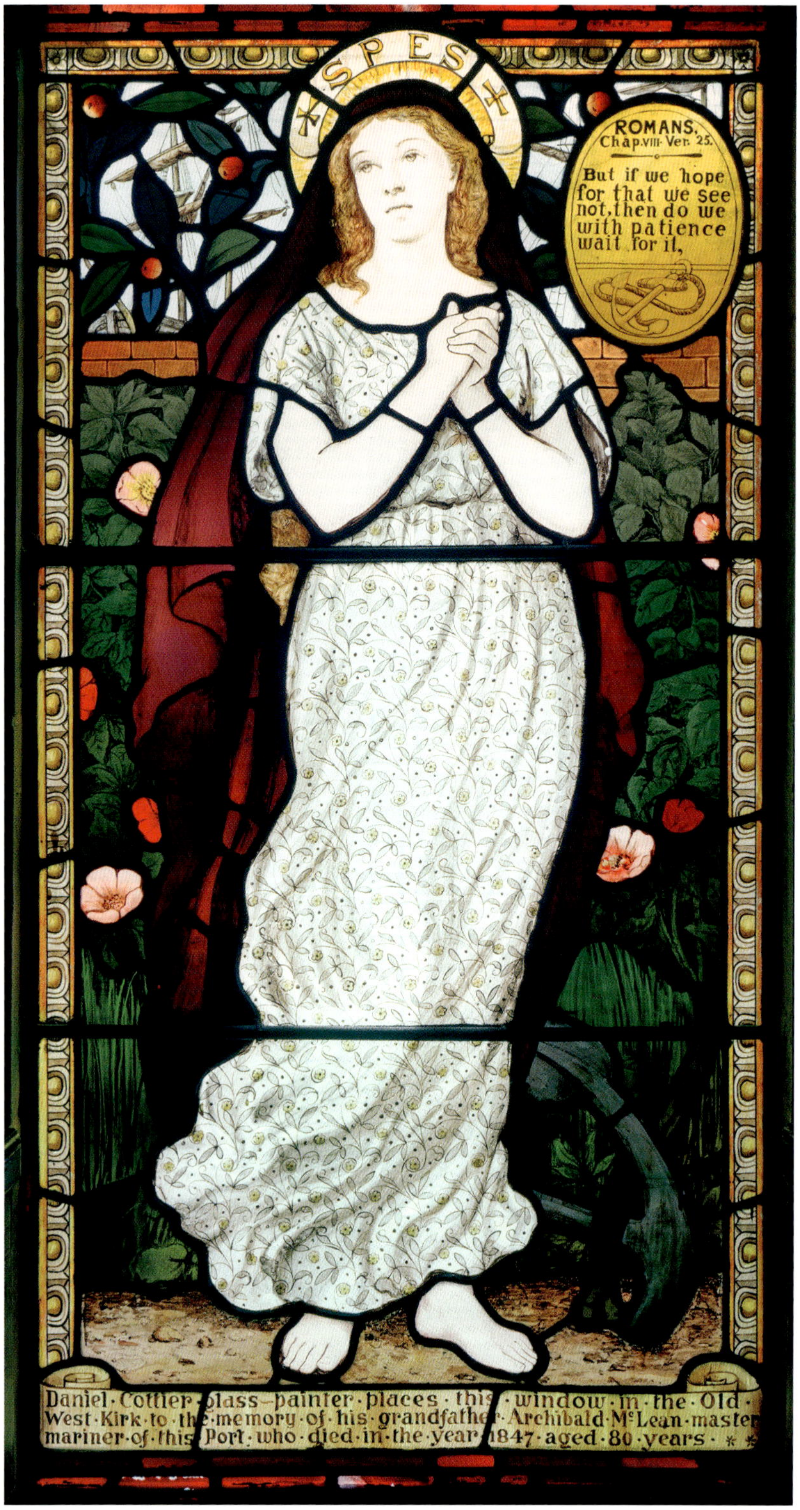

32 *Spes* (Hope), Old West Kirk, Greenock, by Cottier & Co., London, 1884. Stained glass

his brother Theo: 'In the middle of one of the windows the portrait of an elderly lady, such a noble face, with the words "Thy will be done" inscribed above; in the other window the portrait of her daughter, with the words "Faith is the substance of things hoped for, the evidence of things not seen".'[91] Van Gogh was intending to become a missionary at this time and the powerful designs may have touched him because they are portraits of the Countess and Lady Margaret imagined in the lush flower- and fruit-filled garden of heaven, endowed with haloes and surmounted by sacred texts in scrolls. Lady Margaret, who was unmarried, holds a lily, a Christian symbol of purity. A billowing gown, a device often employed by the Cottier studio, dramatises her figure and suggests the authorship of Hart, whose style has similarities to that of Sandys. Van Gogh later observed of Cottier that 'if there's a certain degree of style in a drawing, he'll be enthusiastic all right'.[92]

During the 1880s the palette of Cottier's glass became moodier and more sombre, which may be attributed to Cottier's increased involvement in art dealing and his predilection for tonal paintings. This tendency can be seen in one of the windows Cottier commissioned in memory of a member of his own family in 1884. It was installed at the Old West Kirk in Greenock and dedicated to his maternal grandfather, Archibald McLean, 'master mariner of this Port', after whom Cottier had named his first son, who died as a baby. The window depicts a figure representing *Spes* (Hope) with an anchor at her feet and ships in the background largely obscured by foliage (fig. 32).[93] While the figure, in its diaphanous sprigged gown, is reminiscent of the Owslebury Lady Margaret of 1876–7, the deeper palette is markedly different and evidence of Cottier & Co.'s windows becoming richer and darker in colour in the 1880s. Given the wide range of Cottier's activities by 1884, it is interesting that the dedication describes him as a 'glass-painter', indicating the aspect of his career for which he himself wanted to be remembered.[94]

The Cottier studio was particularly active in Scotland from the 1880s to the early 1900s, making dozens of windows for cathedrals and churches.[95] In

33 *Architecture*, *Painting*, *Sir Henry Raeburn* and *George Jameson*, design for Dundee Royal Exchange by Cottier & Co., London, *c.*1887. Watercolour on paper, 24.3 × 13 cm. Private collection

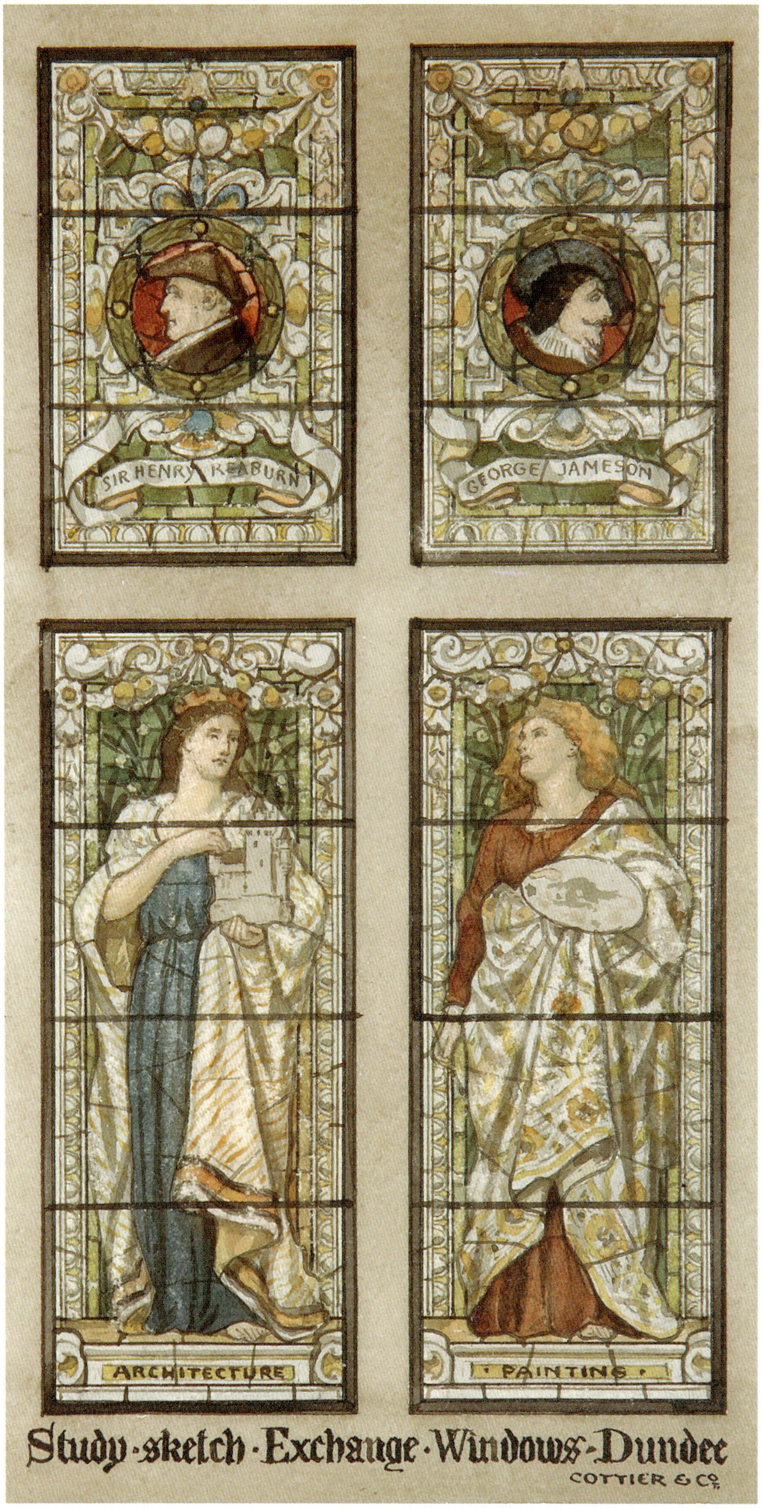

1880 the *Glasgow Herald* noted that the new Cottier windows at Bothwell Parish Church had been 'supplied by Mr W. Craibe Angus, Glasgow, their [Cottier & Co.'s] Scottish agent'.[96] The showroom of William Craibe Angus opened at 159 Queen Street in Glasgow in 1874; in 1886 John Lamb Lyon recorded seeing 'a good deal of Cottier's stuff and stained Glass' when he visited Angus.[97] Another fruitful source of commissions in the 1880s was the miller and collector R. T. Hamilton Bruce (1846–1899). In 1886 Cottier & Co. installed the large west window at St Giles' Cathedral in Edinburgh, depicting ten prophets, in memory of his wife, Fanny (replaced). That same year Bruce and Cottier's other supporters in Edinburgh lobbied for a memorial to the city's former Lord Provost, Sir George Harrison, to take the form of another window in the cathedral, to be made by Cottier.[98] Although this campaign ultimately failed, Bruce met with more success in promoting Cottier's work at Peebles Old Parish Church, where he was presumably behind Cottier's being awarded the commission for the chancel window in 1887 (extant). In 1890 Bruce commissioned for the same church a painted memorial screen for the chancel, made and decorated by Cottier & Co.[99] The screen has been removed, although fortunately a further twenty-six windows, supplied by Cottier & Co. until the early 1900s, remain *in situ*.

As time progressed, Cottier & Co.'s portfolio of designs grew and these were increasingly modified for commissions in Britain and the United States as well as Australia. For example, the figures of the theological Virtues originally designed for the *Painters' Window* in Aberdeen in 1874 (see fig. 28) were adapted for Leiper's Camphill United Presbyterian Church in Glasgow (1876; extant) and many other churches.[100] Although this was common practice among stained-glass studios, Cottier was criticised on one occasion for the way figures were reused. In 1886 the artist George Aikman, responding to William Hole's and Bruce's praise of the window commissioned by Bruce at St Giles' Cathedral, criticised its colouring and the way in which some of the figures, adapted from previous commissions, had been cropped: 'it struck me that the design had not been originally made for its present place, there being evidence of cutting which never occurred in any of the great windows that I ever saw.'[101] Bruce had written to *The Scotsman* newspaper describing the window as 'one of the most beautiful and successful pieces of modern art that has come under my notice ... in my opinion, Mr Cottier is almost alone in his supreme mastery over colour.'[102]

From about 1879 Cottier & Co. also made many windows from designs based on wood engravings by the brothers George and Edward Dalziel after drawings of Christian parables by the Pre-Raphaelite artist John Everett Millais (1829–1896). Originally published in 1863 in Strahan & Co.'s *Good Words* magazine, they were published collectively in *The Parables of Our Lord and Saviour Jesus Christ* by Routledge, Warne & Routledge the following year and the book continued to be advertised by the publisher throughout the 1870s. Cottier's friend Reid was an ardent admirer of Millais and Cottier may have seen Millais's adaptations of the designs for Kinnoull Parish Church, Perth (1870)[103] or, more likely, those made by Adam & Small for Bellhaven United Presbyterian Church in Glasgow (1877). In 1880 a three-light window incorporating parables was installed in Bothwell Parish Church, mentioned earlier, and many other examples are known, especially in the United States (see Chapter Four, pp. 123–4).

As well as church windows, notable Scottish public commissions from the 1880s included several in and around Dundee, possibly connected with the fact that White moved there in 1877. Among these were four windows for the Dundee Royal Exchange in 1887 (*in situ*; fig. 33) and six for the Council Chamber of the Town House in Dundee in 1888. The latter series depicts famous Scots such as James V and the Duke of Argyll, six more being designed by Burne-Jones and installed by Morris & Co. in 1889.[104] The Cottier and Morris windows were removed prior to the demolition of the Town House in 1932 and are now in the collection of Dundee City Council.

CHURCH DECORATION

During the 1870s the decorating side of Cottier's business was active, fulfilling commissions in churches and public buildings throughout England and Scotland, most of which have been overpainted or demolished.[105] These contracts could sometimes prove difficult to win and often depended on personal contacts. J. J. Stevenson's friend the architect Edward Robert Robson (1836–1917), then the Surveyor to the Corporation of Liverpool, assisted Cottier in obtaining the commission to decorate his newly built Church of St Anne (demolished). By the time of the church's dedication in November 1871, Cottier had painted the walls and ceiling in what was described by the local press as a 'highly florid style'; the ceiling was green, decorated with gold spots, 'whilst the other parts of the interior are stencilled in what might be called almost extravagant minuteness.'[106]

Cottier's decorating business appears to have faced two challenges: first the general preference to use local firms and second the difficulty of adapting the style of decoration Cottier had successfully initiated in Glasgow in the mid-1860s to other contexts, primarily because the palette was considered too dark. In 1871, again with Robson's help, Cottier tried to win a commission to decorate the council chamber and luncheon room of Liverpool Town Hall. Although the town council's finance committee recommended that Cottier's tender, for £600, should be accepted, one member of the council thought the colouring 'far too dark' and another that a local firm should be engaged as a matter of civic pride.[107] These sentiments were echoed in a letter published in the *Liverpool Mercury* and written by 'an encourager of home talent' who argued that:

The advocates of Mr. Cottier's design appear to have been unaware that the town hall is Italian; the council room, if anything – perhaps it will puzzle most men to say what – is Italian; and the plans of Messrs. White and Messrs. Jeffery are Italian, and therefore perfectly in harmony with the building; whilst that of Mr. Cottier is Gothic ... Why this love of running to London by the corporate authorities for whatever they may require to have done that has the least importance attached to it?[108]

As a result of this controversy, the town council deferred its decision and there is no record of Cottier undertaking the work; it has not been established whether Cottier was finally awarded this commission.

In Aberdeen Cottier had no problem gaining commissions as he could rely on the support of White and his circle for patronage. Nevertheless, Cottier's decoration of the East Parish Church or East Kirk faced criticism because he was not a local artist and on account of its style. Cottier's men decorated the church in distemper colours for three months over the summer of 1871 and the church reopened on 17 September.[109] No visual record has been located but descriptions of 'Egyptian' decoration suggest it was similar to that employed successfully at Townhead and Queen's Park churches in Glasgow. However, one observer thought that 'Mr Cottier's Egyptian forms and tracings are not very well suited for the decoration of a Gothic edifice.'[110] Another critic thought that the decoration:

gives one the feeling of being enveloped in midnight darkness, or of entering into the valley of the shadow of death. By the bye, that cart-blue ceiling of his, with its Dutch metal star-fish scattered over it, gives a ghost of a suspicion that Mr Cottier supposed it to be in the mediæval style. A little more study on the subject would have prevented him from falling into such a grievous error ... He has stencilled up a good deal of ornament indeed, but of so thoroughly an unecclesiastical character that it would have been much more suitable in the Music Hall ... [111]

The critic, possibly a business rival, also thought that the work should have been done in oil paint, rather than in distemper, 'but being only a glass-stainer, he [Cottier] could not be expected to be acquainted with these minutiae'.[112] In response, one of Cottier's supporters advised that 'if he turns to Dresser's "Art of Ornamentation," he will find on plate XV. an illustration of a dark-blue ceiling, with stars and star-fishes in silver and gold, with the remark that this is given as an example of "the power of decoration to move the feelings, according to the treatment of the middle ages."'[113] This is interesting because some of the motifs used in Cottier's earlier interior decoration (see figs 17 and 18) suggest that he found inspiration in Dresser's designs from the same source. In October 1874 Cottier's decoration at the East Kirk, together with a memorial window, were destroyed when fire gutted the building, forcing members of the congregation, ironically, to worship in the city's Music Hall.[114]

Despite the controversy surrounding his East Kirk decoration, in 1875 Cottier won the commission to decorate and glaze the adjoining West Kirk, which had narrowly missed being destroyed by the fire.[115] Reid was keen that alterations to the building, designed in the mid-eighteenth century by the renowned Aberdonian James Gibbs, should be handled with great sensitivity by a decorator who 'can understand, appreciate and sympathise with the architecture of the building. Decorators of this class are by no means common ... I have told Mr Walker that should the proposal to decorate be favourably received at once to propose Cottier as the only man fit to do the work well.'[116] Several letters from Cottier to William Smith, the Aberdeen City architect, survive (see fig. 24). Cottier advised that the ceiling should be painted 'as one in good blue with gold stars – nothing can look so grand and simple. I have seen it often abroad' and advocated the use of oil paint, rather than distemper, because 'if its [*sic*] new plaster I am afraid it will eat away our blue – it has done so – so after that I am afraid to do Blue in water except its [*sic*] in an old Church. Oil would cost a bit more but be more safe.'[117] As it turned out, the church authorities would not pay for oil paint, so Cottier's men painted the fresh plaster ceiling in distemper in 'a rich blue bespangled with gilt stars.'[118]

One decorative scheme of the 1870s for which visual documentation exists is that executed by Cottier & Co. for the private chapel of John and Emily Gordon at Cluny Castle, Aberdeenshire, in 1872.[119] Cottier's decoration was overpainted after a fire in 1926 but fortunately a watercolour by the artist John Mitchell survives, showing the lavish decoration on the walls and ceiling (fig. 34). Described as 'very rich and sparkling with gold', the ceiling was decorated with panels of sunflowers and bands of rich scrollwork, while inscriptions and a tree of life enlivened the walls. Cottier & Co. also made stained glass (some remaining

34 John Mitchell, *Cluny Castle Chapel, Aberdeenshire*, 1873, showing the painted decoration and furnishings supplied by Cottier & Co., London. Watercolour and bodycolour on paper, 71.7 × 54.9 cm. Private collection

in situ) and a carved oak altar table, pulpit, reading desk and benches.[120]

STAINED GLASS FOR HOMES

At the same time that Cottier & Co. was producing memorial windows, its studio also designed and made domestic stained glass, often as part of larger decorative schemes. As described in Chapter One, in the 1860s Cottier had made a name for himself by exhibiting to critical acclaim two armorial windows in the Renaissance Revival style at international exhibitions in London and Paris, and such windows are sometimes found in his domestic commissions of the 1870s. They were usually positioned in hallways or staircase landings and might incorporate the monograms of the owners, their coats of arms and figurative panels. One example is the upper part of a large window on the staircase landing at Cairndhu House, Helensburgh (*c.*1873; fig. 35). As with the church windows, the figures were worked up from sketches (some, no doubt, by Cottier) by artists such as Hart, who conveyed Cottier's style, which tended towards muscular figures. Subject matter included the Seasons (see fig. 194), popular in Aesthetic interiors, Roman goddesses (fig. 36), literary or artistic figures, panels of birds, foliage, fruit and flowers (see fig. 194), townscapes and seascapes. These panels were framed by glass quarries decorated with motifs painted in silver stain (silver nitrate), a device often used by Morris & Co. and other Aesthetic designers, particularly in their domestic glass. In addition to more or less stylised botanical motifs, which were most common, Cottier & Co. used butterflies as well as boats, another reference to Cottier's maritime ancestry. Quarries probably served a practical purpose in admitting more light into home interiors than was perhaps generally required in churches, although they were also employed in churches where this may have been a consideration.[121]

Good examples of Cottier's domestic stained glass can be found at Coll-Earn, a house designed by Leiper in Auchterarder, Perthshire, for Alexander Mackintosh (1821–1901), a businessman involved in textiles and a friend of White. In 1870, while Coll-Earn was being built, Mackintosh invited Reid to Perthshire to complete family portraits, including those of his daughters Dorothy and Lucy, aged eight and six, sitting by a pool.[122] In 1871 Cottier's artists used Reid's portraits as the model for portrait windows of the girls for the drawing room at Coll-Earn, while another window features allegories of 'Morning' and 'Night' designed by Holiday and made by another London studio, Heaton, Butler & Bayne. Further commissions in Scotland included fine sets of windows for the distiller Robert Stewart (1825–1909) at Ingliston House, near Edinburgh, in the early 1870s (see fig. 36), and in England for Tennyson.[123] Cottier also made stained-glass windows for the London home of his friend the painter William Ewart Lockhart (1846–1900), some of which is visible in the background of a portrait of his daughter Theodora (see image on p. ii).[124]

As was the case with memorial windows, the palette of Cottier's domestic glass changed and darkened in the 1880s and, although many windows continued to feature quarries with individually painted motifs, lending them a 'medieval' character, there was an increased tendency to paint quarries with large swags and ribbons in the Renaissance Revival style (see fig. 103). A good example of this later style are the windows made in 1893 to complement the lavish interiors supplied by the Edinburgh firm of Scott Morton & Co. for the home of a whisky baron and wine merchant, Arthur Sanderson, at 25 Learmonth Terrace, Edinburgh. These windows are in a late style, with panels representing the Seasons and eighteenth-century scenes executed in a rich golden and brown palette, swags of flowers including chrysanthemums and sunflowers, leitmotifs of Aestheticism.

INTERIOR DECORATION

In Britain little of Cottier's domestic interior decoration appears to have survived, although there is enough evidence to gain some impression of the kind of interiors he was creating. In 1872 Haweis wrote an article in *Saint Pauls Magazine* in which she described Cottier as an artist, on a par with Owen Jones and William Morris:

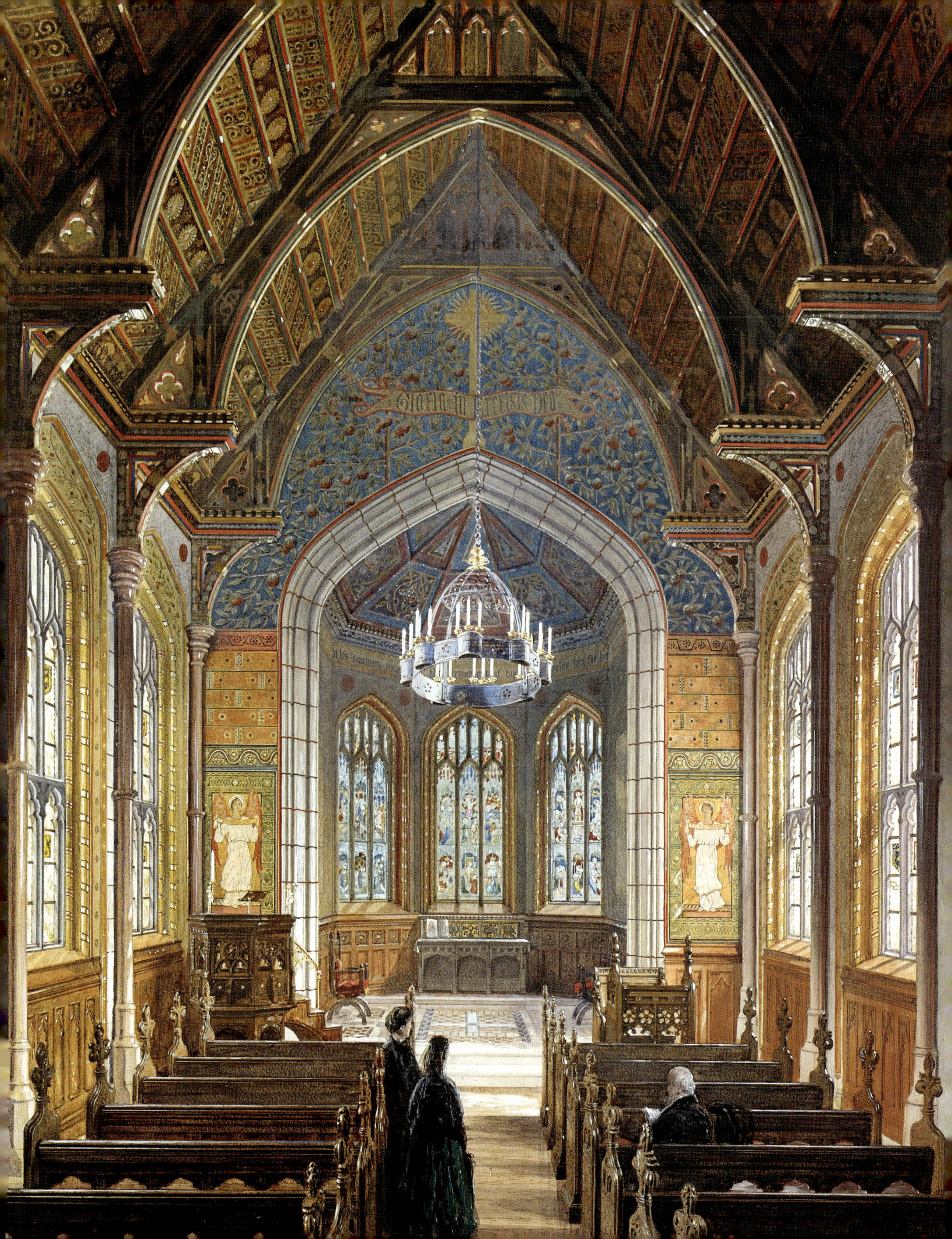

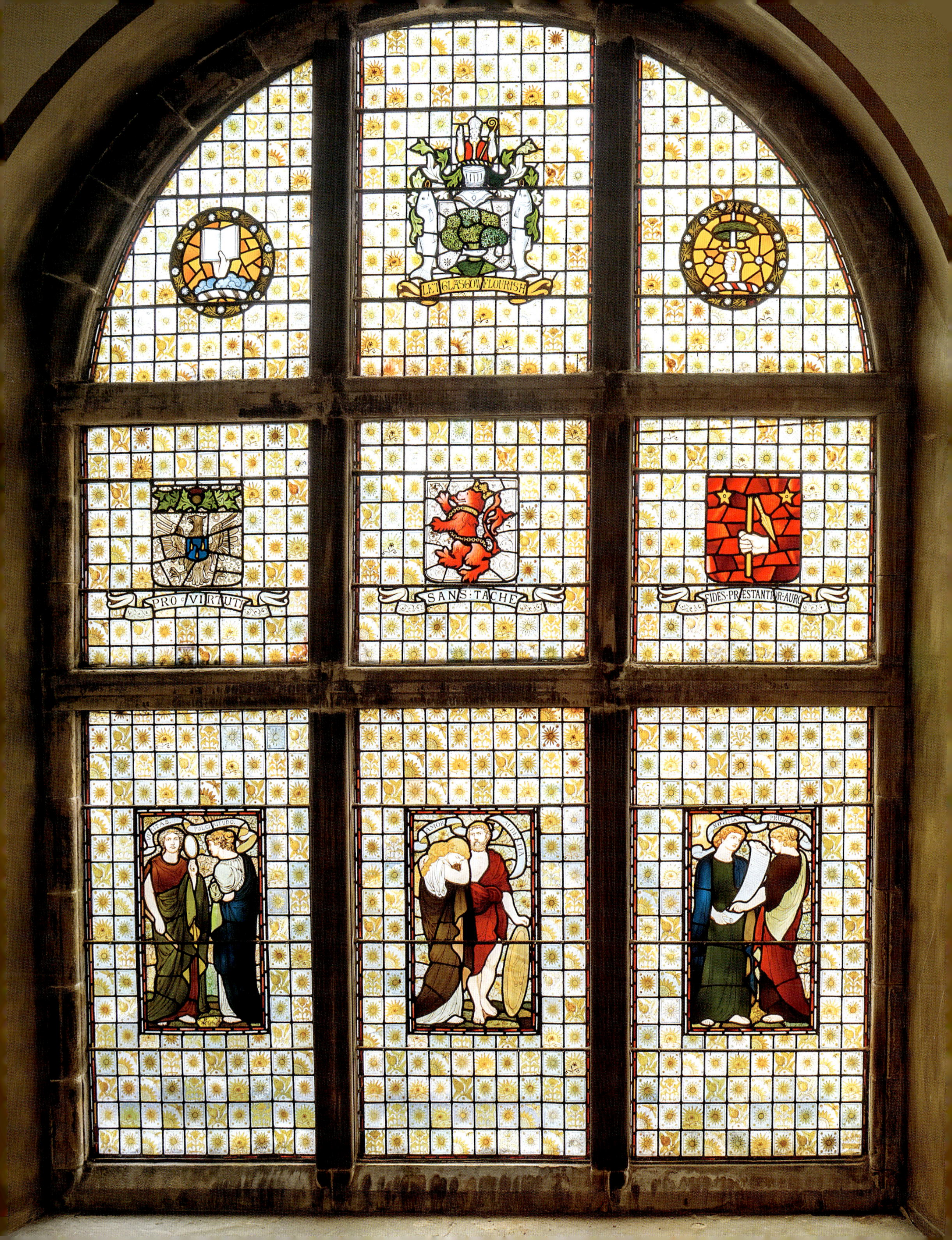
LET GLASGOW FLOURISH
PRO VIRTUTI
SANS·TACHE
FIDES·PRÆSTANTIOR·AURO

35 Staircase window in Cairndhu House, Helensburgh, Argyll and Bute, by Cottier & Co., London, *c.*1873. Stained glass. In the lower right panel, *Notitia* holds a scroll signed by several Cottier & Co. employees.

36 *Pomona*, staircase window in Ingliston House, Midlothian, by Cottier & Co., London, *c.*1870–5. Stained glass

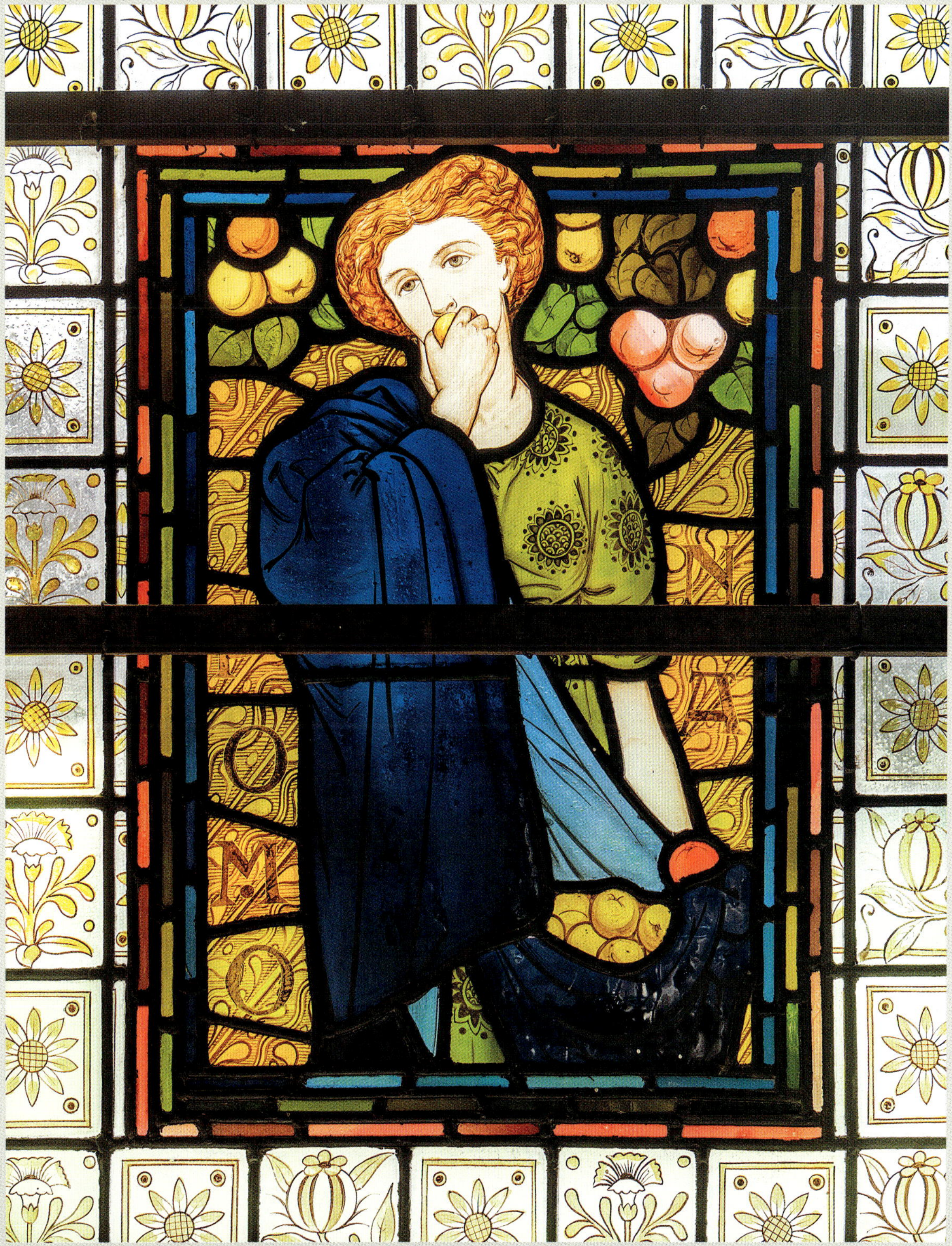

37 Dining room of Kepplestone House, Aberdeen, decorated and furnished by Cottier & Co., 1875. Alexander Mollinger's *Meerkerk, clearing up after Rain* (fig. 60) can be seen to the upper left of the corner. Photograph *c.*1880. Aberdeen Art Gallery and Museums

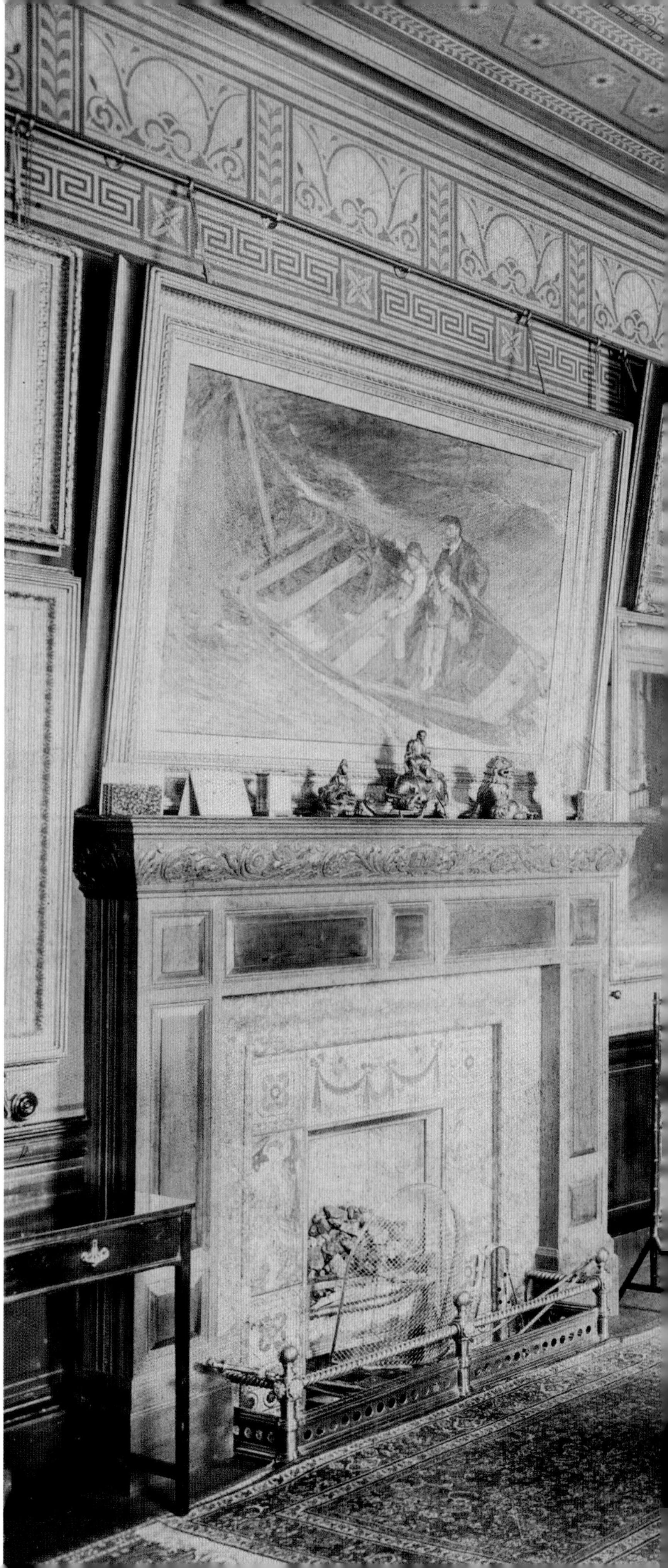

To Mr. Owen Jones, Mr. Morris, Mr. Cottier, and a few other intelligent artists and architects, we owe a debt of gratitude. These gentlemen, especially Mr. Cottier, a pupil of Ruskin's, have lavished their great gift of an 'eye' for form and colour in the direction of mural and room decoration – the stained glass, the ceilings, and stencils designed by them are quite perfect.[125]

Haweis described this group as using 'forms ... studied and adapted from the finest examples in old Roman and Greek decoration'.[126] Two photographs of Kepplestone House (demolished), the Aberdeen home of Alexander Macdonald, a collector and owner of a granite quarrying and sculpting business, decorated in 1875, give a glimpse of the 'forms' (figs 37 and 38) if not the colours which, according to Haweis, were:

all exquisite in themselves and exquisitely harmonised. Queer blues, that are neither blue, nor green, nor lilac; queerer greens and yellows, and all variations of tertiary hints, are tenderly united and mixed; at rare intervals a small bit of raw colour is introduced with peculiarly brilliant effect. Very little gold is employed; but what there is, is most craftily managed. Many colours are clouded or gradated in tint, in one pattern; black comes in well, or invisible greens or browns.[127]

The decoration in public rooms such as the dining room would have provided a foil for Macdonald's impressive collection of contemporary paintings (Millais's *Bright Eyes*, 1877, Aberdeen Art Gallery, is visible in the photograph). While these photographs cannot convey the colours described by Haweis, they illustrate the fact that in the 1870s Cottier was creating interiors painted with motifs similar to those used by Thomson in his architecture and interiors, in tandem with Greek-style furniture (discussed shortly). A well-preserved example of this kind of decoration is at St Leonard's Hall, Edinburgh, built for the publisher Thomas Nelson Jr (1822–1892).[128] Surviving ceilings combine Greek details with other motifs popularised by Morris & Co., such as foliage with fruit against a dark background, possibly the work of Cottier (fig. 39). Morris had used similar panels in the dining room at the South Kensington Museum in the 1860s and they

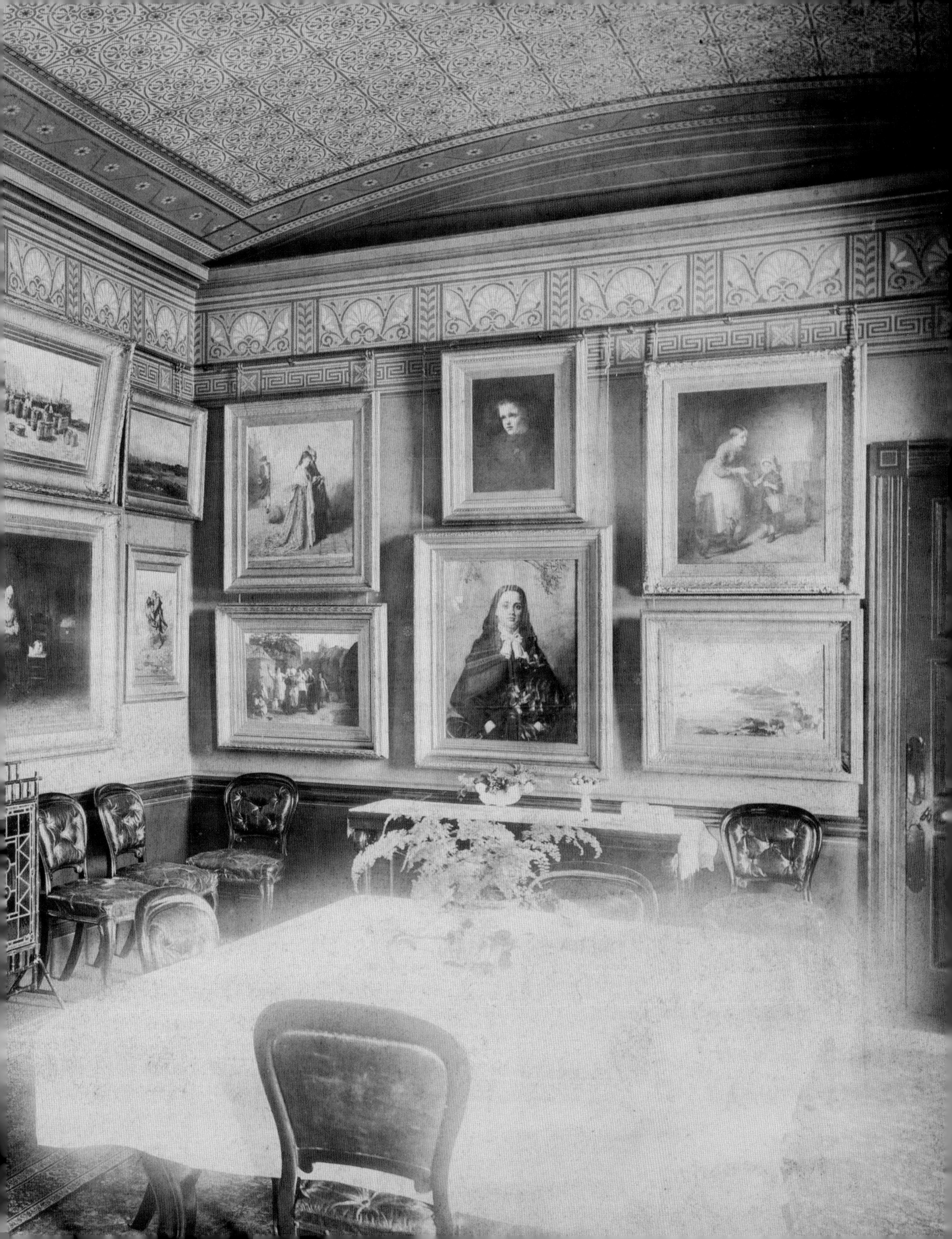

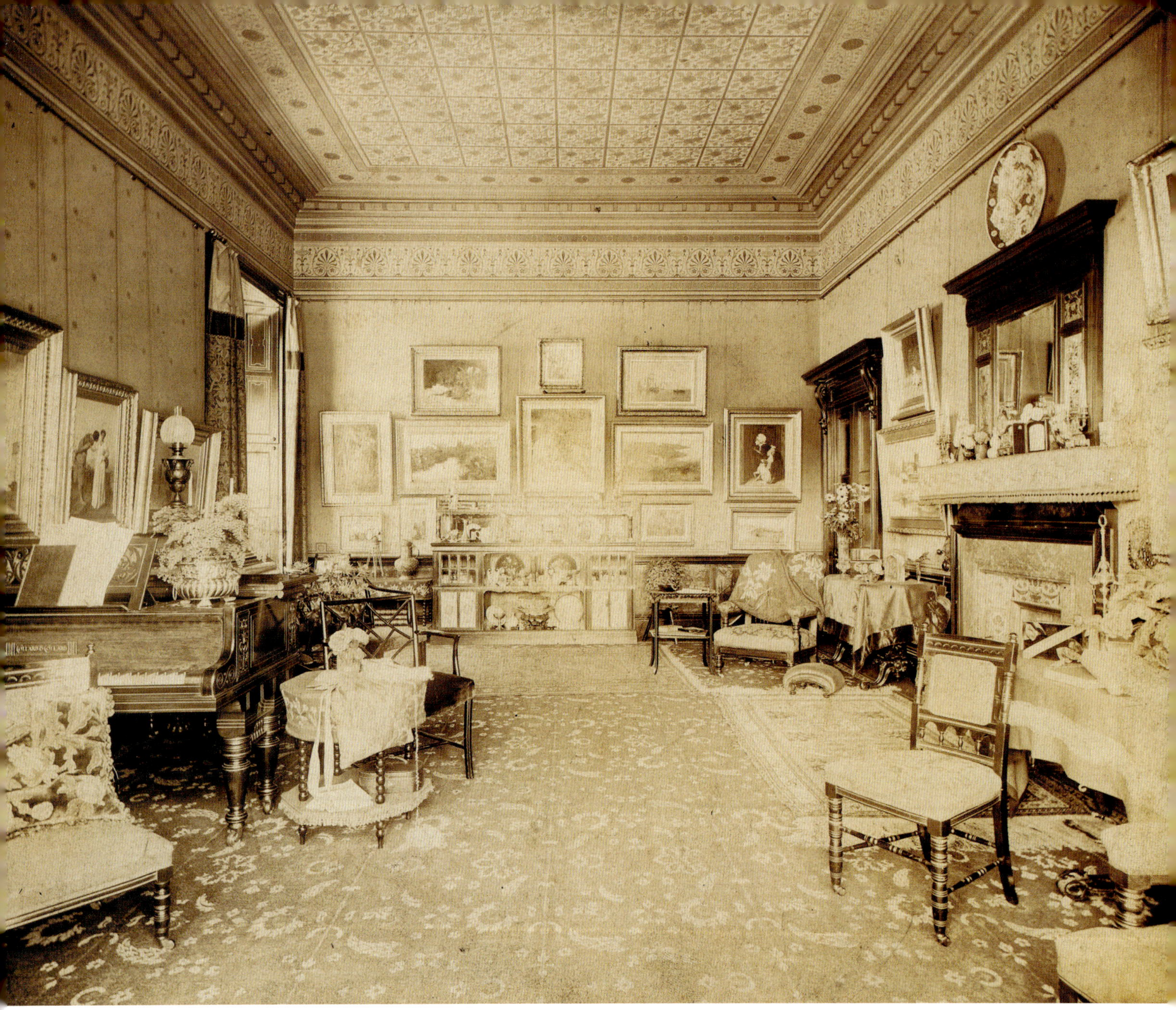

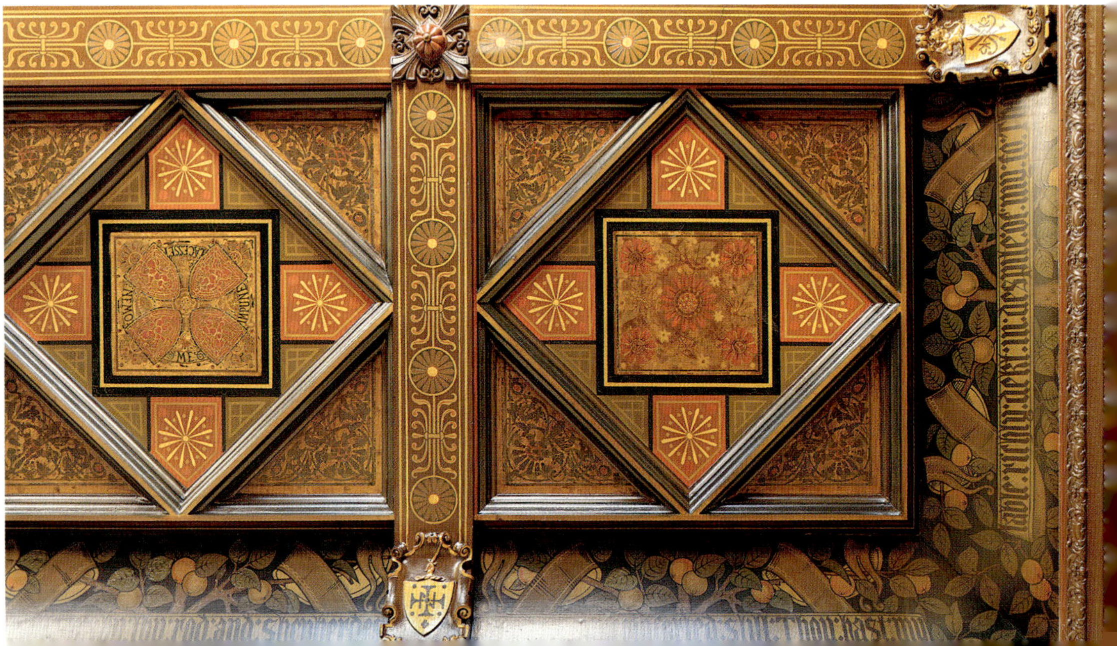

38 Drawing room of Kepplestone House, Aberdeen, decorated and furnished by Cottier & Co., 1875. Photograph *c.*1880. Aberdeen Art Gallery and Museums

39 Ceiling in St Leonard's Hall, Edinburgh, painted decoration attributed to Cottier & Co., *c.*1870–5

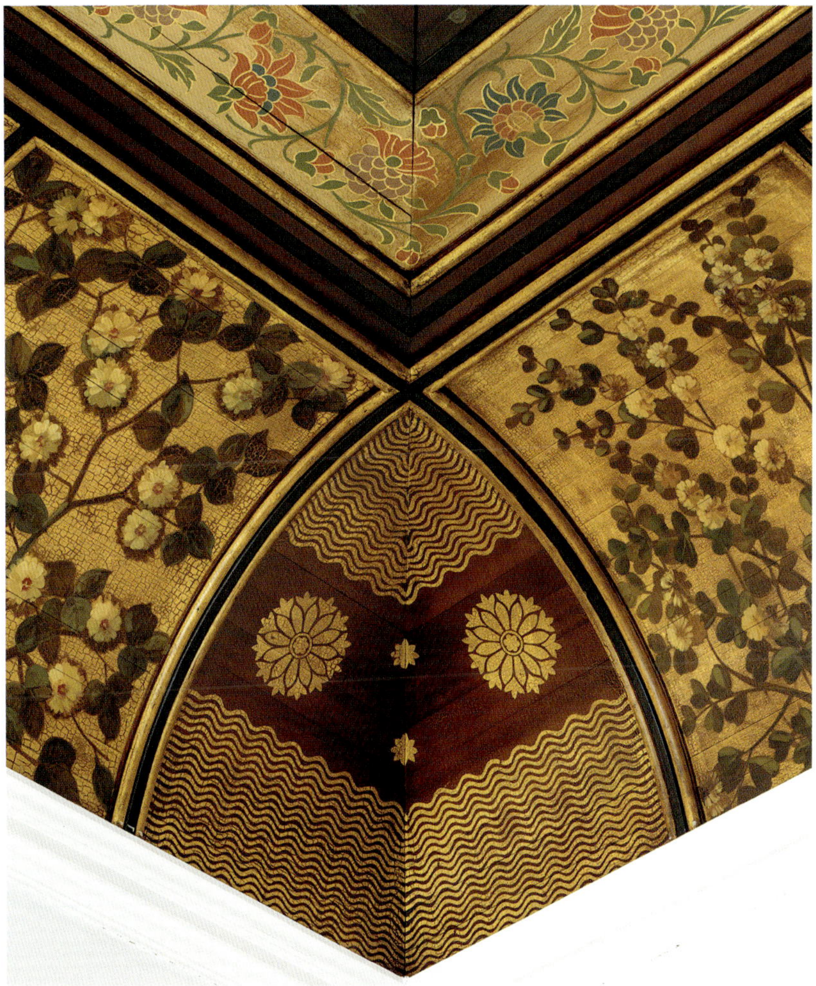

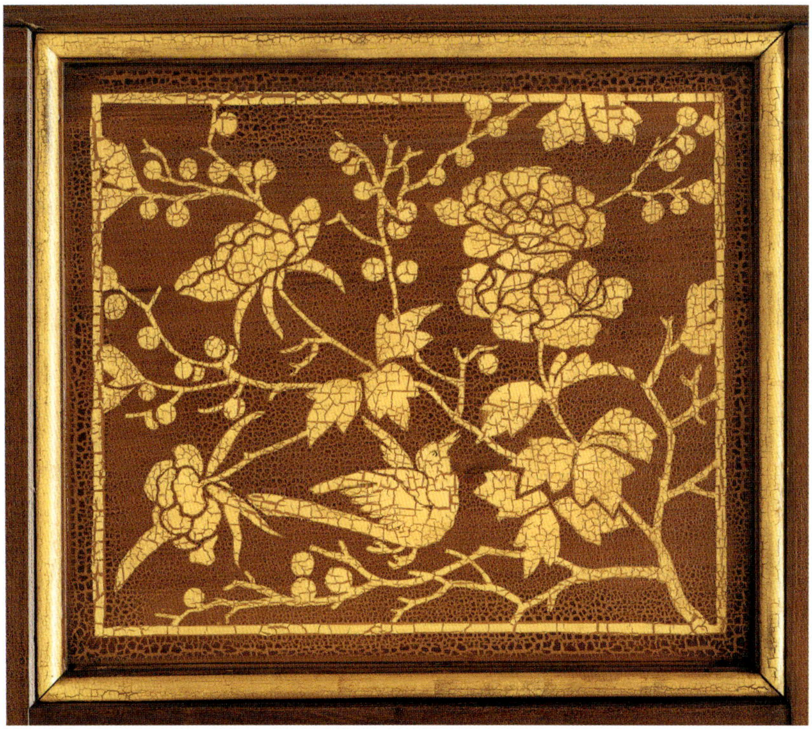

40 Drawing-room ceiling, Cairndhu House, Helensburgh, Argyll and Bute, painted by Cottier & Co., *c.*1873

41 Drawing-room ceiling, Cairndhu House, Helensburgh, Argyll and Bute, decorated by Cottier & Co., *c.*1873

became popular in the 1870s, as in the interiors of Norman Shaw's Cragside, Northumberland, decorated by Heaton.

In 1871 Alexander Thomson observed that Heaton, Butler & Bayne was among the London stained-glass and decorating companies that 'seem to be adapting Japanese art to their Gothic things with great success'.[129] The interest in Japanese art, which had been growing among British architects and designers since the 1862 International Exhibition in London, has already been noted in relation to Cottier's stained glass. It also manifested itself in his interior decoration. At Cairndhu House, Helensburgh, a substantial house designed by Leiper for a miller and art collector, John G. Ure (1824–1901), Cottier provided painted decoration, stained glass and ceramic tiles (see figs 35, 40–43 and 45), contributing to interiors described by the *British Architect* as 'strong and picturesque in style'.[130] The drawing-room ceiling is bordered by coving divided into panels of alternating gold stencilling on the varnished wood and naturalistic leaves and flowers on gold grounds (figs 40 and 41), a design strongly influenced by Japonisme and similar to a ceiling designed by Talbert.[131] In the hallway, which also has a richly stencilled ceiling (figs 42 and 43), a pair of painted and gilded wooden panels flank the overmantel mirror, designed by Henry Stacy Marks. Part of a series of scenes depicting the Seven Ages of Man, the figures represent a man in the 'Sixth Age' admiring a young woman.[132]

Cottier designed a more eclectic interior for White, who commissioned him to add a purpose-built gallery to the back of his house on Union Street in Aberdeen and to refurbish the interior, just after 1870.[133] Cottier supplied ebonised and stencilled furniture, some of it in the Greek style (see pp. 62–4),[134] as well as a fireplace surround and overmantel embellished with tiles illustrating the months of the year and incorporating an oil on canvas portrait by Reid of Mrs White wearing white with a camellia at her breast.[135] Reid wrote to White:

If you did rightly you would throw your house open to the whole of the house painters in Aberdeen – or in the North of Scotland if they wished it. Let them go and sit in it for a

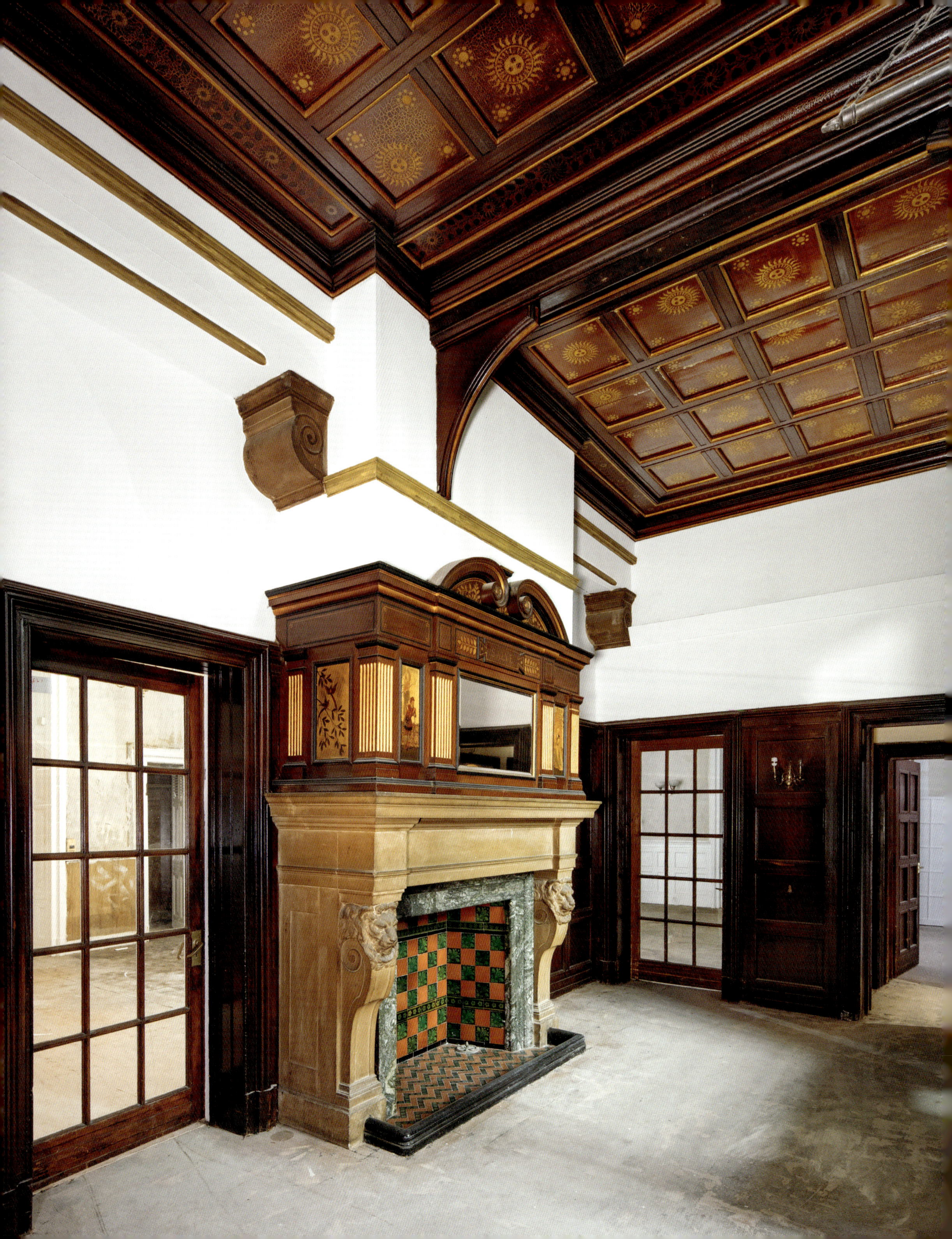

42 Mantelpiece in the entrance hall, Cairndhu House, Helensburgh, Argyll and Bute, decorated by Cottier & Co., *c.*1873. Carved, painted and gilded wood

43 Hallway ceiling, Cairndhu House, Helensburgh, Argyll and Bute, decorated by Cottier & Co., *c.*1873. Painted and gilded wood

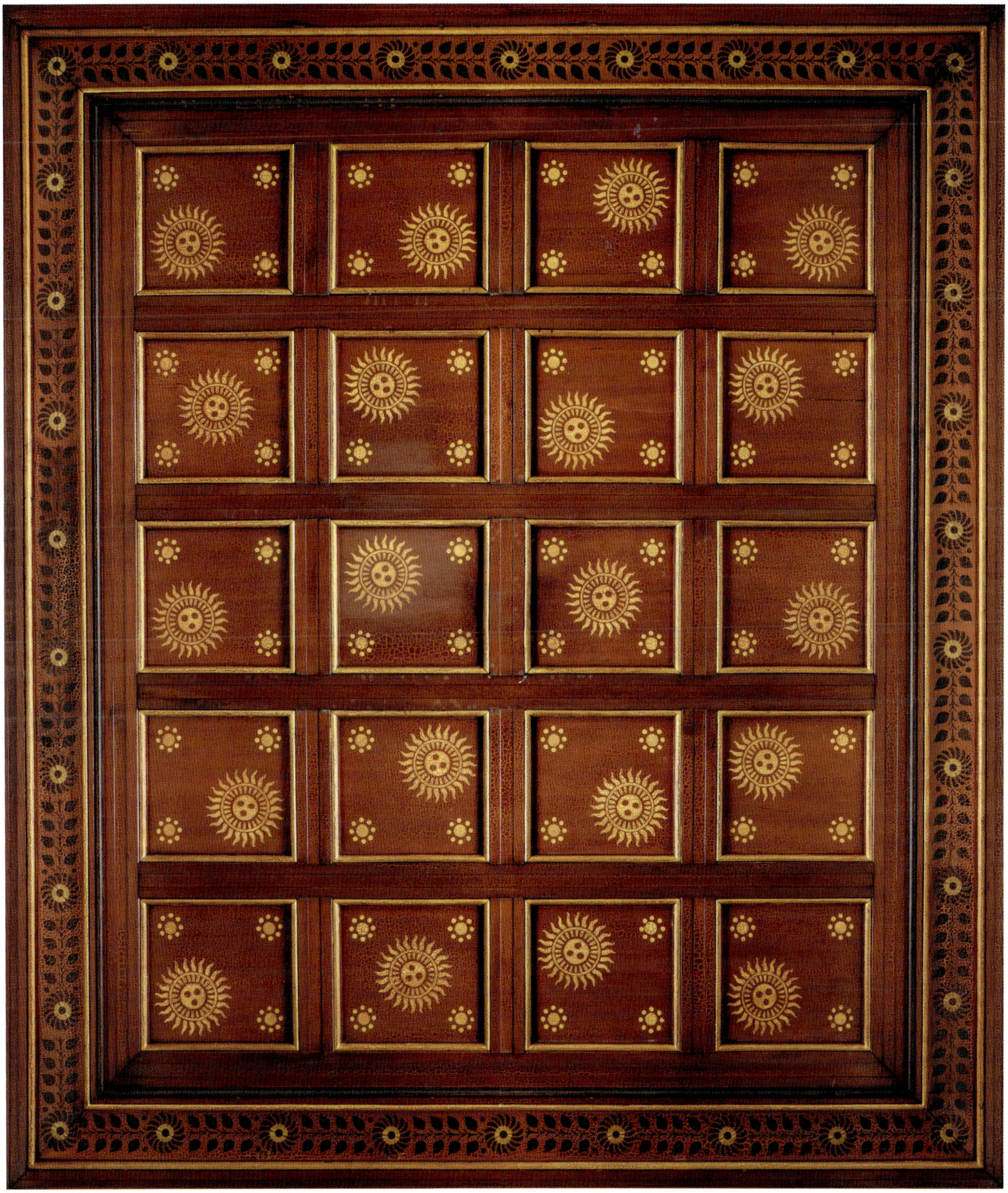

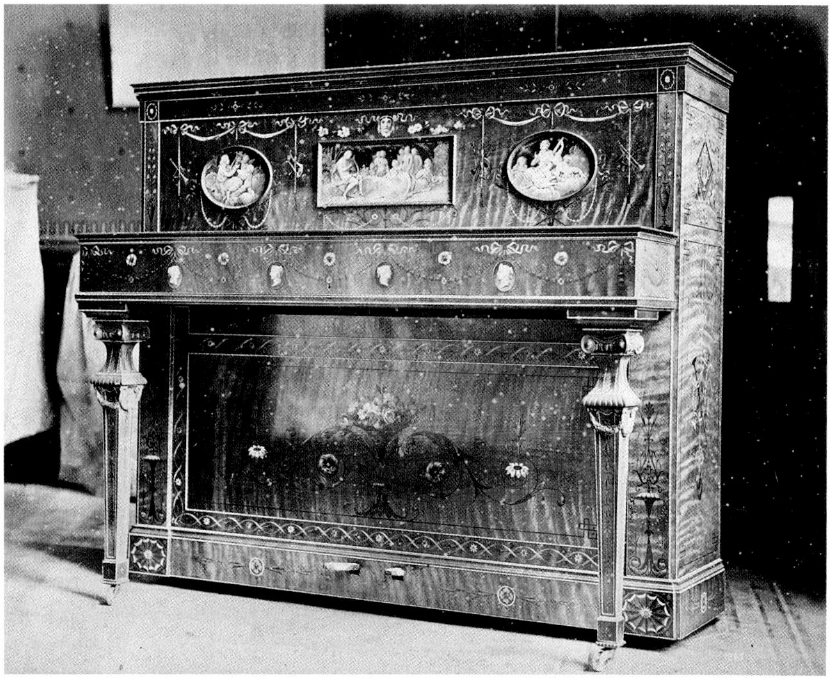

44 Pianette at 3 Chesterfield Gardens, Mayfair, London, the painted decoration attributed to Cottier & Co., 1876. Photograph by Bedford Lemere & Co., 1876. Albumen print. Historic England Archive, Bedford Lemere Collection

fortnight – let them study and consider and if needs be copy every bit of colour and detail about it – and let them do their best to reproduce it in every house they paint – you would be none the poorer, Cottier none the worse.[136]

Cottier decorated the home of another Aberdeen merchant, John Moir Clark, on the Garthdee estate in Aberdeenshire, described in 1877 as having 'been painted and done up internally in a style exceptionally elegant, by Cottier, of London'.[137] But it seems that some of the criticisms levelled at Cottier's preference for dark interiors in public buildings were also held by several of Clark's visitors. Writing in 1935, an Aberdeen lawyer, Lachlan Mackinnon, recalled that

The change-over to the 'severe Cottier' style of house decoration with its subdued dull reds and blacks took place in the 'seventies. I was first introduced to it at Garthdee House, just then built, when its owner, Mr. John Moir Clark, gave a house-warming dance, and the dancers ... discussed the unwonted sombre surroundings in which they pirouetted to the strains of Strauss ... [138]

Surviving evidence of Cottier's house decoration in England remains scarce. In London, Cottier decorated the study of the minister and novelist George MacDonald (1824–1905).[139] From 1867 MacDonald lived in a house on Hammersmith Mall, until in 1877 Morris took on the lease of the house, renaming it Kelmscott House. The designer William de Morgan was unimpressed by the blood-red flock wallpaper, ebonised bookcases and 'a ceiling of azure blue, dotted with gilt stars, considerably tarnished', while Rossetti described the room as 'fearful to the eye'.[140] Cottier's decoration vanished when Morris converted the study into his dining room. Although most of Cottier's house decoration suffered a similar fate, the identity of many of his clients is known thanks to a prospectus for Cottier & Co., published in London for the New York gallery between 1876 and 1881 (see fig. 70), which lists recent commissions including those in the affluent London districts of Belgravia, Kensington, Mayfair and Marylebone.[141] Among them was a Conservative MP, Colonel Edmund Hegan Kennard, who moved into the newly built 3 Chesterfield Gardens, Mayfair, London, with his family in 1876. Two photographs of the interior taken that year by the leading photographer Bedford Lemere show an elaborately painted satinwood pianette case standing against newly painted walls (fig. 44), as well as a boudoir ceiling in a French eighteenth-century style, a rare visual record of Cottier's decoration 'after the French'.

Another name in the prospectus is that of the Spanish merchant José de Murrietta, of 11 Palace Gardens, Kensington, a house also boasting interior decoration designed by Alfred Stevens and Walter Crane.[142] It is possible that Cottier decorated the ballroom and art gallery, which were added to the south side of the house by a Queen Anne architect, Edward John Tarver, in 1873. Other clients included well-known London figures, such as the auctioneer C. T. Christie, of the auctioneers Christie, Manson & Woods, and the property developer Cyril Flower, later first Lord Battersea.[143] In the absence of identified interiors it is difficult to know how Cottier's British interiors developed in the 1880s, although some of the lighter, Adam Revival interiors executed by the Australian branch may give some clue (see fig. 144). On a visit to London from Sydney in 1886 Lyon described the bedroom of Cottier's daughter Isabella at 3 St James's Terrace, which suggests that Cottier had largely moved away from the Japonisme fashionable in the 1870s to embrace more sumptuous effects: 'I had Ella's bed room which was done up quite

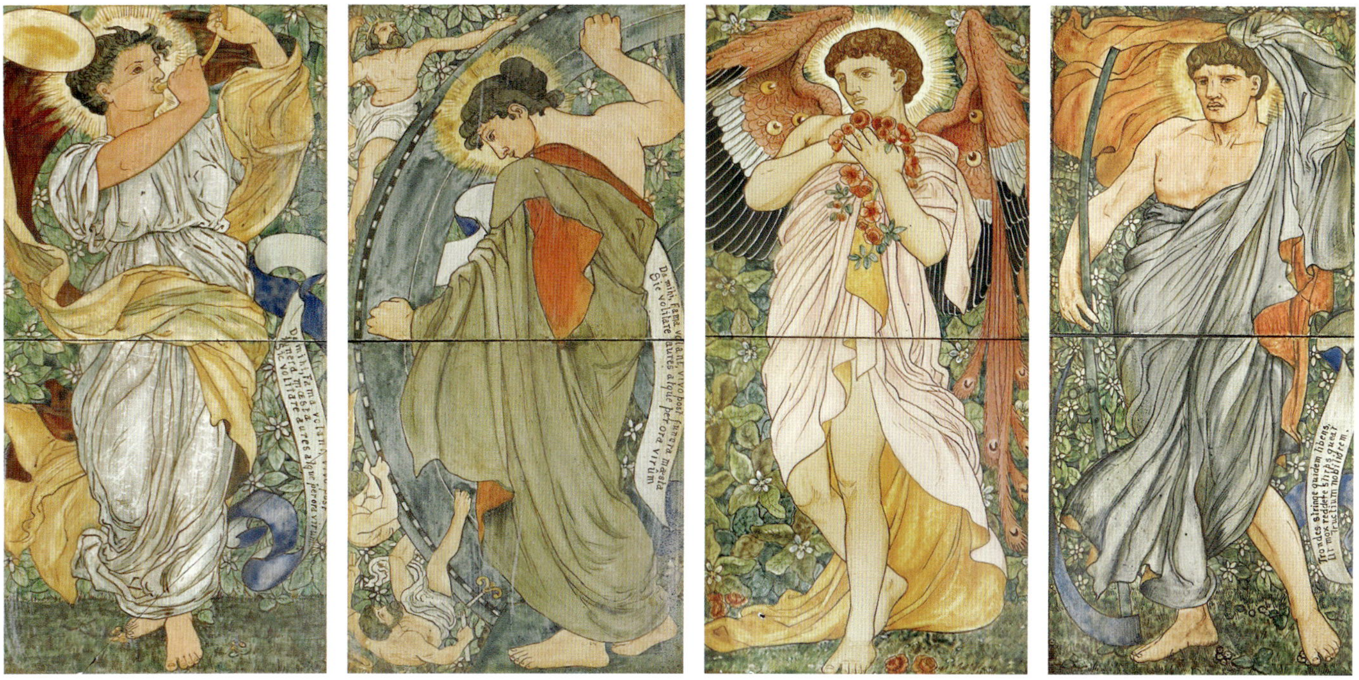

45 *Fame*, *Fortune*, *Love* and *Death* made for Cairndhu House, Helensburgh (removed), by Cottier & Co., London, *c.*1873. Underglaze colours on earthenware tiles manufactured by Minton, Hollins & Co., Stoke-on-Trent, Staffordshire, each panel 41 × 20.5 cm. Private collection

46 Portrait charger by Cottier & Co, *c.*1880. Underglaze colours on earthenware blank manufactured by Minton & Co., Stoke-on-Trent, Staffordshire, d. 39 cm. Four Acres Charitable Trust

47 Charger with chrysanthemums by Cottier & Co., *c.*1882. Underglaze colours on earthenware blank manufactured by Minton & Co., Stoke-on-Trent, Staffordshire, d. 39 cm. Private collection

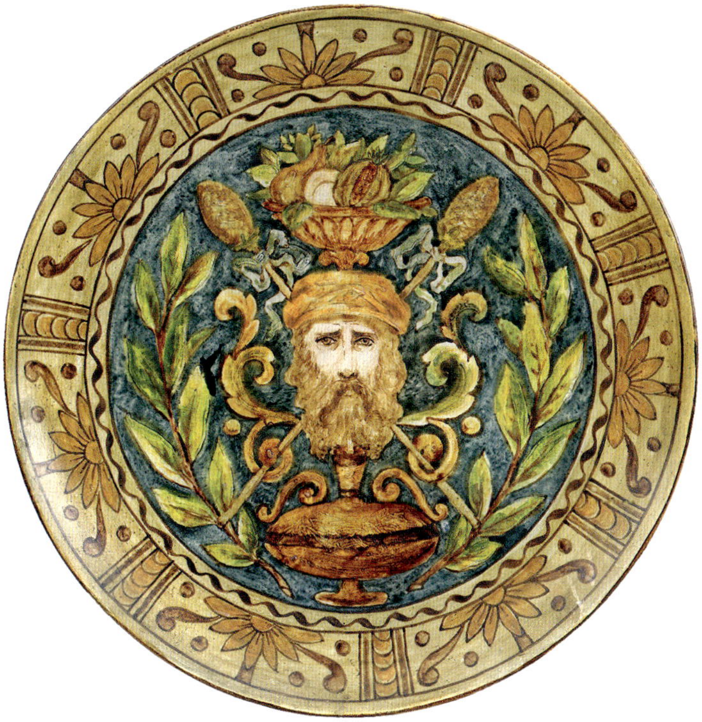

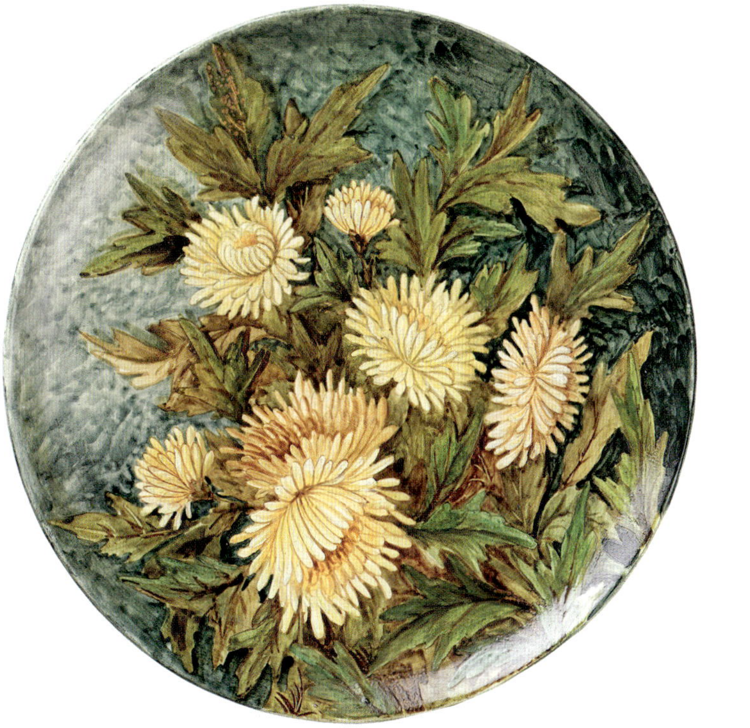

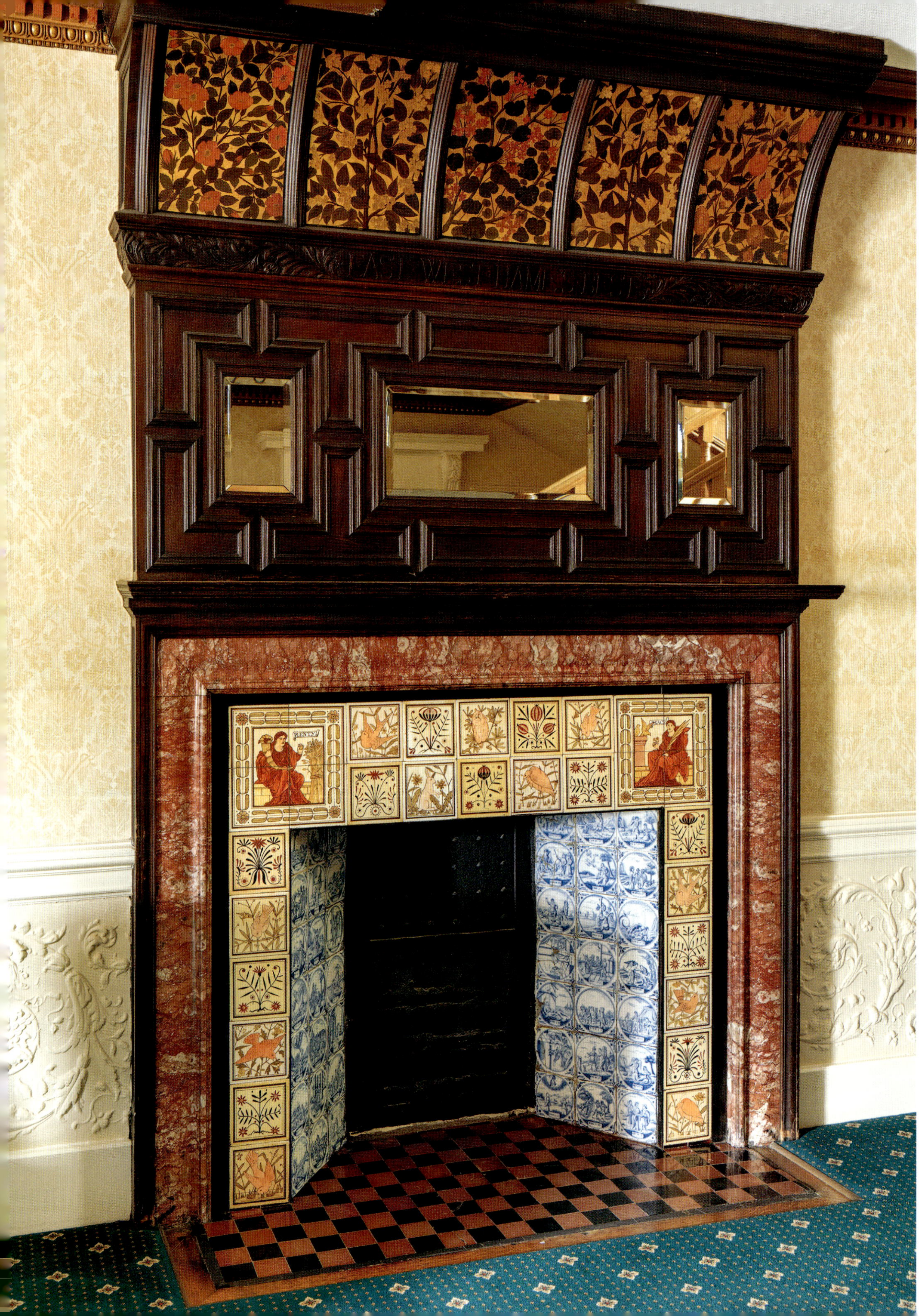

48 Hallway fireplace, Links House, Montrose, Angus, by Cottier & Co., London, *c.*1870–3. Carved, painted and gilded oak. Links Hotel, Montrose, Angus

unique, panelled gold ceiling, wood all painted gold bronze, yellow satin hangings, turkey carpets, venetian brass gasalier, furniture satin wood, Embroidered Japanese quilt and neat bric a brac, Cottier has banished all the Japanese stuff He used be so fond off. He now dislikes it so fashions change'.[144]

In addition to painting ceilings and walls and designing and producing stained glass, Cottier & Co. decorated ceramic tiles, plaques and chargers to embellish interiors (figs 45–8). In 1873 Cottier & Co. sent examples to the Vienna World's Fair, where an American delegate observed:

Plain white or buff tiles may be decorated with figures or flowers, by painting upon the glaze. There are artists who devote their efforts to this work, and the variety of subjects is great. Cottier & Co., the celebrated decorators of interiors, publish a list of classical and allegorical figures, among them such as Pomona, Flora, the Seasons, Industry, etc., and a series of heads of poets, painters, composers of music, discoverers and philosophers.[145]

Some surviving tiles are known to have been painted on Minton, Hollins & Co. blanks. These were probably fired in the same kilns used for stained glass. Minton was one of the firms which encouraged the decoration of ceramics in the 1870s, notably with the establishment of an Art Pottery Studio in Kensington Gore in 1870, and the annual exhibitions of china painting held by Howell & James. From about 1877 Cottier's studio also decorated ceramic chargers – fifteen-inch blanks supplied by Minton in Stoke-on-Trent: Cottier's artists deliberately obliterated the impressed 'MINTON' name by placing the stock (horizontal bar) of the firm's anchor logo across it (see fig. 24); the Minton date cyphers provide approximate dates for their decoration. Their subjects range from designs inspired by Japanese and Iznik wares to female heads and flowers (see figs 46 and 47), while another is inscribed on the reverse with a dedication from Cottier to the art dealer Tripp and his wife.[146] Many of these ceramics are extant in the United States, to where they were probably exported during Cottier's lifetime.

In Britain and the United States, Cottier tiles and plaques can be found in many of the houses in which he worked. The dining-room mantelpieces at Cairndhu House originally incorporated tiles decorated in the Cottier studio (later removed; see fig. 45). Dating from about 1873, they depict personifications of Fame, Fortune, Love and Death, identified by Latin verses in scrolls. Identical figures appear in stained glass in the house[147] and tiles depicting Love and Death are just visible in the dining-room fireplace at Kepplestone House (see fig. 37), as well as on penwork furniture (see fig. 53). In Montrose, Angus, Cottier supplied decoration, stained glass and a painted and tiled fireplace around 1870–3 for Links House, the home of a mill owner and collector, James Middleton Paton (1808–1878), much of which survives (fig. 48 and see fig. 194).[148] In other commissions connected with Cottier, tiles decorated by other makers were used, such as the series depicting the months designed by Albert Moore, under whom Hart had trained: these were framed into the panelling above a fireplace at Coll-Earn (1871).

'AN ARTIST, IN FURNITURE AS IN GLASS'

During the 1870s Cottier & Co. established a reputation for making 'art furniture', a term in use by the late 1860s to denote furniture designed by artists and architects.[149] In 1874 the firm advertised the manufacture of 'Furniture of Special Design, in Best Workmanship, and at Moderate Cost', words echoed by one of their rivals in this field, Collinson & Lock, which promised prospective clients 'good taste, sound workmanship, and economy'.[150] In contrast with Collinson & Lock, Cottier's furniture was rarely marked or stamped and only since the late 1990s has a body of mostly unprovenanced work been identified, often on the basis of shared characteristics with signed stained glass and ceramic designs.[151]

As suggested earlier in relation to stained glass, Cottier may initially have produced furniture designs for others to work up. Many of his designers – John McKean Brydon, William Wallace, James Inglis and Frederick Vincent Hart – had trained or practised as architects, a profession increasingly involved with furniture design during the second half of the nineteenth century.[152] The architectural quality of

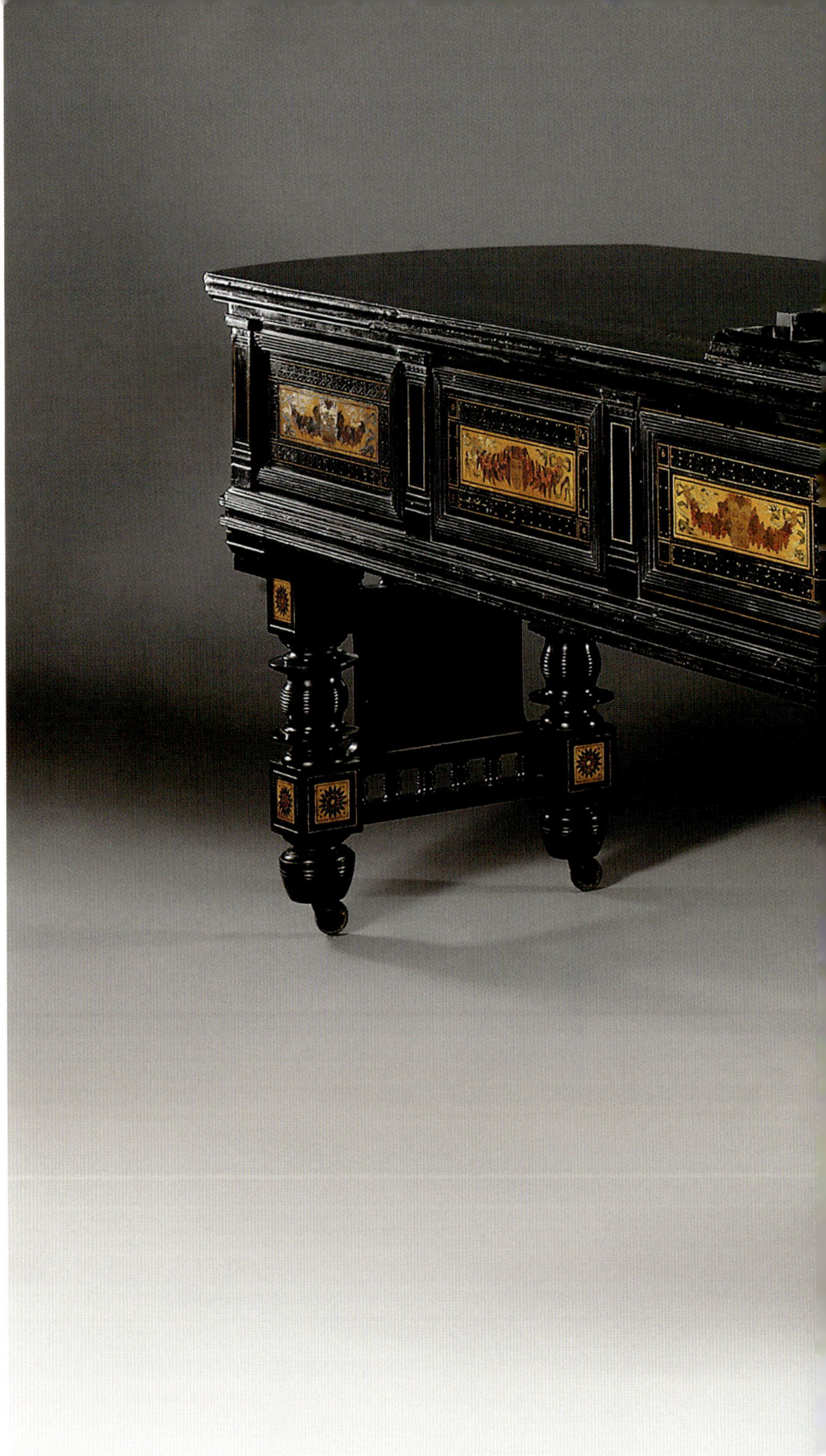

49 Grand piano manufactured by John Broadwood & Sons, London and decorated by Cottier & Co., London, 1872–3. Ebonised, painted and gilded mahogany. Private collection

much Cottier & Co. furniture reflects what George Gilbert Scott junior described as a 'certain masculine character'[153] and finds parallels in some of the furniture designed by Richard Norman Shaw, with whom Brydon had trained.

Following the lead of William Burges and Morris & Co. there was a growing fashion for painted medieval-style furniture, and the display of an ebonised and painted 'art' cabinet designed by the architect Thomas Collcutt for Collinson & Lock's section at the 1871 London International Exhibition helped to popularise this method of decoration.[154] Most of Cottier's identifiable furniture is ebonised and painted, which is unsurprising given that Cottier employed a large number of highly skilled artists and painters. It is likely that the same artists who painted stained glass and ceramics painted the furniture; indeed, furniture was often enriched with the same figure designs used for stained glass, tiles and plaques.

Some of the most distinctive furniture made by Cottier's workshop was embellished with Greek architectural forms and decorative motifs which recall the buildings and interiors designed in Glasgow by Alexander 'Greek' Thomson. Like Cottier, John Moyr Smith[155] knew and admired Thomson's work and in 1869 he suggested that furniture 'might be very effectively treated in dark or even ebonised wood, the ornament being incised and gilt after the manner introduced some years ago by Mr. Alexander Thomson, of Glasgow, in his Greek buildings'.[156] In 1875 the *Building News* published a page of designs by Moyr Smith of 'Ancient Ægyptian Furniture', illustrating the type of furniture which inspired many artists, architects and designers during this period, including Ford Madox Brown, Holman Hunt and Alma-Tadema.[157] It is not known whether Moyr Smith designed furniture for Cottier but it is possible as he designed a chair with Hart in 1871.[158]

Cottier's Greek-style furniture, usually made of mahogany and ebonised, painted and gilded, would have found a place within the unified eclecticism that characterised Aesthetic interiors. One of the few well-documented pieces in this style is a grand piano in a private collection (fig. 49). In 1872 the case, made by John Broadwood & Sons to a Cottier studio design, was sent to Langham Place where it was ebonised, painted and gilded with elaborate Greek decoration. It was given by the political scientist (later Sir) Thomas Hare to his daughter Alice Westlake, whose husband had helped establish the Working Men's College where Cottier studied.[159]

Some furniture was undoubtedly intended to form part of Greek-style interiors decorated by the firm,

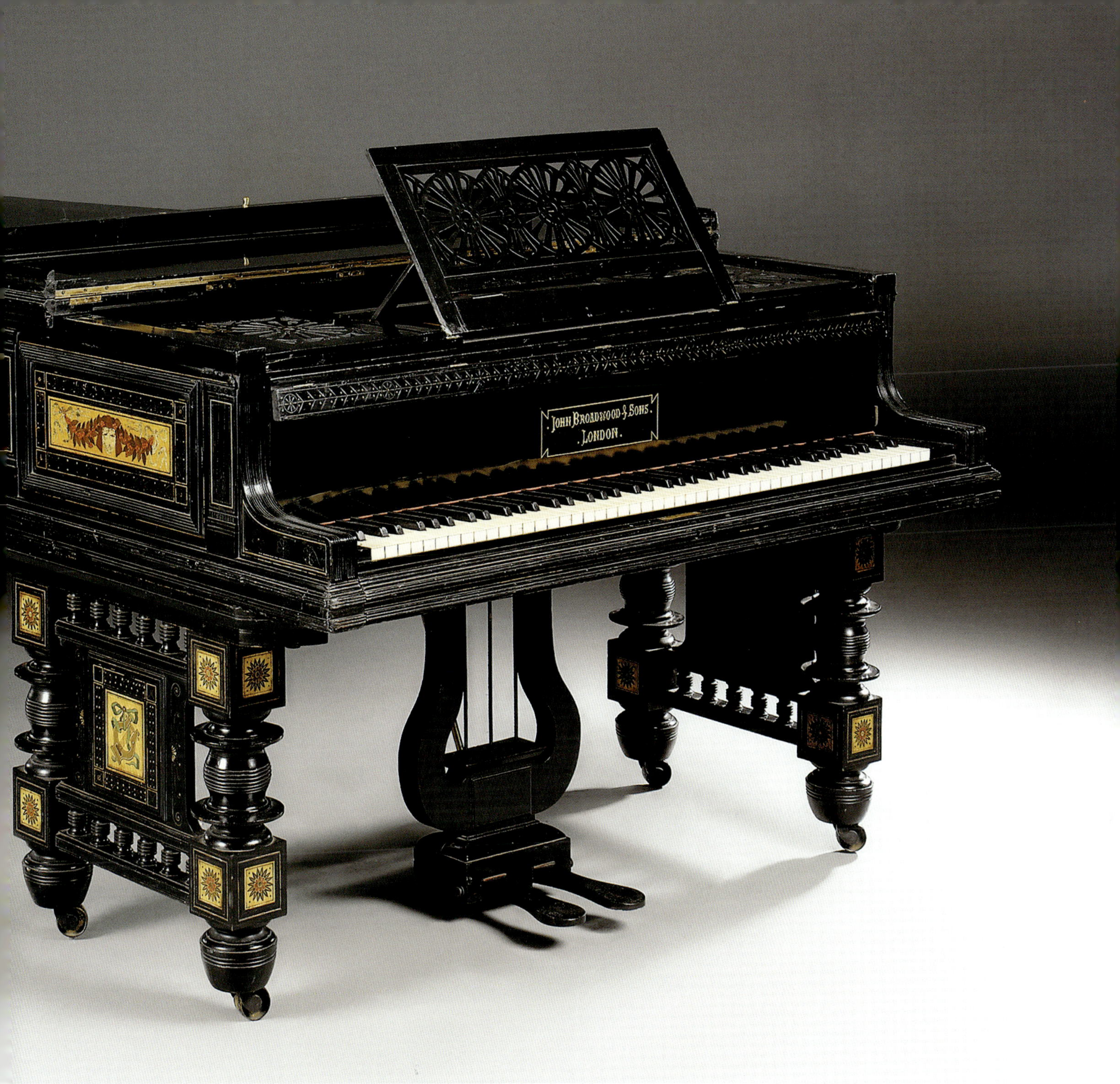

such as Kepplestone House, where ebonised furniture including an overmantel with gilded panels painted with flowers and masks is visible in a contemporary photograph (see fig. 38). An elaborately painted and gilded cabinet of Greek architectural form and Pompeian-style decoration (see fig. 23), dating from the 1870s, suggests the sort of colours which Cottier may have chosen for such interiors. Part of the decoration on the cabinet can also be compared with the lavish interiors devised by Moyr Smith for Holloway Sanatorium, Virginia Water, Surrey, which has stained glass by Cottier & Co.[160]

Cottier & Co. made a range of elegant drawing-room chairs incorporating Egyptian forms and Greek decoration in the 1870s, painted with fine lines of off-white and sometimes orange paint and gilded mouldings (fig. 50). The upholstery on the example illustrated is a modern copy of the original gold, red

50 Chair by Cottier & Co., London, *c.*1870–5. Ebonised, painted and gilded mahogany, with reproduction silk and wool upholstery, 83.5 × 46 × 53.6 cm. Victoria and Albert Museum, London

51 Cabinet by Cottier & Co., London, *c.*1870–5. Ebonised, painted and gilded mahogany, 195.5 × 187.5 × 51 cm. The lower doors are painted with the Greek mythical figures Sappho, Medea, Penelope and Helen. Private collection

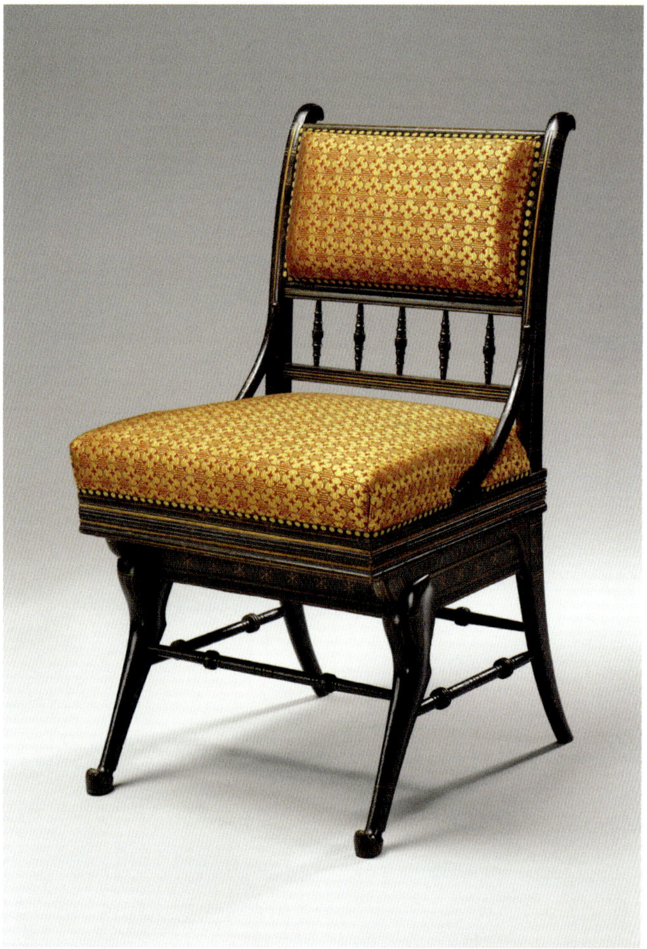

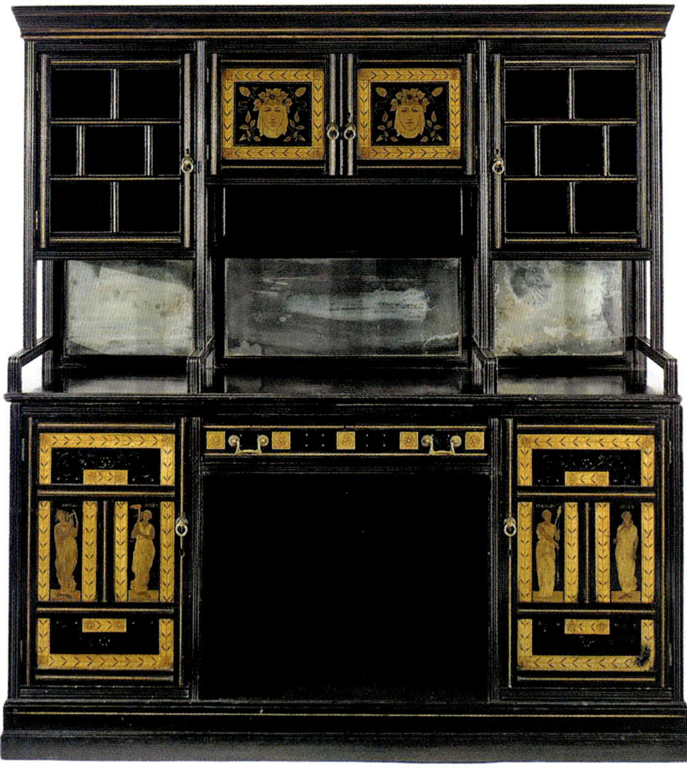

and brown woven wool and silk which was found on a chair that probably formed part of a similar set depicted in the drawing room of John Lamb Lyon's house, Joylen, Sydney (see fig. 168).[161] Although there is little evidence of this aspect of his business in Britain, upholstery and furnishing fabrics played an important part in Cottier's decorative schemes, such as the curtains with silk and stamped velvet panels at Kepplestone House supplied by Cottier in 1875 (see fig. 38). They recall a description of a curtain displayed in the New York gallery in 1875, made of 'russet-brown and gold of closely-woven silk, with worsted figures' and 'stripes of stamped velvet': the curtain depicted a tree rendered with 'botanical analysis'. Described as particularly Japanese in character, it was 'beautiful enough to make a portion of one of Alma-Tadema's or Armstrong's paintings.'[162]

As discussed earlier, Cottier was drawn to Japanese art in the 1870s and many pieces of Cottier furniture from this period incorporated structural forms drawn from the 'Anglo-Japanese' furniture repertoire pioneered by the influential architect designer E. W. Godwin, as well as details such as the ring-handles Godwin often specified.[163] These Japanese details were usually combined with other sources, such as Greek decoration, as is the case with a cabinet with a Japanese-inspired fretwork gallery running around the top (fig. 52) and another with fretwork supporting the upper structure (fig. 51), both of which are painted with Grecian ornaments.[164] Illustrations of Godwin's overmantels provide further examples of the appropriation of his Anglo-Japanese designs by Cottier's circle: they were originally published in the *British Architect* in 1874 and copied by Inglis in New York to accompany Clarence Cook's articles in *Scribner's Monthly*.[165] Also illustrated by Cook was Cottier's sturdy version of a coffee table, after a Godwin design.[166] Collectively published in New York under the title *The House Beautiful* in 1878, the illustrations in Cook's articles (see fig. 85) were also reproduced in *The Dining-Room*

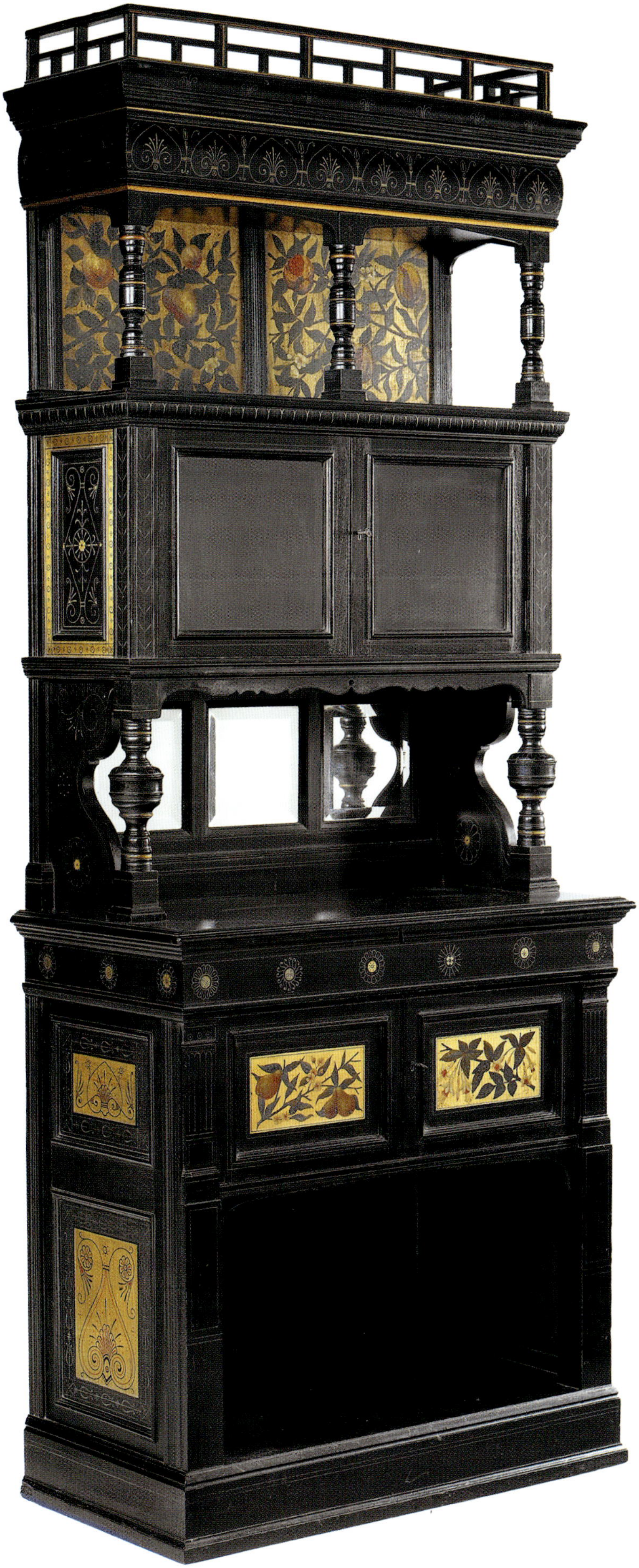

52 Cabinet by Cottier & Co., London, *c.*1870–5. Ebonised, painted and gilded mahogany, 239 × 97 × 49 cm. Private collection

(1878), published in London by Macmillan as part of their 'Art at Home' series. The author, 'Mrs Loftie' (Martha Jane Loftie, 1838–1914) was J. J. Stevenson's cousin. Although Loftie's text does not mention Cottier, by illustrating items such as an ebonised sideboard she helped to promote his versions of the Anglo-Japanese style.[167]

In the later 1870s Cottier & Co. advertised its 'Artistic Furniture of the Queen Anne period, and of the Italian and French Renaissance.'[168] This group of Cottier's furniture produced in the 1870s and early 1880s incorporated structural motifs and decorative devices taken from Renaissance and Queen Anne furniture, a source for many designers in the mid-1870s including Scott junior for Watts & Co. and Rhoda and Agnes Garrett.[169] A richly carved fireplace and overmantel made by Cottier & Co. for Craigtay, Dundee, the home to which White moved in 1877, is typical of this style (fig. 56). Craigtay (now a hotel, much altered), stood behind a flour mill built by White, for which Cottier had designed the façade in 1875.[170] Cottier sometimes combined northern Renaissance motifs with Anglo-Japanese structural devices in furniture which was ebonised with Greek decoration (see fig. 52). Others were enriched with the penwork technique, in which a light wood, sometimes sycamore, was decorated with ink and coloured washes (figs 53 and 55). Often the designs of the figural panels match those found in stained glass and ceramics, such as those at Cairndhu House (see fig. 45). Penwork was employed on a number of pieces, including a cottage piano made by Broadwood and decorated in Cottier's studio with Renaissance Revival motifs for the artist W. E. Lockhart in 1878.[171] Yet another style is represented by the Adam Revival decoration of a pianette, or small piano (see fig. 44), almost certainly decorated by Cottier & Co. for Kennard (discussed earlier), and probably intended for his wife or daughter.

Many surviving examples of Cottier's carcase furniture incorporate panels painted with figures (figs 54 and 55) or with panels depicting fruiting boughs silhouetted against gilded backgrounds (fig. 52). These panels recall those designed by Morris for

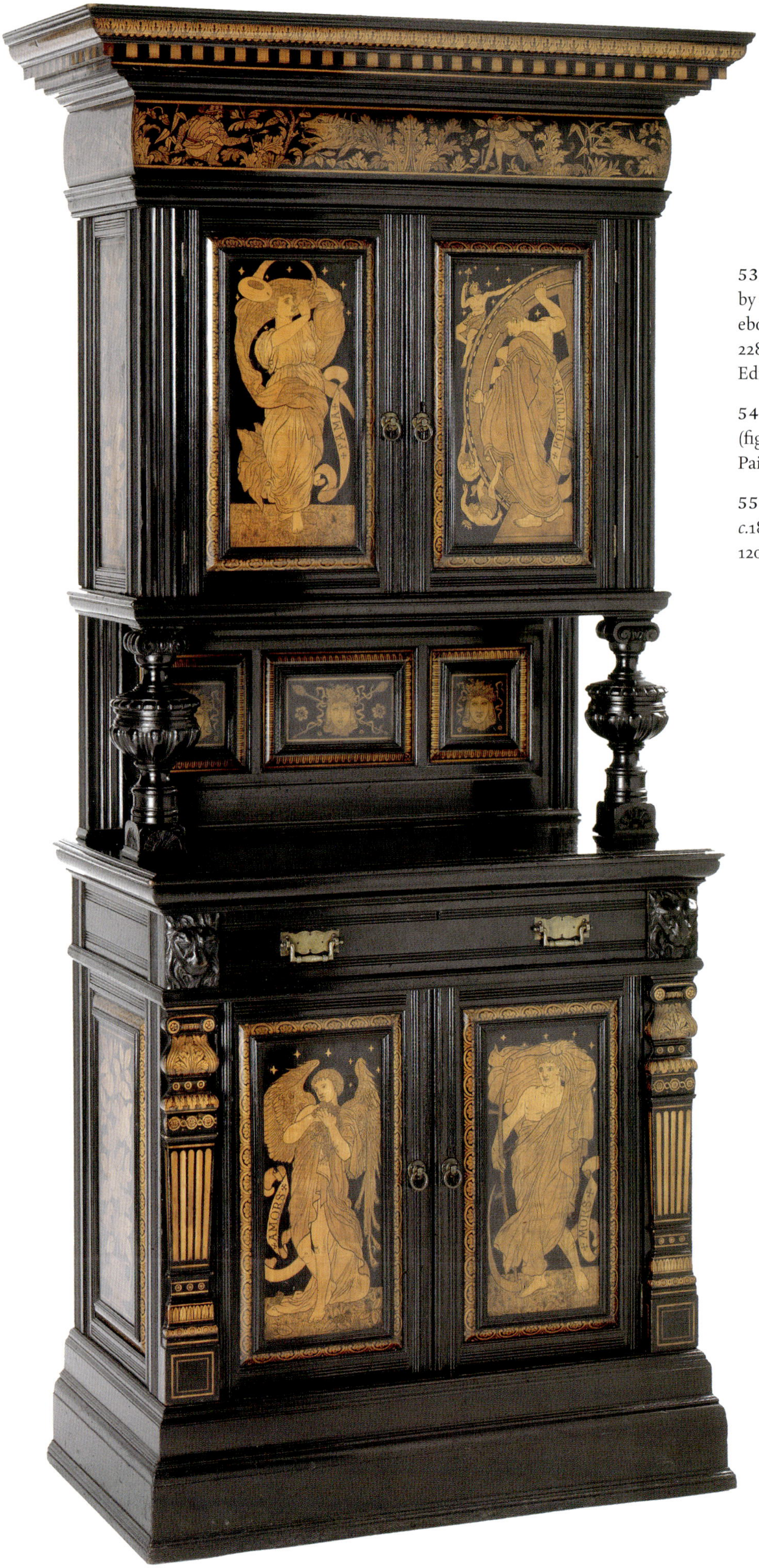

53 Cabinet with *Fama*, *Fortuna*, *Amor* and *Mors* by Cottier & Co., London, *c.*1878. Sycamore with ebonised and penwork decoration, ash and pine, 228 × 117 × 61 cm. National Museums Scotland, Edinburgh

54 Panel from the left side of a music cabinet (fig. 55) by Cottier & Co., London, *c.*1870–5. Painted and gilded mahogany. Private collection

55 Music cabinet by Cottier & Co., London, *c.*1870–5. Ebonised, painted and gilded mahogany, 120 × 49.6 × 39 cm. Private collection

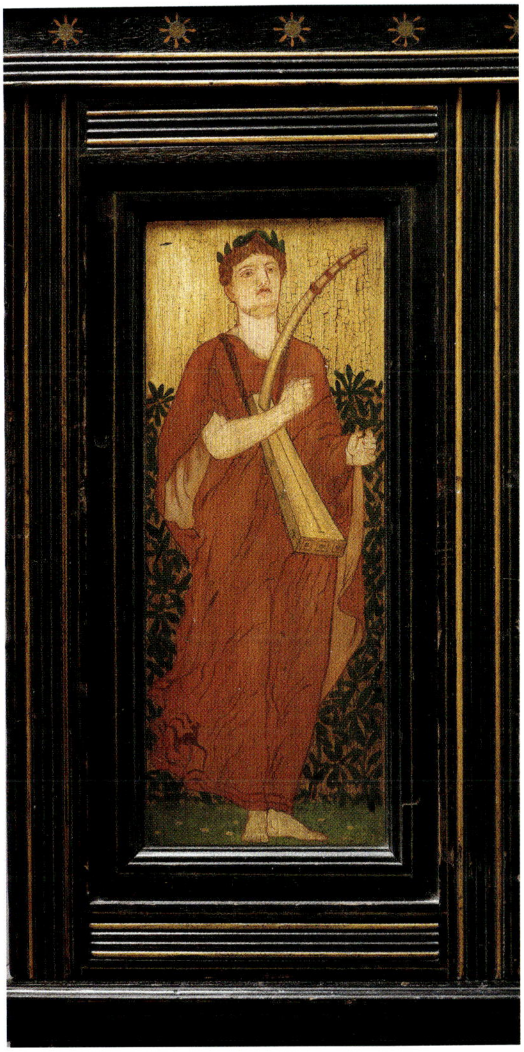

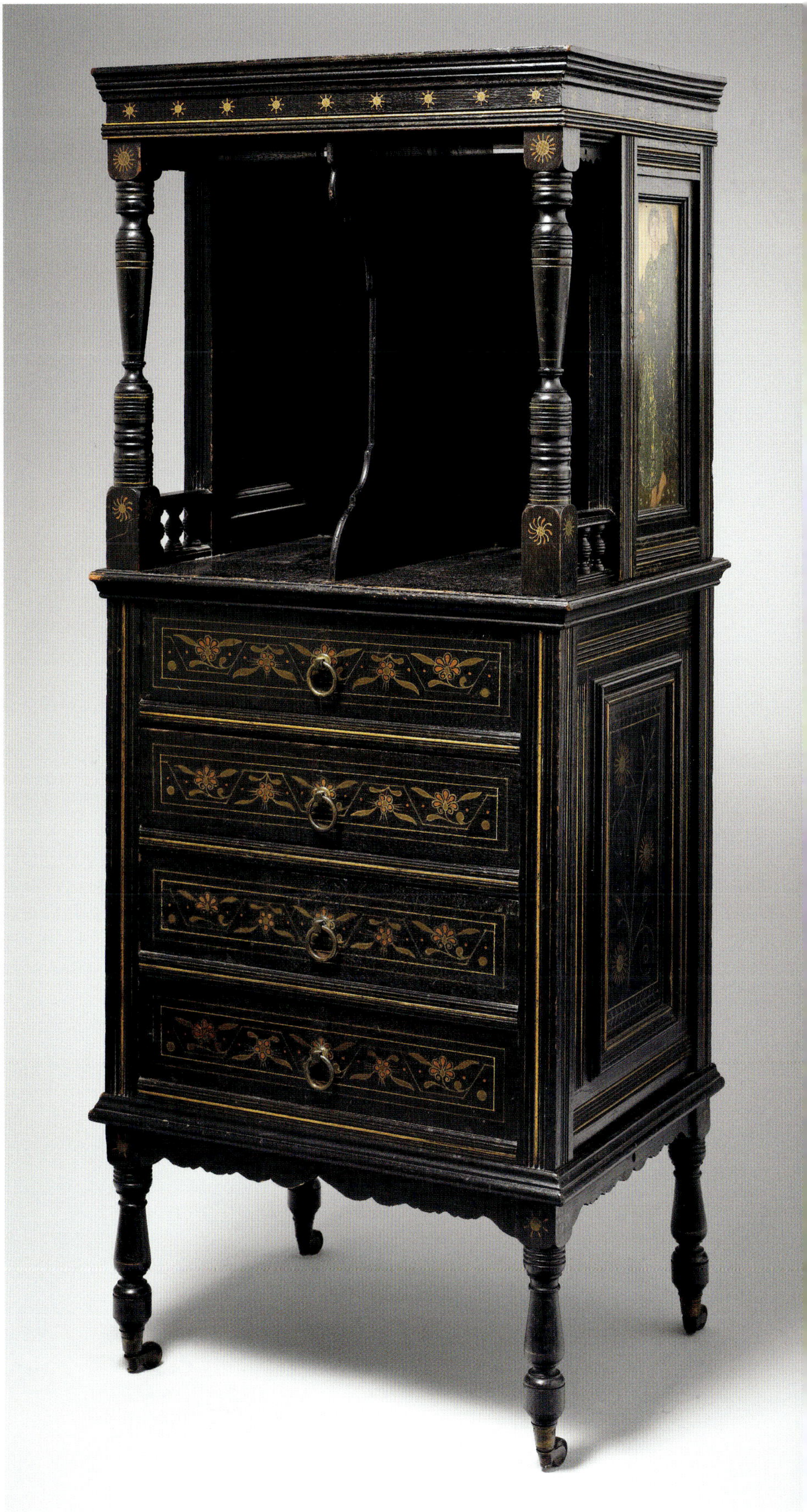

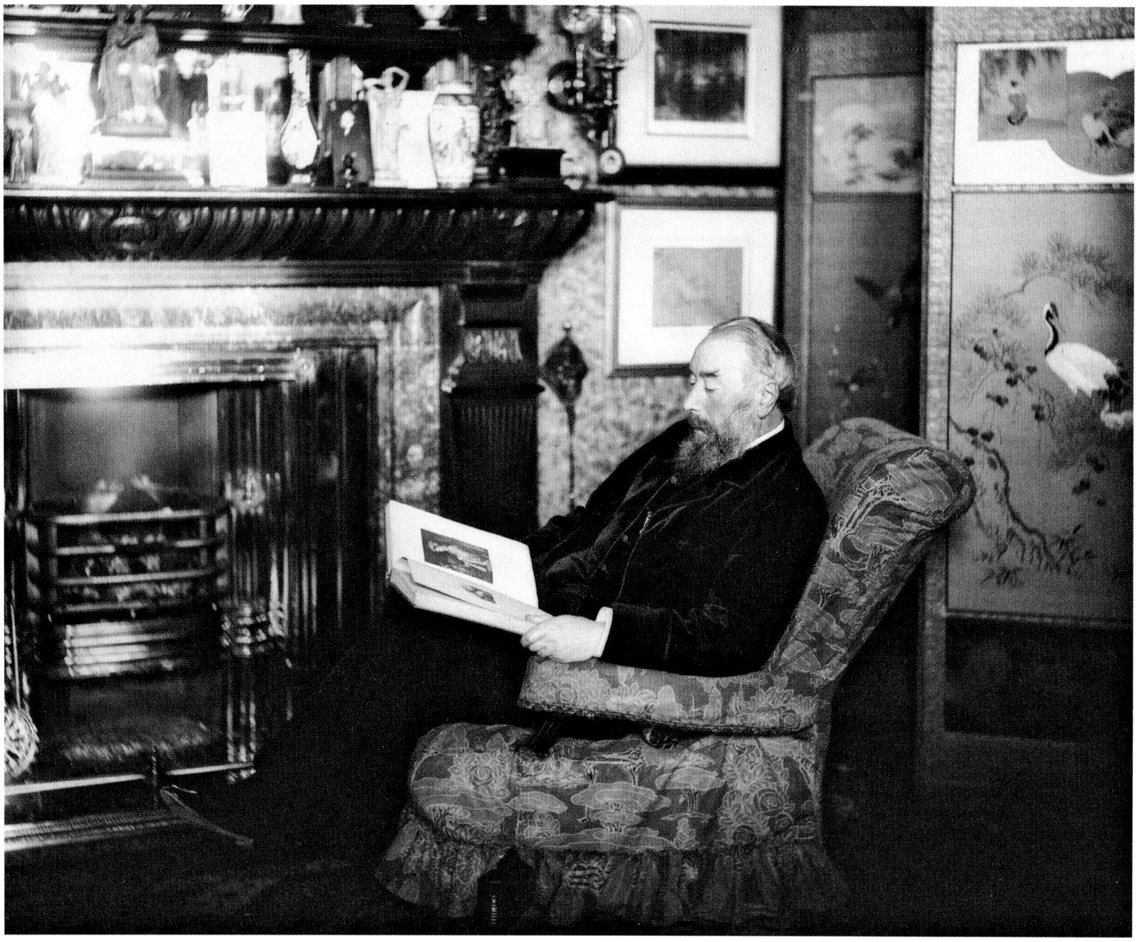

the panelling of the refreshment rooms at the South Kensington Museum between 1866 and 1867, and similar panels also survive in Cottier interiors, such as the decoration attributed to him at St Leonard's Hall, Edinburgh (see fig. 39). Another fashion of the 1880s was to incorporate actual drawings into furniture or panelling, which were glazed to protect them; in 1883 van Gogh wrote to Theo about two drawings by him of peat-diggers and labourers, noting: 'I also thought that these drawings might perhaps be something for Cottier. I imagine they'd lend themselves to being placed, as one sometimes sees in England (and elsewhere too), in the panels of a large cabinet, above a fireplace, in panelling, in short in woodwork.'[172] No examples of furniture incorporating glazed drawings have been identified in Britain, although there is evidence in the United States, where Hart's watercolours were incorporated into a folding screen (see fig. 93).

'Art' furniture often incorporated tiles and plaques, an American delegate noting when discussing Cottier's ceramics in Vienna in 1873, 'Large numbers of tiles are now used for decorating furniture'.[173] Although Cottier & Co. decorated ceramic tiles, it often used tiles decorated by other firms, as with an ebonised Greek overmantel mirror (whereabouts unknown) decorated with tiles representing the months of the year, designed by Albert Moore in about 1870.[174] Cabinets sometimes incorporated glazed panels with gilded leading.

In the absence of business records, a few newspaper accounts indicate the range of furniture supplied by Cottier in the 1870s and the type of customer who bought furniture from his firm. A newspaper advertisement of 1881 describes a forthcoming auction of the 'Artistic Contents' of 28 Upper Grosvenor Street, Mayfair, the home of the recently deceased businessman Thomas Greenwood Clayton and his widow Emily.[175] They included: 'valuable ART FURNITURE (principally of Messrs. Cottier, of Pall-mall), including a mahogany bed-chamber suite, birch, mahogany, and japanned chests of drawers, washing and dressing tables, iron bedsteads and bedding, a 7-octave oblique pianoforte, by Collard, elegant drawing-room appointments, pier glasses and over mantels, dining-room furniture in carved

56 John Forbes White at Craigtay, Dundee, *c.*1900. Photograph by Elliot & Fry. Aberdeen Art Gallery and Museums, presented in 2013 by Jennifer Melville

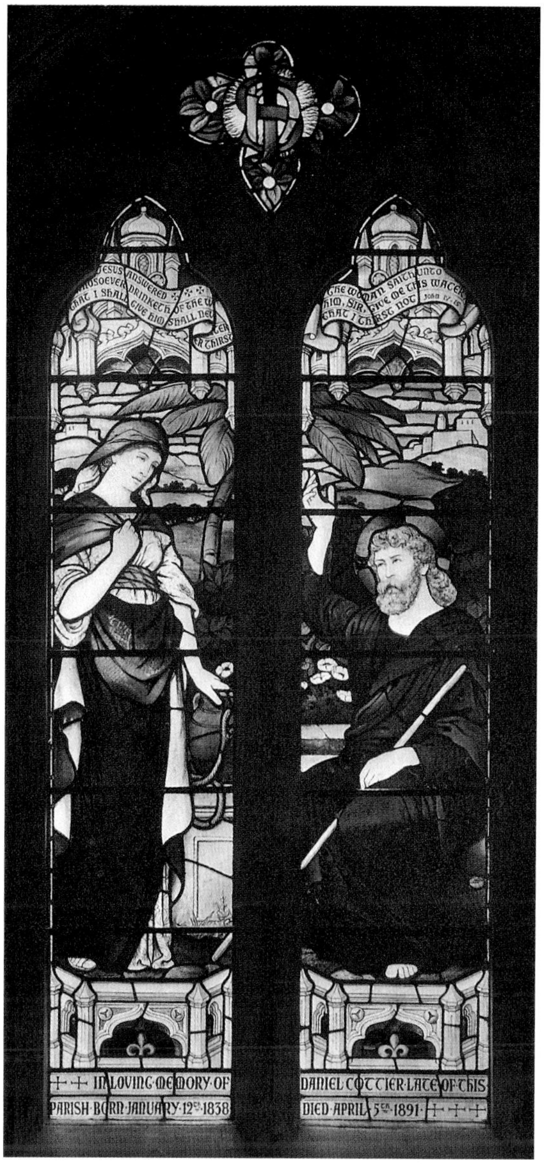

57 Cottier's memorial window (probably destroyed) in St Stephen the Martyr, London, made by Cottier & Co., London, 1891. Photograph *c.*1891. Private collection

oak.'[176] Another newspaper advertisement published in 1881 describes a five-day sale of the stock-in-trade of the Glasgow gallery of Craibe Angus, including:

> *Art Furniture, chiefly designed by Cottier, of London ... a small drawing-room suite, ebonised and gilt, very fine grand cabinet pianoforte, the case also designed by Cottier; walnut bedroom furniture, two cheval screens with stained-glass panels 'after the Antique'. Second day of sale devoted to the furniture and objects; Dog Grate, with Tile Coving and Carved Mantelpiece; Persian Rugs, Ornaments, &c.*[177]

Apart from a few pieces of furniture which can be dated to the early 1880s, no information has come to light about this aspect of Cottier & Co.'s activities in the 1880s and 1890s, apart from a newspaper advertisement in 1897, when the contents of the London workshop were auctioned. A brief description provides a snapshot of the kind of furniture and fittings they held in stock: '5ft. ebonised cabinet, 5ft. Arabian bedstead, the hand-carved fittings and linings of a hall', in addition to an antique brass chandelier.[178] Nevertheless, it is clear that during the 1870s and early 1880s at least, Cottier & Co. was one of the leading and most innovative 'art' furniture makers operating in London.

AFTERMATH OF COTTIER & CO. IN LONDON

At the time of Cottier's death in April 1891, the London foremen of Cottier & Co. were William J. Nelson, the artist who had worked for his firm for at least thirty years, and Charles Gillard. Cottier bequeathed each of them £100 in his will and requested that the services of his brother-in-law and 'confidential clerk', Alexander Innes, should be retained by the company.[179] Cottier & Co. continued to manufacture its stained-glass windows and furniture until 1897 and, although it continued to design windows, it apparently sold off some of its watercolour designs in the early 1900s.[180] The London branch is last listed in the London Post Office Directory as at Grafton Street in 1908. In January 1914, when Marion died in New York, 3 St James's Terrace remained the family home.[181] The house narrowly escaped destruction during the London Blitz in the Second World War but was subsequently demolished and the site is today occupied by an apartment block. However, a fragment of Cottier's connection with the neighbourhood remains, in a photograph of his own memorial window (fig. 57), installed by Cottier & Co. at the church of St Stephen the Martyr, Avenue Road, near the family home. Depicting Christ and the woman of Samaria, the Christ figure is clearly a portrait of Cottier, possibly based on a drawing by the artist William Hole (1846–1917), which captures something of 'his shrewd and humorous eyes'.[182] The memorial itself was probably lost during the Second World War, or when the bomb-damaged church was later demolished.

Suzanne Veldink

CHAPTER THREE
THE ART MARKET IN BRITAIN

Daniel Cottier was introduced to Dutch and French contemporary art by the wealthy John Forbes White from Aberdeen, for whom he regularly did decorative work from about 1859 onwards (see Chapter One, pp. 25–6). Cottier witnessed first-hand White's burgeoning love for the Dutch school of landscape painting and the explosive growth of his collection that followed. White had so many paintings that, just after 1870, he commissioned Cottier to build an art gallery to accommodate his collection.[1]

White was not a typical, passive art buyer who took his cues from dealers; instead he maintained direct contact with artists and his actions influenced their careers. He corresponded with Willem Roelofs (1822–1897), Jozef Israëls (1824–1911) and David Artz (1837–1890), visited their studios in the Netherlands, commissioned works for his own collection and arranged commissions for other collectors in his circle such as James Walker (fl. 1869) and Alexander Macdonald (1837–1884). Roelofs, Israëls and Artz also visited White at Seaton Cottage, just north of Aberdeen, and during these stays they may have met Cottier.[2] In 1865 White even arranged for work by the Utrecht landscape and genre painter Alexander Mollinger (1836–1867) to be shown at the Royal Academy of Scotland's annual exhibition, an event that enticed many other Dutchmen to try their luck abroad (fig. 60). Unfortunately, Mollinger died prematurely in 1867 before he could travel to Scotland.[3] On this tragic event White immediately decided that he would sell the contents of Mollinger's studio in Scotland and sent the profit to the artist's family.[4]

In 1868 White and George Reid (1841–1913), a Scottish artist and Cottier's friend, published their thoughts on contemporary Continental art in a pamphlet, writing under the pseudonym *Veri Vindex* (Claimant of Truth). In their writings the two paid tribute to French and Dutch contemporary landscape painting. They especially praised the choice of realistic subject matter and the emphasis on tone rather than colour. It was in the stimulating White-Reid environment, with ready access to the paintings of the Barbizon and Hague Schools, that Cottier's own views on art developed. To White's preferences he added his personal love for artists who worked in a broad manner and had a visible and discernible hand.

58 David Artz, *Le Bonheur d'une Mère*, 1869. Oil on canvas, 61 × 44 cm. Aberdeen Art Gallery and Museums, Alexander Macdonald Bequest, 1901

A NEW GENERATION OF COLLECTORS

Thanks to White's efforts, around 1870 interest in contemporary Continental art was spreading throughout Scotland with collectors in Dundee, Edinburgh and Glasgow.[5] Cottier realised the potential of this growing fashion early on and decided that, by adding paintings, drawings and etchings to the items supplied by his business in Glasgow, he could offer his Scottish clientele complete interior advice. Often, these collectors kept houses in Edinburgh or Glasgow, the Scottish countryside and in London. According to Robert Thomas Hamilton Bruce (1846–1899), an Edinburgh art collector and Cottier's close friend and client, paintings formed an integrated, decorative part of interior schemes and should not attract too much attention. In 1888 he stated: 'a great picture never violently asserted itself, and in a carefully selected collection repose is one of the most striking features' (fig. 59).[6] Given his emphasis on the tonal, unobtrusive art of the Hague and Barbizon Schools, Cottier shared this aesthetic. Although as a young man he had briefly moved in the same artistic circles as Ford Madox Brown and Dante Gabriel Rossetti and shared their love of the sumptuous colours used by the Venetian Renaissance artists, he did not favour contemporary

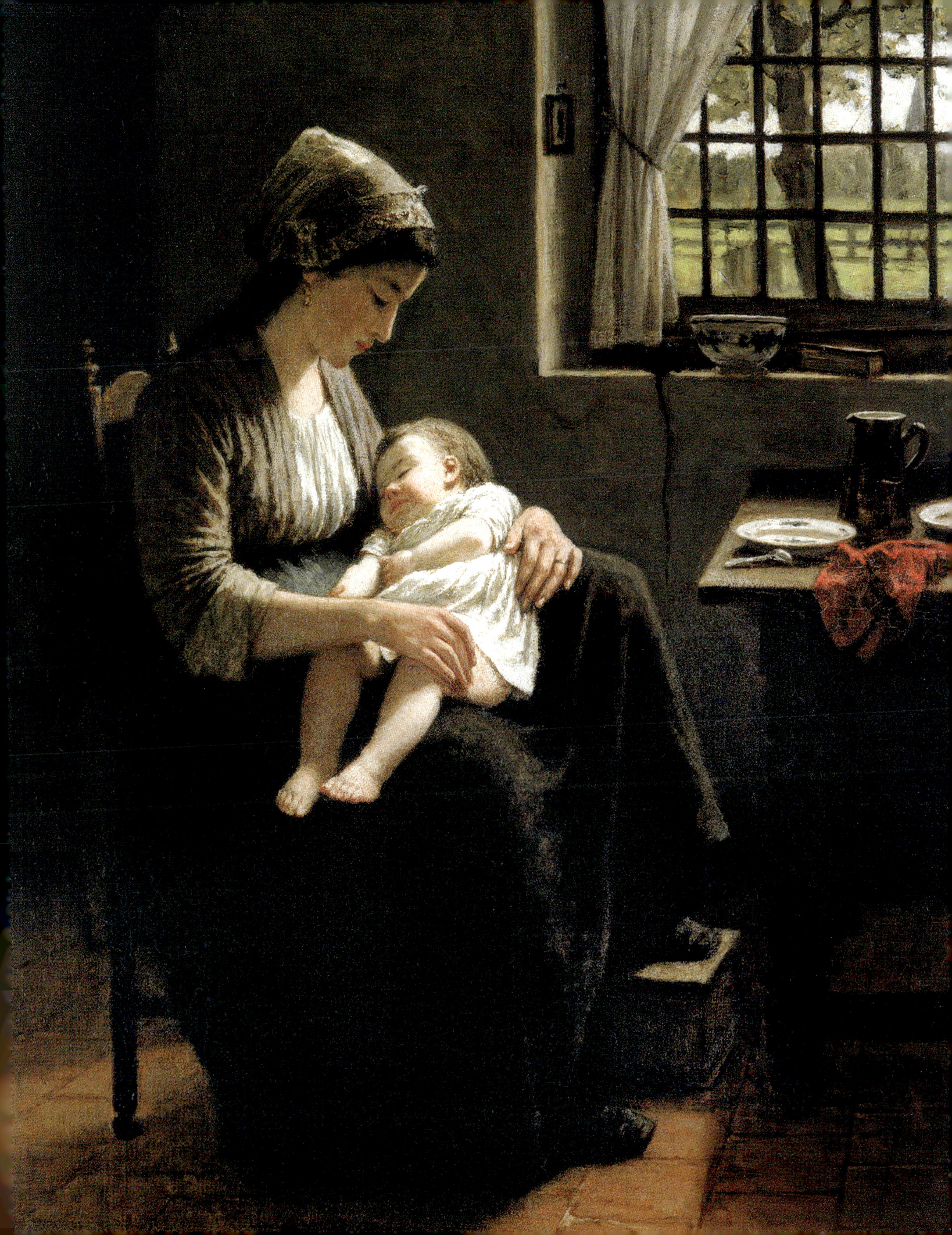

59 Robert T. Hamilton Bruce's collection of French and Dutch art, The Grange, Dornoch. Photograph *c.*1900. Camille Corot's *An Evening in Normandy* can be seen on the far wall, bottom row. Private collection

60 Alexander Mollinger, *Meerkerk, clearing up after Rain*, 1866. Oil on canvas, 41.8 × 68 cm. Aberdeen Art Gallery and Museums, Alexander Macdonald Bequest, 1901

British art. Cottier probably found it polished and not personal enough.[7]

Cottier noticed that White exemplified a new generation of art collectors: largely self-made men who had amassed their fortunes in Scotland's coal, iron, milling or shipbuilding industries and who, by purchasing contemporary Continental art, were giving a modern, self-confident expression to a traditionally aristocratic pursuit. For them, investing in something as durable and elevated as high culture contributed to a public identity that blotted out the stench, din and ugliness of the industry from which they had amassed their capital. Moreover, assembling an international art collection suited their cosmopolitan lifestyle. While in Aberdeen, Cottier had witnessed that this new elite was assertive. They made the most of the opportunities to display the latest addition to their collections and kept a constant eye on the competition. Cottier's future clientele differed from White in only one aspect: as a rule, art buyers did not have the time to travel to the Continent unless their business already took them there. This new generation of collectors, therefore, trusted the taste and knowledge of their dealer. Cottier's commercial instinct, charismatic personality and constant fresh supply of artworks would do the rest.

FROM THE PARISIAN ART MARKET TO THE DUTCH STUDIO

Cottier started his career as an art dealer in a traditional fashion, by buying art from the Goupil & Cie gallery in Paris (hereafter, Goupil's). In July 1867, when Cottier bought his first painting from this gallery, Goupil's had become a wealthy multinational business, with branches in Paris, London and The Hague, and a large distribution network consisting

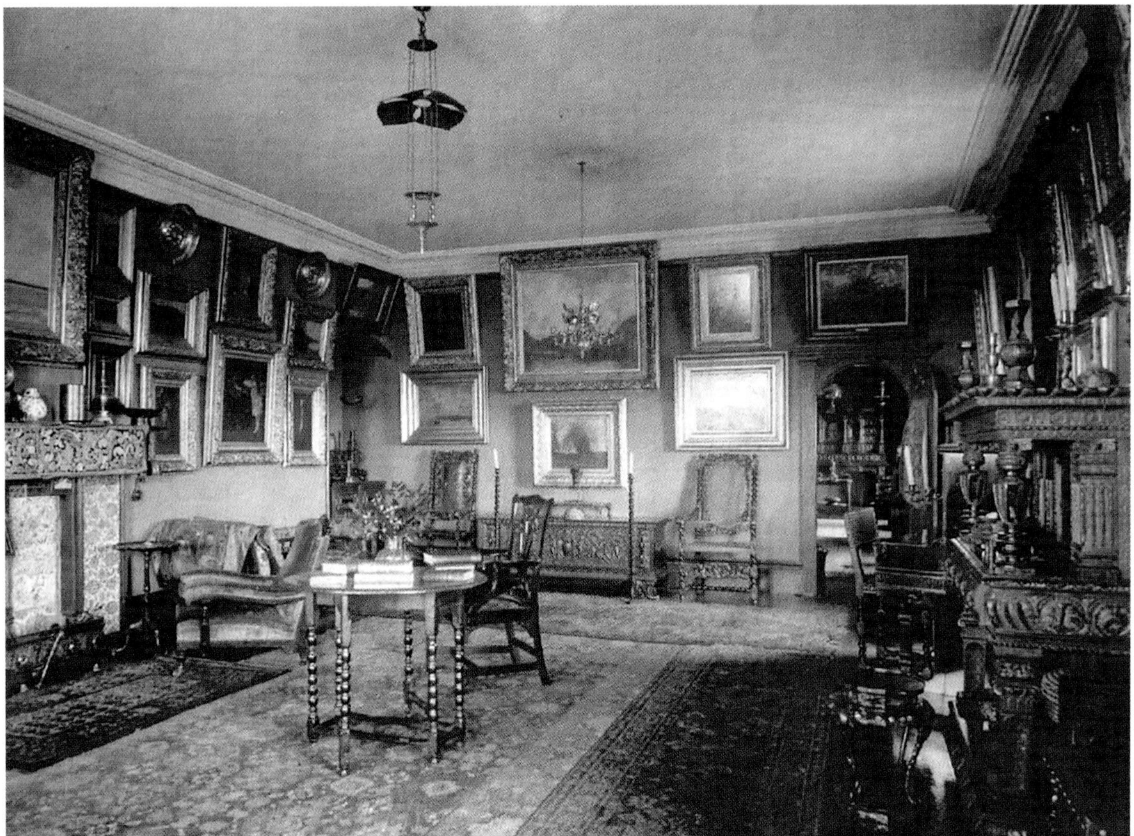

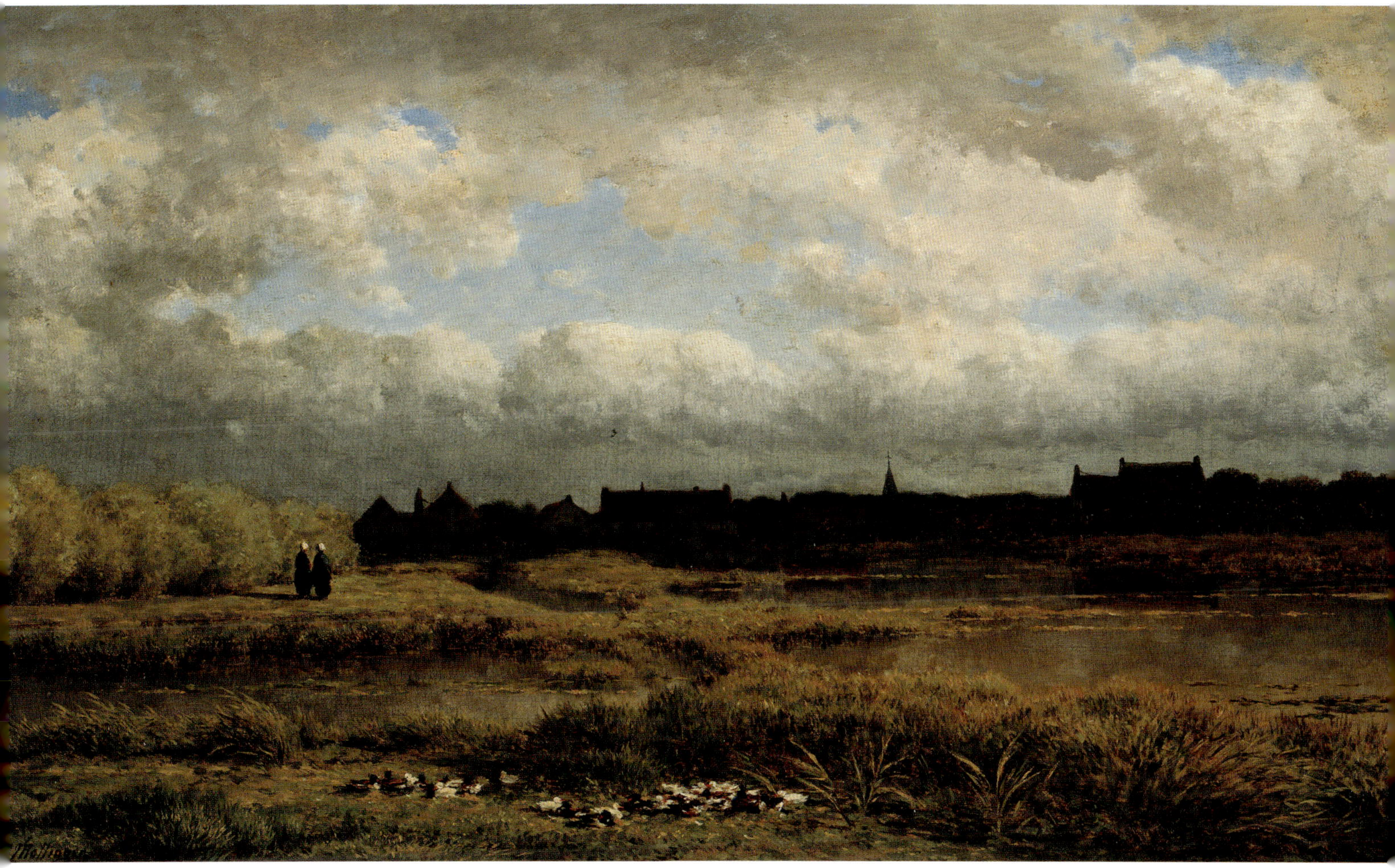

of collectors and fellow dealers. Cottier must have looked on this gallery as one of his most formidable opponents but also as an important source of inspiration. During the 1860s the uncle of Vincent van Gogh (also Vincent; 1820–1888) acted as the manager of the Parisian branch. Thanks to his contacts, he had succeeded in signing exclusive contracts with a number of young, promising Dutch artists who lived in the French capital. These included Jacob Maris (1837–1899), the brother of the artists Willem and Matthijs Maris (discussed later in this chapter), and others who were obliged to sell their work exclusively through Goupil's; the gallery probably also had a large say in the subject matter they depicted.

Artz was among the Dutchmen living in Paris but he refused to be signed by Goupil's. He had already established a name for himself in Britain: in 1868 one of his paintings was exhibited at the Royal Scottish Academy and in the same year he sold some work through the French Gallery in London. Also in 1868 Cottier began acting as his informal agent in Scotland and England. The contact between Cottier and Artz was probably established through White, who already owned a genre painting by Artz and had also interested his friends Walker and Macdonald in the artist's work. According to Reid, Cottier and Artz made a good team. In 1868 he wrote that the artist was 'almost completely cleared out at the present. Cottier has been a good friend to him'.[8] In 1869 Artz travelled to Scotland and England. He returned with so many commissions that he was unsure if he could manage to finish everything in time (see fig. 58).[9] It is not known how Cottier profited from these commissions. Artz, meanwhile, benefited not only financially but also artistically for, after years of searching for his own style and subject matter, he finally decided to focus on what sold well in England and Scotland – meticulously painted pictures of the daily life of the Dutch fishing community.

Cottier continued to sell Artz's work until the mid-1880s, sourcing paintings directly from the artist or from the secondary market.[10] Besides their business relationship, the two remained close friends until Artz's death in 1890; they regularly visited each other

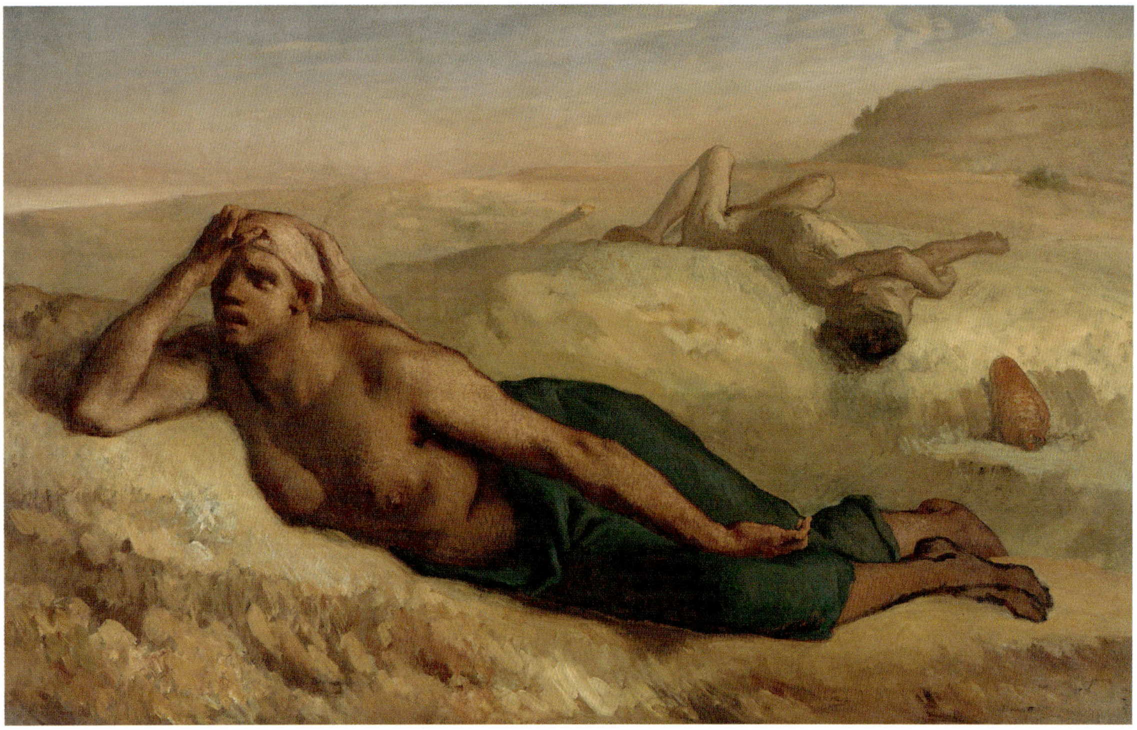

in London and The Hague, wrote lively letters and, when Artz was decorating his new atelier, Cottier supplied him with oriental carpets and lamps.[11] Thanks to Artz, who had an extensive social network, Cottier probably also met the Dutch artists Bernard Blommers (1845–1914), who once referred to Cottier as 'my old friend',[12] Johannes Bosboom (1817–1891) and Matthijs Maris (see also Chapter Two). The marine painter Hendrik Willem Mesdag (1831–1915) might have met Cottier in the 1870s through Lourens Alma-Tadema (1836–1912) – more commonly known to the English-speaking world as Sir Lawrence Alma-Tadema – who was Mesdag's cousin and one of Cottier's neighbours in St John's Wood in London.[13] Alma-Tadema was a highly successful painter of classical scenes, executed in a precise, academic manner, who worked exclusively for the French Gallery in London. Mesdag not only sold his marine paintings through Cottier but also purchased a number of French artworks from him for his private collection, such as Jean-François Millet's painting *Hagar and Ishmael* (1848–9; fig. 61). Millet (1814–1875) never finished this large canvas and this aspect probably appealed to Mesdag and Cottier as they both preferred unpolished painting styles.[14] Cottier maintained friendly relationships with these artists but, according to the Dutch journalist H. L. Berckenhoff, never forgot that making a good deal was his main goal: 'Artists in our country [the Netherlands] who had dealings with him (he crossed the Channel every year and visited studios to purchase art, destined especially for the American market) told me he was a *clever fellow* of whom you had to be careful'.[15] Buying directly from artists was advantageous for Cottier: he did not have to pay a middleman, he became friendly with young Dutch artists and was able to hand-pick the best works for his clientele. This, in turn, gave Cottier's customers the idea that by buying from him they came as close to the source as possible.

WILLIAM CRAIBE ANGUS, COTTIER'S AGENT IN GLASGOW

Towards the end of 1869 or at the beginning of 1870, Cottier and partners launched Cottier & Co. as art furniture makers, mural decorators and glass and tile painters. But his successful cooperation with Artz soon lured him further into the world of art dealing. In 1874, while he concentrated on his branches in Sydney and New York (both opened their doors in 1873), Cottier made the Dutchman Elbert Jan van Wisselingh (1848–1912) head of the fine art section of his London gallery, which from 1875 onwards was located at 8 Pall Mall (see fig. 70). They had met in the late 1860s at Goupil's in Paris, where van Wisselingh had worked as a trainee manager (fig. 62). In the same year, 1874, Cottier helped the Aberdonian William Craibe Angus (1830–1899) to set up shop in Glasgow, selling paintings, armour, antiques and ceramics (fig. 63). The next

61 Jean-François Millet, *Hagar and Ishmael*, 1848–9. Oil on canvas, 147 × 236.5 cm. Mesdag Collection, The Hague

62 Marinus van der Maarel, *Portrait of the Art Dealer E. J. van Wisselingh*, c.1880–1912. Oil on panel, 33.3 × 24.6 cm. Rijksmuseum, Amsterdam, gift of A. M. de Jong-Hug, Naarden

63 Alphonse Legros, *William Craibe Angus*, 1879–80. Drypoint, 30.6 × 25.5 cm. Aberdeen Art Gallery and Museums, presented in 1880 by the artist

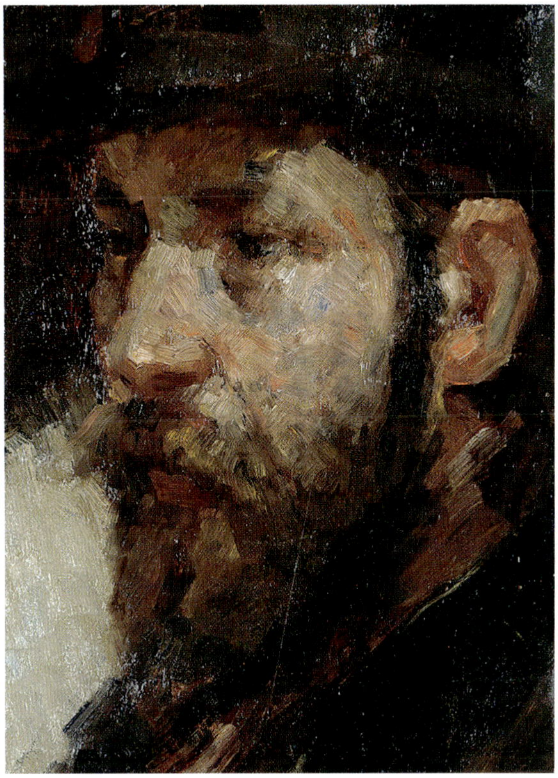

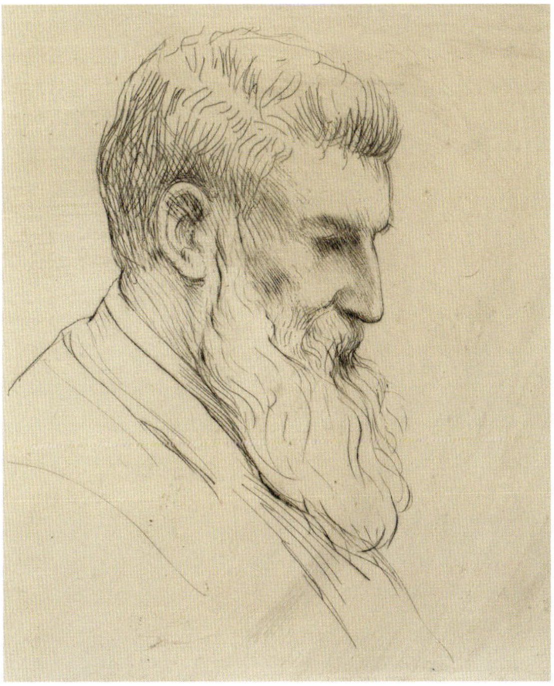

year, in November, Angus sold his stock to 'confine his attention to pictures.'[16]

Through Angus, Cottier decided to regain a foothold in Glasgow (rather than in Edinburgh, the Scottish capital) because of the industrial city's progressive artistic climate that had nurtured his talent in the 1860s. This progressive climate was also reflected in the artworks shown at the Royal Glasgow Institute of the Fine Arts' annual exhibitions. Thanks to the participation of dealers, the Royal Glasgow Institute was able to offer a far more varied and more international selection of artworks than Edinburgh, where submissions were welcomed only from artists themselves or their collectors. Angus's main competitor in Glasgow was Thomas Lawrie, who was instrumental in forming the art collection of John McGavin (1816–1881), followed by Kay & Reid, which mainly dealt in Scottish contemporary art.[17] With Cottier's financial aid, Angus was able to rent a beautiful gallery space at 159 Queen Street, in the heart of the city's business district, and to live on a grand scale in Dormouth House. Several rooms in the house were decorated with French and Dutch art and art furniture produced by Cottier & Co.[18] In this way Angus's home served as an extension of his gallery. His stock consisted of paintings he received in consignment from Cottier, whom he visited regularly in London,[19] and works bought at Goupil's in Paris and The Hague and the Lefevre Gallery in London.[20]

From 1877 the watercolours of Bosboom, Jacob and Willem Maris and Anton Mauve (1838–1888; fig. 64) formed the core of Angus's stock.[21] The favourable prices of works on paper were interesting to Scottish collectors who did not wish to pay dearly for paintings by artists who had not yet proven their market value. He also offered work by Camille Corot (1796–1875), Antoine Vollon (1833 1900), Israëls, Millet, Adolphe Monticelli (1824–1886) and Alphonse Legros (1837–1911), who etched Angus's portrait (see fig. 63).[22] Between 1874 and 1880 Angus counted among his clientele all the well-known collectors of his day: Bruce in Edinburgh and in Glasgow the tobacco merchant James Carfrae Alston (1835–1913), John G. Ure (1824–1901) and Andrew Maxwell (1828–1909).

64 Anton Mauve, *Felling Timber (Deux Boucherons)*, *c.*1877. Watercolour and bodycolour on paper, 27.9 × 47 cm. Burrell Collection, Glasgow Museums

65 Camille Corot, *The Little Bird Nesters*, 1873–4. Oil on canvas, 66 × 90.2 cm. Columbus Museum of Art, Ohio, Museum Purchase, Derby Fund

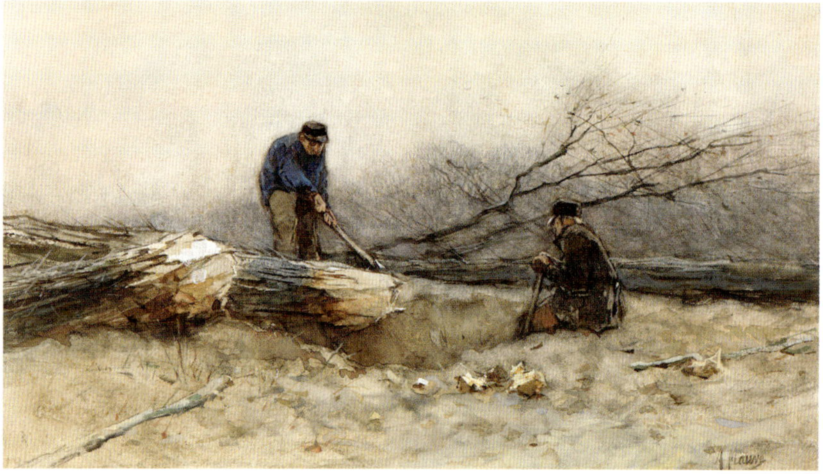

Maxwell bought Camille Corot's *The Little Bird Nesters* (fig. 65) from Angus for £400.[23] Unfortunately, Angus not only suffered greatly from the collapse of the City of Glasgow Bank in October 1878 but also, according to one of his contemporaries, lacked Cottier's 'pecuniary shrewdness'.[24] Despite Bruce's financial support, the dealer's monetary problems soon spiralled out of control and in 1880 he was forced to file for bankruptcy (see Chapter Two, pp. 68–9, for the subsequent sale of Angus's stock).

CONTEXT AND COMPETITION: THE FRENCH GALLERY, JACOB MARIS AND JOZEF ISRAËLS

In Scotland, Cottier and Angus did not experience stiff competition but things were different in London. Cottier's main competitors were Goupil's London branch, which organised annual exhibitions of Dutch and French contemporary art, and the French Gallery situated at 120 Pall Mall.[25] Since 1867 the French Gallery's manager, Henry Wallis (1805–1890), had stocked a mixture of genre and history paintings, including works by established Barbizon artists and by young Dutch talents. With this selection Wallis was following in the footsteps of his predecessor Ernest

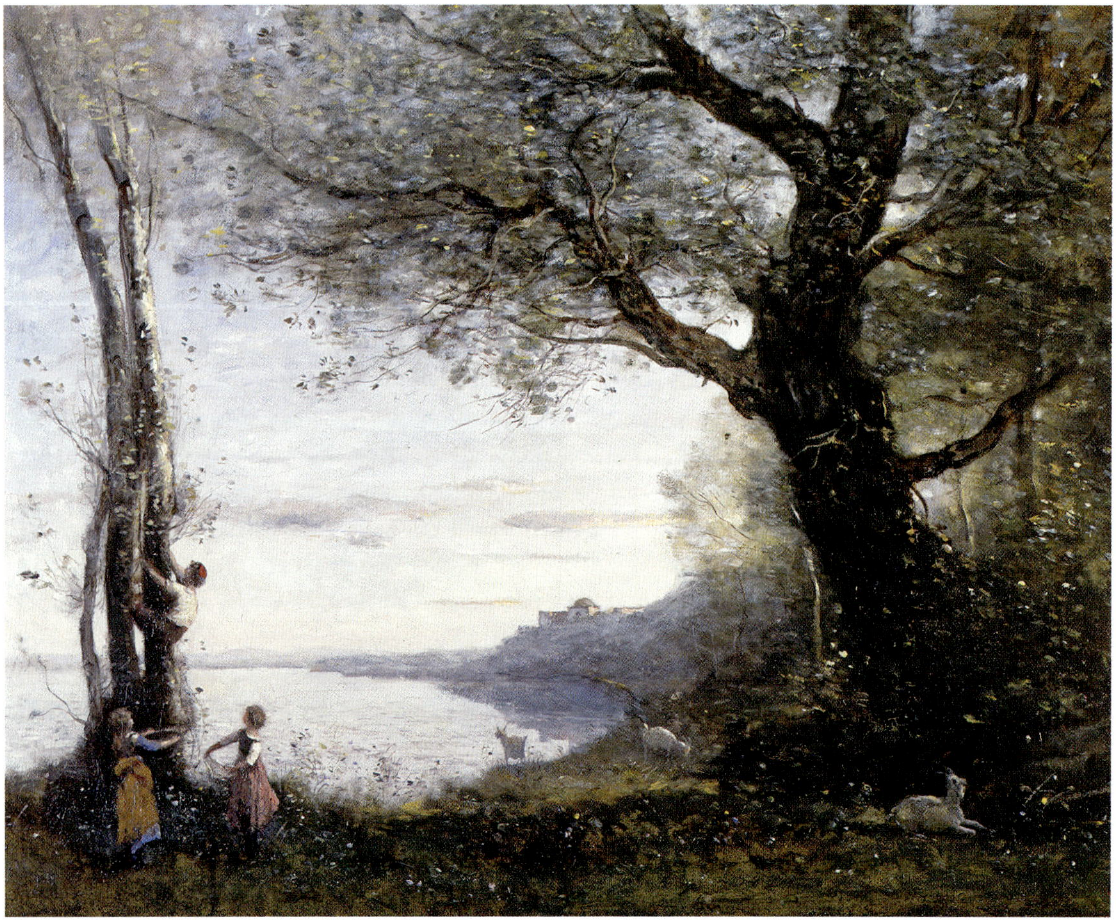

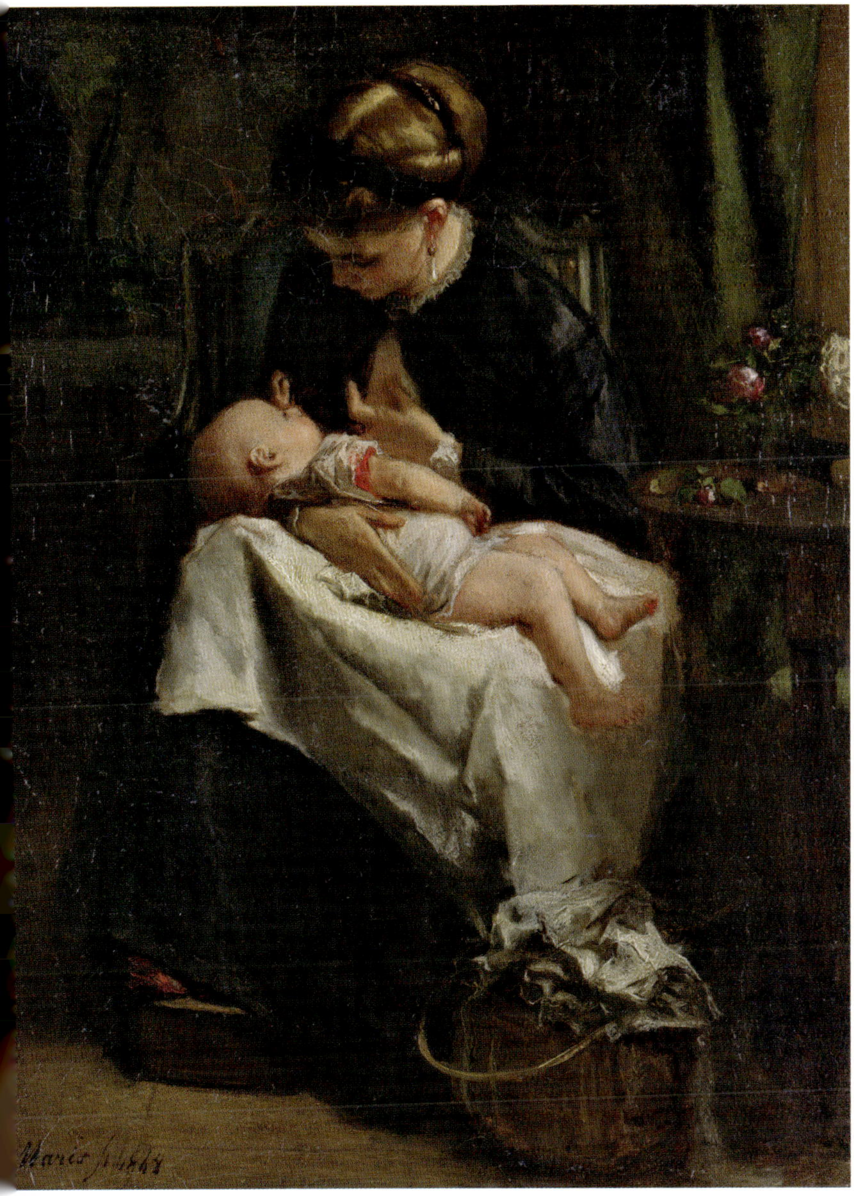

66 Jacob Maris, *A Young Woman nursing a Baby*, 1868. Oil on panel, 29.1 × 22.8 cm. National Gallery, London, presented by J. C. J. Drucker, 1910

Gambart (1814–1902), who was interested in Dutch artists of the Romantic era, such as Barend Koekkoek and Andreas Schelfhout, but who also invested in young artists such as Israëls and Bosboom.[26] According to a letter of February 1869 from George Reid, Wallis's strategies were similar to Cottier's: 'he [Wallis] was here [in Paris] about a fortnight since making his round of the studios (especially of the young fellows) and picking up everything that was worth buying – provided it was cheap enough'; this included commissioning two paintings from Artz, Cottier's protégé, and purchasing work by Jacob Maris.[27] Wallis must have been especially taken by Maris, for between April 1867 and 1871 he purchased twenty-nine of his paintings through Goupil's in Paris.[28] From 1864 to 1875 Wallis mainly offered work by Israëls and Jacob Maris. To this selection he added paintings by Mauve, Willem Maris, Mesdag, Roelofs, Blommers and Paul Gabriel (1828–1903).[29]

Despite (or maybe because of) Jacob Maris's popularity, Cottier decided against investing in this artist – he wanted to distinguish himself from the competition. Only in June 1874 did he purchase his first Jacob Maris painting, *View of Schiedam* (whereabouts unknown) for 3000 francs, mainly because he was asked to do so by John Forbes White.[30] Later in the same year Cottier bought *A Young Woman nursing a Baby* (fig. 66) from Goupil's in London. This intimate painting depicts the artist's wife, Catharina Hendrika Horn, breastfeeding their son Guillaume. In 1868 Wallis had been the first owner of this work. Wallis certainly was successful in promoting Jacob Maris's art, because Cottier paid Goupil four times the price for which Wallis had purchased it six years earlier.[31] Unfortunately, it is not known to whom Cottier sold the painting.

Cottier was not particularly interested in Israëls either, despite his art being favoured by British collectors and, again, Wallis.[32] Israëls's work was definitely available to Cottier. In 1876, for example, his paintings and watercolours were offered for sale at the McLean Gallery, the French Gallery and Agnew & Sons and were included in the Winter Exhibition of the Institute of Painters in Watercolours. By excluding Israëls Cottier was probably simply following his own taste: he did not favour anecdotal art.

MEANWHILE, IN THE NETHERLANDS

From 1875 onwards the Hague School grew increasingly popular in the Netherlands. Herman Tersteeg (1845–1926), the manager of Goupil's branch in The Hague, could easily find buyers for Hague School paintings and he maintained good relationships, especially with Israëls, Mauve and Jacob Maris.[33] Despite Cottier's existing network, it became more difficult for him to purchase work directly from these artists and to react appropriately to changes in the Dutch art market. At the end of October 1875 Cottier enlisted the help of van Wisselingh's father, Hendrik

67 Gustave Courbet, *Portrait of H. J. van Wisselingh*, 1846. Oil on panel, 57.2 × 46 cm. Kimbell Art Museum, Fort Worth, Texas

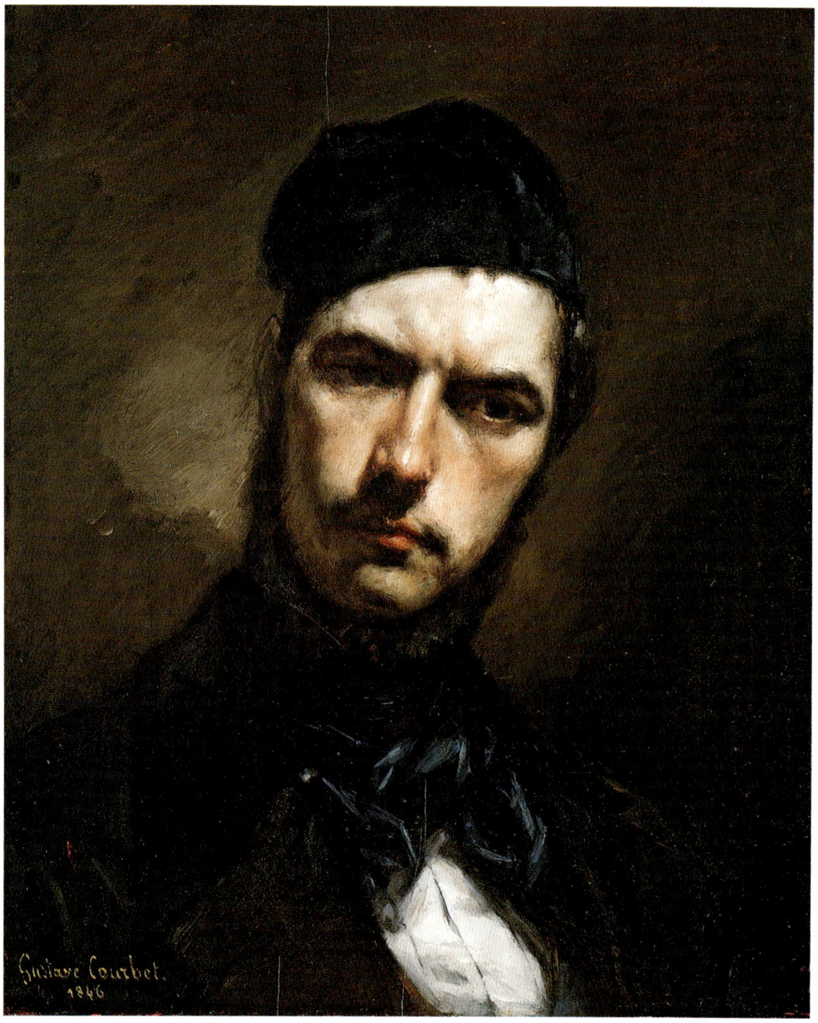

Jan (1816–1884). For £100 per month van Wisselingh senior became Cottier's Dutch agent, tracking down suitable Hague School works and sending paintings and works on paper to London and Glasgow.[34] He also organised selling exhibitions on behalf of Cottier in his own gallery in The Hague.[35]

Within two years, Cottier became a successful art dealer in three European cities: Glasgow, London and The Hague. This success was partly due to the collaboration with van Wisselingh senior who, in the course of his long career, had built contacts with numerous Dutch as well as French artists. These contacts were often intimate: Gustave Courbet (1819–1877) had painted his portrait in 1846 (fig. 67) and Mauve had even lived in his house for a few months in the late 1860s. Young artists not only approached Hendrik Jan van Wisselingh to sell their art but would also visit his gallery to study his extensive collection of Barbizon art – then one of the few French art collections in the Netherlands. Despite his great network, even van Wisselingh sometimes had to turn to Goupil's in The Hague. In 1876 he purchased fourteen works – the largest number he ever bought from them – followed by eleven in 1877. Artz and Mauve were each represented by nine works. A number of these purchases were possibly shipped to Cottier's gallery in New York, where they were auctioned off in April 1878. Then in the years 1878–80 he purchased only a handful of works at Goupil's. Perhaps he had found another source for Dutch art? In 1881, the last year he was active in The Hague, van Wisselingh senior's purchases at Goupil's reached their former level: he bought eight paintings and watercolours, half of them by Jacob Maris. After 1881, the year in which Cottier's gallery moved out of 8 Pall Mall, Cottier's name appeared only sporadically in Goupil's stock books but a letter to Artz of August 1888 reveals that he continued to make use of the services of this gallery: 'will [you] do me a favour by calling on Mr Versteegh (Goupils) and pick me out some cheap cheap water colours £1–£1.10, so on water colors [*sic*] by anybody or everybody – just to pin up in my room to make the walls brighter. send by parcel ... and I will return what I can't take'.[36]

FINDING A NICHE MARKET FOR FRENCH ART: COROT AND DAUBIGNY, DIAZ DE LA PEÑA AND MONTICELLI

By about 1870 French Barbizon artists such as Corot, Millet and Charles Daubigny (1817–1878) were already highly successful and coveted by several international dealers and collectors. To acquire their work Cottier could not simply visit their ateliers, as he had with the Hague School artists. Instead, he had to turn his attention to the secondary art market. In London he had to compete in an already established market for French art: Gambart – and later Wallis – had been showing Barbizon art since the late 1850s, and between 1872 and 1876 Paul Durand-Ruel organised a series of ambitious exhibitions that included some thirty paintings by Daubigny, as well as work by Claude Monet, Édouard Manet and Camille Pissarro. Corot and other French artists had also explored the British market themselves by sending work to the Royal Academy of Arts in London and Daubigny had stayed in the British capital on a few occasions.[37] During the

68 Camille Corot, *Brook in the Dunes*, *c.*1854. Oil on panel, 46 × 55.5 cm. Mesdag Collection, The Hague

Franco-Prussian War (1870–1) London provided a safe haven for many French artists. James Tissot (1836–1902) even made the city his permanent residence, as one of Cottier's close neighbours.

Even within the existing British market for Corot's work, Cottier managed to create a niche, selling at least twenty-five paintings by this artist in the course of his career as a dealer (fig. 68). In 1875 he organised the largest selling exhibition of Corot's work in London, followed by a smaller show a year later.[38] The former opened weeks after the sale of Corot's studio following the artist's death; indeed, it is possible that Cottier purchased the lion's share of his stock there. It was the perfect time to focus on the Barbizon School because, after the deaths of both Millet and Corot in 1875 and their subsequent estate sales, the Parisian market for landscape painting had collapsed.[39] Besides the financial benefits that came with buying at estate sales, these auctions offered the type of art that Cottier loved: intimate studies and unfinished paintings. In April 1876 he also purchased a sketch from Corot at Goupil's in Paris, *Paysage effet de matin*, which was listed in Goupil's stock books as 'Étude signée'.[40]

In 1876 a female journalist writing for *The Aldine* visited the smaller Corot exhibition at Cottier's gallery and was overwhelmed by the effect of his well-observed sketches on her senses. She wrote: 'They are a haze, peering through which we come at last to life

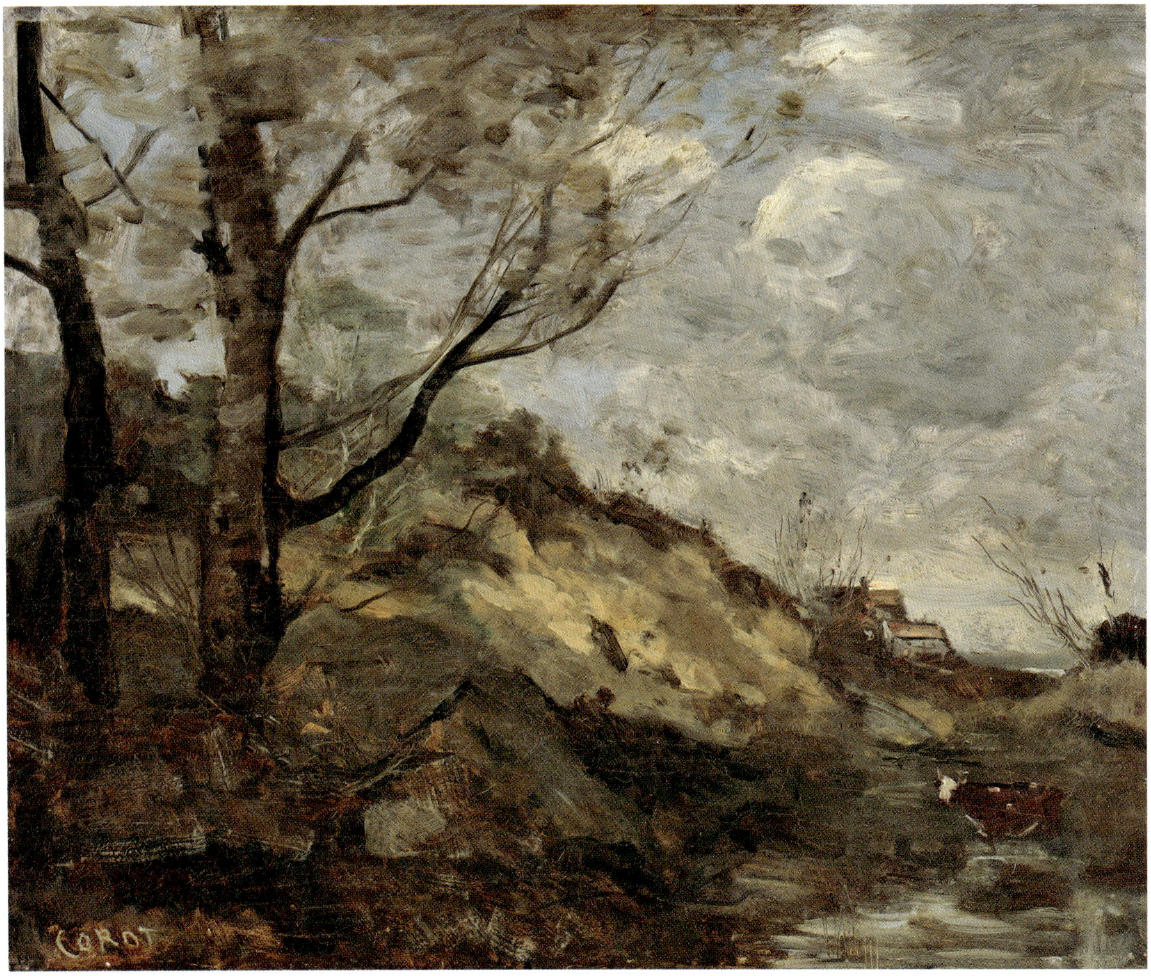

69 Charles Daubigny, *Boats on the Thames*, *c.*1866–7.
Oil on panel, 40.8 × 67 cm. Mesdag Collection, The Hague

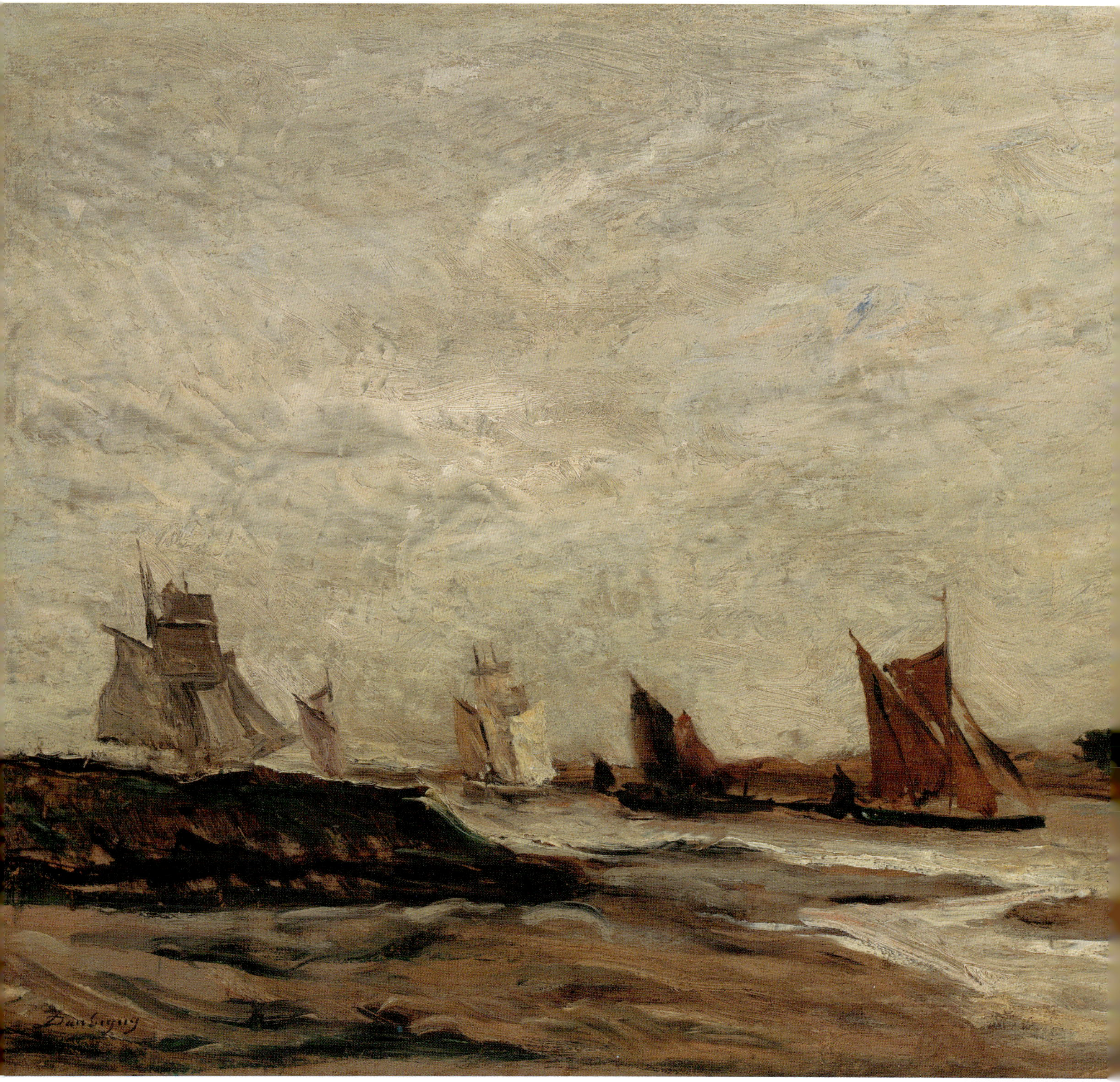

70 Back cover of a Cottier & Co. prospectus published in London, *c.*1876–81. Historic New England, Boston, Massachusetts

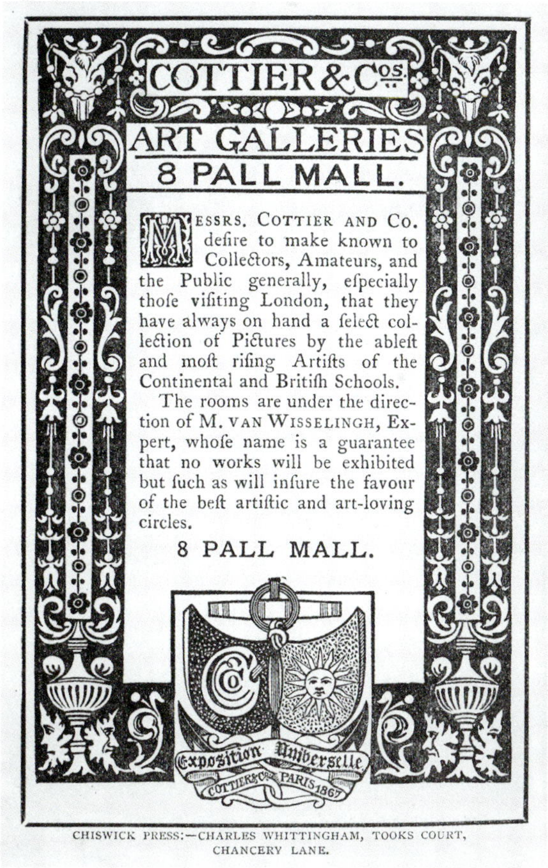

COTTIER & CO'S.

ART GALLERIES

8 PALL MALL.

Messrs. Cottier and Co. deſire to make known to Collectors, Amateurs, and the Public generally, eſpecially thoſe viſiting London, that they have always on hand a ſelect collection of Pictures by the ableſt and moſt riſing Artiſts of the Continental and Britiſh Schools.

The rooms are under the direction of M. van Wisselingh, Expert, whoſe name is a guarantee that no works will be exhibited but ſuch as will inſure the favour of the beſt artiſtic and art-loving circles.

8 PALL MALL.

CHISWICK PRESS:—CHARLES WHITTINGHAM, TOOKS COURT, CHANCERY LANE.

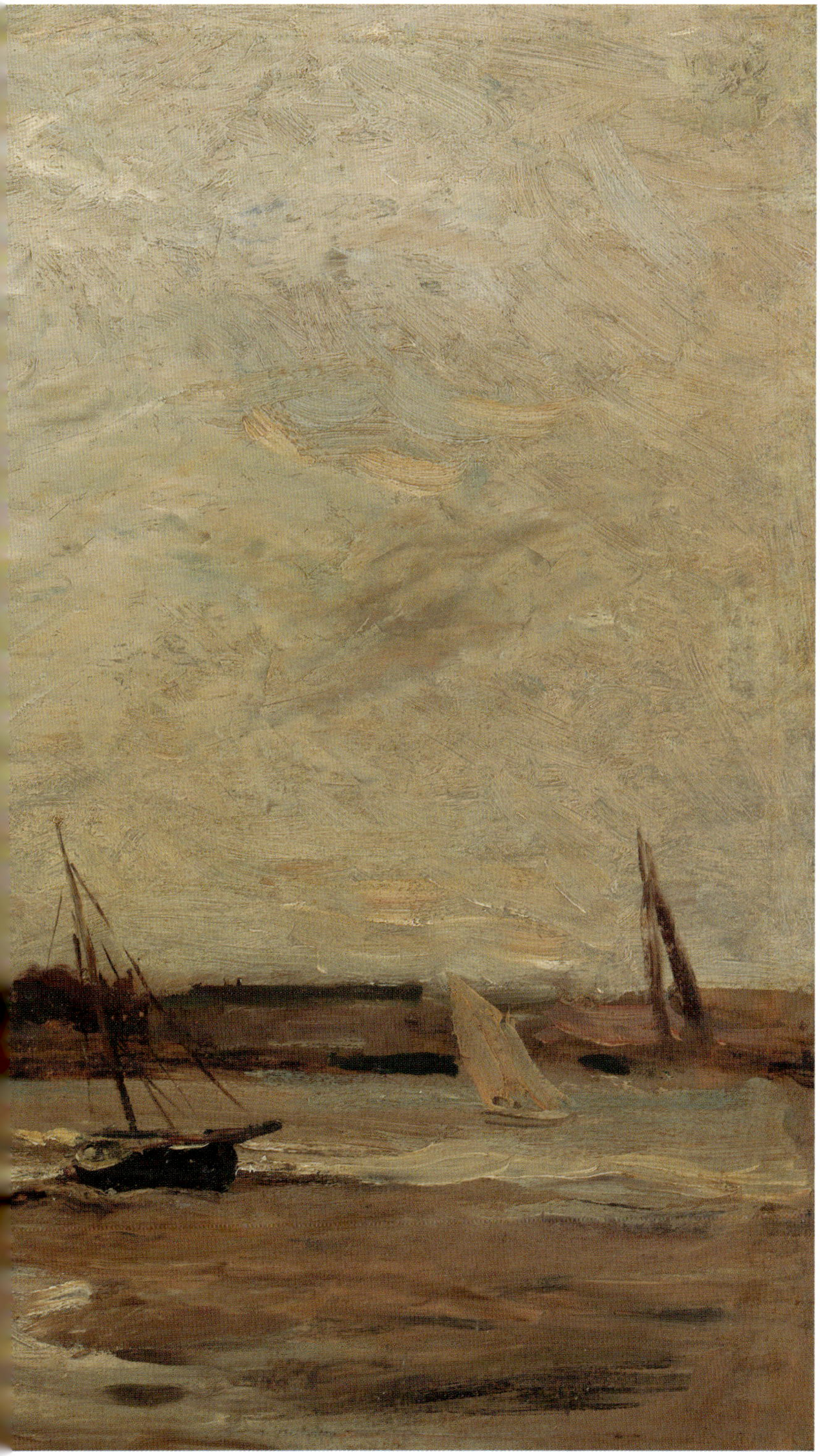

and nature's self. The breeze blows in them, the trees wave and whisper, the sun has a gentle warmth, the water is cool.'[41] One of the paintings in this exhibition, *An Evening in Normandy* (see fig. 59), was purchased by Bruce. Cottier's selection of Corot's art differed essentially from the prevailing taste in Britain. Far more popular were the artist's figure pieces such as *La Toilette*, in the collection of the Scot James Duncan (1834–1905), and his fantasy landscapes filled with nymphs.[42] For instance, John Forbes White had bought *Pastorale: Souvenir d'Italie* (Kelvingrove Art Gallery & Museum, Glasgow) in September 1874. At some point between 1875 and 1877, even Cottier followed White's example and acquired Corot's *The Sleep of Diana* (whereabouts unknown). He later shipped the painting's counterpart, *Orpheus greeting the Dawn*, to New York (see Chapter Five, p. 126 and fig. 115).

Daubigny was another French artist in whose work Cottier invested during the 1870s. From 1875 onwards Cottier bought Daubigny's work from the Austrian dealer Charles Sedelmeyer and from Goupil's in Paris and London – both parties were in direct contact with Daubigny. To these paintings he added pieces he purchased at Arnold & Tripp in Paris. Shortly after Daubigny's death in 1878, Goupil could ask more than

71 Narcisse Virgile Diaz de la Peña, *Roses*, *c.*1870–76. Oil on canvas, 81.2 × 66 cm. Perth Museum & Art Gallery, bequeathed by Robert Brough, 1926

72 Matthijs Maris, *The Nieuwe Haarlemse Sluis at the Singel*, known as *Souvenir d'Amsterdam*, 1871. Oil on canvas, 46.5 × 35 cm. Rijksmuseum, Amsterdam, gift of the heirs of W. J. van Randwijk, The Hague

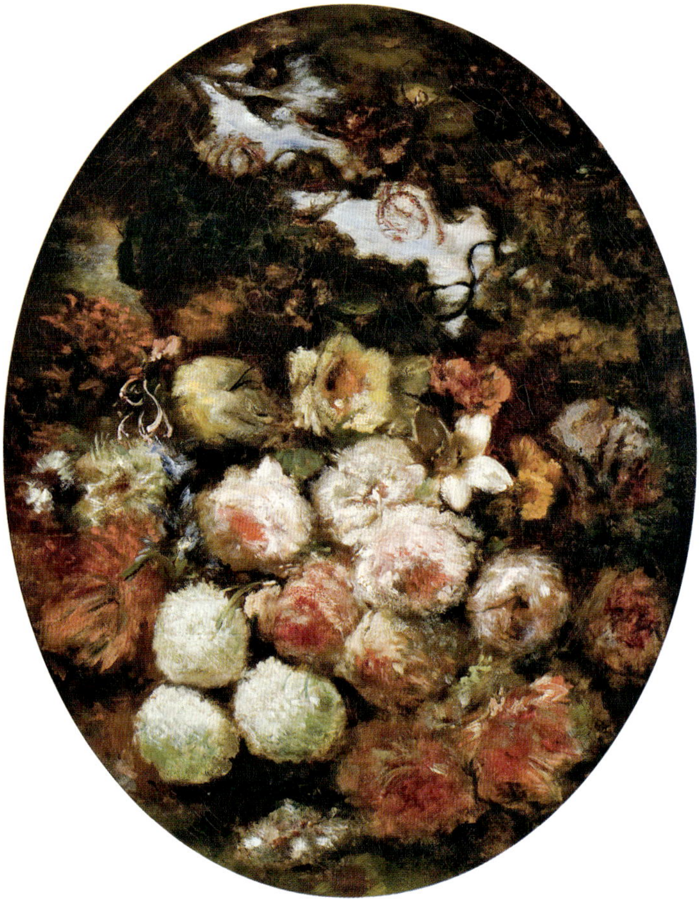

8000 francs for a single painting by the artist, whose riverscapes became especially sought after.[43] Cottier is known to have owned four, two of which were originally commissioned by Sedelmeyer.[44] *Boats on the Thames* (fig. 69) was in Cottier's possession from at least 1886 onwards. This schematic study on panel was painted by Daubigny in 1866 or 1867, most probably outdoors. Given its subject matter, Cottier probably had an English buyer in mind but in 1892, following Cottier's death, it was purchased by the Dutch marine painter Mesdag.[45]

In 1875 Cottier sold White a still life with roses by Narcisse Diaz de la Peña (1807–1876). The painting, oval in shape, is colourful and painted in thick impasto (fig. 71); White himself described it as 'fresh and juicy'.[46] It was different from both the industrial environment in which White made his money and from the idyllic rural scenes painted by the Hague School. In a bold move away from Dutch and towards French art, White agreed with Cottier to exchange five paintings, including the aforementioned townscape by Jacob Maris and one by Mauve, for the Diaz.[47] Other clients, who had trusted Cottier earlier when he had advised them to buy Hague School work, followed suit: John McGavin and Andrew J. Kirkpatrick (d.1900) both acquired work by Diaz, probably through Angus. In 1880 and 1881 the paintings belonging to these collectors were on show at the Royal Glasgow Institute.[48]

While Daubigny, Corot and Diaz were commercially successful artists, Monticelli, Diaz's follower, was not. Around 1875 his paintings of young women in woodland settings, executed in rich colours and thick impasto, were mainly popular among other artists. This did not deter Cottier from investing in his work. He purchased from the artist directly and, between 1878 and 1882, also asked van Wisselingh to buy Monticelli's work from the Parisian dealer Gérard.[49] It is possible that he also bought from Joseph Delarebeyrette, another dealer in Paris, who worked with an agent stationed in Monticelli's home town of Marseille. By 1879 Cottier had amassed enough examples of his work to organise Monticelli's first solo exhibition in London.[50] Around the same time he also sent Monticelli's *Legend* (whereabouts unknown) to Angus; in 1880 this work was valued at £300.[51] Cottier succeeded in interesting collectors such as Maxwell, Bruce and Arthur Sanderson in Monticelli's work, while at the same time, according to a journalist writing for the Dutch newspaper *Het nieuws van de dag*, he kept the best examples for himself. It was only at the sale of Cottier's collection in 1892 that the same art critic learned that 'Monticelli also painted something completely different from canvases looking like pieces of gobelins [French tapestries].'[52]

MATTHIJS MARIS AND DANIEL COTTIER, 1872–1887

Work by the Dutch artist Matthijs Maris, Jacob's younger brother, was a cornerstone of Cottier's stock from 1872 onwards. The two met that year in Paris, where Maris lived at the time, probably through Artz. Artz also helped Cottier to purchase his first painting by Maris directly from the artist, *The Nieuwe Haarlemse Sluis at the Singel*, known as *Souvenir d'Amsterdam* (fig. 72). Maris painted this

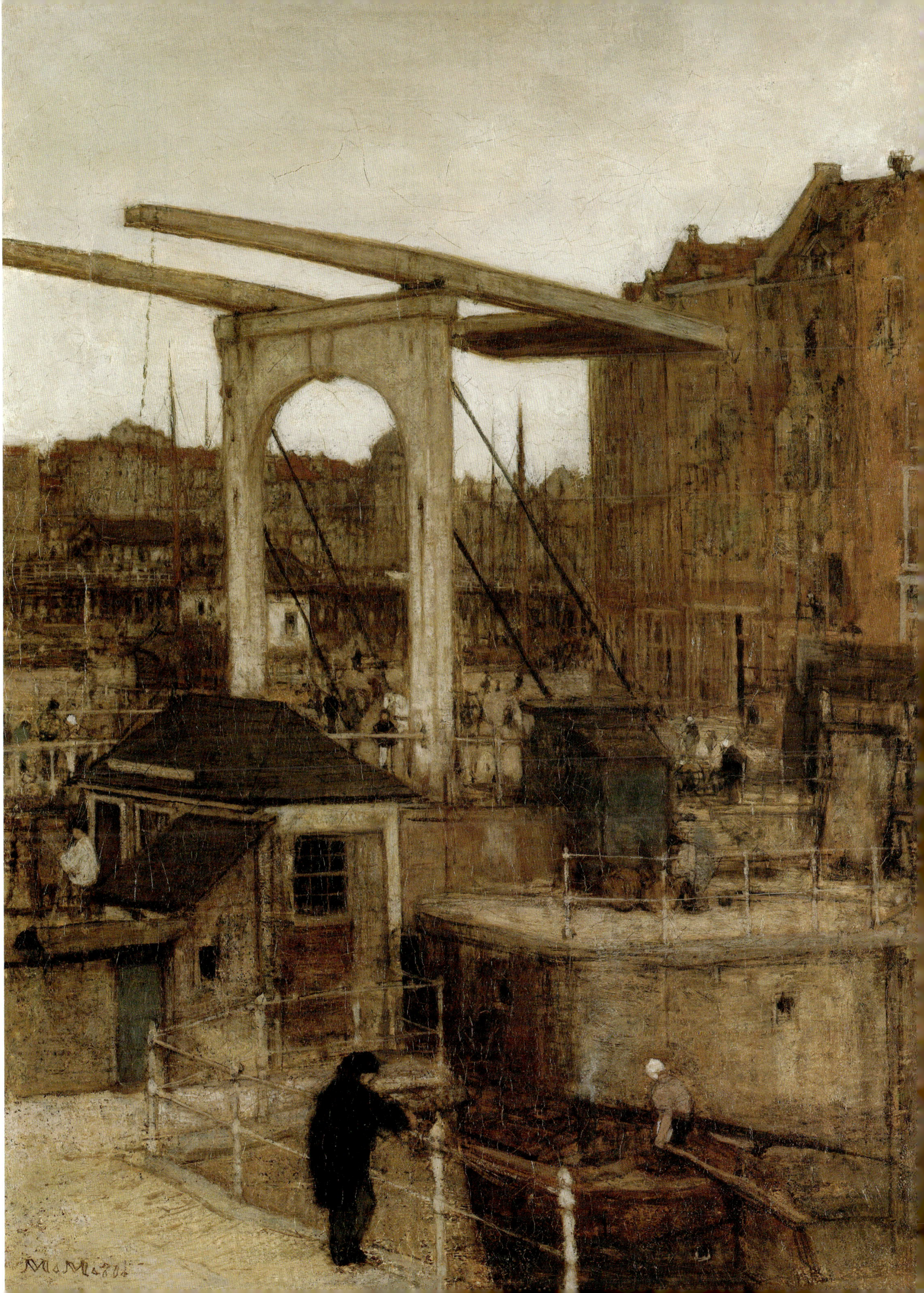

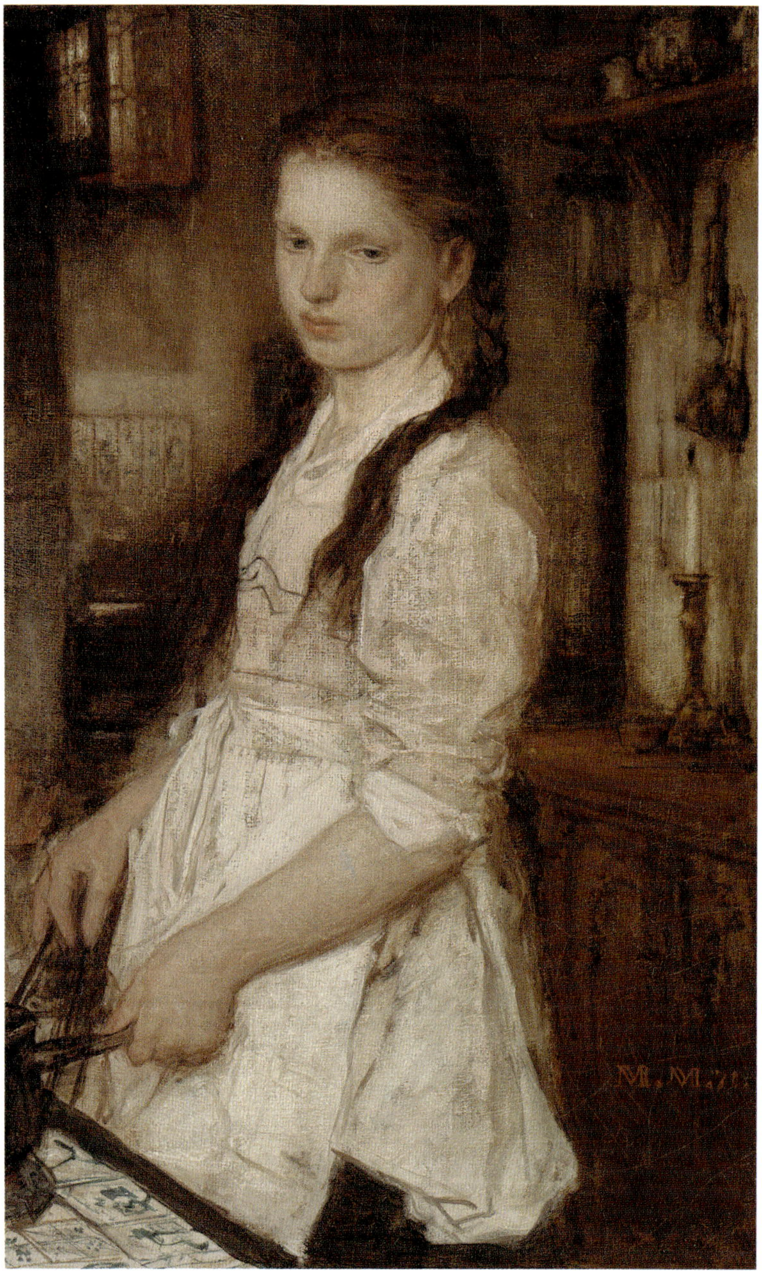

73 Matthijs Maris, *The Young Cook*, 1871. Oil on canvas, 33 × 21 cm. Private collection

Dutch townscape from a stereoscopic photograph which he had acquired during a visit to Amsterdam, while the tall buildings in the background were inspired by Parisian houses. In that same year, 1872, Cottier purchased at Goupil's in Paris another piece by Matthijs Maris, *The Young Cook* (fig. 73). This painting retained traces of the artist's working process. Maris had chosen a canvas with a coarse structure that remained visible even after paint was applied. He painted the girl quickly, probably in a single session, and the green paint used to lay down the figure is visible in her face. The acquisition of both paintings not only marked the beginning of Cottier's lifelong fascination with Maris's work but also represented an expansion of his artistic interests – a taste for poetic art in addition to his previous interest in landscape impressions painted by Jacob Maris and Mauve or the somewhat sentimental figure paintings by Artz.

As with Artz some years earlier, Cottier met Maris in Paris during a highly productive time in the latter's career. His international fame was growing and the prices for his works were rising from 250 to an average of 1000 francs, depending on their size. Although Maris did not sign a contract with the gallery, his most important customer during his Parisian days was Goupil; from July 1871 until October 1873 he sold eighteen paintings to this gallery. Four of them were immediately shipped to American firms and nine to England, where Cottier was the main buyer. In 1873 Goupil also ventured into the Scottish art market by sending the large city view *St Ouen* (private collection) to the Royal Glasgow Institute; shortly after the exhibition closed, it too was bought by Cottier. It was only a matter of time before Cottier purchased all work that entered the market, either through Goupil's or from the artist himself, such as *Quarry at Montmartre* (Burrell Collection, Glasgow). Cottier sold it to Charles Porter, whose dining room he had recently decorated.[53]

Maris listened to Cottier's advice. In 1874, in a bid to please his 'Scotchman', as the artist put it, he changed the colours of *He is Coming!* (National Museum of Wales, Cardiff) to make the painting look more like a stained-glass window.[54] Through Angus the painting became part of Bruce's collection. Despite this success, Maris later labelled the works he made in Paris as 'potboilers', commercial art made merely to earn money. This negative stance was fuelled by his aversion to the art market and the fact that the works fetched higher prices than he himself had ever received for them. Maris described what he wanted to make as 'conceptions'. In other words, he did not want to copy models in nature; he wanted to give shape to inner images that he devised for himself. He later likened this action – getting his 'conceptions' onto the canvas – to singing and poetry.[55]

74 Matthijs Maris, *The Lady of Shalott*, *c.*1879–81.
Oil paint on leaded glass, 52.1 × 29.8 cm. Burrell Collection, Glasgow Museums

75 Matthijs Maris, *The Lady of Shalott*, 1879.
Oil on canvas, 55.9 × 30.7 cm. Burrell Collection, Glasgow Museums

76 Matthijs Maris, *The Lady of Shalott*, 1879.
Oil paint on leaded glass, 56 × 31.8 cm. Private collection

In 1877 Maris's close friendship with van Wisselingh finally convinced him to leave Paris for London.[56] The artist knew that Cottier had bought a large number of his paintings from Goupil's and was confident that Cottier understood his art and would let him work in freedom. He was even given his own rooms in Cottier's home in St James's Terrace, overlooking Regent's Park. According to Maris, while in Paris Cottier lived like a king: 'He was staying in the Grand Hotel, and money was nothing to him, came down one day to fetch me with two of his friends in a swell carriage from the Hotel, and had a drive to Versailles, and feasting no end.'[57] But when he arrived in London the artist found Cottier was having financial troubles. Maris even saw bailiffs at his door.[58] Because money was needed, Cottier burdened him with assignments such as designing stained-glass windows and sprucing up paintings that the firm had bought cheaply, particularly work by Monticelli.[59] Some of these works had been damaged during transport while others were of lesser quality to begin with: according to Maris, Monticelli painted them during a period of artistic crisis and the Dutchman referred to them as 'mad things'.[60] Maris greatly revered Monticelli as an artist and therefore felt uneasy when Cottier sold paintings as by Monticelli-Maris or Maris-Monticelli. He later rejected the idea of co-authorship: 'I had no right to retouch his work, one has to respect it, even when it's bad ... The clothes make the man, not the tailor. So they are not entitled to place the restorer on an equal footing.'[61] It is probable that Cottier got more for the paintings than the £200 he paid Maris for restoring them.[62]

Cottier also expected Maris to produce colourful and romantic works like those he had made in Paris. However, the artist had already set course on another path. He met Cottier's wishes but grew increasingly frustrated. Whether some form of agreement existed between them remains vague. On this topic, Cottier later wrote to Artz:

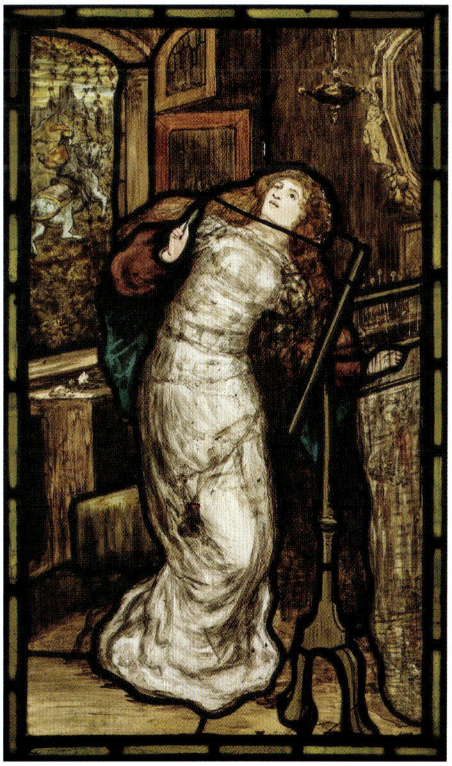

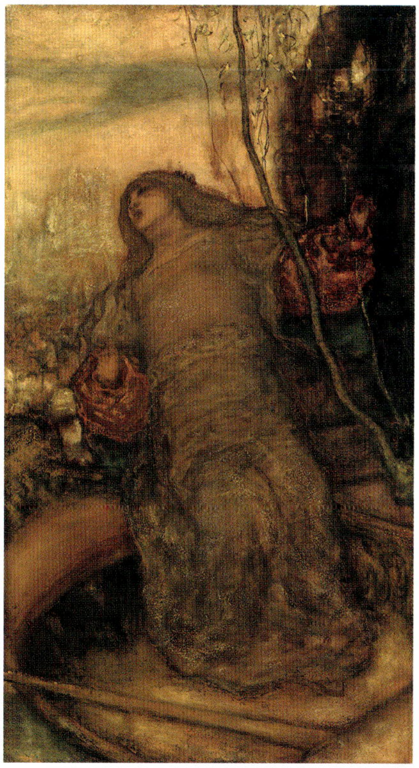

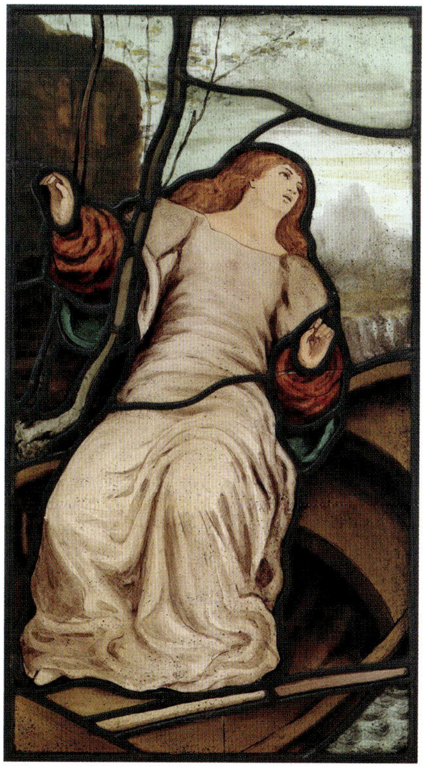

I never tried in any shape or form to have dealings with Maris. I gave him a room to work in at Pall-Mall but left him alone to do what he liked. I saw it would never do to bother with such a man so I left him alone ... Now he never was mine[,] did not arrange with me. I never was his keeper although I kept him.[63]

In his opinion he simply provided Maris with a roof over his head and money when needed. The fact of the matter, however, is that from the moment Maris moved to London he stopped selling to Goupil, or to any other dealer for that matter, and all his output went directly to Cottier.

Like his English contemporaries, Maris was spellbound by Alfred, Lord Tennyson's 1832 poem 'The Lady of Shalott', a subject that Cottier may have suggested to him. It is the story of a chatelaine who lives in a tower under a fatal curse against looking directly at the world: she must only view it reflected in a mirror. Maris probably felt a connection with this tragic heroine because, like her, he did not feel part of society. When the Lady of Shalott does peer out of the window to catch a glimpse of the knight Lancelot, the curse falls on her. Maris depicted this passage in a stained-glass window, the only glass he both designed and executed, except for the leading which was probably done in Cottier's workshop (fig. 74). He had difficulty working on the fragile support:

I could not handle it ... De [sic] shadows had to be done with some kind of watercolour, but that slid over the glass with 'eyes'. Then [Cottier] told me that I should add some turps, but that burned in the fire. So the only thing that exists done by me I painted with oil paint against the light. I do not know how often it came down and broke in pieces. One has to be made for it.[64]

Maris treated the glass like canvas and applied the paint with visible strokes. Thanks to this unorthodox technique the window is not as translucent and delicate as other windows produced by Cottier's workshop. In 1879 Maris depicted another moment in the poem, this time using oil on canvas. We see the Lady as she steps into a boat (fig. 75), shortly before Lancelot finds her lifeless body. Both Maris's window (now in the Burrell Collection, Glasgow) and his canvas painting, individually or combined together, served as templates for dozens of stained-glass windows on the same subject made in Cottier's workshop (see Chapter Four, p. 112). In the case of Maris's canvas and the Cottier window, they are almost the same size and when they are superimposed the match is fairly precise, with only small deviations such as the position of the right foot. This part of the composition had to be moved in the window to accommodate the leading.[65] In the catalogue of the 1913 Cottier sale these Lady of Shalott windows were mentioned as 'originally designed and painted by Matthew Maris.'[66] However, compared with Maris's 'painted' window in the Burrell Collection, the skill of Cottier & Co.'s craftsmen who executed those windows is evident in the successful translation of Maris's design into another medium, visible in the stylisation of the figure, the fine lines of lead and the transparently painted glass (fig. 76).

Despite the time Maris spent on Cottier's commissions, the artist also succeeded in making a fair amount of 'free' work – etchings, images of dreamy female figures and children's portraits – but not enough to his liking. Ultimately Maris felt too curtailed and broke with Cottier after ten years, in 1887.

THE FOREIGN LOAN EXHIBITION OF 1886, EDINBURGH

In May 1886 Cottier wrote to Artz that it was 'poor times for the pictures'.[67] But change was coming. After almost ten years, Scotland was in the process of recovering from an economic depression and Cottier had cultivated a small but influential group of contemporary art lovers with his enthusiasm and perseverance.[68] From 6 May to 30 October the first Scottish International Exhibition of Science, Industry and Art was held in the Edinburgh Meadows and attracted almost three million visitors. Part of this large-scale event was the so-called Foreign Loan Section which featured 106 French and 84 Dutch art works, all lent by Scottish and English collectors. Bruce organised the exhibition but Cottier probably played an important role in the background.[69] Not only did he lend fourteen paintings from his inventory but it is highly

77 Jules Dupré, *The Headland*, c.1881–6. Oil on canvas, 72.4 × 91.4 cm. Glasgow Museums, bequeathed by James Donald, 1905

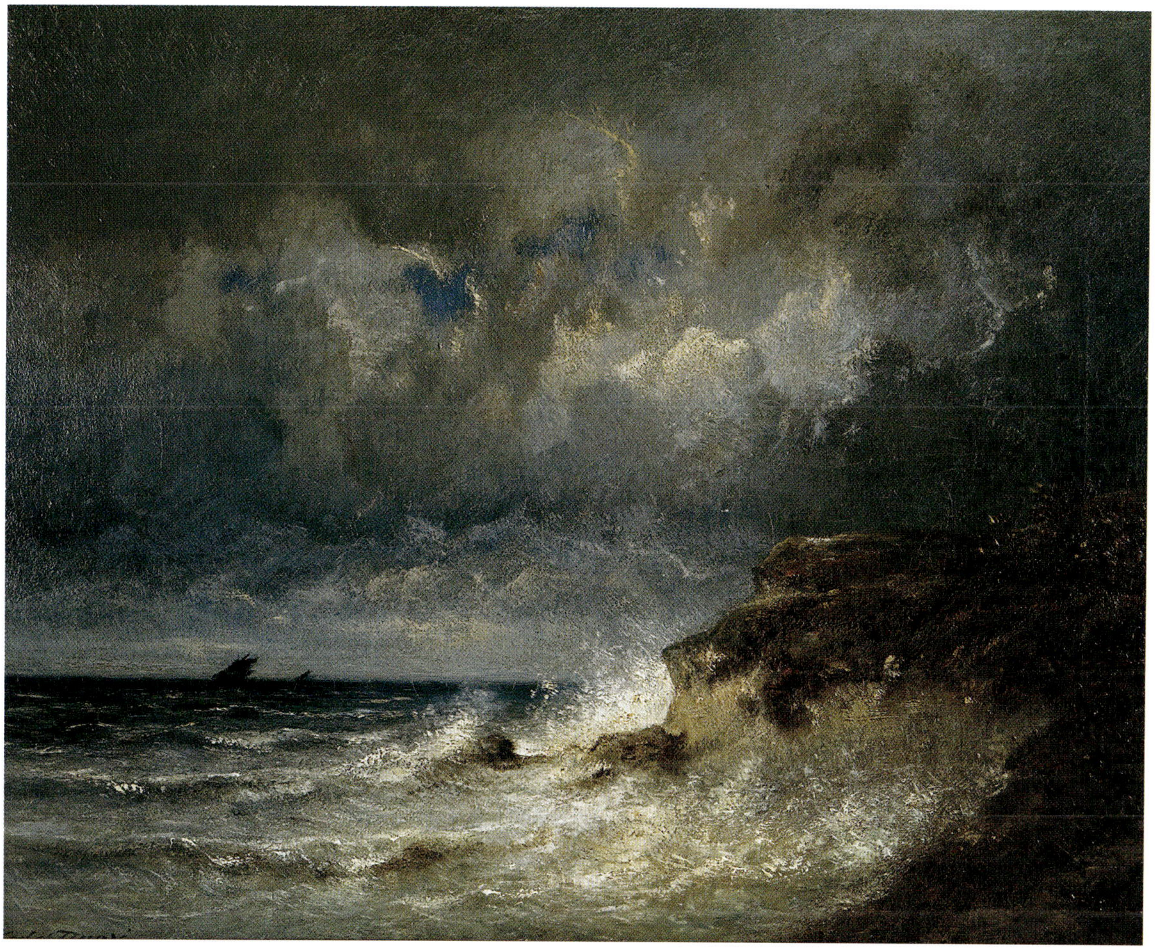

likely that he also pointed Bruce towards interesting pieces belonging to his clients. The Edinburgh exhibition was a reflection of Cottier's clientele and of the aesthetic he propagated: the French painters of the Barbizon School, such as Jules Dupré (fig. 77), Corot, Daubigny and Diaz, contemporary Dutch realism (fig. 78), with the exception of Israëls's narrative paintings and the symbolism found in the work of Matthijs Maris and Monticelli (who died in his birthplace, Marseille, during the exhibition). A *Memorial Catalogue*, richly illustrated, was written by the renowned art critic William Ernest Henley (1848–1903) and included essays on the Barbizon and Hague Schools as well as biographies of all the artists involved. Henley also introduced the term 'Romantic Realism' to describe the French and Dutch works, explaining that 'the foundation of the two schools is the exact and faithful study of nature with a view to the passionate and romantic expression of experience'.[70] This term was subsequently adopted by other art critics.

This successful exhibition became a catalyst for the collecting of Dutch and French art, in Scotland as well as in England. Cottier had started investing in these artists more than a decade earlier and by this time was ready to turn his investments into profits. In 1888, for example, the Goupil Gallery in London organised the first exhibition dedicated to the work of the three Maris brothers and out of the seven works exhibited by Matthijs, two came directly from Cottier: *The*

78 Jacob Maris, *Souvenir of Dordrecht*, c.1884–5. Oil on canvas, 71.1 × 124.5 cm. Burrell Collection, Glasgow Museums

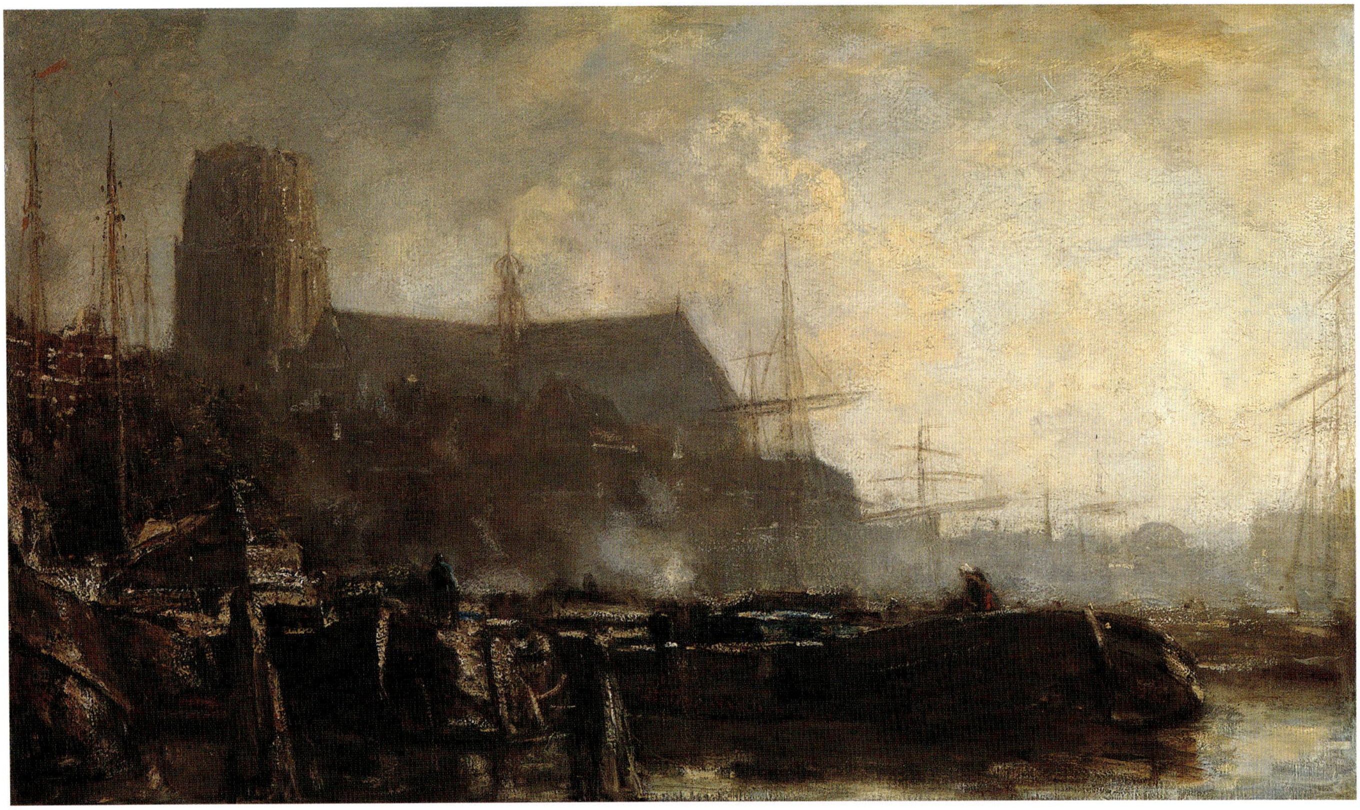

Nieuwe Haarlemse Sluis and *The Young Cook*, on show in Edinburgh in 1886 (see figs 72 and 73). Cottier had been the first owner of both. Also in 1888 Dowdeswell & Dowdeswell organised a Monticelli exhibition consisting of seventy-five works. Interest in Monticelli had increased dramatically after his death and prices had multiplied from 50–100 francs per painting in 1886 to almost 500 francs in 1888.[71] The catalogue that accompanied the exhibition referred to Cottier's role as a tastemaker for Monticelli in both Scotland and America but without mentioning him:

American and Scotch eyes and purses have been to the fore in appreciating Monticelli's works ... History repeats itself in Art as elsewhere, and the story of Monticelli's pictures is further proof that Englishmen, and even this artist's compatriots, must give way before Scotchmen and Americans in swift and unhesitating understanding of a new and felicitous pictorial interpretation of Nature's facts.[72]

Cottier's name is missing from the catalogue's list of participating dealers. His place had been taken by van Wisselingh and Alexander Reid (1854–1928).

THE BEGINNING OF THE END: 'DULL DAYS AND PAINFUL SLEEPLESS NIGHTS'

The 1886 exhibition in Edinburgh was a personal victory for Cottier but his European empire was slowly crumbling. In the previous six years business had been slow in Glasgow and Angus had been forced to file for bankruptcy in December 1880. This unfortunate event led to a disagreement between Angus and Cottier regarding the ownership of twenty paintings in Angus's gallery and numerous Cottier & Co. items destined for Dormouth House. Cottier had sent these objects from London on the understanding that they would either be sold by Angus or returned. So, were they part of Angus's household effects, which were to be auctioned off, or were they Cottier's property?[73] In

February 1881 agreement had been reached and all the disputed objects were shipped back to London; Cottier agreed to guarantee Angus's last payment to his creditors.[74] For five years – from 1881 to 1885, the year in which he opened a new shop in Glasgow – Angus's whereabouts and the nature of his relationship with Cottier are unclear. From notes by Cottier's partner John Lamb Lyon, it is known that Angus was working again as a Glasgow agent for Cottier in 1886 (see Appendix, p. 209). But it was not long before he would trade in Cottier for a new partner, his son-in-law Elbert Jan van Wisselingh.

Van Wisselingh had left Cottier in 1882 to establish his own business in Paris. With his departure, the collaboration between Cottier and van Wisselingh senior also ended. In 1884, after the death of his father, Elbert Jan van Wisselingh closed his shop in Paris and took over the family business in The Hague, naturally continuing to make use of his contacts in Scotland and England. For example, in 1886 he sold Matthijs Maris's painting *Butterflies* from 1874 (Burrell Collection, Glasgow) directly to Angus without Cottier's intervention. Cottier must have been furious, because in the 1870s he had missed out on purchasing this masterpiece when Tersteeg beat him to it. Angus sold the painting to Thomas Glen Arthur from Edinburgh. In 1887 van Wisselingh further tightened his grip on the Scottish market by marrying Isabella Murray Mowat Angus, Angus's daughter, and by taking Matthijs Maris under his wing. In exchange for an allowance, Maris gave van Wisselingh exclusive rights to sell all his drawings and paintings. Cottier did not live long enough to witness the opening of van Wisselingh's Dutch Gallery in London in 1892.

The art market was changing and, while British collectors slowly warmed to French Impressionism, Cottier stuck to his ways, leaving their promotion to a new generation of specialised art dealers, among them Alexander Reid in Glasgow. Cottier equally ignored new developments in Scottish art, such as the rise of the Glasgow Boys, a group of young artists who saw the Hague School as their greatest source of inspiration.[75] According to the artist Robert Macaulay Stevenson, the exclusion of Scottish art at the 1886 Foreign Loan Section was part of a intricate scheme designed by Bruce and Cottier to drive up prices of Dutch and French art and subsequently to 'run down all the Scottish art'.[76] For young collectors such as William Burrell (1861–1958), the work of the Glasgow Boys formed an interesting alternative to the now overpriced Hague School art. Perhaps, at this stage of his career, Cottier was no longer interested in helping and promoting young artists, whose works sold at a fraction of the prices the works of the older generation commanded. His clientele had become older and richer and more conservative.

The biggest setback Cottier experienced from the mid-1880s onwards was his declining health, resulting from the rheumatic fever he had contracted in the late 1860s. It affected his liver and kidneys and he could not walk without crutches.[77] The aggressive letters he received from Matthijs Maris did not help either.[78] In February 1886 he even described his life to Artz as 'full of dull days and painful sleepless nights'.[79] During the months he spent in Aachen, Aix-les-Bains and even Cairo for treatment, there was hardly any time left for the work he loved. But every so often, glimpses of the old, fiery Cottier are visible in his letters, especially when he sensed a good business opportunity. After Mauve died in 1888, for example, Cottier wrote to Artz: 'Is Mrs Mauve left well off. has she plenty of money. is there no sale of his estate same as you did with Mollinger's.'[80]

Cottier died in Florida in 1891 and a year later his private collection was auctioned in Paris. The sale included work from all the Dutch and French artists whom he had energetically promoted and among the buyers were his main customers, competitors and successors. Above all, it symbolised Cottier's skills and courage as a dealer: within twenty years he had dramatically changed the British market for contemporary European art.

Petra Chu

CHAPTER FOUR
NEW YORK 1873–1915

On 5 September 1873 Cottier and his friend James S. Inglis arrived in New York aboard the SS *Baltic*.[1] Born in Edinburgh and some five years younger than Cottier, Inglis had trained as an architect under Richard Norman Shaw (1831–1912) in London. Although it is possible that he first met Cottier in Scotland, the two young men had bonded in London where, according to Inglis's obituary, they 'devoted themselves to the designing of interiors, and to their enrichment with pictures and art objects'.[2]

Soon after their arrival in New York, Cottier and Inglis established a branch of Cottier & Co. at 144 Fifth Avenue. The exact opening date is not known but the firm was already listed in the 1874 *Wilson's Business Directory of New York City* under 'Artists, Decorative' and 'Glass Stainers'.[3] Like the London business, Cottier & Co. in New York focused on home furnishings,'artistic' furniture and stained glass, for both ecclesiastic and secular use, as well as ceramic tiles and plaques (and later, chargers). In time, it would also provide interior design services and sell antiques and works of art.[4] Indeed, Cottier's success in New York was closely bound up with his art gallery, which, at least during his lifetime, may have been the most lucrative part of his business there (see Chapter Five).

Cottier returned to England in late October 1873,[5] leaving Inglis as the manager but returning regularly to New York for longer or shorter periods, both to check in with Inglis and to bring over new inventory.[6] It is difficult to determine how often Cottier visited New York. Through New York Passenger and Crew Lists, we know that he travelled to New York on at least four occasions (not counting the 1873 visit), including three times with his entire family.[7] Undoubtedly, he came more often. Given the time and expense involved in travel, it can be assumed that each trip, like the first, was for two months or more. However, Inglis was responsible for the day-to-day operation of Cottier & Co. in New York and after Cottier's death he continued the business until he died in 1907. The sculptor Olin Levi Warner's (1844–1896) portrait bust of Inglis of 1878 (fig. 80) suggests the qualities that, nearly thirty years later, were highlighted in Inglis's obituaries: geniality, sophistication and wit.[8] Comparing this portrait with Warner's bust of Cottier, of the same year (fig. 81), we gain some insight into the complementary characters of these two men. Cottier was enthusiastic, energetic, restless and impulsive; Inglis was laid-back, thoughtful and sensitive; both played their part to make Cottier & Co. in New York a success.

79 Front cover of Clarence Cook, *The House Beautiful*, 1878. Printed and gilded cloth, 25.5 × 20 × 3.4 cm. Cover design by Daniel Cottier. Ingalls Library, Cleveland Museum of Art, Cleveland, Ohio

SHOWROOM AND WORKSHOP

The building at 144 Fifth Avenue in which Cottier & Co.'s showroom was located has survived to this day (fig. 82). Originally constructed perhaps in the 1850s as a spacious townhouse, the five-storey Italianate brownstone was converted, probably by Cottier and Inglis, into a retail space. Its entrance stairway or 'stoop' on the right was removed and the ground floor turned into a street-level store.[9] The original front door, which would have given access to the first-floor parlour, was replaced by a window. A 'new' façade was framed by two cast-iron pilasters, reaching to the top of the second storey. Also added were two cast-iron plaques bearing cartouches with elaborate strapwork frames, inside which whimsical lettering spells out the street address (fig. 83).[10] Construction work at ground-floor level in May 2017 allowed one to see the remnants of white and gold paint on the cast-iron pilasters; it can be assumed that the two plaques were

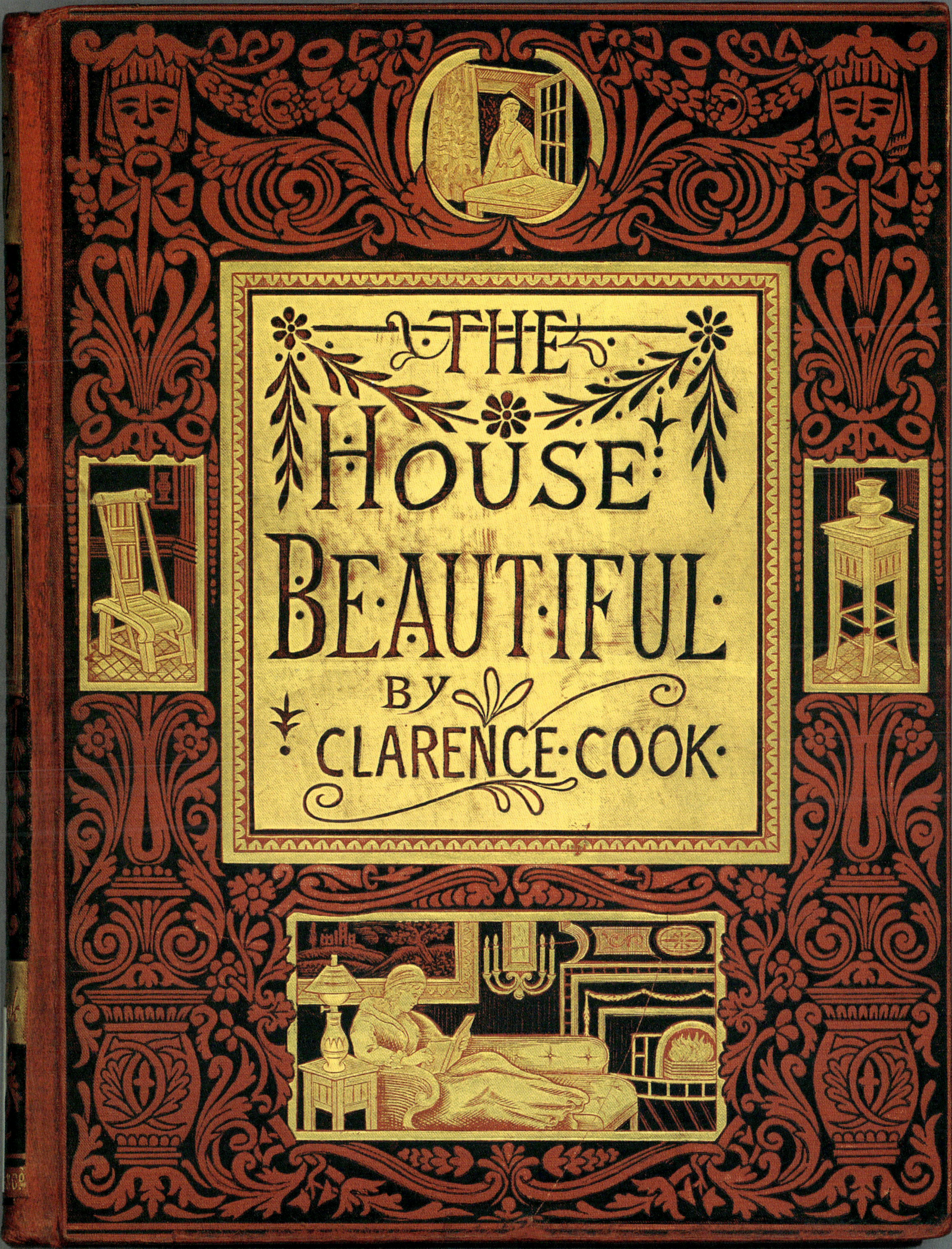
THE
HOUSE
BEAUTIFUL
BY
CLARENCE·COOK·

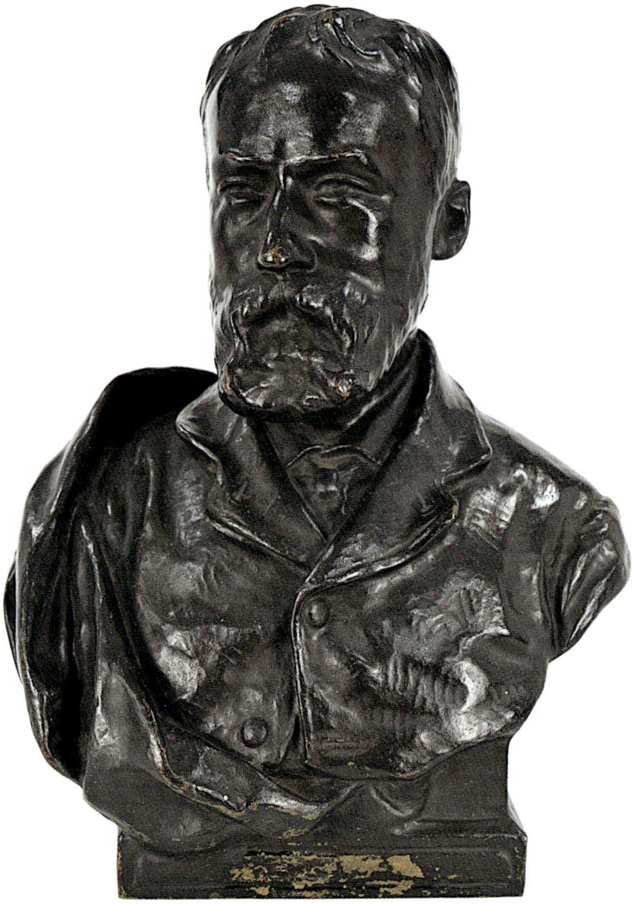

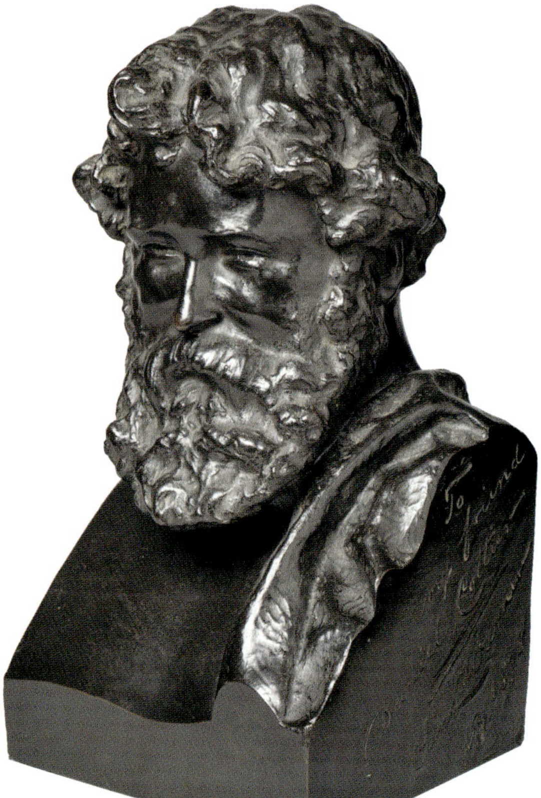

80 Olin Levi Warner, *Portrait of James Inglis*, 1878. Bronze, h. 33 cm. American Academy of Arts and Letters, New York

81 Olin Levi Warner, *Portrait of Daniel Cottier*, 1878. Bronze, h. 28.5 cm. Manx Museum, Douglas, Isle of Man

likewise painted in contrasting colours. With its tinted cast-iron elements – and without the ugly fire escape that was probably added in the early twentieth century – the building must have presented a rich and elegant frontage.

Little is known about the interior but an anonymous note in *Scribner's Monthly* of August 1874 describes the experience of entering Cottier & Co. as something akin to a revelation:

There can hardly be a more delightful surprise for the lover of rich color and beautiful form than to pass directly from the dull uniformity and architectural ugliness of the Fifth Avenue into the showroom of Cottier & Co. This room seems as strange in New York, as a rose-bed with nightingales and a fountain would be, come upon in the back yard of a First Avenue tenement-house.[11]

The reviewer goes on to say that what set Cottier and Co.'s showroom interior apart from those of two established and prestigious cabinetmakers and decorators, Léon Marcotte & Co. and Herter Brothers ('shopkeepers whose business is only to exchange their tawdry for the rich man's money'), is 'the effect of this apartment, so splendid and yet so quiet, exhilarating and yet soothing'. Whether this initial splendid quietness continued throughout Cottier & Co.'s existence is questionable. When Cottier's Australian partner, John Lamb Lyon, visited the shop in New York in 1886, he wrote in his journal that the showroom was 'sumptious [*sic*] and contained 'fine furniture and hangings, Gasliers [*sic*] ...' (see Appendix, p. 208). This remark seems to reflect an increased focus, discussed shortly, by Cottier & Co. on selling high-end luxury goods.

Cottier & Co. occupied the entire building at 144 Fifth Avenue, which the firm had either bought or leased. By 1877 the floor above the street-level showroom was adapted to serve as a Gallery or 'Art Rooms' (see Chapter Five). The three other floors were probably let, used for storage or both. We know that around 1876 Cottier and Inglis lent working space in the building to Olin Warner. He had his studio there until the autumn of 1879, when he wrote to another sculptor, Truman H. Bartlett, that

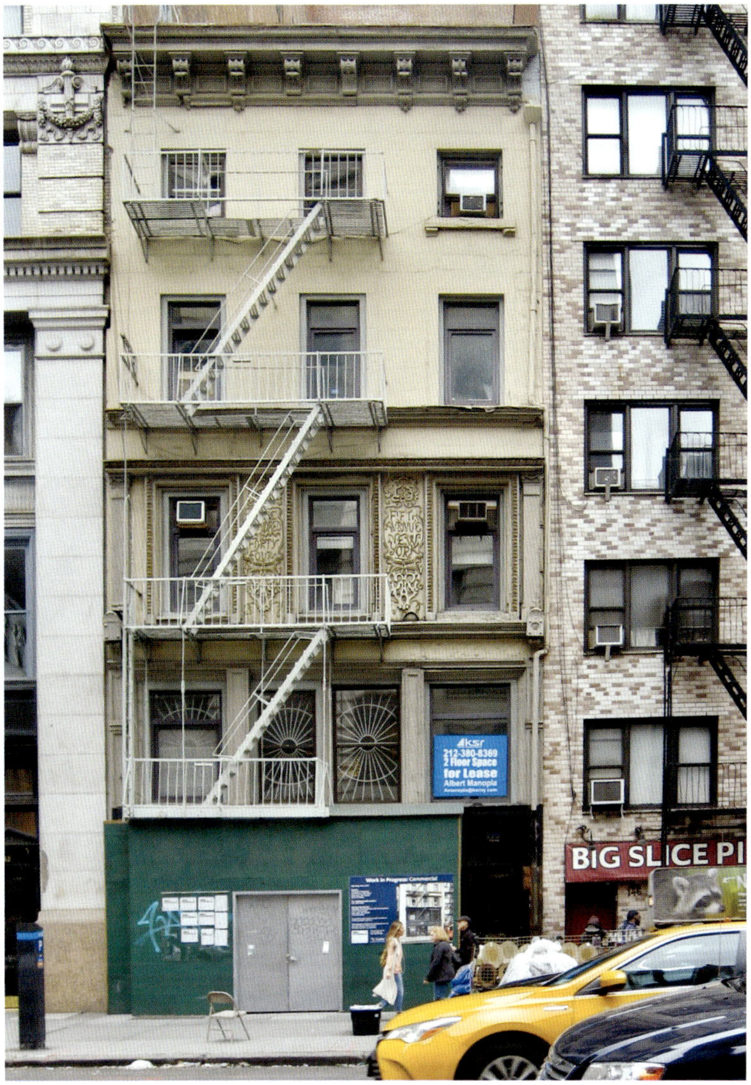

82 Cottier & Co.'s former showroom and gallery at 144 Fifth Avenue, New York. Photograph 2020

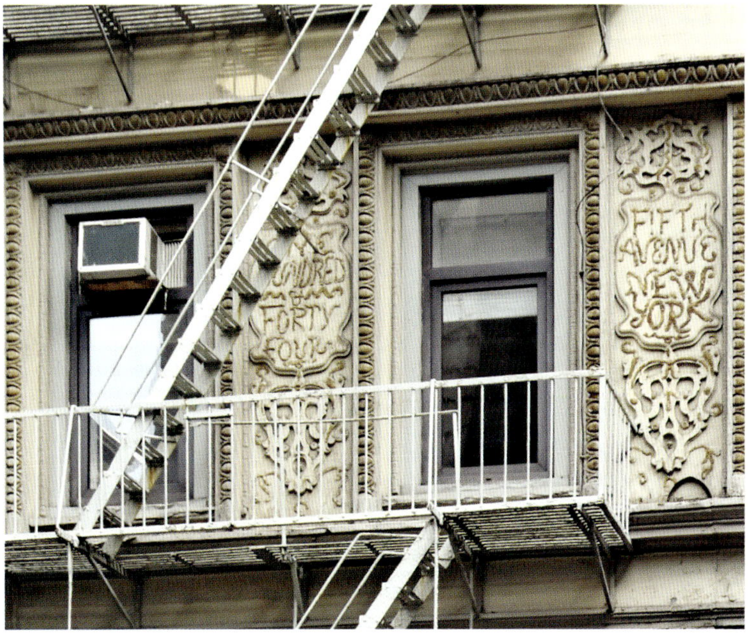

83 Cast-iron plaques at 144 Fifth Avenue, New York

'Cottier's business is increasing so that they must have the room I occupy sooner or later.'[12]

On their initial trip to New York, Cottier and Inglis must have brought a complete inventory in order to waste no time in setting up shop. Time and money were needed to establish an atelier and Cottier and Inglis did not want to wait. Stained glass and ceramics continued to be made in, and sent from, London for decades. They were relatively inexpensive to ship to the United States and, by concentrating the glass and ceramic production in London, Cottier & Co., presumably, benefited from an economy of scale. Just as important, this set-up benefited from a highly skilled workforce in London. In contrast, bulky furniture was more complicated and expensive to transport and, due to the differences in climate, pieces produced in Britain apparently had to be overhauled soon after their arrival in the United States.[13]

As early as 1874 Cottier & Co. seems to have rented or bought manufacturing premises on West 31st Street,[14] which probably focused on the production and decoration of furniture. After moving the workshop around to several locations,[15] the firm eventually opened a large workshop on 223 West 28th Street where, by 1888, according to a notice in *Illustrated New York: The Metropolis of Today*, it employed no fewer than 110 'skilled hands and talented workmen'.[16] These must have included workers with a variety of skills, from machine operators, carpenters and woodcarvers to painters and upholsterers.

In 1886 Lyon described the 28th Street workshop as 'very spacious' with 'room to do a lot of work'. He commented on the 'very fine machinery, the power is got from an engine in an adjoining building' (see Appendix, p. 208). Lyon's mention of machinery is notable. Like its rivals in New York, Cottier & Co. used a hybrid manual and machine technology. Clive Edwards, in his excellent study of the technology and design of Victorian furniture, wrote that most if not all small and mid-sized New York furniture workshops 'employed new techniques and steam-powered machinery (lathes, routers, etc.) in conjunction with traditional craft skills to maintain their position at the top end of the market'.[17]

COTTIER & CO. FURNITURE

Discussion of Cottier & Co. furniture manufactured in America is hampered by the fact that few original pieces unquestionably made in the firm's New York workshop have come to light, even though its production must have been substantial. Much of the uncertainty is related to the complete oblivion into which Cottier & Co. fell after its closure in 1915.[18] Not only does it explain a lack of interest on the part of museum curators and collectors in the firm's products but also their frequent misattribution to other firms. Except for grand pianos, Cottier & Co.'s furniture was rarely signed and as a result its connoisseurship is still in its infancy. The following discussion will rely heavily on prints and photographs of Cottier furniture dating from the time when the firm was still in existence. The first three sections deal with Cottier furniture in general, from around 1875 to 1910; the fourth with painted furniture, which was something of a Cottier & Co. speciality.

Cottier & Co. Furniture from the 1870s

As early as 1878, five years after the firm's establishment, the well-known American domestic architect Henry Hudson Holly mentioned that, when it came to interior decoration and home furnishings, Cottier & Co. was 'among the foremost houses in New York', along with L. Marcotte & Co., Herter Brothers, Pottier & Stymus and Cox & Sons.[19] It is notable that the founders of all these firms had roots in Europe: Marcotte & Co. and Pottier & Stymus in France, Herter Brothers in Germany and Cottier & Co. and Cox & Sons in Britain. According to Holly, this was because there were few skilled artisans in America who could do the kind of woodworking and upholstery work that fine furniture required.[20] It must therefore be assumed that many of the skilled workmen who worked for these companies were brought from Europe to New York.[21]

Cottier's rapid rise to fame in New York owed much to his promotion by the well-known art critic Clarence Cook (1828–1900). Cook was a Ruskinian and the co-founder of the Society for the Advancement of Truth in Art, a group of artists and writers akin to the Pre-Raphaelites in Britain.[22] He was interested in interior design and, probably inspired by the popular success of the British writer Charles Eastlake's *Hints on Household Taste*, wrote a series of articles in *Scribner's Monthly* called 'Beds and Tables, Stools and Candlesticks', beginning in June 1875.[23] Anticipating Oscar Wilde's famous American lecture tour of 1882, Cook's articles were a catalyst for the 1880s vogue of Aestheticism in America. Departing from Eastlake's advocacy for a modern English Gothic style, Cook advocated a more eclectic style of decorating that was adopted by Harriet Prescott Spofford in the United States (*Art Decoration Applied to Furniture*, 1878) and Mrs Haweis in Britain (*The Art of Decoration*, 1881).

Cooks's articles in *Scribner's Monthly*, especially the early ones, frequently mention Cottier & Co. and reproduce a number of the firm's designs. When Cook gathered the articles for publication in book form in 1878, he wrote in the prefatory note that, since he had begun writing, he had been 'constantly indebted for advice and practical help' to Cottier, 'friend and artist', as well as to Inglis.[24] What is more, the first edition of the book, called *The House Beautiful: Essays on Beds and Tables, Stools and Candlesticks*, had a binding designed by Cottier (see fig. 79) and illustrations that were drawn by, among others, James Inglis and Francis Lathrop (1849–1909), a close associate of Cottier.[25]

All our information about the furniture Cottier & Co. sold and produced in New York in the 1870s comes from Cook's publication. Not a single New York-made piece from this decade is known to be extant today.[26] Cook clearly admired the firm's products, which combined simplicity and charm, as well as 'usefulness and beauty'.[27] From the descriptions and illustrations in his book, we learn that, like the furniture Cottier made and sold in London in the 1870s, the New York inventory was initially much influenced by the work of E. W. Godwin. 'Chair and Table from Cottier's' (fig. 84), reproduced in Cook's book, is representative of the furniture that was to the critic's liking. The engraving shows a hexagonal table resembling some of Godwin's Anglo-Japanese tables,[28] together with an upholstered chair which, according to Cook, repeats 'a pattern made some time

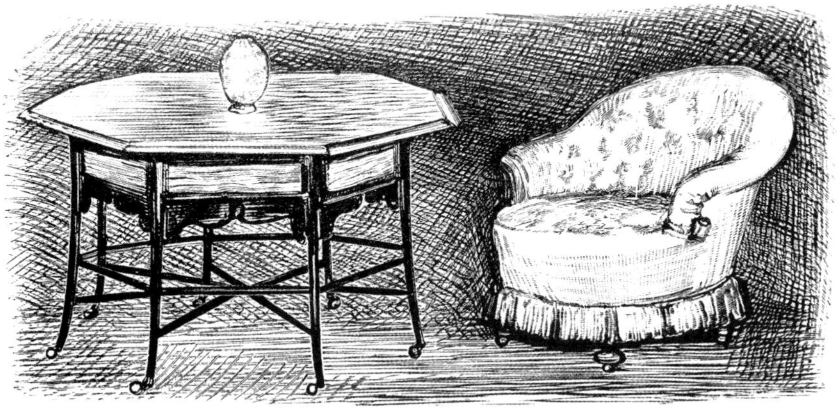

84 'Chair and Table from Cottier's', wood engraving after a drawing by Francis Lathrop in Clarence Cook, *The House Beautiful* (New York, 1878), p. 72

85 'The Children's Quarter of an Hour', wood engraving after a drawing by Francis Lathrop in Clarence Cook, *The House Beautiful* (New York, 1878), p. 223

ago by Cottier'.[29] Cook praises the chair's small size (perfect for New York apartments) but ample comfort; as well as the 'elegance of its lines' and the prettiness of its upholstery – golden-yellow damask and yellow silk fringe with a touch of red (though Cook argues that the chair could look as pretty when covered with a good chintz). Both pieces are marked by a certain daintiness that suited Cook's taste for furniture that would not clutter up living spaces but would leave open space for their inhabitants to move about. Cook also admires Cottier & Co.'s ebonised sideboard (fig. 85), 'from their own designs', which is 'one of the best modern sideboards' that he has seen and one that 'deserves to be recommended as a model'.[30] According to his description, it is 'made of hard-wood, stained black and then polished. The drawers and the doors have key-plates and handles of brass, of that fine gold-color which is now given to it.' Cook applauds the absence of carvings and moulding, observing that the beauty of the piece will come from its use: 'when fruit and flowers, and glass and silver, are busy "making reflections" on the gleaming surface'. While praising the simple sideboard, Cook is ambivalent about a 'Hanging Shelf and Cabinet' (illustration no. 37), which he admires for its design but criticises for the use of mirrors and bevelled glass, which 'add splendor, but splendor not of a sort to please a true taste' and which make the piece unnecessarily expensive.[31]

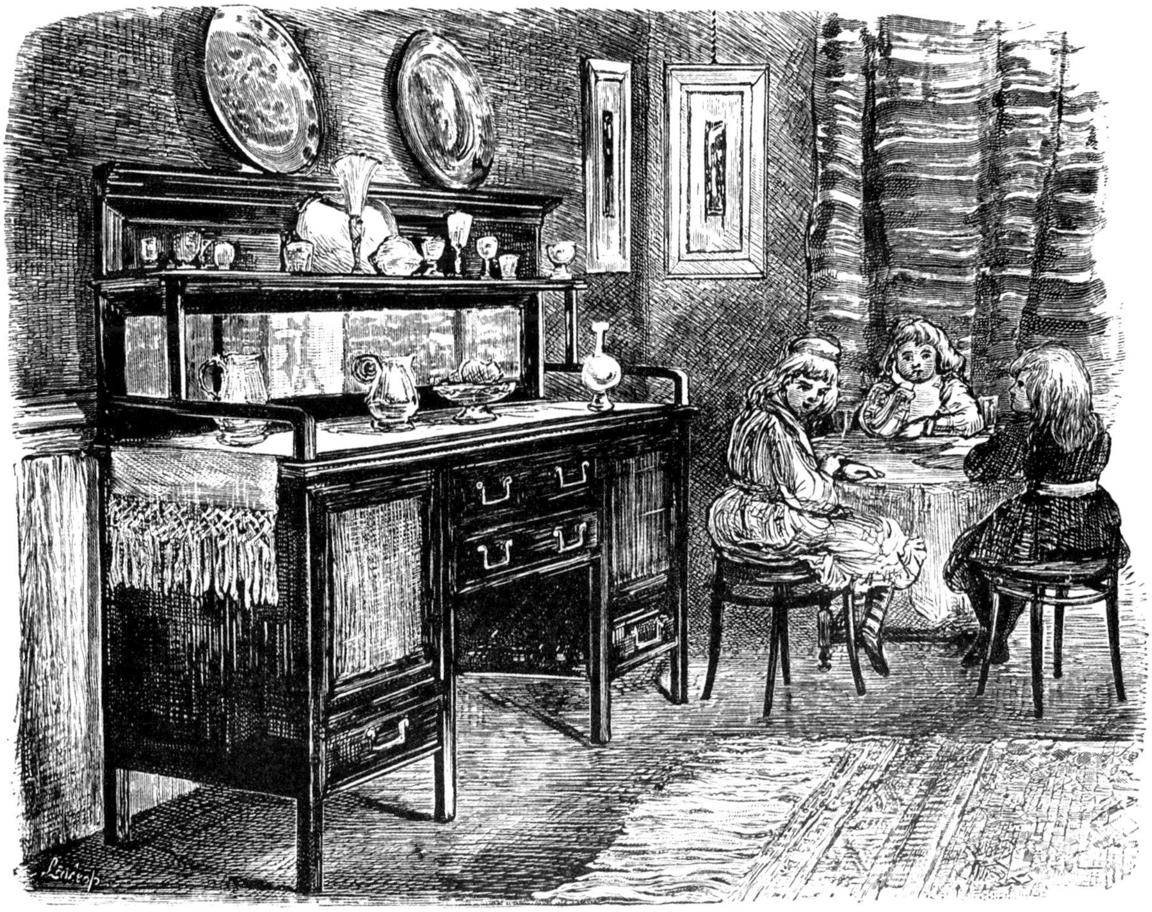

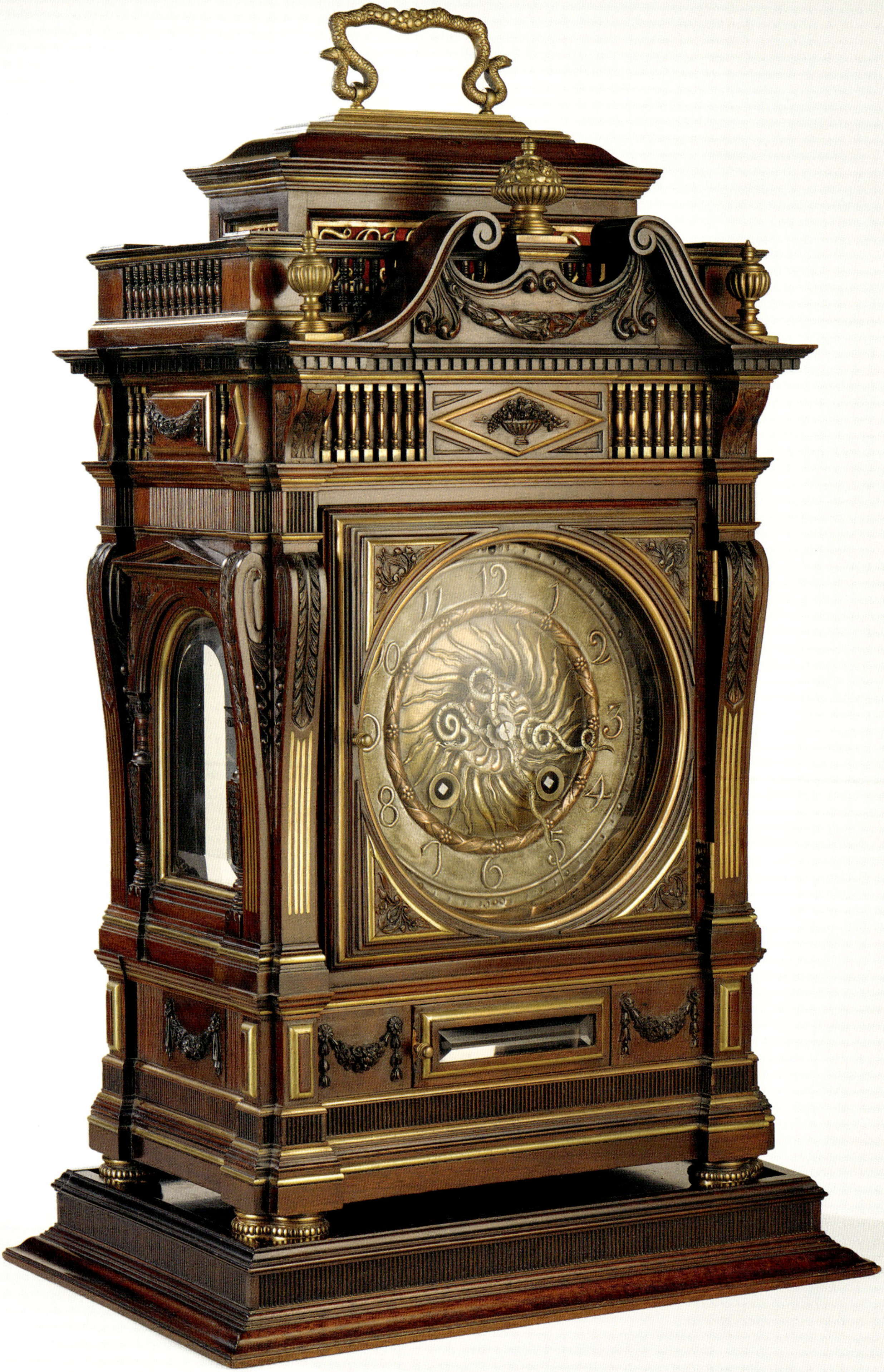

86 Mantel clock by Cottier & Co. and Tiffany & Co., New York, for Ichabod Williams, 1883. Comino mahogany, brass, other metals, glass, 61 × 39.1 × 27.3 cm. Brooklyn Museum, New York, Marie Bernice Bitzer Fund

Cottier & Co., Ichabod Williams and Furniture Production in the 1880s

While no Cottier & Co. piece of furniture from the 1870s attributed with certainty to the New York workshop has been preserved, there are at least two extant pieces from the early 1880s, both mantel clock cases. The earliest one, in a private American collection, is a mahogany and ebonised pearwood case in the William and Mary style, made in the Cottier workshop and stamped with the maker's name, J. Linton. It is dated 1881 in one of the spandrels of the clock face. The dial and the movement of the clock were furnished by Tiffany & Co.[32] Joseph Lindauer (1835–1897), the supervisor of the clock department, designed the dial, which presents a silvered image of the sky, with golden stars and a comet, as well as the capriciously shaped hands, which incorporate a golden sun and moon respectively.

A similar clock case (1883; fig. 86) was designed in Georgian Revival style, complete with broken pediment, volutes and garlands. It boasts gilded feet and finials as well as other gold accents and has a brass handle at the top. Like the 1881 clock, it is a far cry from the Godwinesque pieces reproduced in Cook's *House Beautiful.* No more Japanese influence, no more daintiness – the emphasis here is on the use of expensive materials and meticulous craftwork, lending an air of decorum and solidity. The clock's face, like that of the earlier clock, is made of different metals and has the same capriciously shaped hands, though here they are set against an image of the sun. An inscription at the bottom of the face informs the viewer: 'I. T. WILLIAMS HAD ME MADE 1883 / COTTIER & TIFFANY MADE ME / NEW YORK' (see fig. 195).

The owner of the clock, Ichabod T. Williams (1824–1899) was Cottier & Co.'s most important patron in New York during the 1880s. Williams and Cottier were connected both professionally and personally. Born in the city in 1824, Williams first joined his father's lumber business, then started his own in 1870, specialising in domestic and imported hardwoods.[33] The firm became famous for its rare comino mahogany, which came from trees growing in Colombia.[34] Cottier probably first met Williams as a customer, buying wood and veneers from the latter's mill in Carteret, New Jersey, for the Cottier & Co. cabinetmaking workshop.[35] Williams's headquarters were located at 220 11th Avenue in Manhattan and occupied an entire block between 25th and 26th Streets. This was in walking distance from Cottier's workshop, located on 28th Street near 7th Avenue. Over time, the two men and their families appear to have become close, to the point where Cottier's daughter Margaret married Williams's son Lloyd in December 1890.

From the catalogue of the auction held after Williams's death,[36] we know that his house at 18 West 36th Street bore Cottier & Co.'s aesthetic stamp.[37] Not only had the firm designed and produced much of his furniture but Williams had also bought the lion's share of his extensive painting collection from Cottier and Inglis, and possibly a good part of his well-known collection of Chinese and Japanese porcelain as well.[38] Cottier & Co. may even have designed the interior of his home. Other than the clock (see fig. 86), none of the pieces Cottier & Co. designed and fabricated for Williams is known to have been preserved. However, the catalogue descriptions give us some idea of what they may have looked like: number 514 describes an 'Oak dining room set. Especially designed by Messrs. Cottier & Co. Comprises sideboard, side table and square dining table with rounded corners.' The next, 515, lists a 'Bedroom suite. Comino wood. With painted decorations of fan panels, bowknots and festoons of flowers. Comprises double bedstead ... bureau, large dressing bureau, wardrobe with mirror door and night stand.' We get an impression of furniture that was sturdy and comfortable, beautifully made of expensive woods and in certain instances enhanced with painted decorations, which was something of a hallmark of Cottier & Co.'s furniture production (painted furniture will be discussed shortly).

The furniture Cottier & Co. designed and made for Ichabod Williams must have dated largely from the early 1880s, if we go by the date of his clock (1883). It must have been characteristic of Cottier & Co.'s production of this decade, marked by historicising designs, expensive materials and expert execution. Among the few surviving pieces of this period, other than the two clocks, is a grand piano (fig. 87) that was sold by Skinner Auctions in the USA in 2016.[39]

87 Model B grand piano manufactured by Steinway & Sons and decorated by Cottier & Co., New York, *c*.1890. Painted and ebonised wood, ivory and ebony. Private collection

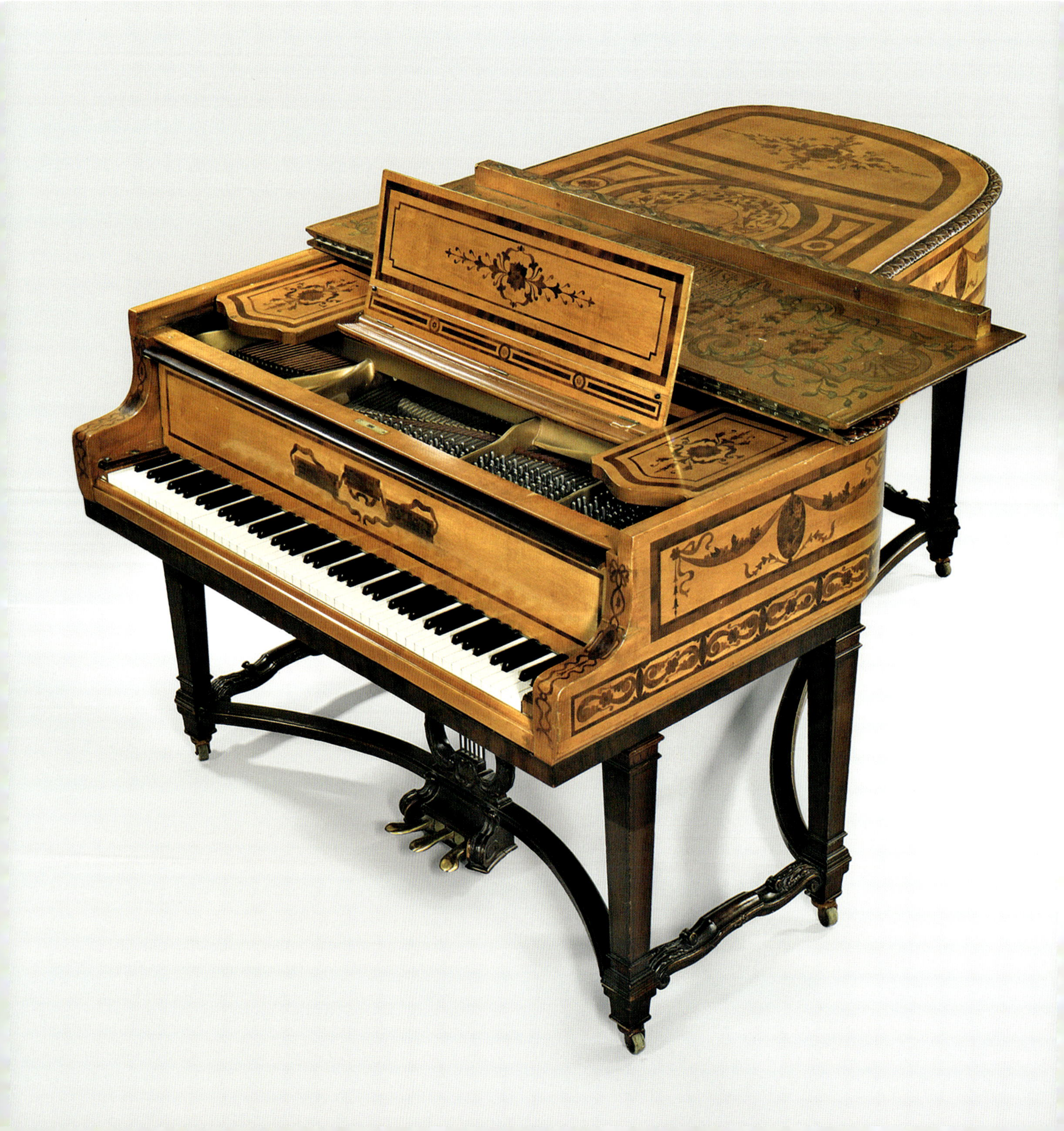

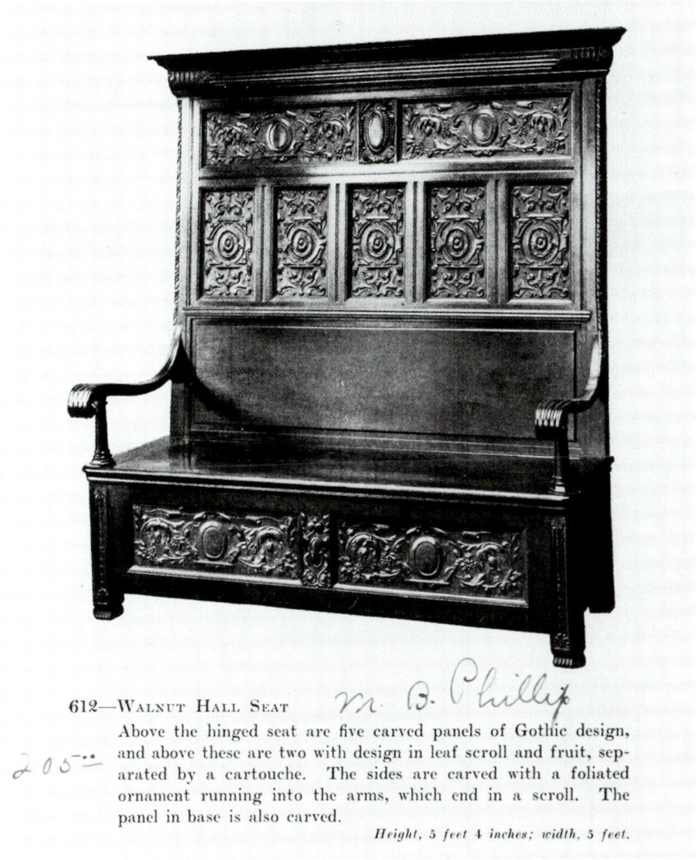
612—Walnut Hall Seat

Above the hinged seat are five carved panels of Gothic design, and above these are two with design in leaf scroll and fruit, separated by a cartouche. The sides are carved with a foliated ornament running into the arms, which end in a scroll. The panel in base is also carved.

Height, 5 feet 4 inches; width, 5 feet.

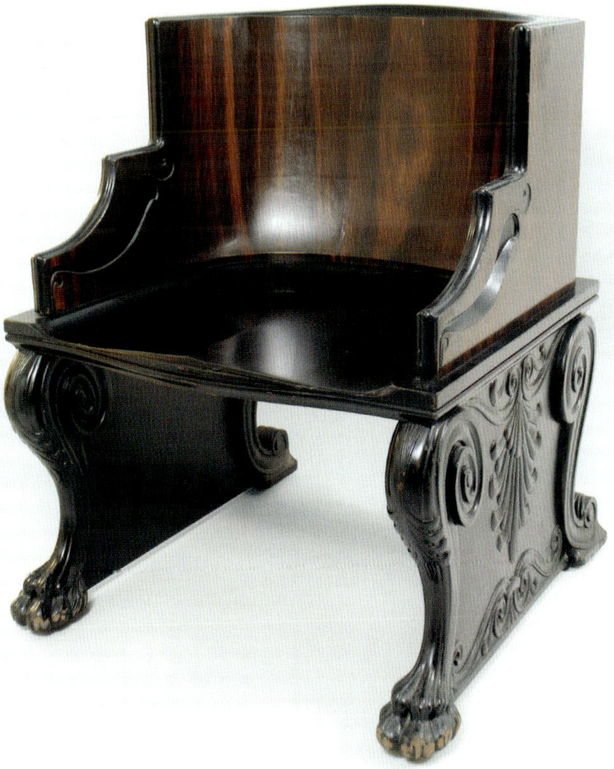

88 Hall seat by Cottier & Co., New York, *c.*1900–10. Carved walnut, reproduced in *The Artistic Property of the Well-Known House of Cottier and Company, New York*, auction catalogue, American Art Galleries, New York, 19–26 November 1913, no. 612

89 'Roman' armchair by Cottier & Co., New York, for Henry Clay Frick, *c.*1905. Probably Macassar ebony and ebonised wood, 84.7 × 66.7 × 62.2 cm. The Frick Pittsburgh

Although actually dating from 1890 (it was delivered by Steinway to Cottier & Co.'s workshop in late November 1890),[40] it still seems representative of the production of the 1880s, as far as we understand it. The instrument is covered with a marquetry veneer forming a variety of decorative motifs – swags, garlands, ribbons, scrolls, vines, masks and others. Inside the front section of the lid is a polychrome inlay of scrolls, festoons and vines centred on a rectangular shield with an inscribed verse, 'CALL IN SWEET MVSIC/ I HAVE HEARD SOFT AIRS/ CAN CHARM OVR SENSES/ AND EXPEL OVR CARES'. The underside of the main lid shows a tonalist painted landscape with two female figures framed by garlands. The piano is signed inside the fallboard 'NEW YORK/ COTTIER & CO. DESIGNERS/ STEINWAY & SONS MAKERS'.[41]

Cottier & Co. Furniture 1890–1910

The 1913 auction catalogue *The Artistic Property of the Well-Known House of Cottier and Company, New York* includes photogravures of numerous late pieces, made after Cottier's death, during the 1890s and the first decade of the twentieth century. All are luxurious, made of fine woods and sumptuously decorated with carvings, marquetry and/or paintings in various historical styles. A walnut hall seat (fig. 88), described and reproduced in the catalogue, is typical of the eclectic style seen in many of Cottier & Co.'s late pieces: the form of the seat with its high back recalls Gothic settles; the carving is inspired by Renaissance designs. While the seat shows the skill of the wood-carvers in the Cottier workshop (who may have used both machines and hand tools to produce it), a settee of comino wood (no. 596) represents the skills of the upholsterers. The design of its frame is simple and the emphasis is on the covering: 'red and gold "St. George" damask ... trimmed with gimp'. Cottier & Co. prided themselves on the upholstery fabrics they carried and the 1913 sale catalogue features numerous lengths of silk lampas, damask, brocade, brocatelle, velvet, plush, as well as upholstery trimmings. It also lists many

90 'A Cupboard of Today' (with doors painted by Francis Lathrop), wood engraving after a drawing by Francis Lathrop in Clarence Cook, *The House Beautiful* (New York, 1878), p. 105

91 Albert Pinkham Ryder, three panels for a screen, *c.*1876. From left to right, *Children playing with a Rabbit, Woman with Deer, Children frightened by a Rabbit.* Oil on gilded leather mounted on canvas, each panel 97.7 × 51.4 cm. Smithsonian American Art Museum, Washington, D.C., Gift of John Gellatly

antique textiles, such as tapestries, altar frontals and table covers, coming from all over the world.[42]

Among the few late pieces of Cottier & Co. furniture that have been preserved are several 'Roman' and 'Greek' chairs sold by Cottier & Co. to Henry Clay Frick (1849–1919) around 1905, some for the gallery in his Fifth Avenue mansion in New York, others for his further homes. Two 'Roman' and two 'Greek' chairs are currently in the collection of the Frick Pittsburgh (fig. 89), housed in his former home Clayton,[43] and five others are known.[44] The Frick item reproduced here is a Roman armchair. An imposing piece of furniture, it has solid sides ending in paw feet and is carved with acanthus scrolls and inverted palmettes. It was almost certainly inspired by an etching in Charles Heathcote Tatham's *Etchings, Representing the Best Examples of Ancient Ornamental Architecture; drawn from the originals in Rome, and other parts of Italy, during the years 1794, 1795, & 1796*, a book apparently still used by furniture designers in the early twentieth century.[45]

The 1913 auction catalogue shows that in addition to furniture that was 'handmade from special designs', Cottier & Co. also sold antique and exotic furniture, which Cottier and Inglis sourced from all over the world. Some of these pieces, like an antique English chinoiserie cabinet (no. 715) are clearly distinct from the pieces manufactured by Cottier and Co.; others, however, like a Chippendale chair (no. 675) are more difficult to distinguish from the products of Cottier's workshops. This raises the question of the different values (aesthetic, emotional and monetary) that Cottier and his clients may have attached to the antique and the newly made furniture sold in his shop. Cook in *The House Beautiful* tells the story of an artist who had his house entirely furnished with antique furniture collected from old farmhouses in the region around his country house. This antique furniture had been much cheaper than anything one could buy at Cottier & Co. or Pottier & Stymus but it had taken many hours and much effort to acquire it. While Cook admires the artist for his diligence in collecting the furniture, he does not express a clear preference for the antique over the modern-made pieces.[46]

Painted Furniture

Cottier & Co. distinguished itself from other furniture makers in New York through its painted furniture, which was frequently produced by 'fine' rather than 'decorative' artists. With an *ante-quem* date of 1875 (the year in which it was published in Cook's series of articles in *Scribner's Monthly*), a corner cabinet reproduced in *The House Beautiful* (fig. 90) is the earliest identified piece of painted furniture sold in America by Cottier.[47] Unfortunately it is known only in reproduction.[48] While still relatively light, and featuring an Anglo-Japanese top rail, stylistically this piece seems to move in a more eclectic and ornate direction. The two top doors, featuring standing female figures painted by the decorative painter Francis Lathrop (1849–1909), are the focal point of the cupboard. Cook goes so far as

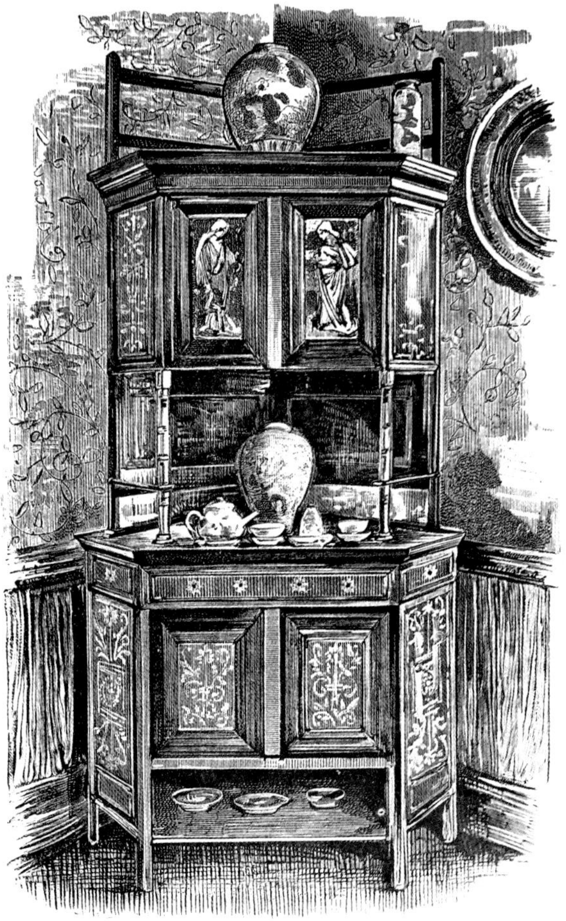

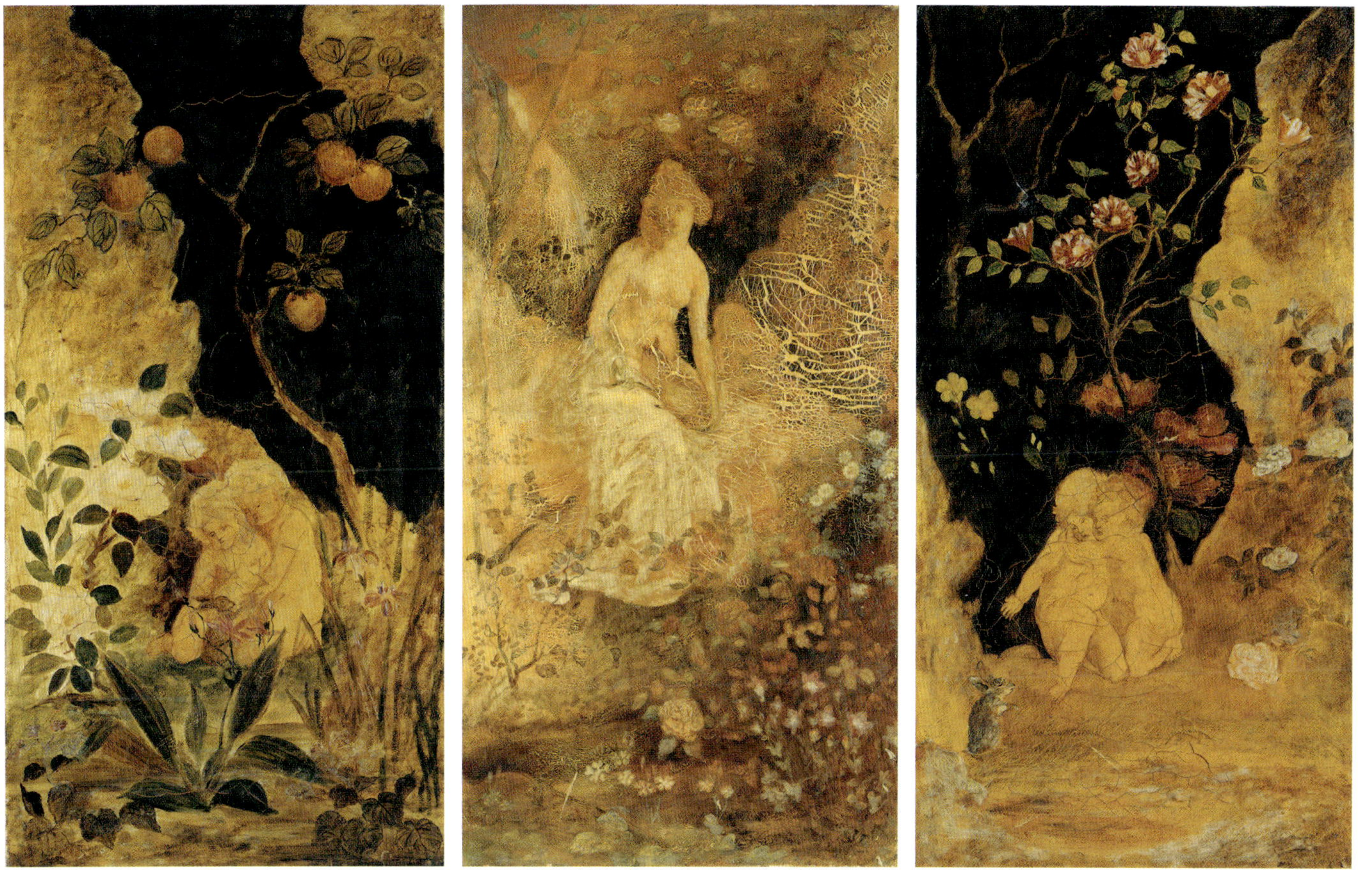

to argue that the cupboard 'mainly ... serve[s] as a frame to the two painted panels' and comments that the rest of the ornamentation of this 'plain enough' cabinet 'painted in gold color, not in gold, on the black ground' is 'kept down as much as possible so as not to interfere with the painting.'[49] Cook's words probably reflected Cottier's attitude towards painted furniture, at least in the 1870s, when he saw it as a way to introduce artworks into aesthetic interiors.[50]

Some eleven years younger than Cottier, Lathrop was the son of an American diplomat. He studied with T. C. Farrer in New York and, briefly, at the Dresden Academy of Fine Arts. Between 1870 and 1873 he lived in England, studying with Ford Madox Brown, James McNeill Whistler and Edward Burne-Jones. Lathrop worked for a while as Burne-Jones's assistant and also assisted William Morris, mostly in the production of stained glass. He doubtlessly had met Cottier in London before he returned to New York in 1873, the same year in which Cottier & Co. New York was founded. In 1876 the two artists both worked in Trinity Church in Boston, assisting John La Farge (on which more shortly). Lathrop initially was at once an easel painter (some of his works were included in the 1875 exhibition of American artists in Cottier's shop; see Chapter Five, p. 139) and a decorative artist but as time went on he focused primarily on decoration.

Another artist who did decorative work for Cottier & Co. during the 1870s was the American Albert Pinkham Ryder (1847–1917).[51] Born in New Bedford, Massachusetts, Ryder was probably still a student at the National Academy of Design when Cottier first met him. Many of Ryder's paintings for Cottier & Co. furniture were done on leather, which was subsequently mounted on screens (the larger paintings) or cabinets and chairs (the smaller ones). Unfortunately, none of Ryder's decorative paintings for Cottier remain on the pieces of furniture for which they were made. Three narrow vertical paintings (fig. 91) must once have decorated a folding screen of the kind that was popular in the late nineteenth century. Painted on gilt leather, the panels were commissioned about 1876.[52] The centre panel depicts a seated female nude cradling the head of a deer, the two side panels nude infants with small rabbits. Elizabeth Broun, who has discussed these paintings in detail, connects them to the legend of Genevieve of Brabant, falsely accused of adultery by her husband, spared by her executioner and rescued by a roe deer in the forest to which she

92 Albert Pinkham Ryder, *The Smugglers' Cove*, *c.*1880. Oil on gilded leather, 25.7 × 70.5 cm. Metropolitan Museum of Art, New York, Rogers Art Fund, 1909

93 Three-panel screen by Cottier & Co., New York, with six watercolours by Frederick Vincent Hart, *c.*1902–13. Comino wood, watercolour on paper, Chinese embroidered silk, 152.4 × 91.4 × 25.4 cm. Reproduced in *The Artistic Property of the Well-Known House of Cottier and Company, New York*, auction catalogue, American Art Galleries, New York, 19–26 November 1913, no. 614. Whereabouts unknown

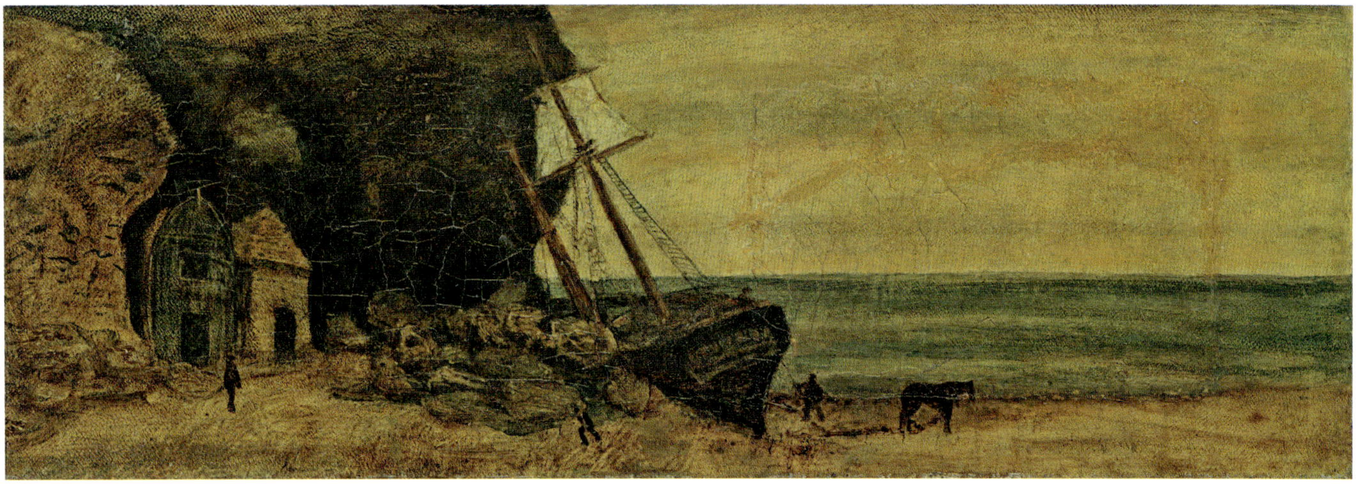

had fled.[53] Broun and others have pointed to the influence of Japanese art visible in the panels, not only in the use of black and gold but also in their asymmetric composition, the craggy rocks and the flowering branches.

In addition to these three sizeable vertical leather panels, Ryder painted a number of landscapes on long horizontal gilded leather panels, which probably once also decorated furniture.[54] Two of these, of approximately the same dimensions, *The Bridge* (25.4 × 67.9 cm) and *Smugglers' Cove* (25.7 × 70.5 cm; fig. 92), can both be traced back to the 1909 estate sale of James Inglis, suggesting that they may have been removed from a sideboard or other piece of Cottier & Co. furniture (both have a Cottier & Co. stamp on the stretcher).[55]

Lathrop, Ryder and perhaps other 'fine' artists appear to have painted occasional panels for Cottier & Co. on wood, leather or possibly other materials which were subsequently mounted on pieces of furniture. During the 1880s and 90s, however, Cottier & Co. also hired painters as employees to decorate furniture in their workshop. Lyon, in the diary entry of his visit to the Cottier workshop in 1886, mentions that he met a painter named Holland, who was decorating a grand piano, made of a golden-toned satinwood, with cupids, roses and ribbons.[56] Another painter employed by Cottier & Co., first in London

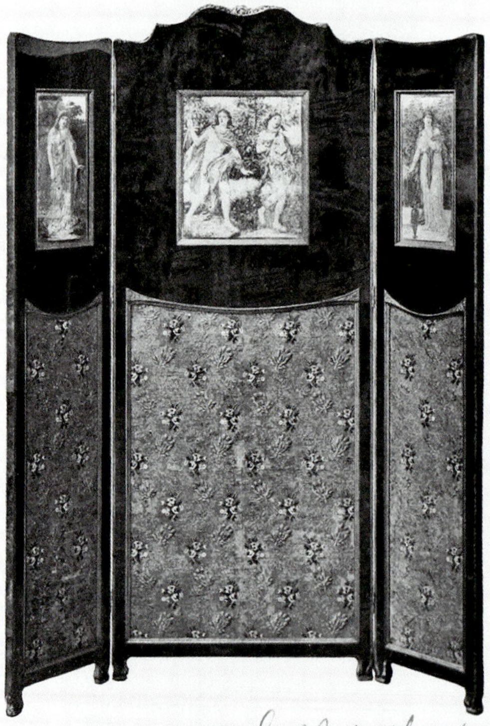
614—Unique Screen C. Winthrop

Comino wood, with top partly carved and gilded. The upper part has six water-color drawings by F. Vincent Hart representing the classical subjects of "Medea," "Cupid and Psyche" and "Cassandra," on one side, and "Proserpine," "Apollo and Daphne" and "Glauce" on the other. The lower part has panels of Chinese embroidery, with bouquet of roses in gold. 400"

Height, 5 feet; length, 3 feet 10 inches.

94 Model D grand piano manufactured by Steinway & Sons and decorated by Cottier & Co., New York, 1894–5. Painted, ebonised and gilded wood and marquetry. Piedmont Piano Company, Oakland, California

and then in New York, was Frederick Vincent Hart, who emigrated to New York in 1902 (see Chapter Two, p. 37). Hart's work for Cottier is known mostly through reproductions. The 1913 sale catalogue of Cottier & Co. lists several pieces he decorated. A three-part screen (fig. 93) of comino wood, with 'panels of Chinese embroidery with bouquets of roses in gold' at the bottom, features six watercolours by Hart at the top, representing Proserpina, Apollo and Daphne, and Glaucus on one side; Medea, Cupid and Psyche, and Cassandra, on the other.[57] More than any piece of furniture, the screen exemplified the global reach of Cottier and Co.'s business. Made of wood from South America and fabric woven and embroidered in China, it was produced in New York and decorated by a painter who had recently emigrated from Europe. The same auction catalogue lists several other pieces of furniture with Hart panels, including two jewellery cases, two stationery stands, a music cabinet and a Persian-style curio cabinet.[58]

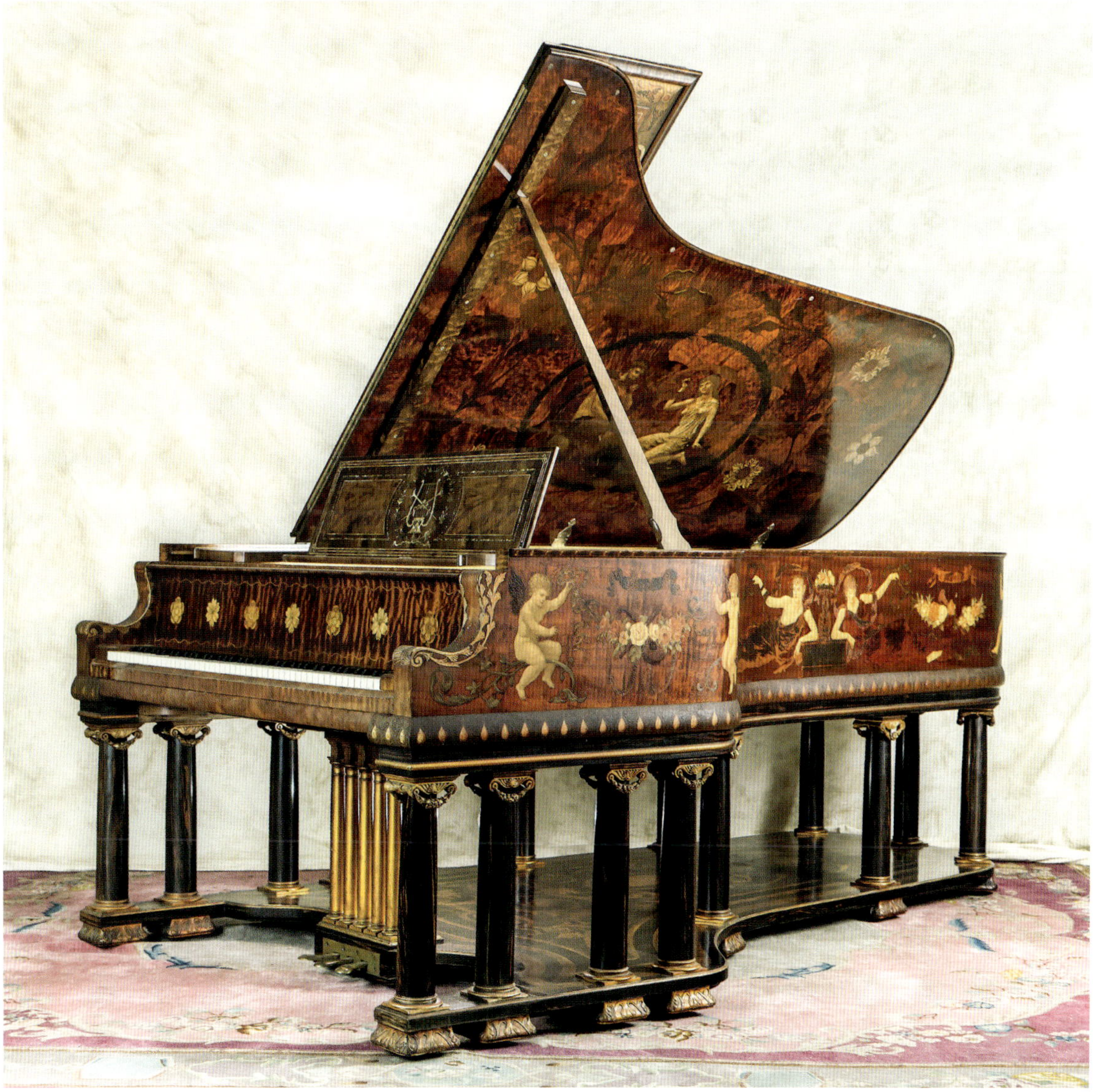

95 (a and b) Music cabinet by Cottier & Co., New York, with painted decoration by Frederick Vincent Hart, for Henry Clay Frick, *c.*1905. Painted walnut, mahogany and pine, 146.4 × 104.1 × 49.2 cm. The Frick Pittsburgh

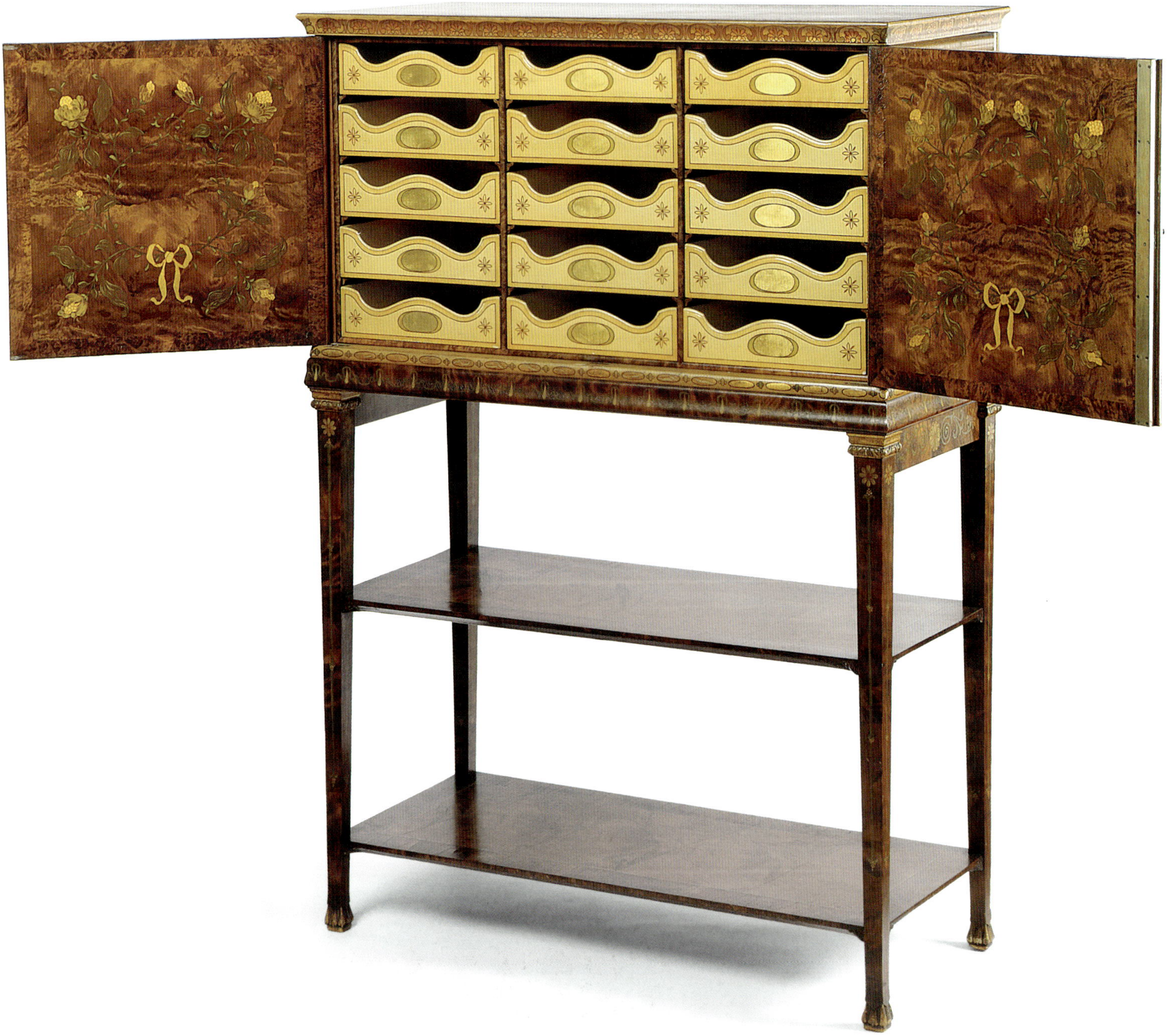

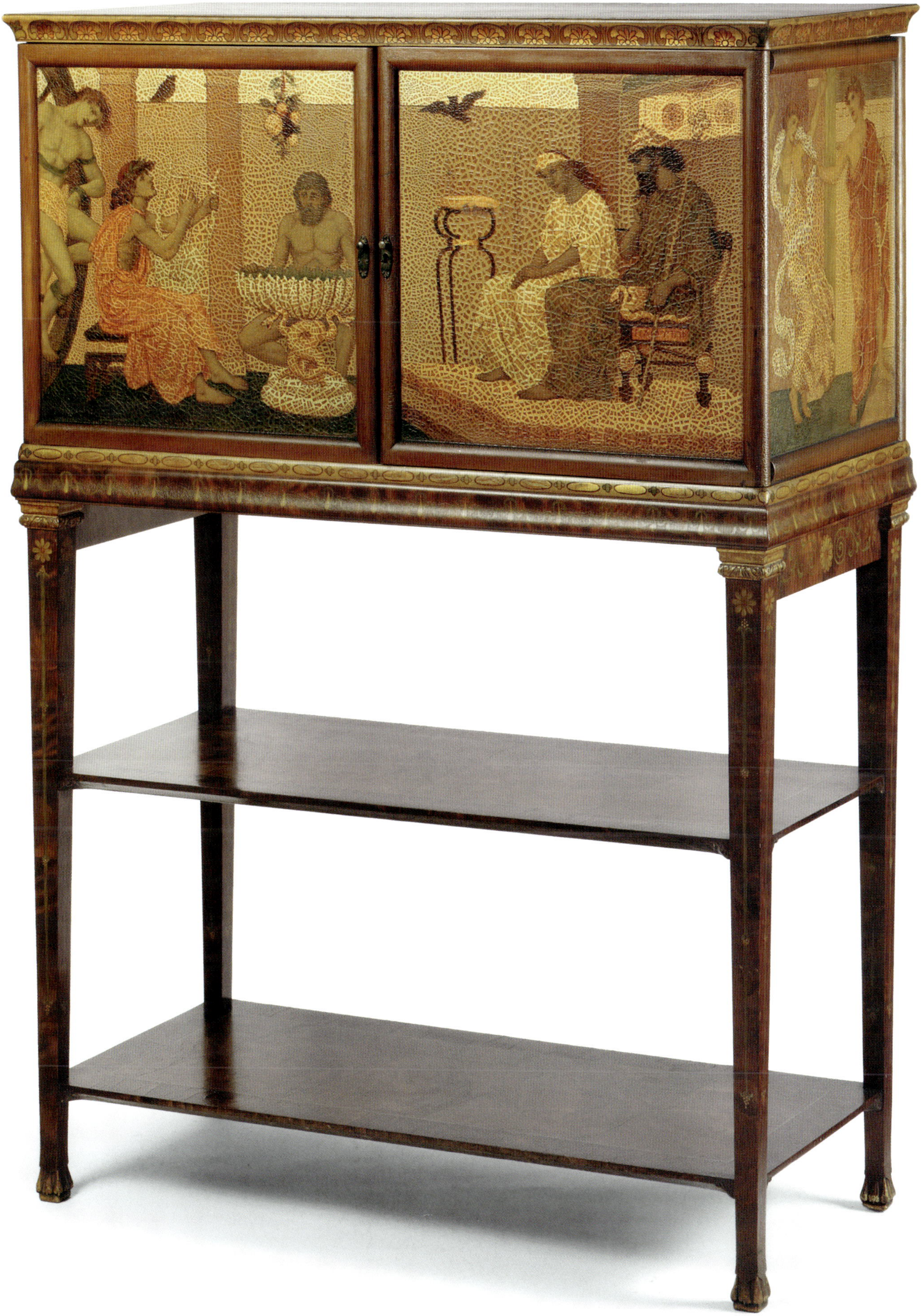

96 Drawing room of the J. C. Phillips House, Boston, Massachusetts (demolished), designed by Cottier & Co. and Richard Codman, reproduced in George William Sheldon, *Artistic Houses*, vol. 2, 1884

None of Hart's pieces reproduced in the 1913 catalogue has been located to date. However, an original example of his work, a music cabinet purchased by Henry Clay Frick from Cottier & Co. for his new residence on Fifth Avenue (figs 95a and b), is now in the Frick Pittsburgh. According to a Cottier & Co. invoice dated 30 December 1905, it originally stood in Mrs Frick's boudoir in New York.[59] Appropriately for a music cabinet, the doors represent Orpheus playing his lyre (left) and Hades and Persephone (right). Stylistically, these paintings are akin to those on the screen and cabinet reproduced in the 1913 catalogue, for all show slender elongated figures dressed in long flowing garments.

By far the most lavish piece of painted furniture from the Cottier & Co. workshop to have been preserved is a Steinway piano (fig. 94), which was decorated by the firm in 1894–5.[60] The identity of the painter or, perhaps, painters is not known. The piano was commissioned by Anna D. Riddle Scott, the widow of Thomas Alexander Scott, the former president of the Pennsylvania Railroad Company, probably for her house in Philadelphia.[61] Cottier & Co. made a marquetry floor for the nine-foot grand piano and replaced the original legs with fifteen dark-stained colonnettes with gilded bases and capitals with gilded decorative trim. The case itself is embellished with inlaid as well as painted decorations. Painted flowers decorate the stained backboard behind the keys and the music rack is inlaid with mother-of-pearl. The top of the lid is painted with two summarily draped putti holding ribbons and garlands of flowers (front) and putti and draped female figures dancing round a large wreath of roses (back). All along its periphery are narrow white-painted strips, possibly with a metallic underlay, inscribed with bars from Bach, Haydn and other composers. The underside of the front lid has a marquetry design of scrolls and vines centred on a shield with the names 'STEINWAY AND SONS, MAKERS' and 'COTTIER AND CO, DESIGNERS'. In the centre of the bottom of the lid is an oval cartouche framing goat-legged Pan and a nymph listening to his music. The sides of the piano are painted with putti holding garlands and with reclining draped female figures. All figures seem to be slightly raised as if they are painted on a layer of gesso.[62] The Scott piano, with its 'over-the-top' decoration, represents Cottier & Co.'s last hurrah. Although Cottier & Co. was still decorating pianos like this in 1906,[63] with the onset of twentieth-century modernism, such furniture soon became outdated and unmarketable.

INTERIOR DECORATION

Of all of Cottier's activities in North America, interior decoration is the one of which we know least. Not a single domestic interior he designed has been preserved intact and only a handful of images and descriptions exist. While painting and stencilling walls had been an important part of the young Cottier's artistic activity in Britain and remained a considerable share of the business of Lyon, Cottier & Co. in Australia, in the United States Cottier & Co. seems to have done none of it, at least not in homes. Instead, American domestic interiors seem to have been wallpapered or covered with expensive wall fabrics, on which occasional paintings were displayed.

That Cottier & Co. was well-known for its decoration in the United States is borne out by the fact that three interiors fitted out by the firm are discussed in the monumental two-volume publication *Artistic Houses*.[64] Published by Appleton and probably the brainchild of the author and photographer George William Sheldon in 1883–4, it presents an overview of the richest and most luxurious interiors on the American East Coast during the early Gilded Age. Sheldon's book contains one photograph each of the drawing and dining rooms in the Boston house of the businessman J. C. Phillips (1838–1888) on the corner of Berkeley and Marlborough Streets.[65] According to the captions, the interiors were designed by 'Messrs. Cottier' and Richard Codman (1842–1928). Codman, like Phillips, was a Harvard graduate, which may explain his involvement. Indeed, it is possible that Phillips had turned to him initially and that Codman asked Cottier & Co. for help, as he was more a designer than a professional interior decorator.[66] It is difficult to draw any conclusions about the nature of the collaboration but it is possible that Codman was responsible for the main

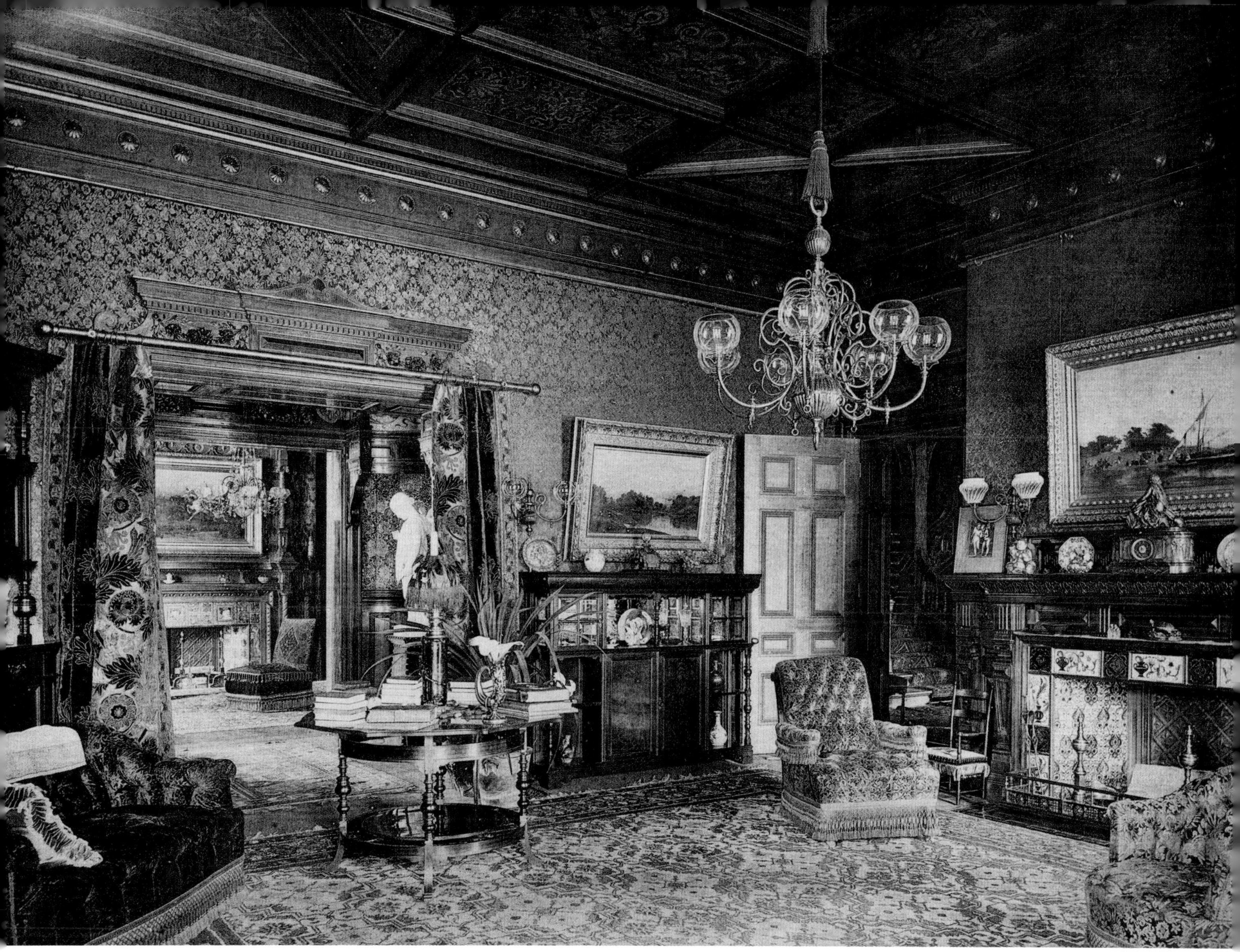

arrangement of the rooms while Cottier & Co. provided the furnishings and perhaps even the art on the walls.[67]

On the right side of Sheldon's photograph of the drawing room in the J. C. Phillips house (fig. 96)[68] is a tiled fireplace. While the tiles do not appear to have been decorated in Cottier's studio, the overmantel with its heavy, curved top moulding is characteristic of his style. At the edge of the photograph is an upholstered armchair closely resembling the one reproduced in Cook's *The House Beautiful* discussed earlier (see fig. 84). Much of the other furniture in the room – the round table; the display cabinet with its simple frame, heavy top moulding and glazed doors; and the sofa and corner cabinet to the left may have been manufactured by Cottier & Co. The floor is laid with a large oriental rug and the wall is covered with damask on which a Nile riverscape by Eugène Fromentin and a landscape by Daubigny, both possibly provided by Cottier, are judiciously hung. Through the beautiful appliquéd and embroidered portières, one looks into another room in which a painting by Adolphe Schreyer is hung above a fireplace with Cottier & Co. tiles.[69]

Sheldon also discussed (but did not reproduce) a parlour that Cottier & Co. designed for the house of New York banker Joseph S. Decker at 18 West 49th Street. According to *Artistic Houses*, it was 'a place of princely but peaceful splendor'. Rose-pink silk damask covered the walls from the wainscot to the frieze which, together with the ceiling, was painted in bronze over a composite surface. There is no mention of paintings on the wall but the room featured a 'very striking mahogany cabinet' with a 'profusion of hand-painted panels'. According to Sheldon, these panels, particularly the ones representing female figures, were so well painted that each was 'good enough to be admitted into an annual pictorial exhibition, and

97 Tiled fireplace with *Guinevere*, in the hallway of Glenview, Yonkers, the tiles decorated by Cottier & Co., London, 1876–7. Earthenware with underglaze decoration. The frieze at the top is lined with Minton fairy-tale tiles designed by J. Moyr Smith. Hudson River Museum, Yonkers, New York

important enough to attract attention in the midst of much more important surroundings.'[70] Sheldon's remark confirms that, in Aesthetic interiors, paintings were more readily accepted when they were part of pieces of furniture than when framed and hung on walls, as they were often seen as marring their elaborately conceived surfaces.[71] The cabinet, almost certainly, was a product of Cottier's workshop.

Traces of Cottier & Co.'s decorating activities may be found in a few extant interiors on the Eastern seaboard but it is not always clear whether the firm merely provided elements, like windows or tile ensembles, or whether its role was more involved. This is the case with the interior of Glenview in Yonkers, New York (now part of the Hudson River Museum), which was built by the Wall Street banker John Bond Trevor in 1876–7. The interiors of the house were largely designed by the Philadelphia cabinetmaker Daniel Pabst (1826–1910) who, for Glenview, chose the Modern Gothic style. This style, also called 'Eastlake', dominated the Philadelphia Centennial Exhibition in May–November 1876, which took place at the time when Glenview was built.[72] Among the original pieces left in the house is the fireplace in the great hall, which is lined with Cottier & Co. tiles (fig. 97).[73] It is not known whether the firm had any involvement in the decoration of the house but it does seem possible that Cottier or one of his designers cooperated with Pabst, since some of the classically inspired details of the house and its furniture were less influenced by Eastlake than by Cottier's early mentor, Alexander Thomson.[74] Cottier may also have been involved in some way in the decoration of Catharine Lorillard Wolfe's cottage Vinland, in Newport, Rhode Island, built by Peabody & Stearns in the early 1880s and decorated by Codman.[75]

While Phillips, Decker, Trevor, Wolfe and Ichabod Williams (whose house Cottier & Co. probably also decorated) were all important clients, probably none spent as much money at Cottier's as Frick. Between 1903 and 1913, Frick employed the firm for the decorating, refurbishing and maintenance of his houses in New York (Fifth Avenue), Pittsburgh ('Clayton') and Prides Crossing, Massachusetts ('Eagle Rock'), as well as the apartments he rented at Sherry's in New York and even his box at the Metropolitan Opera. Over ten years, Frick spent several hundred thousand dollars at Cottier's on furniture (new and antique), wall coverings, draperies and curtains, rugs, paintings, 'bric-à-brac' (Chinese vases, Italian maiolica, bronze statuettes and so on), re-upholstering chairs, cleaning decorated ceilings and other home-related goods and services. Cottier & Co.'s willingness to meet Frick's every and often extravagant demand appears to have been one of the firm's assets. A telegram from one of Frick's assistants to Cottier & Co. says it all: 'Mr. Frick wants rugs here [at Clayton in Pittsburgh] tomorrow morning.'[76] We assume Cottier & Co. obliged.

In addition to domestic interiors, Cottier & Co. also became involved in large projects for libraries and clubs. As was fashionable in the 1880s and 90s, when variety became more important than unity, these projects involved numerous designers.[77] One such project was the Union League Club in New York, its third home since its foundation in 1863. In 1881 the Club acquired a building on Fifth Avenue and West 39th Street (later demolished) and had the interior decorated by an army of designers, painters and sculptors including Louis Comfort Tiffany, Frank Hill Smith, Cottier & Co., John La Farge, Will Hicok Low, Saint-Gaudens and Olin Warner. Cottier & Co. designed and furnished the library, described in *Frank Leslie's Illustrated Newspaper* in 1881 as 'a fine, high-ceilinged room, with light-colored glass in the upper windows, a carved-wood chimney piece ... two other cozy fireplaces ... "high-art" decorative curtains, and a general air of comfort and substance.' The article also describes the room's colour scheme: 'The ceiling is dead-gilt, with brighter, flower-shaped ornaments distributed, and at either end olive-blue, with conventional gilt stars and deep stenciled borders of dead-gilt, light yellows, and light browns.'[78]

Finally, like other decorating companies, Cottier & Co. designed the interior of at least one yacht. An article in the July 1879 issue of *Forest and Stream* informs its readers that the interior of the schooner yacht *Frolic*, launched in that year, was designed by Cottier & Co.[79] Built in Islip, Long Island, by the boat

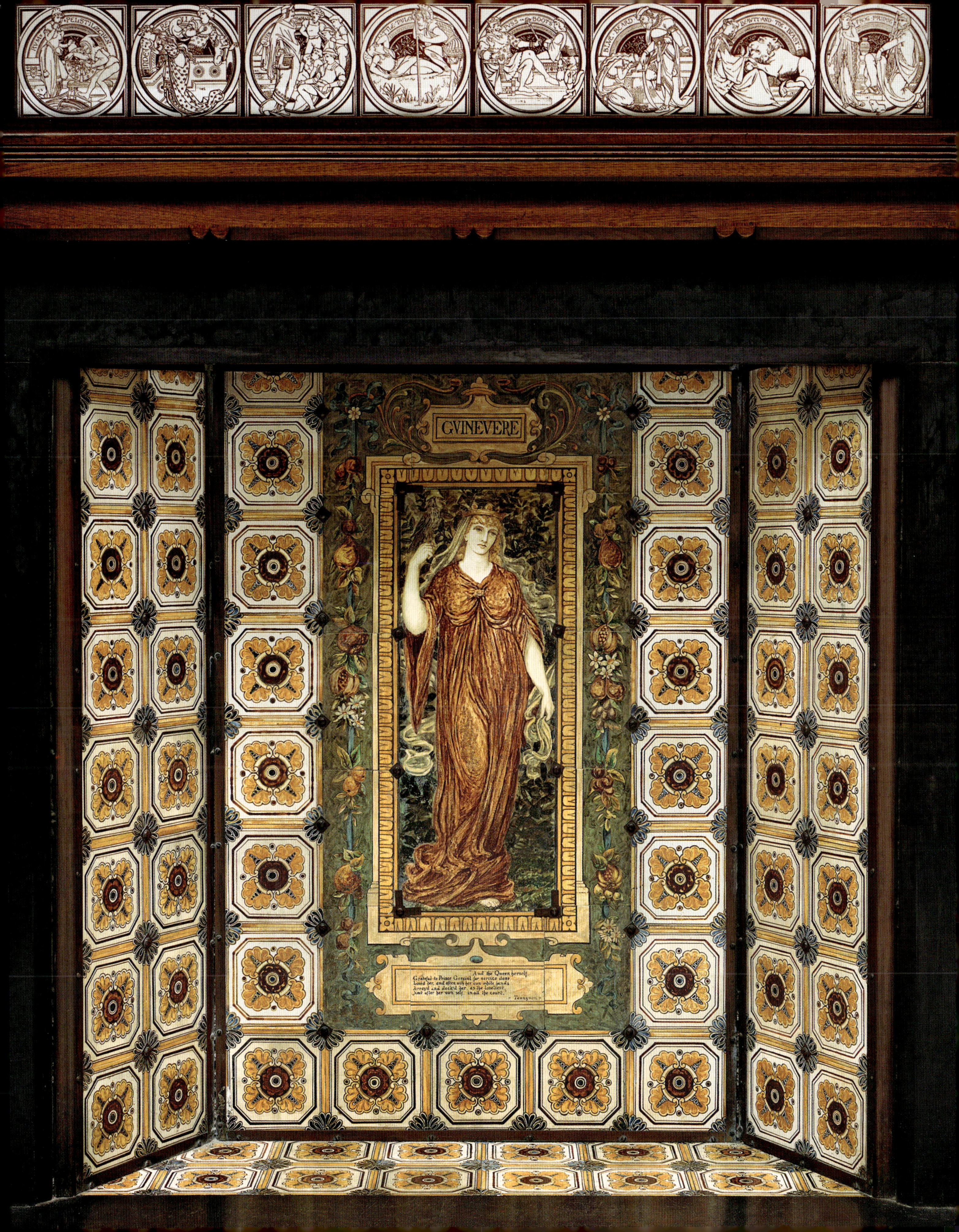
GUINEVERE
"And the Queen herself,
Grateful to Prince Geraint for service done
Loved her, and often with her own white hands
Arrayd and deck'd her, as the loveliest,
Next after her own self, in all the court."
Tennyson

98 *Arch Street Wharf circa 1800 and Seal of Philadelphia*, tile panel by Cottier & Co., London, *c.*1875. Painted in underglaze colours on earthenware tiles, 45.7 × 63.5 cm. Private collection

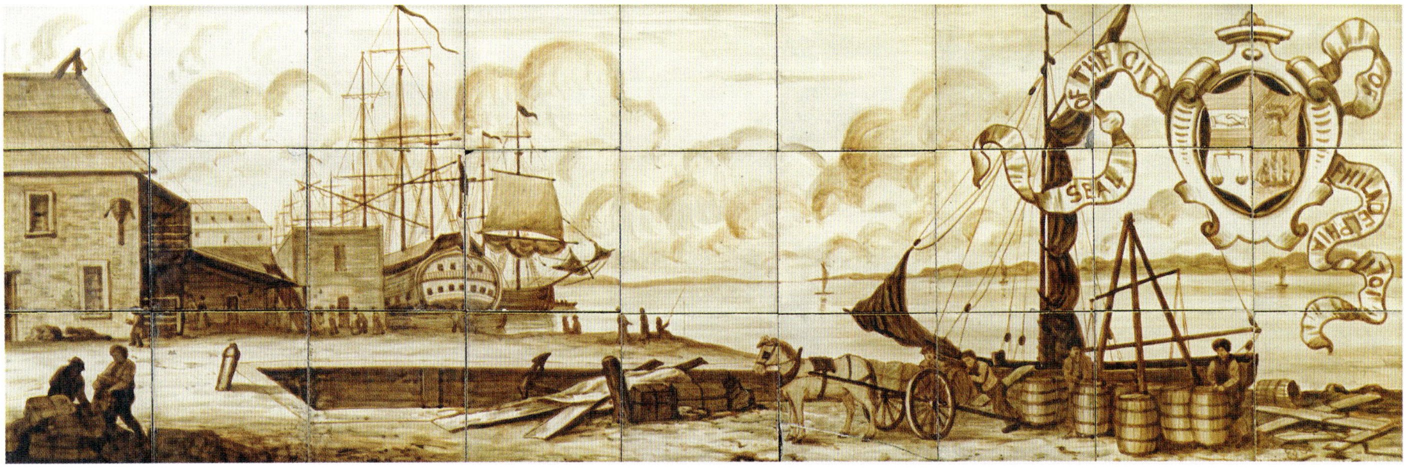

99 'Old Dutch ship, surrounded by eighteen panels illustrating ships, windmills, horsemen and sheaves of wheat', by Cottier & Co., London, *c.*1880–97. Leaded glass (19 panels), centre panel 73.7 × 51 cm, surrounding panels 12.7 × 12.7 cm each. Reproduced in *The Artistic Property of the Well-Known House of Cottier and Company, New York*, auction catalogue, American Art Galleries, New York, 19–26 November 1913, no. 948

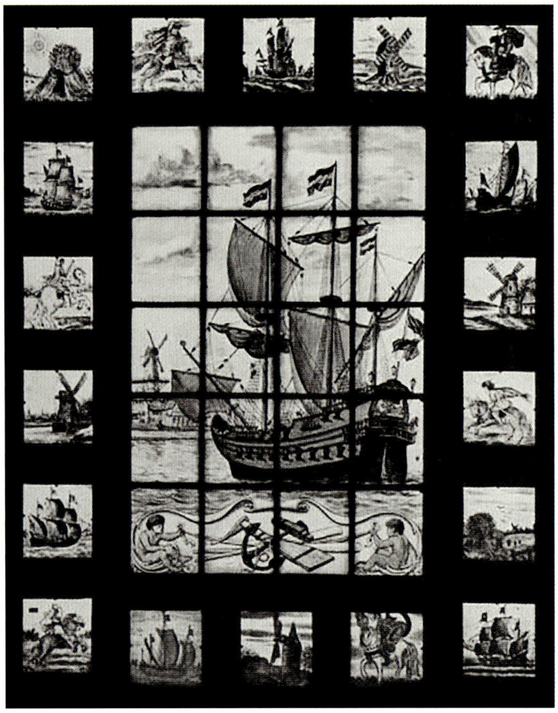

builder Alonzo Smith, the yacht was owned by Joseph Gardiner Cassatt (1849–1911),[80] the younger brother of Mary Cassatt and a member of the New York Yacht Club. Unfortunately, no visual information about this or any other yacht interior designed by Cottier & Co. has come to light.

DOMESTIC STAINED GLASS

The production and sale of stained glass for private homes was an important aspect of Cottier & Co.'s interior decoration business. Indeed, in the classified advertisements for the firm, 'high class interior decoration' and 'artists in stained glass' were often joined.[81] In 1879 the author of an article in *Harper's Magazine*, entitled 'Painted Glass in Household Decoration', argued that stained glass was an eminent form of home decorating: 'Certainly the translucence of glass enables the art collector, if he carefully and fittingly use it, to surpass all the other decorations of his room in special attractiveness.'[82] The article goes on to mention numerous examples of domestic stained glass, even in the homes of the not-so-rich: 'A Brooklyn residence, of ordinary dimension, possesses an extension dining room with four windows representing the Seasons, and in the library casements are four charming medallion portraits of Bryant, Longfellow, Dickens, and Shakespeare.'[83]

Cottier was clearly taking advantage of the popularity of domestic stained glass in America. He sent large quantities to New York, some the result of commissions, others to be exhibited in his shop for sale. The catalogue of the 1913 auction of Cottier & Co. lists no fewer than 242 lots of domestic stained glass, many containing numerous panels (from two to twenty). Much of the glass that was shipped to New York was similar to what was sold in London,

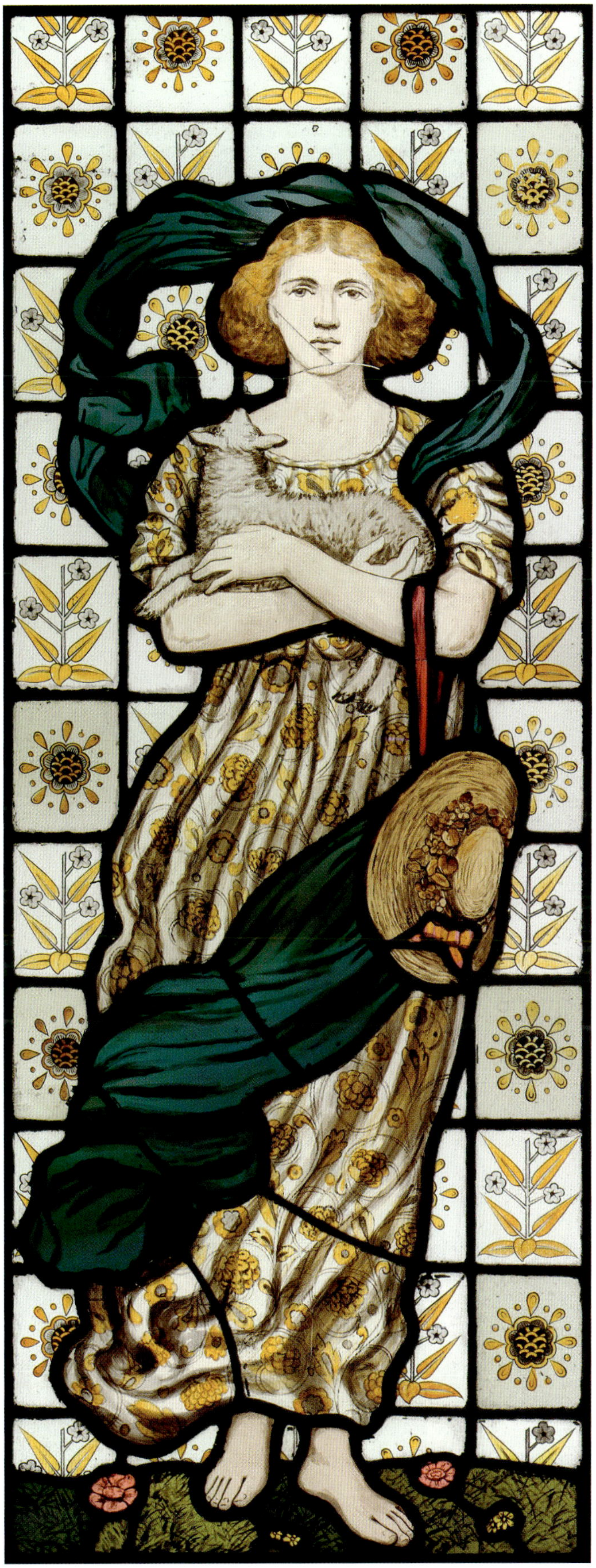

100 *Spring*, by Cottier & Co., London, *c*.1873–85. Stained glass, 133.7 × 76.2 cm. Metropolitan Museum of Art, New York, Gift of the Estate of Virginia Guard Brooks and the Guard family, 2007

although some appears to have made specifically for the American market. For instance, two windows in the catalogue were devoted to Philadelphia themes, including a composite window of stained and leaded glass panels showing a 'Landscape with stream, surrounded by fifteen panels illustrating old Philadelphia, horsemen, ships, windmills, and other subjects.'[84] Not a single Philadelphia-themed window is known today but a surviving tile panel representing the city's Arch Street Wharf is marked Cottier & Co. (fig. 98). The existence of a Cottier tile panel on a theme similar to a Cottier stained-glass window reminds us that the designs for both could be and were used interchangeably. This connection between windows and tilework is also clear when looking at the reproduction of a window in the 1913 catalogue (no. 948; fig. 99) described as 'Old Dutch ship, surrounded by eighteen panels illustrating ships, windmills, horsemen and sheaves of wheat'. Both the central panel and the eighteen surrounding panels are clearly influenced by Dutch or English Delftware tiles, the latter probably available for sale in Cottier's shop. The 1913 catalogue lists numerous other composite windows with Dutch sailing boats and windmills. All these were probably intended for residences in New York, where the city's beginnings as New Amsterdam were much celebrated during what Annette Stott described as the 'Holland Mania' of the late nineteenth and early twentieth centuries.[85]

Few domestic Cottier windows are known in the United States and even fewer can be traced back to specific homes. The Metropolitan Museum, New York, owns a Cottier & Co. window representing Spring (fig. 100), depicting a young woman with auburn hair and windblown flowering dress, set against a background of quarries with stylised plant motifs. It was probably once part of a set of the Four Seasons which may originally have decorated the house of Cottier's son William Field Cottier, who married and settled in New York.[86] Related to this panel, but from a different set, are two panels representing Autumn and Winter, now in the Columbia Museum of Art, South Carolina.[87] Each is framed by quarries and surmounted by a small square panel

101 *The Lady of Shalott* by Cottier & Co., London, after a design by Matthijs Maris, *c.*1875–83. Stained glass, 205.7 × 94 cm. Metropolitan Museum of Art, New York, Gift of E. William Judson and Stephen H. Judson, 2016

102 *Morning Glories* by Cottier & Co., London, *c.*1877–8. Six-panel window from the William Watts Sherman House, Newport, Rhode Island. Stained glass, 280.6 × 182.8 cm. Museum of Fine Arts, Boston, gift of James F. and Jean Baer O'Gorman

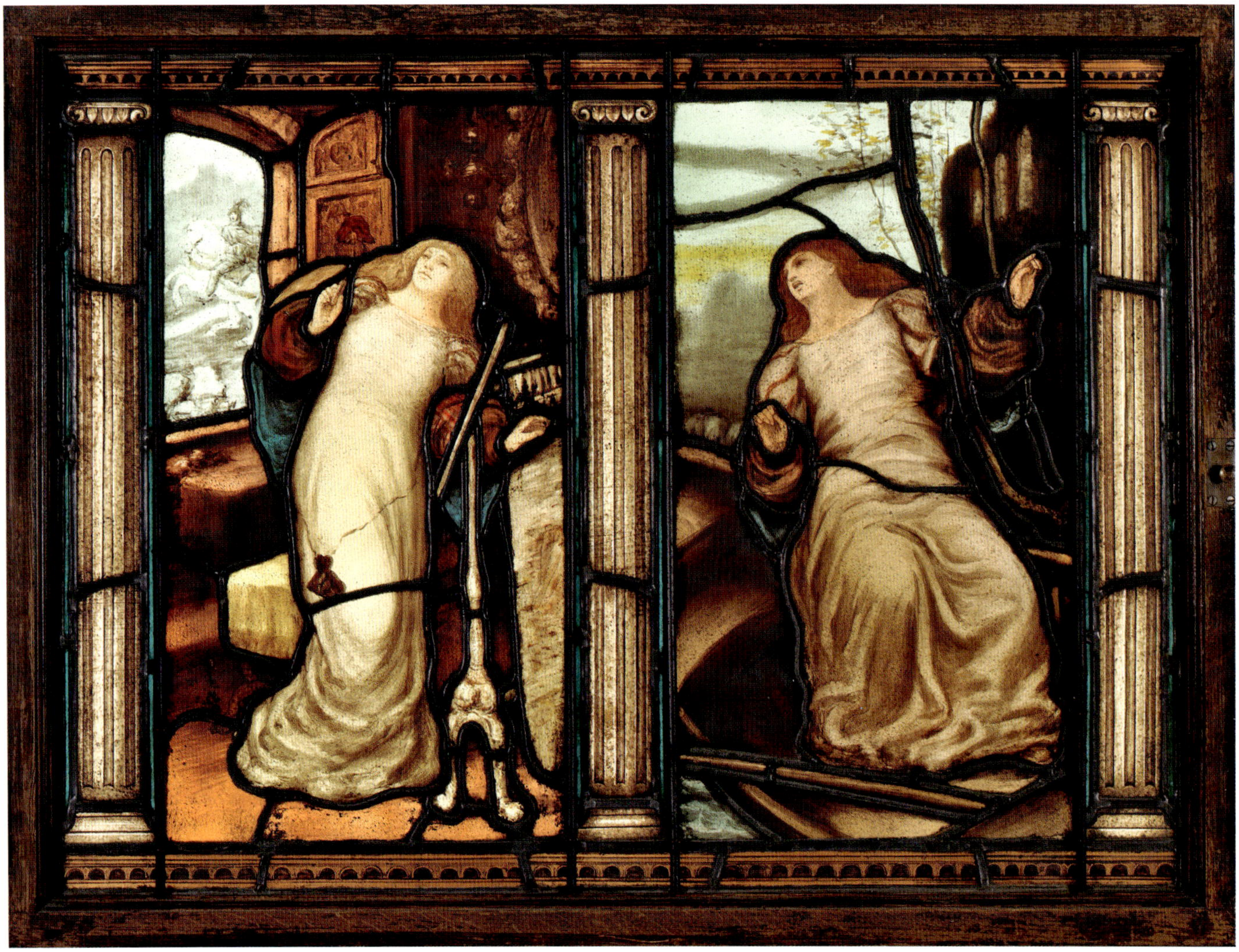

representing a bird (a goose and a partridge, respectively), a typical arrangement of Cottier windows that was influenced by the domestic glass made by Morris & Co.

The Metropolitan Museum also possesses a large rectangular window with the two scenes of Tennyson's 'Lady of Shalott' originally conceived by Matthijs Maris (see Chapter Three, pp. 85–6, and figs 74 and 76) side by side in one pane, separated by a painted column (fig. 101). This panel comes from a house in New York City and its composition must have been popular in America for the 1913 catalogue lists no fewer than twelve panels representing 'two scenes from *The Lady of Shalott* ... originally designed and painted by Matthew Maris'.[88] The popularity of this window in America is also attested by a review in the *New York Times* of an exhibition of Cottier & Co. glass panels organised by Walter Fearon some six months before the 1913 auction, in what was then called the Cottier Galleries. The (anonymous) reviewer singles out the Maris window which is reproduced at the top: 'With the tact of the supreme masters the painter has produced a design absolutely appropriate to the material in which it is to be carried out, one that lends itself

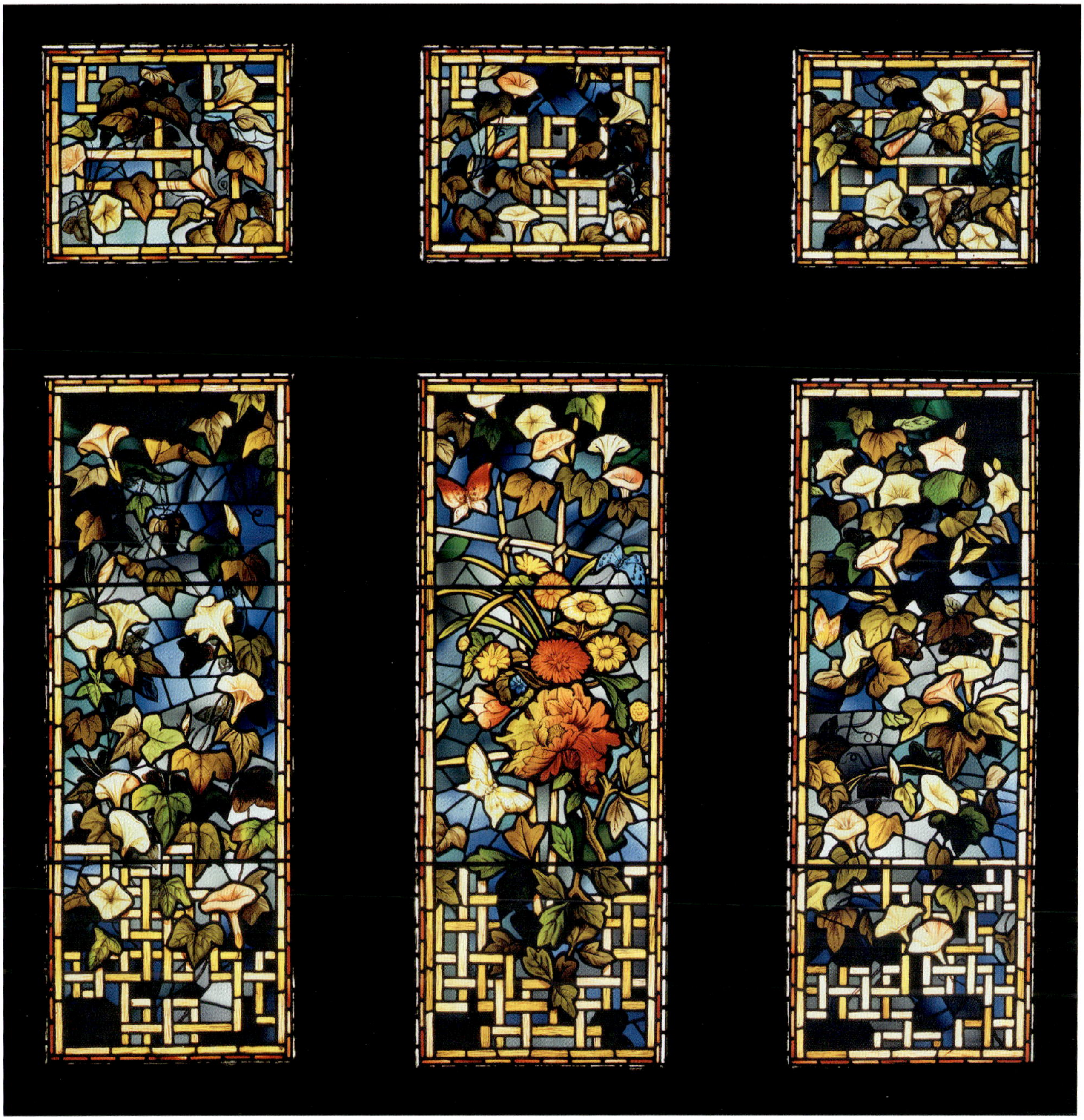

to the use of broad, brilliant masses without elaborate gradations of color or tone'.[89]

Among other domestic Cottier stained glass preserved in museum collections is the beautiful *Morning Glories* window (fig. 102), consisting of three vertical panels, each surmounted by a smaller panel. Once attributed to John La Farge,[90] the window was produced around 1877–8 for the house of a New York banker, William Watts Sherman, in Newport, Rhode Island, built a few years earlier by H. H. Richardson, who may have secured the commission for Cottier. Although the house still stands, the windows were removed and donated to the Museum of Fine Arts, Boston. A late example of Cottier & Co. domestic windows still *in situ* is the set of four on the landing of Clayton (fig. 103), Frick's Pittsburgh home. The set, for which Frick paid $2000 in 1903,[91] shows four standing female figures, identified as the protagonists of four famous literary works: Miranda from Shakespeare's play *The Tempest*, Isabella from Keats's poem 'Isabella; or The Pot of Basil', Marguérite from Alexandre Dumas's novel *The Lady of the Camellias* and Madeline from Keats's 'The Eve of St Agnes'. Representing the final phase of glass produced by Cottier & Co. in

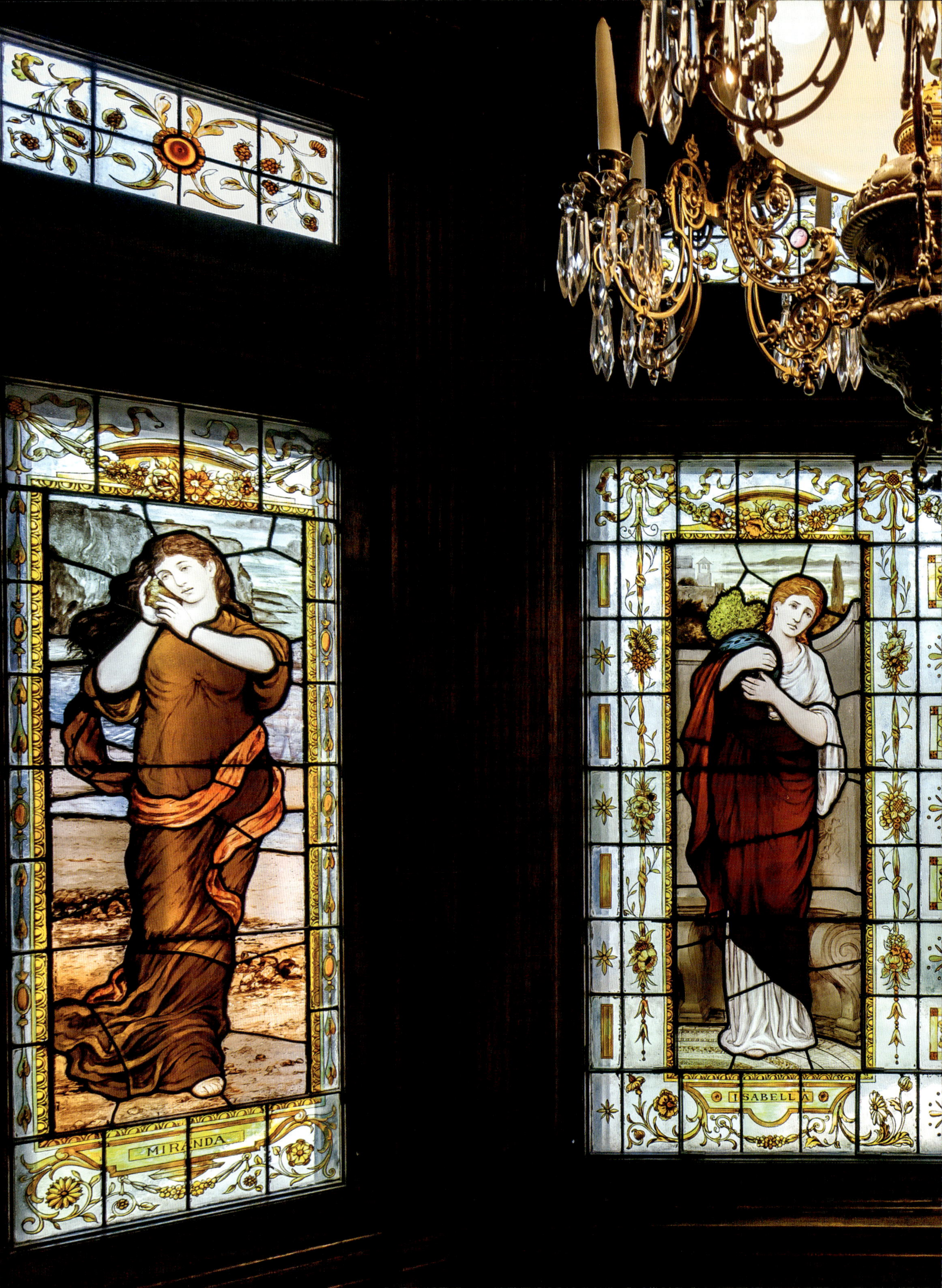
MIRANDA
ISABELLA

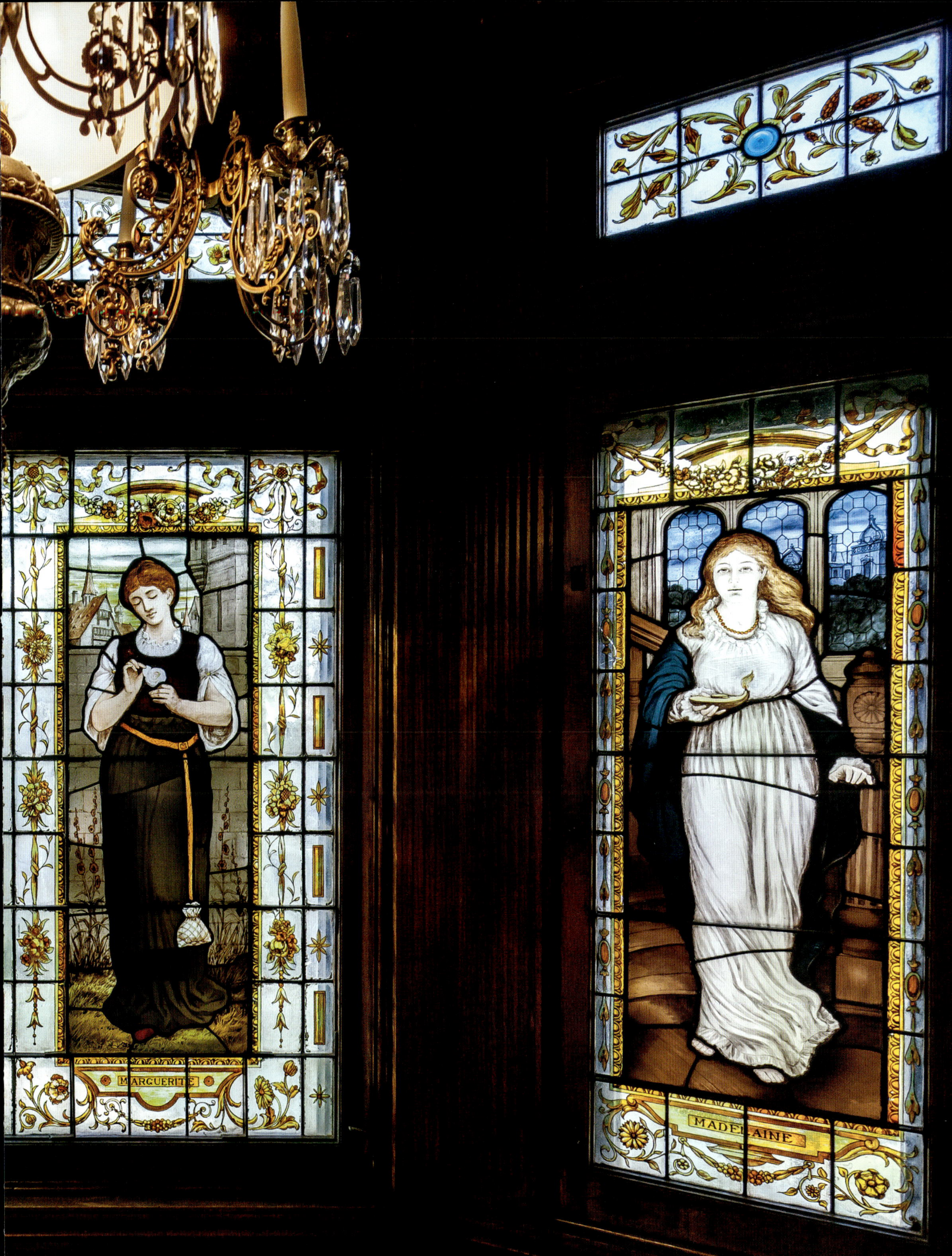
MARGUERITE
MADELAINE

previous pages
103 *Miranda, Isabella, Marguérite* and *Madeline* [note: window legend has Madelaine]. Windows on the staircase landing of Clayton, Pittsburgh, by Cottier & Co., probably London, 1903. Stained glass, The Frick Pittsburgh

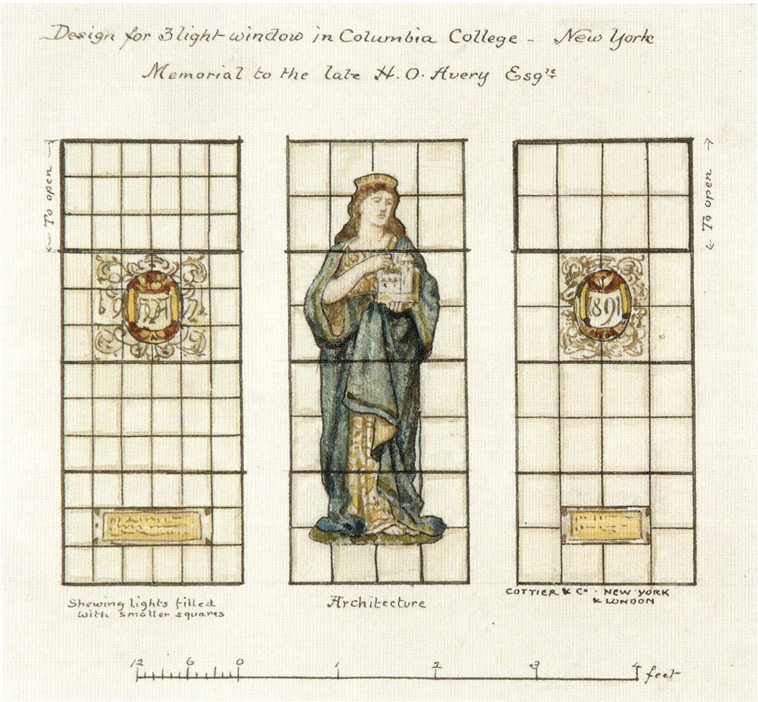

Britain following the closure of the London workshop in 1897, the figures carry on female types first established in the 1870s but they are slenderer and more subdued. The colour is restrained, largely tonal and lacking strong accents.[92]

The 1879 article in *Harper's Magazine* cited earlier informed its readers that stained glass was not only found in homes and 'flats' but also in shops and 'even in the dépôts of the elevated railway.'[93] Cottier's glass panels were no exception. Some of them found their way into libraries and others may have decorated different public spaces. One example is the window Cottier & Co. produced around 1878 for the Green Memorial Alcove in the Society Library in New York. The decoration of the alcove was a gift to the library by a trustee in honor of John Cleve Green, who had left an endowment to the library after his death in 1875.[94] Although neither the window nor the memorial alcove has been preserved,[95] a reproduction in *Harper's Magazine* shows that the window was centred on a vertical panel with two full-length figures, *Notitia* (Knowledge) and *Prudentia* (Prudence). The design of the panel corresponds closely to that of a panel in the large landing window in Cairndhu House in Helensburgh, Scotland (see fig. 35), showing yet again that, in common with the practice of other stained-glass makers, Cottier & Co.'s designs were freely recycled if the subject matter lent itself to the commission. The Society Library panel was set in a rich frame of flowered branches, which in turn was surrounded by painted quarries, while the four corners contained portraits of Homer, Virgil, Dante and Chaucer, also frequently reused subjects.[96]

Another window by Cottier & Co. made for a public space, again a library, dates from the end of Cottier's life. Cottier personally donated this window to the Memorial Library at Columbia founded by his long-time friend Samuel P. Avery in memory of his son, the architect Henry Ogden Avery, who had died on 30 April 1890 aged thirty-eight. Cottier himself died before the window was installed in the initial Avery Library space on the 49th Street campus of Columbia College. The library later moved to the 116th Street campus and the present whereabouts of the window, if it still exists, is unknown. A preliminary design by one of the artists in Cottier's London studio (fig. 104) shows that the central window featured a female allegorical figure of architecture, carrying a model of a castle in her hands; the two side windows showed cartouches inside decorative frames, of which the left cartouche has the initials HOA, the right the date 1891, marking the inauguration of the library.[97]

MEMORIAL WINDOW

When Cottier and Inglis came to New York, American stained glass was still in its infancy, especially when it came to large church windows, and much ecclesiastical glass was imported from Europe.[98] Episcopal and Presbyterian churches usually turned to British manufacturers while Roman Catholic churches tended to patronise French and German studios. However, a few young American artists saw a future in stained glass, both for ecclesiastic and domestic use. Some of these, like Lathrop and John La Farge, were initially in Cottier's orbit but eventually distanced themselves and went their own ways. La Farge in particular revolutionised stained-glass art in the United States through the introduction of opalescent glass, for which he obtained a patent in 1879. He showed some of his early experiments to Tiffany, who took out a slightly different patent two years later.[99] The work of these two artists, who experimented with all kinds of special effects in glass, became immensely popular in

104 *Architecture*, design for three-light memorial window to H. O. Avery in Columbia College, New York, by Cottier & Co., London, 1891. Pen and watercolour on paper, 22 × 26 cm. Private collection

America, denting though by no means eliminating the European competition. Cottier & Co. received its most important commissions early on, before La Farge and Tiffany had become serious competitors, but the firm continued to receive commissions for church windows, most for Episcopal and Presbyterian churches, until the early 1900s.

Ecclesiastical windows in America were often larger than those in Britain, reflecting the greater scale of many of the new churches and cathedrals being constructed. Cottier & Co.'s earliest known memorial window commission, for Trinity Church in Boston, was also an important one. Trinity Church was a much watched architectural project in the 1870s and as early as 1886, in a poll by *American Architect and Building News*, it was voted the best contemporary building in the United States.[100] When the church building was consecrated in 1877, it had only one stained-glass window but over the next five years twenty-four windows, many of them memorials paid for by parishioners, were added. Cottier & Co. contributed four windows, the same number as La Farge and as Morris & Co., the latter employing designs by Burne-Jones.

The connection between Cottier and Trinity Church and its architect H. H. Richardson was probably made by La Farge. La Farge had been included in an exhibition of works of young American artists that Cottier held on his premises in 1875 (see Chapter Five, p. 139) but the two may have met earlier. As noted, La Farge was a friend of Richardson and had volunteered to paint the interior of Trinity Church, a project he began in 1876.[101] He needed other artists to help him in this effort and in October he contacted Cottier, who had ample experience with church decoration in Britain. The nature of Cottier and his firm's contribution is not clear. Clarence Cook, writing in *Scribner's Monthly* in February 1878, acknowledged that Cottier's assistance had been crucial in the practical realm of 'the control of assistants made adepts in the mixing and applying of colors by long experience'. But he also gave Cottier more credit than most for his artistic and conceptual role in the project: 'When all the panels, spandrels, and wall spaces shall have been filled with the pictures that now are in such a slim minority, the obligation to Mr. Cottier will be more plain than ever.'[102] The sculptor Augustus Saint-Gaudens, however, in a letter to Stanford White written in March of the same year, disagreed with Cook:

I don't think, or at least I don't see what La Farge would have done without him [Cottier] in the mixing of colors, direction of men &c. &c., and all the practical part. But on the other hand as regards art I know there isn't a bit of Cottier in the whole church. La Farge had every bit of Cottier's work changed to suit himself ... [103]

Whatever the relationship between Cottier and La Farge and between Cottier and Richardson may have been, artistically and personally, Cottier received commissions for four memorial windows in Trinity Church between 1878 and 1879.[104] Perhaps the most successful of the four is the window of *The Five Wise Virgins* (fig. 105), presented to the church by Abby Matilda Loring in memory of her eponymous aunt. The imagery in the window is inspired by Christ's parable in Matthew 25, which tells of five virgins who brought extra oil for their lamps so that they could join the bridegroom at the wedding feast. The window represents the best of Cottier & Co. windows in the 1870s: the simplified largely lead-outlined forms of the statuesque women dressed in long flowing gowns perfectly fit the available square space, while the suggestion of a large colonnaded banqueting room filled with small figures in the back gives the illusion of depth. The inscription underneath, 'THEY THAT WERE READY WENT IN WITH HIM TO THE MARRIAGE', is a direct reference to the heavenly destination of the deceased Loring, who, according to one source, had been a 'liberal benefactor of the poor'.[105]

Cottier & Co.'s next documented stained-glass commissions were for two composite windows in Harvard University's Memorial Hall.[106] Intended to commemorate and honour Harvard alumni who had died in the Civil War, the Gothic-style building, designed by William Robert Ware and Henry Van Brunt, was dedicated in 1870. In the following years, different Harvard classes commissioned windows for the hall on a generally agreed broad theme of

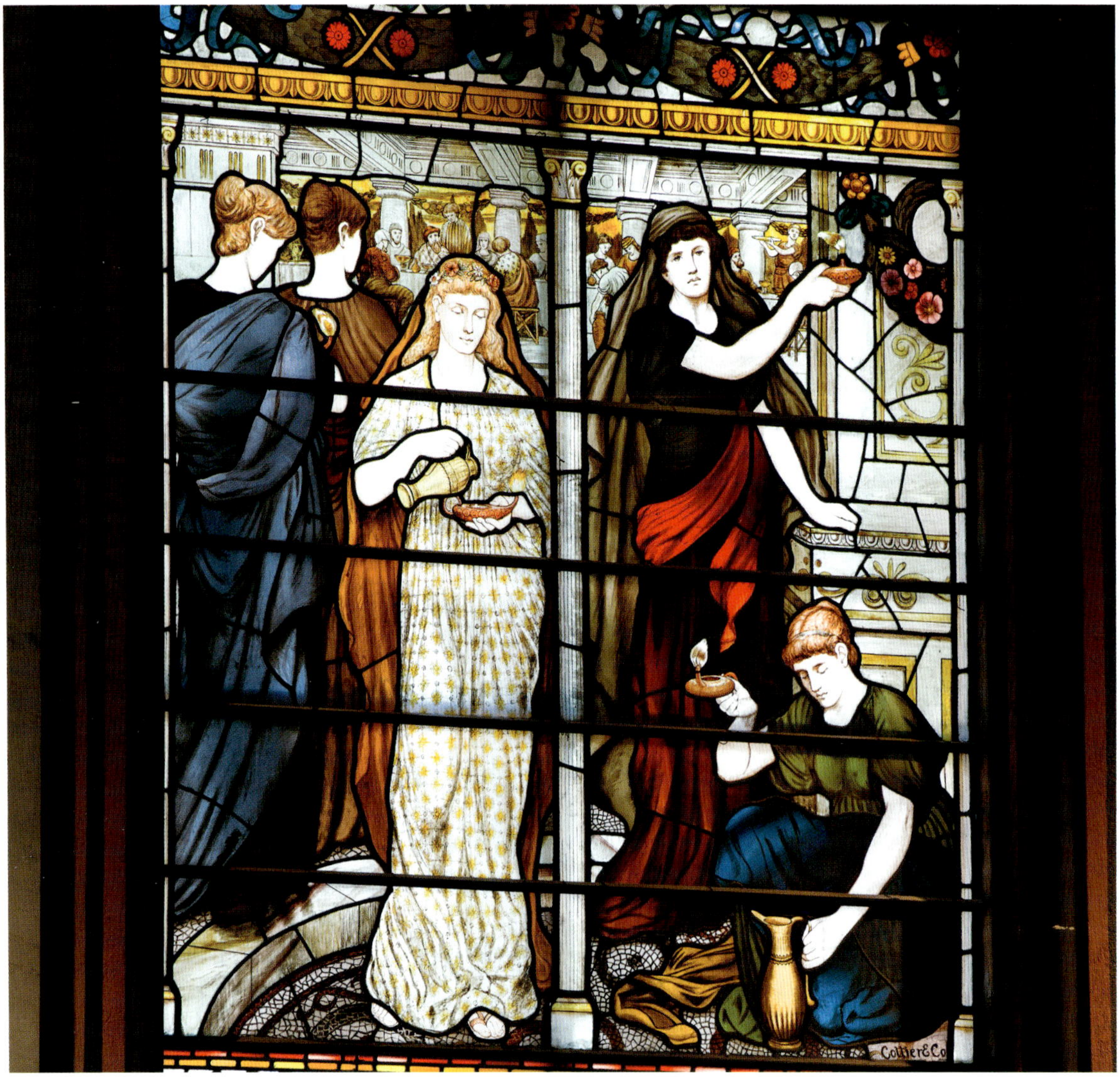

outstanding scholars and valiant heroes in history. The Class of 1857, which was among the first to do so in 1874, commissioned a window from La Farge, representing the English Elizabethan poet and courtier Philip Sidney and the Theban statesman and general Epaminondas, to illustrate, according to the Class of 1857 report in 1882, 'the character of the scholar and the soldier'.[107] Both had died in battle and therefore were appropriate subjects for the Memorial Hall. For each panel, La Farge made several preliminary drawings, two of which were later reproduced in an article on the artist in *Scribner's Monthly* of February 1881 (fig. 106).[108] However, La Farge failed to produce the window and after four years the commission was rerouted to Cottier & Co., whose windows at Trinity Church several members of the class may have seen and admired. Having spent $795.60 on La Farge's designs, the class was pleased to see Cottier's window installed in May 1879 at the cost of $1980 (fig. 107).[109] In April, between their arrival from England and their installation in the chapel, the panels were on display in Cottier's gallery in New York, where they attracted the attention of a critic writing for *Art Interchange*, who deemed them 'beautiful'.[110] But compared to Cottier's own windows for Trinity Church (especially the *Sower and Reaper* window, which likewise shows two male standing figures[111]), the Sidney and Epaminondas window seems unexciting, the figures stiff in their strict frontality, their gestures somewhat awkward. While the difference in quality between Cottier & Co.'s windows can, of course, be attributed to the workshop production of the firm, it may also have arisen from the detailed instructions the firm received from the Class of 1857,[112] which left little room for creative freedom. This is not true for the panels below the figures, illustrating a scene from

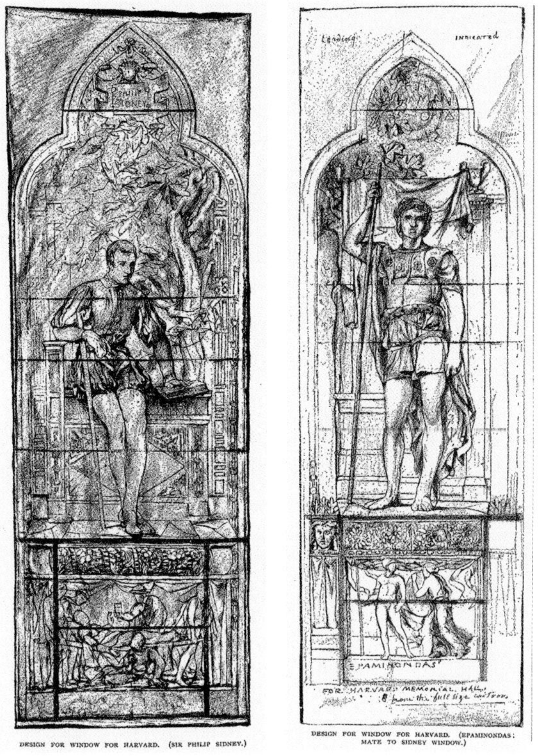

105 *Five Wise Virgins*, Abby Matilda Loring memorial window, Trinity Church, Boston, Massachusetts, by Cottier & Co., London, 1878–9. Stained glass

106 John La Farge, *Philip Sidney* and *Epaminondas*, designs for a two-light window for Harvard Memorial Hall, Cambridge, Massachusetts, 1874. Reproduced in *Scribner's Monthly*, February 1881, 510 and 508

the end of Sidney's life and Plutarch's Spartan mother handing her son Epaminondas his shield with the words: 'Son, either this [his shield] or upon this'.[113] These little panels are remarkable for their balanced compositions, restrained colours and slightly abstract representations of the figures.

In 1882 Cottier & Co. produced a second composite window for Harvard Memorial Hall, this one commissioned by the Class of 1858 (fig. 108). Representing John Hampden, a member of Parliament who challenged the authority of Charles I, and Leonidas, the hero of the ancient Battle of Thermopylae (two more heroes who had died for causes they believed in), the window with its poised figures, closely framed by classicising pilasters, is more typical of the Cottier style. The gestures are less contrived, the drapery is more convincing. Both windows show the warm saturated colours commonly seen in Cottier & Co. windows of this period.

One of Cottier's most extensive commissions was for the Unitarian Church of the Messiah in St Louis, Missouri. The church was planned by its founder William Greenleaf Eliot, the grandfather of the poet T. S. Eliot.[114] It was designed by Peabody & Stearns in 1879–81[115] and entirely glazed by Cottier & Co., which delivered four large three-light windows.[116] Cottier & Co.'s commission for the windows may have been the result of a recommendation of Peabody & Stearns, with whom the firm had recently worked in the house of J. C. Phillips in Boston, as described earlier. It is also possible that Eliot, who came from a Massachusetts family and must have travelled to Boston frequently, had seen Cottier's work in Trinity Church and perhaps Harvard's Memorial Hall and was impressed with it. In 1907 the Unitarian congregation moved to a new building designed by Mauran, Russell & Garden and Cottier's windows, with the exception of the one in the south transept, moved with it.[117] In the Mauran church, the Cottier windows are placed in the chancel, the north transept and the nave. Several windows in the church adapt designs used in Britain since the early 1870s. The two angel musicians in the memorial windows for Susan A. and Edward Y. Ware in the nave, for example, had first appeared at St Machar's Cathedral, Aberdeen.

In one case, however, the adaptation is more original. The 'Reaper and the Flowers' window for Georgiana C. Louderman (fig. 109), who died on 6 March 1875 aged thirteen, is no doubt based on the same design as the window for St John the Evangelist in Birtley, Tyne and Wear (see fig. 30). But the differences are important and change the window's significance and effect. Instead of a full-grown woman, the angel here lovingly carries up a small sleeping girl (too small, indeed, for a thirteen-year-old) in order to emphatically express the tragedy of a child's death. The window seems to be particularly inspired by the last lines of Longfellow's poem: 'Oh, not in cruelty, not in wrath,/ The Reaper came that day;/ 'T was an angel visited the green earth,/ And took the flowers away.'[118]

following pages

107 *Philip Sidney* and *Epaminondas*, memorial window funded by the Class of 1857, Harvard Memorial Hall, Cambridge, Massachusetts, by Cottier & Co., London, 1879. Stained glass

108 *John Hampden* and *Leonidas*, memorial window funded by the Class of 1858, Harvard Memorial Hall, Cambridge, Massachusetts, by Cottier & Co., London, 1882. Stained glass

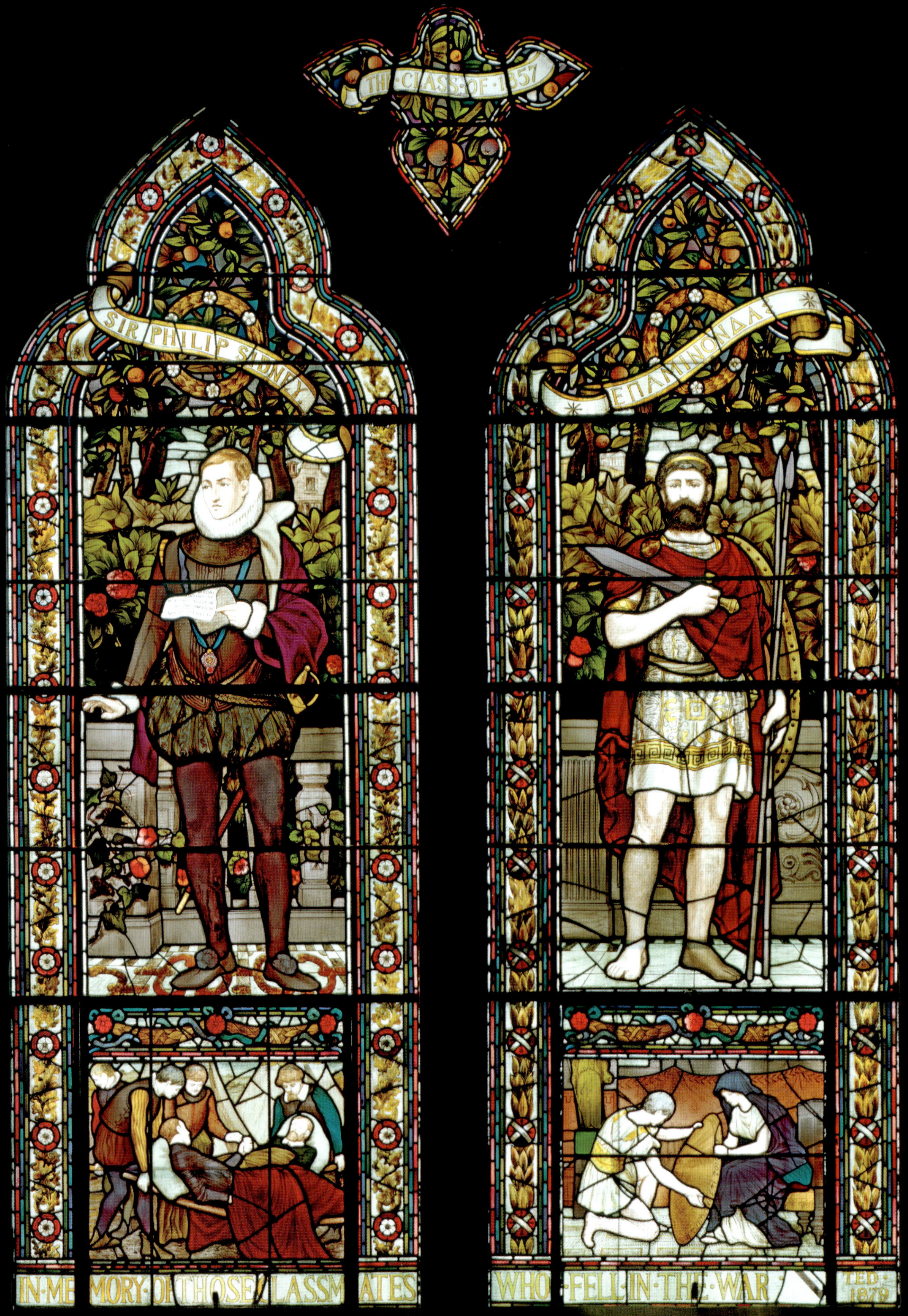
THE·CLASS·OF·1857
SIR PHILIP SIDNEY
ΕΠΑΜΙΝΩΝΔΑ
IN·MEMORY·OF·THOSE·CLASSMATES
WHO·FELL·IN·THE·WAR
T.E.D. 1879

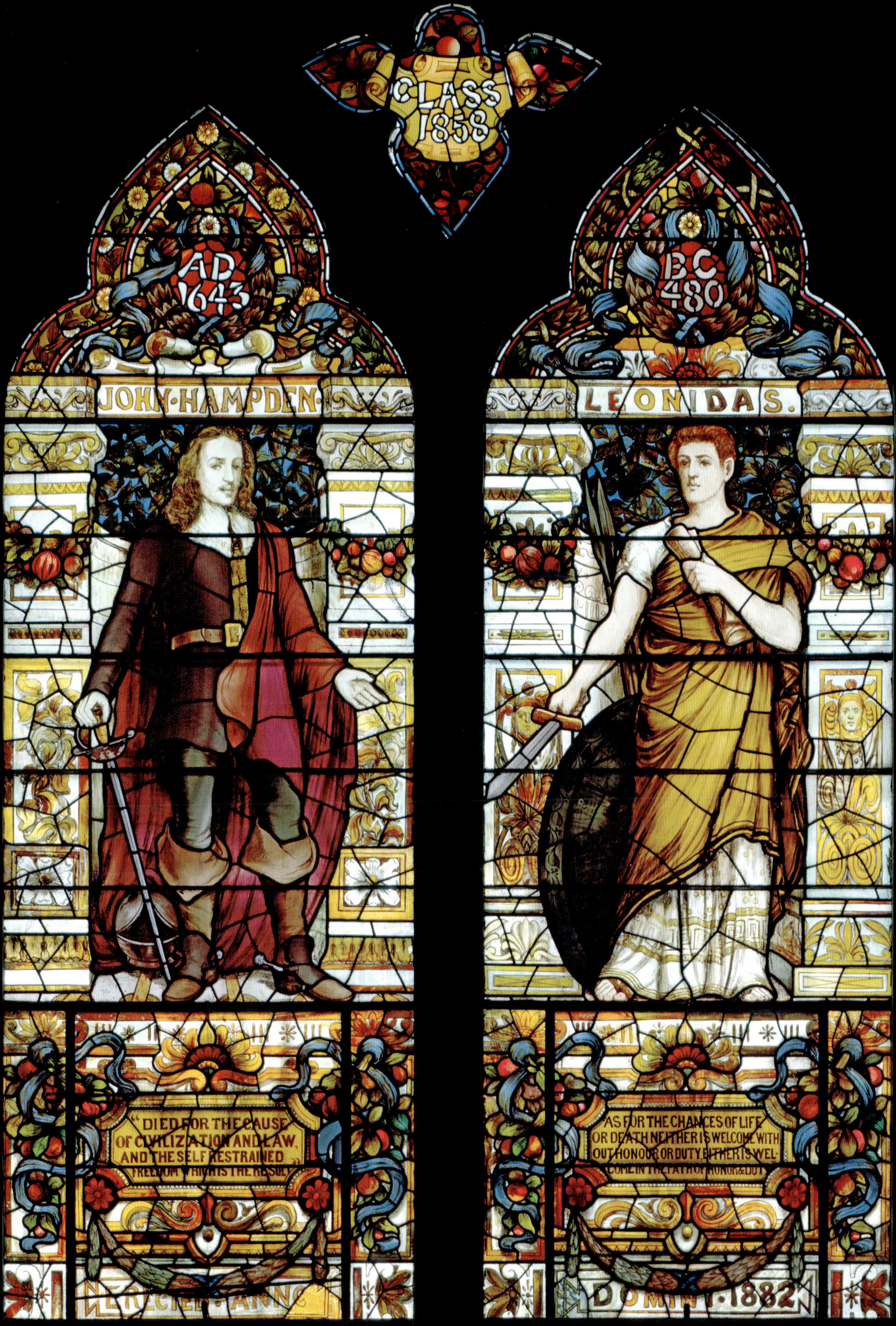
CLASS
1858
AD
1643
BC
480
JOHN·HAMPDEN·
LEONIDAS.
"DIED FOR THE CAUSE
OF CIVILIZATION AND LAW,
AND THE SELF RESTRAINED
FREEDOM WHICH IS THE RESUL
"AS FOR THE CHANCES OF LIFE
OR DEATH NEITHER IS WELCOME WITH
OUT HONOUR OR DUTY, EITHER IS WEL-
COME IN THE PATH OF HONOR & DUT
ERECTED · ANNO
DOMINI · 1882

109 *The Reaper and the Flowers*, Georgiana Louderman memorial window, Salt Covenant Baptist Church (formerly Unitarian Church of the Messiah), St Louis, Missouri, by Cottier & Co., London, *c.*1880. Stained glass

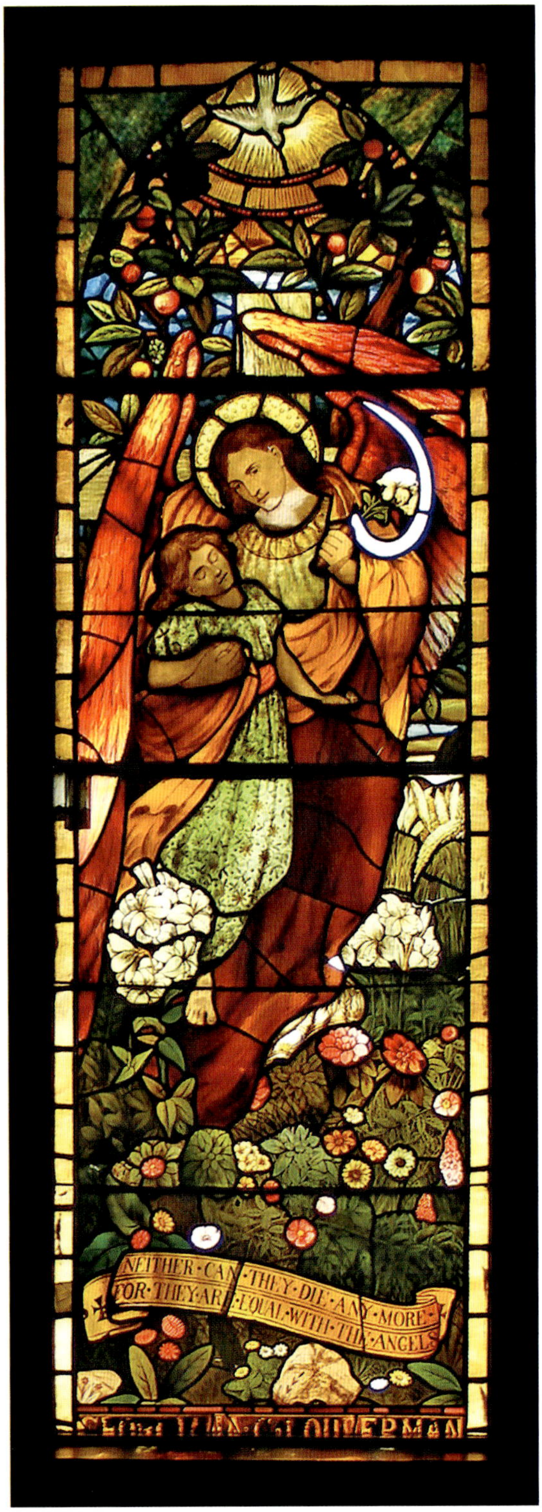

Four of the panes in the chancel windows in the Mauran church are based on the illustrations to *The Parables of Our Lord and Saviour Jesus Christ*, engraved by the Dalziel brothers after drawings by Millais and published by Routledge in 1864 (see also Chapter Two). Exceptionally – as Cottier & Co. mostly used designs by in-house artists – these extremely popular images served as models for several other Cottier & Co. commissions in the United States. The first of these was the commission the firm received in 1879 for a large composite window in the south transept of St John's Episcopal Church in Canandaigua, New York.[119] The window, which shows seven parables, commemorates Watts Sherman II, the father of William Watts Sherman, for whose house in Newport, Rhode Island, the firm had recently provided the *Morning Glories* window (see fig. 102). Comparing one of the panels, representing the Parable of the Lost Coin with the illustration of the same subject in the Dalziel print, it is clear how closely the model was followed (figs 110 and 111). Other examples of Parable panels are found in a memorial window in the Battell Chapel at Yale University (1883)[120] and in a three-lancet window in Calvary Episcopal Church in New York (1897).[121]

The most important example of a Millais-inspired Cottier & Co. window with no fewer than eight parable scenes, separated by a row of Virtues, is found in the apse of the Sage Chapel at Cornell University in Ithaca, New York (fig. 112). Built in 1874 with funds donated by Henry W. Sage (1814–1897),[122] the chapel was twice rebuilt, most drastically in 1898, when the entire eastern part was demolished and replaced by a double transept and an apse flanked by two porches. The Cottier & Co. parable window, a memorial to Sage's wife Susan E. Linn (died 1885), was transferred from its original location in the old chapel to the apse. At that time, four additional windows were commissioned from Cottier & Co. in London. On the right, two windows show, respectively, an allegorical figure of Hope and an image of Christ as *The Light of the World*, after William Holman Hunt's famous painting in Keble College, Oxford.[123] On the left is an allegorical figure of Youth next to Christ as the Good Shepherd, after an unidentified source. It is known

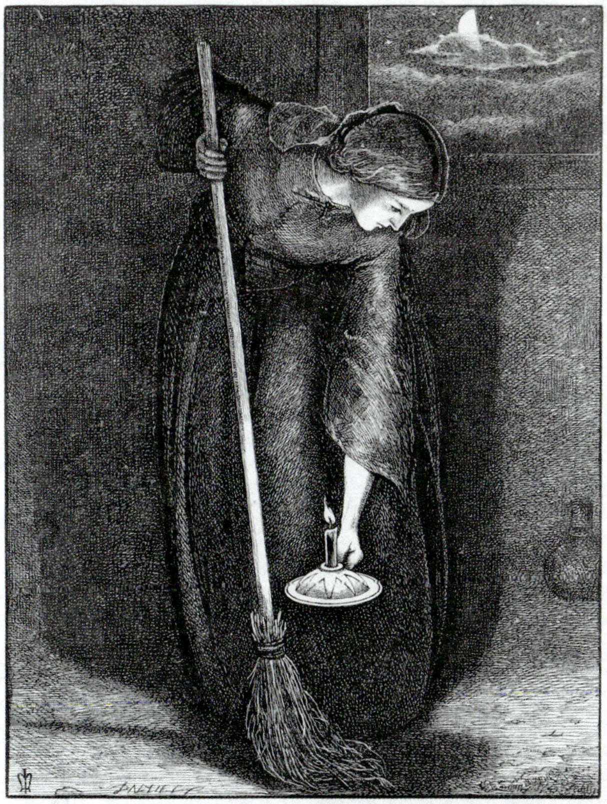

110 *The Lost Coin*, Dalziel Brothers after John Everett Millais, 1864. Wood engraving published in *The Parables of Our Lord*, London, 1864

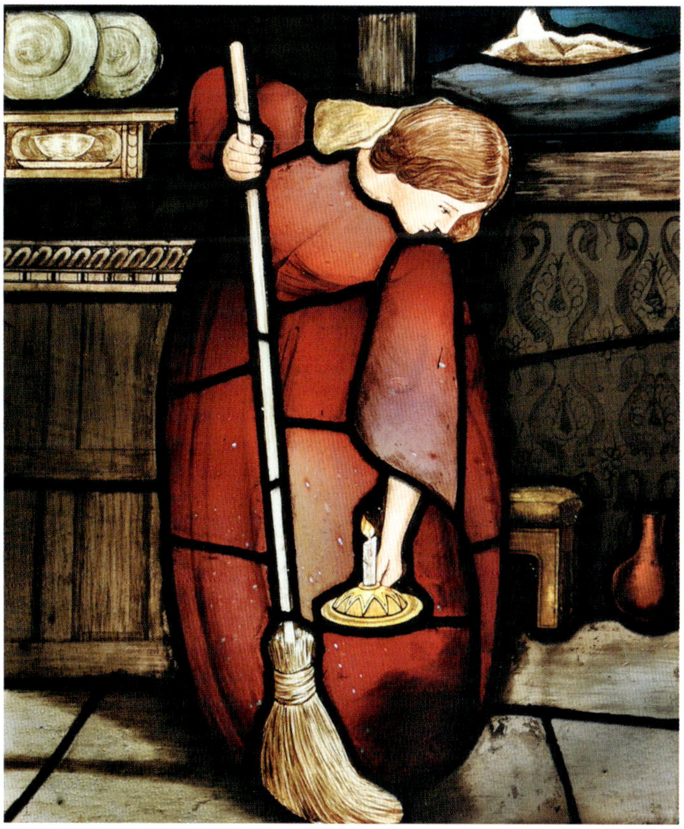

111 *The Lost Coin*, detail of Watts Sherman II memorial window, St John's Episcopal Church, Canandaigua, New York, by Cottier & Co., London, 1879. Stained glass

from two preliminary pencil drawings that the two allegorical figures were newly designed in the Cottier & Co. workshop.[124] When the rebuilding of the chapel was finished, some time around 1900, the ceiling was painted by Cottier & Co., in all likelihood by artists from the New York workshop (fig. 113).[125] Describing the decoration in a lecture of 1904 Professor Clark S. Northup stressed the symbolism of the decorations:

Ecclesiastical symbolism pervades the decoration of the central chapel ... the ceiling paintings include the temple and ship, symbols of the church; the anchor, representing hope and patience; the lamp for piety and wisdom, and the lamb and pennant for Christ. The colors are also symbolic – white for innocence and life; red for creative power and divine love, blue for truth, green for immortality.[126]

It is not known whether the symbolism outlined in Northup's lecture was dictated by the patron's brief or conceived by the Cottier & Co. artists. Be that as it may, the decoration of the Sage Chapel is remarkable as a late example of the kind of overall decoration of walls and windows first seen nearly four decades earlier in Cottier's work in Dowanhill Church (see Chapter One, pp. 15–19).

After the mid-1880s, the number of commissions for church windows decreased. This was probably due, at least in part, to the growth of the American stained-glass industry, which made it unnecessary to commission windows from abroad. Nonetheless, Cottier & Co. and other British stained-glass studios, including those of Henry Holiday and Morris & Co., continued to receive commissions, particularly from Presbyterian and Episcopal churches. For the Church of the Incarnation, in the Murray Hill section of New York, Cottier & Co. made a double window with a representation of Christ feeding the multitude below

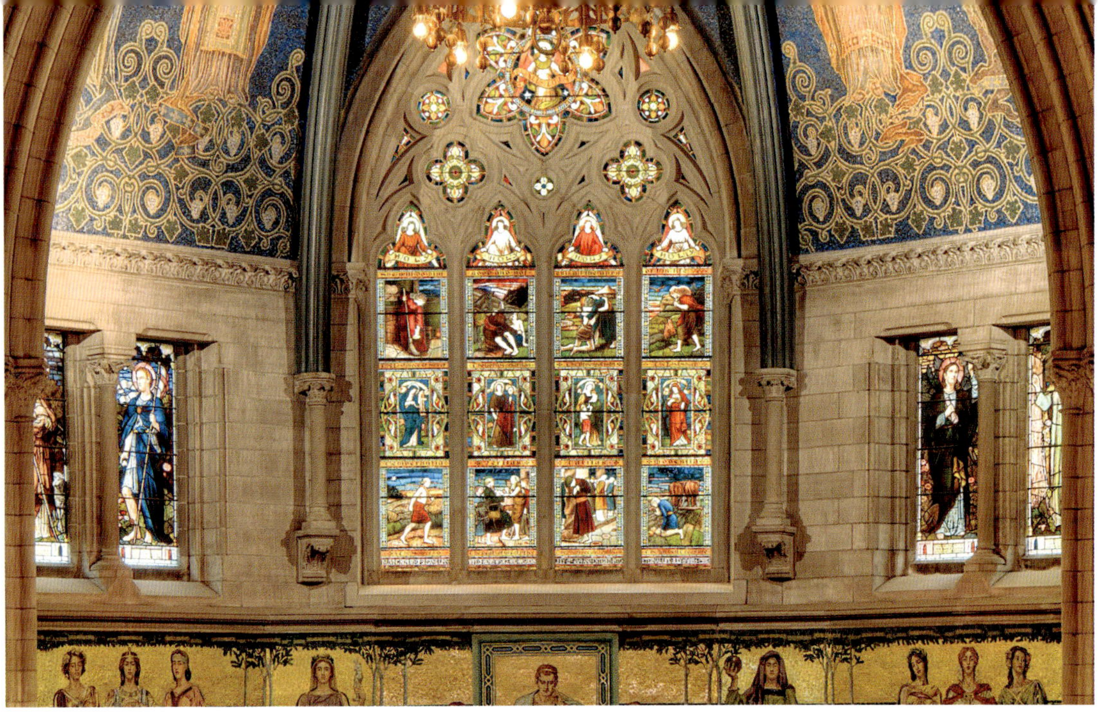

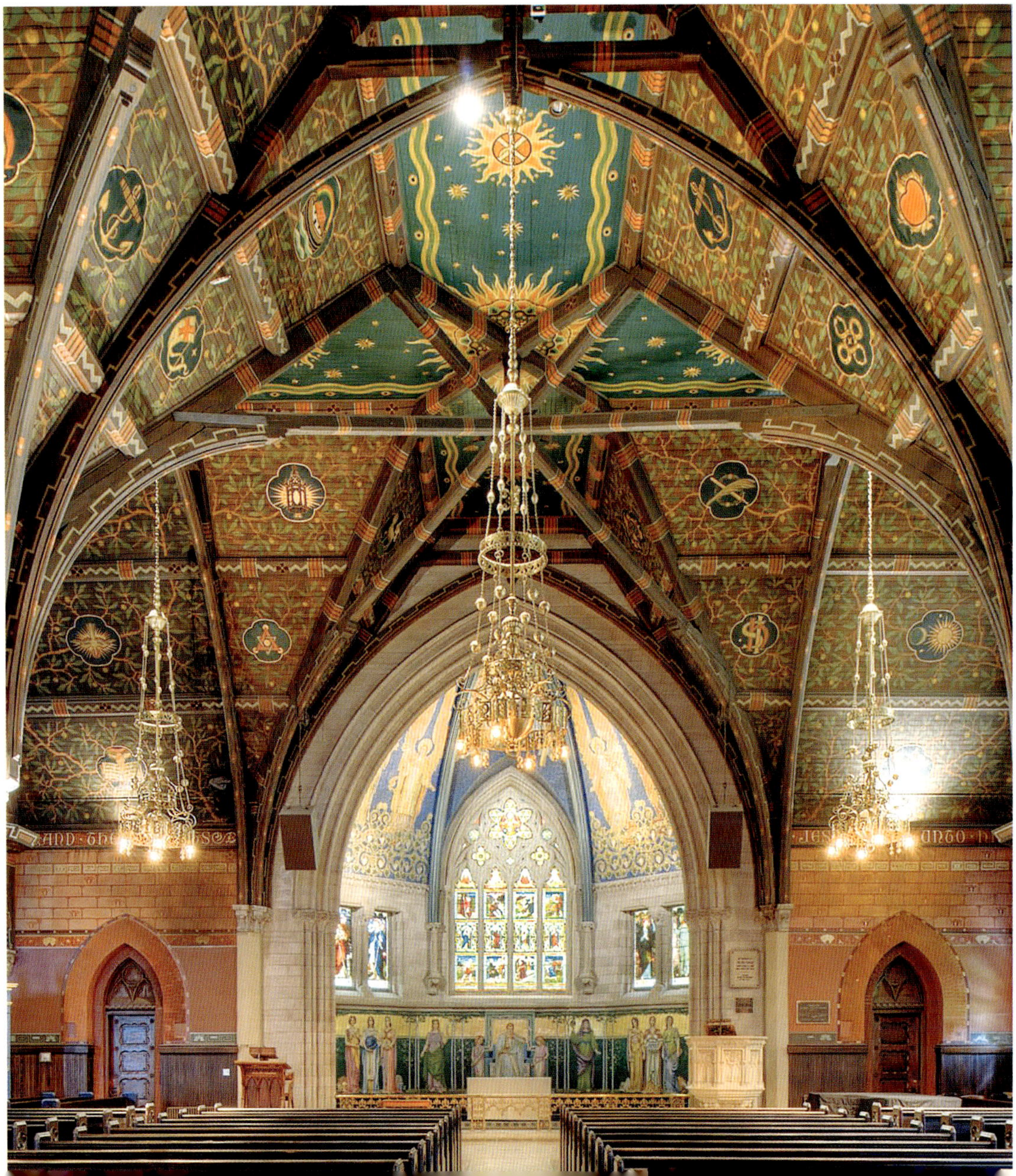

112 Sage Chapel, Cornell University, apse with windows by Cottier & Co., London, second half 1880s (Susan E. Linn memorial window in the centre) and *c.*1900 (windows on either side). Cornell University, Ithaca, New York

113 Painted interior of Sage Chapel, Cornell University, Ithaca, New York, by Cottier & Co., New York, *c.*1900

114 *Christ feeding the Multitude*, bottom lights of a two-tiered window on the theme of the Eucharist (top lights show Moses and the Israelites eating Manna in the Wilderness) by Cottier & Co., London. Church of the Incarnation, New York *c.*1885–90. Stained glass

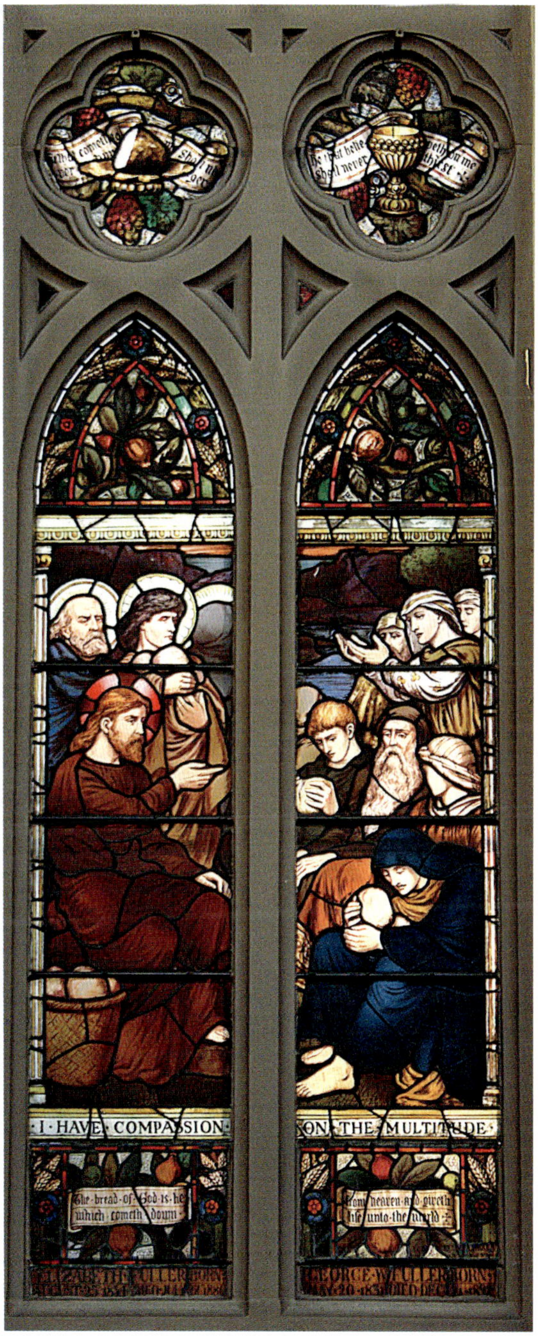

the scene's Old Testament prototype, Moses and the Israelites eating manna in the wilderness (fig. 114). The window is much darker than earlier Cottier windows, a trend observable in other late windows that can be plausibly related to Cottier's art-dealing activities and his predominant interest in tonalist painting.[127] The Church of the Incarnation also features windows by three well-known London firms, those of Henry Holiday, Clayton & Bell and Morris & Co., as well as by American studios including J. & R. Lamb, La Farge and Tiffany. Additionally, it boasts wall paintings by La Farge, sculptures by Daniel Chester French (1850–1931) and Saint-Gaudens and a memorial monument designed by H. H. Richardson. That Cottier & Co.'s work was included in this panoply of well-known artists and art firms suggests the firm's continued reputation as a producer of stained glass.

The likely reasons for the decline in Cottier & Co.'s glass production and quality after the mid-1890s are numerous: they include Cottier's failing health and eventual death in 1891; a falling demand for imported stained glass; and the continued shift of focus within Cottier & Co. from ecclesiastical art to interior decoration and art dealing. Nevertheless in the late 1880s there was a final flowering of glass: Cottier & Co. provided stained glass for two other New York churches, both in Brooklyn Heights. Grace Episcopal Church boasts a window representing the three theological Virtues Faith, Hope and Charity (1890). The figures are close copies of those in the *Painters' Window* of 1874–5 in St Machar's in Aberdeen (see fig. 28), indicating once again that Cottier & Co. continued to reuse designs many years after they were originally conceived.[128] The First Presbyterian Church in Brooklyn Heights has a window representing Christ and the Children (1887) memorialising 'the children of this church who in infancy or in early youth have left us and are with Christ in Paradise'. It is especially striking for its realistic representations of flowers.

Petra Chu

CHAPTER FIVE
THE ART MARKET IN NEW YORK

On 1 March 1877, a little less than four years after the opening of Cottier & Co.'s interior decoration and furniture business in New York, the Cottier Gallery (also referred to as the Cottier Art Rooms) was launched on the first floor of the firm's showroom at 144 Fifth Avenue. In opening the New York gallery, Cottier followed the business strategy initiated in London, where he had begun with a decorating and furnishing business and later added an art gallery. He would try the same in Sydney but with little success. By contrast, in New York the Cottier Gallery thrived and, at least for a time, was a trendsetter in the contemporary art market in New York by introducing the public to the works of artists as yet unknown in North America. For beyond featuring in his gallery the paintings of Barbizon School artists, which could also be found in other New York galleries, Cottier was the first to show works by the painters of the Hague School, including David Artz, Bernard Blommers, Théophile de Bock, Johannes Bosboom, the brothers Maris (Jacob, Matthijs and Willem), Anton Mauve and Hendrik Mesdag.[1] He also launched the works of the eccentric French artist Adolphe Monticelli in New York. Thanks in large part to Cottier, these artists became exceedingly popular in America during the last two decades of the nineteenth and first decade of the twentieth century.

THE COTTIER GALLERY

On the night before the opening of the Cottier Gallery, there was a small but choice reception, attended by 'gentlemen more especially interested in art, artists, members of the press, and others'.[2] Among them was a critic for the *New York Times*, who wrote a lengthy and laudatory review, which, in the absence of Cottier & Co. archives, is the major source of information about the exhibition.[3]

Declaring the exhibition 'not large' but 'very remarkable', the anonymous *New York Times* reviewer gave a room by room description of its content. On entering the large room in the rear of the first floor, he wrote, one was confronted by a 'magnificent specimen' of Charles Daubigny, a 'superb painting' that, by gaslight, yielded 'even greater charms than by day, for the gas penetrates the deepest shadows under the heavy mass of foliage and above a sleeping pond'. Another major work in the exhibition, hung on the left wall of the same room, was Camille Corot's *Orpheus greeting the Dawn* (fig. 115), a tall painting that long remained a fixture, even a hallmark, of the New York Cottier Gallery.[4] Corot had painted *Orpheus* and its companion piece *The Sleep of Diana* (whereabouts unknown) as decorations for the newly built Paris townhouse of Prince Pavel ('Paul') Demidoff in 1865 but the two panels had been sold at auction in 1868, when Demidoff relinquished the house.[5] After changing hands many times, they were purchased by Cottier at some point between 1875 and 1877.[6] Cottier initially kept *Diana* in London but *Orpheus* was sent to New York (see also Chapter Three).[7]

In addition to the large paintings by Corot and Daubigny, the room included a smaller work by Corot, as well as 'sketches' by Théodore Rousseau, Jean-François Millet and John Constable. In what the reviewer called the 'main room' were works by Dutch and French artists including de Bock, one of the Maris brothers, Corot, Narcisse Diaz and Louis Mettling. The only work by an American artist in the show was a painting of a cow by Albert Pinkham Ryder (fig. 116).[8] Finally, a huge watercolour 'some ten feet by four', by the French-British artist Jules Lessore was hung in a curtained off area in the front room of the gallery. It represented the lower part of Manhattan island seen from a point in Brooklyn.[9]

115 Camille Corot, *Orpheus greeting the Dawn*, 1865. Oil on canvas, 200 × 137.3 cm. Chazen Museum of Art, University of Wisconsin, Madison, Gift in memory of Earl William and Eugenia Brandt Quirk, Class of 1910, by their children (E. James Quirk, Catherine Jean Quirk and Lilian Quirk Conley)

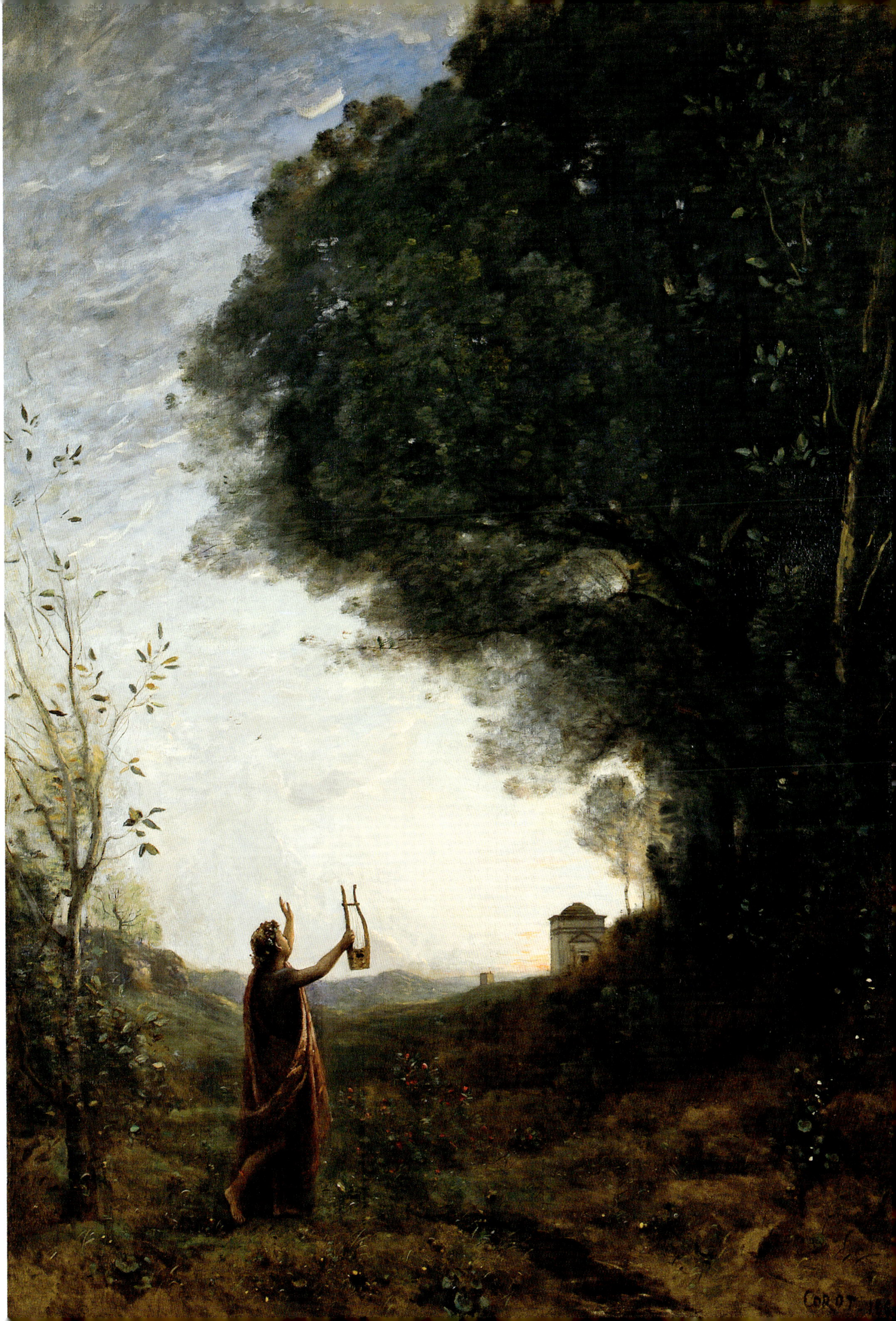
COROT

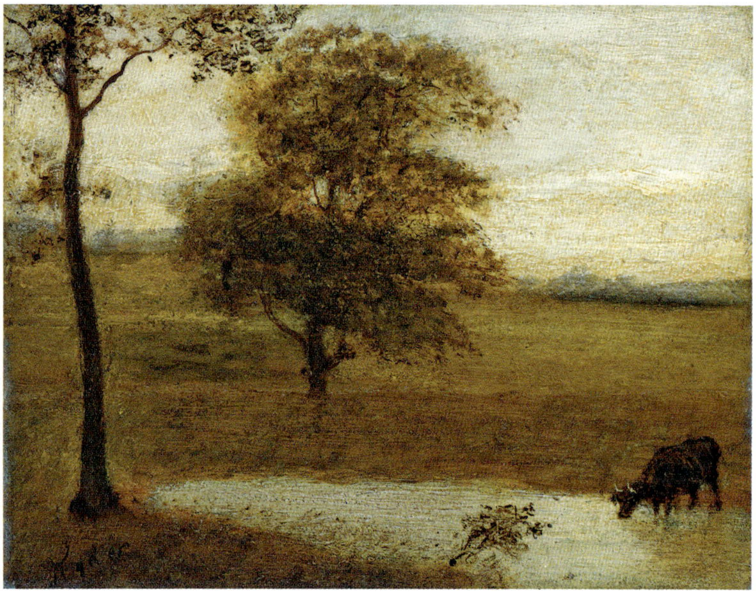

116 Albert Pinkham Ryder, *The Watering Place* (previously called *The Wandering Cow*). Sotheby's Sale N09350 (May 20, 2015), lot 78

Whether Cottier continued to organise formal exhibitions with opening receptions in the years after 1877 is not clear. But his art rooms appear to have had changing displays, depending on pictures that were bought and sold and new art shipments that came in. Judging by newspaper reviews of Cottier's art rooms, it appears that he did invite the press whenever such shipments were received. In April 1878 a review in the *New York Times* featured a lengthy article devoted to Cottier's 'new collection imported for the present season'.[10] After complimenting the previous year's exhibition ('a greater show of admirable modern paintings than anything of the kind hitherto exposed'), the reviewer went on to lavishly praise the new show, which prompted him to 'congratulate New-York on her good luck. It is rare, indeed, that the same firm, as happens to be the case with this one, unites the good taste which selects to the large means necessary to purchase such beautiful works of art'. It is noteworthy that the *New York Times* critic was aware of the cost involved in bringing over paintings from Europe. Aside from the purchasing cost, dealers had to pay for shipping and, after 1883, for tariffs, all of which made importing European paintings an expensive proposition.[11] Hence, the arrival of a new shipment of works of art in a New York gallery was, indeed, newsworthy.

The painting that was singled out by the *New York Times* critic in the 1878 shipment was Monticelli's *Don Quixote and Sancho approaching the Duchess and her Friends*, probably the painting called *Don Quixote and Sancho Panza*, now in the Musée des Beaux-Arts of Tourcoing (on loan from the Musée d'Orsay; fig. 117).[12] He waxed eloquent about this painting, calling it a heroic effort to fuse the styles of the 'much decried "impressionist" school' with that of the 'particularists', a group that he associated with Ernest Meissonier. 'It would be a great loss', the critic concluded, if this 'extraordinary feast of color should leave this country and be lost to the young artists of New-York'. Another review of the exhibition, in the *Art Journal*, highlights a painting by Jules Dupré ('the very best Dupré that we have seen'), hung, 'deservedly', in a room of its own.[13] The review also provides information about additional works in the show by the French painters Corot, Diaz, Charles Jacque, Georges Michel, Millet, Ferdinand Roybet and Constant Troyon, as well as by the Dutch and Belgian painters Bosboom, Mauve and Henri Stacquet. Corot, once again, was represented by his *Orpheus*, though other works by the artist were shown as well. Like the 1877 exhibition, this one included a single American work, a sculpture by Olin Levi Warner.[14]

Only months after receiving his second major art shipment from Europe, on 23 and 24 April 1878 Cottier organised a public auction of his art stock at Leavitt Art Rooms, then at the corner of Broadway and 12th Street.[15] The sale took place 'under the direction' of the New York art dealer Samuel Putnam Avery, whose gallery was nearby at 86 Fifth Avenue.[16] The *New York Times*, which featured a lengthy review of the collection offered at the auction, called it 'by all odds the finest collection of modern masters ever brought together in this country'. And the reviewer went on, 'It is no little thing to have a firm in New York which exhibits so much taste in the selection of pictures as Cottier & Co.; if the report that they intend to give up this part of their business be true, the news will cause much regret among artists and lovers of art in New York'.[17] This remark in the *New York Times*, which was confirmed in the introductory pages of the auction catalogue,[18] raises the question of Cottier's reason for the auction. Although we now know that he did not give up his art gallery, why did he put what seems like his entire inventory on the auction block barely more than a year after opening his gallery? Had he over-extended and consequently run into cash-flow problems? Perhaps. Yet it is also possible, even

117 Adolphe Monticelli, *Don Quixote and Sancho Panza* (previously called *Don Quixote and Sancho approaching the Duchess and her Friends*), 1865. Oil on canvas, 96.5 × 130 cm. Musée d'Orsay, Paris

likely, that Cottier saw the auction as a way to at once publicise and reduce his stock before acquiring and shipping over new paintings from Europe. As Thomas Bayer and John Page have shown in their writings about the nineteenth-century art market, 'the business of retailing in luxury goods demanded the continuous refreshment of a well-diversified inventory'.[19] Other dealers also periodically organised auctions to trim down their stock.

From Avery's annotated copy of the auction catalogue, now in the Metropolitan Museum in New York, we know that of the 163 works at auction, approximately two thirds were retained or bought back by Cottier or his representatives.[20] This has led several scholars to interpret the auction as a failure, even an 'utter disaster'.[21] However, if the auction was indeed intended as a way to gain publicity and reduce (but not eliminate) his stock, its outcome may have been exactly what Cottier intended. In addition, the auction may have been a way to set some baseline prices for the works of artists who were still relatively unknown in the United States.

It is not clear whether the Cottier art rooms closed, temporarily, after the 1878 auction. But in September 1879, the critic for *Art Interchange* reported on the arrival of several new paintings at Cottier & Co., including a 'fine Monticelli' entitled *An Oriental Scene*, two paintings by the Swedish painter Carl Fredrik Hill, a distant follower of Corot; *Forest Scene* by Diaz, *Ville d'Avray* by Corot and *Milking Time* by Anton Mauve.[22] An article in the *New York Times* of 1 September focused in particular on the paintings by Monticelli and Diaz.[23] The reviewer claimed that Cottier & Co. was the first dealer to 'have had the audacity to import specimens of the handicraft of Monticelli, a painter as mysterious as any of his mysterious pictures'. At the end of the review, the critic also referred to some of the other pictures in

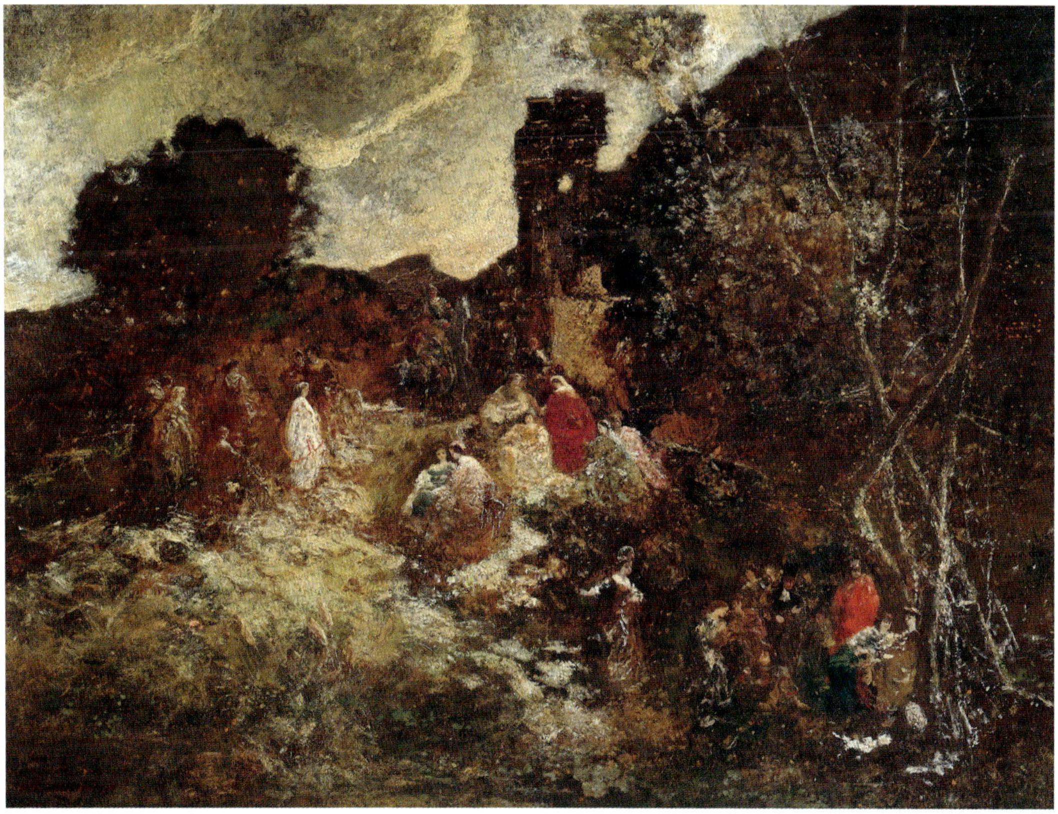

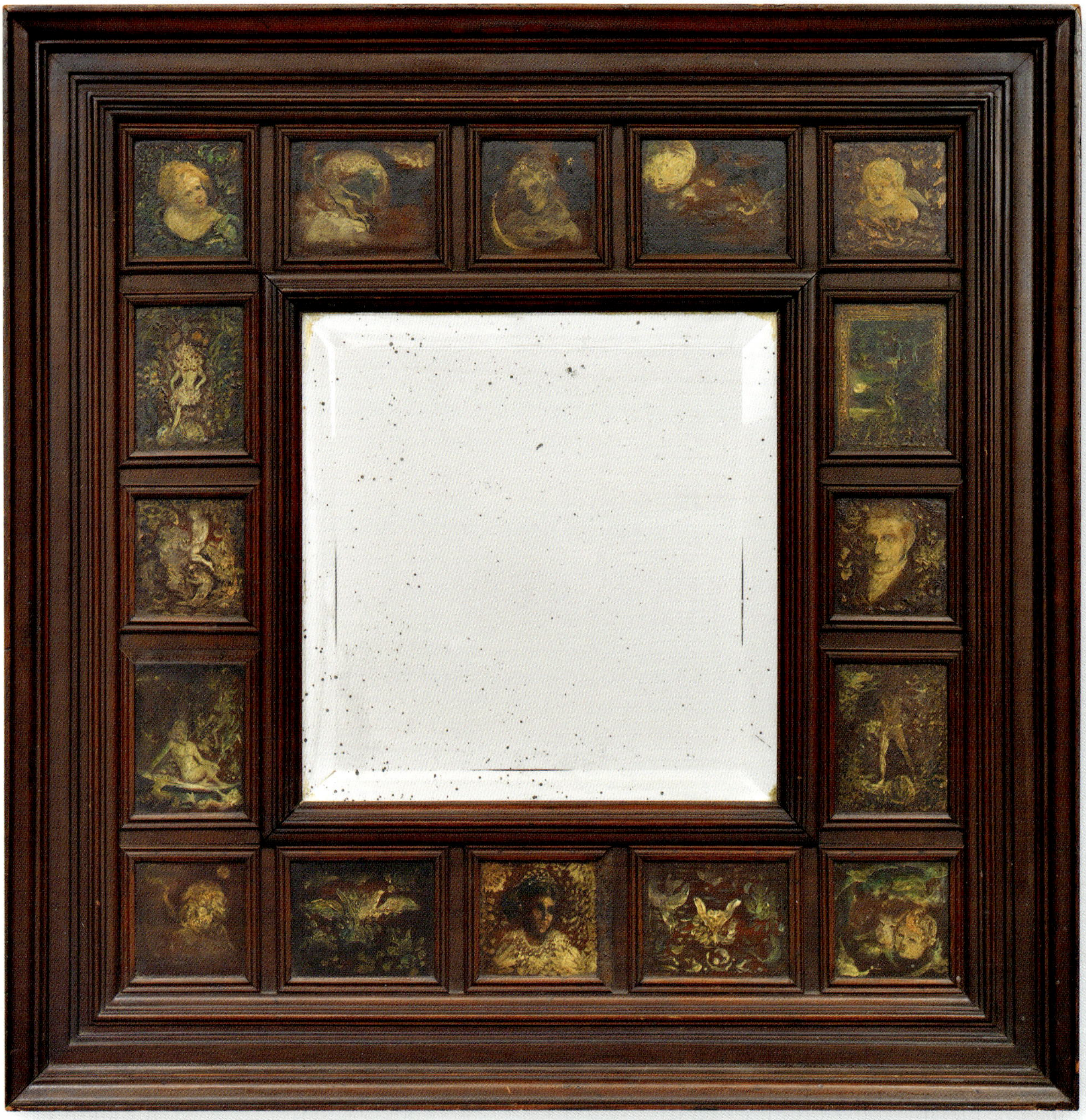

the exhibition – a 'melancholic' landscape by Georges Michel, a view of the 'Zuyder Zee' by Théophile de Bock – and, last but not least, a mirror in a frame decorated by Albert Pinkham Ryder with little painted panels, 'each remarkable for its individual fantastic charm'. This is no doubt the frame entitled *The Culprit Fay* (fig. 118), commissioned by Cottier on behalf of the writer Charles de Kay. The latter had ordered the framed mirror as a present for the sixtieth birthday of his mother, Janet Halleck Drake de Kay. The scenes painted on the mirror frame were inspired by *The Culprit Fay*, the famous narrative poem by Janet's father, the poet Joseph Rodman Drake (1795–1820), who is portrayed on the right side of the mirror frame.[24] The presence of this object in Cottier's art rooms deserves to be mentioned firstly because it was the token American work in the exhibition and secondly because it was a useful domestic object decorated with miniature paintings, thus connecting Cottier's two businesses, the fine and decorative arts.

In 1883 Cottier sent sixty-eight paintings to the Pedestal Fund Art Loan exhibition at the National Academy of Design in New York (nos 86–143 and 184–93). This exhibition, composed of loans of fine

118 Albert Pinkham Ryder, *The Culprit Fay*, 1878–9. Mirror frame, oil on wood, 51.4 × 51.6 cm. Whitney Museum of American Art, New York, Joan Whitney Payson Bequest

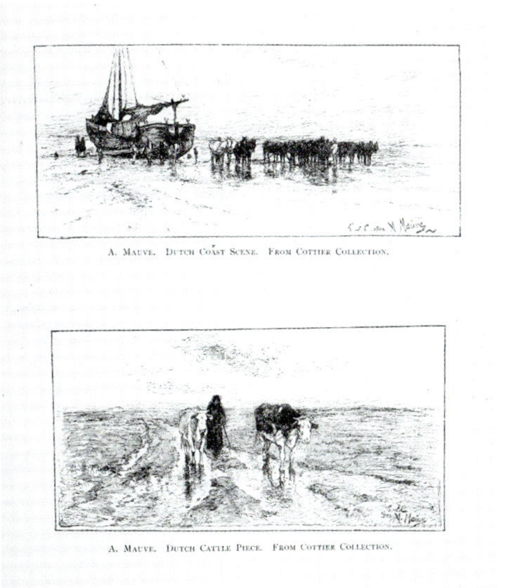

119 Catalogue of the Pedestal Fund Art Loan Exhibition, New York, 1883, p. 25

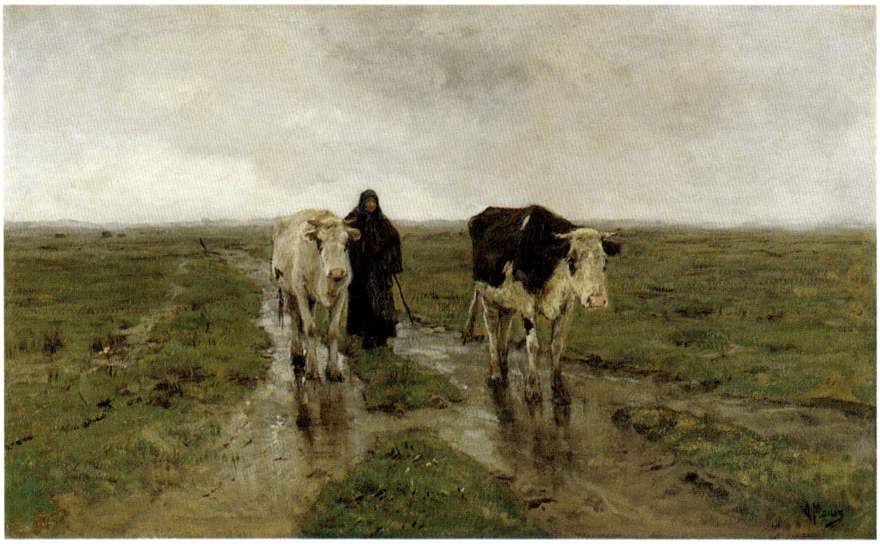

120 Anton Mauve, *Changing Pasture* (previously called *Dutch Cattle Piece*), early 1880s. Oil on canvas, 61 × 100.6 cm. Metropolitan Museum of Art, New York, bequest of Benjamin Altman, 1913

and decorative arts, was organised to raise funds for the pedestal of the Statue of Liberty. Cottier had many contacts among the organisers of the exhibition. Serving on the executive committee were a number of artists he had befriended, including William Gedney Bunce, John La Farge and Olin Warner. The last also served on the painting and sculpture committee, together with Augustus Saint-Gaudens and J. Alden Weir, who were likewise among Cottier's friends (more on them shortly). Any one of these could have approached him to loan works to the exhibition, something Cottier may have been eager to do as it meant publicity for his art rooms. What is more, Cottier may have been instrumental in convincing Ichabod Williams, a major client, to lend works to the exhibition as well. A third major lender was the collector Erwin Davis, a friend of Weir, whose bachelor party that same year was attended by Davis, as well as by Cottier, Inglis, Charles McKim, Saint-Gaudens and Warner – a small world, indeed. Together, Cottier, Davis and Williams lent 120 paintings to the Pedestal Fund exhibition, nearly two thirds of the total number of works shown.[25]

A *New York Times* review of the exhibition in December 1883 called the picture show the most 'impressive' part of the Pedestal Exhibition.[26] The critic compared it with an exhibition of '100 modern masterpieces lately shown in Paris' (in the Galerie Georges Petit)[27] and called the Pedestal Exhibition 'not far behind that in interest'. In certain ways, he argued, New York surpassed Paris, particularly in the strong presence of the work of Monticelli. His paintings, according to the reviewer, 'cannot be seen in France because Mr. Daniel Cottier has a practical monopoly of his work'. The *New York Times* reviewer also specifically mentioned the importance of Williams and Davis as lenders to the show. Thanks to them and a few other lenders, like Avery, Catharine Lorillard Wolfe, Richard Morris Hunt, William Schaus and Albert Spencer, the painting room, according to the reviewer, was 'occupied by the pictures of men whom the best French critics now agree to call the greatest masters of the century'.

The works that were present in the exhibition are difficult to identify on the basis of the catalogue entries, which for the most part give generic titles and provide no dimensions. A small number of paintings, nine to be exact, were reproduced in the form of etchings in the catalogue (fig. 119). Six of them were Cottier loans. They included Mauve's *Dutch Cattle Piece*, now called *Changing Pasture* (fig. 120),[28] and two paintings called *Dutch Coast Scene* by the same artist, which cannot be identified.[29] Among the works loaned by Cottier that can be identified on the basis

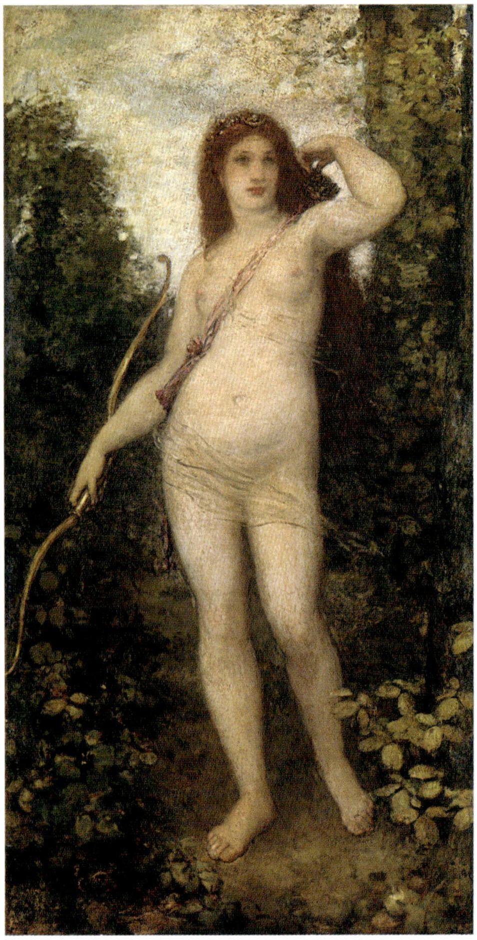

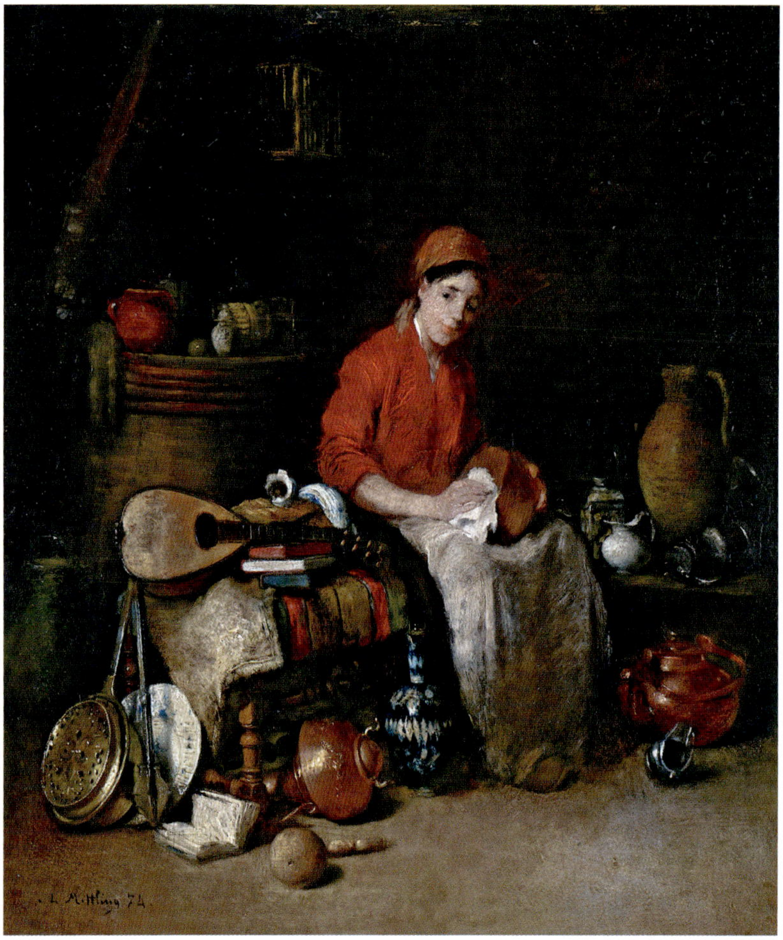

of their titles and descriptions in newspaper reviews was the large *Diana* by Georges Bellenger, 'enhanced' by Matthijs Maris (fig. 121). Corot's *Orpheus*, by 1883 emblematic of Cottier's New York gallery, was also in the exhibition, as were Monticelli's *Gateway to a Fort* (fig. 123) and Mettling's *Among the Curios* (fig. 122).[30]

After 1883, Cottier's Art Rooms received less attention in the press. The reasons for this are difficult to determine. Cottier and Inglis may not have been as active in promoting the gallery because it was by then established and well known. It is also possible that the firm imported fewer new paintings from Europe due to the increased tariffs imposed on art imports in 1883.[31] Moreover, by 1883, Cottier & Co. was no longer alone in promoting the Hague School artists and Monticelli since other dealers such as Knoedler & Co. and Schaus Art Galleries had caught up with him. Nevertheless, as late as 1888, on the occasion of the death of the Hague School artist Anton Mauve, whose reputation Cottier had launched in America, the critic Montague Marks ('Montezuma') summed up Cottier's importance for New York. Marks acknowledged Cottier's essential role in introducing Americans to the art of Mauve and the painters of the Hague School: 'Cottier ... was the first to introduce into the United States the work of this charming painter, as he was also the first to make us acquainted with Mauve's compatriots, Mesdag and the brothers Maris, to say nothing of Corot and Monticelli, for whom he was the American entrepreneur.'[32]

THE COTTIER GALLERY'S STOCK IN THE NEW YORK CONTEXT

In the absence of Cottier & Co. archives, we cannot form as clear a picture of what works came through the Cottier Gallery as we can in the case of dealers like Avery, Goupil & Cie or Knoedler & Co., whose stock books and/or archives have been preserved.[33] However, the catalogue of the auction mentioned in the previous section and those of the exhibitions to which Cottier & Co. loaned works,[34] as well as newspaper reviews of the works that could be seen in his gallery, all give a good idea of the artists whose works the firm promoted in North America. Among them, foremost, were the painters of the Barbizon School, especially Corot and Daubigny.[35] In this respect, Cottier was no

121 Georges Bellenger and Matthijs Maris, *Diana*, *c.*1878–83. Oil on canvas, 199.4 × 103.8 cm. Glasgow Museums

122 Louis Mettling, *Among the Curios* (currently known as *Cleaning Pots*), 1874. Oil on canvas, 44.5 × 38.7 cm. National Gallery of Canada, Ottawa

123 Adolphe Monticelli, *Gateway to a Fort*, *c.*1867. Oil on canvas, 40 × 60.6 cm. Musée des Beaux-Arts, Montreal, Adeline Van Horne Bequest

innovator. Other New York dealers, including Avery, Knoedler and Schaus, sold works by these artists as well, though perhaps not with the same conviction. By contrast, Cottier virtually launched the reputations of the artists of the Hague School in the United States.[36]

In addition to the works by artists of the Barbizon and Hague schools, most (though not all) of whom concentrated on landscape paintings, Cottier also favoured the works of a number of genre painters, specifically, Bonvin, Mettling, Monticelli, Roybet and Théodule Ribot. Among these, Monticelli was the artist Cottier promoted most vigorously. For several years he had a monopoly on the sale of his works, both in London and New York.[37] As seen in Chapter Three, he sourced Monticelli's paintings from a Paris dealer by the name of Gérard and possibly as well from Joseph Delarebeyrette, who acquired Monticelli's paintings through Pierre Piquet, a friend of the artist in Marseille. It is possible that Cottier himself also visited Monticelli there, buying paintings directly from the artist. Several of Monticelli's paintings that Cottier brought over to America were substantially touched up by Matthijs Maris, probably because they were unfinished or damaged in transit from Paris (or Marseille) to London. These works were sold as Maris-Monticelli or as 'Monticelli and Maris', much to Maris's chagrin (as noted in Chapter Three).

Cottier did not show many works by British artists in his New York gallery. Exception must be made for the French-British watercolourist Jules Lessore (1849–1892), whose father, Emile Lessore, was a well-known ceramic artist working for Minton's. Occasionally, works by other artists from Britain went through his hands. The catalogue of the Pedestal exhibition lists works by W. Reynolds, William E. Lockhart and Hugh Cameron.[38]

A rare essay by Cottier on the art he favoured is found in the catalogue of the auction he organised in New York in 1878. There Cottier stressed that his collection had been formed over many years, though

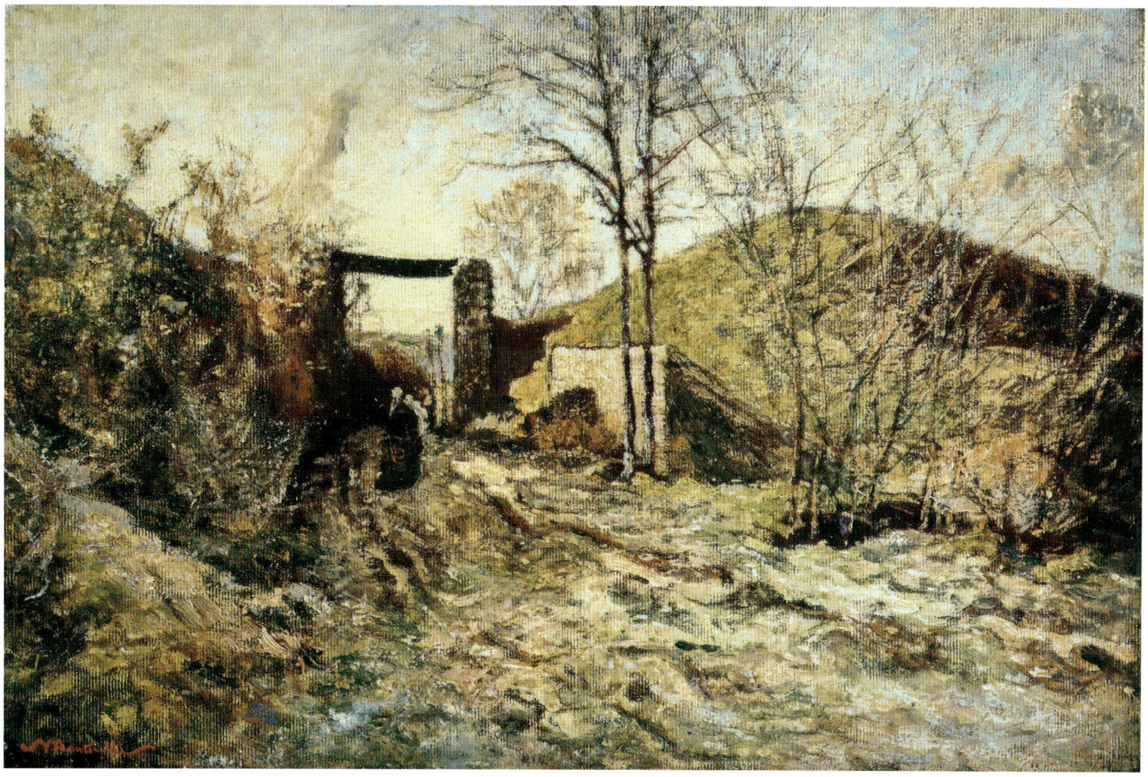

124 Matthijs Maris, *Christening at Lausanne*, 1873. Oil on canvas, 66.3 × 50.5 cm. Centraal Museum, Utrecht

it had recently been enriched by paintings bought at the famous Sensier sale.[39] The best works in his stock were by what he called 'the great modern classic painters departed' – Millet, Corot, Diaz, Michel, Troyon and Daubigny – 'upon whose works ... [the] stamp of genius rests securely'. Added to these were paintings by contemporary artists – Roybet, Ribot, Mettling, Charles Jacque, Dupré, Hill, Vollon and Bonvin – 'living men ... [who] give us the hope that art will rise anew'. Cottier also stressed the importance of Dutch contemporary art: 'Certainly in no land save Holland stands there such a phalanx of true painters'. Having learned at once from the French and from their own painting traditions, many contemporary Dutch artists, according to Cottier, 'stand as first in the art of painting' and, like the younger generation of French artists, 'are bound to bring an earnest revival in true art'.[40]

Throughout his career as a dealer, Cottier stuck closely to his initial choices – Barbizon School, Hague School, and Monticelli. He knew what he liked and was a proselytiser of his own taste, so much so that, as Henley remarked in his introduction to the catalogue of the 1892 posthumous sale of Cottier's collection, 'As a critic he could see no more than what appealed to him, and would underrate good work enough if it lacked the qualities he loved'. Henley characterised this taste as 'Let the colour be right, the arrangement large in purpose and effect, the handling quick and free and essential'.[41] Indeed, Cottier appears to have liked works that were loosely and rapidly painted. As for the 'right colour', with the exception of Monticelli, Cottier preferred paintings done in dark and muted hues, such as the tonal landscapes of the Hague School; the dark Riberesque palette of Ribot, the silvery landscapes of Corot. These, as already mentioned in Chapter Three, seemed to have suited the interiors that Cottier designed and furnished.

A group of three 'business card' advertisements in *The Critic* of 17 January 1885 promote 'Messrs. Cottier & Co., Domestic Artistic Furniture makers', 'Messrs. Cottier & Co., High-class interior Decoration. Artists in Stained Glass' and 'At Messrs. Cottier & Co.'s, Imported pictures highest class'. All three list the same address, 144 Fifth Avenue. This suggests that Cottier's three businesses, though separate, were also intimately connected. As an interior designer and furnisher, as well as a dealer, Cottier must have been aware of the challenge presented by the integration of paintings in the interiors of the last twenty years of the nineteenth century, when Aestheticism dictated elaborate panelled or sometimes papered dadoes, walls that were stencilled or covered with richly patterned wallpapers and colourful friezes and cornices. It is perhaps for that reason that he shied away from paintings with bright colours and illusionistic perspective, which could easily clash with their surroundings, and instead focused on loosely painted tonal paintings. A photograph of an interior designed by Cottier & Co. (with Richard Codman) for John Charles Phillips (1838–1885), a businessman in Boston (fig. 125), shows a single rural scene with peasants and sheep that is in the manner of the Barbizon painters. It is not known whether the painting was bought from Cottier but it looks like the kind of rural scene in tonal colours that he promoted. Displayed against an ornate wall covering, and hung right above the dado, the painting is set in a simple frame, quite different from the heavy Baroque frames that were popular in America in the middle of the nineteenth century. Clearly, the painting and its frame were carefully selected to harmonise with their surroundings.

COTTIER AND CO.'S ART CLIENTELE

Little is known about the identity of the collectors who bought art at Cottier's. Like most dealers, Cottier seems to have done a certain amount of business with other dealers, such as Avery and Knoedler.[42] The absence of stock books makes a general overview of the private clients who bought art from him difficult. Avery's annotations in the 1878 auction catalogue of Cottier's stock indicate that most buyers were living in New York and, it seems, not far from Cottier's gallery.[43] Cottier had chosen his location carefully, in the downtown area of New York which was then inhabited not by the super-rich but by the well-to-do businessmen and industrialists who could afford the art that he was selling.

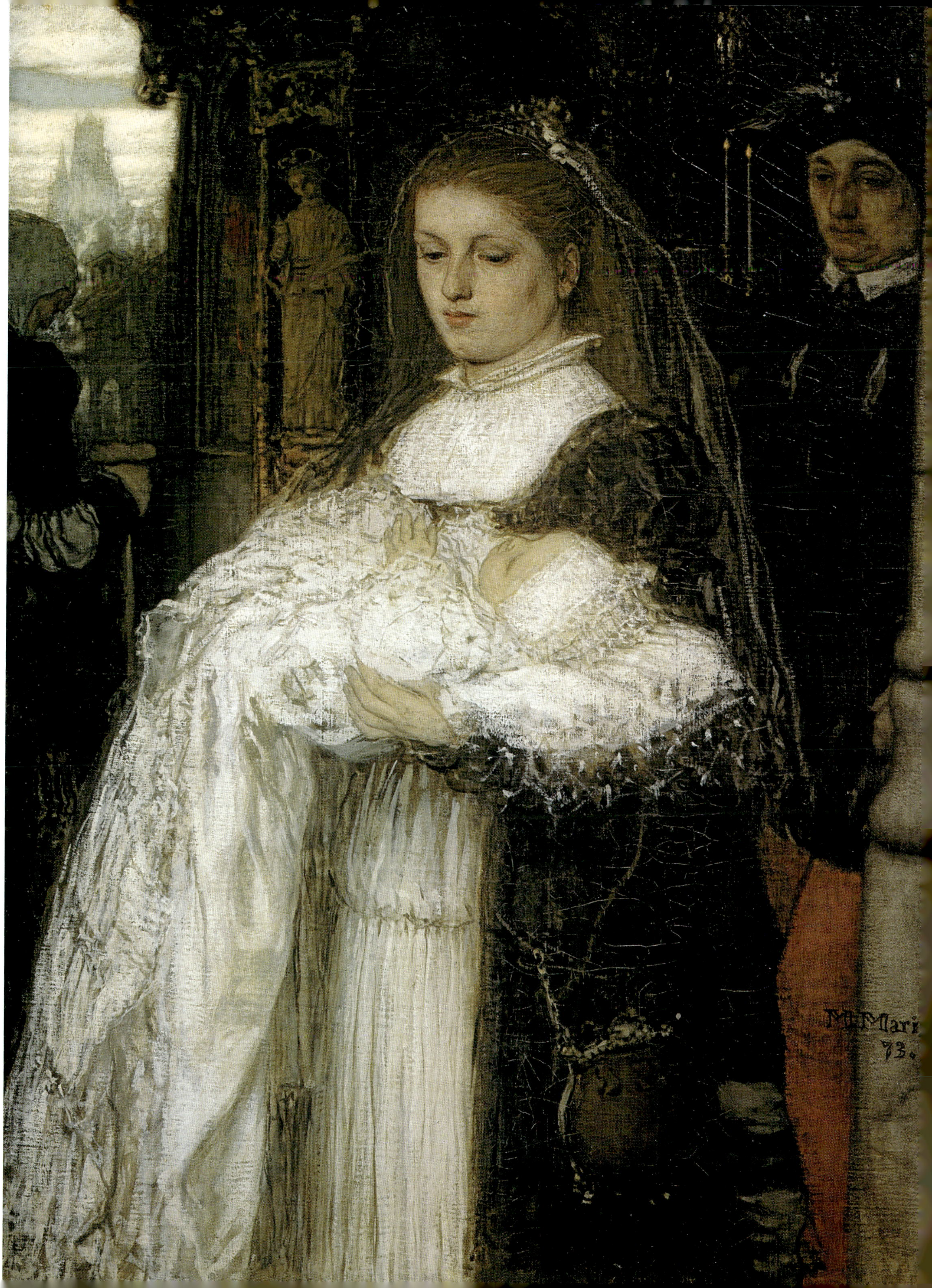
Mari
73.

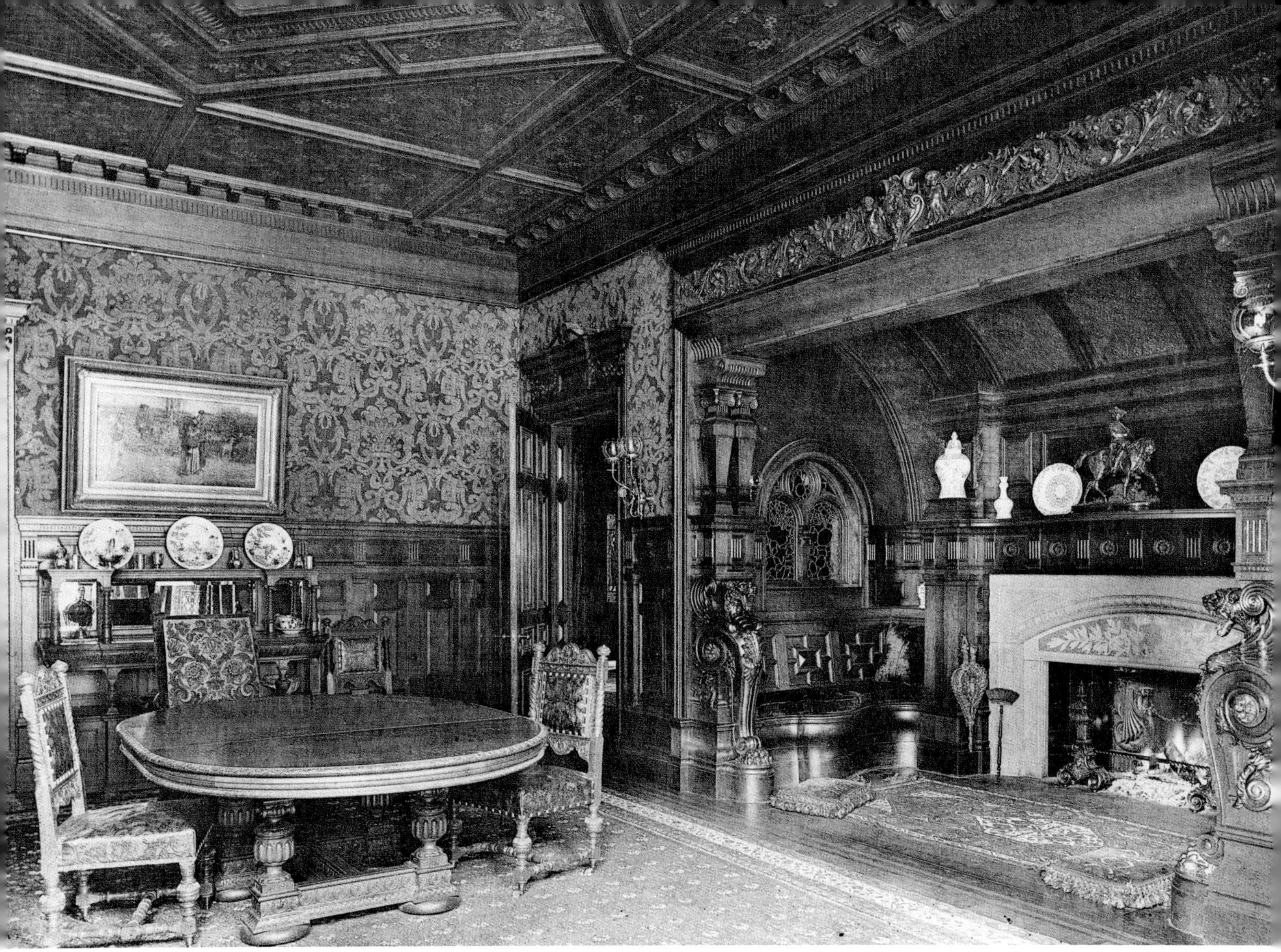

Indeed, while Cottier is known to have sold works to the great, wealthy collectors of the time, such as the Havemeyers (to whom, in 1888, he sold two pendant portraits by Rembrandt for the extraordinary sum of $60,000), John G. Johnson,[44] and Mary J. Sexton Morgan, his major client, Ichabod T. Williams was affluent (but not extremely so) and, like most of Cottier's clients in Britain, largely a self-made man. As described in Chapter Four, Williams was a supplier of wood to the Cottier cabinetmaking workshop and became Cottier's close friend; his son Lloyd married Cottier's daughter Margaret. It is not known when Williams became interested in buying art from Cottier but it was probably soon after Cottier launched his gallery. Williams eventually acquired a substantial collection of contemporary paintings. These were auctioned off by his heirs in 1915, sixteen years after his death.[45] Of the 117 paintings offered for sale, 54 were bought 'from the late Daniel Cottier', according to the catalogue. Another 23 were bought from 'Messrs Cottier & Co.', which probably means that they were acquired after Daniel Cottier's death in 1891. While it is remarkable that Williams bought almost two thirds of his collection from one gallery, it is equally remarkable that mention of this is made in the auction catalogue, as in most such catalogues of the period the provenance of the works is not mentioned. It suggests that even in 1915 the fact that the paintings had gone through the hands of Cottier or Cottier & Co. was still seen as a value-adding factor. The paintings bought from 'the late Daniel Cottier' were characteristic of Cottier's stock: the majority were by painters of the Barbizon and Hague Schools and by Cottier's favourite French figure painters – Bonvin, Mettling, Monticelli, Ribot and Roybet. Only 11 out of the total of about 80 paintings that had been bought from Cottier or Cottier & Co. were American, including 4 by Henry Muhrman, 3 by George Fuller and 2 each by Bunce and Ryder.

125 Dining room in the J. C. Phillips House, Boston, designed by 'Messrs. Cottier' and Richard Codman, reproduced in *Artistic Houses*, vol. 2, 1884, p. 231

Williams's strong reliance on Cottier to build his collection is striking but not entirely unusual. Several collectors of the turn of the century relied heavily on one or a few dealers to form their collections. Perhaps not all had such a close relationship with those from whom they bought their art. The sea captain John Robinson, in *Art in America* of June 1925, recalled a gathering at Williams's house that suggests the intimacy that existed between Williams and Cottier, as well as James Inglis and some of Cottier's artist friends:

In those days, Mr. Ichabod Williams used to like to have Mr. Cottier and some old friends to visit him on Sunday evenings, amongst whom would be Mr. Jas. S. Inglis, Olin Warner, and Albert Ryder; and on a few occasions I was asked with them. Williams entertained us in his splendid picture gallery (he had a very fine collection).[46]

The description is interesting not only because it suggests Williams's close friendship with Cottier but also because it shows that Williams had his artworks concentrated in a single gallery space, rather than hung all over the house. In this he may have been inspired by the example of more famous American collectors of his day, such as William Vanderbilt. It is also possible that he was advised to do so by Cottier, who had designed a gallery for the collection of John Forbes White in Aberdeen (see Chapter Three, p. 70).

We know little about other major clients of Cottier & Co. An article in the *New York Times* of 5 February 1905, reviewing the sale of five collections, mentions that a Mrs Sarah Conklin, the deceased owner of one of the collections, 'had the benefit of the advice of the late Daniel Cottier in many of her purchases and was introduced by him to the modern Dutch school'. The collection included works by Artz, Jozef Israëls, Mauve and the Maris brothers, as well as by the French artists Corot, Harpignies, Millet and Vollon. It also featured three small Ryders, 'paintings ... not likely to fetch much because the artist is still living, still painting, still finishing a painting now and then', according to the critic.[47] Conklin may have been the typical Cottier client – not an important collector but someone who liked to decorate her home with contemporary art.

Although Cottier's clientele was concentrated in New York, he did have customers elsewhere. Unlike New York collectors such as Ichabod Williams and Sarah Conklin, who heavily relied on the firm for advice, many of those outside New York were wealthy collectors who cast a wide net in building their collections, buying from numerous dealers in Europe as well as America. Mention has already been made of John G. Johnson, who lived in Philadelphia. Another customer in that city was Peter A. B. Widener, who in 1894 bought Manet's *Dead Toreador* (*c.*1864; National Gallery of Art, Washington D.C.) from Cottier & Co.[48] The firm also had customers in Canada, especially Montreal, though it is not always clear whether the Canadian collectors dealt with the London or the New York branch or both. It is known that Cottier & Co. in New York had multiple dealings with William Cornelius Van Horne, Montreal's biggest collector, whose interests included fossils, Japanese ceramics and contemporary and Old Master paintings. As the Van Horne family archives in Toronto make clear, Van Horne bought from multiple dealers in London, Paris, the US and elsewhere. He appears to have turned to Cottier especially for contemporary French paintings, buying among other works Monticelli's *Gateway to a Fort*.[49] Cottier also introduced Van Horne to Ryder, from whom the collector bought three works.[50] Van Horne continued to have periodic contacts with Cottier & Co. even after Cottier's death. The Van Horne Family Archive in Toronto contains letters to James Inglis as well as Walter Fearon.[51]

While Van Horne was interested in French art, especially the Impressionists, the industrialist and amateur scholar Edward Black Greenshields, also in Montreal, focused nearly exclusively on Hague School painting, even writing a book about the subject.[52] By the time he started collecting in the early twentieth century, Montreal had several contemporary art dealers and Greenshields bought many works from a local dealer called William Scott & Sons. However, his most famous Hague School painting, *The Christening at Lausanne* (see fig. 124) by Matthijs Maris, was bought from Cottier & Co. in 1906.[53]

126 Olin Levi Warner, *Portrait of Isabella ('Ella') Cottier*, 1882. Plaster, h. 51.7 cm. Smithsonian American Art Museum, Washington, D.C., Gift of Mrs Carlyle Jones

127 (a and b) Invitation to the exhibition at Cottier & Co. of 'works of some of the most noted, as well as some of the younger artists of New York and Boston', 1875. Richard Gilder papers, New York Public Library

COTTIER AND CONTEMPORARY AMERICAN ART

Like most of his dealer colleagues in the 1870s and 80s, Cottier had few American paintings in his stock, despite the fact that he had a number of American painters among his close friends, including Bunce, Ryder and Weir. Many if not all of these artists at one time or another lived in the Benedick Building, an apartment block on Washington Square.[54] It is tempting to think that Cottier may have had a pied-à-terre there himself, where he could have stayed during his extensive visits to the United States. His involvement with the inhabitants of the building is clear from the fact that he decorated Weir's first New York studio in the Benedick, described later by the American author C. E. S. Wood as follows:

Weir had a studio in the Benedick Building which was inhabited by a group such as Bunce, Eaton, Low, Saint-Gaudens, and Warner. This was about 1882. As Weir and I have looked around the bare studios of his later years – warm gray walls, a chair for the model on the movable platform, one easel, a perfectly plain folding screen, and nothing else, we have laughed at the luxurious studio of the young man just back from Paris fitted up by Cottier – velvets, tapestries, brocades, Gothic cabinet, Louis Quatorze chairs, a couch, rugs, armor, a full length copy of a Velasquez by Weir himself over the mantel, and a great yellow Venetian glass bowl filled with goldfish and hung by brass chains from a rough ceiling of darkest blue studded with stars of varying magnitudes and one impossible comet all exceedingly decorative.

Weir had colored his windows to imitate stained glass and altogether it was a studio out of a French novel, but I need not say that, though elegant, luxurious, even sensuous, it was in perfect taste.[55]

Cottier was also friendly with two sculptors living in the Benedick, Augustus Saint-Gaudens and, especially, Olin Levi Warner. From 1877 to autumn 1879, Cottier gave Warner the use of a room as a studio on the premises of Cottier & Co. At the time, Warner made two portrait busts of Cottier and Inglis (see figs 80 and 81) Later he also modelled the heads of his two daughters Isabella ('Ella', 1882; fig. 126) and Margaret ('Peggy', 1890).[56] Alden Weir painted several family portraits, including *Portrait of Miss Cottier*, 'a piece of perfect workmanship', shown at the 1881 Academy exhibition.[57]

While Cottier seems to have had several close American artist friends, whom he helped in numerous ways, he does not appear to have shown many of their works in his gallery. We have seen that a token American work might be present in his exhibits but few American works were part of his stock. This is the more interesting as in April 1875, two years before the opening of the Cottier Gallery in 1877 and not long after he had established Cottier & Co. in New York, he temporarily ceded space in his building to a group of young American artists, who had become dissatisfied with the exhibition policies of the American Academy

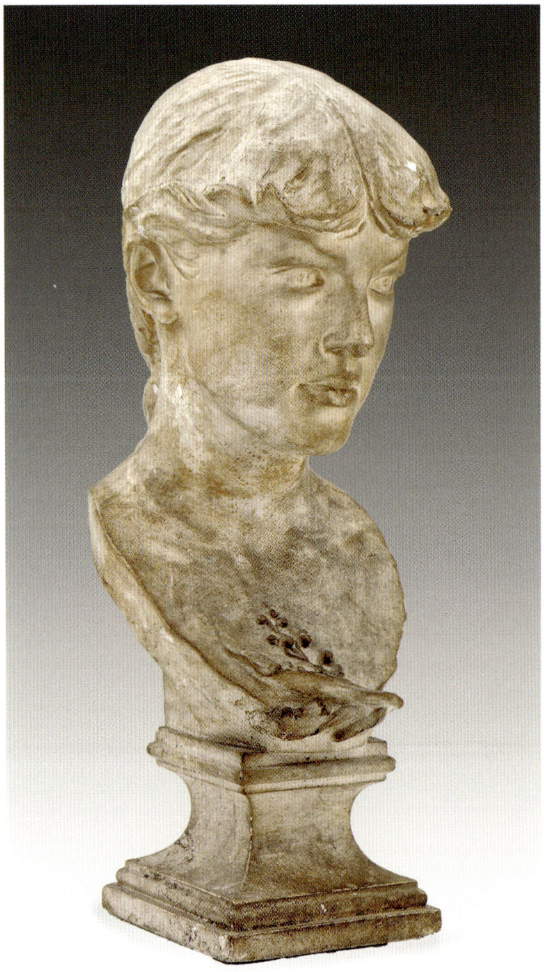

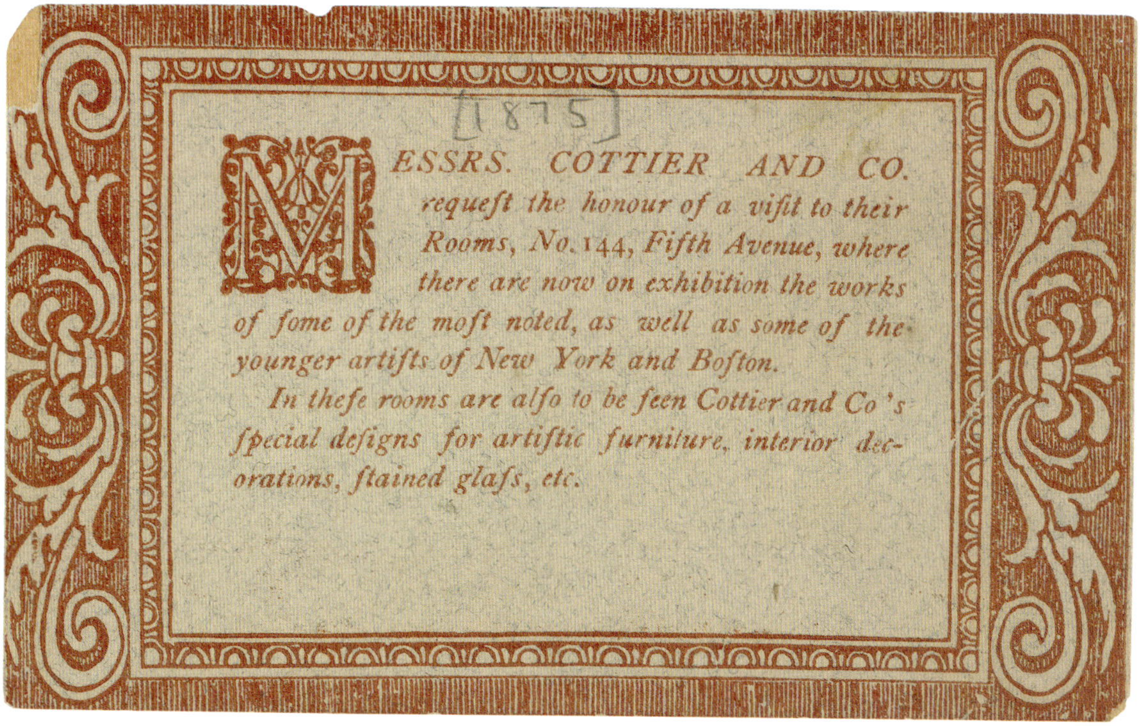

[1875]

MESSRS. COTTIER AND CO. requeſt the honour of a viſit to their Rooms, No. 144, Fifth Avenue, where there are now on exhibition the works of ſome of the moſt noted, as well as some of the younger artiſts of New York and Boſton.

In theſe rooms are alſo to be ſeen Cottier and Co.'s ſpecial deſigns for artiſtic furniture, interior decorations, ſtained glaſs, etc.

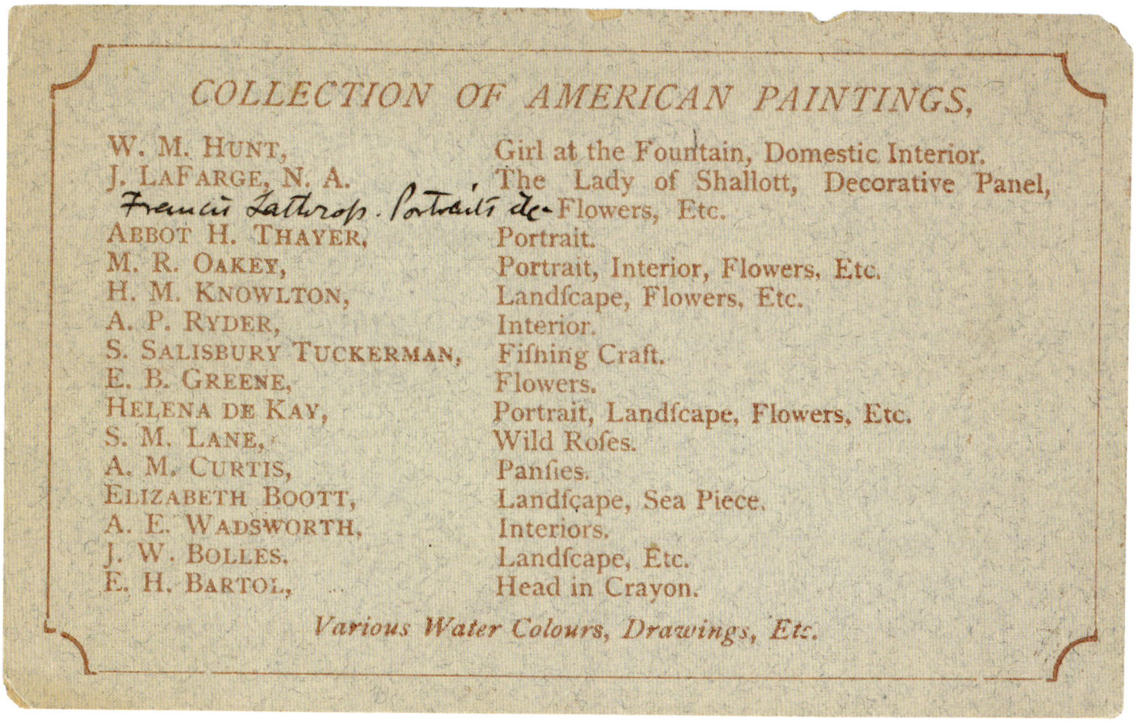

COLLECTION OF AMERICAN PAINTINGS,

W. M. HUNT,	Girl at the Fountain, Domestic Interior.
J. LAFARGE, N. A.	The Lady of Shallott, Decorative Panel,
Francis Lathrop. Portraits &c.	Flowers, Etc.
ABBOT H. THAYER,	Portrait.
M. R. OAKEY,	Portrait, Interior, Flowers, Etc.
H. M. KNOWLTON,	Landſcape, Flowers, Etc.
A. P. RYDER,	Interior.
S. SALISBURY TUCKERMAN,	Fiſhing Craft.
E. B. GREENE,	Flowers.
HELENA DE KAY,	Portrait, Landſcape, Flowers, Etc.
S. M. LANE,	Wild Roſes.
A. M. CURTIS,	Panſies.
ELIZABETH BOOTT,	Landſcape, Sea Piece.
A. E. WADSWORTH,	Interiors.
J. W. BOLLES,	Landſcape, Etc.
E. H. BARTOL,	Head in Crayon.

Various Water Colours, Drawings, Etc.

of Design. His motivation may have been dual, to attract attention to his furniture showrooms and help young artist friends. Indeed, the invitation card to the exhibition (figs 127a and b) informed recipients that they would be able to see the works of 'some of the most noted, as well as some of the younger artists of New York and Boston'; they were told as well that 'In these rooms are also to be seen Cottier and Co.'s special designs for artistic furniture, interior decorations, stained glass, etc.'.[58] The group was largely composed of the students of two European-trained artists, William Morris Hunt (who himself had studied with Jean-François Millet) and John La Farge (a student of Thomas Couture) and included, in addition to Hunt and La Farge themselves, such New York artists as Susan Carter, Helena de Kay Gilder, Francis Lathrop,

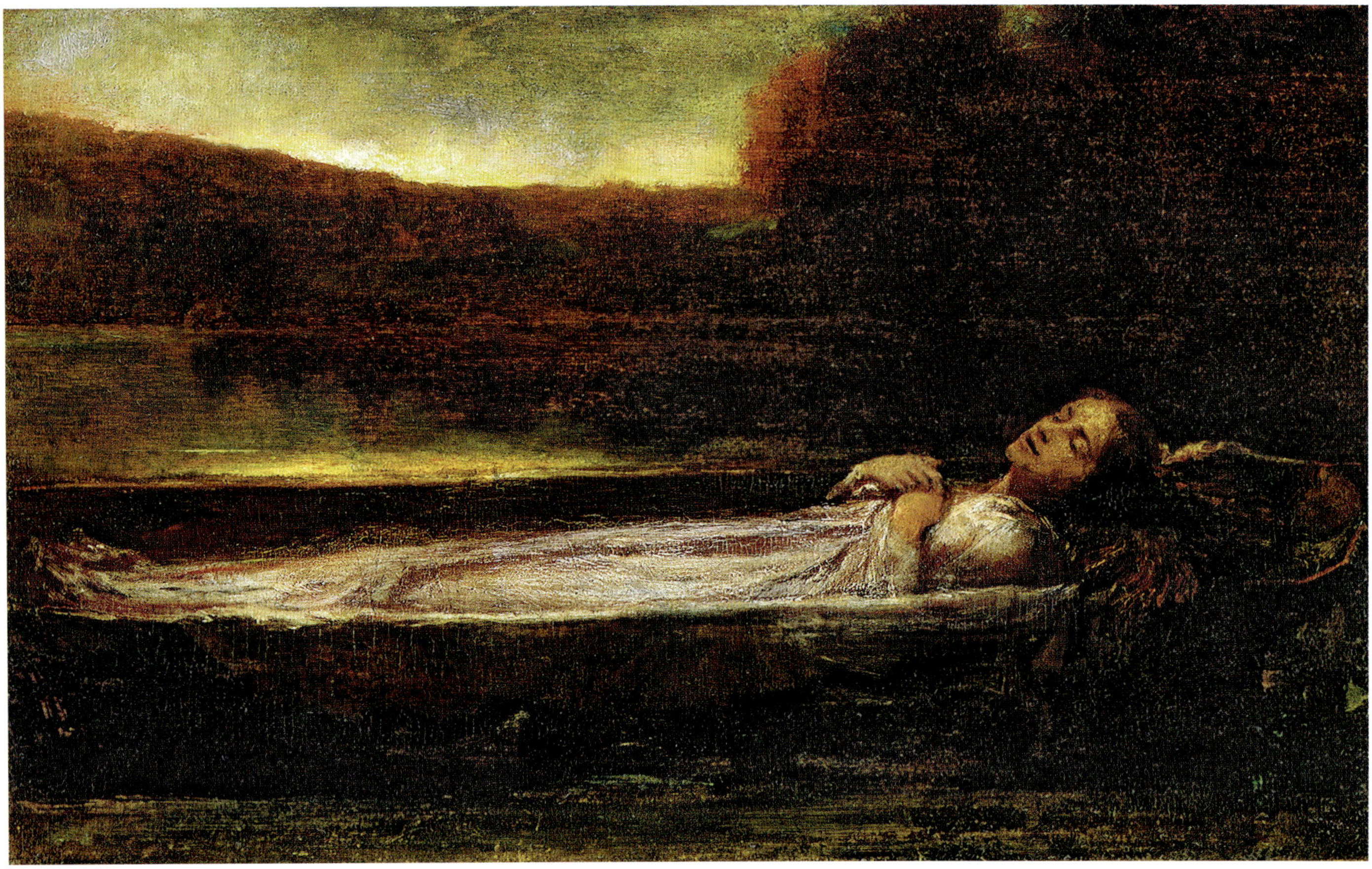

Maria Richards Oakey and Albert Pinkham Ryder, who were the instigators of the show, and a group of Boston artists, all students of Hunt and most of them female, including Elizabeth Howard Bartol, John W. Bolles, Elizabeth Boott, Alice M. Curtis, Elizabeth B. Greene, Helen Mary Knowlton, Susan Minot Lane, S. Salisbury Tuckerman and Adelaide Wadsworth.[59]

Among the paintings in the exhibition that can be traced is La Farge's *Lady of Shalott* (fig. 128), which was especially mentioned in Cottier's invitation to the opening.[60] The painting was widely reviewed, in some cases enthusiastically: a critic writing in *Scribner's Monthly* called it 'a serene and solemn picture-poem; to our thinking, no less important and individual than the poem with which it is associated'.[61] Others were more reserved: 'Mr. La Farge's "Lady of Shalott"', wrote a critic for the *New York Times*, 'is uncanny and repulsive; but perhaps the Tennyson fancy cannot be otherwise'.[62] La Farge also showed a decorative panel entitled *Fish* (Fogg Art Museum, Cambridge, Massachusetts), which he had previously exhibited at the National Academy of Design (1867).

Hunt showed a freely painted head study called *Priscilla* (which an anonymous critic writing in the *New York Evening Post* called 'unfinished'[63]). His *Girl at the Fountain* (fig. 129) may have been another work shown in the exhibition. It corresponds closely to the title and a description of a work mentioned in the *New York Times* review. In addition to these two works by the older artists in the group, the exhibition included numerous flower still lifes, a genre much practised by the women artists, as well as portraits and landscapes. Few of these can be identified with any certainty.

The exhibition was widely and positively reviewed, thanks in part to the efforts of Helena de Kay Gilder's husband, Richard Watson Gilder, who was an editor of *Scribner's Monthly* and had many contacts in the publishing world. The art critic of *Appleton's Journal* argued that the exhibition represented 'a new and fresh development of American art'[64] and his colleague at the Boston *Saturday Evening Gazette* went so far as to claim that the exhibition represented 'one of the most important art movements of the day'.[65] Clarence Cook, writing in the *New York Daily Tribune*, expressed the hope that 'before they [the works in the show] are removed they will have been visited by everyone in our city who is interested in the prosperity of Art in America'.[66] All critics saw the exhibition as a fresh new

128 John La Farge, *The Lady of Shalott*, *c.*1862. Oil on wood panel, 23.2 × 37.5 cm. Museum of American Art, New Britain, Connecticut, Harriet Russell Stanley Fund

129 William Morris Hunt, *Girl at the Fountain*, 1852–4. Oil on canvas, 116.8 × 90.2 cm. Metropolitan Museum of Art, New York, bequest of Jane Hunt, 1907

alternative to academic painting. Cook predicted that the Academy thenceforth would be more accepting of the young artists whose work had been shown in Cottier's space.[67] It did not quite turn out that way and the same year the group seceded from the Academy and formed the Society of American Artists.[68]

Despite Cottier's early support for young American artists and his friendship with many of them, he did not actively deal in their art, though he and Inglis did buy and commission works from them for their private collections, as noted earlier, and convinced some of their collector friends such as Williams to buy their works. Ryder's obituary in 1917 in *American Art News* clearly makes this point: 'The late Daniel Cottier was one of the first to appreciate Ryder's work and was long his sincere and earnest patron. Connoisseurs influenced by Mr. Cottier later became patrons, and all grew to be enthusiastic admirers of his art'.[69] The obituary, in particular, stresses the influence of Cottier and Inglis on collectors in Montreal, mentioning Van Horne, Greenshields and the Scottish-Canadian collector Richard Bladworth Angus.[70]

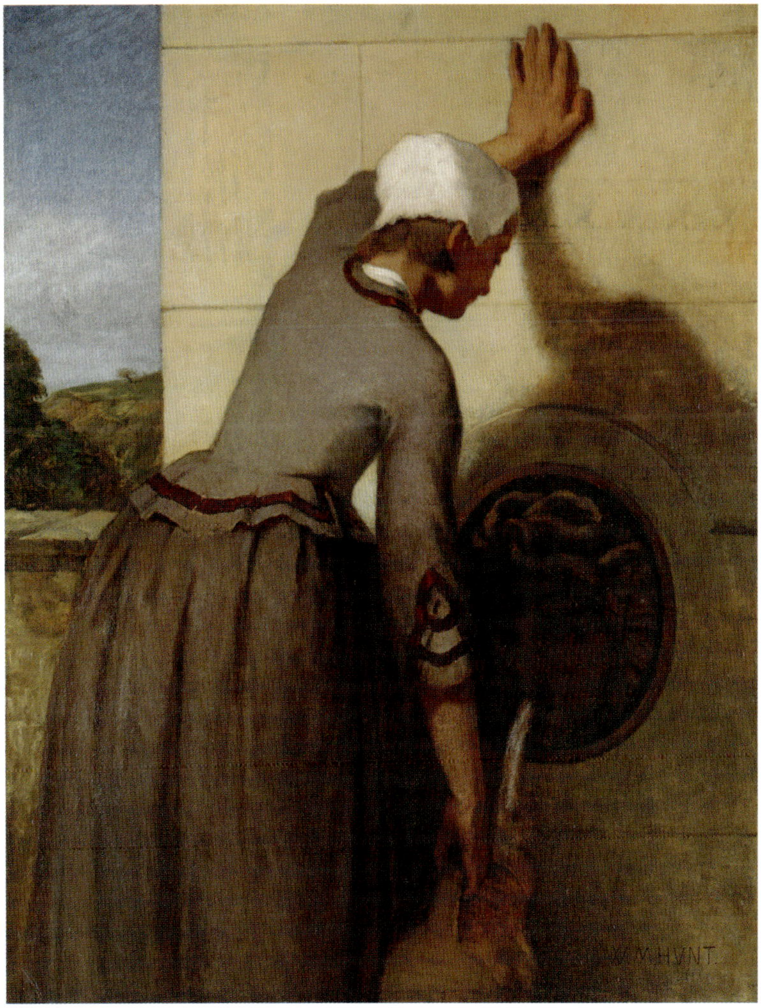

Ultimately, it seems, Cottier and his clientele did not think of contemporary American art as ready for the market. Inasmuch as they may have been sympathetic to young American artists and perhaps even interested in their artistic experiments, they did not see it as collectible, particularly from an investment point of view.

DEALER COLLECTOR

Rapid turnover was the name of the game in the nineteenth-century art market but Cottier often held on to works for a long time. Corot's *Orpheus greeting the Dawn* (see fig. 115), for example, first seen in the 1877 exhibition, was still in his possession at the time of his death. The reason for this 'holding on' is that Cottier was a dealer collector. From everything we know, he loved the works he acquired and was loath to part with them. However, there was another reason as well. As mentioned earlier, he was suffering from rheumatic heart disease and hoped that his collection could be a nest egg for his family: rather than investing in the stock market about which he 'knew nothing', he 'laid out such moneys as he could command in the wares in which he was most competent to deal – to be a provision for his wife and children'.[71] Thus Cottier at once bought and sold artworks and kept others for his private collection. In the absence of a Cottier archive, it is unclear how, administratively, he separated his private collection from the stock of Cottier & Co. But it appears that for the works he did not want to sell, he charged such high prices that no one in their right mind would buy them. When Lyon visited the New York gallery in 1886, he was astonished that for Corot's *Orpheus* Cottier asked £6000,[72] the equivalent of more than £785,000 in 2020.[73]

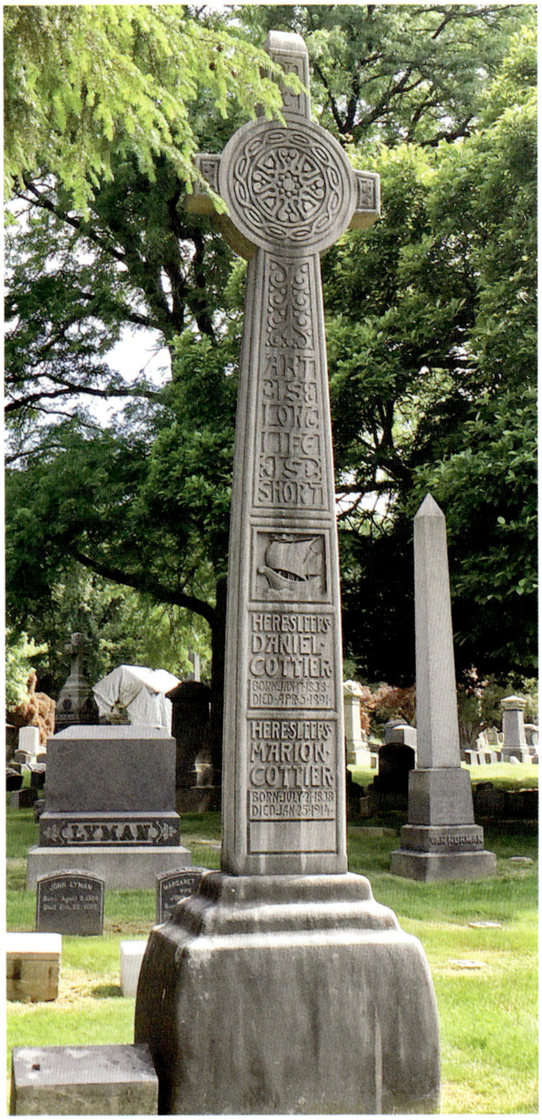

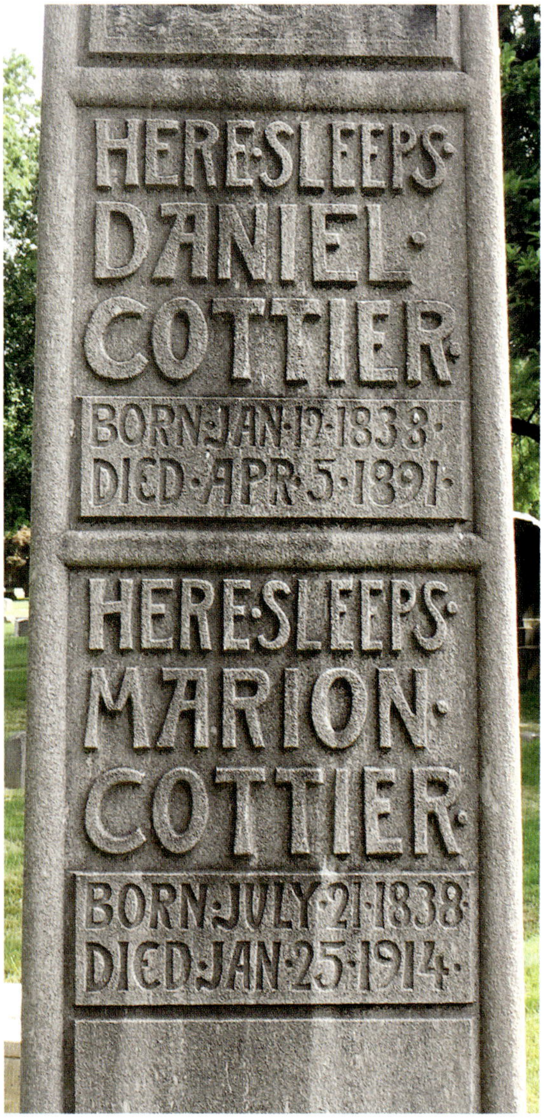

Cottier's pessimism about his lifespan proved justified. On 5 April 1891 he died from acute heart failure in Jacksonville, Florida.[74] He was buried in Woodlawn Cemetery in the Bronx, New York (figs 130a and b). A year later, a major auction of his collection was held in Paris under the auspices of the Durand-Ruel Gallery. The sale was accompanied by a beautiful bilingual catalogue with multiple photogravure reproductions and Henley's biographical essay on Cottier (fig. 131).[75] The catalogue also featured a portrait of Cottier by the Scottish artist William Brassey Hole, perhaps commissioned especially for the occasion. The auction drew an international clientele of knowledgeable buyers, including the Dutch painter William Mesdag, who bought Millet's unfinished *Hagar and Ishmael* (see fig. 61) for his choice collection of contemporary paintings. According to a review of the sale in *The Collector*, the auction 'realized a total of nearly $115,000, from two sessions'. The modern equivalent of this amount would be well over three million dollars.[76]

The death of Cottier did not spell the end of Cottier & Co. In New York the business continued under the direction of its manager, James Inglis, who at some point had become the partner and finally owner of the firm.[77] Inglis moved the showroom to 5 East 34th Street in 1895 and then to 3 East 40th in 1905,[78] perhaps because the New York art business was slowly moving uptown. When he died, on 13 December 1907, the direction of Cottier & Co. was assumed by Walter P. Fearon, who had already assisted Inglis in the later years of his life. On 11–13 March 1909 Fearon organised an auction of 'paintings and watercolors of old and modern masters and other property' in order to 'facilitate the settlement of the estate of the late James S. Inglis of Cottier and Company'. The sale, conducted by Thomas E. Kirby of the American Art Association,

130 (a and b) Gravestone of Daniel and Marion Cottier, Woodlawn Cemetery, 1891–1914. Bronx, New York

was substantial. It included nineteen watercolours and ninety-four paintings, as well as 'artistic house decorations' (antique glass, ceramics, porcelains, bronzes and textiles) and furniture, most of it fabricated by Cottier & Co. The sale brought in $102,270.[79] While Cottier's preferences – paintings and watercolours by Barbizon and Hague School artists and personal favourites like Lessore and Monticelli – were still well represented in the sale, it also included a number of works by Old Masters, representing a corner of the art market in which Inglis had become increasingly interested.[80]

Fearon kept the New York branch of Cottier & Co. running until 1915, when the firm went bankrupt. On 12 March a bankruptcy sale of 'paintings, art objects, books, fixtures, and artistic furniture, comprising the entire stock of Cottier & Co.' was held by order of Fearon in the Anderson Galleries in New York.[81] It was an odd assortment of goods. Paintings and watercolours, (allegedly) by such diverse artists as John Singleton Copley, Asher B. Durand, Domenico Feti, Frederik Hendrik Kaemmerer and Rubens, in addition to several now completely forgotten turn-of-the-century painters (W. P. Leenders, George C. Groll, G. Vizzotto, C. E. Swan and others) were auctioned off with a handful of works by artists who had been part of Cottier & Co.'s traditional cohort, including Colman, Hart and Ryder. An equally odd assortment of 'etchings, carbon prints, and photogravures' included prints by or after Corot, Diaz, John Hoppner, A. Lançon, Millet and Joseph Pratt. The items in the section of 'art objects, textiles, fixtures, artistic furniture' were even more incongruous and included everything from 'a pedestal covered with olive plush' to a small bronze copy of the classical Discus Thrower, from an eighteenth-century Italian mirror to two electrical fans. These were the dregs of the firm that forty years earlier has been one of the leading purveyors of fine furniture and art in New York.

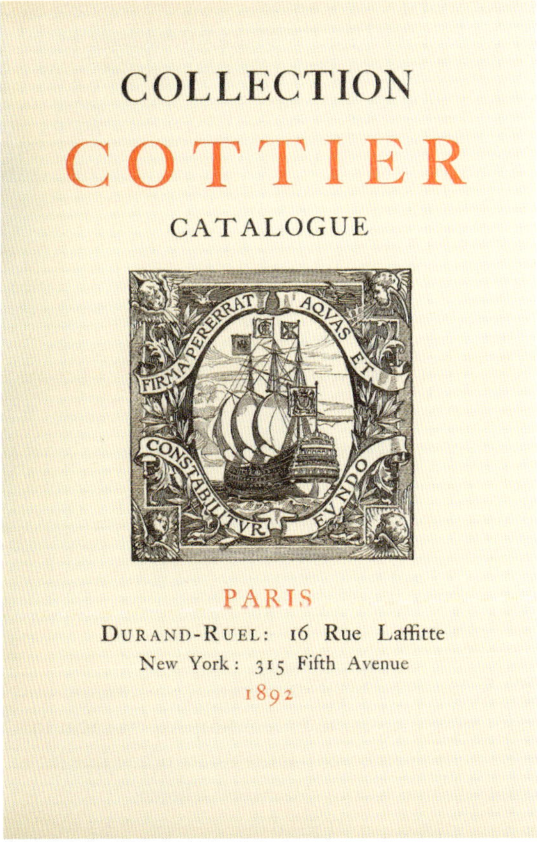

131 Title page of the catalogue of the Cottier Collection sale, *Catalogue of Ancient and Modern Pictures ...*, Durand-Ruel, Paris, 1892

POSTSCRIPT

Walter Fearon recovered from the bankruptcy and a few years later established Fearon Galleries on 25 West 54th Street. In the advertisements for that gallery, he continued to mention his association with Cottier & Co. but, while publicising his pedigree, Fearon had a business model and a stock that were entirely different from Cottier's. His was exclusively an art gallery and his specialty was Old Master paintings rather than contemporary art. Moreover, his focus was on British rather than French art.[82] According to his obituary in the *New York Times* in March 1935, his greatest claim to fame was the formation of a collection of British eighteenth-century portraits for Cyrus H. K. Curtis, the publisher of the *Ladies' Home Journal* and the *Saturday Evening Post*.[83]

Andrew Montana

CHAPTER SIX
SYDNEY 1873–1886

As Daniel Cottier was crossing the Atlantic to launch the New York branch of Cottier & Co., his longtime friend John Lamb Lyon (1836–1916; fig. 133) established Lyon, Cottier & Co. in Sydney in August or September 1873.[1] The son of an upholsterer,[2] Lyon, like Cottier, was born and raised in Glasgow. By 1851 he was apprenticed to the prominent Glasgow stained-glass maker and decorator John Cairney, to whom Cottier may have been an apprentice at about the same time. Lyon is said to have worked in London later in the 1850s for the well-known stained glass company Ward & Hughes.[3] During this time he may have renewed his acquaintance with Cottier, who was also in London in the late 1850s and possibly also worked for Ward & Hughes (see Chapter One, p. 10).

In December 1860, following the death of his first wife, Lyon married Elizabeth Gillespie (née Pearson) in Glasgow. Soon after, they emigrated to Australia, arriving in March 1861. The couple initially lived in Maldon, Victoria, a gold-mining town near Bendigo. John's father James had emigrated to Maldon some years previously with his wife Jane and was a storekeeper there. In late 1861 Lyon became a designer for the Melbourne stained glass company of Ferguson & Urie, becoming a partner in 1866.[4] Travelling back to Britain with his wife and young family in 1870–1,[5] Lyon called on Cottier in London. The two enterprising Scotsmen undoubtedly discussed the prospect of establishing an Australian branch of Cottier & Co. at this time, for after his return to Australia Lyon relinquished his partnership with Ferguson, Urie & Lyon (August 1873)[6] and relocated with his family to Sydney to set up his own firm with the backing of Cottier. The showroom and decorating studio of Lyon, Cottier & Co. were located in Pitt Street from 1873 until 1877, at which time Lyon moved them to Liverpool Street to a building that also could accommodate his family residence.[7]

LYON, COTTIER & CO.'S PURVIEW

Given Melbourne's prominence over Sydney during the last quarter of the nineteenth century, why did Lyon and Cottier not establish their branch in Melbourne? The colony of New South Wales was much larger than the colony of Victoria and, inland from Sydney, in thriving agricultural and mining areas, towns had sprung up which were eventually connected by railways. Growing prosperity in these towns and in Sydney itself offered the possibility of commissions to decorate new private homes, churches and government buildings. Moreover, in Melbourne and Victoria generally, Ferguson & Urie took the lion's share of the decorating business, making it ill-advised for Lyon to establish a rival firm there. But, while Ferguson & Urie received church commissions from as far away as Tasmania, Queensland and South Australia and was known in New South Wales, the firm undertook few jobs around Sydney. In that city there was little competition in the field of painted decoration or, for that matter, in stained glass. Indeed, there was only one glass painter, the Glaswegian John Falconer, who after 1875 formed a partnership with Frederick Ashwin from Birmingham.[8]

Lyon, Cottier & Co. quickly received important public commissions, especially for painted wall and ceiling decorations. In addition, many members of the affluent upper-middle class in New South Wales (and later in other Australian colonies) began to patronise the firm for the painted decorations of their homes. Even as the number of skilled art decorators increased throughout Australia by the late 1870s and into the

132 Advertisement for Lyon, Cottier & Co., *c.*1877. Caroline Simpson Library and Research Collection, Sydney Living Museums

179 LIVERPOOL STREET, HYDE PARK, SYDNEY.

8 PALL MALL, LONDON.

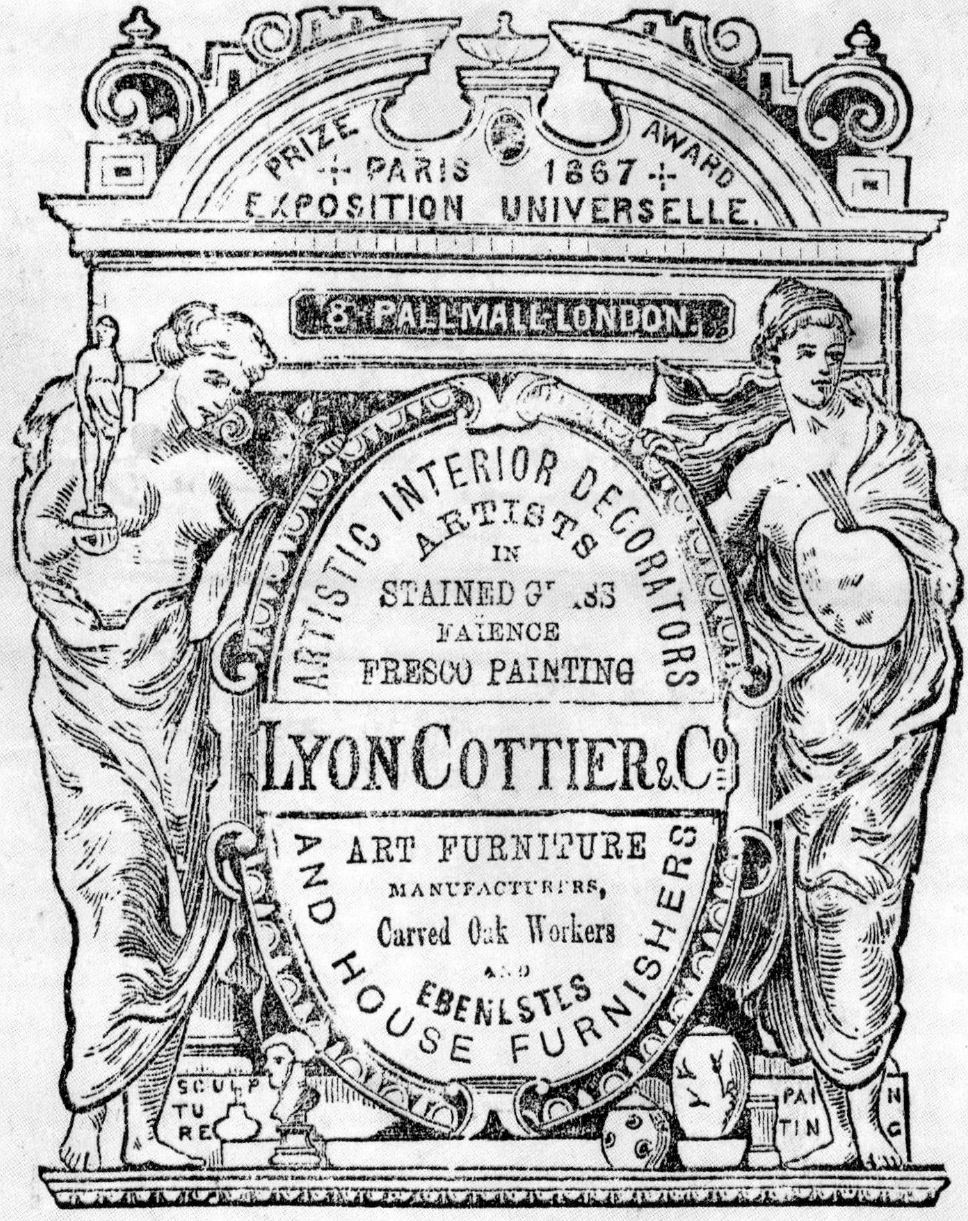

144 FIFTH AVENUE, NEW YORK.

STAINED GLASS WINDOWS,

MEMORIAL AND THANKSGIVING WINDOWS, STAIRCASE WINDOWS,

And every description of Leaded Lights made to order for Churches and Public and Private Buildings. Hand-painted Tiles, Artistic Frescoing. Churches and Houses painted and decorated.

Prize Awards—London, Paris, and Intercolonial Exhibitions.

133 Achille Simonetti, *John Lamb Lyon*, *c.*1885. Plaster, h. 33 cm. Private collection

134 Design for large twelve-light window for a music room (for 'Mr. Miles'), by Lyon, Cottier & Co., *c.*1875. Pencil and watercolour on paper, 47 × 35.5 cm. Mitchell Library, State Library of New South Wales, Sydney

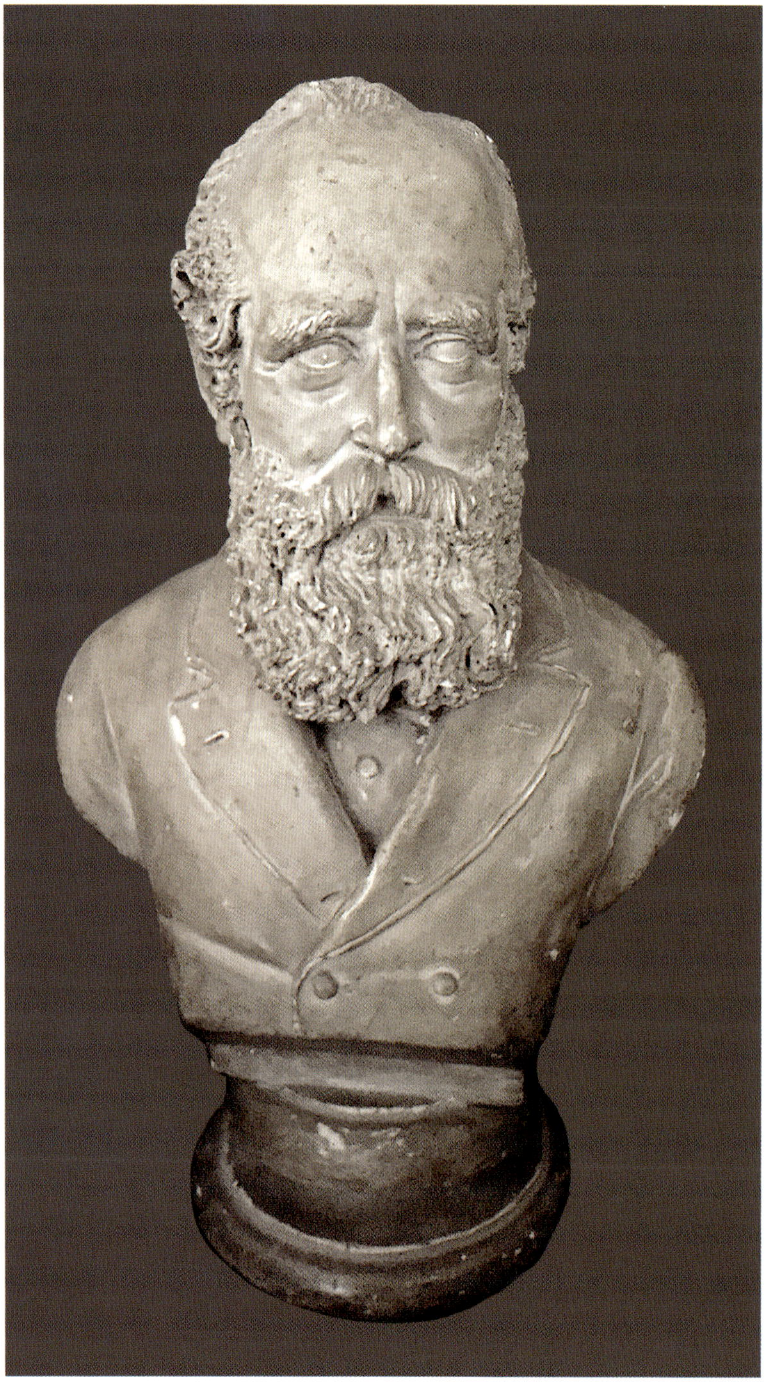

1880s, Lyon, Cottier & Co. remained the firm of choice for those wanting painted decoration. Lyon was responsible for bringing to Australia many of the designs created in Cottier's London studio and adapting them to his stained-glass, ceramic and decorating commissions. He also employed some of Cottier's most talented artisans, men who had worked with him in Britain, such as the stained-glass artist Charles Gow (1847–1893; of whom more shortly) and the decorator Andrew Wells (1845–1918; see Chapter Seven). However, Lyon was more than simply a conduit for Cottier's brand of Aestheticism. An entrepreneur and an artist in his own right, he adapted Cottier's designs to Australian tastes and introduced new decorative motifs, often inspired by the local flora and fauna, to cater to the burgeoning market for decorative arts in late nineteenth-century Australia.

Initially, it appears that Lyon, Cottier & Co. imported some stained-glass panels for the opening of the business in 1873. However, making stained-glass windows in London and sending them to Australia was presumably more expensive and time-consuming than shipment to New York, so from 1874 a workshop was established in Sydney. By the early 1880s Lyon, Cottier & Co. had installed kilns at the back of the Liverpool Street premises where it fired stained glass as well as ceramic tiles, which the company apparently saw as a growth area in the 'artistic interior decoration' that was the focus of its business. By the late 1880s, at the height of the building boom in Sydney, the firm employed thirty to forty workers, some of whom had emigrated from Britain, while others were born in Australia.[9] Another reason why Lyon, Cottier & Co. designed and made its own stained glass was, no doubt, that Lyon himself was trained as a stained-glass painter. He sometimes used Cottier designs and cartoons sent from London and other times designed (or had his assistants design) his own windows. Indeed, a considerable number of designs for windows as well as for wall decorations by Lyon, Cottier & Co. (and Lyon, Wells, Cottier & Co. from 1887 to 1895) have been preserved, distinguishing the Australian Cottier branch from those in London and New York, whose design archives have all but disappeared.[10] For church windows, Lyon's preference (and that of his Australian clientele) seems to have been for the Gothic Revival style, unsurprising given that he had trained with Ward & Hughes. In both church and secular windows Lyon, Cottier & Co. showed a predilection for puce, pale blue and purple, colours found far less frequently in Cottier's London windows. A design by the Australian branch for a large twelve-light window

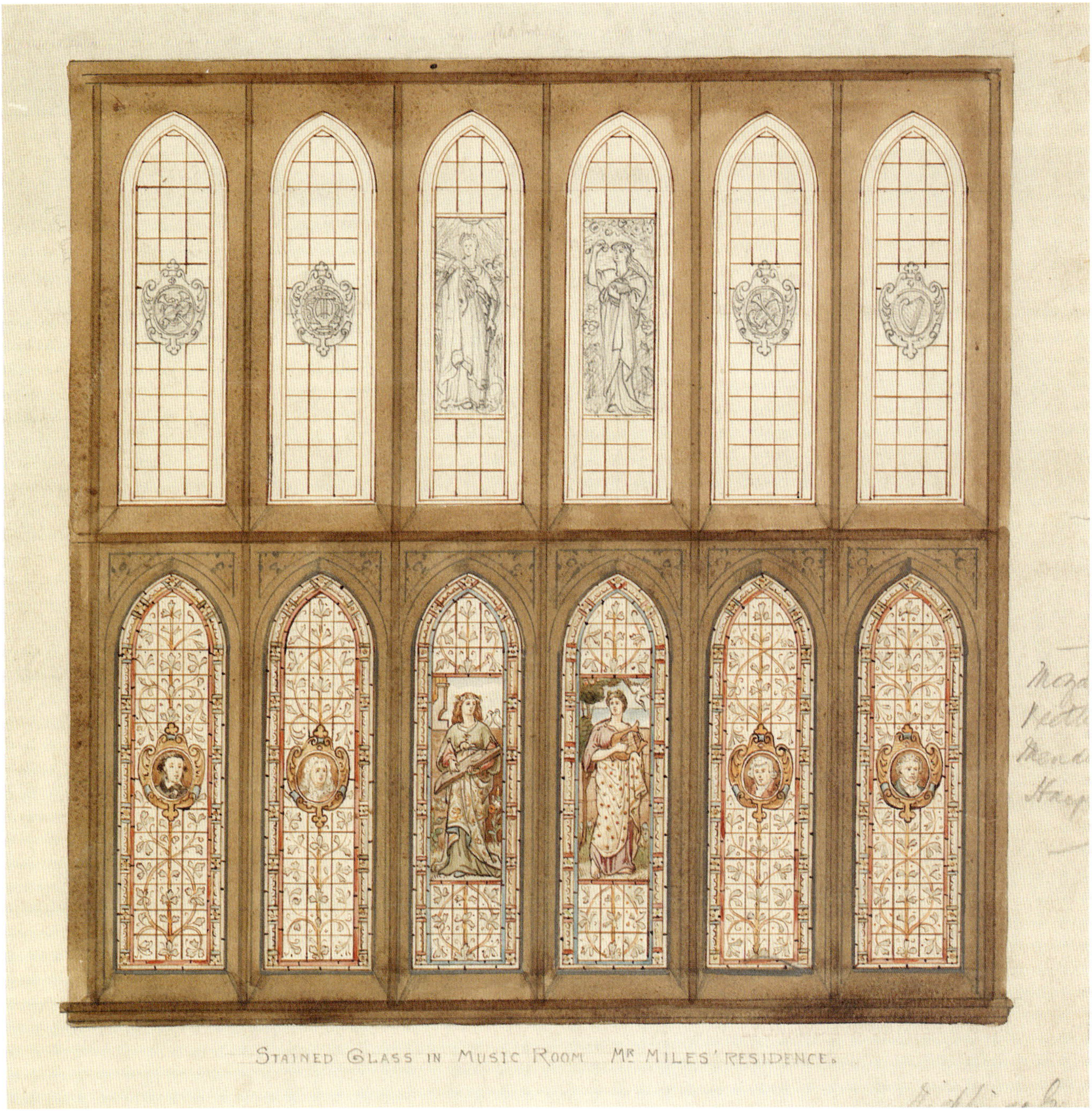

for a music room (for 'Mr. Miles'; fig. 134) may serve as an example of the firm's deployment of colour.

An advertisement of around 1877 (see fig. 132) promoted Lyon, Cottier & Co. as 'Artistic Interior Decorators and House Furnishers', with proficiency in stained glass, ceramics and 'fresco painting' as well as the manufacture of 'art furniture', oak carving and cabinetmaking.[11] However, furniture, although central to Cottier & Co.'s reputation in the United States and Britain, was not an important part of Lyon, Cottier & Co.'s business. At the 1875 Metropolitan Intercolonial Exhibition in Sydney, the firm exhibited a much admired 'decorated cabinet'[12] supplied by Cottier's London branch, probably to show the quality and type of furniture Lyon, Cottier & Co. could provide. The firm continued to advertise its 'art furniture' into the late 1870s and a walnut dresser by Cottier with painted tiles was sold in the auction of a private collection of art and furniture in Melbourne in the early 1880s.[13] But the furniture business never took off. Colonial taste favoured carved furniture in various historicist styles, of the kind that was manufactured and sold

135 (a and b) *Flora* and *Pomona*, Glenyarrah, Double Bay, Sydney, by Cottier & Co., London, *c.*1873, installed 1875–6. Stained glass

in London on Tottenham Court Road and in the Finsbury district in London by cabinetmakers such as William Smee & Son and W. Walker & Sons. Such furniture was also, and more cheaply, produced by local manufactories staffed by experienced immigrant furniture makers and carvers from Britain and the European continent. Even when, in the 1880s and 90s, lighter, ebonised furniture with painted and inlaid decoration became fashionable in Australia, Cottier's imported furniture was too expensive for most clients, who preferred to buy locally produced pieces.

It is remarkable that Daniel Cottier sent oil paintings and watercolours from European artists to Lyon, Cottier & Co. in Australia almost three years before he started dealing from his New York art gallery in 1877. At the end of 1874, and throughout the first half of 1875, shipments of oil paintings and watercolours selected by Cottier's manager Elbert Jan van Wisselingh were sent from the 'London House', as one advertisement in a Sydney paper described it,[14] and exhibited in Lyon, Cottier & Co.'s showroom. But, although it was advertised in the press, no individual artwork was mentioned and no catalogue has surfaced. It is also unknown how well these works sold, if at all. Nevertheless, Lyon, Cottier & Co. are known to have lent an oil painting to the exhibition of art and photography organised by the New South Wales Academy of Art held at the Sydney Post Office as a part of this building's opening celebrations in September 1874. Depicting the subject of Sancho Panza before the Countess from Miguel de Cervantes's *Don Quixote*, it was said to be worth 500 guineas.[15] This painting, by the French artist Charles-Henri Pille (1844–1897), was later shown with some others lent by Lyon to the National Gallery of Victoria in the Public Library complex in Melbourne.[16] Lyon may have done his best to circulate some of the paintings sent from London but there is no record of a single sale. It is possible that he lacked Cottier's talent for art dealing or did not have a passion for the art that Cottier admired. As late as 1886, when Lyon visited Cottier's gallery in New York, he wrote this about what he saw (punctuation added, spellings retained):

The chief picture is Corot, Apollo [actually, Orpheus greeting the Dawn], a landscape. At first sight the picture is disapointing and £6,000 seems a large sum to ask. The most of the pictures seem curious, chosen more for their manner and painting rather than subject. Montichelo [Adolphe Monticelli] is good in color but some of them look like panels covered with the scrapings of the pallette yet undoubtedly he is a genius.[17]

Lyon's backhanded compliments to the artists Cottier admired hardly seem to make him the ideal spokesman for their art.

Given the lack of commercial success of the art trade in Australia, it seems surprising that in 1882 Cottier sent another shipment of forty paintings to Lyon, Cottier & Co. This time a report indicated that the works were predominantly by 'Flemish' (actually Dutch) and French artists and included paintings and watercolours by Victor Leclaire, Mauve, Mesdag, Mettling, Neuhuys (Menhuys in the newspaper), François Pieter Ter Meulen, and Petrus van der Velden, who emigrated to New Zealand in 1890. A 'vivid study' by the Scottish painter William Ewart Lockhart was also part of the shipment, which was exhibited in Lyon, Cottier & Co.'s shop.[18] The following year they were exhibited in an art gallery established by the leading printing and photographic firm of John Sands in George Street, Sydney. In an article in the *Illustrated Sydney News* of November 1883, it is noted that forty works 'judiciously selected by Mr. Cottier of London, from the principal home and Continental studios', were displayed at Sands Art Gallery with examples of colonial painting, decorative objects, statuary and reproductive prints, some of the latter after the paintings of well-known Royal Academicians.[19] Whether these works were for sale or merely on display is uncertain because Sands Art Gallery was both an exhibition and a commercial gallery. It seems likely that, like the first shipment, the paintings were returned to Cottier, because there is no trace of them in Australia, nor are any mentioned a year later in the press notice advertising John Sands's refurbished art gallery, 'tastefully decorated by Lyon, Cottier & Co'.[20]

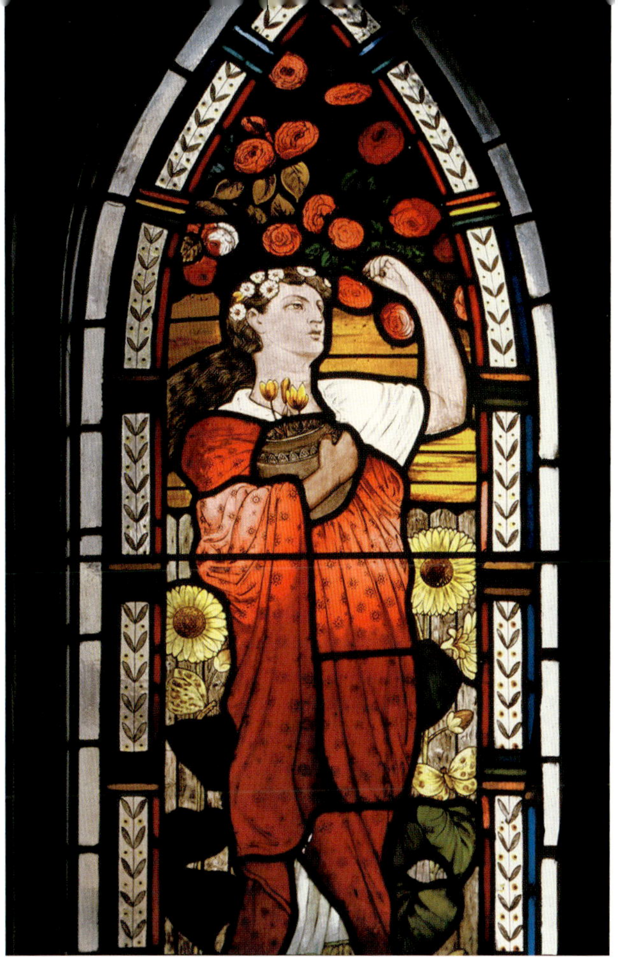

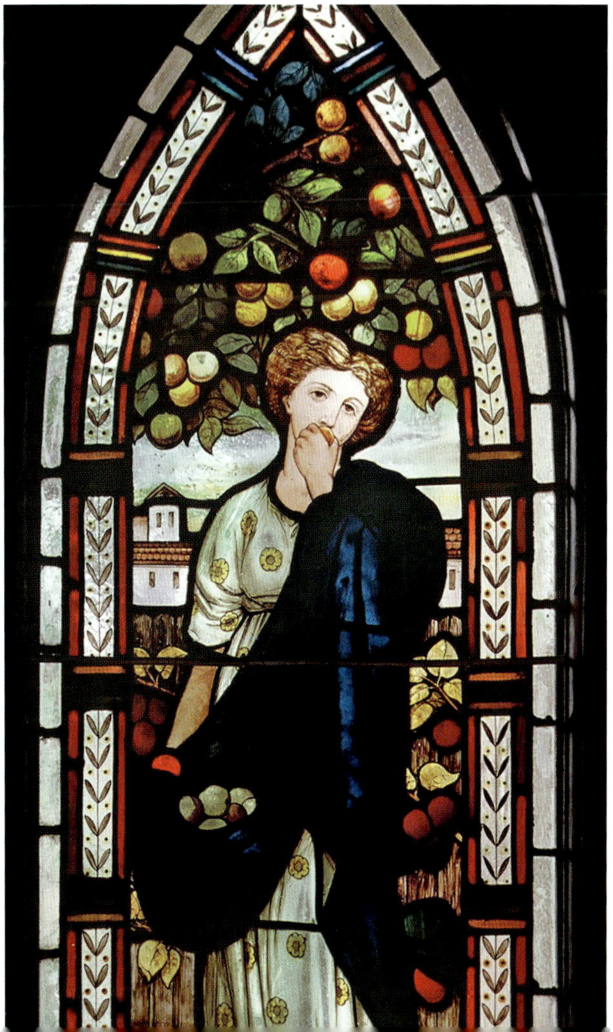

CHARLES GOW AND THE EARLY COMMISSIONS FOR PAINTED INTERIORS OF PUBLIC BUILDINGS

When Lyon went to Sydney to establish Lyon, Cottier & Co. in 1873, he was joined by the talented Charles Gow. The son of a glass stainer, Gow had been apprenticed to a stained-glass maker in his native Glasgow and is first recorded as working for Cottier in London in the early 1870s. Expected to help Lyon with getting the Sydney business started,[21] Gow worked in Australia from 1873 to 1876.[22] His presence in the first three years of Lyon's new business venture was crucial when it came to introducing Cottier & Co.'s 'house style' to Australia, particularly the use of Greek and Roman ornamental vocabulary. Undoubtedly, Gow supervised the decoration of the first Sydney showroom, in what Lyon called 'the latest London style'.[23] A reporter for the *Illustrated Sydney News* described it in detail in 1874:

Messrs. Lyon, Cottier, and Co. ... have opened an establishment at 333 Pitt-street, and as a specimen of their new style of decoration, have painted their showroom. The ceiling is an elaborate design, containing allegorical heads of the seasons, festoons of foliage, grotesque animals, birds, butterflies, &c. The frieze is an adaption of the Greek honeysuckle and lotus pattern, on which are let in heads of the Greek heroines, painted in colours on gold ground ... the aim has been to get a quiet harmony of colour, avoiding all that is loud, raw, or gaudy. The windows contain specimens of their stained glass. One window has the figures of Flora and Pomona in the richest antique glass; the other is very light, having no colour but that produced by the yellow silver stain; the groundwork is little circles like the old German roundlets. Messrs. Lyon, Cottier and Co. are also makers of art furniture, encaustic tile painters, and importers of real Venetian glass and oriental carpets.[24]

Nothing is left of this showroom but it is possible that the figures of Flora and Pomona in one of the windows mentioned in the review were similar in design to the two lights representing the same goddesses acquired by Lyon's client the merchant, pastoralist and politician Samuel Deane Gordon (1811–1882) in 1875 for his mansion Glenyarrah (Double Bay, Sydney), where they remain *in situ* (figs 135a and b). Almost certainly imported from London, the two figures are variants of designs Cottier & Co. used for the hallway windows

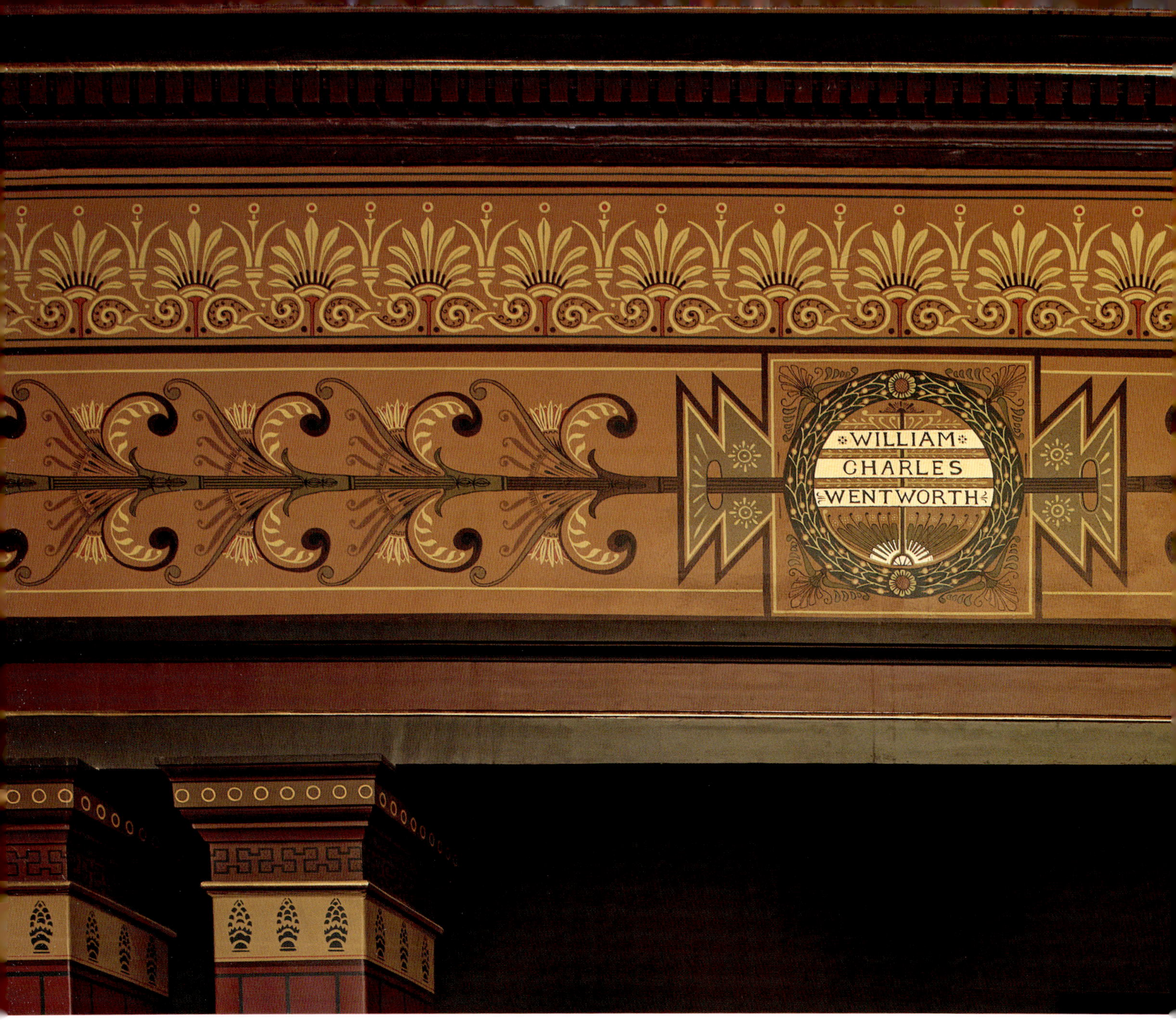

of houses including Coll-Earn House, Auchterarder, and Ingliston House, near Edinburgh, Scotland, in the early 1870s (see fig. 36). The full-bodied classicising figures are typical of the 'Cottier style' of the early 1870s, which, one assumes, also governed the painted decoration of the showroom.

The success of Gow's Pitt Street showroom may have been instrumental in securing prestigious government contracts for Lyon, Cottier & Co. almost immediately on the firm's launching. Before Lyon set up shop in Sydney, painting and stencilling were rarely used in Australia as decorative treatments of walls and ceilings in either private dwellings or public buildings and halls. If deployed, they were used in the corners of ceilings and walls, which might be decorated with sprays of flowers, Italian linework and other light classicising ornament. The walls and ceilings of theatre auditoria generally received more elaborate and polychromatic decorative treatments. Lyon's new business venture revolutionised the decoration of walls and ceilings by covering surfaces entirely.

Lyon, Cottier & Co.'s first commission entailed the decoration of two of the interior spaces of the newly built General Post Office in Sydney.[25] The Scottish-born government architect James Johnstone Barnet (1827–1904) designed the landmark building, made of local Pyrmont sandstone in a Classical Revival style. The building, later enlarged, still stands but the

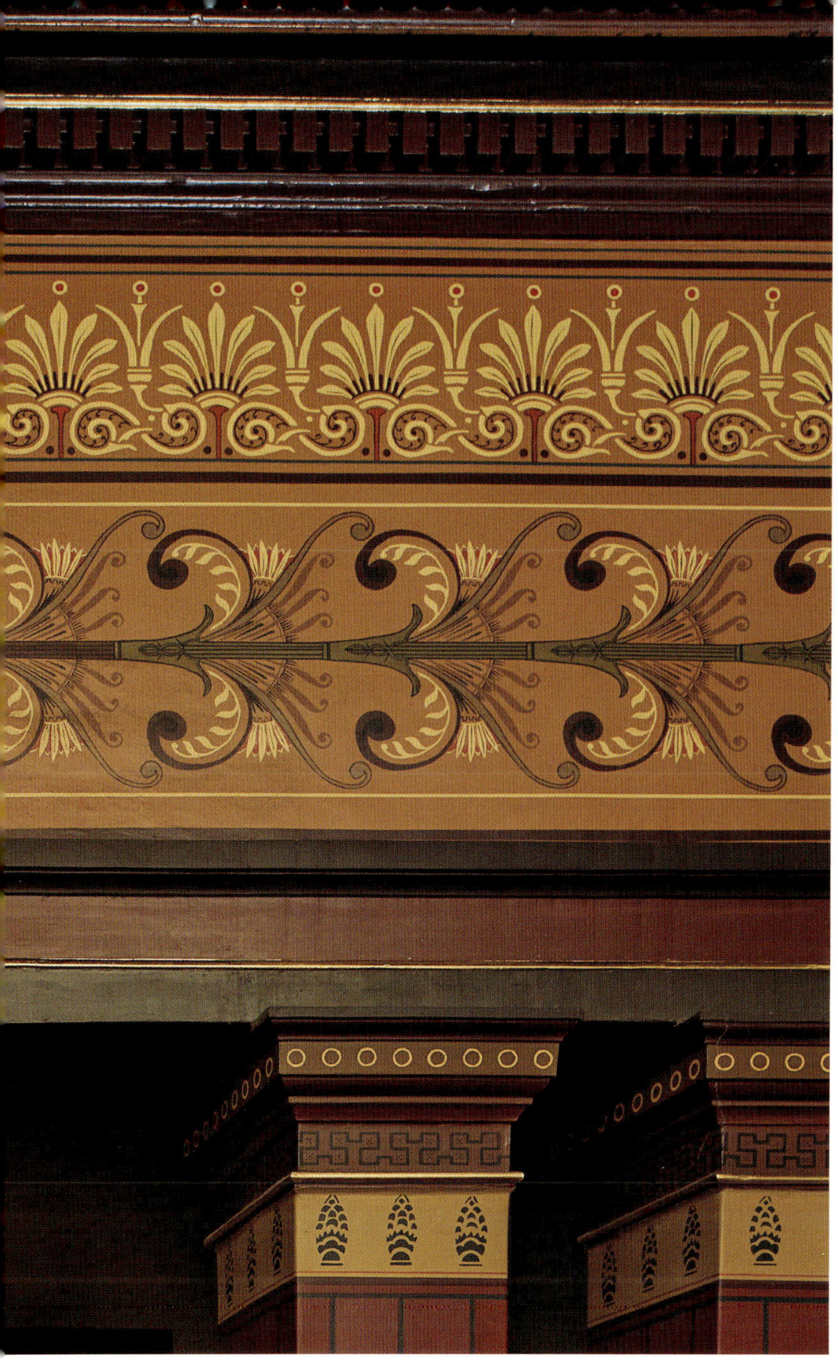

136 Frieze and column decoration in the vestibule of Parliament House, Sydney, by Lyon, Cottier & Co., 1875

decorations of the Postmaster-General's room are no longer extant. The *Sydney Morning Herald* gave this description:

*...the Post-master-General's room ... has been decorated and fitted up most elaborately. The ceiling of the principal room is decorated by Messrs. Lyons [*sic*], Cottier, and Co., of Pitt-street, upon a plan now much in vogue in England. It is technically known as 'frescoing', and is intended to supersede paperhanging, although at present only adopted in large public buildings or private mansions, where everything is intended to be* en regle. *The colours are soft and in harmony, and the walls are stencilled. The carpet is, in pattern, appropriate to the decoration of the ceiling, and rich hangings depend from massive gilt cornices over the windows. The anteroom has been treated in a similar style ...* [26]

It is clear from this account (as in the case of the description of Lyon, Cottier & Co.'s showroom) that the new firm was seen as innovative and original, importing the latest British styles, classical rather than Gothic, into Australia.

In the light of this, it is not surprising that the Post Office commission was followed, in 1875, by one for Parliament House, Macquarie Street, Sydney, which included the decorations of the vestibule and refreshment room. Partially uncovered and reconstructed in the late twentieth century, the decoration of the vestibule is dominated by greens and burgundy and has a strong Greek and Egyptian flavour. Decorative motifs include meanders, palmettes and a frieze in which papyrus-like sedges are strung sideways on horizontal rods (fig. 136). In the centre of the frieze, each rod pierces through a silver-grey cartouche that frames a foliate wreath, inside which the name of a deceased member of the Legislative Assembly is inscribed on gold.[27] The decorations for the refreshment room have not been preserved. They were described in the press as being in the 'Queen Anne' style, a term that in the nineteenth century could mean many things; they may have reflected an eclectic Adam Revival style that would have provided a counterpoint to the more formal decoration of the vestibule. It appears that these early commissions exemplified Lyon, Cottier & Co.'s signature style in painted decorations: in 1876 the firm produced its first advertising brochure that emphasised: 'the ornamentation used, having all the beauty of Ancient Roman and Greek decorations, never fails to give pleasant satisfaction'.[28]

NEW SYDNEY PREMISES AND NEW PUBLIC COMMISSIONS FOR PAINTED DECORATIONS

In the second half of 1877, Lyon, Cottier & Co. relocated to larger premises at 179 Liverpool Street, Sydney.[29] The building (no longer extant) that housed the showroom and workshop, as well as Lyon's family, was attached to a long row of elegant three-storey

137 Sketch for proscenium, School of Arts, Sydney, by Lyon, Cottier & Co., 1878. Pencil on paper, 25.5 × 36 cm. Mitchell Library, State Library of New South Wales, Sydney

138 Drawing-room ceiling decoration, Government House, Sydney, by Lyon, Cottier & Co., 1879

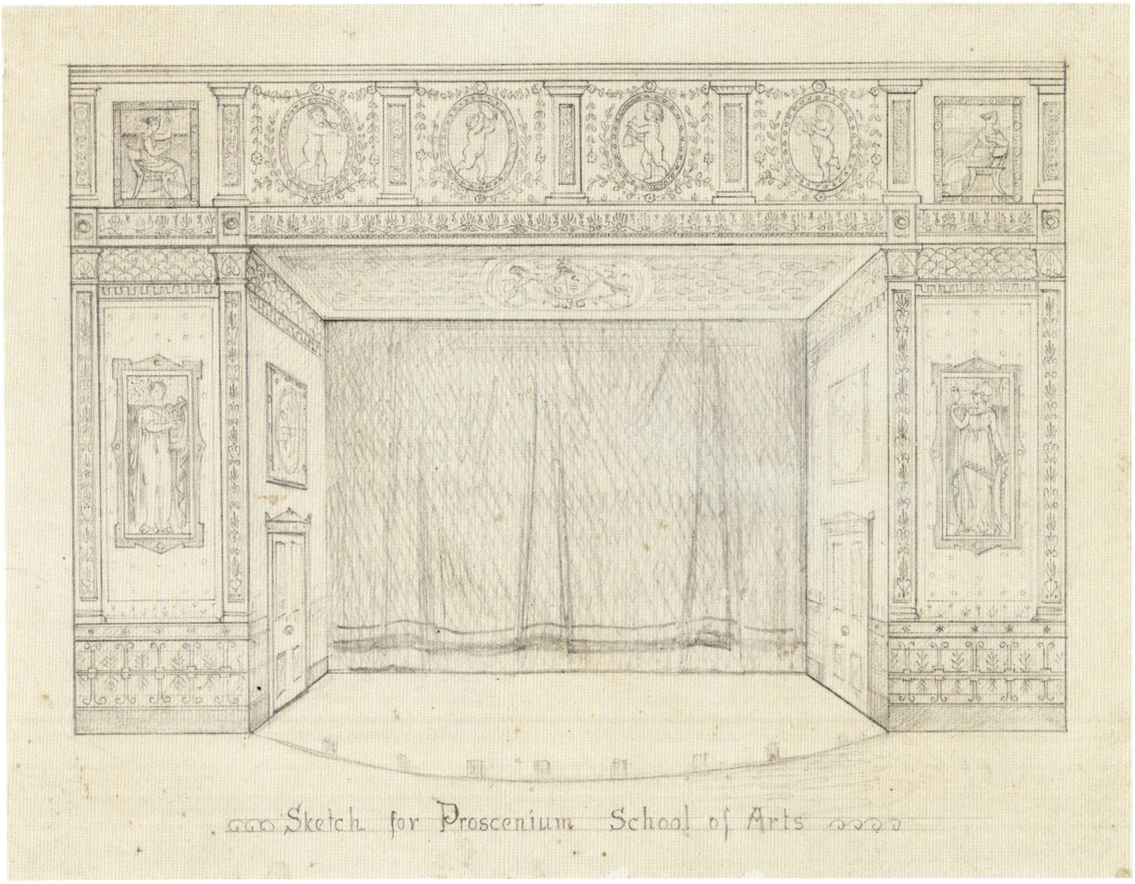

terrace houses, built in the 1840s and inhabited by members of Sydney's professional class. Gow had returned to Scotland on 10 December 1876 and two years later, at the beginning of 1879, Cottier and Lyon dissolved their business partnership in Sydney, although Cottier's name, undoubtedly a selling point, was retained in the firm's title.[30] Lyon, Cottier & Co. thereafter traded under Lyon's sole ownership but retained strong connections with Cottier, continuing to import stained-glass windows and designs for decoration throughout the 1880s.

The move to Liverpool Street appears to have led to renewed commissions. An early one, in 1878, was for the decoration of the newly extended School of Arts auditorium in Sydney. The decorative ensemble was described as the 'most elaborate display of decorative painting in Australia'.[31] Although it has not survived, a concept drawing of the proscenium (fig. 137) and a description in the *Evening News* give some idea of what the decorations looked like. Large panels painted in oils, depicting Apollo and Minerva, flanked the auditorium's proscenium. It was crowned by a group of allegorical panels depicting agriculture, mining 'and other industries' (the preparatory drawing shows only two allegorical panels in addition to panels with putti). The south side of the hall was decorated with life-size figures of Pomona, Bacchus, Euterpe and Clio and the north side with figures of Camilla, Hebe and Flora.[32]

The arrival of the new governor, Lord Augustus Loftus (1817–1904), prior to Australia's first International Exhibition due to open in September 1879, led to a commission from Barnet for the interior of Government House. Lyon, Cottier & Co.'s decorations for the vestibule, drawing room,

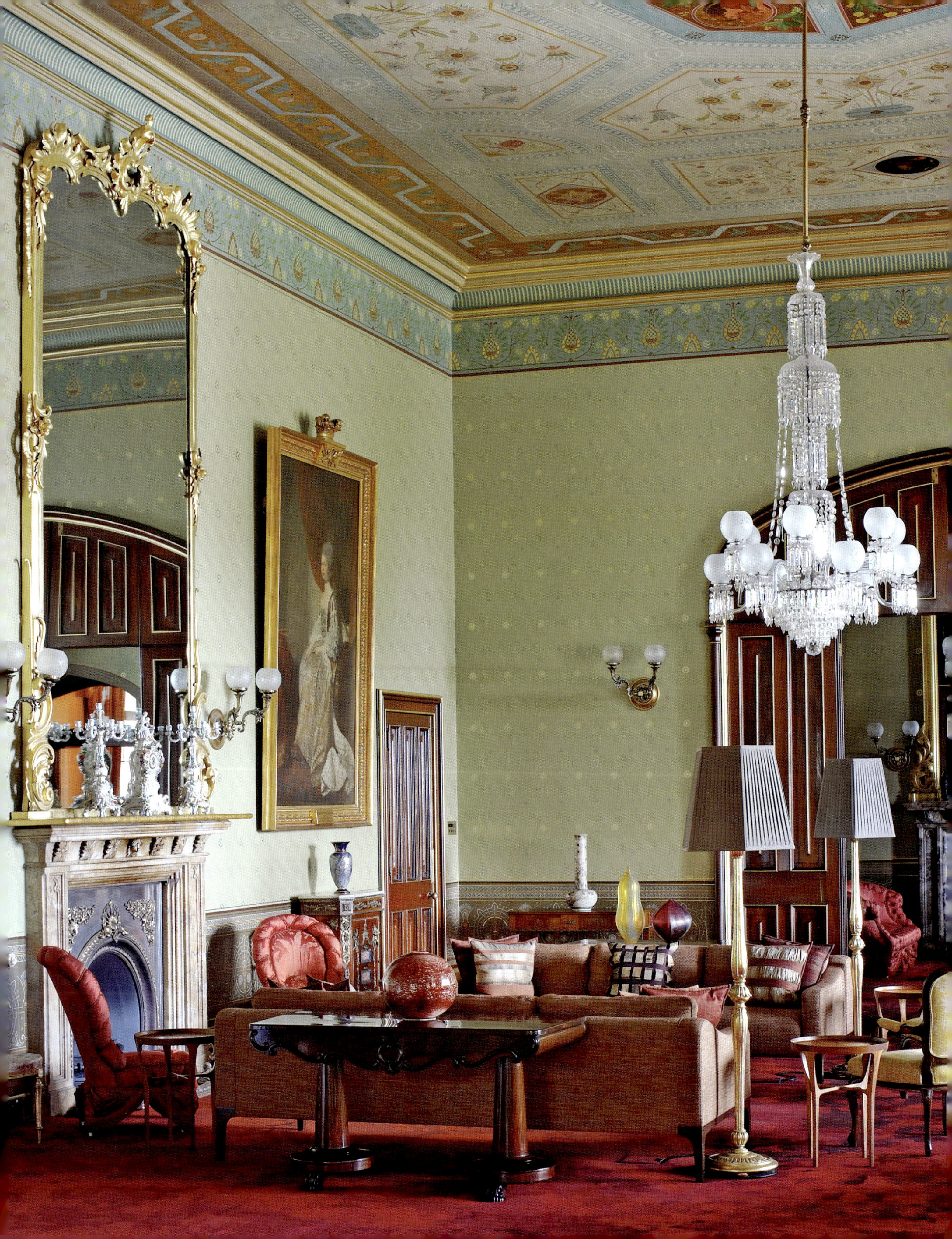

139 Drawing room in Government House, Sydney, by Lyon, Cottier & Co., 1879

140 Stencilled dado in the drawing room, Government House, Sydney, by Lyon, Cottier & Co., 1879

anteroom, dining room and ballroom were executed in conjunction with the building of the long sandstone cast-facing verandah designed by Barnet and carved with Australian waratahs, New South Wales's floral emblem. The rooms at Government House have stencilled friezes, dadoes and walls and painted ceiling decorations in a style best characterised as eclectic, as they comprise Egyptian, classical and medieval motifs, many of them floral.

All the ceiling decorations are centred on octagons, which are elaborated in various ways. In the drawing-room ceiling (fig. 138), for example, the octagon surrounds a circle and is divided by a cross in four fan-shaped parts, which contain medallions with allegories of the Four Seasons. Additional medallions with allegories of Night and Day are found on the two short sides of the ceiling. The use of these medallions, which were also present in the ceiling decoration of Lyon's showroom on Pitt Street, exemplifies the adaptation by Lyon, Cottier & Co.'s painters of designs from the London studio. Indeed, the ceiling paintings appear to be based on designs for some of the stained-glass windows made for Cairndhu House, Helensburgh, and Links House, Montrose, in the early 1870s (see fig. 194). In the corners of the central decoration of the ceiling are the shamrock for Ireland, the thistle for Scotland, the rose for England and the

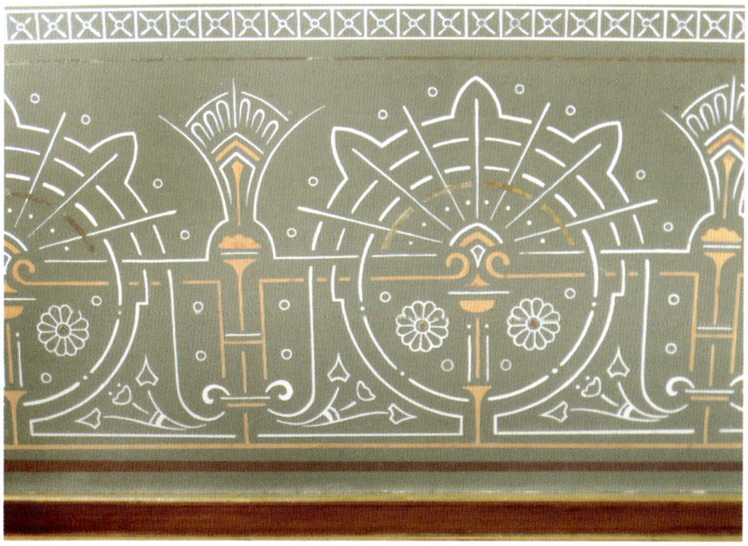

red waratah of New South Wales. The drawing room has a painted taupe-coloured dado (fig. 140), on which a geometric motif of vaguely Egyptian inspiration (and recalling the designs of Cottier's contemporary, Christopher Dresser) is stencilled in white and salmon pink. The furniture suite in the room (fig. 139) was covered in crimson damask with lush ferns and leaf motifs. Crimson window drapes in the same fabric and a figured crimson carpet created a striking ensemble (recreated in a recent restoration), all of it coordinated by Lyon, Cottier & Co. The original decoration of the ceiling of the anteroom, off the drawing room, also survives. Its central octagonal panel, painted in green, is articulated in the same way as the octagon in the drawing room but the four fields are filled with stylised plant ornaments painted in green on a gold ground.

Lyon, Cottier & Co. was also involved in the decoration of the Garden Palace, the 1879 Sydney International Exhibition building designed by Barnet.[33] Located in the large Domain near Government House and the Botanic Gardens, Barnet's vast domed building, intended to house international arts and industries, comprised a long nave, intersected by a transept and ending in pavilion towers. Scheduled to open in September 1879, the building was still under construction when Lyon, Cottier & Co. commenced working on the decoration.[34] The firm required a large team of workers and it is likely that the Glasgow-trained decorator Walter G. Marshall joined Lyon, Cottier & Co. at this time, if not earlier,[35] as well as the South Kensington-trained Benjamin John Grice (1861–1916), who emigrated with his family to Sydney in 1876 and worked with the firm from the late 1870s into the early 1880s.[36]

The Garden Palace was destroyed by fire three years after it was built but some idea about the decorative work done by Lyon, Cottier & Co. may be gained from a preliminary drawing, contemporary photographs and descriptions in papers and reports. At the intersection of the building's nave and transept was a huge dome with a lantern, for which Lyon, Cottier & Co. designed the skylight. A watercolour in the firm's design archive (fig. 141), probably by Lyon himself,

141 Design for the dome lantern light of the Sydney International Exhibition building (Garden Palace), by Lyon, Cottier & Co., 1879. Pen, pencil and watercolour on paper, 25.5 × 17.5 cm. Mitchell Library, State Library of New South Wales, Sydney

142 Interior showing nave and transept under the dome, Sydney International Exhibition (Garden Palace). Photograph 1879. National Library of Australia, Canberra

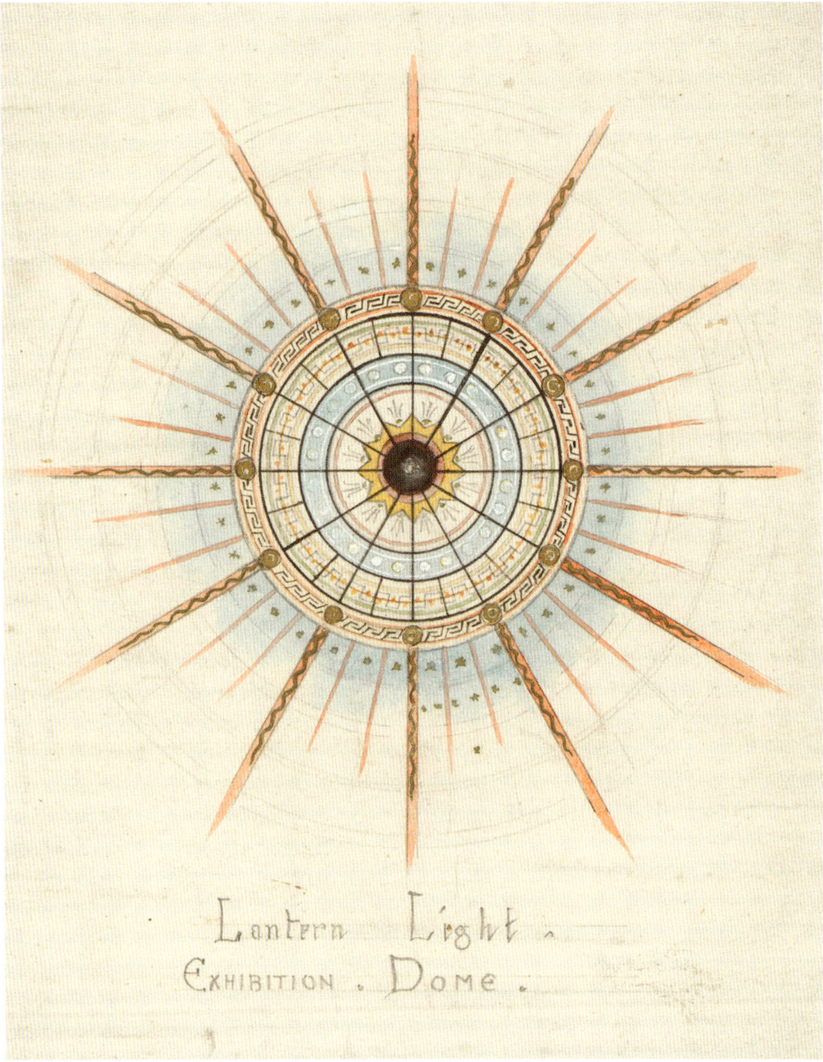

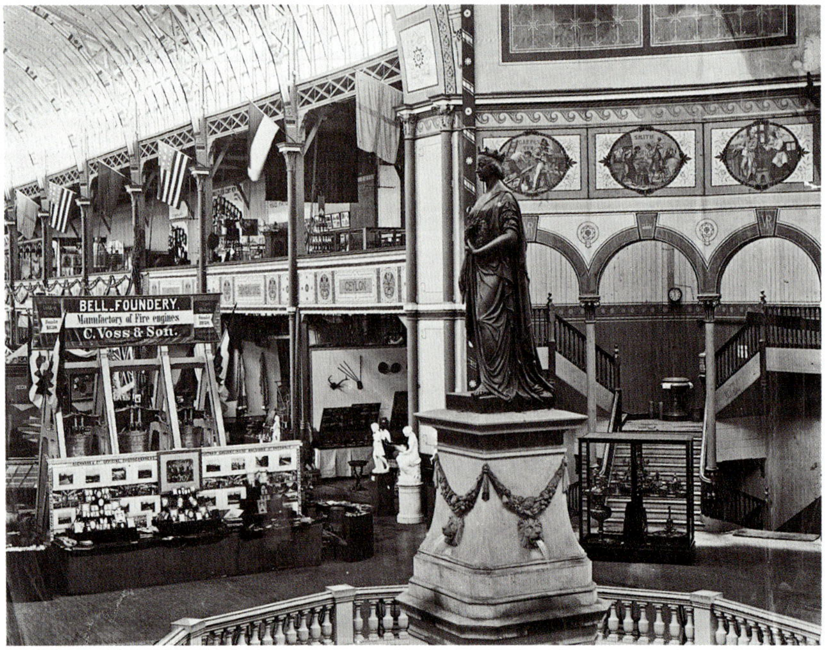

shows that the light was centred on a golden yellow star, which was surrounded by a series of concentric bands, off-white, buff or powder blue, decorated with a variety of motifs, including white dots, meanders and golden stars; radiating from the points of the central star were ribs that held the light together.

It is likely that Lyon and his assistants painted the twelve large oval medallions representing industries that decorated the dome rotunda, which are visible in a photograph taken in 1879 (fig. 142).[37] Contemporary sources relate that the firm also provided cloth friezes painted with stylised flowers: 'the Rose, Thistle, Shamrock, Waratah, Cornstalk, and Southern Cross, respectively'[38] were placed along the upper fronts of the court galleries and beneath the open gallery walkways above. On the nave wall, circular medallions showing sunflowers on gold backgrounds flanked rectangular shields bearing the names of the country, town or city exhibiting in the spaces behind them. The capitals of the nave columns were painted with gold fleurs-de-lis on a vermilion ground surrounded by gold stars. Barnet himself believed that Lyon's firm had 'done their work with true artistic taste'.[39]

Lyon, Cottier & Co. not only worked on the decorations of the exhibition building but also displayed inside the exhibition cartoons for wall decorations and stained-glass designs, in pencil and crayon, gouache and watercolour.[40] Possibly as a result, commissions for decorative painting and stained glass increased. With the ongoing construction and refurbishment of offices, banks, hotels, entertainment halls, hospitals and churches, Lyon, Cottier & Co. decorated buildings designed by leading Sydney architects and were referred to as the 'decorators, of this city'.[41]

WALL AND CEILING DECORATIONS OF PRIVATE RESIDENCES

The International Exhibition may also have helped Lyon, Cottier & Co. to land more commissions for the decoration of private villas and townhouses. It is true that some of these commissions predate the

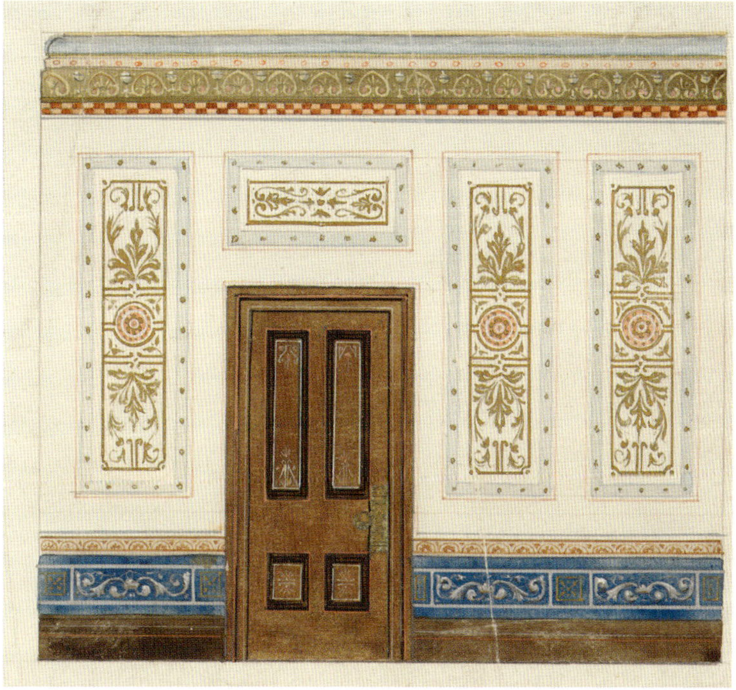

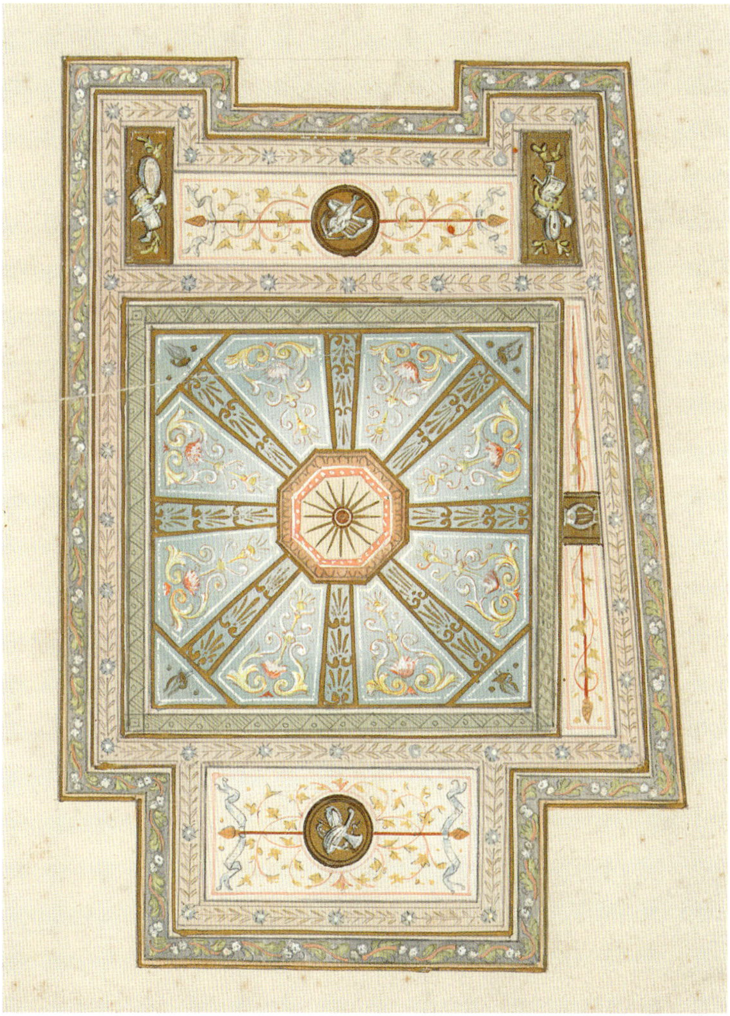

143 (a and b) Designs for decoration of boudoir wall and ceiling, Clarens, Potts Point, Sydney by Lyon, Cottier & Co., *c.*1878. Pencil and watercolour on paper, wall: 21.4 × 26.5 cm; ceiling: 24 × 33.4 cm. Mitchell Library, State Library of New South Wales, Sydney

exhibition, which certainly was not the only catalyst. Some patrons of the firm seem to have been inspired by the work they saw in public buildings that were decorated by Lyon, Cottier & Co., while others were convinced to hire the firm by the architects who built their homes. Indeed, many domestic commissions came to Lyon, Cottier & Co. through Sydney's leading architects, who recognised the company's ability to enrich the interiors of their buildings. These architects included but were not limited to Barnet (Lyon, Cottier & Co. decorated his residence), Edmund Blacket, William Wardell, John Horbury Hunt, Thomas Rowe and later Walter Liberty Vernon and John Sulman (Sulman & Power). The style of Lyon, Cottier & Co.'s domestic decorations was generally classicising but, as Lyon's medieval-style decorations of the Abbey (discussed shortly) indicate, the firm could adapt to its patrons' requirements.

Few of the mansions Lyon, Cottier & Co. decorated have survived. However, in some cases, photographs can give an idea of what their work looked like, while in others preliminary designs in the Mitchell Library, Sydney, provide visual clues. Sir James Martin (1820–1886), thrice premier of New South Wales and chief justice from 1873 to 1886, was one of the firm's high-placed clients. In 1853 he had bought Clarens, a mansion built by Joseph Hyde Potts in an area called Woolloomooloo Hill, before long renamed Potts Point. An admirer of classical antiquity, Martin aimed to create a new antique world in Australia, laying out a garden at Clarens with Italianate sandstone balustrading, tiered steps and replicas of antique statuary and monuments, said to rival 'the garden of an archon of ancient Greece'.[42] Martin also remodelled and redecorated the house, which was unfortunately demolished in 1966. Lyon, Cottier & Co.'s designs of around 1878 for the wall and ceiling decorations of the boudoir of Clarens (fig. 143) show that in the house antiquity also reigned supreme. The design shows classical botanical motifs such as palmettes and acanthus leaves, as well as antique musical instruments. Befitting a boudoir, the colour scheme is light – pinks, olive greens, gold and light blue – except for the baseboard, which is shown as saturated blue.

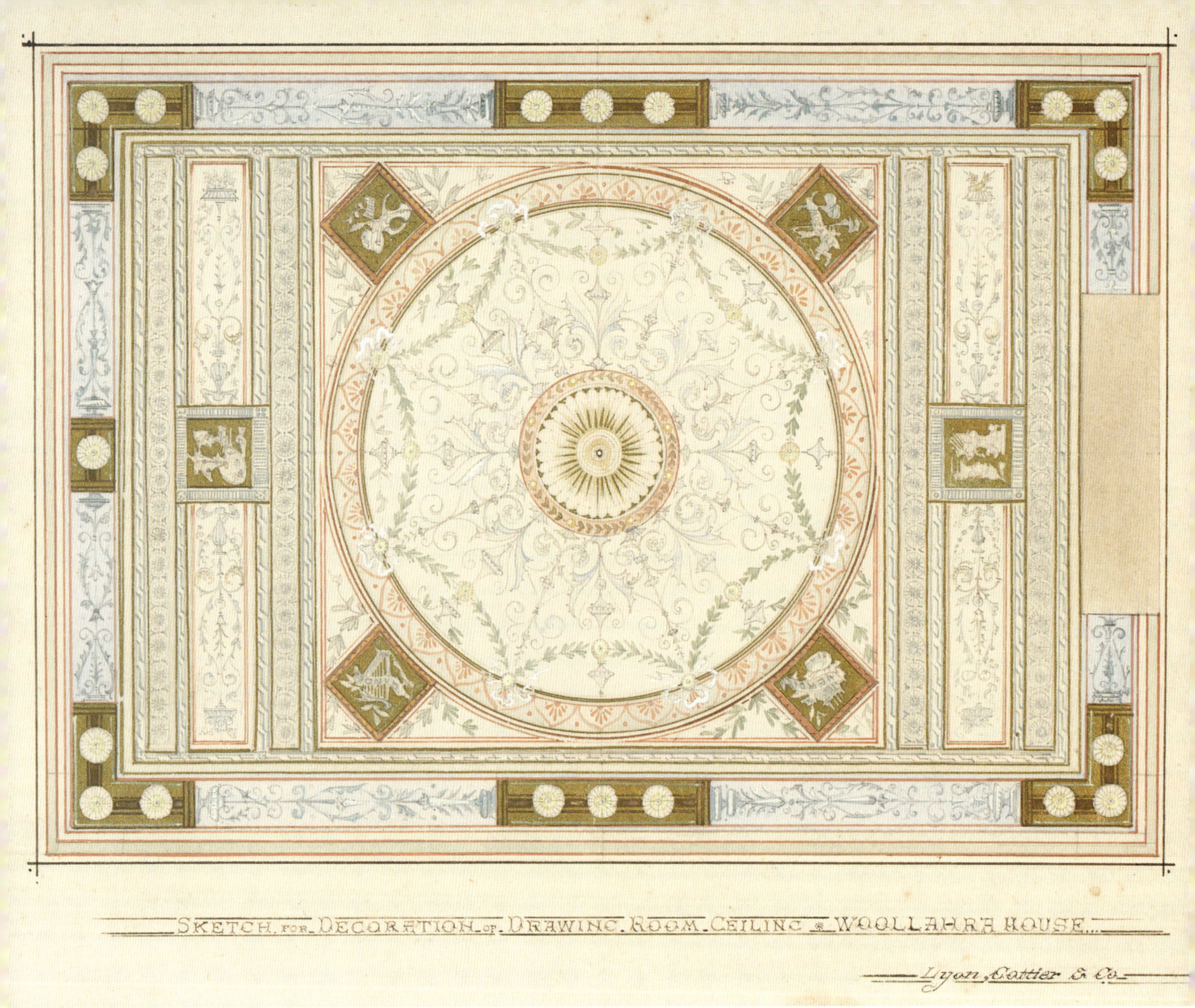

The Mitchell Library archive also contains a design for the drawing-room ceiling of the residence of William Charles Cooper (1851–1925), Woollahra House at Point Piper, near Darling Point, Sydney (1886; fig. 144). This design continues the Adam Revival style of Gow's ceilings in Government House. Here an octagon formed from garlands is set in a circle with four square tablets at the corners, each depicting musical instruments, draped by a banner with a composer's name. Perhaps the most original feature of the pastel-coloured ceiling is the peripheral light blue border, which in the four corners and in the centre of each side show strips of dark brown decorated with yellow flower heads, which frame the composition.

Glenleigh, located near Penrith, west of Sydney, is among the few surviving homes of the late nineteenth century that retains most of its original decoration. The mansion was built in the early 1880s on the initiative of the prosperous Scottish businessman James Ewan (1843–1903). William Wardell designed the house in a modified Scots baronial style;[43] the interior is almost certainly the work of Lyon, Cottier & Co. The wide entrance door is surrounded by stained-glass windows, coloured in yellow, red and powder blue. A tripartite overdoor is centred on Ewan's coat of arms with the motto *cito tuto et jucunde* (quickly, safely and pleasantly) followed by Ewan's initials, all set within a wreath and flanked on both sides by stylised plant motifs.

144 Design for decoration of drawing-room ceiling, Woollahra House, Sydney, by Lyon, Cottier & Co., 1886. Pencil and watercolour on paper, 31.5 × 40 cm. Mitchell Library, State Library of New South Wales, Sydney

145 Window framing rear doorway, Glenleigh, Penrith, NSW, attributed to Lyon, Cottier & Co., *c.*1884. Stained glass

146 Library ceiling decoration with portrait medallion of Sir Walter Scott, Glenleigh, Penrith, NSW, attributed to Lyon, Cottier & Co., *c.*1884

147 Ceiling decoration in the dining room, Glenleigh, Penrith, NSW, attributed to Lyon, Cottier & Co., *c.*1884

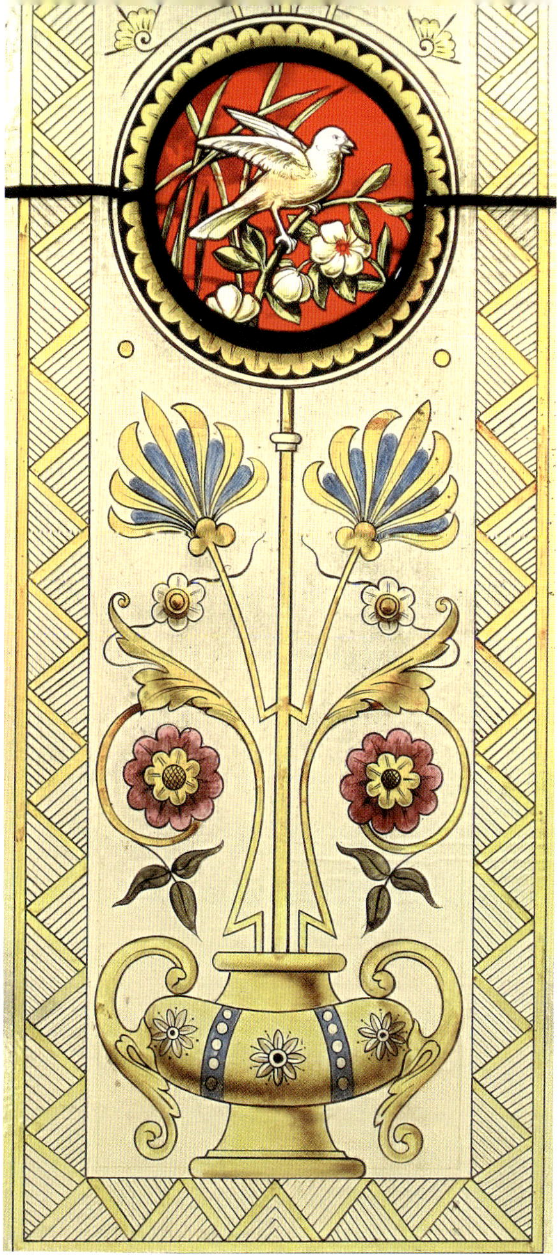

On either side of the mansion's back entrance are two vertical windows, which are centred on roundels with birds (fig. 145). As for the painted decoration, all the ceilings of the principal rooms on the ground floor are treated in the firm's usual way, whereby a geometric framework structures stylised plant motifs, which in Glenleigh are painted mostly in soft pink salmon, blue and gold. Each room, moreover, features painted medallions, sometimes set in cartouches, with subjects appropriate to the use of the room. The ornamental borders on the ceilings of the library, for example, frame portrait medallions of Sir Walter Scott (fig. 146), Shakespeare and Milton, adapted from the firm's stained-glass repertoire of literary figures. The drawing-room ceiling is divided into ornamented frames enclosing portrait medallions of classical and medieval women; the composers Haydn, Mozart, Mendelssohn and Beethoven are featured in the adjoining music room.

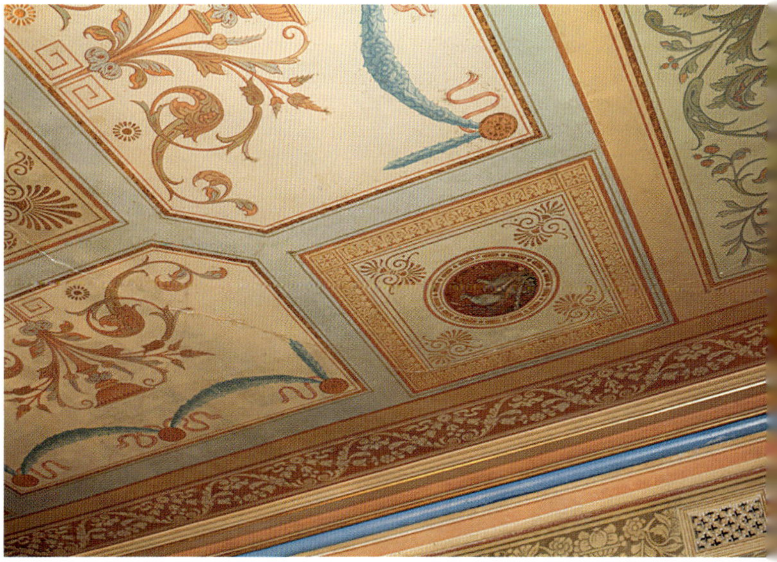

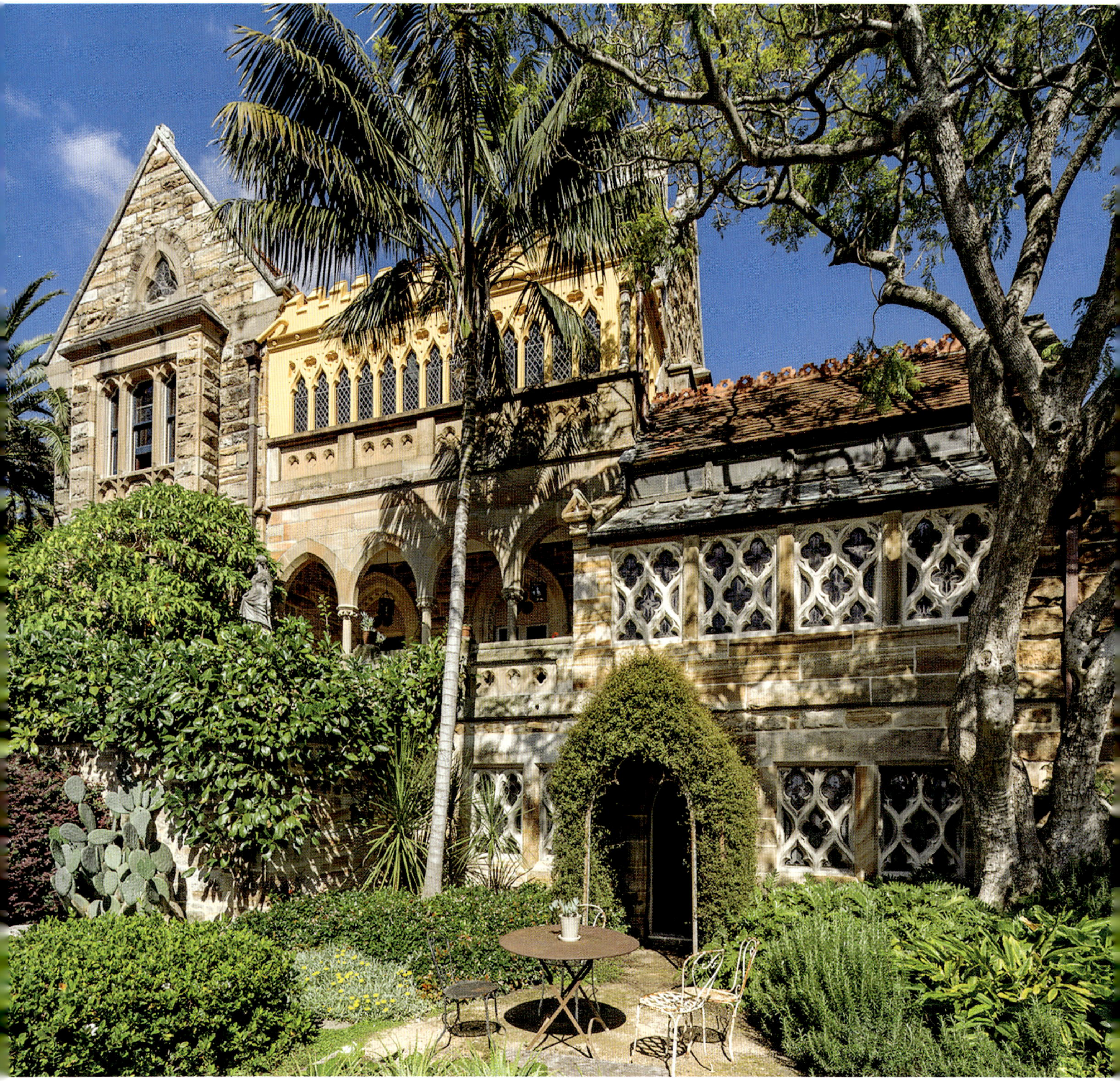

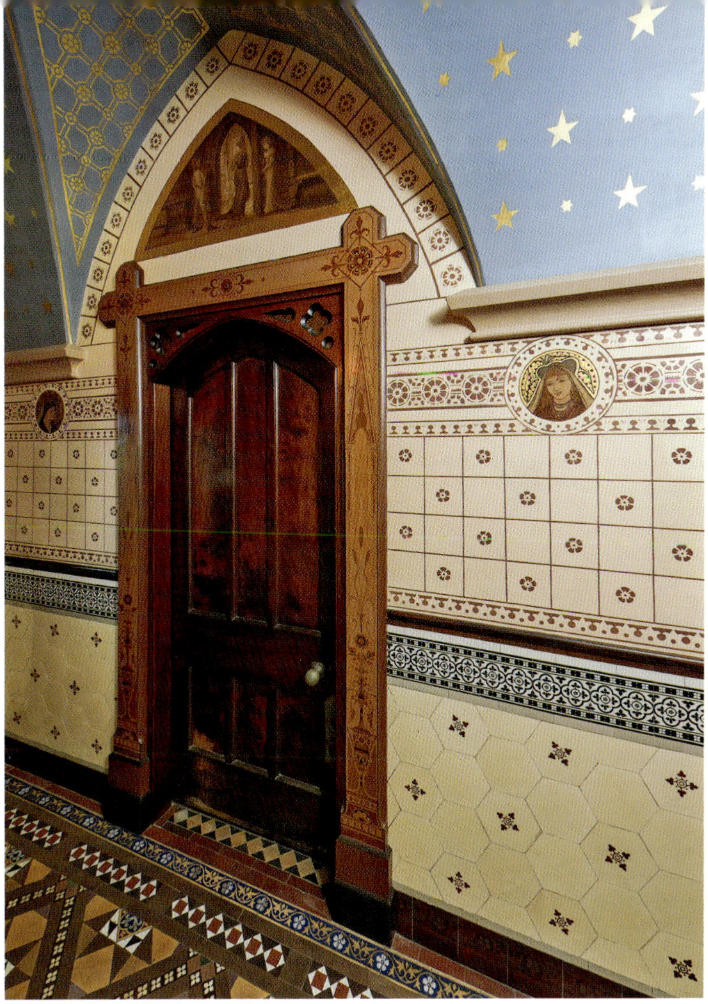

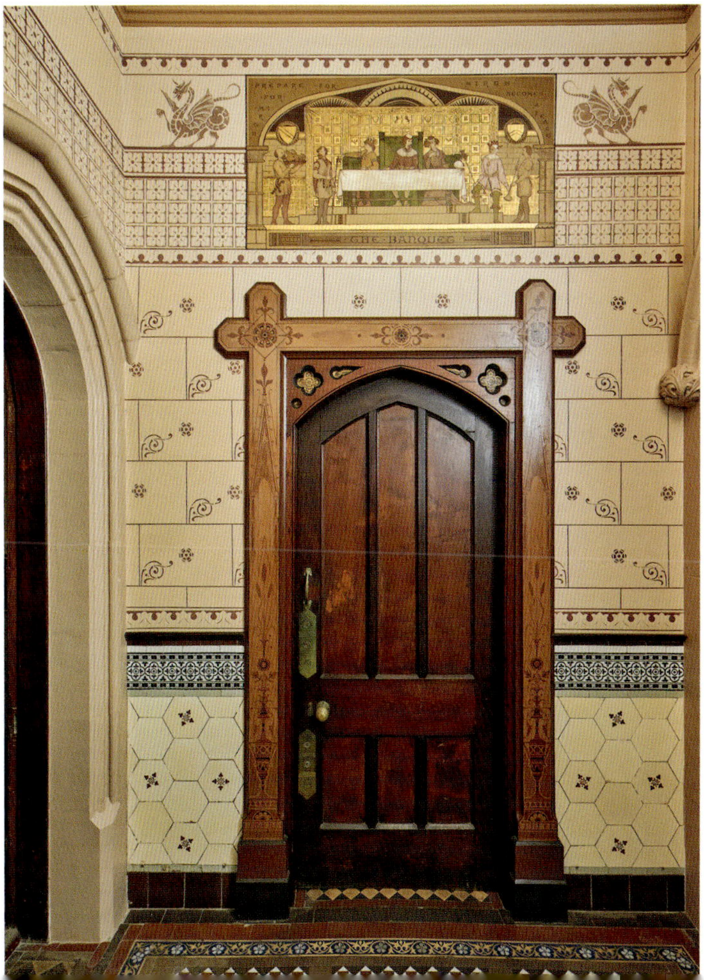

149 Decoration in the entrance hall, The Abbey, Annandale, Sydney, by Lyon, Cottier & Co., *c.*1883

150 Entrance hall wall with overdoor painting of a medieval banqueting scene, The Abbey, Annandale, Sydney, by Lyon, Cottier & Co., *c.*1883

The dining-room ceiling features gold medallions with (edible) animals (fig. 147). That room's wall fill is stencilled with a repeating pattern of pomegranates and foliage and is separated from the frieze by a yellow band with a red meander.

Among the securely attributed, surviving (though much restored) decorations by Lyon, Cottier & Co. are those for the Abbey, in Annandale, Sydney (fig. 148), designed and constructed for John Young (1827–1907), a well-known building contractor, politician, freemason, alderman and later mayor of Sydney who, however, never lived in it.[44] Built between 1881 and 1883 of rock-faced concrete, the Abbey exemplifies the Victorian free Gothic style, which combines features of different phases of Gothic. At the end of the decade, when the house was for sale, an advertisement described it as a 'charming interesting residence ... with 5 sitting rooms, 8 bedrooms, ballroom, smoking room, all richly upholstered, dadoed, fitted with cabinets, wardrobes, cornices, facias &c'.[45]

The decoration of the Abbey marks a departure from Lyon, Cottier & Co.'s usual (classicising) work and shows that the firm could adapt when other styles were requested. Extensive decoration of the walls, ceilings and built-in furniture throughout the house helped to create a medieval fantasy in Sydney.[46] In the entrance hall (fig. 149) the vaulted ceiling is painted blue with golden stars of different sizes. The walls are stencilled to suggest tiling; a frieze with stencilled flowers is interrupted at regular intervals by medallions showing the heads of women and men in medieval attire painted against golden backgrounds and reminiscent of the style of John Moyr Smith, on whose designs they may have been based. Paintings over the doors leading to the dining room and a drawing room show a banqueting scene (fig. 150) and a scene of chivalric romance, possibly indebted to Henry Stacy Marks. In the rooms, dadoes are made of glazed Minton tiles; elaborate wooden doors sport medieval-style hardware. The dining room features an inglenook with an iron stove, flanked by painted and figured tiles. In a small study off the hallway, the gold-lined dado rail is interrupted at regular intervals by pointed arches inside which are pictures of Australian

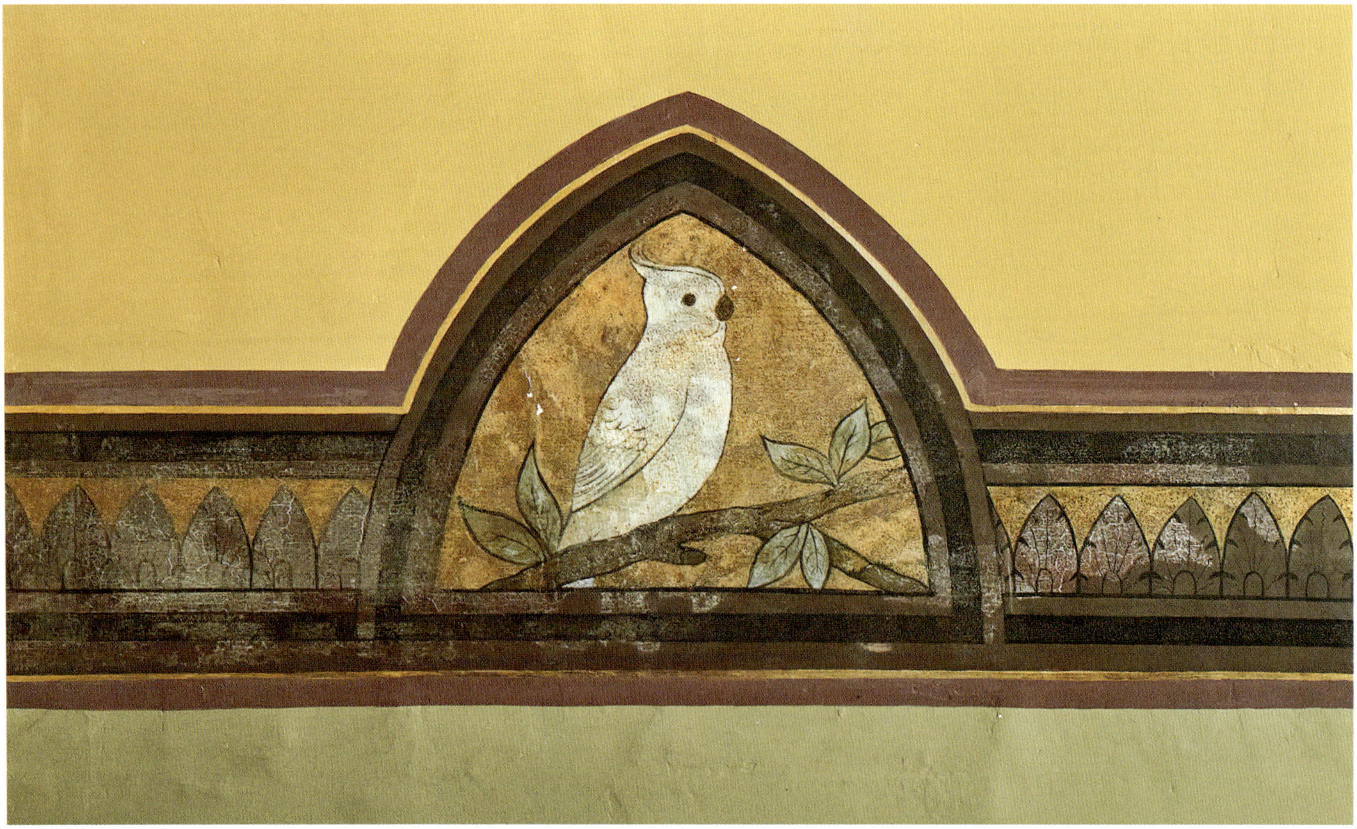

birds (fig. 151). Built-in furniture is decorated with Minton's well-known Shakespeare tiles designed by Moyr Smith in 1872. Gothic Revival bedroom furniture and overmantels with medieval crenellations and crockets are painted with vignettes and birds.[47]

LYON, COTTIER & CO.'S STAINED GLASS

Stained glass was an important part of Lyon, Cottier & Co.'s business and the firm exhibited both religious and secular stained-glass windows in their Sydney showroom and in the intercolonial and international exhibitions held throughout the east coast of Australia during the 1870s and 80s. Designing church windows similar to those produced during his former partnership in Melbourne with Ferguson & Urie, Lyon clearly catered to the Australian taste for high Victorian Gothic Revival stained glass. In his domestic windows, however, Lyon rarely followed his former partners' preference for 'painterly' windows and was more inclined to follow Cottier's abstracting example. Critics recognised the originality of Lyon, Cottier & Co. windows. At the 1875 Victoria Intercolonial Exhibition in Melbourne, which presented a preview of works to be shipped by Australia to the Philadelphia Centennial Exhibition of 1876, Ferguson & Urie showed four domestic windows, including two made for Rupertswood, the newly built country mansion in Sunbury, Victoria, of the landowner, stud-breeder and philanthropist Sir William Clarke (1831–1897).[48] One window, according to the press, was centred with a faithful copy of Edwin Landseer's *The Stag at Bay*, which was (somewhat incongruously) surrounded by images of Australian birds.[49] The subject of a second window was described in the catalogue as 'Chillingworth [*sic*] Wild Cattle', possibly based on Landseer's *Wild Cattle of Chillingham* of 1867 (Laing Art Gallery, Newcastle upon Tyne). Chiding Ferguson & Urie for ignoring the 'true principles which should be kept steadily in view in this development of art', a Melbourne reviewer of the 1875 Intercolonial Exhibition praised, by contrast, Lyon, Cottier & Co.'s Captain Cook window as being 'of quite a different but at the same time more boldly artistic school'.[50]

The Captain Cook window was a large staircase window designed by Lyon to commemorate Captain Cook's voyages in the Pacific and his 'discovery' of Australia. After being shown by Lyon, Cottier & Co. at the 1875 Melbourne Intercolonial Exhibition, it was shipped to the Philadelphia Centennial Exhibition of 1876,[51] furthering the international reputation of Cottier's enterprise which, surprisingly, was not represented at Philadelphia by either the London or

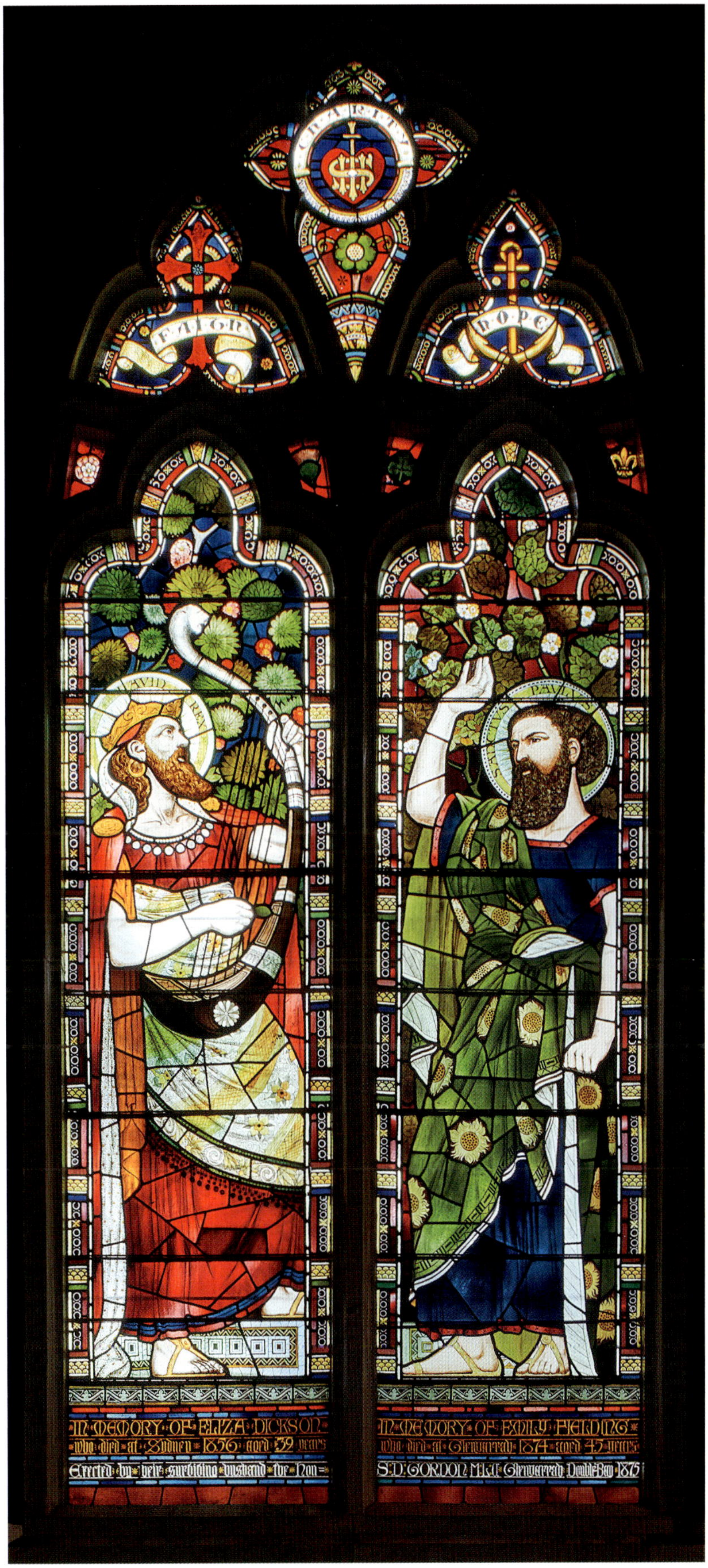

151 *Cockatoo* on the dado in the ground-floor study, The Abbey, Annandale, Sydney, attributed to Parnell Wressell Johnson for Lyon, Cottier & Co., *c.*1883

152 *King David* and *St Paul*, in St Andrew's Scots Presbyterian Church, Rose Bay, Sydney, by Cottier & Co., London, 1875. Stained glass

New York branches of the firm. Another version was shown at the Metropolitan Intercolonial Exhibition in Sydney in 1878.[52] The current location of either version is unknown but in 1878 the press described the figure of Cook as seated at a table 'in deep meditation … quadrant in hand, and nearby a globe with his latest achievement – Australia – conspicuously brought out.'[53] Cook apparently had his hand on the globe, showing Australia as a new colonial possession. Quarries with depictions of native Australian animals (kangaroos and possums) and birds painted in bright colours surrounded this central figure.

Church Commissions

From the beginning, Lyon, Cottier & Co. received commissions for stained-glass windows from religious institutions as well as from individuals wishing to memorialise loved ones by donating a window to their church. By the end of 1876, the firm had produced a brochure in which it advertised a selection of their church commissions around Sydney and New South Wales, listing windows executed for St Andrew's Scots Presbyterian Church, St Peter's Woolloomooloo, Sydney, and All Saints Cathedral, Bathurst, the last being the largest of their church commissions to date.[54] While many of these commissions came from Presbyterian and Episcopal churches and individuals, other churches and even a synagogue were among the firm's clients as well. Its breadth of practice and willingness to work within the budget of the customer or donor ensured the ongoing success of Lyon, Cottier & Co. over the decades.

Enlarged and revamped in 1875, St Andrew's Scots Church in Sydney featured a two-light window depicting King David (*David Rex*) playing the harp and Saint Paul (*Sanctus Paulus*) preaching (fig. 152), which had been commissioned from Lyon, Cottier & Co. by Samuel Deane Gordon in memory of his two deceased wives, and made in the London studio. The church was demolished in the early twentieth century and the window was redeployed in the new church building located in Rose Bay, Sydney, in 1913. After it was originally installed, a reporter for the *Sydney Morning Herald* described it as 'an exact reproduction … of a

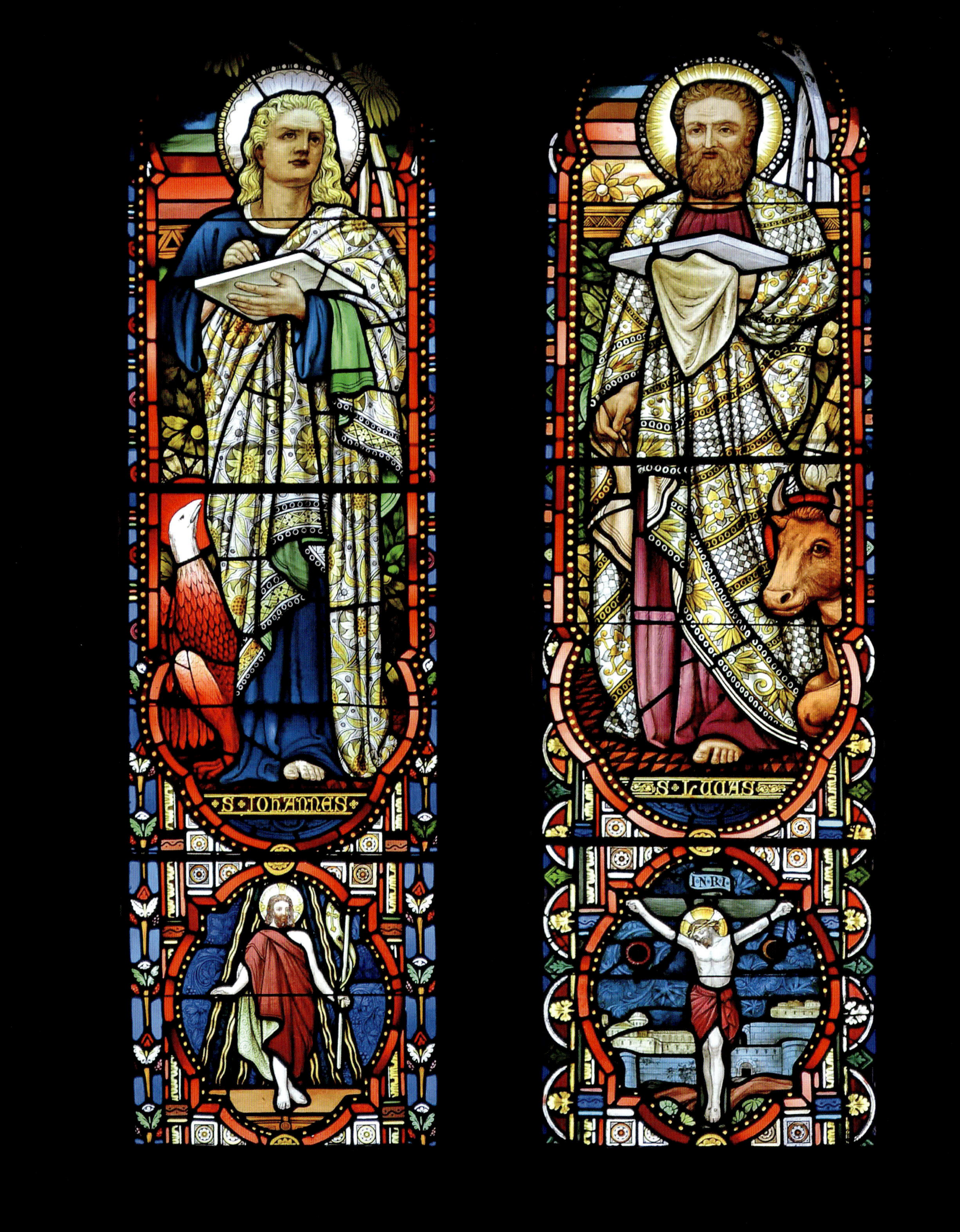
S. IOHANNES
S. LUCAS
I.N.R.I.

153 Two of the *Four Evangelists* in the vestry, All Saints Anglican Cathedral, Bathurst, NSW, by Lyon, Cottier & Co., 1874. Stained glass

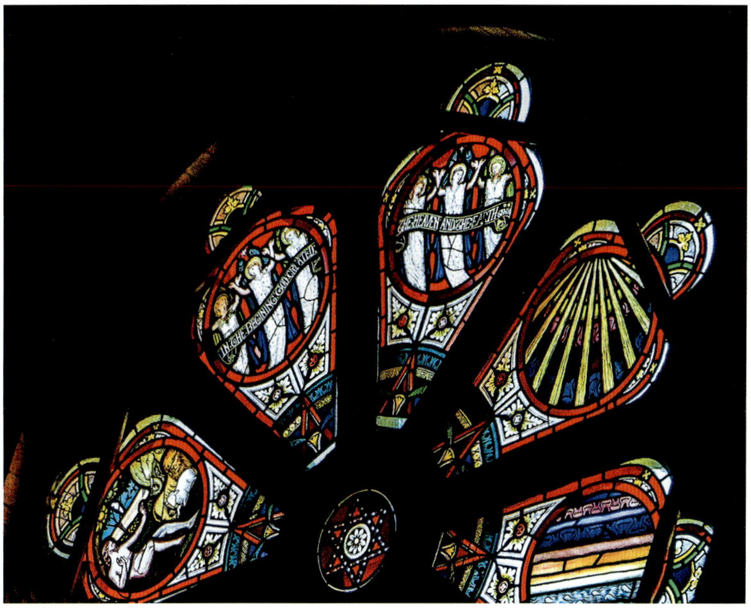

154 *The Six Days of Creation* (detail), rose window in All Saints Anglican Cathedral, Bathurst, NSW, by Lyon, Cottier & Co., *c.*1875. Stained glass

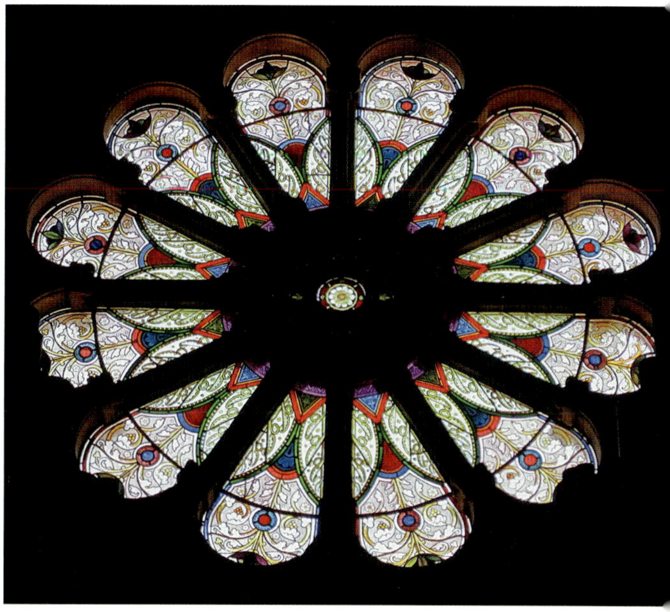

155 Rose window in the south transept, St Thomas' Anglican Church, North Sydney, by Lyon, Cottier & Co., *c.*1882. Stained glass

memorial window erected by Queen Victoria to the memory of Prince Albert and of the Rev. Dr. Norman Macleod, in the Presbyterian Church at Crathie'.[55] The St Andrew's window, indeed, aligns with the description of that originally installed at Crathie Parish Church, Aberdeenshire, in 1873, which was swiftly removed and replaced by another version at Queen Victoria's command (see Chapter Two, pp. 40–1).[56] In the circumstances it seems surprising that Lyon, Cottier & Co. should have allowed the new window to be publicised in this way but perhaps a royal association was too good to waste. The design was reused by the London studio for St James Episcopal Cathedral, Chicago, *c.*1880.

The reporter for the *Sydney Herald* also remarked that the artist who designed King David's costume had 'evidently availed himself of the results of modern research into the antiquities of Assyria'.[57] This comment was astute. Like the David and Miriam windows in Dowanhill Church (see figs 13 and 14), the two figures in the St Andrew Scots window, seen in near-profile, are reminiscent of Assyrian reliefs; costume details (especially in the case of the David), resemble the illustrations of Assyrian clothing shown in nineteenth-century publications, while the bow shape of the harp may be Egyptian rather than Assyrian. Altogether, however, these bold archaising figures hark back to Cottier's time in Glasgow and his cooperation with Alexander 'Greek' Thomson.

In the second half of the 1870s and the early 1880s, Lyon, Cottier & Co. supplied numerous windows for All Saints Anglican Cathedral, Bathurst, New South Wales. Originally built as a parish church, All Saints became a cathedral in 1870 and on that occasion was enlarged by the architect Benjamin Backhouse (1829–1904). The reconstructed and newly extended cathedral was described as 'partaking in the Norman style' of architecture when it opened for worship in 1875.[58] Torn down in the early twentieth century, a new church was built, which eventually was also partially demolished and another cathedral was built on the same site in the 1970s. The original Lyon, Cottier & Co. windows were redeployed throughout this new church.

All Saints and its parishioners were major patrons of Lyon, Cottier & Co. for well over a decade. The iconographic scheme of the chancel windows in the original cathedral's eastern end, as seen in a line engraving published in the press in 1877,[59] comprised a centre light depicting the Ascension of Christ,

156 *Angel playing on an Organ*, detail of window in the inner vestry, St Thomas' Anglican Church, North Sydney, by Lyon, Wells, Cottier & Co., *c.*1888. Stained glass

157 Wheel window in The Great Synagogue, Sydney, by Lyon, Cottier & Co., 1878. Stained glass

158 Three-arched window surmounted by three oculi in the women's gallery, The Great Synagogue, Sydney, by Lyon, Cottier & Co., 1878. Stained glass

159 Tabernacle window in The Great Synagogue, Sydney, by Lyon, Cottier & Co., 1878. Stained glass

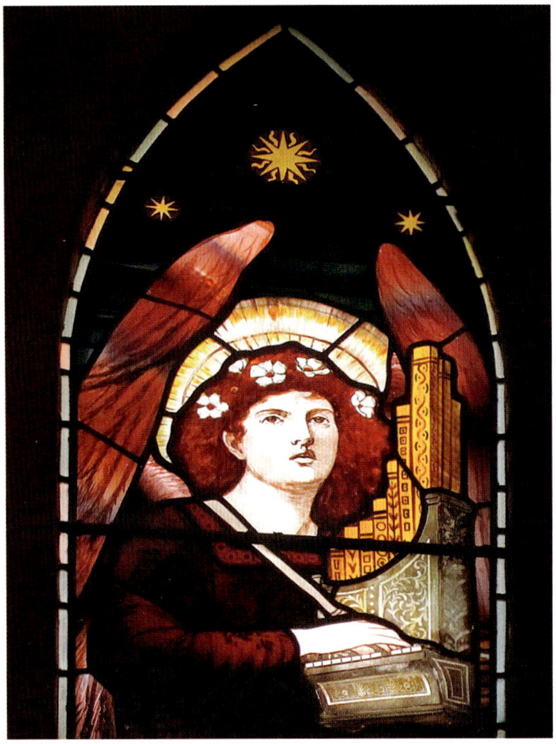

flanked on each side by two lights showing the four Evangelists and their symbols, each one surmounting a small oval medallion representing a Gospel scene (fig. 153). In the rebuilt cathedral, the Evangelist windows are in the vestry. While the figures appear to be based on cartoons from the London studio, and share Cottier's love of patterned drapery, they are more Gothic Revival in style and colouration than windows produced in Cottier's London studio at this time and show the way in which Lyon, Cottier & Co. forged its own visual identity in stained glass. Around 1875–6 Lyon, Cottier & Co. also completed a large rose window for the façade of All Saints that features the Creation and is composed of roundels set in petals depicting the six days of creation in clockwise direction (fig. 154). The two top roundels depict figures clad in white gowns with their arms raised as if in prayer or adoration, placed behind undulating banners inscribed with the opening line of the Book of Genesis.

Lyon, Cottier & Co. also created windows for the enlargement of St Thomas' Anglican Church, North Sydney.[60] Incrementally enlarged between 1878 and early 1880, the church underwent rebuilding and was completed in 1884 under the direction of the Gothic Revival architect Edmund Blacket. Built in rough stone in an Early English Gothic and Venetian style, the church incorporates several Lyon, Cottier & Co. windows,[61] including two large rose windows, one for the southern transept installed around 1882 and gifted by the children of the parish and one in the western end of the church installed in 1884.[62] The rose window in the south transept (fig. 155) is unusual in that it is purely decorative: each petal of the rose window looks like a fan or peacock feather emanating from the point of a star. At its centre is what looks like a peacock feather's eye, alternately coloured in red or blue. The window may be compared with the rose designed by Cottier for the West Free Church, Aberdeen, in 1868. By the end of the 1880s, parishioners had installed a memorial window to a deceased chorister in the inner vestry, depicting an angel playing on an organ (fig. 156). Based on designs made in the London studio, Cottier's music-making angel had first appeared in a window in St Machar's Cathedral, Aberdeen, in 1871.[63]

THE GREAT SYNAGOGUE, SYDNEY

One of the most important religious building projects in Sydney in the second half of the 1870s was the construction of the Great Synagogue in Elizabeth Street. Two Jewish congregations came together to raise the funds for the new building, which became one of the finest Victorian buildings in the city. It was designed in 1874 by the well-known architect Thomas Rowe (1829–1899), who consulted with local rabbis and perhaps also with other architects who had built synagogues in Australia or England. Some of the most prestigious firms in Australia, North America and Britain were commissioned to execute it: Aaron Loveridge was responsible for the masonry, William Coleman for carpentry and joinery, the Fletcher Brothers for the decorative cast iron, Lewis & Steel for the decorative plaster, Cornelius & Co. of Philadelphia for the gas fixtures, Minton, Hollins & Co. for the tiles, P. N. Russell & Co. for the cast-iron columns and Lyon, Cottier & Co. for the stained glass.[64]

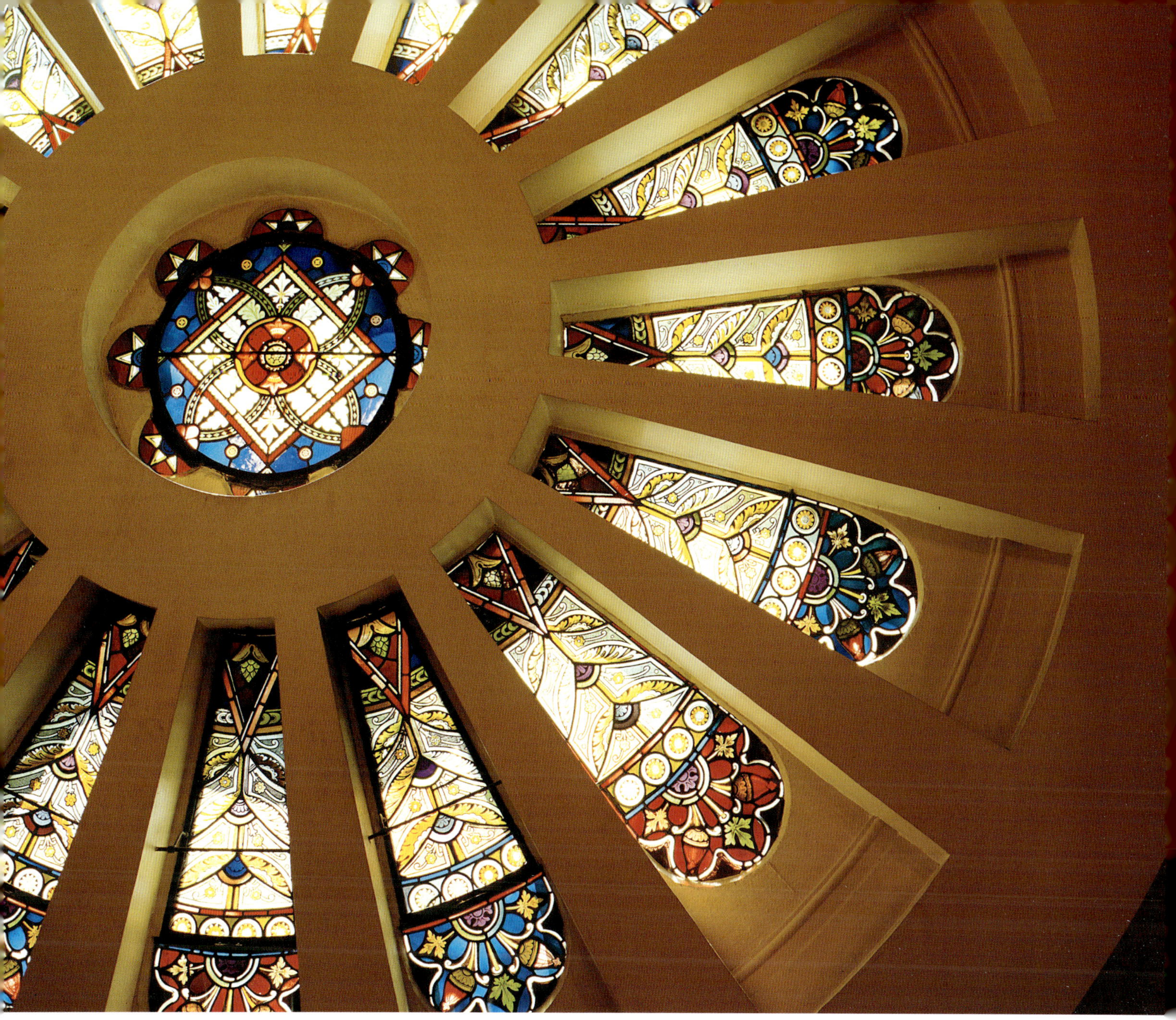
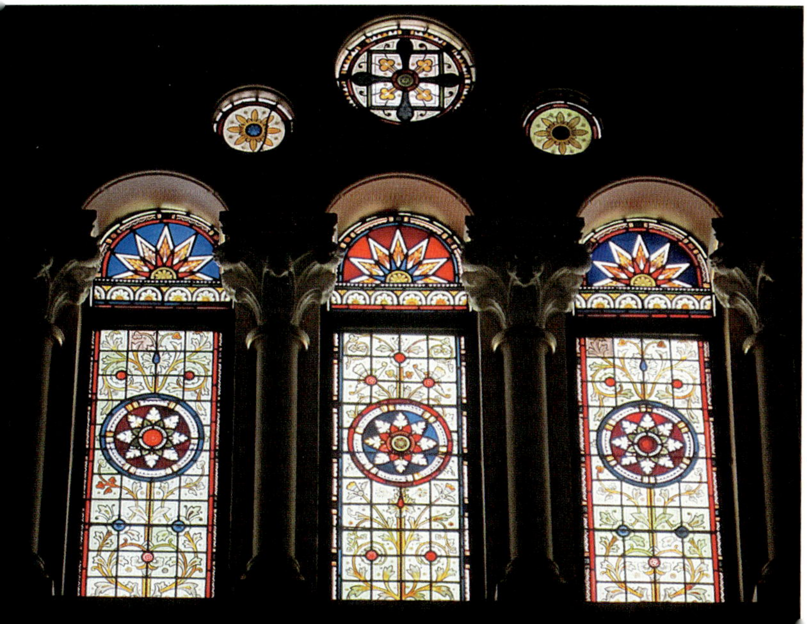
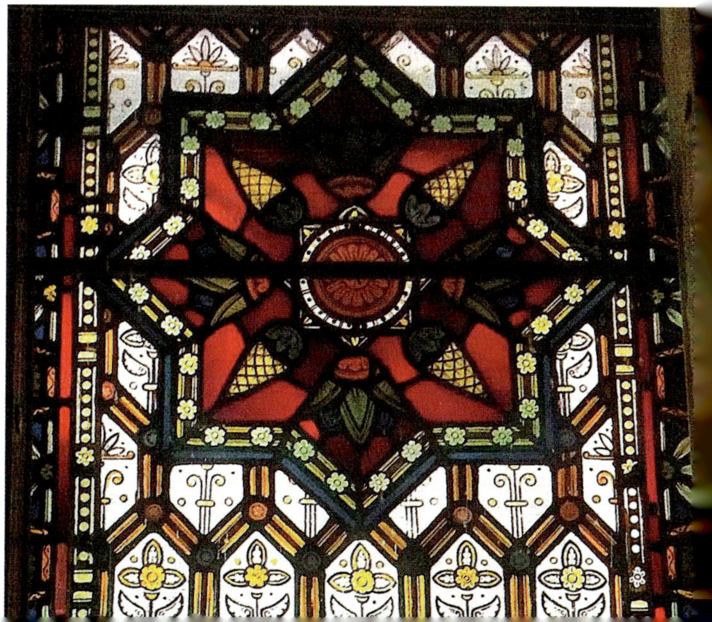

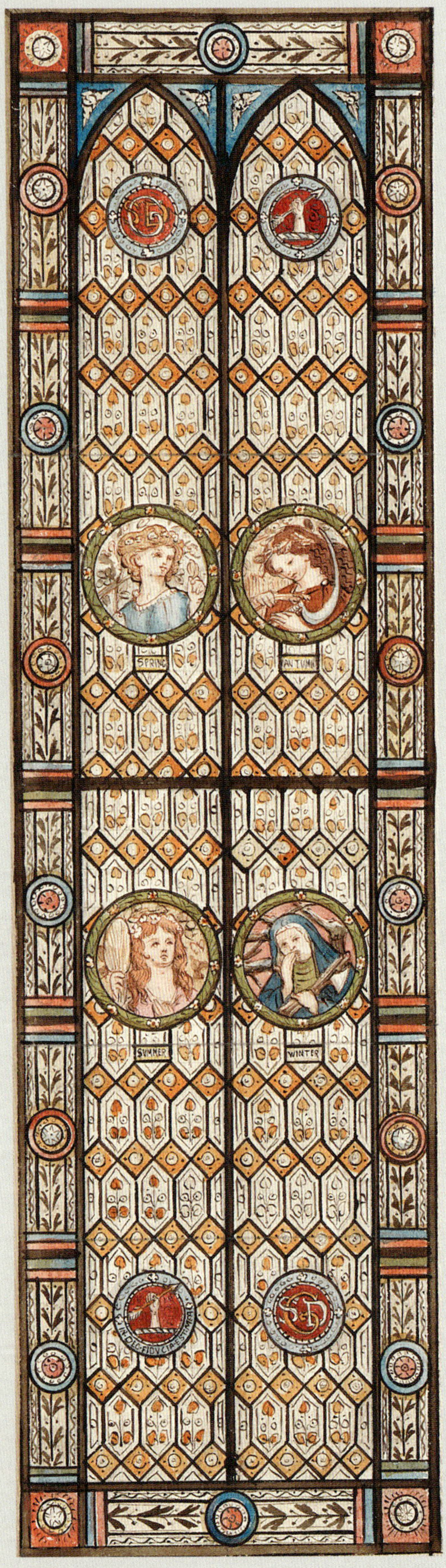
AUTUMN
SUMMER
WINTER

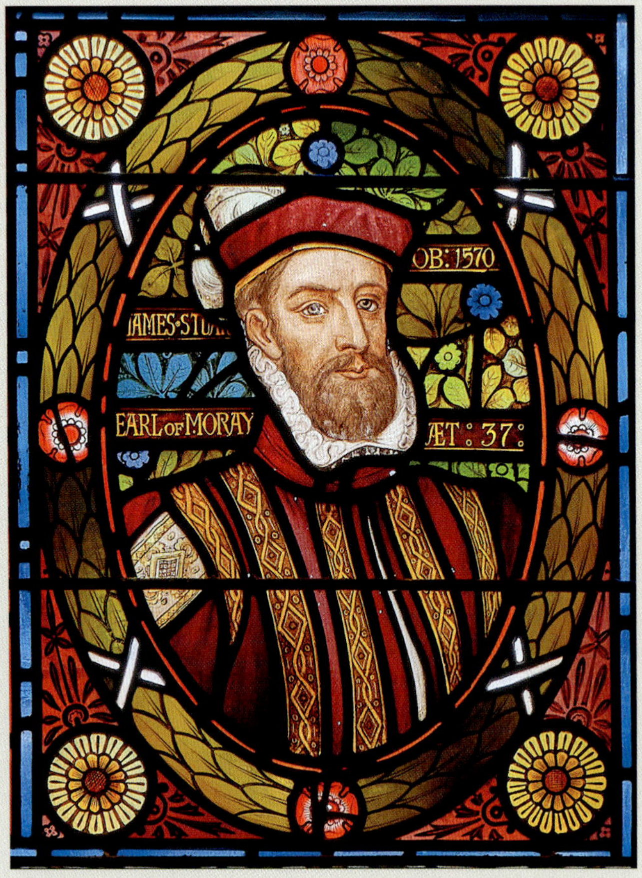
OB: 1570
EARL OF MORAY
ÆT: 37

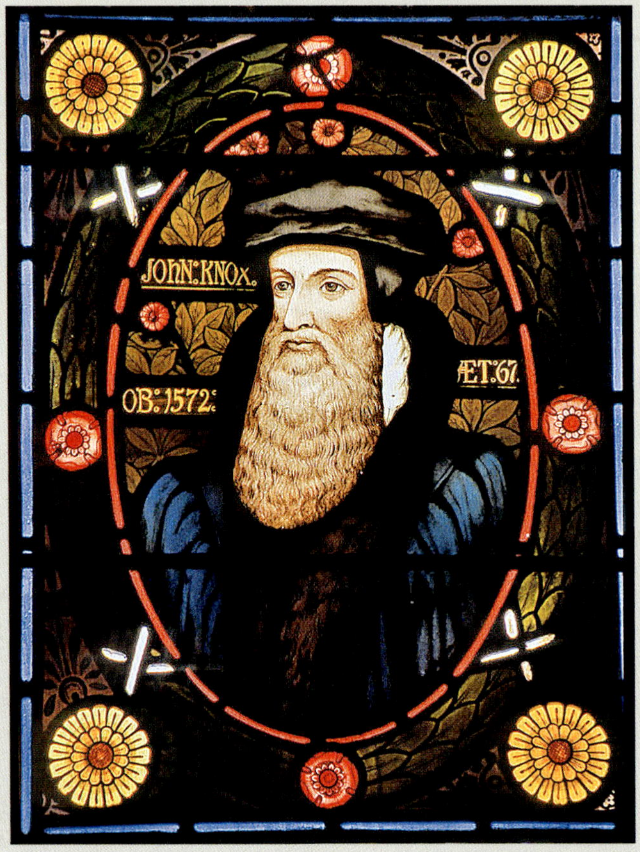
JOHN KNOX
ÆT.67
OB. 1572

160 Design for staircase window, Glenyarrah, Double Bay, Sydney, by Lyon, Cottier & Co., 1875–6. Pencil and watercolour, 42 × 26.5 cm. Mitchell Library, State Library of New South Wales, Sydney

161 (a and b) *James Stewart* and *John Knox*, hall windows in St Andrew's College, University of Sydney, by Lyon, Cottier & Co., *c.*1877. Stained glass

While the Great Synagogue was designed to conform to Jewish ritual and religious rules, stylistically both the façade and the interior show a mixture of Byzantine and Gothic elements. The Gothic aspect is clearly expressed in the abundance of stained-glass windows in the lower level, the halls and the women's gallery. For the latter, Lyon, Cottier & Co. designed three vertical rectangular windows centred on eight-pointed stars, surmounted by semicircular arched windows with sunbursts, perhaps a reference to Judges 5:31, in which those who love the Lord are compared with the sun (fig. 158). The use of the eight-pointed star, now generally associated with Islam, was not uncommon in nineteenth-century synagogues and can be found, for example, in the Dohány Synagogue in Budapest (1854–9). It was not until the end of the nineteenth century that Jews settled on the six-pointed star as the emblem *par excellence* of Judaism.[65] The eight-pointed star is also seen in the tabernacle windows (fig. 159), in which the points are alternately filled with pine cones and triple leaves. The large east-facing wheel window (fig. 157) was shown by the firm at the Sydney Intercolonial Exhibition in early 1877 before being installed in the synagogue later that year when the east end of the building had been completed.[66] At the centre is, once again, the eight-pointed star while the abstract decoration of the petals somewhat resembles that of the petals of the rose window in St Thomas' Anglican Church.

SECULAR WINDOWS

Like Cottier & Co. in London, which supplied domestic glass for commissions throughout Britain and the United States, Lyon, Cottier & Co. designed and made a variety of secular glass. The firm's design portfolio in the Mitchell Library shows drawings for fanlights in a hotel in Newcastle, near Sydney, staircase windows for Her Majesty's Theatre in Sydney, a window design for the Liverpool Arms bar, a staircase window for a bank and numerous designs for windows for private homes. Only a handful of these windows have been preserved. Among them is the staircase window for Glenyarrah in Double Bay, Sydney, the residence of Samuel Deane Gordon. Designed in the mid-1870s (the design is in the Mitchell Library; fig. 160), the two-light window remains in the house, much changed today as it was split into apartments. Largely composed of silver-stained diamond-shaped and hexagonal quarries, the windows feature four roundels with allegories of the Four Seasons in the centre and smaller roundels with Gordon's initials and his emblem, a hand holding up an arrow, at top and bottom. The roundels of the Four Seasons are adaptations of some of Cottier's stained-glass designs from the London studio, found, for example, at Cairndhu House, Helensburgh and Links House, Montrose, Scotland in the early 1870s (see fig. 194). As noted earlier, the same designs were used in the drawing-room ceiling at Government House. Glenyarrah also features two porch windows representing Flora and Pomona, which, as mentioned, may have come from Lyon, Cottier & Co.'s first showroom in Pitt Street.

By far the most important commission for secular windows came to Lyon, Cottier & Co. from St Andrew's College at the University of Sydney. The men behind the commission were three patrons of the college – Samuel Deane Gordon, co-founder and one of the councillors of the college, John Frazer (1827–1884), a businessman and philanthropist, and Captain Charles Smith (1816–1897), a wealthy shipping merchant. Gordon commissioned stained glass and painted interior decorations between 1876 and 1878, including a group of windows in the hall with portraits of famous Scotsmen, set in oval wreaths surrounded by sunflowers (figs 161a and b). The large windows in the College's stairwell were donated by Gordon and Frazer and the three-lancet bay window in the upstairs library was commissioned by Captain Smith (fig. 163).[67] These lancets feature full-length images of Dante, Homer and Chaucer, based on designs from the London studio, surrounded by quarries filled with yellow sunflowers and thistles and surmounted by roundels featuring portraits of the Scottish poets James Hogg, Sir Walter Scott and Robert Burns.[68]

Lyon, Cottier & Co. also decorated the ceiling of the college library, composed of twelve compartments, painted a greenish blue and studded with golden

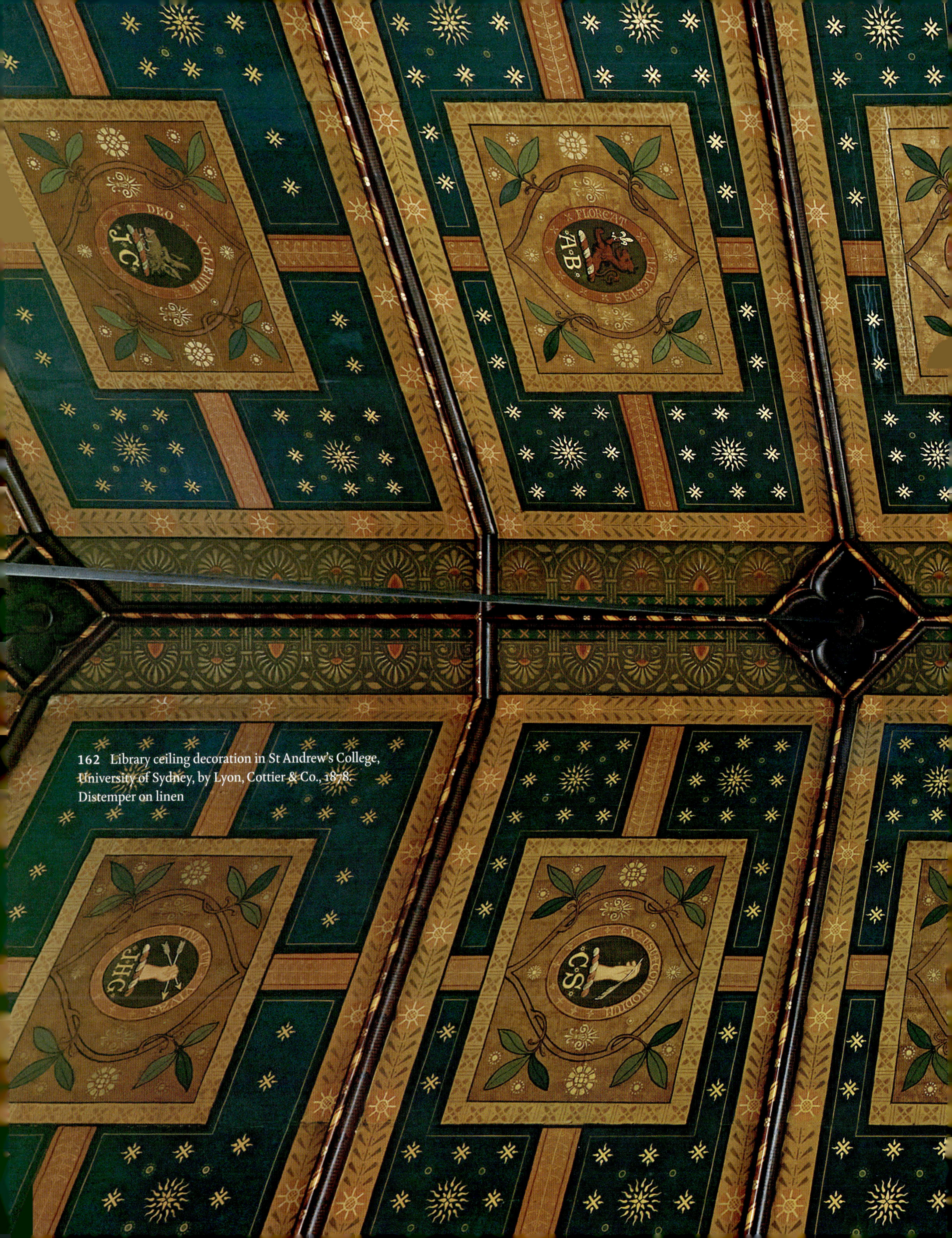

162 Library ceiling decoration in St Andrew's College, University of Sydney, by Lyon, Cottier & Co., 1878. Distemper on linen

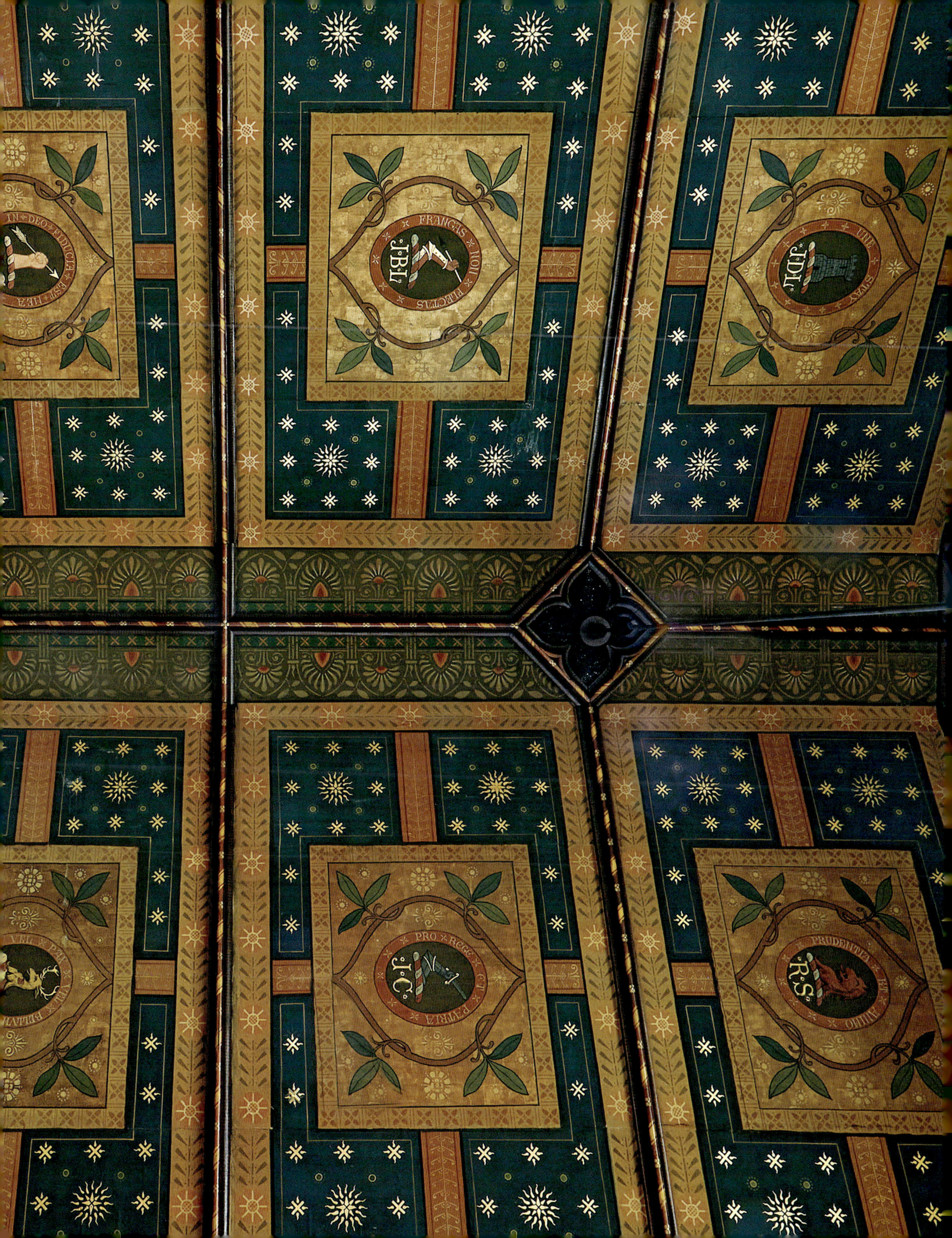
FRANCAS NON FLECTES
PRO REGE ET PATRIA
J.C.
R.S.

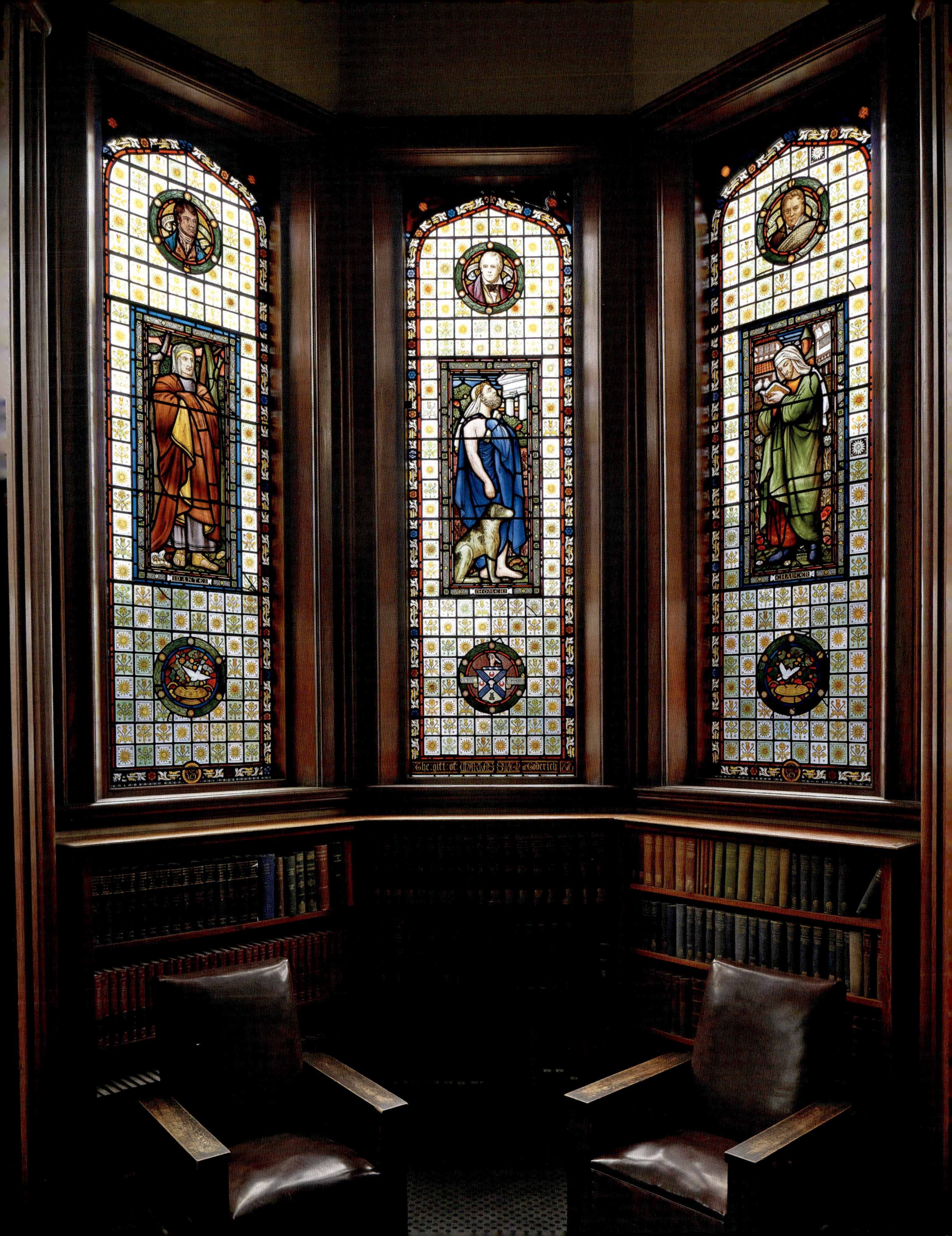
DANTE
HOMER
CHAUCER
The gift of CHARLES

163 *Dante*, *Homer* and *Chaucer*, three-lancet bay window in St Andrew's College library, University of Sydney, by Lyon, Cottier & Co., 1878. Stained glass

164 *Allegory of the Arts* and the *Four Seasons*, three windows in the auditorium of Callan Park Hospital for the Insane, Sydney, by Lyon, Cottier & Co., *c.*1883. Stained glass

stars (fig. 162). Each compartment is divided into four parts and at the intersection of the dividing bars is the crest and the initials of one of the councillors.[69] All the decorations are painted in distemper on linen.[70] The firm also decorated the students' dining hall, which featured a stencilled dado, frieze and lightly stencilled ceiling.

Another public commission came from the Callan Park Hospital for the Insane in Sydney, around 1883. It was for three windows placed behind the stage of the asylum's auditorium, its walls and ceiling stencilled by Lyon, Cottier & Co., which was used as a church, theatre and for public entertainments (fig. 164). The large light in the middle is centred on an allegory of the arts – a woman playing the lyre (music), with a bust on a shelf in the upper left (sculpture), a palette and brushes (painting) and books (poetry) at her feet.[71] Above this panel are small square panels with griffins and heraldic motifs. Together they are framed by an arch composed of small panels that collectively represent vines and around it is another arch of narrow rectangular panels with geometric motifs. The two lights on the side are centred on the encounters of fashionable young women with young men. The paired figures are based on images of the Four Seasons designed by Walter Crane (1845–1915) and published as a set of chromolithographic greeting cards ('Time's Garland for the Year') by Marcus, Ward & Co. around 1878. These are among the few examples of Cottier windows directly based on designs generated outside the company. As described in Chapters Two and Four, other examples

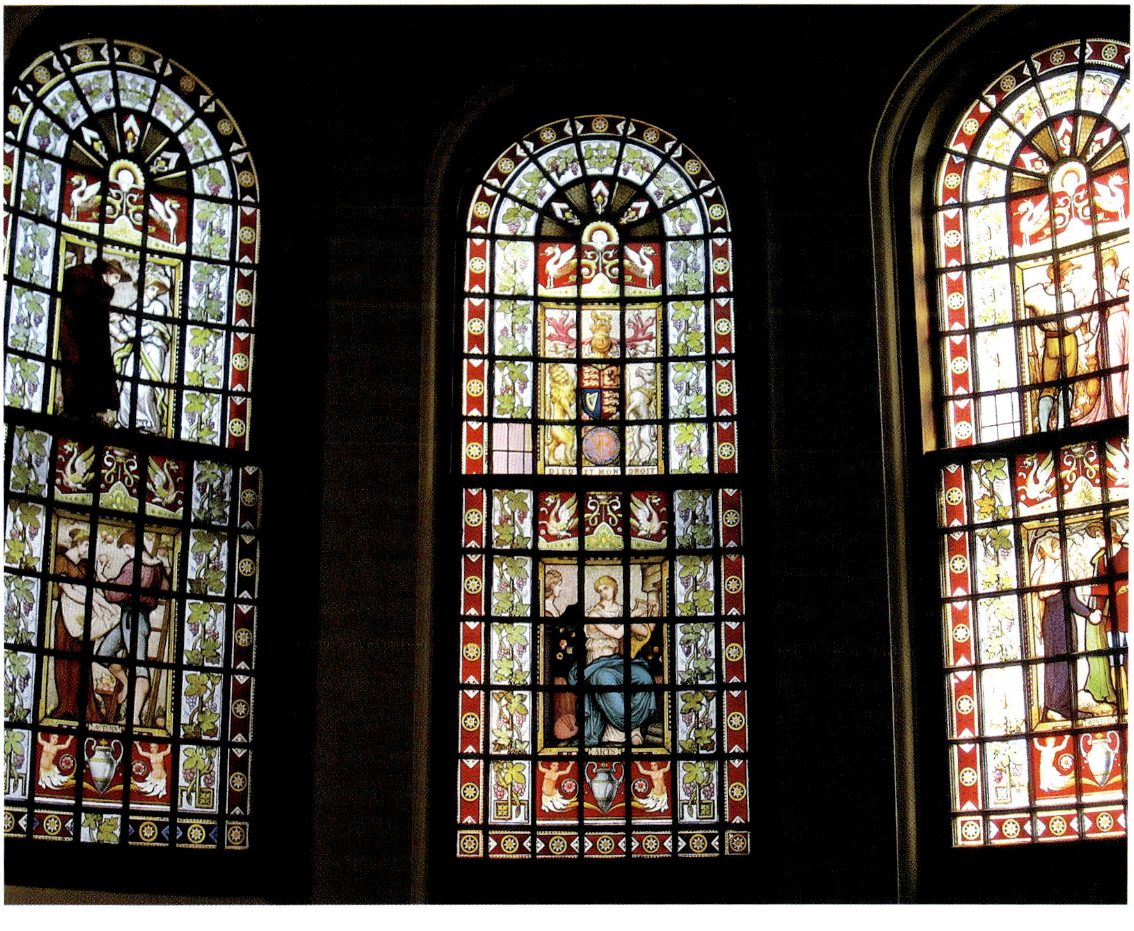

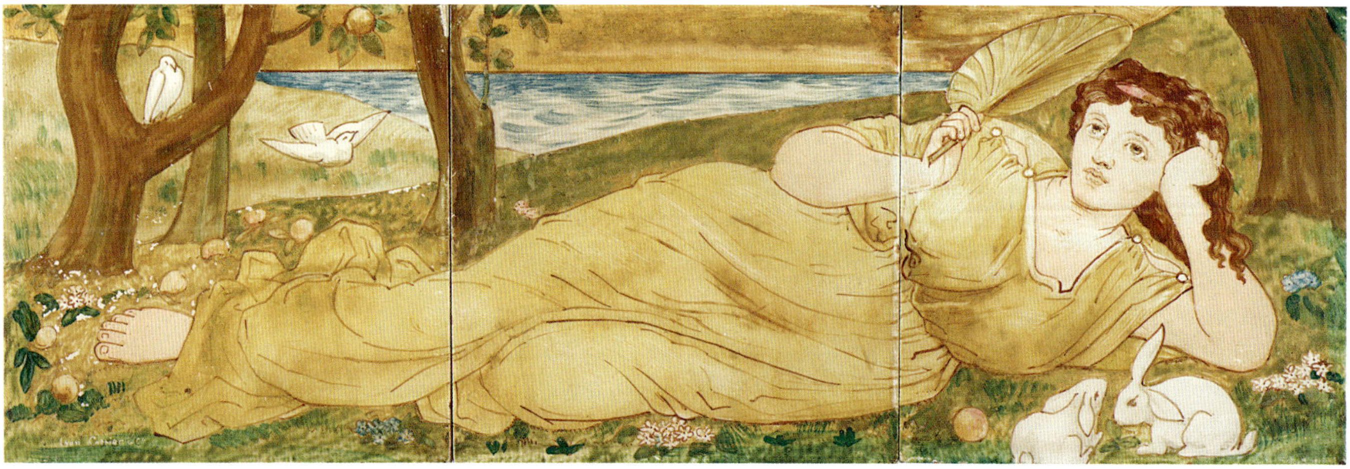

165 *Reclining Woman*, designed by Cottier & Co., London, and decorated by Lyon, Cottier and Co., Sydney, *c.*1878. Underglaze colours on earthenware tiles manufactured by Minton, Hollins & Co., Stoke-on-Trent, Staffordshire, 15.2 × 45.7 cm. Caroline Simpson Library and Research Collection, Sydney Living Museums

include the panels depicting parables based on the Dalziel brothers' prints after Millais and used for many church commissions in Britain and the United States in the 1880s.

CERAMIC PAINTING

If painted ceramics played an important part in Lyon, Cottier & Co.'s production, this arose in large part from Lyon's personal interests. A talented easel and portrait painter, Lyon frequently exhibited with the Art Society of New South Wales, established in 1880. In addition to oil paintings, he also produced ceramic plaques. A newspaper review of the 1881 Society Exhibition mentions that he exhibited a large plaque depicting the face of a young girl with 'a very pretty pre-Raphaelite head' and flowing chestnut hair, placed against the boughs of a blossoming tree on a gold ground.[72] Two hydria-shaped vases, depicting portraits of Joseph Banks and Captain Cook respectively, were painted by Lyon and exhibited at the same Art Society exhibition. The vase depicting Banks, the only one to have survived (Museum of Applied Arts and Science [MAAS], Sydney) was decorated further with painted and enamelled red waratahs.[73]

The firm advertised hand-painted tiles to be used in interiors,[74] as well as ceramic doorplates with waratahs and other Australian flora,[75] but little of this work has survived. A rare extant example is a three-tile panel, painted on Minton, Hollins & Co. blanks, depicting a woman reclining in a landscape and holding a fan (fig. 165). The design is almost certainly the same as that used in a three-tile panel on a mantelpiece decorated by Cottier & Co. in London, in about 1873, for Cairndhu House, Helensburgh, where it appeared with other tiles, including two two-tile panels depicting *Fame* and *Fortune* (see fig. 45).[76]

As in Britain and North America, in the 1870s and 80s it became particularly fashionable for young women in Australia to practise china painting in addition to such artistic pursuits as watercolour painting and needlework. Influenced by the writings of Mary Eliza Haweis, Cottier's acquaintance, the 'Art at Home' book series published by Macmillan, and the numerous similar publications of the last quarter of the nineteenth century, many women regarded house decoration as a moral imperative and their pursuit of beauty 'like a religion'.[77] While for most women such work was a polite pastime, for some it was a form of precarious employment. Fostering talent and ambition, Lyon, Cottier & Co. acted as an agent for women interested in learning fabric and china painting[78] and encouraged the use of their kiln for firing.[79] Known as the only firm in Sydney to stamp or fire china designs, Lyon, Cottier & Co. were recommended to one young hopeful female amateur because they 'are true decorators in every sense of the word, and would doubtless appreciate your artistic suggestions'.[80] Lyon encouraged the pursuits of young women, including

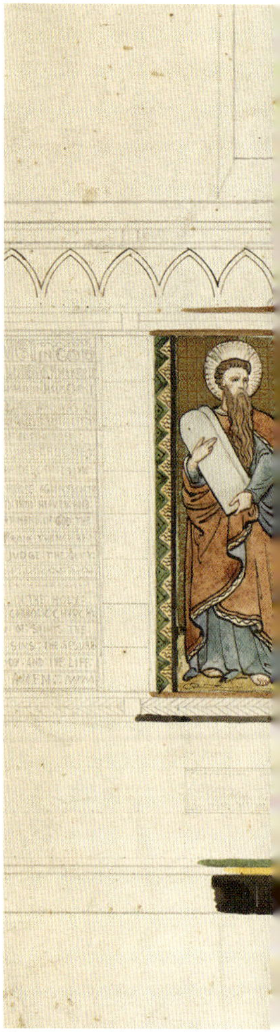

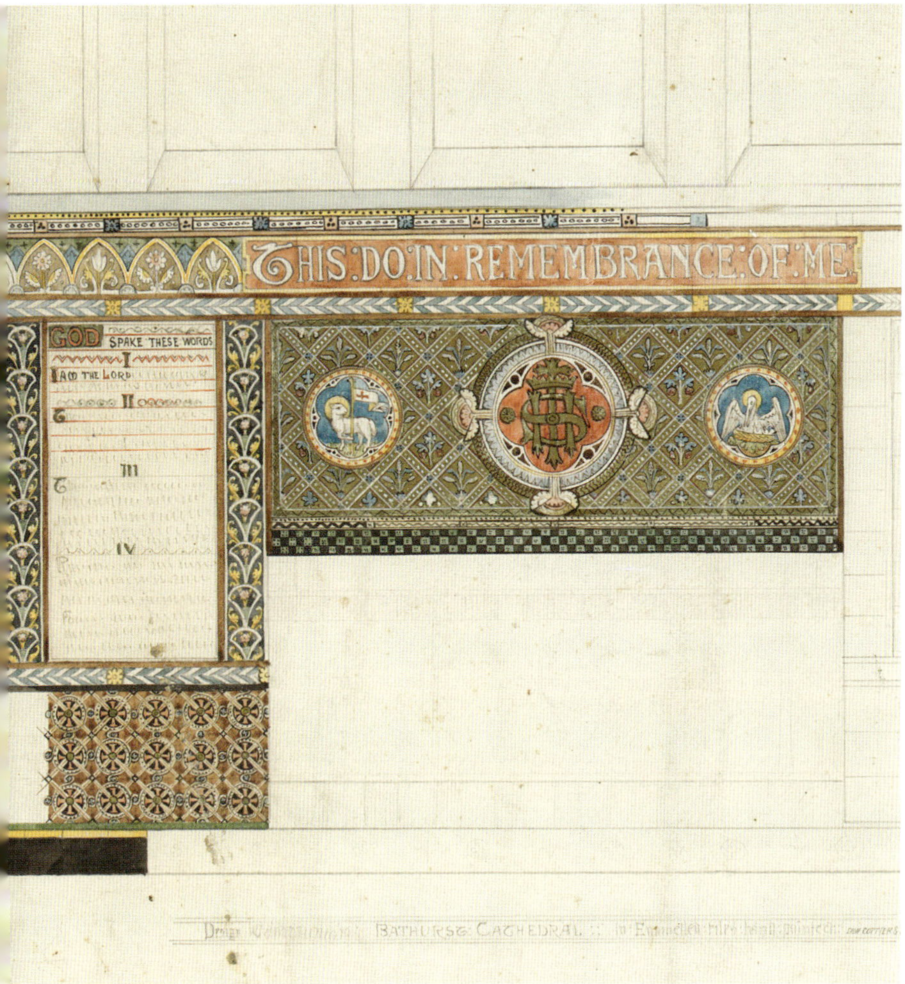

166 Design for tiled reredos, All Saints Anglican Cathedral, Bathurst, by Lyon, Cottier & Co., 1877. Pencil and watercolour on paper, 59.5 × 62 cm. Mitchell Library, State Library of New South Wales, Sydney

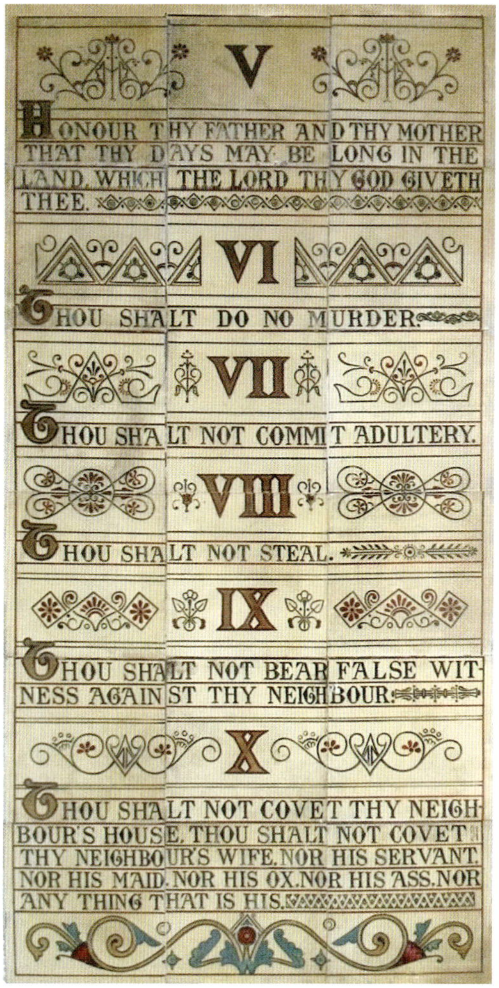

167 Fragment of the tiled reredos, All Saints Anglican Cathedral, Bathurst, by Lyon, Cottier & Co., 1877. Underglaze colours on earthenware tiles. All Saints Cathedral Archive, Bathurst

his own daughter Margaret who painted china for the Melbourne International Exhibition in 1880.[81]

Lyon, Cottier & Co.'s most important work involving ceramic tiles was a large reredos, installed in 1877 at All Saints in Bathurst for which the firm had also provided numerous windows (see figs 153 and 154). Dedicated to the memory of the recently deceased Reverend Canon Thomas Sharpe, who was largely responsible for establishing the Anglican church in Bathurst, the reredos was over 2.7 metres high and nearly 8 metres wide. Unfortunately, only fragments of this monumental altar screen survive but a partial sketch among Lyon, Cottier & Co.'s surviving designs (fig. 166) suggests that the reredos showed, on the left, a full-length figure of Moses holding the tablets of the law, next to the text of the first five of the Ten Commandments. The central part of the reredos, which would have risen above the altar, was covered with decorative tiles surrounding three medallions: a central one with the monogram 'I.H.S.' flanked by medallions showing the Lamb of God and the pelican. The iconography of the right part of the reredos showed the last five commandments and another figure, possibly St Peter (not illustrated), while the lintel at the top featured Christ's words, 'This do in remembrance of me'. As surviving tiles from this reredos (fig. 167)

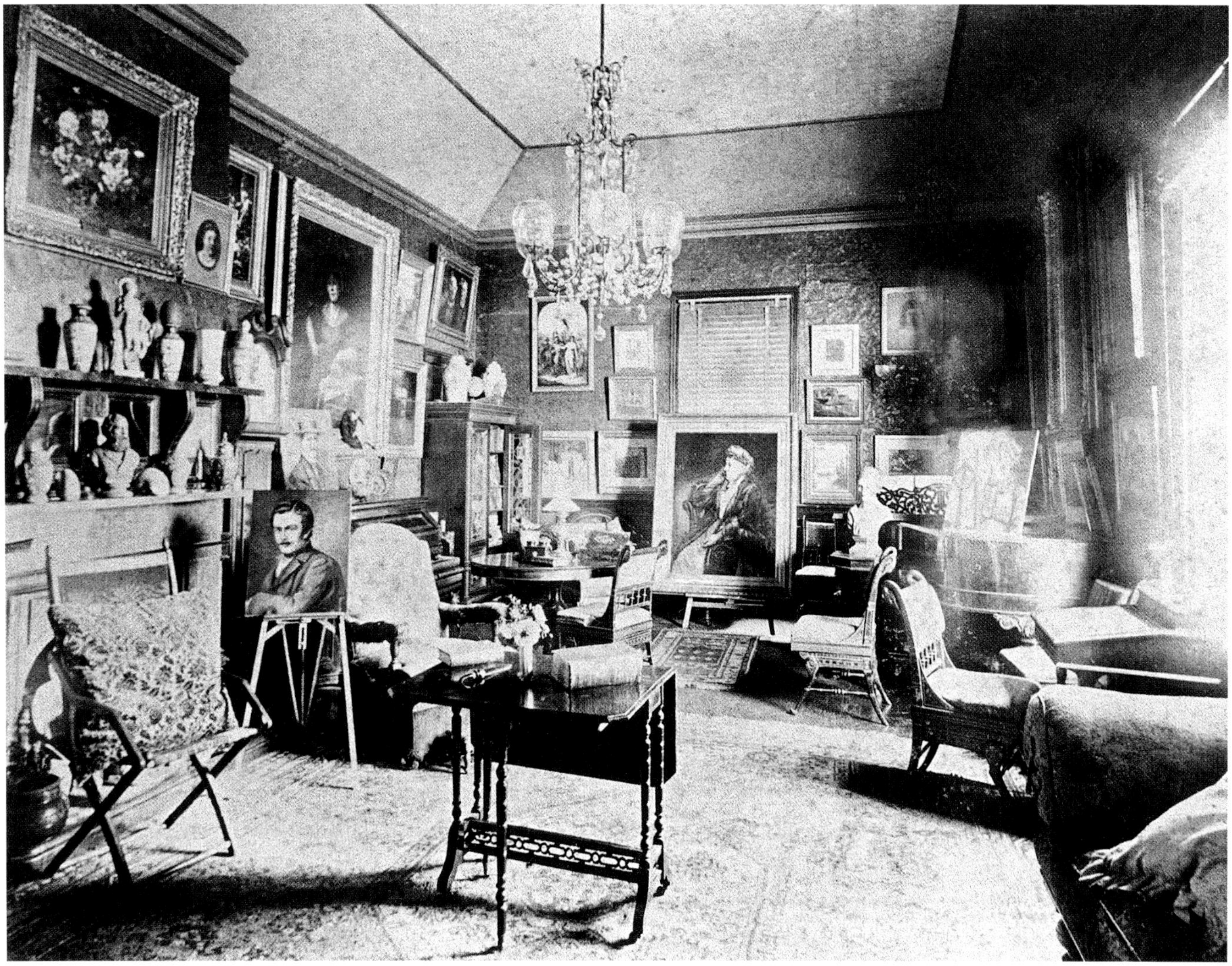

held in the cathedral's archive show, the text and ornaments were painted in enamels and glazed. Before the reredos was installed it was exhibited in Lyon, Cottier & Co.'s showroom in Sydney, suggesting that the firm considered it among its proud achievements and one that could potentially attract further orders.

VILLA JOYLEN, THE 'AUSTRALIA' WINDOW AND LYON'S PLANS TO VISIT COTTIER

After ten prosperous years, in early 1884 Lyon moved with his family to a new brick villa called Joylen at Birchgrove near Balmain. The waterfront residence, with seven large rooms, was unfortunately demolished in 2005, but some photographs and a set of windows survive. A photograph of the interior of the drawing room gives evidence of Lyon's activity as a painter, as pictures are everywhere, not only hanging on the walls but also leaning against furniture (fig. 168). His portrait bust by the Italian, Sydney-based sculptor Achille Simonetti from the 1880s centres the mantelpiece (see fig. 133). Lyon's study featured a large, six-light stained-glass window from Lyon, Cottier & Co., now in MAAS in Sydney (fig. 169). Three vertical panels include roundels with the portraits of the Venetian Renaissance painter Titian, the Dutch sixteenth-century glass stainer Wouter Crabeth and the Spanish Baroque painter Diego Velázquez, set in wreaths punctuated by flowers.[82] Similar to designs made by Cottier in Scotland for John Forbes White at Seaton Cottage (see figs 15 and 16), the roundels are surrounded by Renaissance Revival strapwork and set into windows composed of glass roundels which are rippled, a treatment seen in a number of Lyon, Cottier & Co.'s domestic windows. Above the vertical panels are three smaller arched panels (not illustrated) which contain the Lyon family crest in the centre and small shields with

168 Drawing room of John Lamb Lyon's family home Joylen, Birchgrove, Sydney. Photograph *c.*1890

169 *Titian*, *Wouter Crabeth* and *Diego Velázquez*, lower section of a six-light study window from Joylen, Birchgrove, Sydney, by Lyon, Cottier & Co., *c.*1884. Stained glass. Museum of Applied Arts and Sciences, Sydney

the initials of Lyon and his wife on either side, both surrounded by Scottish thistles. Across the bottom of these three upper panels is the motto, taken from the book of Psalms 31:1, 'In Te Domine Speravi' (In Thee, O Lord, have I put my trust).

Joylen also featured, in one of its rooms, the large Australia window that Lyon, Cottier & Co. had made for the Colonial and Indian Exhibition held in London in 1886.[83] The window was destroyed in a storm in 1955 but from the catalogue of the London exhibition and reports in the Sydney press, we know it was centred on an 'emblematic' figure of Australia standing before a trellis entwined with fruit vines. Her head was surrounded by the rising sun and her right hand rested on a shield emblazoned with the coat of arms of the Australian colonies. Her left arm supported a cornucopia, resting on a ram's head, alluding to New South Wales's thriving pastoral industry. Beneath this figure was a group after the famous Sydney Cove medallion designed by the English sculptor Henry Webber (1754–1826), and first modelled in clay taken from Sydney Cove at Wedgwood's Etruria at the end of the eighteenth century. It depicted Hope visiting Sydney Cove, attended by Peace, Art and Labour. The window was inscribed with a quotation from Erasmus Darwin's prophetic verses, commissioned by Wedgwood, of the future greatness of New South Wales.[84] The borders of the window contained small sections filled with depictions of Australian flora and fauna, including possums, parrots, lyrebirds, waratahs and native roses. Exhibited in Lyon, Cottier & Co.'s Sydney showroom before it was sent to London, the window's theme was clearly conceived in anticipation of the upcoming centenary of Australia's colonisation in 1888 and portrayed the natural bounties the continent had contributed to the wealth of the British Empire.[85] As for Lyon, Cottier & Co., it showed how the firm was positioning itself, over a decade after its foundation, as the promoter of a new Australian art, rooted in the European tradition but with its own iconography, supporting an ideology of Australia's unique place within the British Empire.

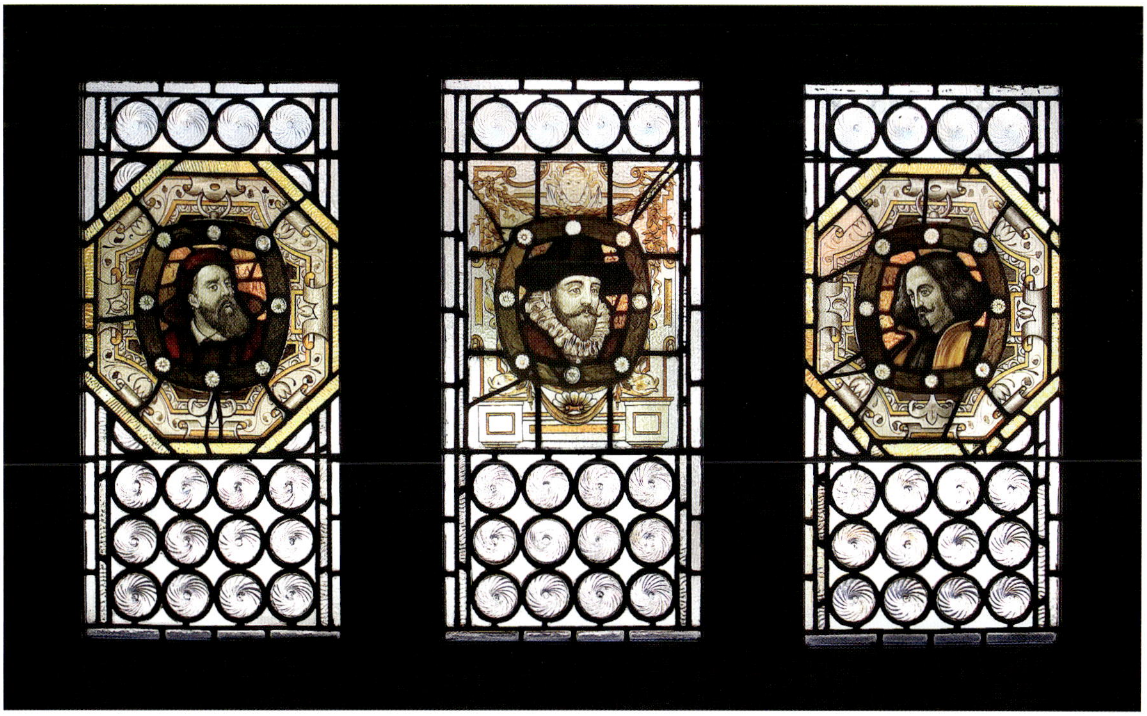

Andrew Montana

CHAPTER SEVEN
SYDNEY & MELBOURNE 1887–1924

170 Design for wall decoration in the banking chamber of the English, Scottish and Australian Chartered Bank, Melbourne, by Andrew Wells for Lyon, Wells, Cottier & Co., 1887. Watercolour on paper, 38 × 43 cm. Mitchell Library, State Library of New South Wales, Sydney

In 1887 John Lamb Lyon went into partnership with one of Daniel Cottier's former assistants, the Scottish decorator Andrew Wells (1845–1918), operating under the name of Lyon, Wells, Cottier & Co. The restructured company lasted until 1895, after which Wells returned to Scotland and formed a new partnership in Glasgow with William Guthrie (in 1898[1]) and the Australian partnership reverted to its former name, Lyon, Cottier & Co.

The arrival of Wells in Australia followed soon after Lyon's journey to the United States and Europe in 1886. The aims of Lyon's trip were to call on relatives and friends and to study the architecture, stained glass and the art and decoration in the cities he visited. His travel journal has been preserved (see Appendix) and contains much interesting information about the New York branch of Cottier & Co. (as described in Chapter Four) and the Glasgow showroom of Cottier's agent William Craibe Angus, as well as St James's Terrace in London, where Lyon was the Cottiers' house guest.

During his stay in Britain, Lyon undoubtedly connected with Wells, whom Cottier may have recommended. Cottier had known the Edinburgh native since the days when they both worked for Field & Allan in the early 1860s and he had brought the talented artist along as an assistant when he set up his own firm as a glass painter and mural decorator in Edinburgh in 1864. In about 1870 Wells had established a business in Glasgow, which lasted until 1886, when he travelled to Australia, apparently for health reasons.[2] Together with his family he embarked on the long voyage towards the end of 1886, about half a year later than Lyon himself, who returned to Sydney on 26 July 1886.

Prior to Wells's departure for Australia, a large farewell party was held at the Pen and Pencil Club in Glasgow in mid-October 1886. The journal *Decoration*, edited by John Moyr Smith, reported that 'About sixty gentlemen associated with painting, sculpture, and architecture, decoration, literature, music, science, and the drama, showed their esteem for Mr. Wells as a man and an artist' and wished him well for his new life in Sydney.[3] Smith had been an admirer of Wells's work for some time; in 1885 he had praised Wells as 'a draughtsman of great skill, taste, and spirit, a bold, original, versatile and harmonious colourist'[4] and a few months before Wells's departure he had published in *Decoration* some of Wells's work for the Glasgow residence of the prominent shipbuilder and MP William Pearce (1833–1888).[5] Smith continued to write about Wells's decorating work even after he went to Australia: in early 1887 *Decoration* covered his work at St Andrew's Hall, an auditorium near Charing Cross, Glasgow, as well as his ceiling and wall decorations for some Glasgow churches.[6]

When Wells arrived in Australia, New South Wales and Victoria were at the height of an urban real estate boom. In Melbourne especially, property values were rocketing, being surpassed within the British Empire only by London.[7] The colonies were also preparing for the celebrations of the centennial of British colonisation in 1888. As a result, there was a healthy demand for the artistic decoration of business premises, clubs, churches and especially residences. In response, the firm opened a branch in Melbourne, with an office located at 16 Collins Street, though the main office remained in Sydney. In 1888 Lyon, Wells, Cottier & Co. were considered to be 'the most representative house in its line in Australia', which 'regularly employed between thirty to forty hands, and at times more.'[8] However, by the late 1880s business must have slowed down because of the onset of a severe

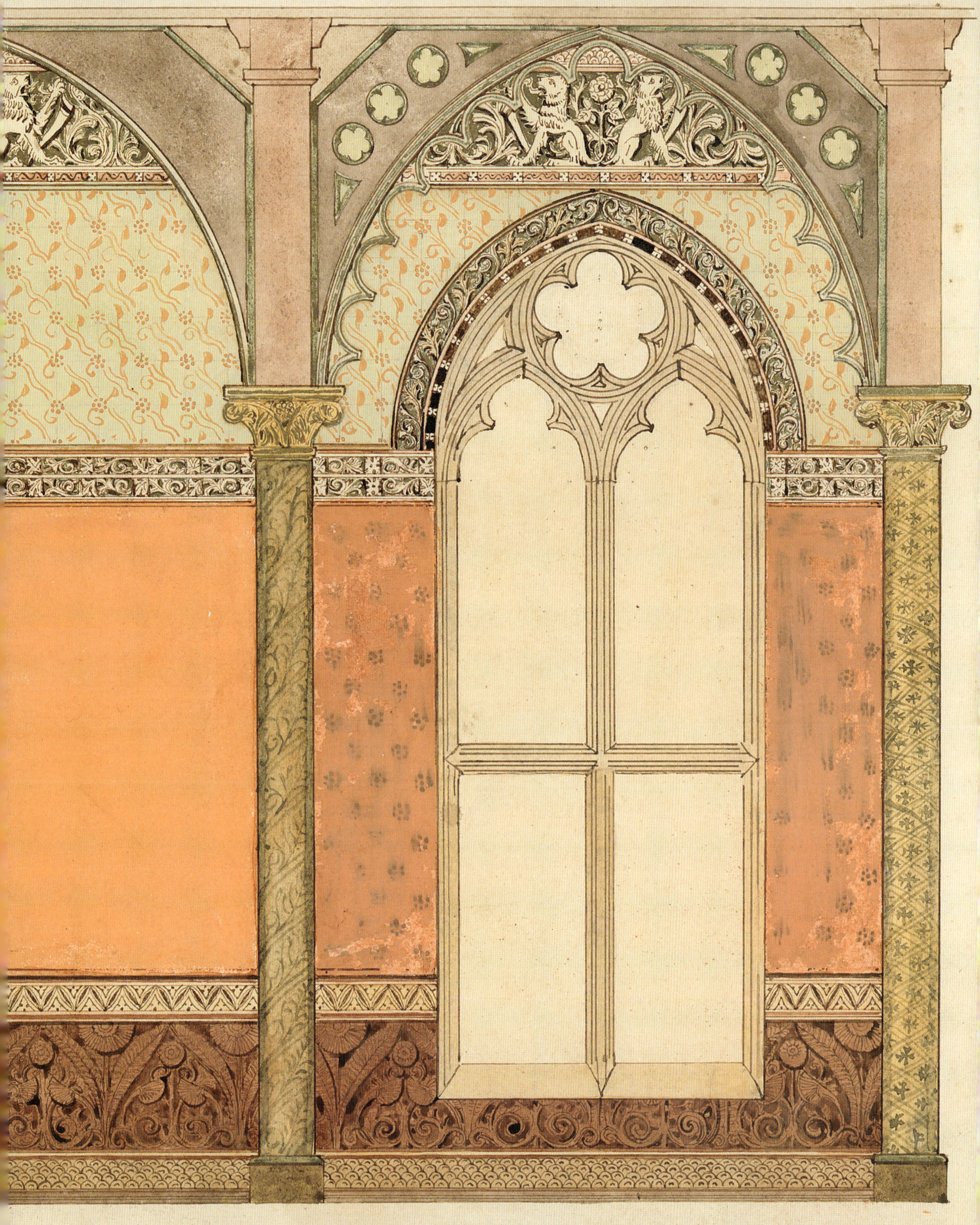

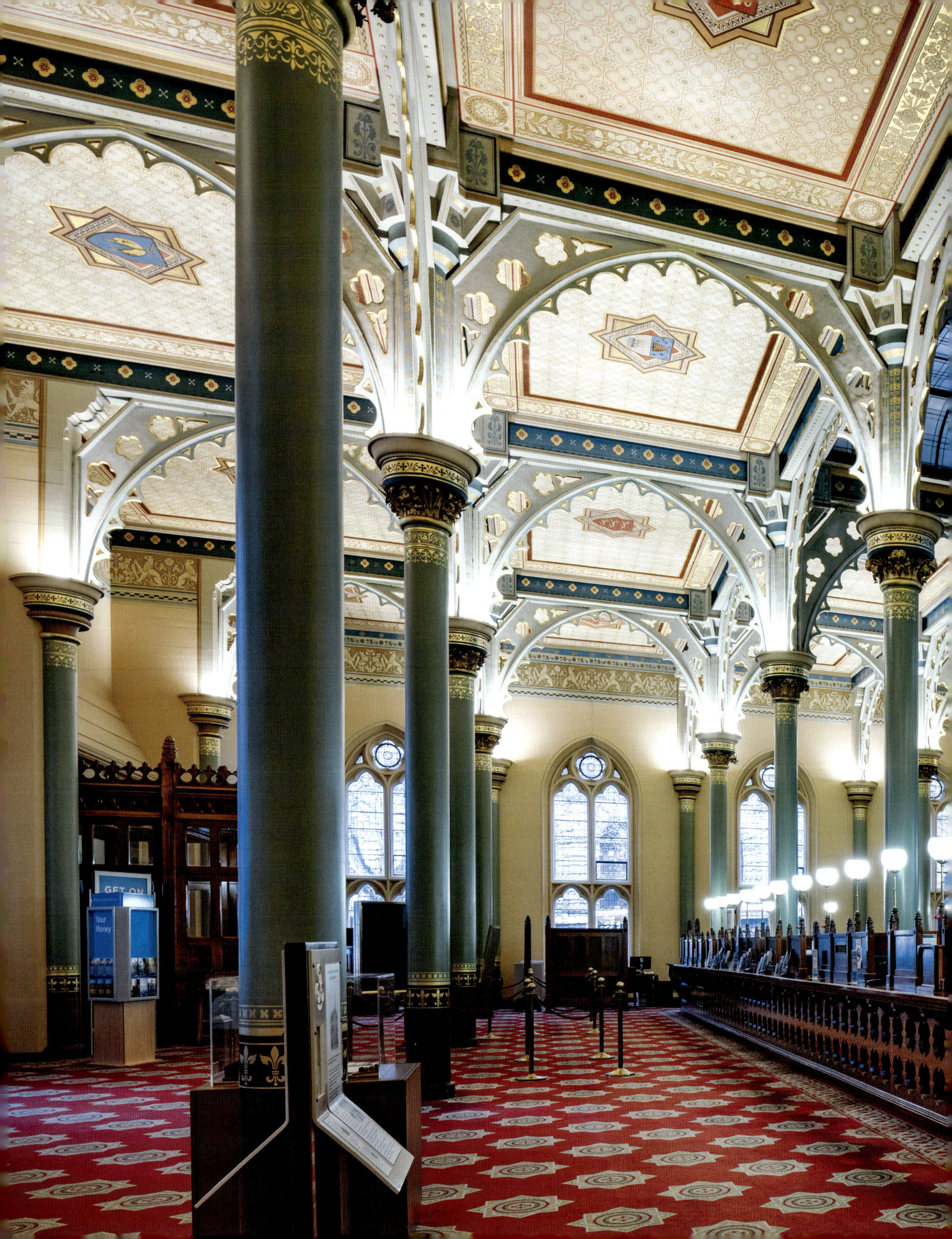
GET ON
Your Money

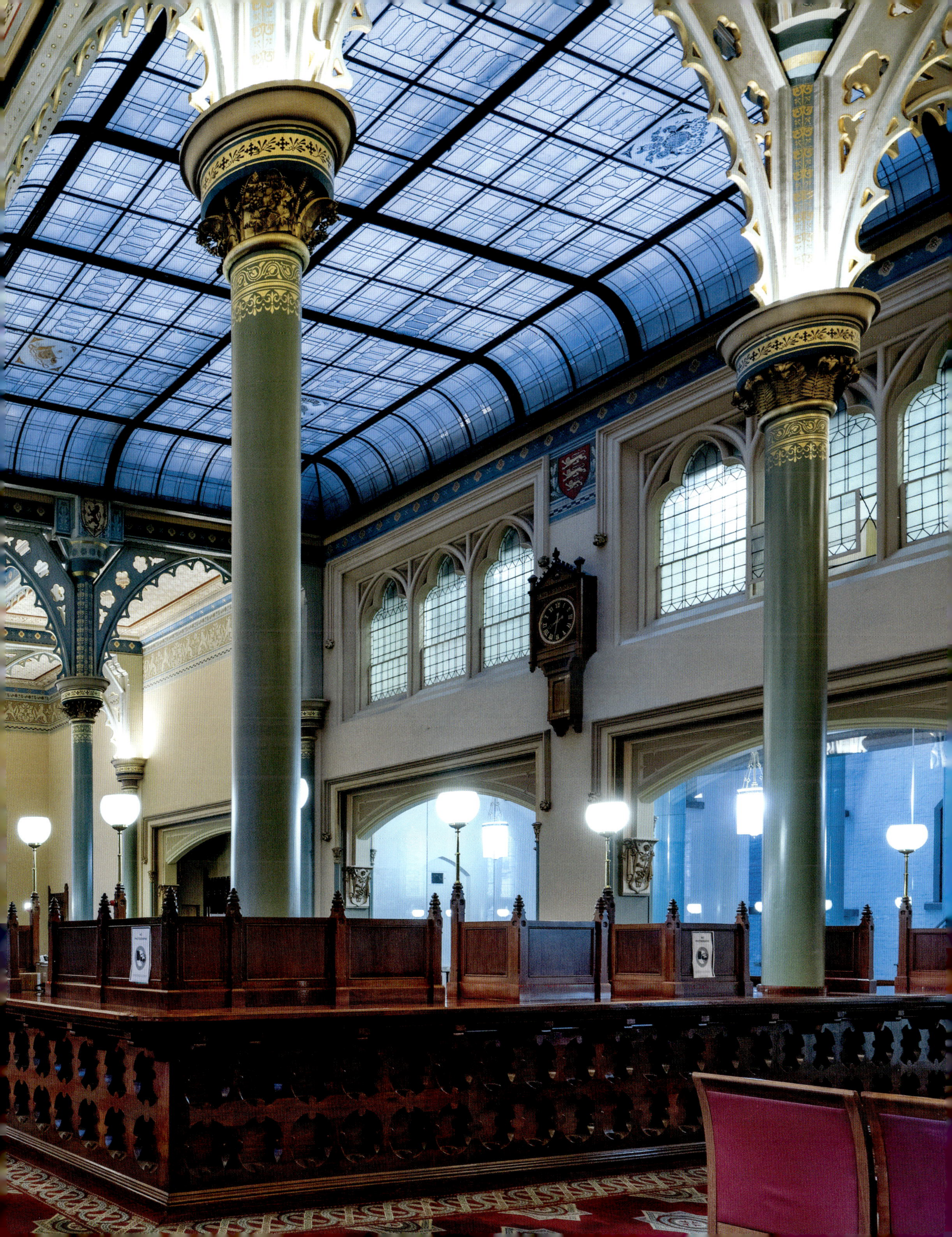

previous pages
171 Painted decoration in the banking chamber of the English, Scottish and Australian Chartered Bank, Melbourne, by Lyon, Wells, Cottier & Co., 1887

this page
172 English, Scottish and Australian Chartered Bank (now the ANZ Gothic Bank), Melbourne, designed by William Wardell, built 1887. Photograph *c.*1925

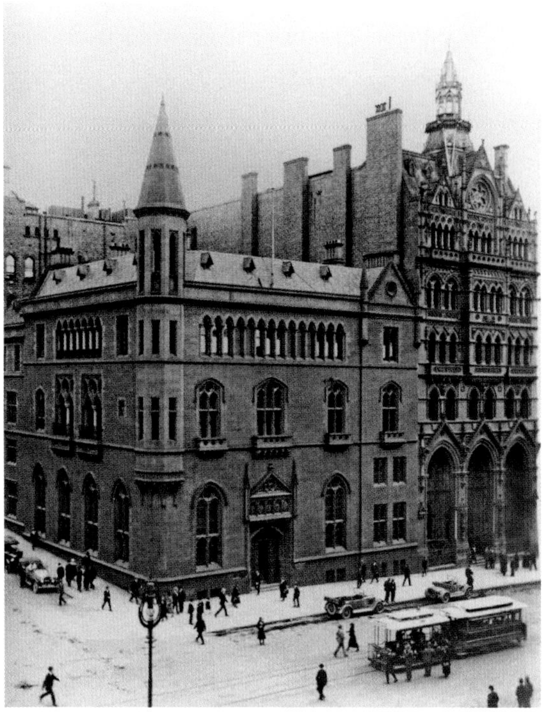

economic depression that hit Australia in the early 1890s. The firm closed its Melbourne branch in 1890 to operate again solely from Sydney.

WELLS AND WARDELL IN MELBOURNE AND SYDNEY

One of the most prominent patrons of Lyon, Wells, Cottier & Co. in Melbourne was the banker and politician Sir George Frederic Verdon (1834–1896), an art connoisseur who from 1883 was the president of the trustees of the National Gallery of Victoria. Verdon had had previous dealings with Lyon, Cottier & Co. He had purchased from the firm a dresser with hand-painted tiles (which he sold in 1882[9]) and in 1880 he had recommended the firm for the interior decoration of the English, Scottish and Australian Chartered Bank in Adelaide (since demolished).[10] Verdon awarded the new partnership one of its early major commissions, the interior decoration of a branch of the same bank in Melbourne, of which he was the manager. The project included his own two-storey residence located above the bank. Wells described the commission in a letter to Smith, which the latter published in *Decoration*:

I have joined the firm which is now Lyon, Wells, Cottier, and Co., Glass Stainers and Decorative Artists. Mr. Lyon manages the glass department, and I the decorative. The second day after my arrival I began the drawings for the decoration of a large bank in Melbourne, for which we were asked to tender against the best Melbourne firms. After three weeks I got the designs and estimates finished, and brought them to Melbourne, with the result that we got the work to do, and in addition the dwelling-house of Sir George Verdon, which is over the bank.[11]

Designed in 1880 in the Venetian Gothic style by the Pugin-trained British-Australian architect William Wardell (1823–1899), the bank on Collins Street was completed in 1887 (fig. 172). The building, its furnishings by James Bell and its painted decorations by Wells for the interior of the banking chamber as well as the rooms and halls of Verdon's residence, have been remarkably well preserved, restored and maintained. The Venetian Gothic banking chamber (fig. 171) is sumptuous yet conveys a sense of gravitas appropriate for a bank. A contemporary reporter for the *Argus* who visited the newly decorated bank had this to say:

The banking chamber is of noble dimensions. Above there is a rich yet well-harmonised glow of blue and gold, of columns ornamented with beautiful capitals representing the fruits of Australia, the grape, the fig and the wheat-sheaf ... The eye wanders forth again from the mirror-like polish of the fittings to the columns and the ironwork of the arching roof, whose supports, even to the rivets, are cunningly made to share in the decoration ... In the spaces between the girders are painted the arms of England, Ireland and Scotland, and of Australia, and other countries with which the bank is associated in its operations.[12]

Today, buff, green, blue and gold are the dominating colours of the bank's interior. Wells's decorations comprise the stencilled griffin frieze and the painted ceilings (see fig. 198), which are centred on large eight-pointed stars, overlaid by the painted armorial shields referred to in the *Argus* article. A preliminary sketch for the wall of the chamber (see fig. 170) shows a different colour scheme (olive green and terracotta) for a wall as well as a much richer wall articulation, complete with painted columns, arches and dadoes. No remnants of this have been discovered during the

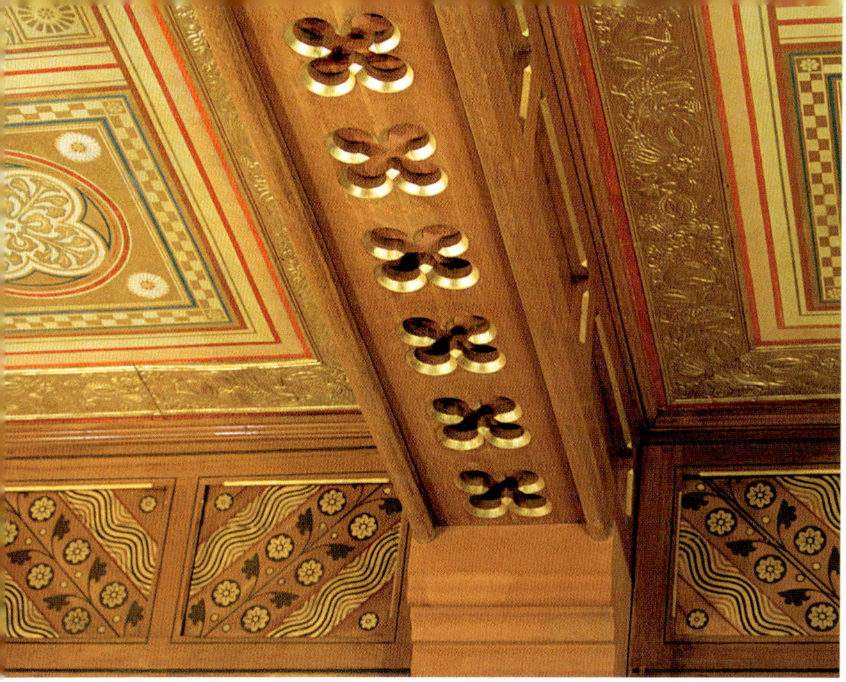

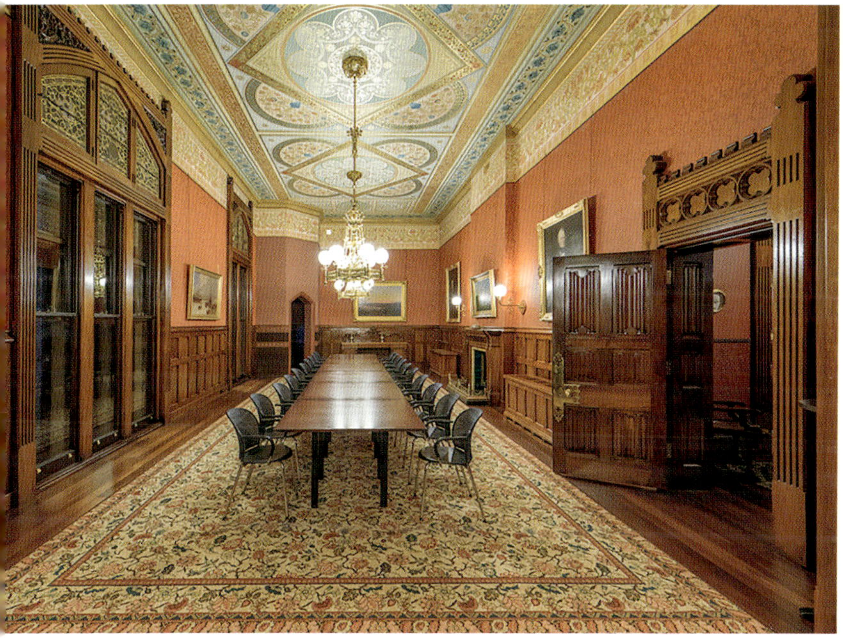

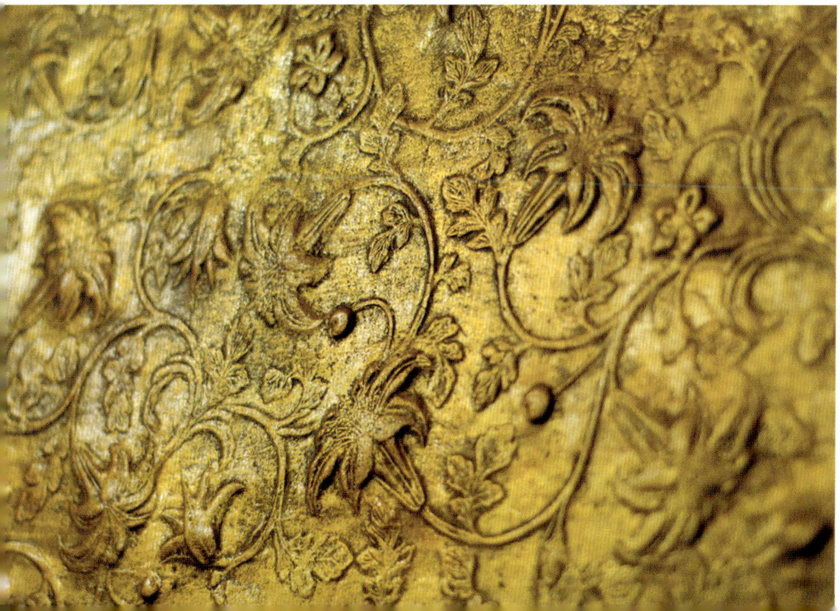

173 Ceiling in the dining room of Verdon's residence above the English, Scottish and Australian Chartered Bank, Melbourne, by Lyon, Wells, Cottier & Co., 1887

174 Drawing room in Verdon's residence above the English, Scottish and Australian Chartered Bank, Melbourne, by Lyon, Wells, Cottier & Co., 1887

175 Gilded Tynecastle Tapestry wall covering in the library of Verdon's residence above the English, Scottish and Australian Chartered Bank, Melbourne, decorated by Lyon, Wells, Cottier & Co., 1887

restoration of the walls. It is possible that the design was one of several that were submitted to Wardell but not selected. The only part of the drawing that was retained was the stencilled griffin frieze.

Verdon's two-storey residence above the banking chamber contains more than seventeen rooms. The architecture is Gothic Revival but the decorations, especially of the ceilings, are more eclectic. Each ceiling shows a different elaboration of the Gothic quatrefoil as the organising theme, which consists for the most part of botanical motifs of classical, medieval and Renaissance inspiration. The colouring is rich and gold is used liberally, especially in the dining-room ceiling (fig. 173). Compared to Lyon, Cottier & Co.'s ceilings of the 1870s, those by Wells are richer and more colourful and their fluid style of painting makes them look less flat. The wall treatments of the rooms range from relatively simple to ornate. Most spectacular are the walls and friezes that are covered with embossed materials and gilded to create a rich and sumptuous effect (figs 174 and 175). Wells was particularly fond of the effects he could achieve with such coverings, which were something of a novelty and were produced by several manufacturers, including the Scottish firm of Scott Morton & Co.[13]

The decorations Wells provided for Verdon's bank and residence delighted both the patron and the architect. Wells noted: 'We have £2600 for the work, and I am making it the finest in this part of the world, and am pleased to say it is giving great satisfaction to Sir George Verdon, the chief of the bank, and the architect, Mr. Wardell.'[14] Indeed, Wardell commended Wells's work and later wrote of him: 'Mr. Wells enjoys one of the best reputations in England and Scotland as a decorative artist. I have always found him willing and anxious to do the fullest artistic justice to what he undertakes and without stint of labour or pains'.[15] It is possible that Wardell liked working with Wells because the latter allowed him the ultimate control;[16]

176 Vestibule ceiling decoration, New South Wales Club, Bligh Street, Sydney, by Lyon, Wells, Cottier & Co., *c.*1887

he procured many commissions for Wells, ranging from modest to comprehensive.[17]

Among the latter was the commission for the decoration of one of the largest and most luxurious mansions in Melbourne, Cliveden. In 1887 Wells wrote to Smith, '[Wardell] told me he had recommended me to Sir William Clark [*sic*], of Melbourne, who is getting a very stately mansion built, costing about £100,000, and, best of all, I have got it to do.'[18] The mansion in question was the grand townhouse in East Melbourne of Victoria's wealthiest landowner, Sir William Clarke of Rupertswood (Australia's first baronet) and his large family. Wells may also have been recommended for the commission by Verdon:

*Sir George Verdon has received from London a book by Moyr Smith, called 'Ornamental Interiors', in which my work is mentioned favourably. He told me to-day he had travelled in the train with Lady Clark [*sic*], and had been speaking of me and told her of the book, which he is going to send to her. So you see the book has done me a good turn, and is likely to be useful to me here.*[19]

Cliveden (possibly named after the Duke of Westminster's Italianate mansion designed by the English architect Charles Barry) was torn down in 1968 to make way for the Melbourne Hilton Hotel but descriptions and a few photographs give some idea of what it looked like.[20] The house was designed and built in the Italian Renaissance style by Wardell in partnership with the English-Australian architect Walter Liberty Vernon (1846–1914), who had arrived in Sydney in the mid-1880s. Completed in 1887, Cliveden was decorated in 1888 both before and after the Clarkes moved in. There was quite a bit of interest in the project on the part of the press. A reporter for the *West Australian* informed his readers that the interior decorations would 'be on a scale unprecedented in Melbourne, a talented artist has been specially imported from Europe to superintend the work'.[21] Wells undertook much of the decorative work for the 28-bedroom mansion and also played the role of interior coordinator, overseeing the work of many skilled artisans and art decorators, advising on the acquisition of wallpapers, furniture and furnishings and generally controlling the artistic effect of the interior. Curiously, the firm was not responsible for the glass, which was provided for the most part by William Montgomery (1850–1886), a recent immigrant from Britain.[22] An early twentieth-century photograph of the hall shows that it was furnished with an Elizabethan Revival oak fireplace (a style favoured by Clarke) and a mantel 'in the sixteenth century style, reaching to the ceiling and elaborately carved.'[23] It also shows friezes with embossed medallions and a Lyon, Wells, Cottier & Co. decorative panel positioned near the large landing window.

While in the mid-1880s Wells worked primarily in Melbourne, he also undertook some projects in Sydney, at least one of which came to him through Wardell. For the New South Wales Club in Bligh Street, Sydney, a large three-storeyed building designed after an Italian Renaissance palazzo by

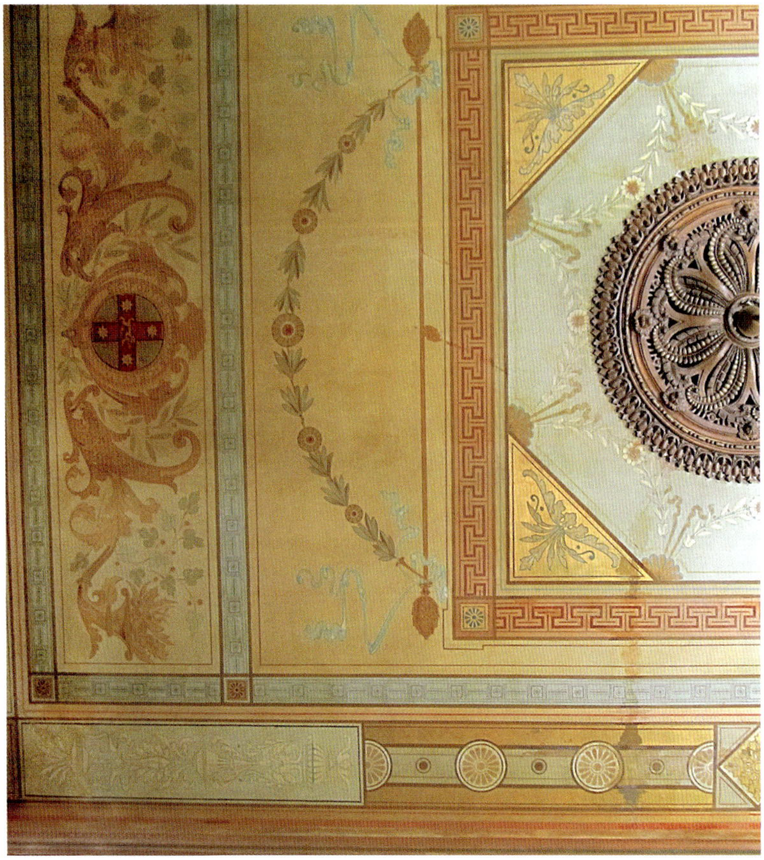

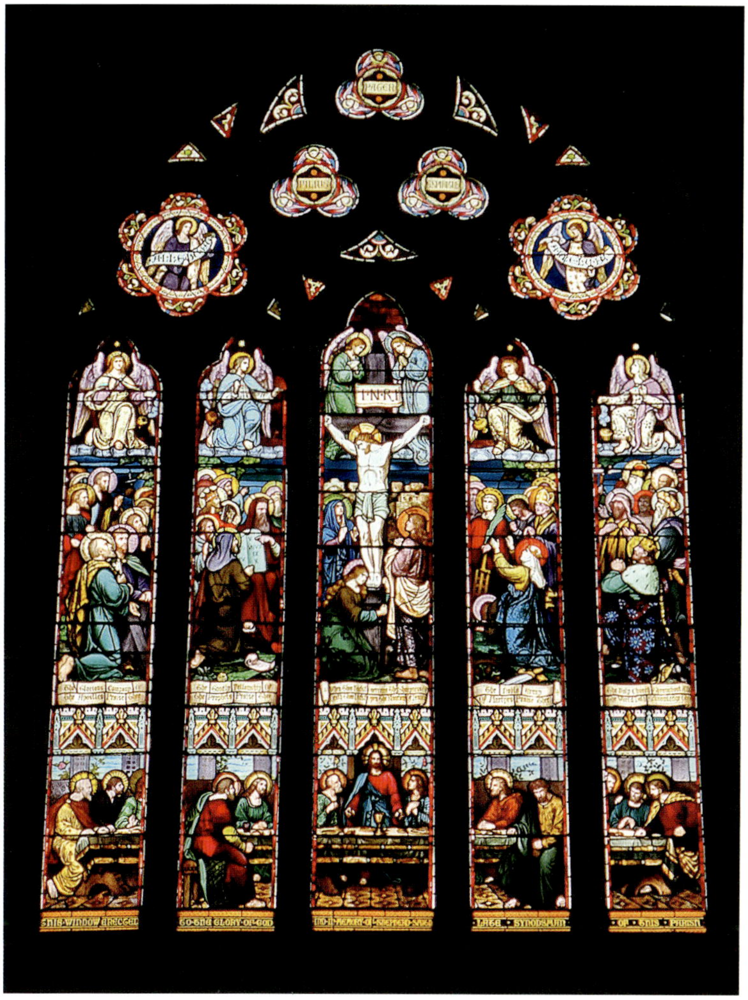

177 *Te Deum Laudamus*, chancel window in All Saints' Anglican Church, Hunter's Hill, Sydney, by Lyon, Wells, Cottier & Co., *c.*1888. Stained glass

Wardell and completed in 1887, Wells decorated the ceiling and walls of the large inner entrance, the vestibule and the dining room. The vestibule's ceiling (fig. 176) is painted in a colour scheme of ochre, aqua and orange and is centred on a three-dimensional painted stucco rose, which is set in an octagon placed in a square. On the short sides of the ceiling the Club's coat of arms – a red cross with a gold lion and gold stars encircled by the Club's Virgilian motto, 'Sic Fortis Etruria Crevit' (Thus Etruria grew Strong) – is set between decorative scrolls that vaguely resemble fish. Like Lyon, Wells was sensitive to the needs of the Australian colonies to develop their own iconography, complete with a newly developed heraldry, rooted in British tradition.

THE 1888 MELBOURNE CENTENNIAL EXHIBITION

In early 1888 Daniel and Marion Cottier and their three children travelled from London to Sydney, where they arrived in February, returning to London in mid-March.[24] It was the centennial year of the British colonisation of Australia and a significant time to visit the colonies, although the Cottiers did not stay for the Melbourne Centennial Exhibition, which opened in August. It is possible, however, that they brought some materials for the Lyon, Wells, Cottier & Co. exhibit.

Held in the large exhibition building in Carlton Garden, designed by Joseph Reed for the Melbourne International Exhibition of 1880, the Melbourne Centennial Exhibition was a major event. Lyon, Wells, Cottier & Co. was well represented, showing both decorative work (Melbourne branch) and stained glass (Sydney branch). Wells served as its representative and promoted the firm in general and the Melbourne office in particular.[25] As for the decorative work, the firm exhibited painted timber panels to show the various decorative surface treatments it was capable of providing.[26] But the main emphasis was on stained glass. In competition with two other prominent stained glass firms in Sydney, Ashwin & Falconer and Goodlet & Smith, Lyon, Wells, Cottier & Co. exhibited a large selection of windows that demonstrated a range of styles and treatments suitable for private, public and church architecture.[27] One of their main exhibits, a large window allegorising Australia, may have been the same one that the firm had exhibited at the Colonial and Indian Exhibition in London in 1886 (see Chapter Six, p. 177). Domestic glass panels included an allegorical window representing 'Music', in addition to 'heads after Holbein', 'figures from Tennyson', 'flower panels' and, appealing to the Scottish immigrant market in Australia, 'views of old Scotch towns [Glasgow, Stirling, Edinburgh and Dumbarton]'. Church windows included 'Hope' and 'Charity', 'Angel with Harp' and windows representing Christ's parables, probably based on the Dalziel Brothers' engravings after Millais (discussed in Chapters Two and Four and see fig. 110). But the *pièce de résistance* of the church window exhibit was a large 'Te Deum' church window (fig. 177). The composite window was inspired by the famous hymn *Te Deum Laudamus* (We Praise Thee, O God) which, in its English translation is an important part of the

178 *St James* and *St John*, Griffiths memorial window, St John's Anglican Church, Ashfield, Sydney, by Lyon, Wells, Cottier & Co., *c.*1888. Stained glass

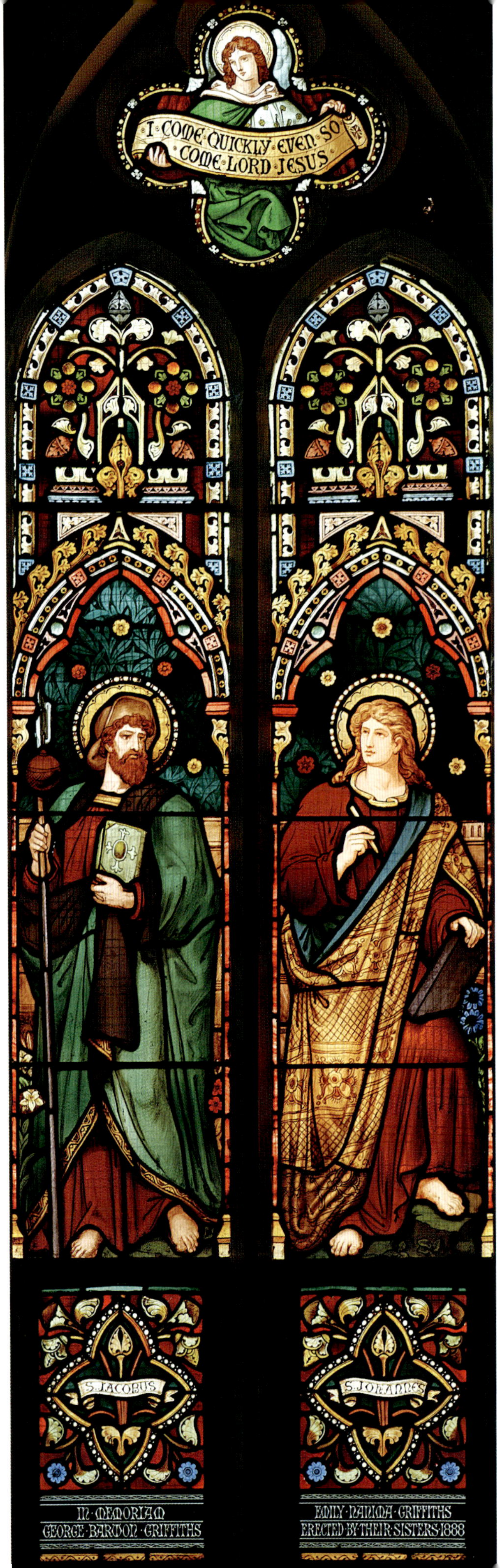

liturgy of the Anglican Church. In the trefoil arch at the top, angels sing God's praise. Below, the central window shows an image of the Crucifixion, flanked by what the hymn refers to as 'the glorious company of the Apostles', 'the goodly fellowship of the Prophets', 'the noble army of Martyrs' and the 'holy Church throughout all the world'. The latter group, in the panel on the extreme right, is particularly interesting. As Jasmine Allen has pointed out, it shows eight figures of different ethnicities, a clear reference not only to the presence of Christianity around the world, lauded in the hymn, but also to the worldwide reach of the British Empire, celebrated in the exhibition.[28]

The five panels at the bottom show a representation of the Last Supper across the window's entire width. Unlike Lyon, Cottier & Co.'s windows of the 1870s, these panels are painterly and seem to be loosely based on late Quattrocento representations of the theme by such artists as Domenico Ghirlandaio. In its compositional reliance on early Renaissance models, it calls to mind the works of the Pre-Raphaelites and their followers, such as the painting of the *Last Supper* by Henry Holiday in St Chad's Anglican Church in Kirkby, Merseyside, England. At the same time, the three-dimensional quality of the figures dressed in voluminous draperies marked by wide dark folds connects the painting with High Renaissance (Leonardo da Vinci) and even Baroque art.

SIGNIFICANT CHURCH COMMISSIONS 1887–1888, SYDNEY

In June 1889 the large *Te Deum* window exhibited at the 1888 Melbourne Centennial Exhibition was installed in the chancel of All Saints' Anglican Church in Hunter's Hill, Sydney, designed by John Horbury Hunt and opened in April 1888.[29] Its installation was followed by several commissions for memorial windows from parishioners, who must have admired its grand conception. In addition, Lyon, Wells, Cottier & Co. executed numerous memorial windows for other Anglican churches in Sydney and its suburbs, such as St John's in Ashfield and St Paul's in Burwood. Several of these windows represent

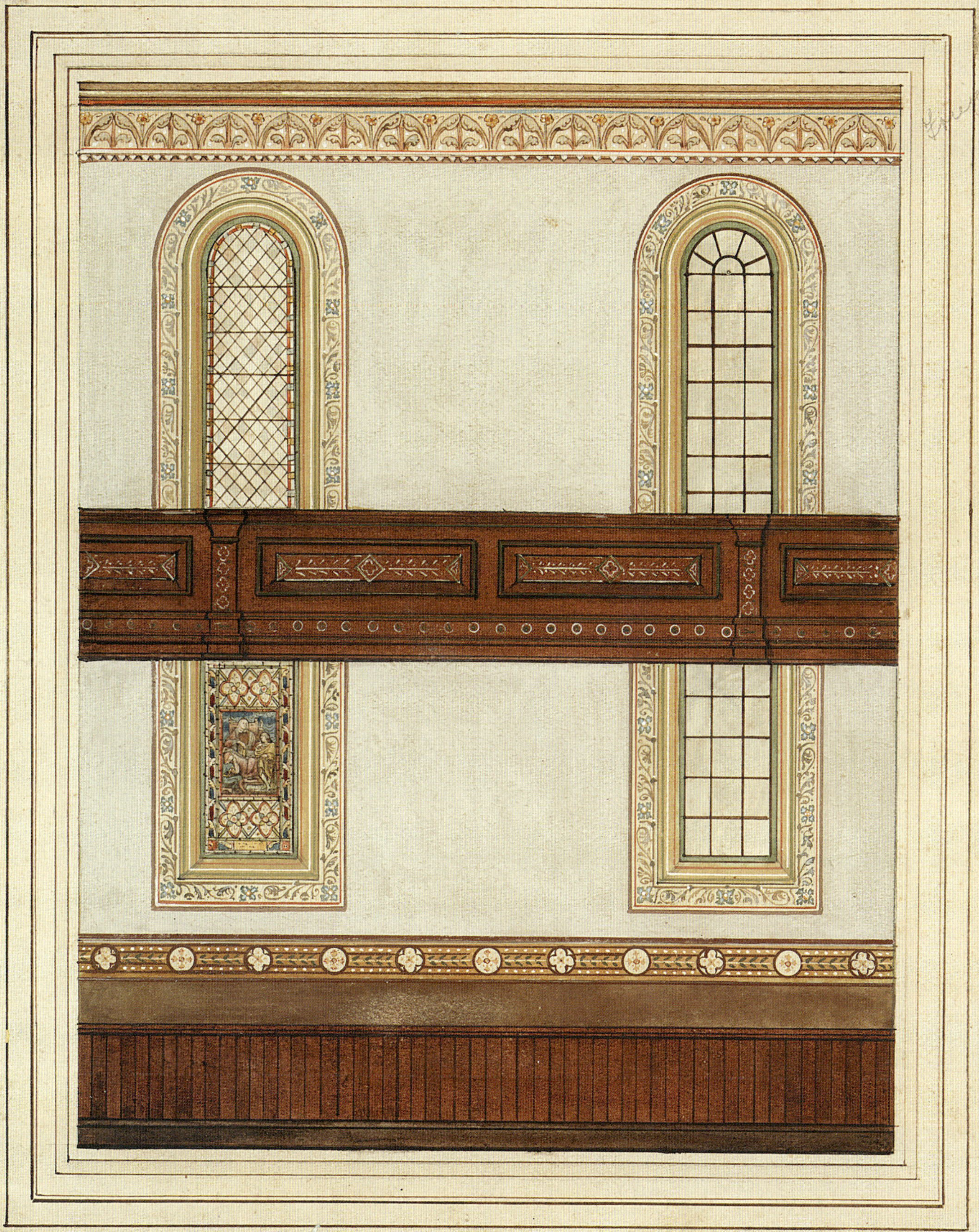

Portion of Wall, St Stephen's Church, Sydney.

previous page
179 Design for painted decoration for St Stephen's Presbyterian Church, Sydney, by Andrew Wells for Lyon, Wells, Cottier & Co., 1888. Pencil and watercolour on paper, 59.5 × 40.5 cm. Mitchell Library, State Library of New South Wales, Sydney

apostles, no doubt reflecting the Anglican reliance on the Apostolic Creed. A two-light window in St John's, Ashfield, memorialising the siblings George Barton Griffiths and Emily Nanima Griffiths, may serve as an example (fig. 178). Two lancet windows representing the apostles James and John with their traditional attributes (the pilgrim's hat and staff and the pen and book, respectively) are surmounted by a quatrefoil showing the half-length figure of an angel bearing a scroll that reads 'I come quickly, even so come Lord Jesus' (Revelation 22:20). Compared with the figures in Lyon, Cottier & Co.'s windows of the 1870s, like the *Four Evangelists* window in the Anglican Cathedral, Bathurst of 1874 (see fig. 153), the figures in the 1880s windows show more volume and dynamism, resembling the figures in the 'Last Supper' in the *Te Deum* window. To what extent this change in style was the result of Wells's influence on the company's designs or a response to market demands for more painterly effects is difficult to tell, but it does seem that the painterly style was marketable.

In 1888 Lyon, Wells, Cottier & Co. was commissioned to decorate St Stephen's Presbyterian Church in Sydney. The firm (probably Wells) designed all the decorative painting and stencilling and the press noted their Glaswegian character: '[The church] has just been repainted and decorated in a style rare among us, but after the example of some Presbyterian and other churches in Glasgow'.[30] Unfortunately, most of the decoration was lost by the 1930s before the building was torn down to make way for a square. In the early 1930s, a crest with the Burning Bush, symbol of the Presbyterian Church, could still be seen above the pulpit (fig. 180). Studded with stars and placed on a St Andrew's Cross, it was framed by the church's motto, 'Nec Tamen Consumebatur' (and yet it was not consumed; Exodus 3:2). Two preliminary designs have been preserved, one for the ceiling, the other for the wall (fig. 179). Both are done in muted tertiary colours and the decoration is light, even whimsical. This is 'Glaswegian' not in the early heavy Cottier mode of the 1860s but in the way in which he (and presumably Wells also) worked in the 1870s. There is a kinship with Cottier's 1875 ceiling at the West Kirk, Aberdeen (1875; see Chapter Two), while the painted decoration of the balcony woodwork recalls that on some of Cottier's furniture of the period.

St Stephen's also had Lyon, Wells, Cottier & Co. stained-glass windows (placed at either side of the pulpit and the Burning Bush crest)[31] representing the preaching and martyrdom of Saint Stephen (fig. 180). These were relocated to the reception hall in the basement of the rebuilt St Stephen's in 1933.[32] The spaces above and below each of these windows are filled with heads of the Four Evangelists framed by laurel wreaths and set in squares, the corners of which are enlivened by colourful glass bubbles (fig. 181). These squares are surrounded by yellow glass panels decorated with scrolling branches.[33] The heads appear to have been executed in Australia; they resemble a set of four drawings of evangelists' heads found in the firm's archive but are less generic and idealised.[34] It is possible that they were done by Lyon himself, who was active as a portrait painter. Indeed, the head of St Luke, shown here, has the specificity of a portrait and may even be a self-portrait. Lyon was, after all, a member of the congregation of St Stephen's, to which he and his wife donated a memorial window after the death of their infant daughter Christina (1873–1876).[35]

DOMESTIC COMMISSIONS IN VICTORIA AND NEW SOUTH WALES

During the late 1880s and before the onset of the depression of the early 1890s, the firm received a number of important commissions for the decoration of large private homes. Some of these were in the suburbs of Sydney and Melbourne, others were in the countryside.

In 1887 Lyon, Wells, Cottier & Co. secured a commission for a large country house called Booloominbah in Armidale, New South Wales.[36] The house was designed by John Horbury Hunt (1838–1904) for the pastoralist Frederick Robert White (1835–1903) and built between 1885 and 1888 (fig. 182). A red-brick, gabled mansion, partly shingled and tiled, Booloominbah is representative of Hunt's forward-looking style, which combines aspects of the American shingle style and early Australian Arts and Crafts

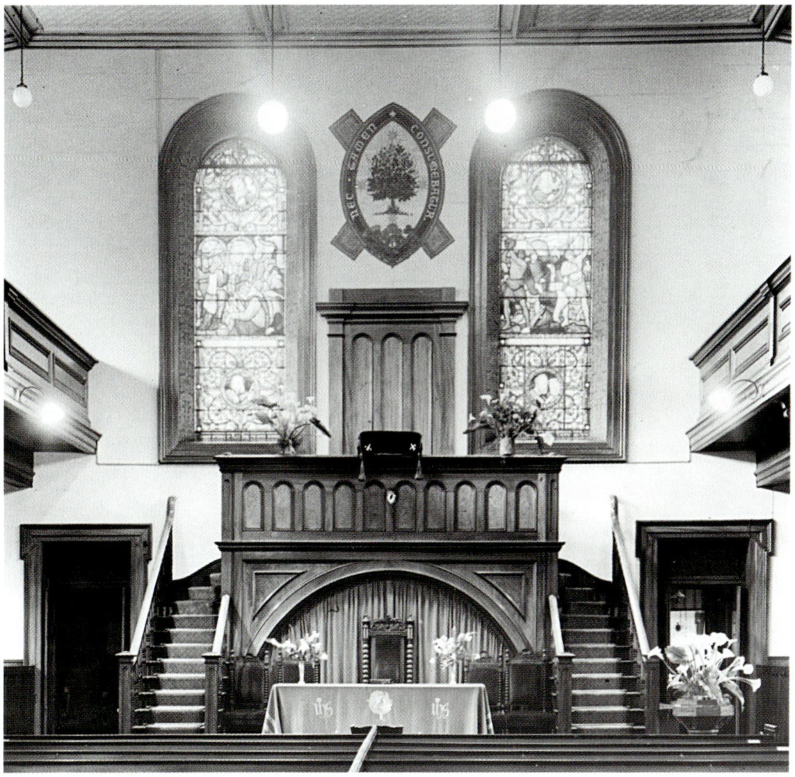

180 *The Preaching of St Stephen* and *The Martyrdom of Saint Stephen*, St Stephen's Presbyterian Church, Sydney by Lyon, Wells, Cottier & Co., 1888. Stained glass. Photograph *c.*1930, Caroline Simpson Library and Research Collection, Sydney Living Museums

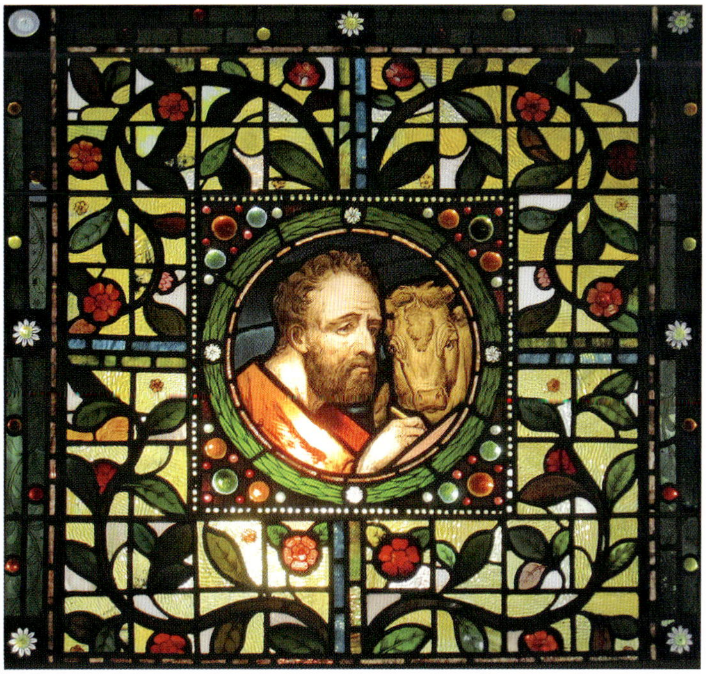

181 *St Luke*, part of the right window illustrated in fig. 180. St Stephen's Presbyterian Church, Sydney. Stained glass

architecture.[37] Substantially altered, the house is today part of the University of New England.

White held many sheep stations around New South Wales and Queensland and, like his brother James White of Cranbrook,[38] was an influential patron of the arts whose commissions carried great weight. The decoration of Booloominbah resulted from a creative synergy of patron, architect and decorators. It reflected White's combined allegiance to Australia (his birthplace), to the British Empire of which it was a part and to Britain, whence his parents had emigrated. Particularly striking are the many painted mottoes expressing White's belief in British-Australian middle-class virtues and values. But the decoration also bore the imprint of Hunt, who was an avid reader of American and British architectural journals and made albums of cuttings of historic and contemporary carvings, furniture, tiles, Arts and Crafts exhibition displays, architectural details and domestic and ecclesiastical stained glass.[39]

Booloominbah's decoration involved wood carving, painting and stencilling but the house is especially known for its stained-glass windows. With the exception of a large staircase landing window, which was made by the London studio of Lavers, Barraud & Westlake,[40] all glass was supplied by Lyon, Wells, Cottier & Co. Stylistically and iconographically the windows vary greatly. The themes chosen for the windows, as well as the mottoes they contain, were selected for their appropriateness to the rooms in which they are placed, probably by White himself. The large composite dining-room window (fig. 185), for example, shows in its four top lights medallions with grisaille renderings of a fish, deer, bull and pheasants, representative, one assumes, of the food served at White's table. Below this are three detailed scenes, perhaps based on contemporary book illustrations, representing the process of turning wheat into bread. Executed in a largely tonal palette of shades of yellow and brown, appropriate to the subject, they are separated by narrow vertical lights representing stalks of wheat, the remainder of the panels showing fruit and vegetables (not illustrated). In the six-light library window (fig. 183), portraits

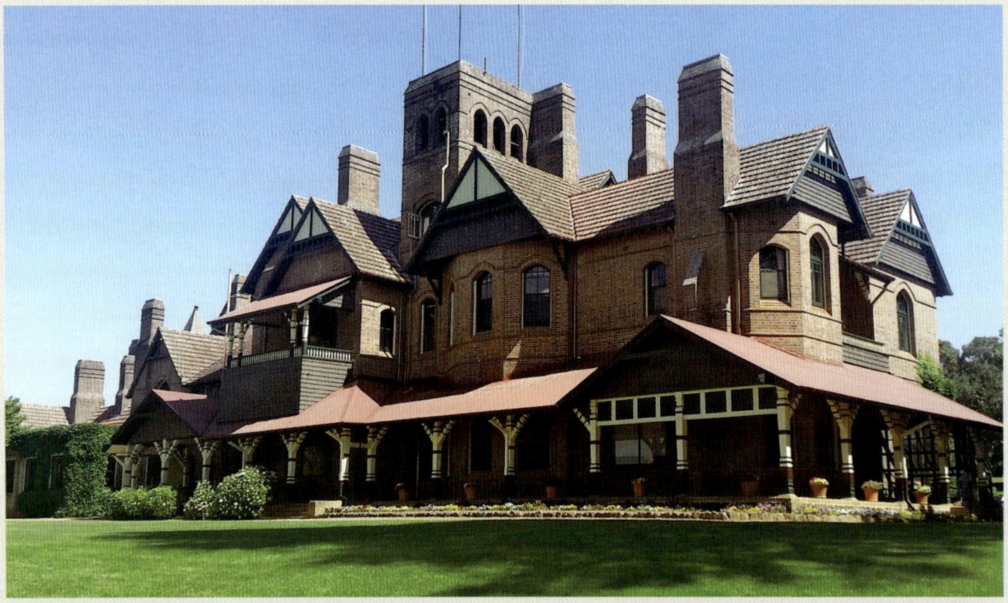

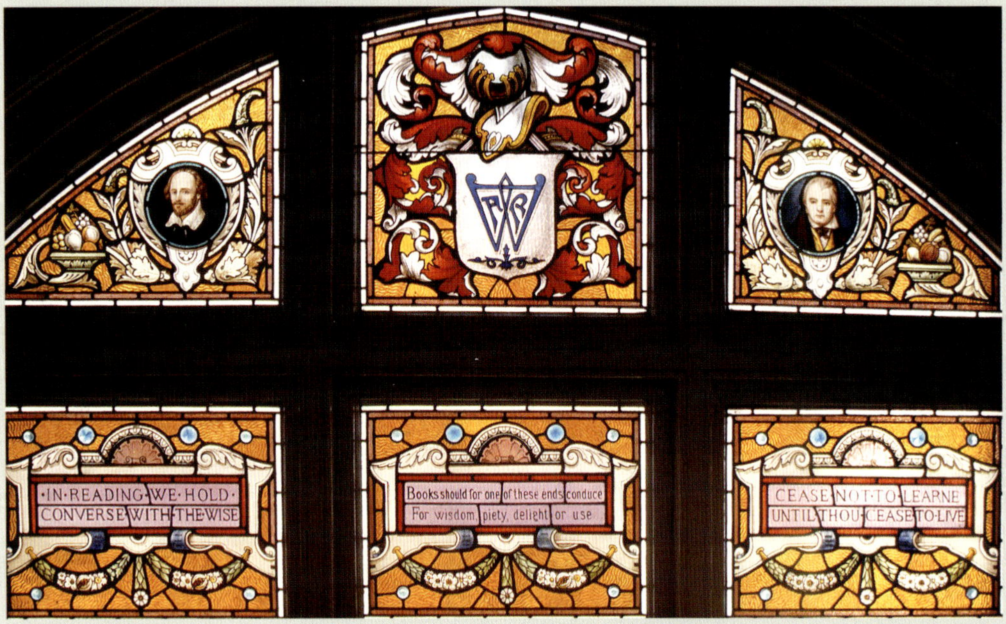

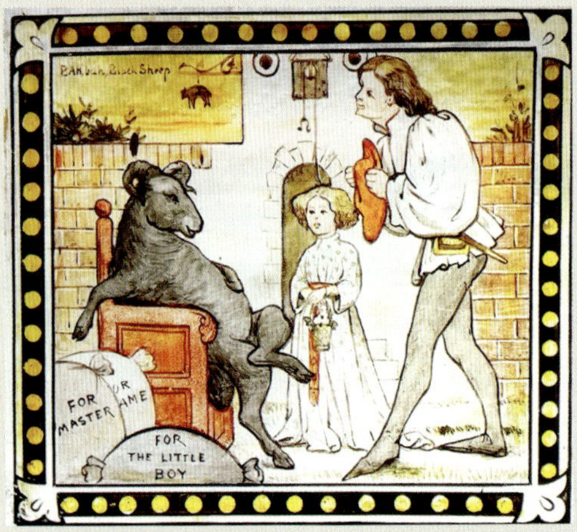

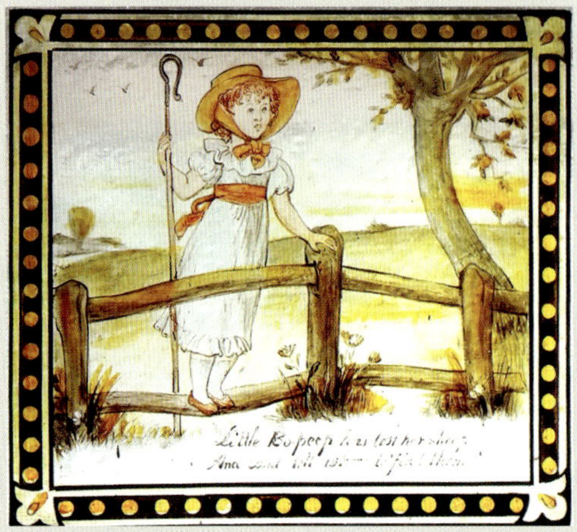

this page
182 Booloominbah, Armidale, New South Wales, designed by John Horbury Hunt, *c.*1884. Now an administrative building of the University of New England

183 Library window with the coat of arms of Frederick Robert White, portraits of William Shakespeare and Sir Walter Scott, and maxims, Booloominbah, Armidale, New South Wales, by Lyon, Wells, Cottier & Co., *c.*1887. Stained glass

184 (a and b) Day nursery windows with images from popular children's books and nursery rhymes, Booloominbah, Armidale, New South Wales, by Lyon, Wells, Cottier & Co., *c.*1887. Stained glass

opposite
185 Dining-room window with scenes of bread-making and animals, Booloominbah, Armidale, New South Wales, by Lyon, Wells, Cottier & Co., *c.*1887. Stained glass

186 Twelve-panel overdoor window with Australian flowers and birds, Booloominbah, Armidale, New South Wales, by Lyon, Wells, Cottier & Co., *c.*1887. Stained glass

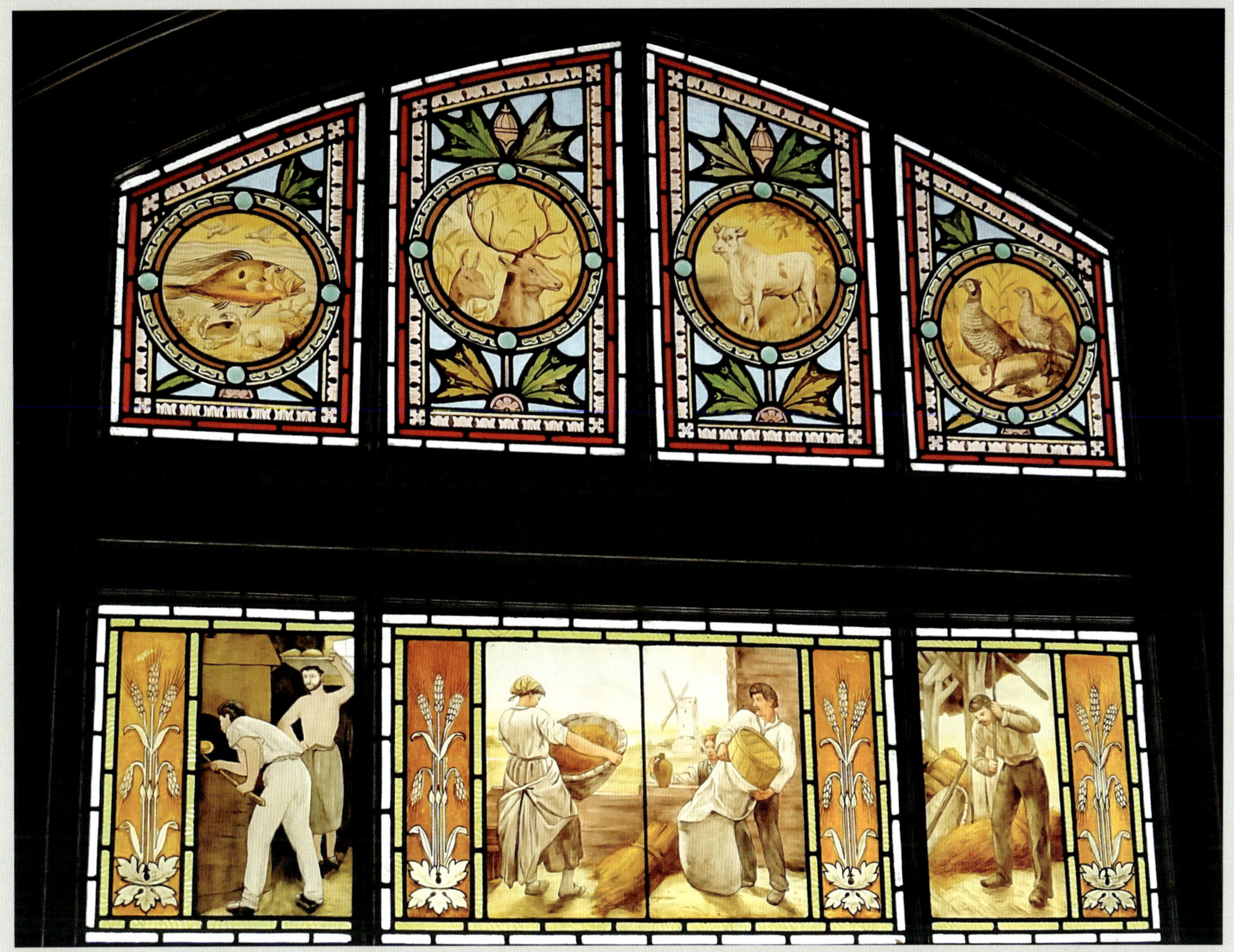

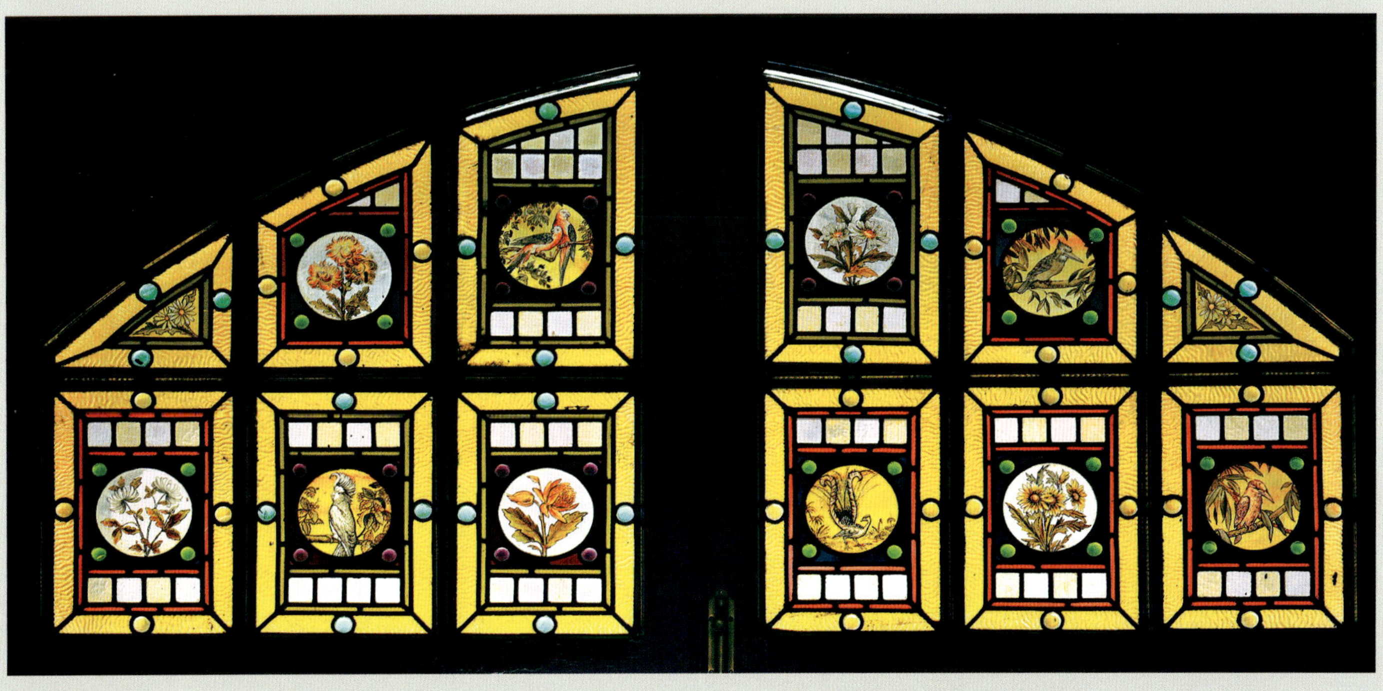

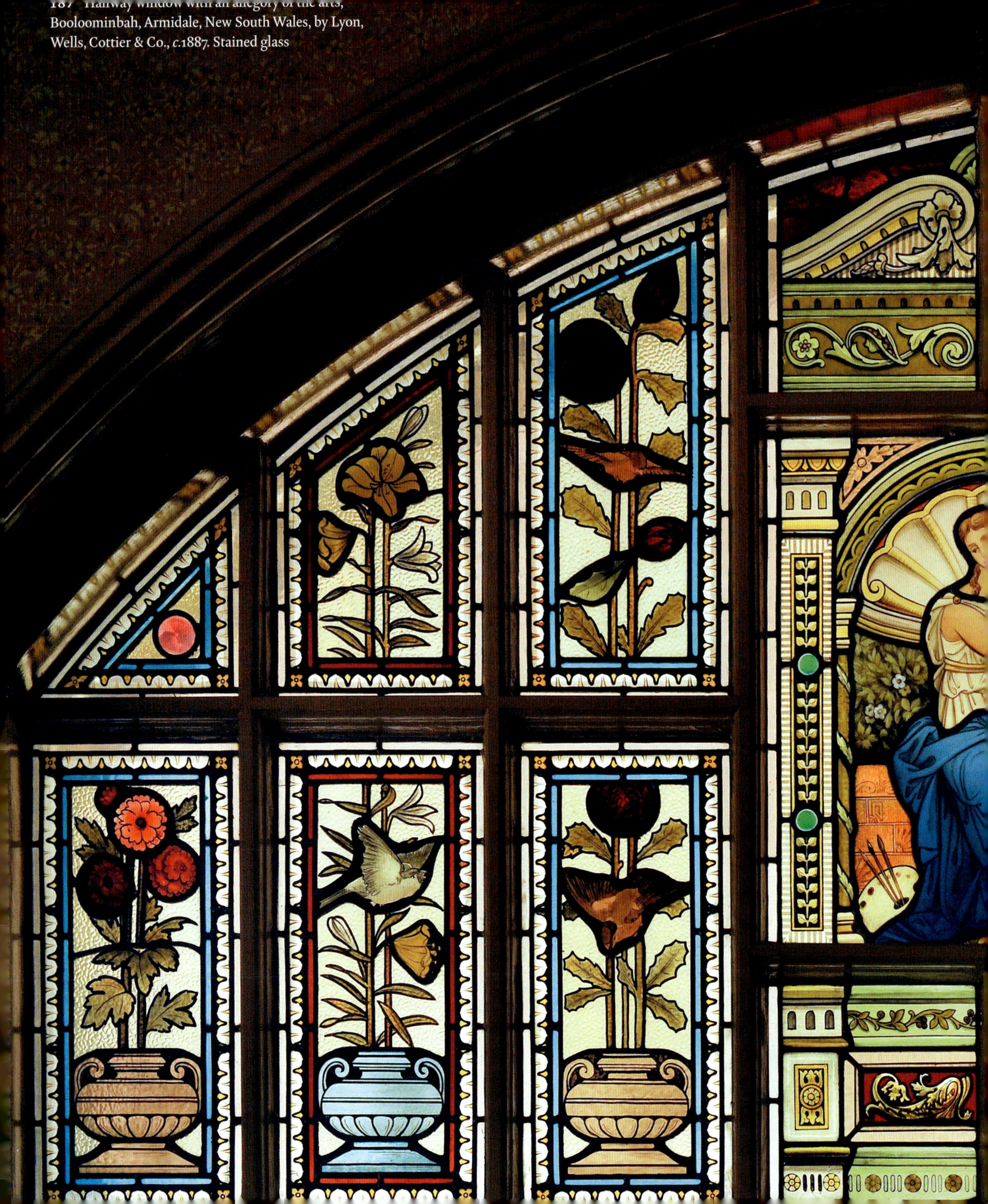

187 Hallway window with an allegory of the arts, Booloominbah, Armidale, New South Wales, by Lyon, Wells, Cottier & Co., *c.*1887. Stained glass

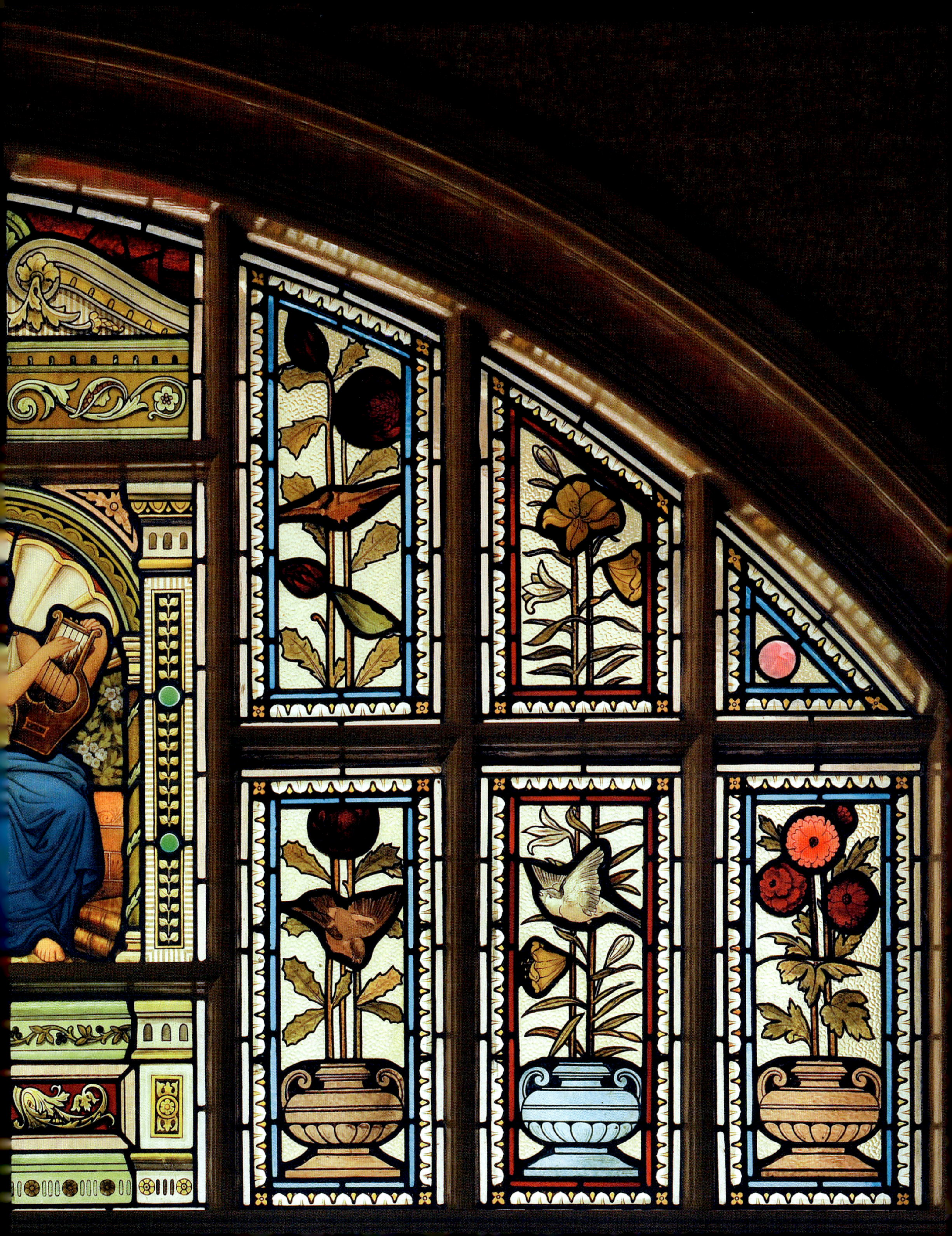

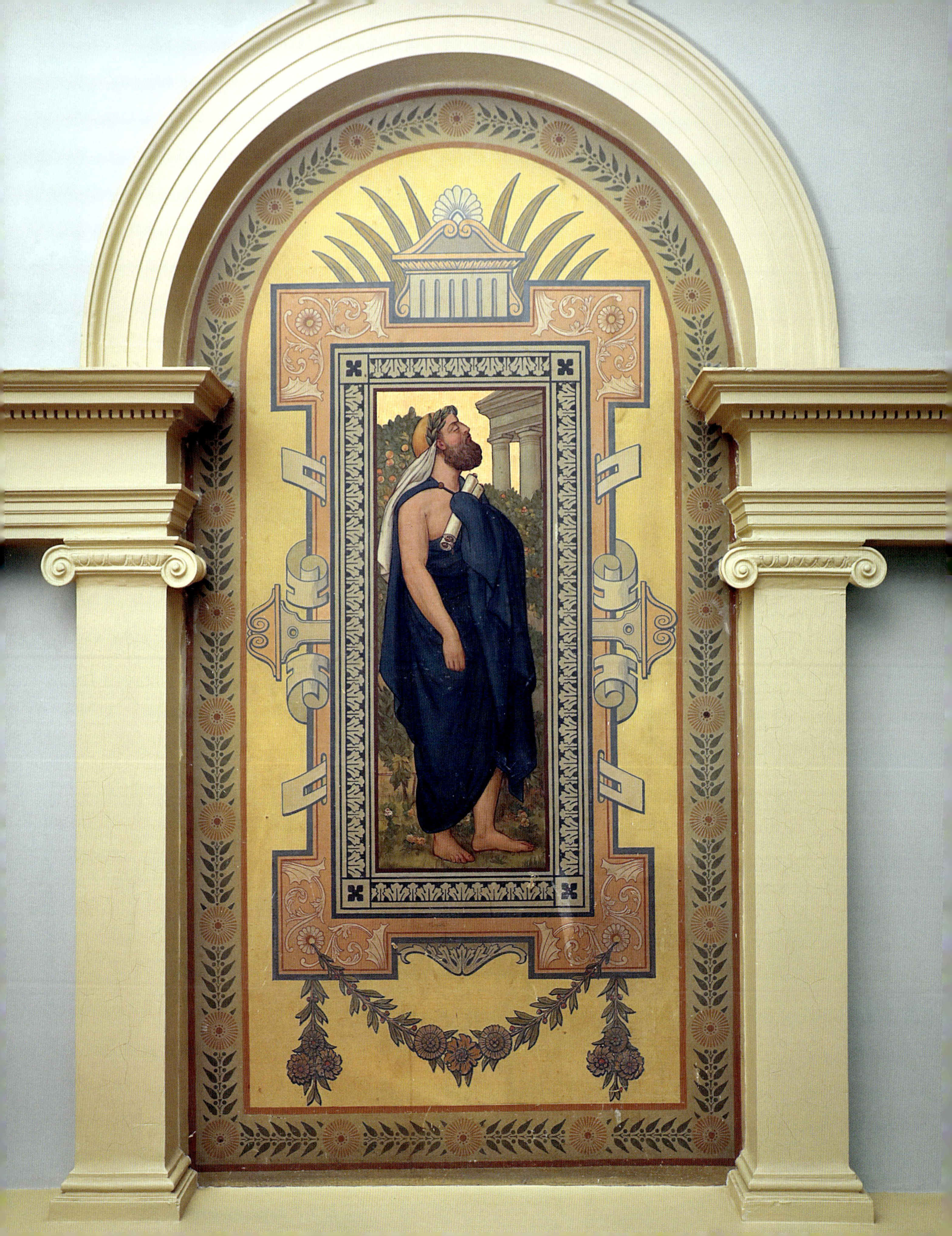

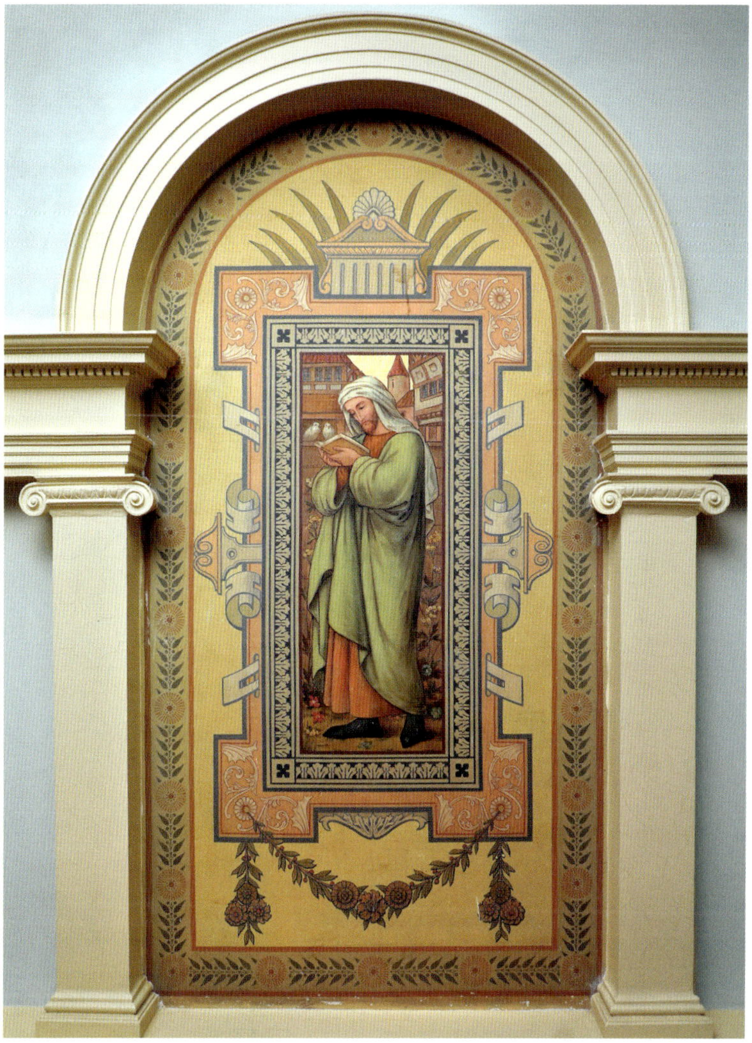

188 (a and b) *Homer* and *Chaucer*, painted decoration in Gowan Brae (now part of Kings School), Parramatta, New South Wales, by Lyon, Wells, Cottier & Co., *c.*1889. Murals

of William Shakespeare and Sir Walter Scott set in Renaissance cartouches flank a white shield with the initials 'F.R.W' in blue, surmounted by a helmet and set in a rich mantling of acanthus and fruit. Below, three rectangular panels contain pink tablets with texts set in white cartouches against golden-yellow backgrounds. The texts, such as 'Cease not to learne until thou cease to live', stress the value of reading. In the day nursery (figs 184a and b), twenty small panels, arranged along the top of the wall, depict images from popular children's books and nursery rhymes,[41] freely adapted from illustrations by the English artists Kate Greenaway, Henry Stacy Marks and Randolph Caldecott, each scene identified by a name of a line in the book from which it was taken.[42]

The windows of the main bedroom feature panels with allegories of the Four Seasons and depictions of Australian flora and fauna. Panels with Australian birds and flowers also fill the arch above the door leading from the hall to the garden (fig. 186). Likewise, in the drawing room, the small glass panels of the window above the glass doors leading out to the garden depict a kangaroo, a kangaroo rat, a bandicoot, a possum, a parrot and other Australian birds. By contrast, the painted decoration of the two jambs of the arched bay window in this room features tall sunflowers and lilies, growing in classical urns against golden backgrounds. The square panels above and below depict birds seated in branches also painted on gold grounds.

Urns with tall flowers – lilies and chrysanthemums – among which birds fly are also found in the monumental window in the hall (fig. 187). They fill ten panels on either side of a large central panel depicting an allegory of the arts – a seated female figure playing a lyre with, at her feet, a palette and brushes (left) and some books (right). Although the exact prototype for the figure is difficult to determine, it is in the tradition of Baroque allegories of music.[43] In their entirety, the windows show a fascinating mixture of subjects and styles, suggesting a strong input from the patron, who may have not only dictated much of the iconography but also provided specific imagery that he wanted Lyon, Wells, Cottier & Co.'s designers to follow.

The firm's next major decorating commission for a private home in New South Wales came from James Burns (1846–1923), a wealthy shipowner. In 1889 his large Italianate mansion Gowan Brae (Scottish for 'daisy-covered hillside'), designed by the largely forgotten architect M. C. Day of Sydney, was completed on a 200-acre estate near Parramatta, west of Sydney.[44] Today, the estate has been subdivided and the sandstone Italianate mansion is owned by the Kings School. While little of the house's original comprehensive painted decorative scheme remains intact, on the first floor are two well-preserved mural paintings representing Homer and Chaucer (figs 188a and b), which were based on designs made in the London studio and previously used for windows in St Andrew's College, Sydney, in 1876–8 (see fig. 163). The two life-size figures occupy elaborate stencilled cartouches, which are set against golden backgrounds surrounded by arches stencilled with a laurel pattern. The firm's archive contains a design for a large Doric-style archway with the initials J. B. and M. B. (Burns'

189 Design for a painted Doric-style archway with *Audentia* and *Notitia* and the initials J. B. and M. B., by Lyon, Wells, Cottier & Co., *c.*1889. Pencil and watercolour on paper, 30 × 52 cm. Mitchell Library, State Library of New South Wales, Sydney

190 Armorial window on the staircase landing, Gowan Brae, Parramatta, New South Wales, by Lyon, Wells, Cottier & Co., *c.*1889. Stained glass

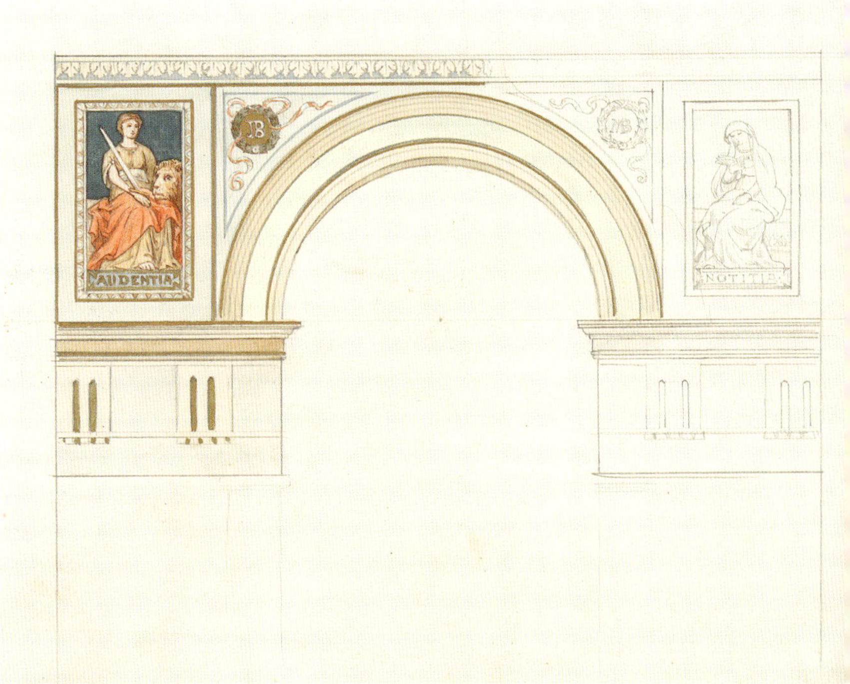

wife, Mary) in the two spandrels (fig. 189). On either side of the arch are two allegorical figures, *Audentia* (Courage) and *Notitia* (Fame). The couple's initials also appear in a stained-glass window, still *in situ* on the staircase landing, a large three-light armorial window with the Burns arms in the central panel (fig. 190). Brightly coloured decorative elements are set against a golden yellow ground stained with decorative patterns, creating the impression of a luminous brocaded gold fabric. Hand-painted tiles depicting a waterfall in the Scottish Highlands and draped female figures flank the marble fireplaces in the reception and dining rooms, respectively, but is not known whether they were the work of Lyon, Wells, Cottier & Co.

In 1888 the firm decorated Mooroolbeek, the gabled red-brick mansion of the parliamentarian Frank Madden (1847–1921) in the affluent Melbourne suburb of Kew. With its open verandahs, the house, built in 1884 largely on the basis of Madden's own designs, exemplified the adaptation of the fashionable Queen Anne style to Melbourne's climate.[45] Mooroolbeek was torn down in 1968 and five rectangular wooden staircase panels are the only surviving pieces (figs 191a and b). Described at the time as 'inlaid',[46] the panels are in fact executed in penwork, a technique used on a number of pieces of Cottier furniture produced in the London workshop (see fig. 53). Presumably by Wells, the panels depict Australian birds such as the kookaburra, parrot, owl, ibis and hornbill and recall the work of the British artist Henry Stacy Marks, whose (figural) designs were also used by Cottier & Co. at Cairndhu House, Helensburgh, in 1873 (see Chapter Two, p. 55). Other Australian bird motifs were apparently also used in the firm's stained-glass windows for Mooroolbeek.[47] This use of Australian fauna (and perhaps also flora) as decorative motifs may have been dictated, or at least encouraged, by Madden himself, who was a hunter and active member of the Field Naturalists' Club of Victoria. He gave talks for its members (one, in fact, about ibises), which were published in the Club's paper, *The Victorian Naturalist*.[48] Of course, Madden was not

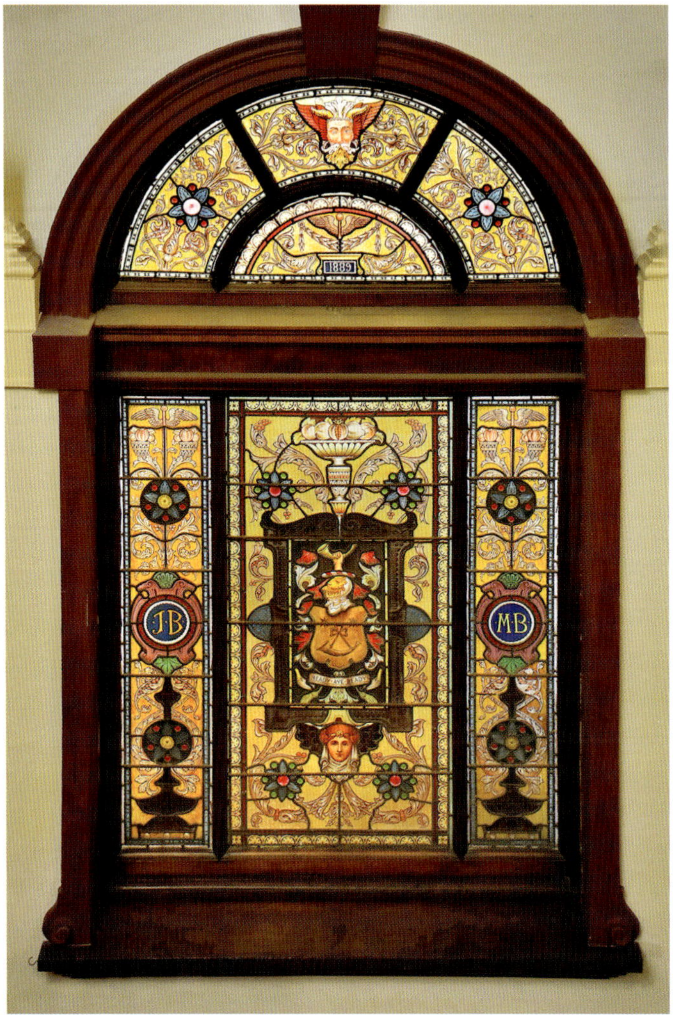

191 (a and b) *Hornbill* and *Ibis*, staircase panels for Mooroolbeek, Kew, Melbourne (demolished), by Lyon, Wells, Cottier & Co., *c.*1888. Penwork on stained wood. Ian Potter Museum of Art, University of Melbourne Art Collection

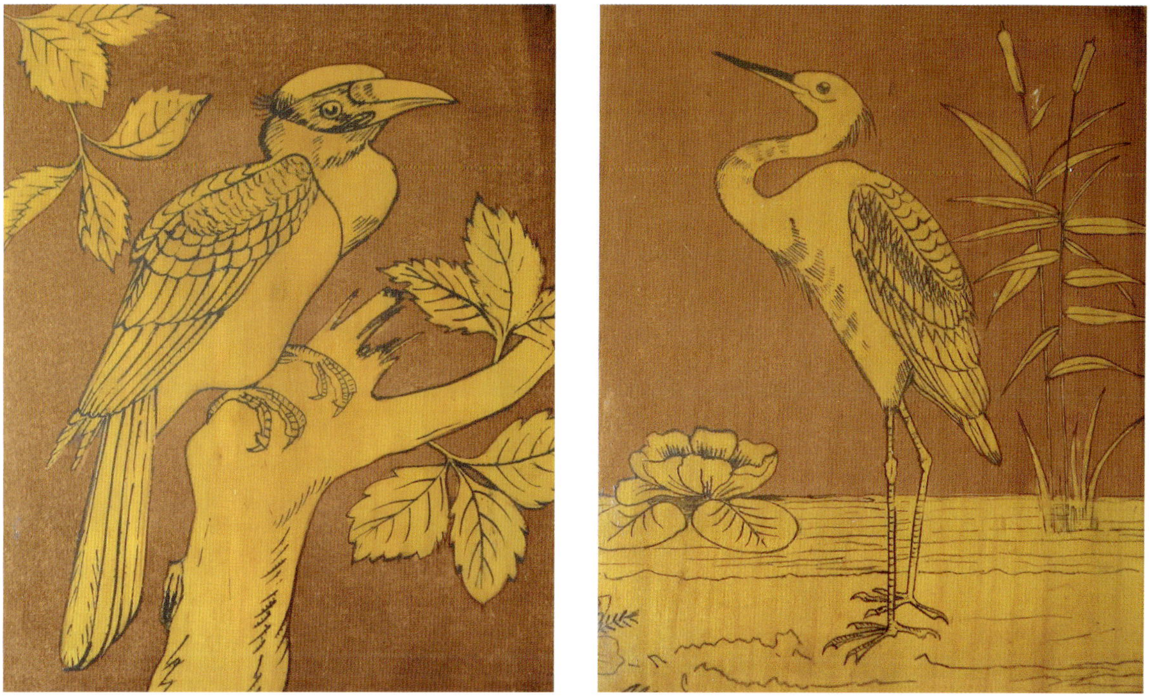

unique in his preference for Australian natural motifs, which are found in many other Australian homes of the period, both painted on walls and in stained-glass windows. As described earlier, Lyon, Wells, Cottier & Co. had already used such native natural motifs in Booloominbah, New South Wales, and in Cliveden, Victoria, William Montgomery had used Australian faunal and floral motifs.[49]

LYON, WELLS, COTTIER & CO.'S PUBLIC FACE

The firm of Lyon, Wells, Cottier & Co. was frequently mentioned in the Australian press, which kept up with the major construction projects – public, ecclesiastical and private – that went on in the colonies, as amply borne out in the many references in the present book to newspaper and magazine articles. This section will not deal with the press received by projects but rather by the publicity generated by statements and lectures of individual partners in the firm, especially Cottier and Wells.

Cottier, his wife and their two daughters made their second trip to Australia in March 1890.[50] Their eldest daughter Isabella was to marry Dr Arthur Marwood, a Melbourne surgeon working in Geelong in regional Victoria.[51] The wedding took place on 3 April at St Matthew's Church, Prahran,[52] ironically a church that featured numerous stained-glass windows that were designed and produced by Ferguson & Urie, some five years after Lyon had left that firm to establish Lyon, Cottier & Co. in Sydney.[53]

When Cottier returned to Sydney, Lyon invited him to an Art Society of New South Wales 'smoking concert' held at the Society's rooms in April 1890. The *Australian Star* reported that at this event Cottier spoke about the growing appreciation of the arts in America and the developing talents of American artists.[54] Cottier was said not to have been impressed by many works in the National Art Gallery of New South Wales (although his early tutor Ford Madox Brown's painting *Chaucer at the Court of Edward III* [1856–68] had been bought from the artist for the collection in 1876). Cottier attributed what he perceived as the weakness of the gallery to a shortage of art patrons in Australia, particularly patrons who would generously donate or bequeath works to museums, where both the general public and young artists could admire them.[55] Another newspaper report introduced Cottier as the 'famous art dealer and *connoisseur* of London and New York',[56] who spoke about the need for one of Sydney's rich men to present a Rembrandt or a Correggio to the city's gallery and thereby follow the lead of rich patrons in New York and Boston. According to the report, Cottier believed that exhibitions in Sydney should include a mix of the best European works with Australian works 'and an upward tendency in art would make itself felt at once.'[57] Cottier's words are the more intriguing as the Australian branch of Lyon, Cottier & Co., as we have seen, had tried to set up an art gallery along the lines of the London and New York branches. Was he hoping to try again or was his speech a case of sour grapes? We will never know as Cottier died a year after his Australian trip. It is clear, however, that he realised that the absence of an art gallery clearly distinguished the Australian branch of the firm from those in London and New York, which were less dependent on the decorating part of the business and perhaps could be a little more selective when it came to the projects they undertook.

While Cottier's presence in Australia was only brief, Wells was an important spokesperson for the firm, particularly in the early 1890s, when he presented several lectures on the history and current state of the decorative arts, which were published in architectural and engineering journals.[58] The aim of the lectures may have been to spur interest in interior decoration at a time when eastern Australia was experiencing an economic depression which affected business, especially when it came to commissions for private clients. In a lecture he gave in May 1892 to the members of the Sydney Architectural Association, Wells presented a short overview of the history of the decorative arts before launching into advice for the decoration of contemporary residences.[59] He began with the embellishment of utilitarian objects by what he termed 'savages', then moved through the ornamental styles of Egypt, Greece and Rome, Byzantium and Gothic and Renaissance Europe. Wells thought that classical and Renaissance ornamentation were superior and should serve as models for the present. 'Now how do we stand in Australia as compared with the Greeks?' he asked, and the implicit and explicit answer to this rhetorical question was, of course, that Australian artists must strive for the beauty and refinement of Greek art. After his historical introduction, Wells went on to instruct his audience on the use of colours and patterns in interiors as well as on the treatments of floors, ceilings and walls. He praised the wallpaper patterns of William Morris but also advocated the use of embossed wall coverings, such as Tynecastle Tapestries, Lincrusta, Anaglypta and Japanese leather papers which produced the 'most pleasing effects' when they were harmoniously coloured.[60] The *Australasian Builder and Contractors' News*, which published a second lecture by Wells before the Sydney Architectural Association on the treatment of stained glass in decoration (6 November), included in its May 1892 publication some illustrations of Wells's Glasgow projects. Wells presented the Association with a copy of Moyr Smith's *Ornamental Interiors* in which some of his work for the house of William Pearce was discussed.[61]

COSMOPOLITANISM AND NATIONALISM, TRADITION AND INNOVATION

The published May 1892 lecture by Wells also illustrated his design for a seal for the short-lived Australian Academy of Art, of which both Lyon and Wells were members. This design showed the goddess Minerva surrounded by waratah flowers and Wells described it as follows: 'The helmet-decked Minerva occupies the central cameo as the Goddess of Wisdom, and around her twines the Australian waratah in loving strength, beneath the pediment which symbolises Architecture as at once the prop and crown of the Fine Arts.'[62] The seal clearly expressed the position of Australian artists and, indeed, Australians in general at the end of the nineteenth century, divided as they were in their loyalties between their homelands and the land to which they had emigrated; between the cosmopolitan British Empire of which at an ideological level they were a part and the provincial

192 Design for ceiling decoration by Andrew Wells, for Lyon, Wells, Cottier & Co., *c.*1892. Pencil and watercolour on paper, 72.5 × 52.5 cm. Mitchell Library, State Library of New South Wales, Sydney

Australian reality in which they lived; and finally between the long European cultural tradition that they had inherited from their ancestors and the desire to create for their offspring a new tradition all their own.

In July 1892 Wells delivered 'The Growth of Ornamental Art' for the Academy of Arts, which was also subsequently published.[63] In this lecture he

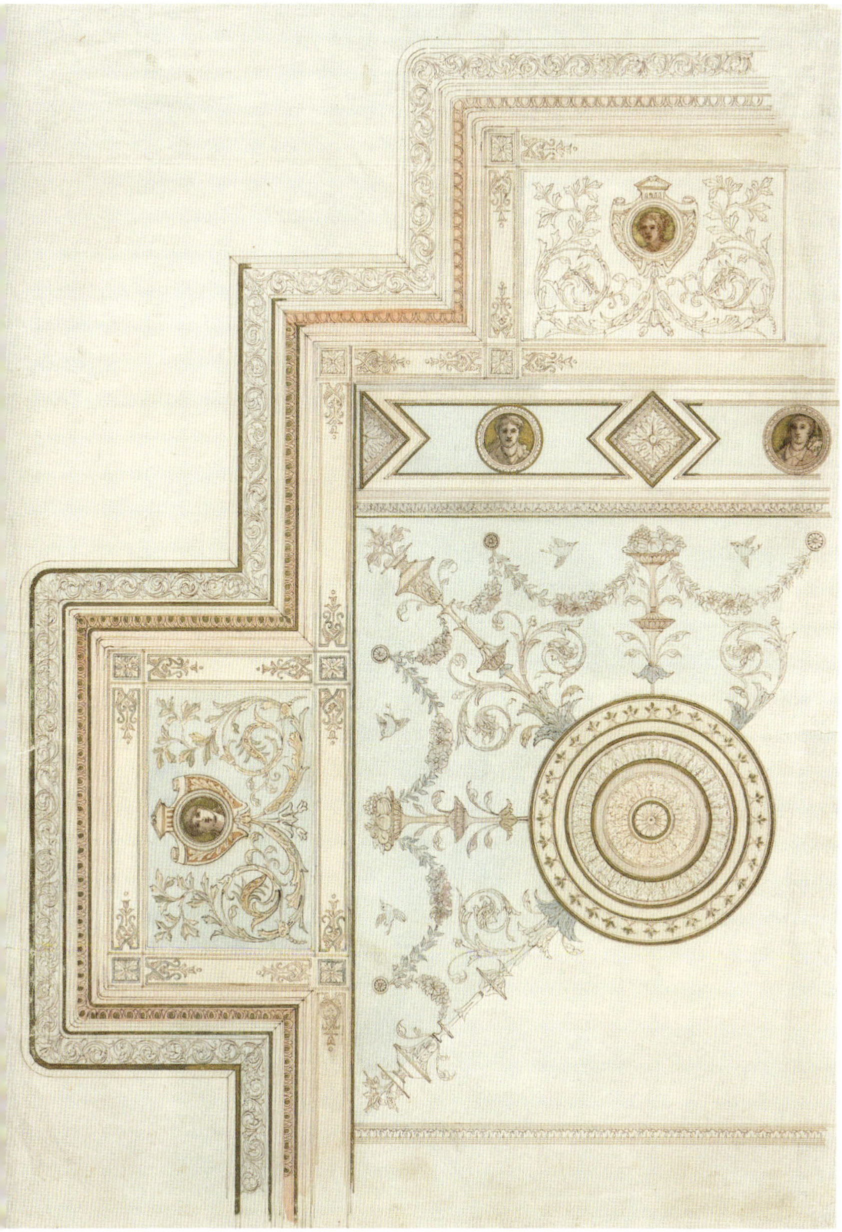

reflected on the cosmopolitanism of the age and the breakdown of national distinctions. 'People of all nations mix so freely', he said, 'or their products are so interchanged, that each country knows what all others are designing and thus it is not likely that local characteristics will continue in their purity, as in times before the introduction of steam communication.'[64] That same month, as if to set store to his words, Wells exhibited some of his work for Lyon, Wells, Cottier & Co. at the annual exhibition of the Academy of Arts of Australia. His submission included four sets of designs for painted ceilings, one of which was Italian Renaissance in style and showed medallions with classical heads painted *en grisaille* on a gold background (fig. 192).[65] It was a design that, with some variations, could have been made anywhere in the Western world, from America to Russia and from Scandinavia to Spain. However, in addition to this kind of generic international design, also seen in some of the decorations discussed earlier, Lyon, Wells, Cottier & Co. followed a trend in Australian design during the period of Federation (1890–1910) of adapting motifs from the Australian natural world into their ornamental schemes. Since this is a tendency more clearly seen in the company's glass than in its mural decorations, it may be ventured that it was Lyon rather than Wells (who lived in the country for less than ten years), who promoted it. Of course, as has been shown, when it comes to the use of Australian motifs patrons cannot be discounted: some, like White and Madden, must have specifically demanded their use.

Lyon, Wells, Cottier & Co. appears to have been especially interested in using Australian motifs in such a way as to express a sense of Australia as a specific territory within the British Empire, bringing Australian flora and fauna together with classical motifs and at times with typically European animals and plants. The firm was active in Australia when the triple allegiance to a cosmopolitan British Empire, Britain, the ancestral country of most Australians, and Australia was much on everyone's mind as the country's large self-governing colonies were working towards the creation of a Federation, which eventually came to pass in 1901.

Several of the firm's decorative projects discussed here show examples of this combination of Australian, British and traditional 'cosmopolitan' motifs and the firm's design portfolio in the Mitchell Library shows many others. Among them is a drawing for a design of a roundel intended for the Sydney Hospital on Macquarie Street, built after a design by Thomas Rowe later modified by John Kirkpatrick. The actual window, still *in situ*, is one of four roundels placed high around the operating theatre's apsidal wall, two of which are reproduced here (figs 193a and b). They are variations on traditional armorial windows, but the centre shields, instead of traditional charges, show flowers – a waratah and a rose. (The other two roundels show the Scottish thistle and the Irish shamrock.) In all the windows, the flowers are placed on a white shield, which is set inside a complex mantling of concentric rings and scrollwork. Instead of a traditional helmet crest, the top of a classical column bears two scrolls crowned by a palmette. Around the coat of arms is a wreath of red mistletoe, coming together at the bottom in a stylised daisy. A series of concentric rings, the widest of which shows an egg and dart motif, frame the window. The design clearly exemplifies the multiple strains of Australian heritage.

THE LAST DECADES

The number of commissions received by the firm decreased after 1890, due to the major depression that started in that year. This was especially true for public commissions, although some work still trickled in. On 15 January 1891 the Earl of Jersey became the new governor of New South Wales. Lyon, Wells, Cottier & Co. was commissioned by Vernon, recently appointed as the New South Wales government architect, to redecorate areas of Government House. On inauguration day, the press noted that nearly 'every part of the large building has been subjected to the transforming influences of the painter's and decorator's art'.[66] The firm repainted and repapered part of the walls on the first floor and created three stained-glass panels featuring the coats of arms and the periods of office of the early governors of the colony commencing with Captain Arthur Phillip (1788–92), as well as three large panels with those of more recent governors, including the incoming earl.

By 1895 Wells decided to return to Scotland with his family. His partnership with Lyon was dissolved on 31 December 1895 and the following January he advertised the sale of his property, Missenden, on Sydney's North Shore.[67] In early March, the contents of his house were auctioned there. They included sets of dining- and drawing-room furniture made by the well-known Edinburgh firm Scott Morton & Co. in Edinburgh[68] and stained-glass panels with subjects of Australian native birds designed and painted by Lyon, Wells, Cottier & Co.[69] Wells left Sydney with his family in late March bound for London.[70]

Following the dissolution of the partnership, the firm reverted to its earlier name of Lyon, Cottier & Co., even though by then Cottier had been dead for five years. Apparently, even in Australia Cottier's name meant something or perhaps Lyon retained his name out of loyalty. Cottier's work and entrepreneurial spirit had inspired Lyon and were directly behind the genesis and rapid success of their joint decorating enterprise. But Lyon was a force in his own right and it was he who was responsible for taking this leading Australian decorating firm into the early twentieth century.

Commissions for the decorations and windows of churches, government buildings and for mansions and villas continued into the early 1900s and the firm carried on exhibiting internationally. To the British-Franco Exhibition in London of 1908 it sent a large window depicting Edward VII in his coronation robes, surrounded by royal insignia. The figure was adapted from Sir John Longstaff's (1862–1941) portrait of the king (1904) in the National Art Gallery of New South Wales (now the Art Gallery of New South Wales).[71] The whereabouts of the window is unknown and much of the late domestic work of the firm no longer exists, unlike its religious glass, which survives in churches throughout New South Wales.[72] Adapting to the times, the firm added to its eclectic repertoire of classical, medieval, Renaissance and Pre-Raphaelite motifs elements of the Rococo revival style, which became increasingly popular in the late nineteenth

193 (a and b) Roundels with a waratah flower and a rose set within shields, Sydney Hospital, by Lyon, Wells, Cottier & Co., 1893–4. Stained glass

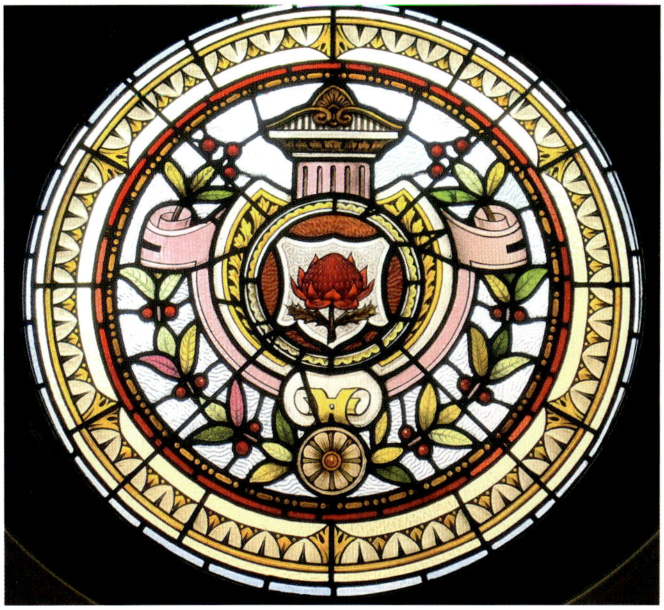

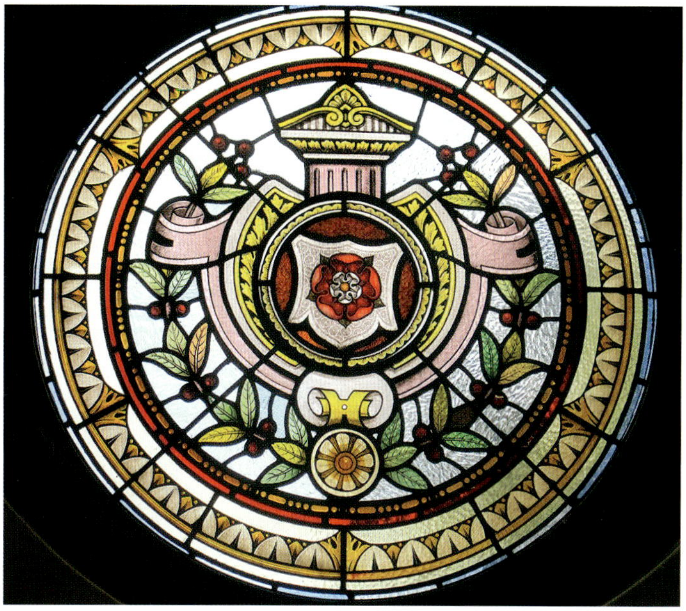

century as one of the sources of Art Nouveau.[73] The firm also continued to use Australian floral and faunal motifs, as at Warinilla, a mansion on Sydney's inner North Shore (demolished), where Lyon, Cottier & Co.'s painted birds encircling clusters of waratahs and roses were wreathed across the drawing-room ceiling.[74] But with the advent of modernism, Lyon, Cottier & Co.'s eclectic style became old-fashioned. Moreover, the introduction of new building technologies such as pressed metal (zinc) ceilings put an end to forms of decoration including ceiling painting for which the firm had been well known.

In about 1913 the headquarters of Lyon, Cottier & Co., then managed by Lyon's son Bertram Fraser (1871–1950), known as Bert, and daughter Lillie (Lillie Janet; b. 1876) were moved from Liverpool Street to Rushcutters Bay, a harbourside suburb of Sydney.[75] John Lamb Lyon died in June 1916[76] but the firm continued painting, decorating and producing stained-glass designs until 1924.[77] The auction sale of the firm's remainders (paints, oils, varnishes, kilns and workshop furniture) cleared Lyon, Cottier & Co.'s stock and the business closed.[78] Lyon's obituary in the *Australasian Decorator and Painter* in 1916 commemorated the firm's achievements, noting that since its beginning it had: 'decorated a large number of important private residences, churches and public buildings throughout Australia, many of which still bear witness to the skill of the firm and its staff, and evidence of the willingness of the public in earlier days to indulge a taste for decorative art.'[79] The obituary also highlighted Lyon's former partner and mentor, Daniel Cottier, emphasising his international reputation as a decorative artist and a collector of pictures. It is further confirmation of Cottier's lasting reputation worldwide and explains why neither Lyon nor Inglis ever dropped Cottier's name, even after his death. Cottier was a quality brand and they knew it.

CONCLUSION

'Surely, then, there is in commerce nothing incompatible with art.'
DANIEL COTTIER, 1866[1]

This book has traced the arc of the career of Daniel Cottier from his beginning as a gifted and original designer to the time of his premature death, when he was the engine and impresario of a comprehensive business empire that stretched across three continents. It is tempting to think of this arc as a bridge between opposite poles – the disinterested pursuit of art at one end and the calculated and mercenary practice of commerce at the other. Cottier himself, as the quotation at the beginning of this chapter suggests, did not see it that way. And while his statement about the compatibility of art and commerce may, at first glance, seem self-serving, to Cottier it appears to have been a deeply held conviction. He brought to commerce the same creativity, originality and passion that he brought to his design work. One might argue that Cottier was a 'design thinker' *avant la lettre.* Loving art in all its forms, he realised its sensual, spiritual, symbolic, as well as pecuniary, value. He saw the promise of bringing art to the public, for its and his own benefit, and designed a business strategy to realise that potential.

Although unique for its geographic reach and its comprehensiveness, the decorating business empire founded by Daniel Cottier in Britain, the United States and Australia was one of many such businesses operating between about 1865 and the outbreak of the First World War. All of them took advantage of what the philosopher and cultural critic Walter Benjamin (1892–1940) has referred to as the nineteenth-century 'addict[ion] to dwellings.'[2] From the 1830s onwards, the home or the apartment became, especially for the middle class, a secluded microcosmos within an increasingly complex and perilous world outside. For men, it was a place to which they could withdraw after a long day's work in the office, for women and children a haven where they would be protected from the dangers waiting in the streets of the new cities. At the same time the home performed an important social function and several of its rooms were designated and designed as spaces and backdrops for gatherings of family and friends. Thus the house was at once a container and a medium through which a variety of messages – aesthetic, psychological, political, economic, cultural – were transmitted.[3]

The bourgeois desire to make of the house a meaningful (in the literal sense of 'full of meaning') world-within-a-world caused artisanal firms that were in the home furnishing business to move away from specialisation in order to create shops where one could buy everything for the home. This allowed customers to think more holistically about the interiors they were fashioning and the messages they wanted to convey.[4] Thus, while at the beginning of the nineteenth century, homemakers would turn to cabinetmakers, upholsterers, painters, glaziers and other specialised artisans to furnish their homes, by the third quarter of the century, firms such as Morris & Co. in Britain or Herter Brothers in the United States would provide everything for the home, including, if desired, decorating advice and coordination. These firms were successful because they operated during the zenith of Benjamin's 'addiction to dwellings', from about 1870 to 1900, a period that coincided with Aestheticism, which was, in many ways, its corollary.

Benjamin, of course, was writing about the European continent and it is perhaps for that reason that he had little to say about the 'house' outside the home that had a special importance in the nineteenth-century Anglo-Saxon world, namely the church. It was here that families gathered for Sunday services, as well as for all important life occasions – birth, marriage,

194 The Four Seasons, birds and flowers, staircase window in Links House (now Links Hotel), Montrose, Angus, by Cottier & Co., London, *c.*1870–3. Stained glass

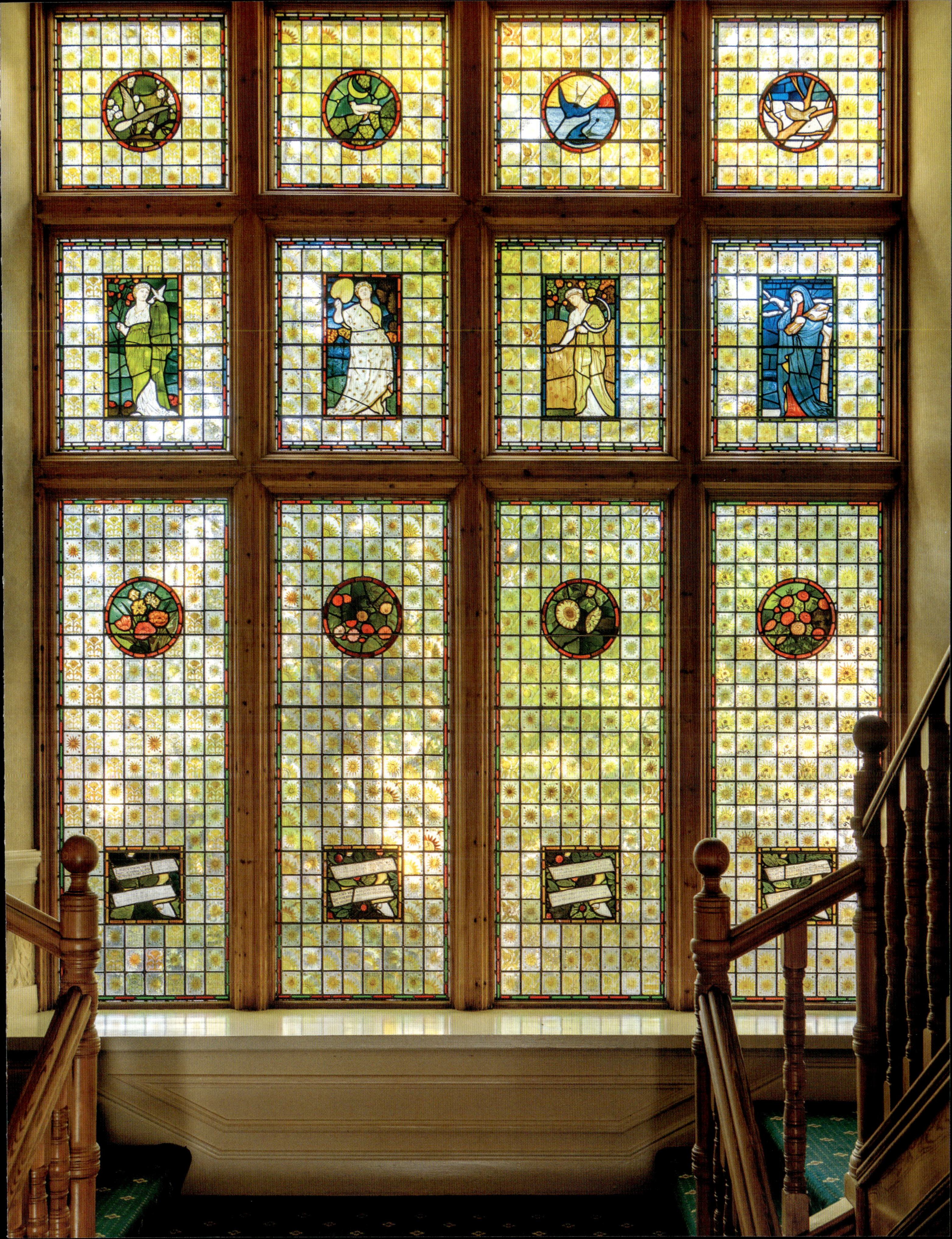

195 Detail of mantel clock by Cottier & Co. and Tiffany & Co., New York, for Ichabod Williams, 1883. Brooklyn Museum, New York (see fig. 86)

death. If not addicted, Victorians were certainly devoted to their 'houses of worship', a devotion that may be measured by the thousands that were built or rebuilt during Queen Victoria's reign in Britain alone. Many of these buildings were enriched with wall paintings, stencilling, woodcarving, metalwork and stained glass, much of it funded by wealthy parishioners. It was common for church members, for example, to pay tribute to their loved ones by donating stained-glass windows to their parish church. Indeed, most nineteenth-century Anglican and Presbyterian churches were glazed with such memorial windows.

Some decorating firms did work for homes as well as churches, especially if, like Cottier & Co. or Morris & Co., they had expertise in stained glass. At the same time, there were firms that specialised in church work. Most of these, like the London firms of Clayton & Bell, James Powell & Sons and Ward & Hughes (for which John Lamb Lyon, and possibly Cottier, worked as young men), specialised in stained glass but others broadened their business by making domestic glass or practising decorative painting. Cottier himself initially privileged church work over domestic decoration but he soon recognised the growing importance and business potential of the home and the increasing capital available for its beautification.

By the time he was in his late thirties Cottier had created a firm that not only provided more services than any other to date but also operated in three continents. The firm's branches in London and New York, its partnership in Sydney and its agent in Glasgow designed and manufactured furniture and stained glass (religious and secular); decorated walls, ceilings and ceramics; supplied wall coverings (papers or embossed) as well as rugs and carpets; upholstered furniture and made window dressings; and, in time, dealt in contemporary and Old Master paintings and retailed antiques both Western (including sculptures and Venetian glass) and non-Western (Chinese and Japanese porcelain). Not all branches offered all these items and services, nor did they operate in identical ways. In each location he and his managers, Elbert Jan van Wisselingh in London and James Inglis in New York, his business partner John Lamb Lyon in Sydney and his agent William Craibe Angus in Glasgow, adjusted the firm's scope to the markets they encountered and perhaps as well to their own preferences and expertise. Thus while the London branch, jointly run by Cottier and van Wisselingh, provided all services, the New York branch, managed by Cottier and Inglis, executed little wall painting but its furniture business thrived and its art gallery, especially in the early years, was considered cutting edge and appears to have been financially successful. In Australia, where the Cottier partnership was headed by Lyon, wall and ceiling painting were a major activity of the firm, which, however, sold little or no furniture, while its attempts at art dealing failed. Finally, Cottier's agent in Glasgow, Angus, concentrated on the art trade, though he also procured commissions for stained glass. While all three branches of Cottier & Co. had their own workshops, the one in New York produced only 'art' furniture and woodwork (panelling, staircases and so on) while other items like stained glass and tiles were shipped from England. The Sydney atelier, in contrast, manufactured stained glass and decorated ceramics but little else. In London, finally, Cottier & Co. designed and made stained glass and decorated ceramics for commissions in Britain, France, the United States and Australia, and made furniture. Cottier and his assistants drew on styles fashionable in the 1870s such as Anglo-Japanese, classical and Renaissance Revival, and Queen Anne, creating from these eclectic sources a strong visual brand which continued to appeal to the growing pool of enthusiasts for Aestheticism in the following decades.

As for the firm's impact, in Britain Cottier created a market for French and Dutch contemporary art, especially in Scotland where there was less competition than in London. In New York, Cottier and Inglis introduced Anglo-Japanese furniture and encouraged an Aesthetic sensibility. The Cottier gallery, moreover, launched the reputation of the Hague School, previously unknown in North America, and of the French painter Adolphe Monticelli. In Australia, the firm initiated comprehensive schemes of wall and ceiling decoration that had previously been unknown there. And in its best stained-glass windows, it introduced a

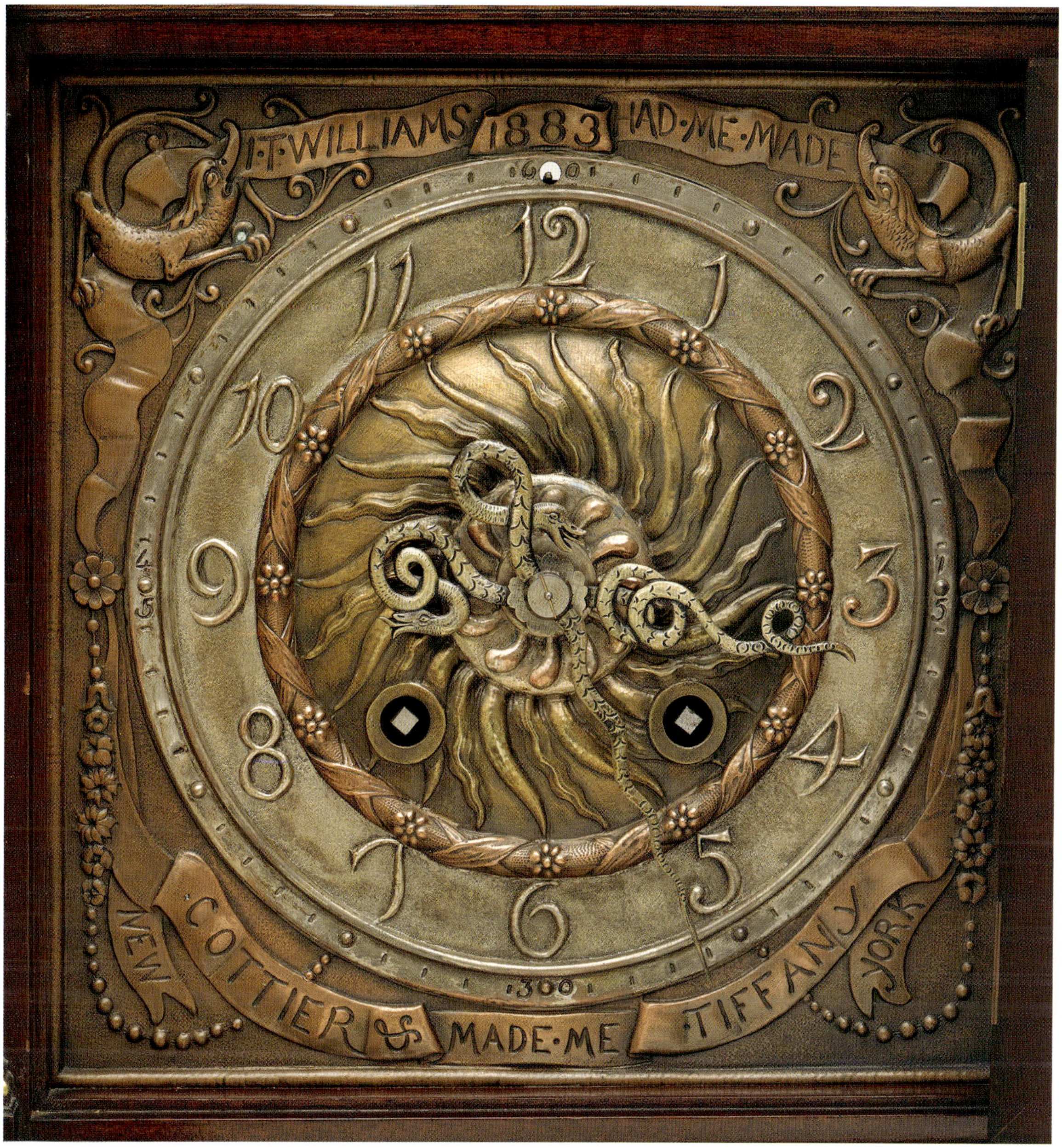

note of Aestheticism into the country's predominantly Gothic Revival output.

Like many, though by no means all, founders of the large decorating firms of the nineteenth century, Cottier had an artisanal training, being apprenticed to a coach painter and then a stained-glass maker (and probably decorator). His business success was due to a number of qualities that helped his rapid rise from an employee in the glazing firm of Field & Allan in Leith and Edinburgh to a global art entrepreneur. These qualities included artistic talent, boundless energy, a shrewd business sense, a uniquely charismatic personality and, most importantly, excellent team-building skills.

While contemporary sources frequently mention Cottier's personal qualities, they remain silent when it comes to the financial aspects of Cottier's business, about which we know very little. How did he finance his ventures – shops and workshops – in three major cities? How did he capitalise the stock of his art galleries? The lack of an archive containing Cottier & Co.'s financial records has been a major impediment to answering these questions and other, related ones, such as how he financed his numerous trips, often in the company of his entire family, as well as the substantial art collection he assembled during his lifetime and which, after his death, was sold for the equivalent of three million US dollars.

196 Bookcase door panel designed by Charles Rennie Mackintosh, made by McCulloch & Co., Glasgow, 1901. Stained glass with modern textile backing. Glasgow School of Art

197 Window made for a house in Cleveland, Ohio (demolished), by Cottier & Co., London, *c.*1877–80. Stained glass, 119.4 × 48.3 cm. Metropolitan Museum of Art, New York, Purchase, Barrie A. and Deedee Wigmore Gift

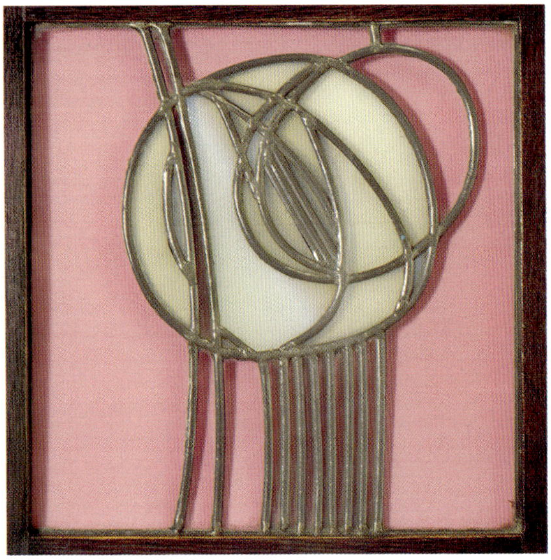

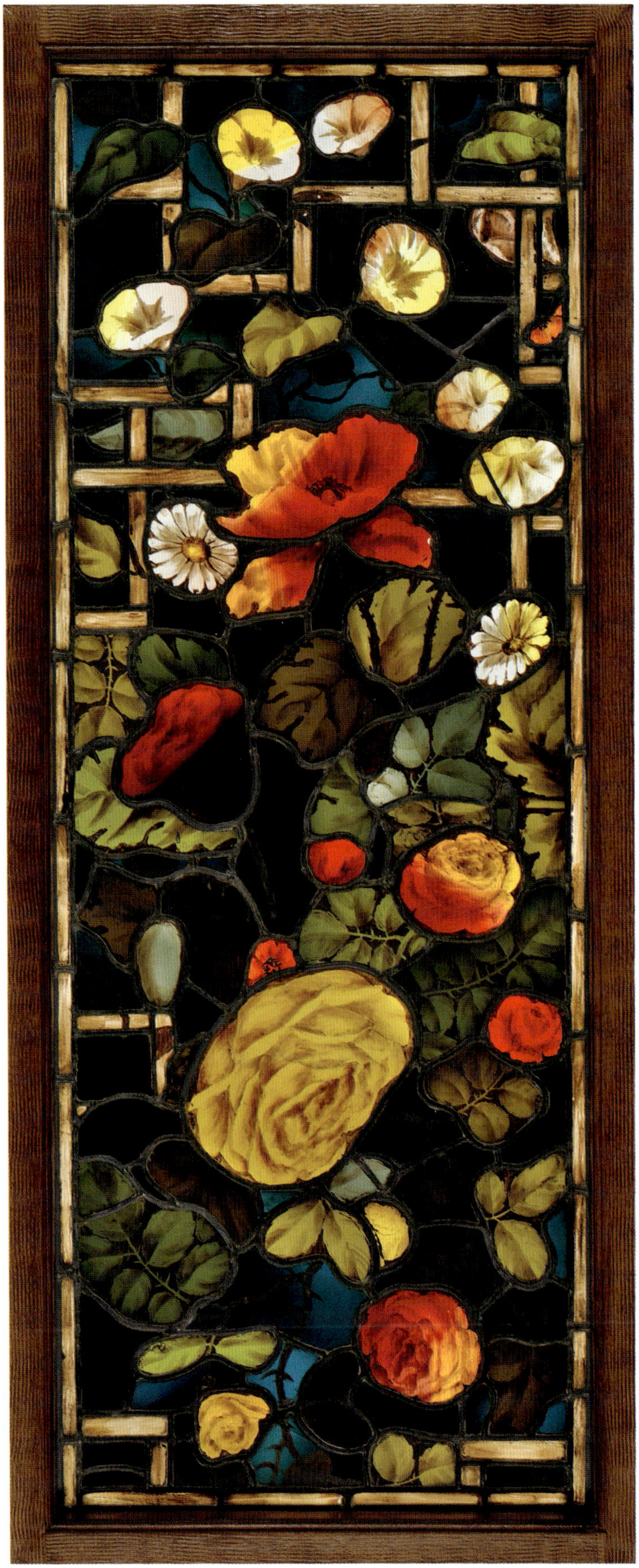

While we may never know how Cottier financed his enterprise, we do have some information about the way in which he built a clientele, which certainly was at the heart of his success. He and his managers and partners in New York and Sydney, all Scots, took advantage of the Scottish diaspora, making inroads through the Presbyterian church and immigrant societies. Cottier was also what today would be termed media savvy. In addition to cultivating writers and journalists, both female and male, he was adept at developing relations with major taste-makers in the countries in which he operated. This is true for Britain as well as the United States; in both countries he befriended 'influencers', including the English writer Mary Eliza Haweis, who praised him in *The Art of Beauty* (1878) as well as *The Art of Decoration* (1881) and the American Clarence Cook. To nurture these connections Cottier sent Haweis a stained-glass window made to her design as a Christmas present, and designed a cover for Cook's bestseller *The House Beautiful* (1878; see fig. 79), which described Cottier and his business in glowing terms.

Given Cottier's success during his lifetime, why was he forgotten so soon after his death? A number of reasons present themselves. Cottier's death in 1891 coincided with the rise of the Arts and Crafts movement, which breathed new life into traditional forms, a direction which those who continued his business did not follow. The Arts and Crafts movement also placed increasing emphasis on the work of the individual craftsperson, which made businesses like Cottier & Co., which subsumed the names of designers and artists under the brand name, seem out of step. Concomitantly, historical revivalism became old-fashioned and, instead of the plenitude of styles appealing to Aesthetic taste, a new generation of artists and designers in the 1890s advocated the creation of a recognisable period style, an *art nouveau*, a 'new art' inspired not by styles from the past but by forms in nature, which were not meant to be convincingly rendered but to serve as a point of departure for a new formal design language. The highly stylised stained-glass panel with a single rose (fig. 196) designed for a bookcase by Charles Rennie Mackintosh (1868–1928), who was thirty years younger than Cottier, is a far cry from a Cottier & Co. window with roses, daisies and morning glories (fig. 197), the realism of which was clearly inspired by seventeenth-century Dutch flower paintings. In architecture and furniture design, moreover, the notion that all art should aspire to music (that is, formal beauty at the expense of subject or function) was replaced by the notion that form must follow function.[5]

By the time the First World War broke out, most of the interiors that Cottier & Co. had planned and coordinated were dismantled as much of the furniture produced by the firm had become outdated; domestic stained-glass windows were often removed, damaged or destroyed. Even the paintings Cottier sold, especially those of the Hague School, fell out of fashion. Some floated on the market for several years before 'disappearing' into private collections; others, donated to museums, ended up in storage. What remained in public view were Cottier's windows in churches and some public buildings, but stained glass itself lost its appeal in the twentieth century when it was associated with religion and religious worship, which likewise fell out of favour with the advance of secularism.

It could be argued that the twentieth-century disregard for objects made in the context of Aestheticism is closely related to the century's 'abuse of beauty' itself.[6] As the pursuit of beauty came to be considered trivial in the twentieth century, objects created with aesthetic pleasure as the dominant goal were disparaged or even seen as kitsch. Only in the last four decades or so, as the interest in beauty has revived, both in art and in philosophy, has there been a renewed attentiveness to Aestheticism and its artistic production. In *Only a Promise of Happiness* (2007) Alexander Nehamas argues that beauty is not in the first instance an individual experience but one which humans want to share.[7] Beauty, therefore, has an important social dimension, a truth that nineteenth-century home owners clearly understood and one on which entrepreneurs such as Cottier capitalised and established their reputations.

APPENDIX SELECTIONS FROM JOHN LAMB LYON'S TRAVEL JOURNAL, 'SHORT TOUR IN EUROPE', 1886

The following excerpts come from John Lamb Lyon's unpublished travel journal, 'Short Tour in Europe', in which he jotted down his impressions of a trip from Australia to North America and Europe in 1886. The manuscript is held in the Mitchell Library, State Library of New South Wales in Sydney (Lyon and Stowe family papers, 1862–1955, MLMSS 1381 / 1).

Lyon left Sydney on 6 February 1886 aboard the steamship *Australia* and arrived in San Francisco twenty-three days later after a stopover in Honolulu. He stayed in San Francisco for a week, then took a train to Niagara Falls. After seeing the falls, he travelled to Chicago and from there to New York, where he visited the sights as well as Cottier's showroom at 144 Fifth Avenue and his workshop. From New York, he took the SS *Circassia* to Greenock, Scotland, from where he took the train to Glasgow. He stayed in his native city for six days, seeing relatives and friends, there and in Rothesay, Isle of Bute. Lyon then went by train to London, where he was Cottier's house guest. He visited Westminster Abbey and St Paul's Cathedral and went to hear the sermons of several famous preachers. After a short excursion to the European continent (Paris, Antwerp, Amsterdam), he returned to Australia.

The selected excerpts focus on New York, Glasgow and London, which are most relevant to the Cottier story. Lyon uses no punctuation and few capitals, as may be expected in a journal that is, essentially, an accumulation of notes. The excerpts have been transcribed as closely as possible to the original. A single slash means the end of a line, a double slash the end of a page. Omitted text is indicated by ellipses, illegible words by ellipses between square brackets.

Short Tour in Europe [New York]

... from Chicago to New / York this is quite up to / expectation the street / buildings are high and / much life and bustle / about I put up at the / Ashland House[1] the Hotels / of N. York are quite magnificent / a great deal of marble / in the Halls brass / hangings decorations every / thing very sumptious fifth / avenue hotel[2] and Delmonico[3] / a fine painting by Bouguereau / of the satyr & nymphs / this especialy lighted / at night rather a luscious / look[4] Theatres are numerous / The Casino[5] is the most / original in the Alhambra / style some fine stores / Cottier's is sumptious / / fine furniture and / hangings, Gasliers, pictures / The chief picture is Corot / Apollo a landscape[6] / at first sight the picture / is disapointing and £6,000 / seems a large sum to ask / the most of the pictures / seem curious chosen more / for their manner and / painting rather than subject / Montichelo [Adolphe Monticelli] is good in color / but some of them look like / panels covered with the / scrapings of the pallette / yet undoubtedly He is a / genius. got introduced / to Mr Ryder[7] an American / artist He is a nice fellow / and a poet as well / He declaimed / "The Wind The Wind"[8] / and other original pieces / / Cottier's manager and / partner Mr Inglis was / very kind his assistants / are Mr Valantine & Mr Kay[9] / in the carpenters shop / the shop is very spacious / and room to do a lot / of work very fine machinery / the power is got from / an engine in an adjoining / building Mr Holland is / the artist and seems / to be good at flowers / on furniture saw a / grand piano, goldy / looking satin wood / the ornament with Cupids / roses and ribbons looks / very rich for a small / log they paid £500 / it is cut up into / / veneers a bed of / the same wood coverlet / yellow satin they / make hangings on / the mosaic system / cutting out all the pattern / say on red satin and / letting in the pattern in / gold satin and outlining / with gold cord it has / a very rich effect must / be very expensive

saw / some being done for the / Vanderbilts it requires / a millionaire purse / for such luxuries / saw a window by Le Farge / of the ascension[10] *done / altogether in a new / kind of opal glass / / except the flesh which is done in antique / the effect of the window / is peculiar and outside / the whiteness of the china / looking glass is bad / still some good effects / may be got in this / glass for domestic / work The central park / in New York is fine / fine drives & walks / a good managerie / and museum*[11] *with a / very good collection / of pictures and other / curiosities the Produce / Exchange*[12] *is a fine / building ... / / [with] / a large tower from which / is a good view of the city / and harbour Brooklyn / bridge is immense / The ferry boats are / immense taking over / heavy drags &c at / sacremento the ferry / boat is the largest in the / world*[13] *it takes on the / whole train Engines / and all it is paddle / each wheel has an engine / to itself so they could / in a small space turn / sailed from N. York / on the Circassia for / Glasgow ...*

[Glasgow and London]

... Landed safely at Greenock / train to Glasgow put / up at "Steel Hotel"[14] *stayed / some 6 days in Glasgow / Friends seemed changed / with various fortunes / but mostly for the worse / saw Mrs. Lamont at Rothesay / also Aunty Kate & Kirsty / Rothsay greatly built / upon but still a / nice easy looking place / Visited Glasgow Cathedral / the windows look rawer / than ever much of the / enamel painting falling / off the Germain work / is a mistake in old Gothic / buildings*[15] *saw a Window / in the west end by Morris / large figures grassaile [grisaille] / pattern top & bottom / five lights*[16] *visited the / new College no rich / windows there yet saw / Charlie Gow,*[17] *D. Dewar*[18] */ Johnie Stewart, W. Kier*[19] */ Tom [?] MacMillan – Mrs Forrester / W. Bertram & family / Mr Frazer and ditto / Pat Pearson's family / / He being up in London / his affairs all crooked / saw Cragie Angus*[20] *a / picture dealer in Queen / St / a very good stock a / good deal of Cottier's stuff / and stained Glass a curious / card himself saw J. N. / Mitchell, E. Wilson J. / Finnie*[21] *visited the place / where I first saw the / light the houses all pulled / down to make way for / the new municipal b / buildings*[22] *extending the / whole block John St / Frederick St George St & / Cochrane Street also little / Hamilton St was in / course of demolition to / make room I heard / / for a Railway took / Train from St. Enochs station / to St. Pancras a new route / to me going through the / midland counties very / nice scenery arrived / in London about 7. o clock / too early in the morning / for Cottier who was not / up when I called– / fifteen years shewed / great changes on the whole / family but after a little / talk you get reconciled / to appearances which / seem to vanish and the / unaltered voice and / manners makes one / feel as young as ever / Ella has grown a rather / tall young lady reserved / / slim and rather good / looking acomplished pianist / and good singer her / sister Peggy is the stronger voice Peggy is quite different / from sister stouter in build / and more strong minded / and girl of the period / style – plays the banjo / still at school as is / also Willie at least he / goes to the university / He seems to be getting a / modern education no / end of subjects Anatomy / Phisiology Phonography / &c &c. rather tall – slim / and of an aristocrats air / rides a bicycle and does / a little soldiering there / is a good deal of quiet / style in Cottier's house / He does not give parties / but His ordinary table is / fit for any visitor that may / come in He has taken / the adjoining house which / when finished and furnished / will make a great establishment / I had Ella's bed room / which was done up quite / unique panelled gold / ceiling wood all painted / gold bronze yellow satin / hangings turkey carpets / venetian brass gasalier / furniture satin wood / Embroidered Japanese quilt / and neat bric a brac / Cottier has banished all / the Japanese stuff He / used to be so fond off / He now dislikes it / so fashions change / / visited Dr Dykes*[23] *church / on Sunday a very curved / congregation never saw / so many people taking / notes in a church He only / preached the sermon another / did the preliminary reading / at Spurgeons*[24] *in the evening / the young one preached / instead of his father who / was unwell the tabernacle / crowded as much as ever / visited the Abbey*[25] *a fine / building but no particular / change there men are / employed restoring the / outside a good window / in St Margarets by / Holloway*[26] *saw the latest / / work of Hughes in St / Mary's le bow*[27] *in his / old manner but improved / visited St Pauls Cathedral / little new in the way of / glass some of the mosaics / in the dome are finished*[28] */ awful dark foggy weather / outside St Pauls from / Ludgate hill is very grand / looks finer than St Peters / heard Dr Fraser*[29] *in his / new church the commandments / and some texts on the / pulpit wall.*

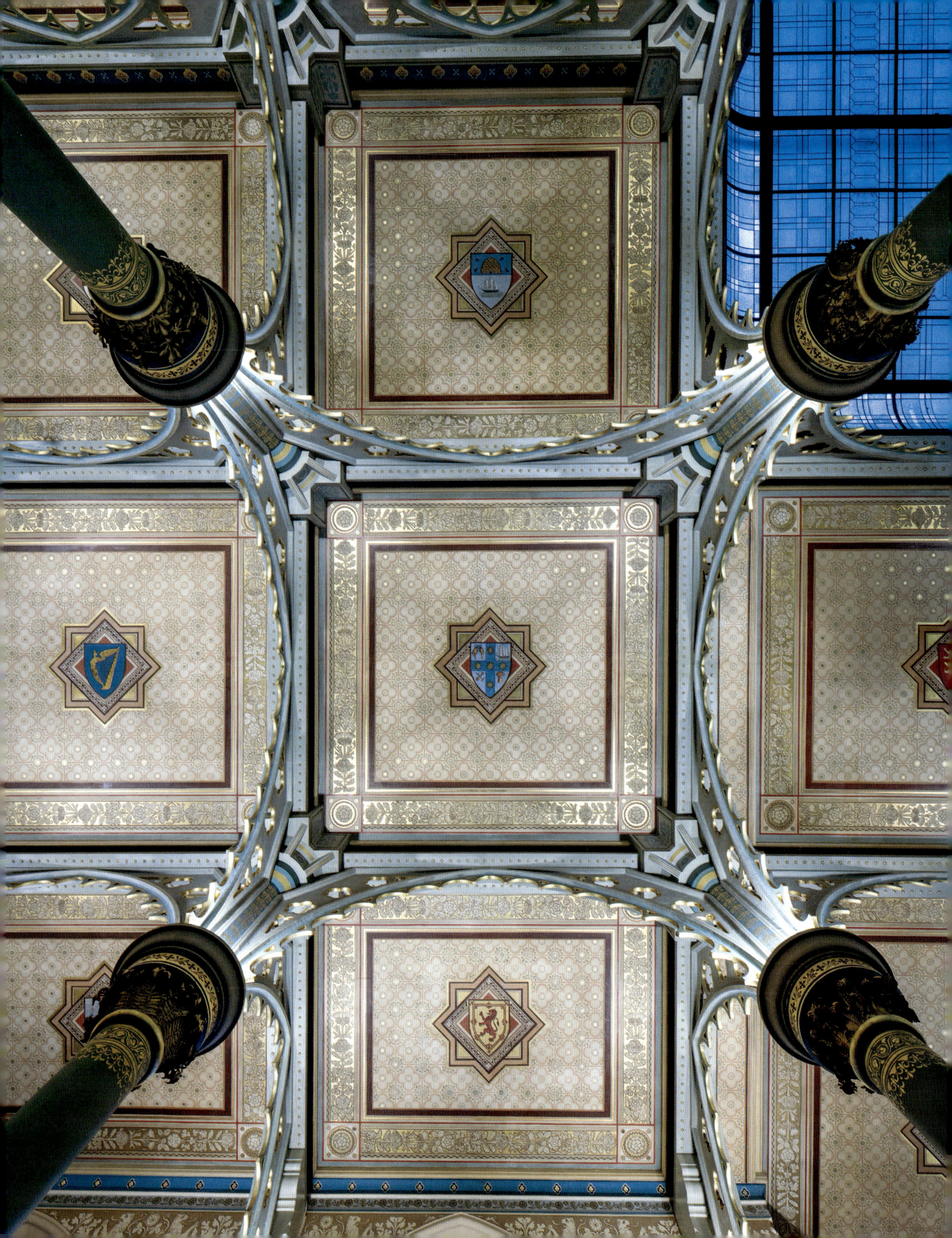

NOTES

198 Painted and stencilled decoration showing the arms of England, Ireland, Scotland and Australia on the ceiling in the banking chamber of the English, Scottish and Australian Chartered Bank, Melbourne, by Lyon, Wells, Cottier & Co., 1887

Introduction *pages 1–7*

1. 'The Cottier Sale', *The Collector* 3: 14 (15 May 1892), 216.
2. Cook 1883, 317.
3. Ford Madox Brown, quoted in the *Evening Times* (Glasgow), 9 October 1893, n.p., requoted in Madox Ford 1896, 364, but omitting 'other modern'.
4. Henley 1892, xii.
5. C. E. S. Wood cited in Millet 1921, 70: 'Wood told me that Cottier could tell a work of art a mile away. It is my great regret that I was not to meet Cottier. He went off the stage of New York Art as I came on.'
6. Grove Art Online, s.v. 'Aestheticism,' via Oxford Art Online, https://www.oxfordartonline.com, accessed 16 July 2020.
7. Walter Pater reminded his readers, 'Each art, therefore, having its own peculiar and incommunicable sensuous charm, has its own mode of reaching the imagination': Pater 1877, 526.
8. Proposition 4 of Owen Jones's *Grammar of Ornament*'s 'General Principles in the Arrangement of Form and Colour, in Architecture and the Decorative Arts, which are Advocated Throughout this Work': Jones 1856, 4.
9. Hamilton 1882, Preface.
10. Burke et al. 1986; Orr and Calloway 2011; *The Cult of Beauty* was shown at the Musée d'Orsay, Paris (2011–12) and the de Young Museum, San Francisco (2012).
11. Victor Cousin quoted in Kelley 2001, 577.
12. On Aestheticism in private homes, see among others Girouard 1977, passim.
13. Dresser 1862a, 29.
14. For a full listing and a brief summary of the essence of colour treatises, see the useful website https://www.colorsystem.com, accessed 16 July 2020.
15. Hay 1836, vii, argues that, just as beautiful music is subject to rules of harmony that are rooted in science, so science-based rules can be articulated for 'agreeable' colour harmonies.
16. Veblen 1912, 129; he warned of a 'sense of costliness masquerading under the name of beauty' and of 'conspicuous wastefulness' becoming a 'constraining norm selectively shaping and sustaining our sense of what is beautiful' (128). See also Cook 1878a, 336, who, in concluding his *The House Beautiful*, strenuously objected to 'measuring beautiful things by a money standard'.
17. See e.g. Dresser 1874–6, 24.
18. Even if Cottier did not attend Ruskin's 'Two Paths' lecture, he may have read it, for it was published in 1859.
19. Ruskin 1859, 91–2.
20. Henley 1892, xii.
21. Lepine 2012, at http://www.branchcollective.org/?ps_articles=ayla-lepine-on-the-founding-of-watts-co-1874, accessed 21 July 2020.
22. Haweis, 1882, 31. In her discussion of the house of the painter Lawrence Alma-Tadema, Haweis suggested that Cottier, William Morris and Owen Jones each had his own distinct style, seen in all the homes they decorated, but Alma-Tadema's house was one of a kind: 'a Tadema picture that one is able to walk through'.
23. Haweis 1872 (*Saint Pauls Magazine*), 190, repr. in Haweis 1872 (*Eclectic Magazine*), 473.
24. Cook 1883, passim.
25. Vincent to Theo van Gogh, The Hague, on or *c.* Tuesday, 5 June 1883: http://vangoghletters.org/vg/letters/let350/letter.html, accessed 16 July 2020.
26. Exception must be made for a short essay about Cottier's preferences in contemporary art (in the 1878 catalogue of the auction of his New York gallery stock) as well as some letters, most notably two groups of letters written to the Dutch artist David Artz, in the Rijksprentenkabinet (the print room of the Rijksmuseum, Amsterdam) and The Hague's Municipal Archive. Partial archives of Lyon, Cottier & Co., the Australian branch of Cottier & Co., are in the Mitchell Library, Sydney.
27. Girouard 1977; Harrison 1980; Michael Donnelly 1981 and 1997.
28. Hobler 1987.
29. Burke et al. 1986.
30. See Alice Cooney Frelinghuysen in ibid., 178.
31. Kinchin, Macartney and Robertson 2011, 14–57.

1 · Scotland 1838–1869 *pages 8–31*

1. The 1841 Great Britain Census, Glasgow, Strathclyde, digital image s.v. 'Daniel Cottier', http://www.scotlandspeople.gov.uk, accessed 29 July 2020.

2. The origin of the family name is English or French and in his brief biography of Cottier the poet and writer William Ernest Henley (1849–1903) noted that 'it has been suggested that the founder of the family was a Huguenot exile': Henley 1892, ix. Henley's account, which was probably informed by Cottier's friend and patron Robert Hamilton Bruce, also stated that Cottier's ancestors 'had been settled for generations in the Isle of Man', an assertion which tallies with 'Discovery of a Cottier Stained-glass Window in Lezayre' 1939, 125, describing Cottier's ancestry: 'This family of Cottier hails from "Nerindale" (Narradale) and Kerrowmoar in the Abbey Lands of Kirk Christ Lezayre. There are records of their holding Nerindale in Monastery times. As far back as 1541 Gilberto MacOtter (Cottier) was tenant of the Abbey, in 1660 the same land was held by John Cottier and in 1703 by William Cottier, so that there is a continuous line recorded for 350 years.'

3. Mary Catherine Cottier, marriage record, 1865, http://www.scotlandspeople.gov.uk, accessed 29 July 2020.

4. Cottier's paternal grandfather, who died in 1803 according to an inscription on a memorial window Cottier donated to Kirk Christ Lezayre (Holy Trinity), Isle of Man, in 1884, was 'a native of Lezayre': *Isle of Man Times*, 31 May 1884, 5.

5. Daniel Cottier and Margaret McLean, marriage record, 1834, http://www.scotlandspeople.gov.uk, accessed 29 July 2020.

6. Isabella Cottier, birth record, 1836, and death record, 1837; Mary Catherine Cottier, birth record, 1840; the 1841 Great Britain Census, Glasgow, s.v. 'Daniel Cottier', http://www.scotlandspeople.gov.uk, accessed 29 July 2020. Cottier's birth certificate has not been traced.

7. Daniel Cottier's death date of 1843 is given on the memorial window donated by Cottier to Kirk Christ Lezayre (see n. 4 above).

8. Before the introduction of compulsory education in 1872, Scottish children either attended schools run by the church or other charitable bodies, or were educated privately. Cottier's wife Marion had also lost her father when she was a child and, according to the 1851 census, she was a boarder at the Trades' Maiden Hospital, an Edinburgh institution founded to educate 'the daughters of decayed tradesmen' where she would have received an education until the age of seventeen: *Black's Picturesque Tourist of Scotland*, 5th edn (Edinburgh: Adam and Charles Black, 1847), 58–9.

9. 'The Late Daniel Cottier', *Glasgow Herald*, 7 May 1892, 4, probably a reference to the firm of A. & W. Paterson, boot and shoe manufacturers, founded *c.*1821.

10. The 1851 Great Britain Census, Glasgow, Strathclyde, digital image s.v. 'Daniel Cottier', http://www.scotlandspeople.gov.uk, accessed 29 July 2020.

11. 'The Late Daniel Cottier', 4.

12. One fact that points towards Cottier training with Cairney was that he apparently 'worked at his art' in Dunfermline, a town near Edinburgh, about this time (Henley 1892, ix), where the local stained-glass artist Robert Boyle Watson acted as an agent for Cairney; see Michael Donnelly 1997, 27.

13. John Lamb Lyon, who emigrated to Australia and became Cottier's collaborator in Sydney, was apprenticed to Cairney: see Ch. 6, p. 144.

14. *A Description of the New Palace of Westminster* (London: W. Warrington & Son, 1848), 10.

15. Donnelly 1997, 27.

16. *The Statistical Account of Edinburghshire* (Edinburgh and London: William Blackwood & Sons, 1845), 705.

17. Hay 1828.

18. See Wainwright 1989, 167–8.

19. The Palace of Holyroodhouse interiors were recorded in watercolour by George Grieg in 1865 (Royal Collection Trust). I am grateful to an anonymous reader for this reference.

20. Morrison 1888, vol. 2, 756. Lyon worked with Cottier in London 'for some years'; see 'Personal: Mr John L. Lyon' 1909, 264.

21. Adding credence to the suggestion that Cottier worked for Ward & Hughes is the fact that at a meeting of the Society of Antiquaries of Scotland in Edinburgh in May 1865, it was announced that Cottier had donated four fragments of medieval stained glass from Lincoln Cathedral to the Society's museum: *Proceedings of the Society of Antiquaries of Scotland: Eighty-Fifth Session, 1864–65*, vol. 6, pt 1 (Edinburgh: Printed for the Society by Neill & Co., 1866), 204; I am grateful to Ross Anderson for this reference. See also *The Scotsman*, 11 May 1865, 5. The glass is in the collection of the National Museums of Scotland, Edinburgh, H.KK 1–4; I am grateful to Jacqueline Moran for showing me it.

22. In 1883 Ford Madox Brown, who taught at the Working Men's College, described Cottier as a former pupil; see report in *Evening Times* (Glasgow), 9 October 1893, n.p.

23. Cottier quoted in Haweis 1872, 473.

24. Harrison 1954, 44.

25. See Madox Ford 1896, App. A, 'Madox Brown as a Teacher', 425, and 159, n. 1, respectively.

26. John Phillips Emslie quoted in ibid., App. A, 426.

27. Emslie quoted in Davies 1904, 52.

28. Ibid. Brown painted *Work* (Manchester City Art Gallery), his most famous painting, from 1852 to 1865 and a smaller version (Birmingham Museum and Art Gallery) from 1859 to 1863.

29. The 1861 Great Britain Census, London, digital image s.v. 'Daniel Cottier', Ancestry.com, accessed 29 July 2020, records Cottier as lodging in a boarding house at 3 Francis Street, Marylebone. His name is followed by that of Alexander Macleure [*sic*], a glass painter also from Glasgow.

30. Hereafter referred to as Morris & Co., the name of the firm from 1875. See Donnelly 1997, 28, who states that Cottier joined Morris & Co. in 1861, citing the fact that 'in 1870 he [Cottier] drew upon the unpublished Morris-Burne-Jones panel *The Lady of Woodbank and her daughters*, executed in 1861 for Woodbank House, Arden, near Bingley, Yorkshire, as a source for his Speirs Memorial window in Paisley Abbey.' The Morris & Co. panel is now in the William Morris Gallery, London, C212ii.

31. William Gibson, 2 Crown Terrace, Dowanhill, Glasgow, to William Young, 4 May 1914, 2, quoting a letter from Andrew Wells in Boscombe, Bournemouth, in which he recalled working with Cottier in Scotland in the 1860s: Young Scrapbooks, vol. 37, p. 70, Mitchell Library, Special Collections, Glasgow Museums and Libraries Collections. William Gibson was a merchant and member of the congregation of Dowanhill Church; William Young (1845–1916) co-founded the Glasgow Art Club in 1867. I am grateful to Clare Thompson for this information.

32. *Building News*, 5 December 1862, 441.

33. After Trinity Church, Irvine, was closed for worship the panel was removed and restored; see Harrison 1980, 48, n. 19. The building is now a travel hub and a restored rose window designed by Cottier incorporating heads of the Four Evangelists remains in the west end.

34. E.g., *Special Exhibition of Works of Art of the Mediæval, Renaissance, and more Recent Periods*, South Kensington Museum, London, June 1862; the *Crucifixion* in All Saints Church, Selsley, Gloucestershire, designed by Ford Madox Brown for Morris, Marshall, Faulkner & Co., London, 1862.

35. *The Scotsman*, 19 April 1862, 2. Cottier was described as the designer and painter of the window.

36. Ibid.

37. Ibid.

38. Sebastian Evans quoted in Mallet and Johnson 1862, 406. More generally, Evans lamented the fact that 'glass painting in non-ecclesiastical styles is very poorly represented in the Exhibition, the best producers having abstained from exhibiting at all.'

39. *International Exhibition, 1862: Medals and Honorable Mentions awarded by the International Juries*, 2nd edn (London: Eyre & Spottiswoode, 1862), 363.

40. *Caledonian Mercury*, 5 April 1864, 2.

41. 'Exhibition of Paintings on Glass, South Kensington Museum', *The Ecclesiologist*, 163, n.s. 127 (August 1864), 189.

42. *Building News*, 27 May 1864, 393–4.

43. Ibid., 5 May 1865, 326.

44. The 1861 Great Britain Census, Edinburgh, Lothian, digital image s.v. 'Andrew Wells', Ancestry.com, accessed 29 July 2020.

45. Gibson to Young, 4 May 1914, 2, quoting Andrew Wells.

46. Daniel Cottier and Marion Field, marriage certificate, Edinburgh, 1866, Ancestry.com, accessed 29 July 2020.

47. Townhead Parish Church's decoration was almost entirely overpainted in the twentieth century and, despite its seminal importance in the history of Scottish architecture and interior design, it was demolished (apart from the tower and spire) in 1997.

48. Girouard 1977, 39. For a biography of Stevenson, see the *Dictionary of Scottish Architects*, 2016, http://www.scottisharchitects.org.uk/architect_full.php?id=200799, accessed 29 July 2020.

49. See Sewter 1975, 80–81.

50. The Morris, Marshall, Faulkner & Co. window at Townhead Parish Church was removed before the church's demolition and is now in the collection of Glasgow Museums (E.1998.10). However, by the time the church was demolished many of the Cottier windows were damaged and only a few fragments were saved.

51. Sally J. Rush, 'Alexander Thomson, Daniel Cottier and the Interior of Queen's Park Church', in Stamp and McKinstry 1994, 182.

52. Report on Cottier's paper 'Colour the Handmaid of Architecture', *Building News*, 2 March 1866, 142.

53. Ibid.

54. Wells 1902, 145.

55. Ibid.

56. *Dumfries and Galloway Standard and Advertiser*, 13 June 1866, 3. The organ was moved to the chancel in the later nineteenth century. In 1993 it was dismantled and removed to St Margaret's Church, Knightswood, Glasgow, where the organ was rebuilt in 2002. About twelve pipes retaining their original decoration of red, turquoise, yellow and red chevrons and diapers were incorporated inside the instrument. I am grateful to Matthew Hynes for this information; see Kinchin, Macartney and Robertson 2011, 129 fig. 108.

57. *Glasgow Herald*, 7 June 1866, 2.

58. *Dumfries and Galloway Standard and Advertiser*, 13 June 1866, 3.

59. 'The Late Daniel Cottier', 4. Baird's brother-in-law, the businessman Alexander Whitelaw, was probably instrumental in directing a significant portion of Baird's legacy towards the new church.

60. *Paris Universal Exhibition of 1867: Catalogue of the British Section* (London: Her Britannic Majesty's Commissioners, 1868), 53, cat. no. 113.

61. For Leiper, see John R. Hume, 'The Scottish Houses of William Leiper', in Ian Gow and Alistair Rowan, *Scottish Country Houses, 1600–1914* (Edinburgh: Edinburgh University Press, 1995), 285–97, and Simon Green, *Architectural Heritage 3: The Age of Mackintosh* (Edinburgh: Edinburgh University Press, 1992), 32–42.

62. In 1984 Dowanhill was sold by the Church of Scotland to the Four Acres Charitable Trust, which in 1994 reopened the building as Cottiers Theatre and has undertaken extensive conservation, including Cottier's decoration and stained glass.

63. Kinchin, Macartney and Robertson 2011, 13. Leiper went to Paris *c.*1875–8, where he studied at the Académie Julian, returning to Scotland to resume his architectural work in 1880.

64. Ibid., 36, fig. 24 A–C.

65. Ibid., 34 fig. 23A; Dickie 1916, 9; see also Dickie 1926, 73.

66. I am grateful to Rosemary Watt for showing me the Dowanhill minister's chair and one of the collecting dish stands. The chair has been repainted and the original embroidered cover replaced, although the stands retain their original paintwork.

67. Report of Cottier, 'Colour the Handmaid of Architecture', 142.

68. Dickie 1926, 73.

69. See Hilary Macartney and Alan Ferdinand, 'Documenting the Painted Decoration', in Kinchin, Macartney and Robertson 2011, Ch. 7, 100–9.

70. Kinchin, Macartney and Robertson 2011, 20.

71. *Glasgow Herald*, 12 November 1866, 4. *Building News* carried a similarly worded account but went further in praising 'Mr. Cottier, to whom no small honour is due for the able manner in which he has furthered the views of the architect': 16 November 1866, 769.

72. Mavor 1923, 227.

73. Thomson designed a new studio for Cairney in Bath Street, Glasgow, 1860–1 (demolished).

74. *Post Office Glasgow Directory*, 1866, 94.

75. *Glasgow Herald*, 20 October 1868, 3.

76. *Greenock Advertiser*, May 10, 1866, 1.

77. 'Greek Thomson', read by Gildard on 30 January 1888 and quoted in *Proceedings of the Philosophical Society of Glasgow* 19 (1887–8), Glasgow: John Smith & Son, 1888, 200.

78. Ford Madox Brown cited in *Evening Times* (Glasgow), 9 October 1893, n.p.

79. Ibid. Thomson's name is misspelt 'Thompson' in the newspaper article.

80. Cottier's workshop was also close to the premises formerly occupied by the stained-glass business of David Kier, at 45 Carrick Street. In 1866, prior to having his own Glasgow workshop, Cottier had had to prepare the designs for the decoration of Townhead Parish Church from his mother's house at 154 Shamrock Street, Glasgow: cited in Gibson to Young, 4 May 1914.

81. Daniel Cottier, 'The Painted Windows of Glasgow Cathedral', quoted in *The Daily Review* (Edinburgh), 8 March 1867, 2–3.

82. Ibid.

83. Ibid.

84. *The Scotsman*, 21 March 1867, 8. I am grateful to Clare Thompson for this reference.

85. *Building News*, 15 March 1867, 197.

86. *Deutsche Bauzeitung* 1: 17 (27 April 1867), 165. I am grateful to Marc Fecker for the translation.

87. Kinchin, Macartney and Robertson 2011, 23.

88. Waters and Carew-Cox 2017, 319.

89. Kinchin, Macartney and Robertson 2011, 37.

90. Ibid., 35.

91. See e.g. the Heaton, Butler & Bayne windows *Feeding the Hungry* in St Peter, Dunton, Norfolk, and *Christ's Passion* in St Mary, Jackfield, Shropshire, both 1863. Both firms showed work at the exhibition of stained glass held at the South Kensington Museum in 1864, which Cottier may have seen, as his *Gentle Shepherd* panel for Field & Allan was also shown there. *The Vision of Beatrice* by Lavers & Barraud, *c.*1864, was one of two panels exhibited by them that the museum acquired (Victoria and Albert Museum, London, 780–1864), in addition to four Morris & Co. panels, including *Penelope*.

92. *Exposition Universelle de 1867 à Paris: Catalogue Général*, 2 vols (Paris: E. Dentu; London: J. M. Johnson & Sons, 1867), pt 1, 174.

93. Kirchhoff 1867, 81–2.

94. *Glasgow Evening Post*, 9 July 1867, 2. Some Cottier windows, e.g. at Coll-Earn House, Auchterarder, and Prudhoe Hall, Northumberland, bear inscriptions referring to the London and Paris awards and as late as 1888 an American writer was noting enthusiastically that 'At the French International Exposition in 1867 Messrs. Cottier & Co. were awarded several first class premiums, medals, etc., for the beauty, quality, and finish, of their art work': *Illustrated New York* 1888, 283.

95. Recalled by White's daughter Ina: Harrower 1918, 31. White's daughter Alice, who remembered Cottier as 'a jovial man with a red beard and a Glasgow accent', maintained that her father met Cottier on a train from London to Aberdeen: 'Daniel Cottier, Artist and Stained Glass Maker' 1938, p. 49.

96. See Gould 1969, 1–2 and 21 figs 6–8.

97. I am grateful to Jane and Bill Church for showing me Glenseaton Lodge in March 2018.

98. Gould 1969, 1.

99. Ibid. and 21 figs 7 and 8, illustrating two panels depicting Raphael and Miranda. By 1969 some glass remained in the drawing room at Seaton Cottage, while other roundels, including these, had been removed and were in the possession of White's children. From the Rembrandt and Emily panels (figs 15 and 16), it is evident that the frames of these panels are similar to those used for a set of the Four Seasons made by Cottier & Co. for Knockderry House, Cove, Argyll and Bute (a house enlarged by Leiper in 1890), and by Lyon, Cottier & Co. for the windows of Joylen, Cottier's house at Birchgrove, Sydney, *c.*1884 (see fig. 169).

100. Cottier is known to have supplied White with several pieces of ebonised and painted furniture, probably made by Cottier & Co. in London in the early 1870s. These included a wardrobe, an ebonised dressing-table with cheval glass, a wash-stand with painted tiles and chairs; see Gould 1969, 2.

101. John Forbes White quoted in ibid. In 1867, another protégé of White, the painter George Reid (1841–1913), enhanced the ceilings of these rooms by designing painted monograms; see Melville 2000, 20.

102. I am grateful to Jane and Bill Church for this information.

103. *Aberdeen Journal*, 16 September 1868, 5, which observed: 'It has been painted in a rather fantastic style, producing withal a pleasing effect ... The grotesque design is indescribable and inexplicable, except that it is in the mediæval style of art, and, as such, it is said to be grateful to an artistic eye; consequently it must be left for people to form their own opinions about it.' It must have been at this time that Cottier designed a cabinet which was made from some removed roof beams from St Machar's: *Aberdeen Evening Express*, 1 March 1881, 2; 10 March 1881, 3.

104. Gildard 1888. Cottier was involved in the installation of painted panels in the first-floor drawing room at Holmwood. Painted by Hugh Cameron (1835–1918), whom Cottier may have known from the Trustees' Academy in Edinburgh, the panels (whereabouts unknown) illustrated scenes from Alfred, Lord Tennyson's *Idylls of the King* and were set into painted Greek key borders, perhaps designed by Cottier.

105. I am grateful to Scott Abercrombie for sharing information about the stencilled wall decoration of 1 Great Western Terrace, Glasgow.

106. See MacDonald 1987, 42; some of the hardware (see p. 61, fig. 3) was removed from 4 Great Western Terrace and is now in Glasgow Museums (PP1985.165.3). It can be compared with the enamelled brass clock case designed by Talbert *c.*1865 and made by Skidmore's Art Manufactures Co., Coventry (Victoria and Albert Museum, London, W.2–1985).

107. These Leiper houses included Kirktonhill in Dumbarton and Woodside Lodge on Loch Goil (both 1867) and Cornhill House, Biggar (1871), a substantial French Renaissance-style house designed for Alexander Kay, who had paid for much of the stained glass at Dowanhill.

108. The genre scenes may be based on the designs of John Moyr Smith and Henry Stacy Marks (discussed in Ch. 2). The *Pittsburgh Post-Gazette*, 30 April 1987, 15, illustrates a near-identical stained-glass panel (to fig. 19) for sale, described as 'one of six in three wooden doors believed to have come from Andrew Carnegie's razed East End mansion'. This may be a reference to Fairfield, the Pittsburgh house that Carnegie vacated in 1867 when he moved to New York and in which his younger brother, Thomas M. Carnegie, lived in the 1870s.

109. E.g., Cottier's firm decorated the club-house of the Tynemouth Amateur Rowing Club in 1867: *Shields Daily Gazette*, 5 February 1887, 3.

110. I am grateful to Juliet Kinchin for this information.

111. The glass at Prudhoe Hall remains *in situ*. It was followed by stained glass for the Church of Our Lady and St Cuthbert, which opened in October 1870. The church windows were removed and incorporated into an enlarged building in 1891, and that building itself was moved a mile into the town of Prudhoe in 1904–5. I am grateful to Fr Paul Zielinski for this information; see Zielinski 2006.

112. *Newcastle Courant*, 9 April 1869, 5; *Shields Daily Gazette*, 3 April 1869, 3.

113. *Glasgow Herald*, 19 December 1866, 3.

114. *Paisley Herald and Renfrew Advertiser*, 30 May 1868, 1.

115. *Glasgow Herald*, 27 May 1868, 5.

116. *Durham County Advertiser*, 11 December 1868, 5.

117. *Durham Chronicle*, 15 May 1868, 7.

118. Harrison 1980, 48.

119. *Newcastle Courant*, 15 May 1868, 5.

120. *Aberdeen Free Press and Buchan News*, 16 February 1869, 2.

121. Ibid. I am grateful to Stephen Muirhead for facilitating access to the interior of the former West Free Church, Aberdeen.

122. The Cottiers' home in Glasgow was at 130 West Graham Street.

123. Henley 1892, x.

124. Kinchin, Macartney and Robertson 2011, 25.

125. Daniel Cottier to David Artz, 3 February 1886, Cottier letters to Artz, Rijksprentenkabinet, Rijksmuseum, Amsterdam, Collection Family David Artz.

2 · London 1870–1908 *pages 32–69*

1. Henley 1892, x.

2. George Reid to John Forbes White, 17 May 1870, Reid letters and papers, Aberdeen Art Gallery and Museum Archive, James McBey Reference Library, Aberdeen.

3. In July 1870 Cottier was convalescing from rheumatic fever in Bad Aachen: John Pettie to Alexander Macdonald, 21 July 1870, Aberdeen City and Aberdeenshire Archives, DD391/13/15/6; and Reid to White, 23 July 1870, Sir George Reid Papers; see also Reid to Macdonald, 25 November 1872, Aberdeen City and Aberdeenshire Archives, DD391/13/5/40. Other references include Cottier's stay at the spa town of Buxton in Derbyshire, presumably to recuperate, in the *Buxton Herald and Gazette of Fashion*, e.g., 30 July 1874, 37. Alexander Walker, a tea and wine merchant whose family were members of the West Kirk in Aberdeen, wrote to William Smith, the architect overseeing the refurbishment of the church, 4 February 1875: 'Mr. Cottier is far from well just now, and isn't personally superintending', Aberdeen City Libraries.

4. *Morning Post*, 22 October 1870, 8. For all Cottier's London addresses see Post Office directories of the period.

5. Reid to White, 12 June 1870, Reid letters and papers, Aberdeen Art Gallery and Museum Archive: 'Cottier is working well but has exceedingly too much to look after ... I went out to Cottiers house at St Johns wood in the evening – a very nice house indeed – he has bought it I believe. Mrs. Cottier and the children have come up from Glasgow it will need some little time to set things to right. Cottier however seems hopeful and happy – and that's good. I go to see him again this afternoon.'

6. G. A. F. Rogers, *The Arts Club and its Members* (London: Truslove & Hanson, 1920), 66; I am grateful to David Robertson for this information. The club's full membership list at this period is given in https://archive.org/details/artsclubitsmembeooroge, accessed 16 July 2020.

7. St John's Wood residents who were Arts Club members during this time included the Clique artists Frederick Walker, Henry Stacy Marks, John Evans Hodgson and David Wilkie Wynfield, as well as Tissot, Eyre Crowe and George Dunlop Leslie.

8. An engraving of the aftermath of the *Tilbury* explosion, showing damaged houses in the background, was published on the front cover of the *Illustrated London News*, 65: 1833 (10 October 1874).

9. Kinchin, Macartney and Robertson 2011, 47, pl. X caption.

10. Alexander Thomson to his brother George, 3 June 1871, quoted in McFadzean 1979, 228.

11. The exterior of Stevenson's Red House is illustrated in *Building News* 27 (18 September 1874), 351.

12. Haweis 1882, 90–8.

13. Haweis 1872, 190.

14. Letter from Mary Eliza Haweis to her mother Eliza Joy, 1 January 1876, quoted in Howe 1967, 132. Haweis was then living at 16 Welbeck Street, Cavendish Square, but the overdoor is today filled with plain glass.

15. Reid to White, 12 July 1870, Reid letters and papers, Aberdeen Art Gallery and Museum Archive. For Brydon see 'Contemporary British Architects', *Building News* 58 (7 February 1890), 221, and his obituaries in the *RIBA Journal*, 22 June 1901, 400–5, and *The Builder*, 1 June 1901, 540–1.

16. *House Furnisher and Decorator*, 1 March 1872, 29. He was possibly the John Bennet born 1841/2 in Leith and described as a 'Decorator & Cabinet Maker' in the London 1871 Census. However, by the time of the 1881 Census he was employed as a 'Woollen Warehouseman' and living in Innerleithen, Peeblesshire.

17. Brydon had moved to London to work for the architects William Eden Nesfield and Richard Norman Shaw. He became a part-time employee in 1869, possibly to assist Cottier in setting up; see *Dictionary of Scottish Architects*, s.v. 'Brydon', http://www.scottisharchitects.org.uk, accessed 2 August 2020.

18. *Morning Post*, 7 February 1872, 8. Talbert has been described as also having briefly been a partner of Cottier & Co.: Burke 1986, 180, 415; however, although Cottier and Talbert undoubtedly knew each other and certainly worked with many of the same people, Talbert's name is not mentioned in this *Morning Post* notice or in other published accounts of the dissolution of Cottier & Co. in 1871.

19. *Morning Post*, 22 April 1874, 6. Wallace and Brydon also entered briefly into a partnership in 1880: *Dictionary of Scottish Architects*, s.v. 'Brydon, John McKean and Wallace, William', http://www.scottisharchitects.org.uk, accessed 2 August 2020.

20. Haweis 1882, 99.

21. Ibid., 90–107. Haweis also praised the interiors of Wallace as well as Cottier and Stevenson: Haweis 1881, 368.

22. The studio at 17 (now 44) Grove End Road is illustrated in *Building News* 26 (15 May 1874), 537.

23. As Girouard 1977, 211, noted, Brydon's association with Cottier was probably behind his being the only British architect to write on the 'Queen Anne' style in the *American Architect*.

24. Harrison 1980, 48.

25. George Gilbert Scott junior to J. J. Stevenson, March 1870, quoted in Stamp 2002, 255.

26. Bettley 2002, 12.

27. For Watts & Co. see Hall 1996.

28. For Heaton see Saint 2010, 196–200.

29. For Collinson & Lock see Edwards 2012.

30. *London Post Office Directory*, 1882, quoted in ibid., 257.

31. Advertisement, *Saint Pauls Magazine* 14 (1874), n.p.

32. Henley 1892, ix.

33. The Garretts were related to J. J. Stevenson through marriage, as John's younger brother Alexander married Margaret Anderson, the sister-in-law of Agnes's older sister Elizabeth Garrett Anderson. For the Garretts, see Crawford 2002 and Ferry 2003.

34. Conway 1882, 169.

35. Vince 1925, 259, quoted in Garrett 2018, 76.

36. In 1875 the Garretts moved their recently founded business to 2 Gower Street where a ceiling they painted survives in a first-floor reception room: with its Adam Revival garlands and swags set with portraits of Old Master painters including Raphael and Titian, it recalls some of the Lyon, Cottier & Co. decoration surviving in Australia; see Garrett 2018, 96–7 and 130 fig. 2.5.

37. See 1905 inventory of Alde House, a Garrett family home in Aldeburgh, Suffolk, listing a sofa by Cottier in the Winter Bedroom, valued at £5: inventory of Alde House, Aldeburgh, Elizabeth Garrett Anderson Collection, Suffolk Record Office, Ipswich, HA436/5/1, cited in ibid., 216 n. 625. Cottier decorated the Andersons' home at 20 Upper Berkeley Street, London: ibid., 75 n. 221.

38. Melville 2000, 92.

39. *Pall Mall Gazette*, 3 June 1875, 14.

40. Ibid., 14 July 1881, 12.

41. Cottier acquired the leasehold of 4 St James's Terrace by 1886, when it was referred

to by Lyon during his visit to London: see App., p. 209. In 1896 when Hart exhibited designs for stained glass at the Royal Academy of Arts, his address was given as 4 St James's Terrace.

42. Daniel Cottier, London, to William Smith, Aberdeen, 16 February and 23 October 1875, Cottier letters to William Smith 1875.

43. *Morning Post*, 8 June 1897, 8.

44. It is possible that following the closure of the studio and workshop Cottier & Co. stained glass was made in Glasgow by J. & W. Guthrie & Andrew Wells, the partnership established in 1898 by Andrew Wells, who had returned to Scotland from Australia in 1887. Another possibility is that Cottier's former foreman, William J. Nelson, and his son, Benjamin (1875–1922), a glass painter and enameller, continued to be involved in the production of Cottier & Co.'s stained glass in London; for details about the Nelsons see Cormack 2015, 102–3. Post-1897 windows include two memorial windows for Hillhead Parish Church, Glasgow, and four windows made for Henry Clay Frick's house Clayton, Pittsburgh, both commissions 1903; for the latter, see Ch. 4.

45. Reid to White, 5 January 1872, Reid letters and papers, Aberdeen Art Gallery and Museum Archive.

46. Henley 1892, xii, xi respectively.

47. Ibid., xii.

48. Cook's studio was at 98 Gower Street, near Cottier's Langham Place premises. In 1873–4 Cook shared these premises with Talbert and from 1876 with Brydon; see Harrison 1980, 56. A stained-glass panel designed by Hart and made by Cook, depicting 'St. Cecily' (St Cecilia), was displayed at the London International Exhibition in 1871: *London International Exhibition of 1871* 1871, 113, cat. no. 2371. It was described by 'J. P. S.', probably the architect John Pollard Seddon, as 'one of the best works in the Meyrick Gallery ... The figure is well drawn and beautifully draped. The left arm, however, which is foreshortened, does not seem right to us. The expression of the head is very good': J.P.S., 'Stained Glass at the International Exhibition', *Building News* 20 (26 May 1871), 414. Hart also designed for Seddon, and an undated watercolour depicting Flora putting flowers in her hair with the Four Seasons in a group of stained-glass designs by Seddon bears the initials FVH: Victoria and Albert Museum, London (D.1723–1896).

49. Augusta Jones's sister Mary Emma, also an actress and model, was Sandys's partner.

50. In 1896, e.g., Hart exhibited 'Windows in Hillhead Church, Glasgow' at the Royal Academy of Arts. This was probably a design for the P. Sandeman Peat memorial window installed by Cottier & Co. in 1893: *British Architect* 40 (20 October 1893), 270.

51. Matthijs Maris, 18 Westbourne Square, Bayswater, London, to W. J. G. van Meurs, Duvenvoordestaat, Haarlem, 29 April 1914, Teylers Museum, Haarlem, Letter 216. I am grateful to Lili Couvée Jampoller for the translation (adapted). 'Henry' may be a reference to Henry Stubbings, who was Maris's studio assistant.

52. W. J. Nelson signed e.g. a pair of plaques depicting Isolt and Morgan Le Fay and his monogram is signed on two chargers, all in private collections in the United States. I am grateful to Walter H. Buck for information about the plaques. Cormack 2015, 102–3 suggests that Nelson was probably also a designer, noting the similarity of a window designed by him *c.*1901 to windows produced in Cottier's studio in the 1880s.

53. Gillard's name is signed with other Cottier employees in a panel depicting *Notitia* and *Prudentia* in the staircase window at Cairndhu House, Helensburgh (fig. 35); William Nelson, Norman McLeod MacDougall and Charles Gow also signed the window.

54. Michael Donnelly 1981, 17.

55. Another Scottish glass and house painter working for Cottier in London, Hugh McCulloch (1843/4–1925), returned to Glasgow in 1874 to establish his own business: ibid., 26.

56. For Stephen Adam, see ibid., 13–15.

57. Cottier to Smith, 16 February 1875, Cottier letters to William Smith 1875, in which Cottier also mentions 'the way I frequently saw churches glazed in italy [*sic*]'. As the West Kirk authorities were not prepared to pay for this, they compromised on Cathedral glass, with borders of Antique green glass and additional portions of Antique ruby glass. The result was judged a success: 'The windows, while letting in plenty of light, serve to bring down the colours, and diffuse them throughout the church, thereby imparting to it a warm and pleasing effect': *Aberdeen Journal*, 8 September 1875, 5.

58. Morrison 1888, 756.

59. The Rushpool Hall commission was presumably for rooms not already completed by the Italian craftsmen employed when it was built in 1863–5, or perhaps alterations to them. Bell's older brother, Isaac Lowthian, who had built Rounton Grange nearby in the 1870s (demolished), was a major patron of Morris & Co., making John's choice of Cottier & Co. all the more interesting. Other Cottier clients in the north-east included J. Wilson of the Wilson Shipping Line in Hull, George W. Rendell of Sir William Armstrong & Co. of Condercum House, Northumberland, Percy Westmacott of Benwell Hall, Northumberland, and a banker, George Fenwick, in Whitburn, Co. Durham; see Cottier and Co. [*c.*1876–81], 7 and 12–13.

60. *York Herald*, 5 April 1873, 10.

61. Cottier to Smith, 31 August 1875, Cottier letters to William Smith 1875. Cottier was referring to windows he had installed in the East Kirk, possibly in 1871 when his workmen decorated the building. In 1872 Cottier & Co. installed a memorial window in the East Kirk commissioned by John Moir Clark: *Aberdeen Press and Journal*, 1 January 1873, 4.

62. E.g. Whiteinch United Presbyterian Church, Glasgow (1877; demolished *c.*1966), which had 'two figure windows' by Cottier & Co. above the choir and was decorated by Andrew Wells: *British Architect* 8: 15 (12 October 1877), 182. Another commission was for the renovated Park Church, Glasgow (demolished 1968), for which Cottier & Co. supplied a large east window in 1889; for the design see Kinchin, Macartney and Robertson 2011, 153 no. 81 and pl. XL (private collection).

63. At the same time a larger window was also unveiled in St Machar's Cathedral, made for John Forbes White: *Aberdeen Press and Journal*, 5 July 1871, 4. In memory of his older brother Adam, a missionary who had died in India, it depicts Saints John the Baptist and Paul.

64. Melville 2000, 64 and n. 83.

65. Ruskin quoted in *The Scotsman*, 20 July 1871, 2.

66. John Ruskin, *The Stones of Venice* (1853), vol. 2 (London and New York: George Allen, 1904), App. 12, 'Modern Painting on Glass', 455–7.

67. Harrison 1980, 48; for the window of *c.*1872 see pl. 21b; see also Waters and Carew-Cox 2017, 313 fig. 506 and 321 fig. 514.

68. *Paisley Herald*, 12 April 1873, 1.

69. *The Times*, 29 May 1918, quoted in ODNB, s.v. 'Strahan, Alexander Stuart', entry by Patricia Srebrnik, 2004 edn, https://www.oxforddnb.com, accessed 6 August 2020. Strahan & Co. also published *Saint Pauls Magazine*, which ran articles by Haweis in 1872

('The Art of Beauty') and in which Cottier advertised in 1874.

70. Queen Victoria's Journal, 3 May 1873, Royal Archives, Windsor Castle, RA VIC/MAIN/QVJ (W) (Princess Beatrice's copies), http://www.queenvictoriasjournals.org, accessed 6 August 2020.

71. *Manchester Guardian*, 18 June 1873, 6.

72. *Building News* 24 (20 June 1873), 718.

73. Queen Victoria's Journal, 14 June 1873, RA VIC/MAIN/QVJ (W) (Princess Beatrice's copies), accessed 16 March 2018.

74. Ibid.

75. *The Builder* 32: 1649 (12 September 1874), 772, noted that 'Messrs. Cottier & Co. recently supplied the memorial windows erected in Crathie Church by her Majesty in memory of the Prince Consort and the Rev. Norman McLeod.'

76. Queen Victoria's Journal, 22 November 1873, RA VIC/MAIN/QVJ (W) (Princess Beatrice's copies), accessed 16 March 2018.

77. Ibid.

78. Glasgow Museums (PP1985.156). The panel of St Paul is in an incomplete state.

79. *British Architect* 2: 33 (14 August 1874), 105. The name of the window is given in ibid. 3: 5 (29 January 1875), 65.

80. Alexander Walker was a Dean of Guild, a town magistrate with responsibility for enforcing building regulations. In 1871 he and his brother James commissioned Cottier to make a window in memory of their parents at St Machar's Cathedral, depicting SS Mary Magdalen and James; see Waters and Carew-Cox 2017, 323 fig. 516.

81. Caption to photograph taken in 1875 of the original design for the window; reproduced in Max Donnelly 2011a, 124, fig. 1.

82. *Aberdeen Journal*, 15 September 1875, 3.

83. *British Architect* 3: 64 (19 March 1875), 162.

84. E.g. a window designed by Harry Ellis Wooldridge depicting the Archangel Michael made by James Powell & Sons for St Michael and All Angels, Weybridge, Surrey in 1876, now in the collection of the Stained Glass Museum, Ely (ELYGM:1973.2).

85. For an outline of Holiday's early career see Bryant 2013, 173–6.

86. For Holiday, see ibid., 177–207; for Morris see Sewter 1974–5.

87. I am grateful to Peter Cormack for sharing this observation.

88. *Aberdeen Journal*, 15 September 1875, 3. The description was republished in *British Architect* 4: 90 (17 September 1875), 157.

89. The Baptist Coats family owned the painting, which Dowling, son of a Baptist minister, painted in London in 1863. Dowling was Australia's first major colonial-trained professional artist and the *Baptism of Christ* was gifted to the Art Gallery of South Australia by the Thomas Coats Memorial Church Trustees in 2019.

90. See Max Donnelly 2011b.

91. Letter from Vincent van Gogh to Theo van Gogh, 8 October 1876, Van Gogh Museum, Amsterdam, inv. no. b90 V/1962: see Leo Jansen, Hans Luijten, Nienke Bakker, eds, *Vincent van Gogh: The Letters* (Amsterdam and The Hague: Van Gogh Museum and Huygens ING), 2009, http://vangoghletters.org, accessed 6 August 2020. The biblical quotation (Hebrews 11:1) van Gogh saw in the Lady Margaret design was replaced with 'Fear not, only believe' in the window itself. Although van Gogh did not see the finished windows, a 'Churchman' visiting St Andrew's on Easter Sunday 1882 described them as 'two very beautiful painted windows, being portraits – one of the late Countess of Northesk, the other of her daughter, the Lady Margaret. They are by Cottier, and are, undoubtedly, of great merit. These amply repaid us for the fatigue of the journey': *Hampshire Chronicle and General Advertiser for the South and West of England*, 22 April 1882, 3.

92. Vincent van Gogh to Theo, 5 June 1883, http://vangoghletters.org, accessed 6 August 2020.

93. The window was reinserted when the Old West Kirk was moved in the 1920s; see Carruthers 2013, 29.

94. Another memorial window, in memory of Cottier's father and paternal grandfather, was installed at Kirk Christ Lezayre (Holy Trinity) Church, Isle of Man in May 1884: see Ch. 1 nn. 2 and 4 above. It consists of a two-lancet window each with four panels, including personifications of Industry, many of the figures adapted from designs used for a memorial window installed in Paisley Abbey in 1873 (see p. 40). At Lezayre Cottier also 'contributed handsomely' to the organ fund: *Isle of Man Times*, 31 May 1884, 5.

95. For details see Kinchin, Macartney and Robertson 2011, App. This included further windows for Paisley Abbey (1886) and St Giles' Cathedral, Edinburgh (1890), as well as windows for Arbuthnot Parish Church (1890), St Mary's Parish Church, Dundee (1891), Ardler Parish Church (1892), St Michael's Parish Church, Linlithgow (1895), Scoonie Parish Church, Leven (1905). In addition to commissions in England, notably Holy Trinity, Leamington Spa (1892; see Waters and Carew-Cox 2017, 332 fig. 529), Cottier & Co. also supplied two further windows to Holy Trinity, Nice (*c*.1887 and *c*.1897), and a window to Christ Church, Rathgar, Dublin (1888).

96. *Glasgow Herald*, 23 March 1880, 3; see n. 103 below for more on Bothwell's window.

97. John Lamb Lyon 1886; see App., p. 209 above.

98. The artist William Hole wrote to *The Scotsman*, praising the Bruce window and describing Cottier as 'a Scotsman whose work is well known and appreciated abroad, but who has not yet, I think, received his due meed of recognition in his native country': *The Scotsman*, 4 August 1886, 9.

99. In memory of Bruce's two sisters, who had died in Peebles, the screen was painted with apples, pomegranates and a central vine, the Ten Commandments and Lord's Prayer in scrolls, with niches above with kneeling figures representing Christian virtues; see *Glasgow Herald*, 11 November 1890, 10.

100. The figures of *Fides*, *Caritas* and *Spes* were adapted for commissions including Camphill Church, Glasgow (1876), St Giles' Cathedral, Edinburgh (1890), Arbuthnot Parish Church (1890) and Grace Episcopal Church, New York City (*c*.1890). A *Caritas* panel was sold when the New York company liquidated its stock in 1913: Cottier & Co. Sale 1913, lot 889 (illustrated).

101. *The Scotsman*, 12 August 1886, 7. Another critic of the window, William S. Black, thought that 'while this [Cottier's] window is a marked contrast and improvement *in colour* to many of those at present in the Cathedral, it cannot be considered either masterly in design or drawing, while there is no trace of religious feeling which many of the others possess'; ibid., 10 August 1886, 7.

102. Ibid., 11 August 1886, 10.

103. Millais himself made watercolour replicas of fourteen of the twenty designs which were translated into stained glass, by the London firm of Lavers, Barraud & Westlake, at Kinnoull Parish Church, Perth, in 1870, a window which Cottier may have seen. The window in Bothwell Parish Church is close in composition to the Kinnoull window, the sections between the parables being filled with roundels containing flowers, set on a background of quarries.

104. See Carruthers 2004, 19–20.

105. E.g. St Enoch's Church, Dundee, which opened for worship on 1 January 1874 (demolished 1964). Cottier & Co. glazed

the church and decorated the nave ceiling with 'gold stars on a greenish blue ground. The walls of the clerestory are divided into three great bands of colour – the upper being yellow, the lower dark green, and the middle neutral – all broken up by lines and diaper ornaments. The walls of the aisles are coloured red and lined in imitation of ashlar work, with a base of black and other dark bands decorated with gilded and coloured ornaments': *Supplement to the Dundee People's Journal*, 6 December 1873, 5.

106. Supplement to the Liverpool *Daily Post*, 17 November 1871, 7.

107. *Liverpool Mercury*, 2 March 1871, 5; a local firm, J. R. Jeffery & Co., was recommended.

108. Ibid., 4 March 1871, 7.

109. *Aberdeen Press and Journal*, 20 September 1871, 8.

110. Ibid.

111. 'G.R.T.', letter to the editor, ibid., 27 September 1871, 6.

112. Ibid. The author appears to have been a 'Mr Taylor who steals Cottier's ideas and designs whenever he can and then speaks of him as "only a glass stainer"': Reid to White, 30 September 1871, quoted in Melville 2000, 235. This may have been G. R. Taylor, a painter, decorator and gilder operating in Aberdeen during this period, whose work encompassed 'church decorations'; see Taylor's advertisement in *Scottish Witness* 1 (January 1868), 2.

113. *Aberdeen Journal*, 4 October 1871, 8. This must refer to Dresser 1862b, 167, which the author of the letter has paraphrased; the title of Ch. 12 is 'The Power of Ornament to Express Feelings and Ideas', in which pl. XV (1), a chromolithograph depicting the globe, is described by Dresser as being surrounded by stars and clouds 'using the form furnished by the middle-ages'.

114. *Dundee Courier*, 12 October 1874, 3.

115. Cottier to Smith, 14 March 1875, letters to William Smith, 1875.

116. Reid to White, 21 October 1874, quoted in Melville 2000, 240.

117. Cottier to Smith, 14 June and 16 February 1875, Cottier letters to William Smith, 1875. Cottier told Smith that 'to divide the main roof into flat painted panels would be to make it common looking and if one was to try to imatate [*sic*] raised panels, it would take a fortune to do. I think the Grand old Ceiling all antique blue with gold stars will keep up well making a kind of nave looking high and going splendidly with the old stone work': ibid., 14 June.

118. For a black-and-white photograph of the ceilings before they were whitewashed in the 1950s see Melville 2000, pl. 28.

119. I am grateful to Cosmo Linzee Gordon for showing me the chapel.

120. *Aberdeen Journal*, 4 September 1872, 5. The side windows in Cluny Castle incorporate shields of the arms of the Gordon family and the initials of Captain John and Mrs Gordon; the chancel windows were by Clayton & Bell.

121. For quarries in churches see e.g. the Church of the Holy Saviour, Tynemouth Priory, Northumberland, *c*.1872.

122. Melville 2000, 57 and pl. 25, Reid's sketch of the composition.

123. Charles A. Cole, 'Painted Glass in Household Decoration', *Harper's New Monthly Magazine* 59: 353 (October 1879), 662. The window for Tennyson consisted of a three-light staircase window with a suitably literary theme, 'in which figures of Dante, Homer, and Chaucer filled the principal lights, having three medallions in the fan-lights of Beatrice, Penelope, and Griselda, and emblematic fruits and flowers in the lower panels.'

124. The roundel depicted in the painting is very similar to one in the staircase window at Links House, Montrose, inverted.

125. Haweis 1872, 190. This article was quoted in the *Aberdeen Press and Journal*, 7 February 1872, 3, presumably with the encouragement of Cottier's supporters in Aberdeen. It was also republished in the United States in the *Eclectic Magazine of Foreign Literature*, n.s., 15: 4 (April 1872), 472–9, helping to prepare the ground for Cottier's arrival in New York the following year.

126. Haweis 1872, 190.

127. Ibid.

128. See Cottier and Co. [*c*.1876–81], 12.

129. Alexander Thomson to his brother George, 3 June 1871, quoted in Sally J. Rush, 'Alexander Thomson, Daniel Cottier and the Interior of Queen's Park Church', in Stamp and McKinstry 1994, 182.

130. *British Architect*, 22 September 1882, 453. The house had become a hotel and nursing home and at time of writing is being converted into flats.

131. Illustrated in Bruce J. Talbert, 'A Study of Decorations and Furniture', *The Architect*, 24 July 1869, between 42 and 43.

132. Henry Stacy Marks sold the designs to Minton's, whose artists painted them on plaques, chargers and tiles: Elizabeth Aslin and Paul Atterbury, *Minton 1798–1910*, exh. cat. (London: Victoria and Albert Museum and Thomas Goode & Co., 1976), 68–9.

133. According to Melville 2000, 21, a local decorator, Tom Baird, was employed to undertake the work; this may have been the firm of the Aberdeen cabinetmaker and upholsterer Thomas Baird.

134. Fyfe and Minto 1970, 11.

135. Melville 2000, 21. Although the location of the painting is not known, the description of it recalls the work of James McNeill Whistler. The overmantel survives in the ownership of White's descendants.

136. Reid to White, 26 August 1872, quoted in ibid., 21–2. White's gallery was later occupied by a photographic studio and part of Cottier's interior was mentioned in *Aberdeen Press and Journal*, 25 January 1895, 4: 'At the end of the same passage in front is the ladies' boudoir, the decorations of which, as in other parts of the building, were the work of Cottier'.

137. *Morning Post*, 10 July 1877, 10.

138. Mackinnon 1935, 67.

139. Originally from Aberdeenshire, George MacDonald was a close friend of White and Ruskin, as well as Strahan and F. D. Maurice, co-founder of the Working Men's College.

140. William de Morgan quoted in MacCarthy 1994, 392; Dante Gabriel Rossetti quoted in *Journal of the William Morris Society* 1–2 (1961), 16.

141. Cottier and Co. [*c*.1876–81]. Another account, in *The Standard*, 3 April 1880, 7, describes a substantial ('compact and convenient') residence in Gloucester Place, with eight bedrooms, four reception rooms and an ante-room, which in 1880 was offered for sale, 'decorated and furnished throughout in the most artistic and substantial manner by Messrs. Cottier'.

142. Dakers 1999, 130.

143. In 1875 Cottier wrote to William Smith describing 'recently finished houses' in London: 'the folks had left town and I believe the Ceilings are all covered, the first time I ever saw folks so careful over our work, the whole rooms are lined with cloth'; Cottier to Smith, 31 August 1875, Cottier letters to William Smith, 1875. Other recent commissions in Cottier and Co., 144, Fifth Avenue *c*.1876–81, 10 and 13 were for clients throughout England including the banker Louis Huth of Possingworth Hall, Sussex.

144. Lyon 1886: see App., p. 209 above.

145. Blake 1875, 79. Tiles of painters include a six-inch tile of Jan Steen, sold Freeman's, Philadelphia, 13 July 2006, lot 177.

146. Ceramic charger formerly in the collection of Geoffrey Godden. I am grateful to Alice Cooney Frelinghuysen for this information.

147. For the Cairndhu window depicting Fortune see Max Donnelly 2001, 920, pl. VII.

148. I am grateful to Allan James for showing me the interior of Links House, now the Links Hotel. Also in Montrose, in 1874 Cottier & Co. installed a five-light window in the chancel of St Peter's Episcopal Church, depicting a life-size Christ flanked by the four Evangelists: *The Builder* 32: 1649 (12 September 1874), 772.

149. See Henley 1892, xi.

150. For the 1874 advertisement see n. 31 above; Collinson & Lock's advertisement appeared in the *Pall Mall Gazette*, 11 May 1870, 50.

151. In one of few references to furniture designs, the artist A. E. H. Miller recalled that his father, a Glasgow cabinetmaker described as being on the fringe of Cottier's circle, had owned 'a number of drawings for furniture painted with decorations': *Manx Journal*, 1938, 64.

152. Another architect-trained designer who worked for Cottier possibly in London and certainly in New York, where he is recorded from 1883, was Thomas Clarkson Wilberfoss (1848–1900), who was apprenticed in the office of the architects J. L. Pearson and then J. Clarke 'but later directed his special attention to designing furniture, metal, and embroidery': *Yorkshire Post*, 1 August 1900, 6.

153. George Gilbert Scott quoted in Stamp 2002, 255.

154. Victoria and Albert Museum, London (MISC.127:1–9-1921).

155. For John Moyr Smith see Stapleton 1996 and 2002.

156. J.[ohn] M.[oyr] S.[mith], 'Pianoforte. – Painted and Inlaid', *Building News* 16 (29 January 1869), 99.

157. 'Ancient Ægyptian Furniture', *Building News* 29 (17 December 1875), after 670, illustrating chairs, stools and tables by Moyr Smith.

158. Chair designed by Moyr Smith and Frederick Hart, made by Collinson & Lock and exhibited at the London International Exhibition in 1871, where it was described as doing 'credit to its designers': 'Furniture at the International Exhibition', *Building News* 20 (19 May 1871), 391.

159. The Broadwood piano's price, £137, was apparently in part exchange for Alice Westlake's old grand piano: Dr A. D. Laurence, John Broadwood and Sons Ltd, London, to Meghan Melvin, Christie's, London, 30 September 2001. I am grateful to Meghan Melvin for this reference.

160. The windows of Holloway Sanatorium, Virginia Water, are similar to those installed by Cottier & Co. in the West Kirk, Aberdeen, in 1875.

161. I am grateful to Penny Williams for this information.

162. *Appletons' Journal*, 14: 343 (16 October 1875), 506. Thomas Armstrong (1832–1911) in 1860 joined the circle of painters associated with the emergent Aesthetic movement. Cottier and Co. [*c*.1876–81], 2, described fabrics 'woven by Foreign and English looms, the exclusive designs and property of Messrs. Cottier and Co.' The rugs visible on the drawing-room floor at Kepplestone House may also have been supplied by Cottier, for his New York gallery carried 'Indian and Oriental Rugs, specially chosen by Mr. Cottier for colour and design': ibid., 4.

163. For Godwin's Anglo-Japanese furniture, see Soros 1999a.

164. The cabinet in fig. 51 has a provenance in the United States dating back to 1917, and that in fig. 55 also surfaced there, suggesting they may be among pieces exported by Cottier in the 1870s.

165. Cook 1876, 349, notes that the drawings for figs 1 and 2, on pp. 342 and 343, were 'copied by Mr. Inglis from wood-cuts in "The Architect"' (the woman in fig. 1 was added by Francis Lathrop) and that two fireplaces and mantels had been 'designed by Mr. Edward W. Godwin, one of the best of the rising English architects'.

166. Cook 1878a. The illustration is after a drawing by Francis Lathrop.

167. Rhoda and Agnes Garrett also promoted the Anglo-Japanese style in *Suggestions for House Decoration*, again in the Macmillan series, in which the frontispiece included another version of Godwin's coffee table, much to Godwin's dismay: see Soros 1999b, 254.

168. Cottier and Co. [*c*.1876–81], 4–5.

169. See Hall 1996, fig. 4, 188, and a walnut cabinet designed by Rhoda and Agnes Garrett for James and Margaret Beale, 1875, Victoria and Albert Museum, London (W.14–2017).

170. Demolished; the flour mill was described as 'Italian style' with a rusticated ground floor surmounted by six pillars, a cornice and entablature: *Dundee Courier and Argus*, 10 January 1877, 4.

171. I am grateful to Christopher Nobbs and Jennifer Melville for this information.

172. Vincent van Gogh to Theo van Gogh, on or *c*.5 June 1883, http://vangoghletters.org, accessed 6 August 2020, describing his drawing *Peat Diggers in the Dunes* and an untraced drawing of a 'team of workmen labouring'.

173. Blake 1875, 79.

174. For the overmantel see Phillips, London, *Art Nouveau, Decorative Arts and Studio Ceramics*, 23 March 1989, lot 348.

175. *Morning Post*, 16 April 1881, 8. Thomas Greenwood Clayton died in 1880.

176. Ibid. The piano, made by the London firm of Collard & Collard, was clearly a particularly fine example of Cottier & Co.'s work, as it was described as a 'Valuable Instrument' with a 'case of the highest taste, specially designed by Messrs. Cottier and Co.'.

177. *The Scotsman*, 16 April 1881, 11. Cottier's furniture continued to be promoted by Craibe Angus: in 1888 Craibe Angus & Son lent a carved oak Cottier table to the Edinburgh Exhibition of Decorative Handwork held in the Royal Scottish Academy Galleries; *Glasgow Herald*, 29 November 1888, 3.

178. *Morning Post*, 8 June 1897, 8.

179. Will of Daniel Cottier, proved 16 June 1891, Principal Public Registry, London.

180. A watercolour design for an unexecuted memorial window to the Aberdeen merchant and benefactor Robert Gordon, proposed for Drum's Aisle in the Kirk of St Nicholas, Aberdeen, in 1879, was sold by the Cottier studio to Robert Gordon's College in 1903: *Aberdeen Daily Journal*, 28 November 1903, 4. The design depicts full-length figures of the prophets Isaiah, Jeremiah, Ezekiel and Daniel, with angels above. I am grateful to Tom Cumming for further information about the design.

181. In 1895 it was noted that 'Mrs. Cottier, of Fifth avenue, New York, who resides in London during the season, has loaned Mrs. Sawyer her house in St James's Terrace Regent's Park, for an At Home, which she will give prior to returning to America', referring to the American singer Antonia Sawyer: *Musical Courier* 31: 1 (3 July 1895), 15. Sawyer later recalled the Cottiers at St James's Terrace: *Songs at Twilight* (New York: Devin-Adair Co., 1939), 75–6.

182. Henley 1892, ix, also describing Cottier's 'big head, his curly red hair'. It is likely that Cottier's portrait appears in earlier windows, such as for the St Peter in the rose window

at Dowanhill Church and Christ in the background of the *Five Wise Virgins* at Trinity Church, Boston (see fig. 105). Ina Harrower asserted, plausibly, that in the Bruce window at St Giles' Cathedral, Edinburgh: 'Cottier put himself in as the prophet Daniel, with red tousled hair and beard!': quoted in *Journal of the Manx Museum*, 1938, 49.

3 · The Art Market in Britain *pages 70–89*

1. Melville 2000, 22.
2. Artz visited White in May–June 1869 and also stayed in Edinburgh and Broughty Ferry: de Liefde-van Brakel 2001, 23. Israëls was in Aberdeen and Edinburgh in June 1870 for his debut at the Royal Scottish Academy: Dekkers 1999, 358. In August–September 1873, in addition to Aberdeen, Roelofs also visited Callander, Edinburgh and the Isle of Skye: Van Heteren 2006, 14.
3. Mollinger mentioned his plan to go to Scotland in a letter to David Artz, 7 July 1867, Municipal Archives, The Hague, 8000–01, Overige Verzamelingen 2: Schildersbrieven.
4. John Forbes White to George Reid, 30 September 1867, Sir George Reid Papers, James McBey Reference Library, Aberdeen Art Gallery and Museum Archive, Aberdeen.
5. The most recent publications on Scottish interest in Continental art are Melville 2000; Fowle 2002; Fowle 2008; Veldink 2009–10; Fowle 2010; Veldink 2015.
6. R. T. Hamilton Bruce, 'The Fine Art Congress at Liverpool', *The Scotsman*, 6 December 1888.
7. Cottier Collection Sale 1892, 9.
8. George Reid to Alexander Macdonald, [1868], Papers of Alexander Macdonald of Kepplestone and his trustees, Aberdeen City and Aberdeenshire Archives, Aberdeen.
9. See Artz's friends Frederik Kaemmerer to Johannes Kaemmerer, 9 July 1869, in Kaemmerer and Versteegh 2001, 117.
10. E.g., in 1873 Artz wrote: 'A couple of days ago a friend from England visited my studio and bought paintings and drawings worth 5000 francs': de Liefde-van Brakel 2001, 46. In May 1886 Cottier thanked Artz for a painting he had sent: 'The picture is first rate just what we all wanted. and its [*sic*] awfully good of you to do so quickly': Daniel Cottier to David Artz, 19 May 1886, Collection Family David Artz, Rijksprentenkabinet, Amsterdam. I am very grateful to Freek Heijbroek for informing me about this group of letters.
11. Cottier to Artz, 19 May 1886, Collection Family David Artz.
12. 'Impressions of America on a Dutch Impressionist', *New York Times*, 1 May 1904, 3.
13. Mesdag first visited Alma-Tadema in London in May or June 1872. At this time – perhaps thanks to Alma-Tadema's intervention – Mesdag was also in contact with Henry Wallis of the French Gallery. In the 1870s the two cousins continued to see one another regularly, both in The Hague and London; see Pennock 1996, 64.
14. Leeman and Pennock 1996, 334–6.
15. Berckenhoff 1917, 103.
16. 'The Late Mr Craibe Angus, by One who Knew Him', *Scots Pictorial*, 15 January 1900, 17–18. The opening of the new shop had been advertised for the first time in *The Scotsman*, 16 February 1874, 8.
17. Fowle 2010, 14–15.
18. At the time of his bankruptcy, in 1881, Angus's house was decorated with furniture and lamps produced by Cottier & Co. worth nearly £1000: Furnishing House Dormouth, W. Craibe Angus, submitted 5 February 1881, Wm Craibe Angus Sequestration Book, National Archives of Scotland, Edinburgh.
19. Matthijs Maris wrote that he regularly saw Angus, to whom he refers as 'the partner' at Cottier's: Maris to Willem van Meurs, 16 July 1914, Teylers Museum, Haarlem.
20. Condescendence for Appellants in Appeal Messrs Goupil & Coy Against David Bird for C.A. Glasgow, Wm Craibe Angus Sequestration Book.
21. See the day register of acquisitions and sales of watercolours for 1861–78, Archive dealer Goupil (The Hague), Netherlands Institute for Art History (RKD), The Hague. The RKD holds all seven day registers for The Hague branch covering 1861–1917.
22. 'The Late Mr John [William's son] Craibe Angus', *The Scotsman*, 29 August 1910, 6.
23. For the sale of Corot's *Little Bird Nesters* see Wm Craibe Angus Sequestration Book.
24. Mavor 1923, 228.
25. For more information on the history of the French Gallery see Maas 1975.
26. In 1864 Jozef Israëls and Johannes Bosboom made their debut at the French Gallery's annual exhibitions; see French Gallery 1864.
27. George Reid to Alexander Macdonald, 27 February 1869, Papers of Alexander Macdonald of Kepplestone and his trustees.
28. See Goupil's day registers for Paris for 1867–71, among fifteen Paris day registers in the Getty Research Institute, Los Angeles: https://piprod.getty.edu/starweb/pi/servlet.starweb?path=pi/pi.web, accessed 12 August 2020.
29. In 1864–75 the French Gallery included eight works by Israëls and seventeen by Jacob Maris in their selling exhibitions.
30. Goupil's day registers for Paris, inv. no. 8619, book 7.
31. Compare ibid., inv. no. 3645, book 4, with inv. no. 9334, book 7.
32. For more information on British collectors of work by Israëls see Dekkers 1999, 101–14.
33. Van Heteren 2003, 65–6.
34. Heijbroek and Wouthuysen 1999, 27.
35. Bionda 2017, 137.
36. Cottier to Artz, 29 August 1888, Collection Family David Artz.
37. Chu 2005, 52.
38. Fowle 2002, 33, mentions the large exhibition; the display of 1876 is discussed in Hawthorne 1876.
39. Ambrosini 2016, 91, n. 104.
40. Goupil's day registers for Paris, inv. no. 11079.
41. Hawthorne 1876, 128.
42. Duncan paid Durand-Ruel more than 10,000 francs for the painting: see Watson 2010, 40.
43. Ambrosini 2016, 88.
44. The two commissioned by Sedelmeyer are Daubigny's *Bank of the Oise near Auvers* (n.d., oil on panel, 31.5 × 52.5 cm) and *The Bank of the Oise* (1872, oil on panel, 34.7 × 58.3 cm), both Mesdag Collection, The Hague: see Leeman and Pennock 1996, 159, 162.
45. Ibid., 155.
46. Melville 2000, 102.
47. Ibid., n. 7.
48. Fowle 2002, 35.
49. Matthijs Maris later wrote that, somewhere between 1878 and 1882, he joined van Wisselingh to see Monticelli's paintings at the dealer Gérard: Matthijs Maris to Willem van Meurs, [postmark 21 January 1914], Teylers Museum.
50. Bionda 2017, 34.
51. Lists of pictures returned by the Bankrupt to Messrs Cottier & Co., Wm Craibe Angus Sequestration Book.
52. Loffelt 1896, 9.

53. For the sale of Maris's *Quarry at Montmartre* see Willem van Meurs, handwritten note, n.d., Archive W. J. G. van Meurs, RKD, The Hague.

54. Matthijs Maris to Albert Plasschaert, [March 1909], Archive Albert C. A. Plasschaert, RKD, The Hague.

55. Matthijs Maris to Willem van Meurs, [postmark 6 July 1914], Teylers Museum.

56. Berckenhoff 1917, 98.

57. Matthijs Maris to H. L. Berckenhoff, 1888, cited in ibid.

58. Matthijs Maris to van Meurs, [postmark 2 April 1914], Teylers Museum.

59. Ibid.

60. Matthijs Maris to van Meurs, [postmark 31 January 1917], ibid.

61. Matthijs Maris to van Meurs, 15 August 1912, ibid.

62. Matthijs Maris to Hélène Artz-Schemel, 20 October 1893, Overige Verzamelingen 2: Schildersbrieven, Municipal Archives, The Hague, 8000–01.

63. Cottier to Artz, 21 January 1889, ibid.

64. Matthijs Maris to van Meurs, 10 February 1910, Teylers Museum.

65. Hermens and Veldink 2017, 60–5.

66. This information was repeated by Bionda 2017, 207.

67. Cottier to Artz, 27 May 1886, Collection Family David Artz.

68. Mavor 1923, 229.

69. Veldink 2009–10.

70. Henley 1888, 37.

71. Fowle 2010, 35.

72. Fowle 2000, 95, n. 16.

73. See List of Claimants and Lists of pictures returned by the Bankrupt to Messrs Cottier & Co., Wm Craibe Angus Sequestration Book.

74. No. 129 of Process, Certificate of Despatch, 10 February 1881, Wm Craibe Angus Sequestration Book.

75. See Veldink 2015.

76. Robert Macaulay Stevenson cited in Fowle 2008, 140.

77. Cottier's rheumatic fever is mentioned in a letter from George Reid to John Forbes White, 23 July 1870, Sir George Reid Papers.

78. Matthijs Maris's angry letters began in January 1889, shortly after he left Cottier, and the quarrel between the two men reached its peak in June that year. According to Cottier, Maris had threatened to smash his head against a stone wall, taking advantage of his weak condition: Cottier to Artz, 17 June 1889, Overige Verzamelingen 2: Schildersbrieven.

79. Cottier to Artz, 3 February 1886, Collection Family David Artz.

80. Cottier to Artz, 28 August 1888, ibid.

4 · New York 1873–1915 *pages 90–125*

1. See Ancestry.com 2010, *s.v.* 'Daniel Cottier', accessed 15 August 2020.

2. Inglis Obituary 1907.

3. *Wilson's Business Directory of New York City* 1874, 17 and 259.

4. In *Taintor's Route and City Guides* 1877, Cottier & Co. is referred to as a 'celebrated art establishment' (p. 27) and is said to offer 'ceramic art, stained glass, and the higher kind of household decorations' (p. 43).

5. See *New York Times*, 26 October 1873, 4, 'Passengers Sailed' lists Cottier as a passenger on the SS *Celtic*, bound for Liverpool.

6. Cottier and Co. [*c.*1876–81], 2, has Cottier arriving in New York from Europe, 'bringing with him artistic novelties in rich and simple stuffs, woven by Foreign and English looms, the exclusive designs and property of Messrs. Cottier & Co'. In addition to these 'stuffs', described in detail, he brought over the firm's 'new designs in rich Flemish and English Brass-work, Candelabra, Chandeliers, Wall Brackets, &c., &c., and their new Venetian Drawing-room Hanging Lights, specially made by their London firm'.

7. The New York Passenger and Crew Lists, 1820–, on Ancestry.com 2010, *s.v.* 'Cottier', indicate that Cottier arrived in New York on 6 September 1880 (with his wife and three children) on the SS *Celtic*; on 6 October 1882 (with his wife and three children) on the SS *Republic*; on 29 September 1884 (with his wife and three children) on the SS *City of Rome*; and on 11 October 1890 on the SS *Eider*. They also record Mrs Daniel Cottier and son William arriving on 11 September 1891, on the SS *Trave*, after Cottier's death. There is little doubt that Cottier came to New York on other occasions. The ship records are far from accurate and it is possible that a David Cottier, age 38, for example, an 'artist' who arrived on 17 October 1877 on the SS *Abyssinia* was in fact Daniel Cottier; a D. Cottier who arrived on 21 April 1879 on the SS *Germanic* may also be identified with him. Cottier may also have arrived at other harbours on the Eastern seaboard or in Canada.

8. In addition to Inglis Obituary 1907 see also Inglis Obituary 1908, which is especially complimentary.

9. This ground floor was called in America an 'English basement', the lowest floor of a townhouse or brownstone, which is partly below and partly above ground level and which has its own entrance separate from the rest of the building.

10. Much of the information about 144 Fifth Avenue comes from Miller 2012.

11. 'Cottier & Co.' 1874, 500.

12. Olin Warner to Truman H. Bartlett, 1879, quoted in Gurney 1978, vol. 1, 75 and 96, n. 18.

13. Cook 1878a, 71 wrote: 'The Messrs. Cottier long since found themselves obliged to give up importing furniture from England, as all the pieces that came from overseas had to be overhauled before they had been many weeks in this country.' In Cottier and Co. [*c.*1876–81], 4–5, Cottier is still said to have brought over from Europe 'the latest designs in their Artistic Furniture of the Queen Anne period, and of the Italian and French Renaissance'. It is not certain whether that means that he brought the designs from Europe or, perhaps, prototypes to be copied in New York.

14. *Wilson's Business Directory of New York City* 27 (1874), 17 lists two addresses for Cottier & Co., 144 Fifth Avenue and 131 W 31st Street.

15. Perusing *Goulding's New York City Directory*, the *Trow New York City Directory* and *Wilson's Business Directory* for 1874–80, I found at least five other locations, all between 26th and 31st Streets on Manhattan's West side, and there may have been more.

16. *Illustrated New York* 1888, 283.

17. Edwards 1993, 159.

18. In such obscurity the firm of Cottier & Co. was, of course, not alone. Much late-Victorian furniture designed and manufactured before the impact of the Arts and Crafts movement made itself felt was largely forgotten until the late twentieth century. When it comes to American Gilded Age furniture, the Metropolitan Museum of Art in New York has played an especially important role in its reappraisal, through such exhibitions as *In Pursuit of Beauty* (1987), *Herter Brothers: Furniture and Interiors for a Gilded Age* (1995) and *Artistic Furniture of the Gilded Age* (2016).

19. Holly 1878, 155.

20. Ibid., 151; see also Edwards 1993, 158.

21. We know little about the employees of Cottier & Co. in New York. In Cottier's will of 1 October 1890, proved 16 June 1891 (Principal Public Registry, London), mention is made of Mr Valentine, the company clerk. Thomas E. Valentine (1840–1925) remained a trusted employee of Cottier & Co. long after Cottier's death. In the New York Court of Appeals Records and Briefs transcribing the 1909 hearings in which the siblings of James Inglis contested his will, Valentine is mentioned as one of the executors as well as a legatee. In his affidavit, Valentine identifies himself as the treasurer of Cottier & Co. and states that he has been working for the company for 28 years, which means that he joined Cottier & Co. in 1881: https://tinyurl.com/y6aludfh, accessed 13 August 2020. Cottier's will also mentions David Kay and Henry Caithness, who served as foremen in the workshop. Lyon, reporting on his visit to Cottier's establishment in New York (see App., p. 208), in addition to Valentine and Kay, mentions a decorative painter named Holland.

22. Georgi 2013, passim.

23. Eastlake 1868, US edn 1872; numerous editions followed in both countries.

24. Cook 1878a, 17.

25. The impressive list of illustrators of Cook 1878a included, besides Inglis and Lathrop, Walter Crane, Maria Oakey Dewing, W. B. Duncan, R. Riordan and Alexandre Sandier. The cover design is not signed and the attribution to Cottier is based on a line in Cook's 'Preface', 17, in which he specifies that Cottier designed it (in later editions this detail is left out). Cottier's cover design was embossed in black and gold on cloth bindings of different colours, including red, blue, green and taupe.

26. Of course, we cannot be sure that all the Cottier pieces reproduced in Cook 1878a were made in New York but Cook's remark quoted in n. 13 above suggests that most probably were.

27. Cook 1878a, 73: 'Next to making simplicity charming, the Cottiers have done us the greatest service, in showing us how to unite usefulness and beauty.'

28. E.g., an octagonal table designed by E. W. Godwin, *c.*1876, Victoria and Albert Museum, London (inv. no. W.54–1980), manufactured by William Watt & Co. or Collinson & Lock. Godwin had been designing this kind of table since *c.*1870.

29. Cook 1878a, 72.

30. Ibid., 224; the Cottier sideboard has constructional similarities with one designed by Godwin, of which the best-known example is in the Victoria and Albert Museum (Circ. 38–1953), repr. http://collections.vam.ac.uk/item/O8380/sideboard-godwin-edward-william, accessed 8 August 2020.

31. Cook 1878a, 99, ill. no. 37, and 100–1.

32. Cottier & Co. mantel clock, 1881 (private collection); movement stamped '123', which corresponds to the number of the commission by Cottier & Co. in Tiffany's clock department's Order Book (1879–1918), New York Historical Society.

33. On Ichabod Williams see Callahan 1985.

34. See 'Comino Trees of Colombia' 1894.

35. The Williams mill was documented by *Historic American Engineering Record* in 1984 but was demolished in 1995; for photographs see Library of Congress, http://www.loc.gov/pictures/item/NJ0121, accessed 13 August 2020.

36. Williams Sale 1915 (2).

37. For Williams's address see Williams Obituary 1899. The house and its neighbour, no. 16, were demolished and replaced by a high-rise building in the early twentieth century.

38. From Cottier & Co. Sale 1913 we know that the firm sold Chinese and Japanese porcelains (cat. nos 172–326), European ceramics (cat. nos 327–97), Venetian glass (cat. nos 1–171) and miscellaneous objects for domestic use and decoration. This is confirmed by the archives of Henry Clay Frick, Frick Collection, New York, which contain numerous Cottier & Co. receipts for Chinese vases, Italian maiolica, small bronzes and other *objets d'art*. It is not known precisely where Cottier sourced all these objects.

39. Skinner Auction 2920M, 274 Cedar Hill St, Marlborough, Mass., 15 July 2016, lot 512, https://www.skinnerinc.com/auctions/2920M/lots/512, accessed 30 September 2019.

40. The Steinway archivist provided the following information to Skinner Auctions: 'serial number 69430 corresponds in our records to a New York Grand Model B Fancy White Holly by Cottier & Company, 7 octaves (85 notes), length 6'10½, completed by Steinway & Sons on October 21, 1890, and delivered to Cottier & Company of New York City on November 29, 1890': ibid.

41. Notable Steinway grand pianos decorated by Cottier & Co. include one commissioned in 1890 by a Scottish-born Canadian businessman, James Leveson Ross (1848–1913), as a wedding gift for his wife, Annie, for their mansion in Montreal's Golden Square Mile. In 1995 it was acquired by the Unitarian Church in Montreal: https://www.ucmtl.ca/music, accessed 3 August 2020.

42. The late nineteenth- and early twentieth-century interest in historic and exotic textiles is a subject that has received little attention. Textiles were used not only for upholstery but also for drapes and portières; in addition, they were hung on walls and draped over tables and chairs. As a case in point, numerous textiles were included in the sale of the collection of the painter Lawrence Alma-Tadema, held in 1913 in London (Hampton & Sons) after the artist's death. For examples of the way these textiles were used in Alma-Tadema's successive homes see Gere 2017.

43. Several Greek, Roman and other chairs are mentioned in Cottier & Co. invoices and receipts kept in the archives of Henry Clay Frick, Frick Collection, New York, most dated to between 1904 and 1906. See Frick Papers, passim. The Frick in Pittsburgh currently owns two Roman armchairs and one Greek chair with an upholstered seat (1970.122, 1970.123, 1985.339). I am grateful to Dawn Reid Brean, Associate Curator of Decorative Arts at The Frick for providing me with information about these chairs.

44. Two Roman armchairs, much like that in fig. 89, belong to H. Blairman & Sons, London. Three other, similar but less decorated, chairs were auctioned in Cleveland, Ohio, in January 2018: https://www.bidsquare.com/online-auctions/cowans/cottier-co-golden-ebony-throne-chairs-lot-of-three-986544, accessed 30 September 2019.

45. We thank Martin P. Levy for this information.

46. Cook 1878a, 318.

47. The cabinet's production history is not clear: it could have been entirely made in England and painted by Lathrop while he was still in London; or made in England and the doors painted in America; or the entire cabinet was made in New York.

48. Several similar corner cabinets by or attributed to Cottier & Co. are still extant. Max Donnelly 2001, 919 has drawn attention to the similarity between that in fig. 90 and a corner cabinet currently in a private collection in the USA; see also Zukowski 2006, 74. Their forms are similar but the decoration is different. Donnelly's reproduction of the latter cabinet shows that it was entirely ebonised; the upper doors each feature a dark-grey bird alighting on a reddish-coloured

leafy branch; the lower doors and the sides of the cabinet are decorated with stylised plant motifs painted in yellowish white on the ebonised ground. The identity of the painter is not known nor whether the cabinet was produced in England or America. A related chest of drawers, made in London *c.*1870–5, was acquired in 2017 by the National Trust for Scotland for Holmwood House, Glasgow.

49. Cook 1878a, 106.

50. The importance of painted furniture for Cottier & Co. is confirmed by the fact that the firm submitted to the 1888 Annual Exhibition of the Architectural League of New York not entire furniture pieces but two sets of 'Cabinet doors painted on ebony': *Catalogue of the Fourth Annual Exhibition* 1888, nos 258 and 262.

51. See Wyatt Eaton (Canadian-American portrait painter) to Scribner's editor, Richard Watson Gilder, 23 September 1879: 'Ryder is doing a good deal of decorative work for Cottier and others'; Gilder papers, New York Public Library, scrapbook no. 2, quoted in Broun 1989, 302, n. 1. Among the 'others', as Gilder must have known, was Charles de Kay, the younger brother of his wife, the painter Helena de Kay. See Ch. 5, p. 130.

52. The panels' date according to the Smithsonian Institution website.

53. Broun 1989, 46; the story was especially popular in the nineteenth century, after being revived by Ludwig Tieck's *Leben und Tod der heiligen Genoveva* in 1799.

54. See James Inglis to C. E. S. Wood, 9 July 1896, with a drawing of four leather panels for a cabinet, to be stained and rubbed with gold by Inglis, Huntington Library, San Marino, Cal., cited in Broun 1989, 206, n. 2. Six of Ryder's panels for furniture are known, though two have not been located: ibid., 48–50.

55. Inglis 1909, nos 59 and 68.

56. See App., p. 208. Nothing is known about Holland and he cannot be firmly associated with any known piece of furniture by Cottier & Co.

57. Cottier & Co. Sale 1913, no. 614 does not indicate on what material the screen's watercolours were painted but it was probably parchment or paper.

58. See ibid., nos 585, 587, 592, 595, 603, 613.

59. Cottier & Co. invoice, 30 December 1905, describes the piece as 'one music cabinet of white holly with trays, decorated by Fr. V Hart showing scenes from the classical history of Orpheus.' It was bought for $2200: Henry Clay Frick Papers.

60. According to Steinway records, it was shipped in November 1894 from the Steinway factory to the Stetson Agency, Steinway's representative in Philadelphia. From there it travelled to Cottier & Co. in New York City: https://www.piedmontpiano.com/all-used-pianos/model-d-1894?rq=1893Steinway, accessed 6 August 2020.

61. Anna Riddle was Scott's second wife and one of the leaders of Philadelphia's fashionable society (portrait by Cecilia Beaux, 1897, private collection).

62. It is difficult to establish exactly what materials and technical processes were used to decorate this Steinway grand. Whatever shellac or finishing material was applied over the paintings, either at the time it was decorated or subsequently, has darkened and cracked. The piano has only been partially restored and in-depth conservation and restoration would be needed not only to return it to its original splendour but also to get a better idea of its multi-layered surface.

63. A figured walnut model B Steinway grand piano was decorated by Cottier & Co. in 1906 for Cara Leland Rogers (1867–1939). She took the piano with her when she emigrated to Britain in 1912 with her English husband, Urban H. Broughton, and it was later moved to Anglesey Abbey, Cambridgeshire, which was purchased by their sons (now National Trust): Kinchin, Macartney and Robertson 2011, 130, fig. 111 (detail) and 160.

64. Sheldon 1883–4.

65. Porter 1888, 6. Phillips had acquired a lot at 299 Berkeley Street, Boston, in 1877 and had a house built on it by Peabody & Stearns: see Back Bay Houses, https://backbayhouses.org/299-berkeley, accessed 16 August 2020, with a photograph of the house.

66. Ochsner 1984, 56. Codman was also a close friend of the architect H. H. Richardson, who may have recommended Cottier & Co. to him. Codman's nephew, Ogden Codman Jr, co-authored Edith Wharton's *The Decoration of Houses* in 1897.

67. The Phillips house's gasolier and beautiful portières may have been supplied by Cottier & Co. as well.

68. A number of photographs in *Artistic Houses*, including this one, were mistakenly printed in reverse. See Lewis, Turner and McQuillin 1987, v–vi. In this book it is printed as it should have been, so that paintings and other objects appear in the correct way.

69. Since many artists in the nineteenth century, made numerous painted versions of the same subject, it is difficult to identify the Schreyer, as well as the paintings by Daubigny and Fromentin, with specific works in museums or private collections, but their attribution leaves little doubt.

70. Sheldon 1883–4, 2, pt. 2, 144–5.

71. The case was most strongly made by Day 1882, 218–48.

72. On the influence of the British designer Charles Eastlake see Madigan 1975.

73. The tiled fireplace surround shows a central tableau of Queen Guinevere, dressed in a dark orange gown, surrounded by a garland of flowers and fruits and flanked by square tiles with stylised floral motifs in orange, green and brown. The queen's name is spelled out at the top; below her is an escutcheon with a brief quotation from 'The Marriage of Geraint' (1857), one of the twelve books of Tennyson's *Idylls of the King*: 'and the Queen herself,/ Grateful to Prince Geraint for service done,/ Loved her, and often with her own white hands/ Arrayed and decked her, as the loveliest,/ Next after her own self, in all the court.' Cottier & Co. no doubt provided tiles for other fireplace surrounds in North America. One example still *in situ* is in the Public Library, Stratford, Connecticut, built 1894–6, where allegories of Fame and Fortune similar to those found at Cairndhu, Helensburgh and Kepplestone, Aberdeenshire (see Ch. 2 above) decorate one of the fireplaces in the main reading room: http://stratfordlibrary.org/about/library-history/, accessed 3 August 2020. We are grateful to Paul Jeromack for this information.

74. See Bradbury 2015, 271–2 and 296.

75. Burke 1986, 415 notes that Cottier & Co. provided some of the furniture for Vinland. This included a piano described by Sheldon 1886–7, vol. 2, 186, as being of 'unusual beauty', its comino wood case 'decorated with painted figures and flowers by Cottier and Company, at a cost of three thousand dollars'. Little is known about the connection between Peabody & Stearns and Cottier but it is known that he was involved with several buildings that the firm designed, including the Church of the Messiah in St Louis, Missouri (see pp. 119 and 122, fig. 109) and the Phillips House in Boston, also with Codman.

76. Jos. Holroyd, Pittsburgh, Penn., to Cottier & Co., telegram 29 May 1905, 9:22 am, Henry Clay Frick Papers, Series: Correspondence.

77. 'Some of the Union League Decorations' 1881–2, 747.

78. *Frank Leslie's Illustrated Newspaper*, 1881, quoted in Burke 1986, 415.

79. *Forest and Stream* 12: 26 (July 1879), 508.

80. *Brentano's Aquatic Monthly and Sporting Gazetteer* 1: 5 (August 1879), 468 states that Joseph Gardiner Cassatt owned *Frolic*.

81. See e.g. *The Critic*, 14 February 1885, iii.

82. Cole 1879, 655.

83. Ibid. For the 'Spring' window see fig. 100.

84. Cottier & Co. Sale 1913, no. 885. These Philadelphian themes confirm that Cottier & Co. had a clientele there, in addition to New York and Boston (see the yacht decorated for Joseph Cassatt, who lived in Philadelphia). It is also known that Cottier & Co.'s Art Rooms sold paintings to John G. Johnson in Philadelphia: see Ch. 5, n. 44 below.

85. Stott 1998.

86. According to the *New York Herald*, William Cottier married Estelle Blain Travis on 4 April 1895: http://nyvagenealogy.homestead.com/1895NYMARRIAGESAPRIL.html, accessed 15 August 2020. The couple appears to have lived in New York or its surroundings. The Metropolitan Museum owns a second window with a different version of Spring. Another version appears in a large six-light staircase window made in 1890 for the home of the lumber merchant Henry M. Thompson on North Lake Drive, Milwaukee, illustrated in Zimmermann 1987, 204 and 206. We thank Annamarie Stapleton for this reference.

87. For a reproduction of the Autumn and Winter panels see https://www.columbiamuseum.org/node/383, accessed 30 September 2019. A set of the Four Seasons was also on offer in Cottier & Co. Sale 1913, no. 858.

88. See Cottier & Co. Sale 1913, nos 744, 776, 778, 783, 843, 863, 865, 875, 895, 909, 951, 952; additional entries name the Lady of Shalott as a window subject but not Maris.

89. 'Fine Examples of Nineteenth Century Painted Glass Panels on Exhibition at Cottier Galleries', *New York Times*, 26 May 1913, section 'Art at Home and Abroad', SM13.

90. The window's attribution to La Farge indicates the oblivion into which Cottier (and Cottier & Co.) fell after his death. On the reattribution to Cottier see Frelinghuysen 2020, n.p. The few known Cottier windows were church windows. Little was known about the firm's domestic glass. However, Cottier & Co. Sale 1913 lists numerous windows with flowers, both in vases and 'on latticework'. The Metropolitan Museum in 2020 acquired such a window (of 1877–80), which shows roses, morning glories and daisies on a brown and white lattice trellis: see fig. 197.

91. Henry Clay Frick Papers, Series: Subject Files (no. 304). The set replaced another one by the English-born Alfred Godwin (1850–1934) in Philadelphia on the theme of 'Love in the Tower'. Two small panels of that window remain in the Frick Pittsburgh.

92. Two panels with 'Isabella' and 'Miranda' are listed in Cottier & Co. Sale 1913 (lot 898); two other panels are identified as 'The Basil-pot' and 'Miranda' (lot 904). The online auction website Invaluable features two panels showing female figures similar to Marguérite and Miranda, though they are not so designated; dated *c.*1890, their colours are brighter than those of the Frick window: https://www.invaluable.com/auction-lot/ca-1890-a-pair-of-late-19th-century-stained-glas-673-c-cca453fba2, accessed 7 September 2020.

93. Cole 1879, 662.

94. According to an inscription on a scroll at the bottom of the stained-glass window in the Green Memorial Alcove, Society Library, New York, reproduced in ibid., 'THIS ALCOVE WAS DECORATED AS A TRIBUTE OF FRIENDSHIP FROM ROBERT LENOX KENNEDY'. The interior of the alcove was designed by Sidney V. Stratton and executed by Léon Marcotte: Gray 2007 and Burke 1986, 415. For contemporary accounts see *Art Interchange* 1 (13 November 1878), 39 and 'Notes', *Art Interchange* 2 (30 April 1879), 191.

95. The room was dismantled when the Society Library moved from 109 University Place to 53 East 79th Street in 1937. It was only partially reconstructed in the new location and the window by Cottier seems to have disappeared.

96. Small panels portraying famous writers or artists were stock items of Cottier & Co., as Cottier & Co. Sale 1913 indicates.

97. Roberto C. Ferrari, Curator of Art Properties, Avery Architectural & Fine Arts Library, Columbia University, New York, email, 12 June 2017, informed me that 'this window was in the original Avery Reading Room in the 49th St. building. When Columbia moved uptown, [the] Avery [library] wound up in one of the rooms that is today an administrative office before moving, and in 1912 it moved into the current McKim, Mead & White building. From what we can gather, the window was never installed in the current Avery Library, and seems to have been likely destroyed, or dismantled and sold, when the 49th St. buildings were torn down in the early 20th century.'

98. In Europe, the old medieval methods of stained-glass making had been revived from about the 1850s: Harrison 1980, 15–25.

99. Eskilson 2018, Ch. 2.

100. 'The Best Ten Buildings in the United States', *American Architect and Building News*, 13 June 1886, 282.

101. For a detailed discussion of La Farge's mural project in Trinity Church, see Weinberg 1974.

102. Cook 1878b, 571. While Cottier did many painted decorations for churches in Scotland, he did little decorative work in America. Other than Trinity Church, where he had a subordinate role, we know of only one instance where he is alleged to have painted decorations for a church: 'Some of the Attractions of New York', *Academy Notes*, 1885, 167, mentions that the chancel of the Episcopal Church of St Mary the Virgin on 5th Avenue and 53rd Street was 'decorated with paintings by Mr. Daniel Cottier with the exception of the central work, an exquisite *Mother and Child* by Matthijs Maris of Holland'. For an old grainy photograph see https://www.stmvirgin.org/historical-photos, accessed 14 August 2020. After Cottier's death, his firm did painted decorations for the Sage Chapel: see pp. 122–5.

103. Augustus Saint-Gaudens to Stanford White, March 1878, quoted in Saint-Gaudens 1913, vol. 1, 257; see also Frelinghuysen, 'A New Renaissance: Stained Glass in the Aesthetic Period', in Burke 1986, 180. T. M. Clark, 'Letter to the Editor of *The Nation*', 31 January 1878, 77 confirmed that Cottier's role was primarily logistical.

104. Either La Farge or Richardson may have served as an intermediary for this commission. The four windows are: *Five Wise Virgins*, in memory of Abby Matilda Loring (1799–1863), presented by her niece who carried the same name; *Sower and Reaper*, in memory of Alexander Cochrane (1813–1865), donated by his son, who carried the same name; *The Angel troubling the Pool*, in memory of Charlotte Troup Winthrop (Mrs Egerton L. Winthrop) (1840–1878), donated by her sister, Mrs Hollis Hunnewell; *Peace, be still (Jesus on the Sea of Gennesareth)*, in memory of John Fenno (1779–1820), who died at sea on the Indian Ocean, donated by his son John Brooks Fenno and his children.

105. Chester 1888, 48.

106. Although Memorial Hall, strictly speaking, is not a religious building, I discuss

it here because the memorial function of the windows is similar to that of most of the church windows Cottier & Co. designed.

107. *Report of the Class of 1857*, 247: https://www.google.com/books/edition/Report_of_the_Class_of_1857_in_Harvard_C/aDPiAAAAMAAJ?hl=en&gbpv=1, accessed 14 August 2020.

108. Lathrop 1881, repro. of *Epaminondas* 508; of *Sidney* 510. For other examples see Stebbins, Orcutt and Anderson 2008, 74, n. 2. The original drawings are lost. According to Yarnall 1990, 32, a colour study for the *Sidney* (watercolour over a photomechanical reproduction of the original drawing) exists in a private collection.

109. Stebbins, Orcutt and Anderson 2008, 74, n. 3.

110. 'Notes', *Art Interchange* 2 (1879), 190–1.

111. For an image of Cottier & Co.'s *Sower* window, Trinity Church, Boston see http://college.holycross.edu/RaguinStainedGlassInAmerica/Boston/Images/B25.Cottier_Trinity%20Boston,%20Sower1.jpg, accessed 16 August 2020.

112. See Stebbins, Orcutt and Anderson 2008, 74, n. 8 and Max Donnelly 2011a, 128–32.

113. Plutarch, *Moralia*, 'Lacaenarum Apophthegmata' (Sayings of Spartan Women): see http://penelope.uchicago.edu/Thayer/E/Roman/Texts/Plutarch/Moralia/Sayings_of_Spartan_Women*.html#note23, accessed 16 August 2020.

114. In Crawford 2015, 40–1 the author ponders the degree to which T. S. Eliot may have been moved by Cottier's window in the church he attended every Sunday as a child.

115. The Unitarian Church of the Messiah in St Louis was well known in architectural circles at the end of the nineteenth century and was one of only five discussed in *L'Architecture Américaine*, 3 vols (Paris: Librarie Générale de l'Architecture & des Travaux Publics, André Daly fils & Cie) 1886.

116. The Messiah commission is not the only one Cottier & Co. received from a Midwestern church. The firm also supplied a window for St James Church (since 1955 St James Cathedral) in Chicago: see Ch. 6, pp. 163–4.

117. On the Mauran church, see the informative application for placement on the National Register for Historic Places, with a full description of all windows, by Mary Stiritz and William Seibert, https://dnr.mo.gov/shpo/nps-nr/13000005.pdf, accessed 7 August 2019. The church now belongs to the Salt Covenant Baptist Church.

118. For the full text of 'The Reaper and the Flowers' see https://www.hwlongfellow.org/poems_poem.php?pid=89, accessed 8 August 2020.

119. The Canandaigua window shows seven parables: 'The Pearl of Great Price' (Matt. 23: 45–46); 'The Lost Coin' (Luke 15: 8–10); 'Wheat and Tares' (Matt. 13: 24–30, 36–43); 'The Good Samaritan' (Luke 10: 30–37); 'The Lost Sheep' (Matt. 18: 12–14); 'The Hidden Treasure' (Matt. 13: 44); and 'The Pharisee and the Publican' (Luke 18: 9–1). The Canandaigua window is nearly contemporary with a Cottier window in Bothwell Parish Church, near Glasgow, which has six panels showing the same parables: see Ch. 2, p. 46 above.

120. The Battell Chapel window was commissioned in memory of the Yale University student Loring William Andrews, who died in his senior year. It shows the Parable of the Lost Sheep, surrounded by four Virtues. The composition is held together by the Tree of Jesse, topped by King David and bears the following inscription (translated from Latin): 'KING DAVID/ CHARITY/ COURAGE/ PATIENCE/ TRUTH. In memory of Loring William Andrews, a senior of this school, who was born on the 26th day of August, A.D. 1861 and died on 21 October, 1882.' Andrews was the son of William Loring Andrews, a prominent book collector, who was the first librarian of the Metropolitan Museum of Art, New York, and a founding member of the Grolier Club.

121. Commissioned by Lucie Bond Robinson, the Calvary Episcopal Church window is composed of three lancets respectively commemorating Robinson's father, the US Congressman (from Ohio) William Key Bond, her mother, Lucie Strong Bond, and her husband, Augustus Robinson. All three lancets have a fruit tree motif in the background; the central Robinson window has the Parable of the Leaven at the bottom and of the Pharisee at the top. In the middle is the figure of Christ the Good Shepherd, dressed in a voluminous blue cloak, his yellow-orange hair surrounded by a strawberry-red halo. The windows on either side show (left) the Good Samaritan and (right) the Good Shepherd. While the central parables are still directly based on the Millais drawings, the other two show new and different interpretations of the theme.

122. The Sage Chapel's architect was Charles Babcock (1829–1913), the first professor of architecture at Cornell. Babcock was a student, as well as the son-in-law, of the well-known architect Richard Upjohn (1802–1878); he not only designed the original chapel but was also responsible for its 1898 enlargement.

123. For a reproduction of these two apse windows in the Sage Chapel see https://digital.library.cornell.edu/catalog/ss:99393, accessed 16 August 2020.

124. Both drawings, private collection in Britain: *Youth* is inscribed at the top with the words 'approved (left)'; *Hope* carries the inscription 'not approved' but, apparently, the design was used anyway, without many modifications. Both drawings show the figures in reverse of the way they are seen from inside.

125. W. P., 'Expand Sage Chapel Facilities: Building has grown with University', *Cornell Alumni News*, August 1940, claims that the interior was painted by Cottier & Co. of London but it is unlikely that artists would have come over from Britain to do the work.

126. Clark S. Northup, 'Sage Chapel, a description', being, in abridged form, an address delivered in Sage Chapel, April 17, 1904, Ithaca, N.Y: Cornell University, 1904, n.p.

127. Harrison 1980, 57. For the changes in Cottier's post-1880 window style see the discussion in Ch. 2, pp. 44–6.

128. On the window in St Machar's see Donnelly 2011a, 123–6 and Ch. 2, p. 41 above.

5 · The Art Market in New York
pages 126–43

1. See Dekkers 1996 and Chu 2009.

2. 'The Fine Arts: Opening of the Cottier Gallery on Fifth Avenue – An Extraordinary Collection of Masters', *New York Times*, 1 May 1877.

3. No New York Cottier & Co. archive has been found, thus far. Moreover, during Cottier's lifetime, no exhibition catalogues were printed. For information about the Cottier Art Rooms, therefore, we are largely dependent on the contemporary press.

4. Cottier kept Corot's *Orpheus* to his death and often exhibited it; see also next note.

5. Paul Demidoff (1839–1885) had commissioned the architect Alfred Feydeau to build a house in Paris at 35 rue Jean-Goujon. He (or perhaps Feydeau) commissioned several artists, including Corot, Jules Dupré, Eugène Fromentin and Théodore Rousseau, to paint decorative panels for the house: see Thompson and Wright 1996, 273–4 and

Sotheby's, New York, sale catalogue, 9 May 2014, no. 77, http://www.sothebys.com/en/auctions/ecatalogue/lot.77.html/2014/19th-century-european-art-n09143, accessed 8 June 2017.

6. Blumenthal 1970, 23 and n. 7.

7. Cottier also held onto the *Diana* all his life. *Orpheus greeting the Dawn* was bought in his posthumous sale in 1892 by Paul Durand-Ruel on behalf of Bertha Palmer (Chicago, Ill.), who bequeathed the work to the Art Institute of Chicago. On 2 March 1944 the painting was sold by the museum via Parke-Bernet Galleries (lot 47) in New York. It was bought, probably, by Vose Galleries in Boston, Mass., which, that same year, sold it to Earl William Quirk (Watertown, Wis.); the work stayed in Quirk's family until 1981 when it was gifted to the Elvehjem (now Chazen) Museum of Art. I am grateful to Andrea Selbig, Collections Registrar of the Chazen Museum for providing this information. *The Sleep of Diana* at some point was shipped to New York and was eventually sold by James Inglis to the Metropolitan Museum, which deaccessioned it in 1981; for a detailed provenance see Sterling and Salinger 1966, 63.

8. In 1890 Charles de Kay, using the pseudonym Henry Eckford, described this painting in *The Century*: 'The moon is half veiled by thin clouds, yet shimmers on a pool before which a cow stands in an attitude of alarm': Eckford 1890, 257. The painting may be identified as *The Watering Place*, auctioned by Sotheby's, New York, in 2015. According to the catalogue, Cottier bought the painting from Ryder. It was subsequently owned by his son William, then by his daughter Peggy: http://www.sothebys.com/en/auctions/ecatalogue/lot.78.html/2015/american-art-n09350, accessed 21 March 2018.

9. I have not been able to trace this huge Lessore watercolour. Two smaller ones, both representing the southern tip of Manhattan, are listed in the sale catalogue of Inglis 1909 (lots 13 and 14), indicating that such watercolours may have been a long-time staple of Cottier & Co.

10. 'The Cottier Collection of Paintings: Its Additional Attraction. The Approaching Sale', *New York Times*, 17 April 1878, 5.

11. See Penot 2017.

12. For the (incomplete) provenance of the painting, see http://www.musee-orsay.fr/en/collections/index-of-works/notice.html?no_cache=1&nnumid=009117&cHash=9c1c231944, accessed 22 August 2020.

13. 'Notes', *Art Journal* 4 (1878), 94.

14. The article in the *Art Journal* does not give the title of Olin Levi Warner's sculpture. It may have been a plaster or bronze cast of *Twilight*, modelled by Warner in a room at 144 Fifth Avenue, which Cottier had placed at his disposal (bronze cast, 1878, Chicago Institute of Fine Arts). In 1879 Warner had the piece carved in marble and sold it to Ichabod Williams (now Metropolitan Museum of Art, New York): see Dimmick, Hassler and Tollis 2000, 206.

15. For the annotated copy of the catalogue held in the Metropolitan Museum of Art, see Cottier & Co. Sale 1878, at https://archive.org/stream/b1469146#page/n23/mode/1up, accessed 21 March 2018.

16. Avery and Cottier appear to have been close. According to his diaries, Avery visited Cottier's premises in London whenever he was in town and, on occasion, visited Cottier & Co. at 144 Fifth Avenue: see Fidell-Beaufort, Kleinfield and Welcher 1979, 2: 76; 3: 8, 61, 112–13; 4: 44, 97, 135; 5: 4, 29, 59, 101, 107, 109, 139, 148 (the index, on p. 850, erroneously gives Cottier's first name as Maurice, as a result of a mistaken identification of the 'Cottier' mentioned in the text with the painter Maurice Cottier). Cottier designed and presented a memorial window to the library Avery founded in honour of his son Henry Ogden: Avery Library 1895, v, illus. The window does not seem to have survived.

17. 'Cottier Collection of Paintings', 5.

18. 'Messrs. Cottier & Co., intending to discontinue this branch of their business, have requested Mr. S. P. Avery to undertake the management of a closing-out auction sale of their entire collection of Oil Paintings and Water Color Drawings': Cottier and Co. Sale 1878, n.p., 'A Unique Gallery of Paintings'.

19. Bayer and Page 2010; on this general subject see also Bayer and Page 2011.

20. Cottier & Co. Sale 1878 lists all the actual buyers but scribbled over many of the entries is the name of Cottier. Among those who bought for Cottier were both people who worked for him, like James Inglis, James Fenton and Elbert Jan van Wisselingh, and friends and colleagues, like Charles Yandell, who owned the furniture shop close to Cottier & Co., at 140 Fifth Avenue.

21. Dekkers 1996, 64.

22. 'Art Galleries', *Art Interchange: A Household Journal* 3: 6 (17 September 1879), 52. None of these paintings can be identified with certainty.

23. 'The Cottier Gallery: Monticelli and his Friend Diaz – Dreams of the Orient – A Tapestry in Paint', *New York Times*, 1 September 1879, 5.

24. See https://helenadekaygilder.org/dekayfam/index.htm, accessed 15 September 2020.

25. O'Brien 1986, 37.

26. 'The Pedestal Art Loan', *New York Times*, 2 December 1883, 2.

27. The *Cent Chefs-d'oeuvre des collections parisiennes*, Galerie Georges Petit, Paris, 1883, was widely reviewed. The catalogue, Wolf 1883, was translated into English and published by Knoedler, New York, in 1883 (with several reprints).

28. Mauve's *Changing Pasture* was donated to the Metropolitan Museum by Benjamin Altman, who had bought it from Knoedler's after it had been on the art market for some time: http://www.metmuseum.org/art/collection/search/437040?sortBy=Relevance&ft=Mauve+changing+pastures&offset=0&rpp=20&pos=1, accessed 31 August 2017.

29. One *Dutch Coast Scene* is close in subject and composition to Mauve's *Scheveningen* in the Burrell Collection, Glasgow, but it is not the same picture.

30. Monticelli's *Gateway to a Fort* and Mettling's *Among the Curios* were identified by O'Brien 1986, 167 and 172. Monticelli's painting was eventually bought by the Canadian collector William Cornelis Van Horne, whose daughter Adaline donated it to the Montreal Museum of Fine Arts. Mettling's was bought by the National Gallery of Ottawa from Cottier & Co. in 1911 and is currently known as *Cleaning Pots*. It had been bought by Cottier, presumably from the artist, by 1883 for his private collection and was acquired by E. J. van Wisselingh at the 1892 Cottier sale. Van Wisselingh may have sold it to Inglis, as it appeared at the Inglis 1909 sale (lot 17, *Le Récurage*), where it must have been acquired by Walter Fearon for Cottier & Co.

31. Penot 2017, n.p.

32. Montezuma 1888, 104. At the death of Matthijs Maris, in 1917, an anonymous short article, 'Matthew Maris', *Art World* 3: 1 (1917), 58, also stresses the importance of Cottier as 'the chief agent in making the landscapes and figure-pieces of the Maris brothers known in America'.

33. Avery papers, Metropolitan Museum of Art, New York; Knoedler Archives, Getty Research Institute, Los Angeles, which also owns the Goupil stock books. For other Goupil international business archives see New York Public Library; Netherlands Institute for Art History, The Hague; Goupil Museum, Bordeaux.

34. These catalogues include the *Pedestal Fund Art Loan Exhibition* 1883 and Henley 1888 (see Ch. 3).

35. Diaz, well represented in Cottier's London stock, was not promoted in the same way in New York.

36. Dekkers 1996, 62 states categorically that '[t]he introduction of the Hague School to the United States actually began with the Scottish art dealer Daniel Cottier', even though admitting that other dealers in New York had occasional works by these artists in their stock before Cottier opened his gallery.

37. On Cottier's early monopoly on Monticelli, see Sheon 1979, 93. Cottier's direct line to Monticelli is borne out by Inglis 1909, which for seven of the Monticelli paintings in the auction (lots 42–4, 80–3) indicates that they are 'From the collection Daniel Cottier, Esq., who bought it from the Artist', and for the eighth (lot 113), 'From the artist'.

38. See O'Brien 1986, 47.

39. Alfred Sensier, well-known collector and writer on art, sale 1877, catalogue: http://gallica.bnf.fr/ark:/12148/bpt6k12403350.texteImage, accessed 20 August 2020.

40. Cottier & Co. Sale 1878, n.p.

41. Henley 1892, x.

42. The point that dealers recycled a large amount of paintings among themselves was first made by Bayer and Page 2010, n.p.

43. See n. 16 above.

44. John G. Johnson bought, among others, John Macallan Swan's *Wild Boars* and Corot's *Street Scene* in June 1891 (for the receipt of purchase see Philadelphia Museum of Art archives), reproduced in Heijbroek and Wouthuysen 1999, 27.

45. Williams Sale 1915 (1), https://archive.org/details/illustratedcataloоamer_0, accessed 8 August 2020.

46. John Robinson cited in Burke 1980, 15.

47. 'Sale of Five Collections', *New York Times*, 5 February 1905, 7.

48. For the complete provenance of Manet's *Dead Toreador* see https://www.nga.gov/collection/art-object-page.1179.html#provenance, accessed 22 August 2020. After Cottier's death, Inglis increasingly broadened the stock of Cottier & Co., both with Old Master paintings and with works by the Impressionists.

49. See p. 132 and n. 30 above.

50. See Knowles 2004, 289–90; also Sherman 1920, 69.

51. E. P. Taylor Research Library & Archives, Toronto, Van Horne Family Fonds SC065; see http://atom.ago.ca/index.php/la-sc065, accessed 22 August 2020.

52. Greenshields 1906, with reproductions of works in the author's collection.

53. Buis 2008, 59, 71, 74.

54. The Benedick Building, Washington Square East, six storeys built in red brick in 1879 by Lucius Tuckerman, was originally intended for unmarried male professionals. It was named Benedick after the bachelor in *Much Ado About Nothing* and attracted many young artists, including, at one time or another, William Gedney Bunce, Wyatt Eaton, Winslow Homer, John La Farge, George Maynard, Albert Pinkham Ryder, Augustus Saint-Gaudens, Olin Levi Warner, J. Alden Weir, and Stanford White. Several of these artists were among the founders and/or early members of the Society of American Artists. See Bienenstock 1983, passim.

55. C. E. S. Wood, 'A Letter', in Millet 1921, 103.

56. For the original plasters of Warner's busts of Isabella and Margaret Cottier see Smithsonian Institution, American Art Museum, Washington D.C., inv. nos 1974.88.4 and 1974.88.12, which also owns the original plaster of the bust of Cottier. Bronze versions of the three busts are in different collections. For more on these works, see Gurney 1978, vol. 2, 359–67 (Daniel Cottier), 500–2 (Isabel), 719–20 (Margaret).

57. For Alden Weir's *Portrait of Miss Cottier* see van Rensselaer 1881, 200. The portrait (impossible to tell whether it represents Margaret or Isabella) is now in the hands of Cottier descendants in the USA, who also own a portrait of Cottier's wife, Marion Field Cottier, and a presumed portrait of Cottier himself, both attributed to Weir. Private correspondence, 2 March 2012.

58. As for the friendships Cottier had formed with young artists when he first came to New York, he may have met some of them through Francis Lathrop, who had studied in England between 1870 and 1873 and, like Cottier, worked in stained glass. By 1875 Lathrop may have already done some decorative work for Cottier: see Ch. 4, pp. 100–01.

59. See Bienenstock 1983, 19–20.

60. The 1875 exhibition at Cottier's did not have a catalogue but the main works on exhibit (probably all oil paintings) and their authors were listed on the invitation card (see p. 139, fig. 127b).

61. 'Culture and Progress', *Scribner's Monthly* (June 1875), 253.

62. 'Some New-School Pictures', *New York Times*, 29 April 1875, 2. For more reviews, see the informative entry by the New Britain Museum of American Art: https://ink.nbmaa.org/objects/149/lady-of-shalott, accessed 21 March 2018.

63. 'A Remarkable Exhibition', New York *Evening Post*, 29 April 1875, 2.

64. *Appleton's Journal* cited in Bienenstock 1983, 22.

65. *Saturday Evening Gazette* (Boston) cited in ibid.

66. Cook 1875.

67. Ibid.

68. Bienenstock 1983, passim.

69. Ryder Obituary 1917.

70. Angus owned Ryder's *The Temple of the Mind*, which in 1918 he donated to the Albright-Knox Art Gallery in Buffalo, N.Y.

71. Henley 1892, xii–xiii.

72. See App., p. 208.

73. By the CPI Inflation Calendar: https://www.in2013dollars.com/uk/inflation/1886, accessed 21 August 2020.

74. Numerous obituaries appeared in American papers, such as the *New York Times*, 8 April, 1891, 5 and the *New York Tribune*, 8 April 8, 1891, 7. Several art journals also featured obituaries: 'Daniel Cottier's Death', *The Collector* 2 (15 April 1891), 141, and 'The Late Daniel Cottier', *The Architect* 47 (13 May 1892), 323–4.

75. Henley 1892, ix–xiii. On Henley see also Ch. 3, p. 87.

76. 'Small Talk and Palaver', *The Collector*, 3: 16 (15 June 1892), 241. For the contemporary equivalent of $115,000 see https://www.in2013dollars.com/us/inflation/1892?amount=1, accessed 21 August 2020.

77. According to Inglis 1909, intro., Inglis was first the manager of the New York branch, then a partner and, after Cottier's death, the owner of Cottier & Co., which had 'its headquarters in New York and a branch in London'. See also Ch. 4.

78. See Inglis Obituary 1907.

79. 'Recent Picture Sales: Cottier/Inglis Sale', *American Art News* 7, 23 (March 1909), 5.

80. Cottier, on occasion, had also bought and sold Old Master paintings. Most important, no doubt, was his acquisition of the portraits of a husband and wife, probably of the van Beresteyn family (Metropolitan Museum of Art, New York), which Cottier bought in 1887–8 from the French framer and dealer Félix Gérard and sold to the Havemeyers for $60,000. Extensive information about Rembrandt's pendant portraits and their provenance can be found on the Metropolitan Museum website.

81. Cottier & Co. Sale 1915.

82. Fearon was born in Newcastle-upon-Tyne and had an art gallery in London before he went to New York in 1902. According to his *New York Times* obituary, his London gallery remained open until three years before his death: Fearon Obituary 1935.

83. Ibid.

6 · Sydney 1873–1886 *pages 144–77*

1. The first advertisement for the new firm appears in the *Sydney Morning Herald*, 16 September 1873, 4.

2. 1851 Census, Glasgow, s.v. 'John Lamb Lyon'.

3. See Rutledge 1986, using the spelling Kearney instead of Cairney.

4. On Ferguson & Urie see https://fergusonandurie.wordpress.com, accessed 7 September 2020.

5. John and Elizabeth Lyon are recorded in the 1871 Census in London, with their daughter Margaret (aged 9) and sons John (3) and Patrick (2). I am grateful to Clarissa Ward for this information. They left from Liverpool on 17 December 1871 on the *Great Britain*, arriving in Melbourne on 21 February 1872.

6. *Government Gazette* (Victoria), 29 August 1873, 1553.

7. While the business premises and decorating studio were in Pitt Street, Lyon and his family lived first in Paddington and then in Bourke Street, Sydney.

8. The firm was initially called Falconer & Ashwin, later Ashwin & Falconer.

9. Morrison 1888, vol. 1, n.p.

10. All but one of the known designs of Lyon, Cottier & Co. and Lyon, Wells, Cottier & Co. are in the Mitchell Library, State Library of New South Wales, Sydney: Lyon, Cottier & Co., *c.*1876–1915, DGD 30, and Lyon, Cottier & Co. and Lyon, Wells, Cottier & Co., 1888–1907, PXD 609 (images for the latter available online); some additional designs have different call numbers.

11. For a printing block for the letterhead of the firm see Mitchell Library, R 816.

12. 'Intercolonial Exhibition', *Freeman's Journal* (Sydney), 17 April 1875, 8.

13. 'Sale of Sir George Verdon's Art Collection', *Argus*, 19 October 1882, 9.

14. Advertisement, *Freeman's Journal*, 12 December 1874, 1.

15. 'Opening of the New Post Office', *Sydney Morning Herald*, 4 September 1874, 3.

16. 'New Pictures in the Public Library', *The Age* (Melbourne), 19 January 1875, 3. The painting by Pille is not known.

17. See App., p. 208 above.

18. 'Fine Arts', *Sydney Morning Herald*, 22 May 1882, 7.

19. 'A New Art Gallery', *Illustrated Sydney News*, 24 November 1883, 14.

20. 'Opening of Mr. Sand's New Gallery', *Daily Telegraph* (Sydney), 27 October 1884, 6.

21. A Mr Gow, almost certainly Charles, is listed as a second-class passenger on the *Superb*, leaving Gravesend, Kent, for Melbourne on 7 May 1873. The voyage took about five to six weeks. Gow's exact date of arrival in Melbourne is unknown but there is a record that he left Melbourne with Lyon for Sydney in late August when both men were listed together departing by ship: *Australasian*, 30 August 1873, 13.

22. Listed under the profession of 'artist', Gow's name and address appear in *Sand's Sydney & New South Wales Directory* 1875, 481. Gow left Sydney on 10 December 1876 for London: *Sydney Mail*, 23 December 1876, 882; he never returned to Australia.

23. 'Personal: Mr. John Lamb Lyon', *Australasian Decorator and Painter*, August 1909, 264.

24. *Illustrated Sydney News*, 28 February 1874, 3.

25. 'The New Post Office', *Sydney Morning Herald*, 25 September 1874, 5.

26. Ibid.

27. *Sydney Morning Herald*, 13 November 1875, 7.

28. For a copy of the 1876 brochure see Mitchell Library, MSS 1381.

29. *Evening News* (Sydney), 29 October 1877, 3; *Sydney Morning Herald*, 10 July 1877, 8, advertised the lease or sale of the shop and premises previously occupied by Lyon, Cottier & Co.

30. *Government Gazette* (New South Wales), 8 August 1879, 3523.

31. *Sydney Morning Herald*, 25 November 1878, 5.

32. 'School of Arts', *Evening News* (Sydney), 16 November 1878, 5.

33. On the history of the Garden Palace see https://www.sl.nsw.gov.au/stories/garden-palace and https://www.records.nsw.gov.au/archives/magazine/galleries/garden-palace-fire, accessed 7 September 2020.

34. Lyon, Cottier & Co. took on the lion's share of the decorations: 'Basement work, Mr. A. Torning and Messrs. Lyon and Cottier; American and Queensland sections, Mr. A. Torning; European sections, nave and transept, Messrs. Lyon and Cottier; British section, Messrs. Palmer and Weekes; Victorian and Tasmanian sections, Mr. Hibble': 'Sydney International Exhibition', *Evening News* (Sydney), 3 July 1879, 2.

35. *Australasian Painter and Decorator*, 1 February 1909, 121.

36. Ibid., 1 June 1909, 203.

37. Ellsmore 2000, 94.

38. 'The International Exhibition', *Sydney Daily Telegraph*, 1 October 1879, 6.

39. James Barnet paraphrased by reporter in *South Australian Register*, 23 September 1882, 6.

40. *Sydney International Exhibition, 1879* 1880, 72, 81, 83.

41. *Sydney Morning Herald*, 22 May 1886, 9.

42. 'The Premier's Residence. Potts Point, Sydney', *Maitland Mercury and Hunter River General Advertiser*, 20 June 1868, 2, quoted in Lennon 1994, 113.

43. *Sydney Morning Herald*, 8 July 1882, 8; I am grateful to Graham Windridge for this reference.

44. Lyon knew John Young for years. Also a draughtsman, Young designed the stone font in Decorated Gothic style for the Medieval Court featuring Ferguson, Urie & Lyon's church work at the 1866 Intercolonial Exhibition in Melbourne: 'Medieval Court,' *Australian News for Home Readers*, 20 December 1866, 10–11.

45. Advertisement for the Abbey, *Sydney Morning Herald*, 19 October 1889, 18.

46. It is unlikely that the firm designed the stained-glass windows, which appear to be the work of the rival Sydney firm of Ashwin & Falconer.

47. Much of the painting was done by Parnell Wressell Johnson (1850–1913), an art teacher at the Sydney Technical College who also did

work for Lyon, Cottier & Co. See 'The Late Mr. P. W. Johnson', *Australasian Decorator and Painter*, 1 June 1913, 220.

48. The window is listed in *Victorian Intercolonial Exhibition 1875, Preparatory to the Philadelphia Centennial Exhibition of 1876* (Melbourne: McCarron, Bird & Co., 1875), 17, 120.

49. *Bacchus Marsh Express*, 31 July 1875, 4.

50. *Argus (Exhibition Supplement)*, 3 September 1875, 3.

51. *Victorian Intercolonial Exhibition 1875*, 1875, 17.

52. *Clarence and Richmond Examiner*, 4 May 1878, 5.

53. Ibid., cited in https://glaasincresearch.wordpress.com/author/bdhughes2012, accessed 3 September 2020.

54. See n. 28 above.

55. 'St. Andrew's Scots Church: Memorial Windows', *Sydney Morning Herald*, 12 July 1875, 5.

56. The window in St Andrew's, Sydney, may be the original Crathie Kirk window, slightly cut to make it fit in its new location. It is also possible that it was based on the same design as the Crathie window and that the original is lost.

57. *Sydney Morning Herald*, 12 July 1875, 5.

58. 'All Saints' Cathedral (Church of England), Bathurst', *Illustrated Sydney News*, 23 June 1877, 5.

59. Ibid.

60. The new chancel and transept of St Thomas' Anglican Church, North Sydney, were completed in September 1880; 'St Thomas' Church, Willoughby', *Sydney Morning Herald*, 20 September 1880, 3.

61. Installed by Lyon, Cottier & Co. in 1880, the large three-light chancel window in St Thomas' memorialising the church's first rector represents in its centre Christ as the Good Shepherd, Saint Thomas examining the wounds of Christ across the lower sections, the parable of the Good Samaritan in the southern light and Jesus and the woman of Samaria in the northern light. Four circular windows depicting the Evangelists are placed at the top and bottom of these southern and northern lights. A large memorial window by the London firm Clayton & Bell was installed in the north transept, also in 1880.

62. 'St Thomas' Church, North Shore', *Sydney Morning Herald*, 13 October 1884, 4. The district names of Willoughby and North Shore in Sydney were interchangeable around this time.

63. The window is illustrated in Waters and Carew-Cox 2017, 332, fig. 531. I am grateful to Max Donnelly for this information.

64. See New South Wales Office of Environment and Heritage, https://www.environment.nsw.gov.au/heritageapp/ViewHeritageItemDetails.aspx?ID=5051584, accessed 3 September 2020.

65. See Berkowitz 2004, 301.

66. *Australian Town and Country Journal*, 14 July 1877, 19; 'The Intercolonial Exhibition', *Sydney Morning Herald*, 1 May 1877, 5.

67. The famed literary figures and portraits in these large windows in the College's library are robust and spirited and the firm used the figures for subsequent interior mural and ceiling paintings. Adapted from paintings and prints, the portrait of Sir Walter Scott owed a debt to Sir Henry Raeburn's then well-known portrait of 1822 (National Galleries of Scotland, Edinburgh): see https://www.google.com/search?q=Henry+Raeburn+portrait+walter+Scott&ie=utf-8&oe=utf-8&client=firefox-b-ab, accessed 3 September 2020.

68. *Illustrated Sydney News*, 23 February 1878, 10; Sherry 1987, 3–4; a fine two-light window by Lyon, Cottier & Co. with portraits of James Watt and George Stephenson and painted quarries of the leek, thistle, rose and waratah was gifted by the early colonist and engineer John Struth in 1884.

69. For a design for St Andrew's College library ceiling see Lyon, Cottier & Co. archive, Mitchell Library, DGD 30 no. 7.

70. Ellsmore 1993, 32.

71. A similar Allegory of the Arts figure was later used in Booloominbah: see Ch. 7, fig. 187.

72. 'Art Society's Exhibition', *Sydney Mail*, 29 October 1881, 773. The location of the plaque is unknown.

73. See Kinchin, Macartney and Robertson 2011, 54, pl. XIV B for the Banks vase.

74. *Freeman's Journal*, 15 April 1882, 2.

75. *Australasian Builder & Contractors' News*, 2 July 1892, 11–12.

76. Another mantelpiece, remaining in the dining room at Cairndhu House, originally contained *Love* and *Death* with a pendant figure to this tile, as well as single tiles depicting artistic or literary figures. The panels of *Fame, Fortune, Love* and *Death*, also painted on 8-inch Minton, Hollins & Co. tiles (see fig. 45), were removed from Cairndhu in the later twentieth century and sold by Woolley & Wallis, Salisbury, 19 June 2018, lot 26. An identical design to fig. 165, inscribed with the title *Evening*, was used for a painted and gilded panel made for an ebonised and painted Grecian-style cabinet made by Cottier & Co. in London *c.*1870–5, in a private collection.

77. *Weekly Times* (Sydney), 16 December 1876, 10.

78. *Sydney Morning Herald*, 3 September 1881, 15.

79. *Sydney Mail*, 4 November 1882, 7, and 10 March 1883, 466.

80. Ibid., 11 December 1897, 1235.

81. Margaret Stowe (née Lyon), diary entry, 23 April 1880, Mitchell Library, Sydney, MSS 1381/1.

82. These and other artists' portrait medallions (of Cellini, Palissy, Rembrandt, Reynolds, Rubens and others), loosely copied after painted or engraved portraits or self-portraits, were stock-in-trade domestic window designs in the Cottier studio and appear in numerous stained-glass lots in Cottier & Co. Sale 1913. They were designed by Cottier in the late 1860s and used in John Forbes White's Seaton Cottage, Bridge of Don, Aberdeen.

83. Stowe, diary entry, 15 December 1885, Mitchell Library, Sydney, MSS 1381/1.

84. See *Official Catalogue of Exhibits from the Colony* 1886, 465, and 'The Colonial and Indian Exhibition', *South Australian Advertiser*, 19 July 1886, 6.

85. *Sydney Morning Herald*, 8 December 1885, 7; *Colonial and Indian Exhibition* 1886, 157.

7 · Sydney and Melbourne, 1887–1924 *pages 178–207*

1. The new partnership, J. & W. Guthrie & Andrew Wells, lasted only until *c.*1903: https://www.mackintosh-architecture.gla.ac.uk/catalogue/name/?nid=GutWel, accessed 23 March 2020.

2. See Juliet Kinchin in Banham 1997, vol. 1, s.v. 'Cottier'.

3. *Decoration*, November 1886, 30; published by Sampson Low, Marston, Searle & Rivington, the journal's full name was *Decoration in Painting, Sculpture, Architecture, and Art Manufactures.*

4. Ibid., September 1885, 39.

5. Ibid., July 1886, 1. Some months later, Smith also highlighted Wells's decorations for the house of John P. Currie in Pollockshields, Glasgow: ibid., October 1886, 22.

6. See ibid., January 1887, 2 and March 1887, 18.

7. Briggs 1993, 278.

8. Morrison 1888, vol. 2, n.p. Like Cottier & Co. in London and New York, the firm must have used workers with different skills but little is known about their identities. One James Ross from Scotland worked with Lyon, Cottier & Co. in the early to mid-1880s as a house painter and also trained at the Sydney Technical College while an employee: *Daily Telegraph* (Sydney), 12 October 1885, 10. A drawing for two stained-glass windows is attributed to Alex Gibbs: Lyon, Cottier & Co. and Lyon, Wells, Cottier & Co., 1888–1907.

9. See Ch. 6, p. 147 and n. 13 on p. 228 above.

10. *South Australian Register (Supplement)* 31 March 1883, 1; 'English and Scottish Banking House', *South Australian Register*, 2 May 1883, 5.

11. Andrew Wells quoted in *Decoration*, 13 (June 1887), 47. Wells had competed against, among others, Charles Monkhouse, who worked for a leading Melbourne art decorating firm, the Scottish-born Paterson Brothers: *Australasian Decorator and Painter*, 1 July 1925, 5.

12. 'English, Scottish, and Australian Chartered Bank', *Argus*, 27 May 1887, 7.

13. The Scottish firm of Scott Morton & Co. in Tynecastle produced Tynecastle Canvas or Tynecastle Tapestry, an embossed leather-like wall covering made of a compound of canvas and paste which could be tinted or gilded. For a short time *c*.1900 the firm had an office in Melbourne. Other embossed wall coverings included Lincrusta, invented by Frederick Walton in 1877, and Anaglypta, a washable product invented by Walton's employee Thomas John Palmer that went into production in the late 1880s.

14. Wells in *Decoration*, June 1887, 47.

15. William Wardell to James Orr, 8 August 1889, in Wardell 1878–1902, vol. 1, p. 867. Orr was the manager of the Union Bank of Australia. Wardell's letter was aimed at recommending Lyon, Wells, Cottier & Co. for the decoration of this bank's new premises in Sydney, which Wardell had designed in 1888.

16. For example, when Lyon, Wells, Cottier & Co. received the tender from Wardell for the extensive decorations of Thomas Allwright Dibbs's sandstone mansion Graythwaite on Sydney's North Shore, the firm was told that the best bedroom must not be commenced until Wardell returned to Sydney: Wardell to Messrs. Lyon, Wells & Cottier, 10 October 1892, in ibid., vol. 3.

17. Among the more modest commissions Wells received for Lyon, Wells, Cottier & Co. in Melbourne through Wardell was one for decorations for St Mary's Catholic Church in East St Kilda, designed by Wardell in the 1860s and enlarged in the early 1870s: *Advocate*, 13 August 1887, 15. Wells's stencilled decorations on the ceiling and walls of the sanctuary are extant today.

18. Wells in *Decoration*, June 1887, 47.

19. Ibid. The work of Wells, especially his decorations for William Pearce's residence in Glasgow, was extensively discussed in Smith 1887.

20. Some fragments of Cliveden – a set of dining-hall doors, a mantelpiece and a window – designed by John William Brown and manufactured in Britain, are in the National Gallery of Victoria, Melbourne.

21. *West Australian* (Perth), 23 February 1887, 3.

22. On William Montgomery and his Cliveden windows, see the excellent https://williammontgomeryartist.com/, accessed 26 August 2020.

23. *Australasian*, 22 September 1999, 9.

24. *Sydney Morning Herald*, 21 February, 6; 14 March 1888, 8.

25. Public Record Office of Victoria, VPRS 840 1888, vol. 3, no. 33, 3.

26. A parallel can be drawn with the display of stained pearwood panels by Cottier & Co. in New York in the Third Annual Exhibition of the Architectural League of New York, 1887–8: see *Catalogue of the Third Annual Exhibition* 1887, 28, no. 334; and a display of decoratively treated mahogany in the League's exhibition in New York the following year: *Catalogue of the Fourth Annual Exhibition* 1888, 35, no. 239.

27. *Catalogue of the Exhibits in the New South Wales Court* 1888, 330.

28. Allen 2018, pp. 173–4.

29. 'New Memorial Windows at All Saints' Hunter's Hill', *Illustrated Sydney News*, 27 June 1889, 35. The window was illustrated as a black-and-white line print and the firm used this in its advertising for the *Australian Anglican Church Directory*, 1891, advertising section; a variant of the 'Last Supper' was later used by the firm in the large stained-glass east window for Hunt's Christ Church Cathedral in Grafton, New South Wales, installed in 1896.

30. 'The Decoration of St. Stephen's Church, Sydney', *Sydney Morning Herald*, 30 June 1888, 15.

31. For a history of the church, see http://www.ssms.org.au/our-history.html, accessed 26 August 2020.

32. St Stephen's Presbyterian Church was relocated from Phillip Street to Macquarie Street, when the new church was built in the 1930s.

33. 'St. Stephen's Church, Sydney', *Australian Town and Country Journal*, 7 July 1888, 9.

34. Four drawings of the Evangelists' heads, Lyon, Cottier & Co., *c*.1876–1915, DGD30, 38.

35. The St Stephen's memorial window to Christina Lyon depicts the parable of the Wise and Foolish Virgins and is part of a series of twelve memorial windows depicting Christ's parables, made by the firm for St Stephen's: *Sydney Morning Herald*, 16 February 1889, 9 and *Evening News*, 20 February 1889, 3. Christina ('Crissy') died at the age of three: Dobson 1973, 6. The window's inscription reads 'In memory of wee Crissy – Jesus called a little child unto him'.

36. The origin of the name Booloominbah is unknown but according to Hunt it came from the Australian aboriginal word for the native apple trees, a myth that became legendary among locals.

37. On Hunt, see Reynolds, Muir and Hughes 2002.

38. For James White's country house at Camden, Kirkham, Lyon, Wells, Cottier & Co. designed a large staircase window depicting horse riders and playful putti within Renaissance-inspired borders. The design survives in the firm's archive (DGD 30, 62) but it was not executed. The firm did produce smaller windows for the house, featuring Australian birds and geometric mandalas, illustrated in Reynolds, Muir and Hughes 2002, 138.

39. Hunt papers 1860–1903.

40. The Booloominbah staircase window depicts scenes from the life of General Charles George Gordon who was thought of at the time as one of Britain's greatest heroes. For images and a discussion of the window see https://www.une.edu.au/research/une-research-priorities/humanities-and-creative-arts-research/research-networks-and-groups/19th-century-studies-network/the-gordon-window, accessed 26 August 2020.

41. Mitchell 1988.

42. Hunt owned a copy of Kate Greenaway's book of nursery rhymes: Reynolds, Muir and Hughes 2002, 32; but probably the glass painter did not copy this and other children's

books directly but worked after tile designs by Stacy Marks for Minton.

43. An earlier version of the same figure may be seen in a large window by Lyon, Cottier & Co. in the Callan Park asylum, Sydney (see fig. 164).

44. *Builder & Contractors' News*, 3 May 1890, 933.

45. For a picture of Mooroolbeek see https://vhd.heritagecouncil.vic.gov.au/places/112820, accessed 26 August 2020.

46. *Australasian*, 14 September 1889, 24.

47. Rogers 1973, 171–3.

48. Frank Madden, 'Notes on the White Ibis', *Victorian Naturalist* 19: 5 (4 September 1902), 72–4.

49. A reporter for the *Builder & Contractors' News*, 9 June 1888, 371, wrote: 'An opportunity has been afforded the writer of seeing some of the beautiful and artistic stained glass that is being produced under the superintendency of W. W. Wardell, Esq. (of Messrs. Wardell and Vernon, Architects), for the town residence of Sir W. J. Clarke in Melbourne. The panels for the large dining-hall are now in their places, and have a most brilliant effect, the treatment being a happy combination of mosaic and painted glass. The subjects are all derived from the Flora and Fauna of Australia, and have been sketched from nature by the artists specially for the work': cited in https://william-montgomeryartist.com/2019/08/25/1888-east-melbourne-cliveden/#_edn2, accessed 26 August 2020.

50. The Cottiers sailed from San Francisco at the end of the winter of 1890: *Sydney Morning Herald*, 7 March 1890, 6.

51. Isabella may have met Marwood in Britain, where he studied medicine in Dublin, Edinburgh and Glasgow: Smith 1904, 444; or on her first voyage to Australia in early 1888, when Marwood was listed as a fellow passenger also travelling first class: *Sydney Morning Herald*, 11 February 1888, 12. On 9 October 1888 Cottier wrote to David Artz in the Netherlands of Isabella's excitement: 'Ella is busy telling all the folks about her engagement to Marwood of Melbourne, Australia': Cottier letters to Artz, Rijksprentenkabinet, Amsterdam. The Cottiers stayed in Sydney before travelling down to Melbourne, returning to Sydney: *Sydney Morning Herald*, 5 April 1890, 10. They left in mid-April for England: *Table Talk*, 18 April 1890, 12.

52. St Matthew's was chosen because it was the parish of Arthur Marwood's stepfather, Dr G. Featherstone, a resident of Prahran, Melbourne. Margaret Cottier and Marwood's sister served as bridesmaids.

53. A reception for *c.*400 guests was held at the Menzies Hotel in Melbourne. In a speech at the reception Cottier expressed his 'earnest wish that amongst his daughter's many new friends, she would find a happy home, though parted from her own family': *Life*, 10 April 1890, 3.

54. *Australian Star* (Sydney), 14 April 1890, 8.

55. *Sydney Morning Herald*, 14 April 1890, 5.

56. *Daily Telegraph* (Sydney), 14 April 1890, 6.

57. It is difficult to establish just how well known Cottier was as an art collector in Australia. In 1889 the *Argus* and *Australasian* in Melbourne reported on Cottier's purchase of two Rembrandt portraits and their subsequent sale to the American Henry Osborne Havemeyer, of the sugar refining firm, for $60,000. These reports noted that Havemeyer intended gifting them to the Metropolitan Museum of Art, New York: *Argus*, 12 January 1889, 13.

58. On 2 May 1892 Wells read a paper, 'Decoration', before the Sydney Architectural Association, published as Wells 1892a; in July that year he presented a lecture, 'Growth of Ornament Art', at the Australian Academy of Art, Sydney, published as Wells 1892b; and the next year, on 6 November 1893, he talked on 'The Treatment of Stained Glass in Decoration' to the members of the Sydney Architectural Association, published as Wells 1893.

59. Wells 1892a, 331–5.

60. Ibid., 333.

61. Ibid., 331.

62. Ibid., 335.

63. Wells 1892b; *Sydney Morning Herald*, 23 July 1892, 11.

64. Wells 1892b, 68.

65. De Libra 1892, 62. Wells also exhibited a collection of wooden panels including 'one with a bird and cherry blossom subject in rich and ruddy brown, another panel of somewhat neo-Grec design' and 'two small cabinet panels bearing female figures representing the Seasons'.

66. *Sydney Morning Herald*, 15 January 1891, 6.

67. *Government Gazette* (New South Wales), 21 February 1896, 1334; *Sydney Morning Herald*, 15 January 1896, 3.

68. *Sydney Morning Herald*, 10 March 1896, 3.

69. Ibid., 7 March 1896, 3. Wells's library included an edition of Ludwig Gruner's *Fresco Decorations and Stuccos of Churches and Palaces in Italy during the Fifteenth and Sixteenth Centuries* (London: John Murray, 1844).

70. *Sydney Mail and New South Wales Advertiser*, 4 April 1896, 681.

71. 'The British-Franco Exhibition', *Evening News* (Sydney), 6 March 1908, 8.

72. A two-light memorial window was also made in Sydney for Holy Trinity Church, Dinting Vale, Derbyshire, in 1904. It is illustrated in 'Australian Stained Glass-Work', *Art and Architecture, Journal of the Institute of Architects of New South Wales* 2: 2 (March–April 1905), 98; the architect Edwin Williams of Sydney, formerly of Dinting, commissioned Lyon, Cottier & Co. to create the two-light window in memory of his daughter, Sarah Mather Williams: 'Memorial Windows', *Daily Telegraph* (Sydney), 28 January 1905, 14. I am grateful to Karla Whitmore for her email communication about Lyon, Cottier & Co.'s later stained-glass work.

73. At times Rococo revival and Art Nouveau are difficult to distinguish, as with the windows the firm made for Canonbury at Darling Point, Sydney, a mansion built for the wealthy theatre entrepreneur Harry Rickards. The mansion was demolished in the 1980s but some salvaged fragments are today in the Museum of Applied Arts & Sciences (MAAS), Sydney, including a window in an interesting style half-way between Rococo and Art Nouveau: https://collection.maas.museum/object/168347#&gid=1&pid=3), accessed 26 August 2020.

74. 'Home and Society: "Warinilla" North Sydney', *Sunday Times* (Sydney), 18 January 1914, 30.

75. *Catholic Press*, 3 December 1914, 36; Bert's role is mentioned in Obituary, 'Death of Mr. John L. Lyon' 1916, and Lillie's role in *The Mirror*, 3 February 1918, 4.

76. *Sydney Morning Herald*, 15 June 1916, 6.

77. Until 1913, when the Australian navy was established, the firm continued periodically to produce heraldic lancet and roundel windows for Admiralty House, Sydney, featuring the coats of arms of the British admirals posted to Australia from 1885 to 1913 to command the Imperial Fleet: D'Apice 2017, 110–13.

78. *Sydney Morning Herald*, 24 May 1924, 26.

79. Obituary, 'Death of Mr. John L. Lyon' 1916, 257.

Conclusion *pages 202–7*

1. Cottier 1866, 142.
2. Benjamin 2003, 220.
3. Brown 2008, 3. On the physical and the spiritual importance of the home in the nineteenth century, see also Muthesius 2009, passim.
4. This trend was catalysed by the gradual replacement of artisanal work by machines.
5. Sullivan 1896, 408.
6. Danto 2003.
7. Nehamas 2007.

Appendix *pages 208–9*

1. Ashland House was at 315 Fourth Avenue.
2. The well-known Fifth Avenue Hotel was located at 200 Fifth Avenue. It opened in 1859 and closed in 1908.
3. Delmonico was a famous restaurant at the corner of Broadway and 26th Street.
4. William Bouguereau's *Nymphs and Satyr*, 1873, The Clark, Williamstown, Mass., was owned by the hotelier Edward S. Stokes, who displayed it in the well-known bar of the Hoffman House Hotel on Broadway and 25th Street.
5. Built in 1882 in Moorish style, the Casino Theatre was located at 1404 Broadway; it had a popular roof garden.
6. No doubt an erroneous reference to Corot's *Orpheus greeting the Dawn*, the pride of Cottier's New York gallery (see fig. 115).
7. The painter Albert Pinkham Ryder; see Ch. 4 above.
8. For Ryder's poem 'The Wind' see https://teachingpoetryandart.weebly.com/ryder--voice-of-the-forest--the-wind, accessed 20 May 2020.
9. For Thomas E. Valentine see Ch. 4; David Kay was named in Cottier's will as one of the company's two foremen in New York.
10. Probably the window installed in 1886 in Trinity Episcopal Church in Buffalo, New York: see http://library.bc.edu/lafargeglass/items/show/180, accessed 20 May 2020.
11. The Metropolitan Museum of Art, New York.
12. The New York Produce Exchange was located at Bowling Green in Lower Manhattan, in the place of the current skyscraper at 2 Broadway. The first building in the world to combine wrought iron and masonry, it was designed by George Browne Post and looked like a gigantic Florentine palazzo with a Palazzo Vecchio-style tower. It was demolished in 1957.
13. Lyon is reminded of the ferry boat *Solano* across the Sacramento River, which he probably took on his way to Niagara Falls.
14. Steel's Hotel at 5 Queen Street was one of the established commercial hotels in Glasgow.
15. Lyon, like most Scottish glaziers, agreed with Cottier that the 1857 controversial decision to award the commission for the windows of Glasgow Cathedral to the Royal Stained Glass Manufactory in Munich had been a major mistake: see Ch. 1 above.
16. Morris & Co. installed a five-light window depicting Christ the Good Shepherd flanked by the four Evangelists in Woodlands Parish Church in 1882: see Sewter 1975, 81–2. The window was removed when the church was sold to another denomination in the 1970s and is now in the collection of Glasgow Museums.
17. For Charles Gow see Ch. 6 above.
18. Probably Duncan Dewar (*c.*1840–1925), a glass-painter from Glasgow, who may have worked for Cottier in Scotland before working in Cottier's London studio; his name is signed on a window at Cairndhu House, Helensburgh (see fig. 35). By the time of the 1881 census Dewar was working as a foreman decorator in Cambuslang, near Glasgow.
19. No doubt the stained-glass painter William Kier who, with his brother James, owned the studio W. & J. J. Kier, founded by their father David Kier (1802–1864).
20. For William Craibe Angus see Ch. 3 above.
21. Perhaps the landscape painter and engraver John R. E. Finnie (1829–1907).
22. The City Chambers, designed by William Young, built between 1882 and 1888.
23. James Oswald Dykes (1835–1912) was a well-known Scottish Presbyterian clergyman who in 1869 had been appointed minister of the Regent Square Presbyterian Church.
24. Known as the 'Prince of Preachers', Charles Haddon Spurgeon (1834–1892) was an English Particular Baptist who was the pastor of the congregation of the Metropolitan Tabernacle (previously the New Park Street Chapel) in London for 38 years. His twin sons Charles and Thomas were preachers as well. The latter moved to Australia, where Lyon may have met him. The former must have given the sermon to which Lyon is referring.
25. No doubt Westminster Abbey.
26. St Margaret's, next to Westminster Abbey. Lyon was possibly referring to the stained-glass designer Charles Edward Holloway, although it is more likely that he meant Henry Holiday, the designer of a window in the south aisle commemorating Lord Frederick Cavendish, who had been murdered in Dublin in 1882. The window was made by James Powell & Sons and remains *in situ*.
27. Henry Hughes (d. 1883) was the partner of Thomas Ward in the stained glass firm Ward & Hughes, for which Lyon (and possibly Cottier) had worked in his youth. The window does not survive as St Mary-le-Bow, City of London, was severely damaged by an air raid in 1941.
28. The eight mosaics in the spandrels of the dome of St Paul's were installed between 1864 and 1892. The long time it took to complete the work was due, in part, to a public debate about adding new decorations to the historic building.
29. Donald Fraser (1826–1892), pastor of Marylebone Presbyterian Church, George Street near Bryanston Square, which had been enlarged and rebuilt in 1874–5: see 'Dr. Donald Fraser's New Church', *The Pictorial World*, 17 July 1875, 337.

BIBLIOGRAPHY

ARCHIVAL SOURCES

Angus, W. Craibe, Sequestration Book, National Archives of Scotland, Edinburgh

Cottier, Daniel, letters to David Artz, Municipal Archives, The Hague, 8000–01 Overige Verzamelingen 2: Schildersbrieven

——, letters to David Artz, Rijksprentenkabinet, Rijksmuseum, Amsterdam, Collection Family David Artz

——, letters to William Smith, 1875, Aberdeen City Libraries, Pamphlet and Ephemera Collection, LoP 941.25 C83

Frick, Henry Clay, Papers, Frick Collection/ Frick Art Reference Library Archives, New York

Geelong Art Gallery Committee Meeting Minutes, Geelong Gallery, Victoria

Glasgow Architectural Society, Minute Books, 1858–68, c/o Fiona Sinclair Architect, Glasgow

Goupil & Cie, Paris, 1846–1919, Stock Books, Getty Research Institute, Los Angeles, http://www.getty.edu/research/tools/digital_collections/goupil_cie/books.html

——, The Hague, 1861–78, Day Register of Acquisitions and Sales of Watercolours, Netherlands Institute for Art History (RKD), The Hague, Archive dealer Goupil (The Hague)

Hunt, John Horbury, papers, 1860–1903, Mitchell Library, State Library of New South Wales, Sydney, MLMSS 7087

Lyon and Stowe family papers, 1862–1955, Mitchell Library, State Library of New South Wales, Sydney, MLMSS 1381

John Lamb Lyon, 1886. 'Short Tour in Europe', Mitchell Library, State Library of New South Wales, Sydney, MLMSS 1381

Margaret Lyon, 1880–6. Diary. Mitchell Library, State Library of New South Wales, Sydney, MLMSS 1381

Lyon, Cottier & Co., 333 Pitt Street, Sydney, London House, 8 Pall Mall, Artistic Interior Decorators, Stained Glass Painters, Etc., *c.*1876. Sydney: Gibbs, Shallard & Co., Mitchell Library, State Library of New South Wales, Sydney, MLMSS 1381/2

Lyon, Cottier & Co., *c.*1876–1915. Designs for stained-glass windows and painted walls and ceilings, Mitchell Library, State Library of New South Wales, Sydney, DGD 30, https://search.sl.nsw.gov.au/primo-explore/fulldisplay/ADLIB110337611/SLNSW

Lyon, Cottier & Co. and Lyon, Wells, Cottier & Co., 1888–1907. Designs for stained-glass windows and painted ceilings, Mitchell Library, State Library of New South Wales, Sydney, PXD 609, https://search.sl.nsw.gov.au/primo-explore/fulldisplay?docid=ADLIB110337625&context=L&vid=SLNSW&lang=en_US&search_scope=E&adaptor=Local%20Search%20Engine&tab=default_tab&query=any,contains,Lyon%20%20Cottier

Macdonald of Kepplestone, Alexander, Private Letterbook, 1874–80, Aberdeen City and Aberdeenshire Archives, DD391/14/12

Maris, Matthijs, 300 letters to Willem van Meurs, Teylers Museum, Haarlem

Principal Probate Registry, London

Reid, Sir George, RSA, letters and papers, Aberdeen Art Gallery and Museum Archive, James McBey Reference Library, Aberdeen

Wardell, William Wilkinson, 1878–1902. Letter Books (5 vols), Mitchell Library, State Library of New South Wales, Sydney, MLMSS 10

SECONDARY SOURCES

Aldrich, Megan, 1990. *The Craces: Royal Decorators 1768–1899*, exh. cat., Brighton: Royal Pavilion, Art Gallery & Museums

Allen, Jasmine, 2018. *Windows for the World: Nineteenth-century Stained Glass and the International Exhibitions, 1851–1900*, Manchester: Manchester University Press

Ambrosini, Lynne, et al., 2016. *Daubigny, Monet en Van Gogh: Impressies van het landschap*, exh. cat., Amsterdam: Van Gogh Museum

Arondéus, W., 1930. *Matthijs Maris: De tragiek van den droom*, Amsterdam: Querido

Avery Library, *Catalogue of the Avery Architectural Library*, 1895. New York: Library of Columbia College

Banham, Joanna, ed., 1997. *Encyclopedia of Interior Design*, 2 vols, London: Taylor & Francis

Bayer, Thomas M., and John R. Page, 2010. 'Arthur Tooth: A London Art Dealer in the Spotlight, 1870–71', Nineteenth-Century Art Worldwide 9: 1 (Spring), http://www.19thc-artworldwide.org/spring10/arthur-tooth

——, 2011. *The Development of the Art Market in England: Money as Muse, 1730–1900*, London: Pickering & Chatto

Beautiful Sydney: Including Newcastle Coalopolis and Fertile Maitland, 1896. Sydney: George Robertson & Co.

Benjamin, Walter, 2003. *The Arcades Project*, ed. and tr. Howard Eiland and Kevin McLaughlin, Cambridge, Mass: Belknap Press

Berckenhoff, Leonard, 1917. 'Matthys Maris (1839–1917)', *Onze Eeuw* 17: no. 4, 92–110

Berkowitz, Michael, 2004. *Nationalism, Zionism and Ethnic Mobilization of the Jews in 1900 and Beyond*, Leiden: Brill

Bettley, James, 2002. '"An earnest desire to promote a right taste in ecclesiastical design": Cox & Sons and the Rise and Fall of the Church Furnishing Companies', *The Journal of the Decorative Arts Society* 26: 8–25

Bienenstock, Jennifer A. Martin, 1983. 'The Formation and Early Years of the Society of American Artists: 1877–1884', PhD dissertation, City University of New York

Bionda, Richard, 2017. *Matthijs Maris*, exh. cat., Amsterdam: Rijksmuseum

Blake, William P., 1875. *Ceramic Art: A Report on Pottery, Porcelain, Tiles, Terra-cotta and Brick, International Exhibition, Vienna, 1873*, New York: D. van Nostrand

Blumenthal, Arthur L., 1970. *19th and 20th Century Art from Collections of Alumni & Friends: Inaugural Exhibition*, exh. cat., Madison, Wis: Elvehjem Art Center

Bradbury, Oliver, 2015. *Sir John Soane's Influence on Architecture from 1891: A Continuing Legacy*, London: Routledge

Briggs, Asa, 1993. *Victorian Cities*, Berkeley: University of California Press, 1st edn 1963

Broun, Elizabeth, 1989. *Albert Pinkham Ryder*, Washington, D.C: Smithsonian Institution

Brown, Julia Prewitt, 2008. *The Bourgeois Interior*, Richmond: University of Virginia Press

Bryant, George B., 2013. 'Frank Furness and Henry Holiday: A Study of Patronage, Architecture and Art', *Architectural History* 56: 169–211

Buis, Alena M., 2008. '*Ut Pictura Poesis*: Edward Black Greenshields' Collection of Hague School Paintings', MA thesis, Concordia University, Montreal, at https://spectrum.library.concordia.ca/976098/1/MR45453.pdf

Burke, Doreen Bolger, 1980. *American Paintings in the Metropolitan Museum of Art*, vol. 3: *A Catalogue of Works by Artists born between 1846 and 1864*, New York: Metropolitan Museum of Art

——, et al., 1986. *In Pursuit of Beauty: Americans and the Aesthetic Movement*, exh. cat., New York: Metropolitan Museum of Art and Rizzoli

Callahan, John C., 1985. 'The Mahogany Empire of Ichabod T. Williams & Sons, 1838–1973', *Journal of Forest History* 29: 3, 120–30

Carruthers, Annette, 2004. 'William Morris and Scotland', *The Journal of the Decorative Arts Society* 28: 8–27

——, 2013. *The Arts and Crafts Movement in Scotland*, New Haven and London: Yale University Press

Catalogue of the Third Annual Exhibition of the Architectural League of New York, 1887. New York: Architecture Press

Catalogue of the Fourth Annual Exhibition of the Architectural League of New York, 1888. New York: Architecture Press

Catalogue of the Exhibits in the New South Wales Court, 1888. *Centennial International Exhibition, Melbourne*, Sydney: Government Printer

Chester, Arthur H., 1888. *Trinity Church in the City of Boston: An Historical and Descriptive Account with a Guide to its Windows and Paintings*, Cambridge, Mass: John Wilson & Son

Chu, Petra ten-Doesschate, 2005. 'The Lu(c)re of London: French Artists and Art-Dealers in the British Capital, 1859', in John House, ed., *Monet's London: Artists' Reflections on the Thames, 1859–1914*, exh. cat., Saint Petersburg: Museum of Fine Arts; Brooklyn: Museum of Art; Baltimore: Baltimore Museum of Art, 39–54

——, 2009. 'Anton Mauve in America', in Saskia de Bodt and Michiel Plomp, eds, *Anton Mauve*, exh. cat., Haarlem: Teylers Museum; Laren: Singer Museum. Bussum, Netherlands: Thoth, 147–65

Clark, Eliot, 'Adolphe Monticelli: 1824–1866', *Art in America* 3, 1915, 14–23

Cockerell, Sydney C., 1915. 'Ford Madox Brown on Art Education', *Burlington Magazine* 28: 152 (November), 66–7

Cole, Charles A., 1879. 'Painted Glass in Household Decoration', *Harper's New Monthly Magazine* 59 (October), 655–64

Colonial and Indian Exhibition, 1886. *Official Catalogue 1886*, London: William Clowes & Sons

'Comino Trees of Colombia (Aniba perutilis, Hemsl.)', 1894. *Bulletin of Miscellaneous Information (Royal Botanical Gardens, Kew)* 91 (July), 197–9

Conway, Moncure Daniel, 1882. *Travels in South Kensington, with Notes on Decorative Art and Architecture in England*, London: Trübner & Co.

Cook, Clarence, 1875. 'Fine Arts: American Pictures at Cottier's', *New York Daily Tribune*, 17 May, 2

——, 1876. 'Beds and Tables, Stools and Candlesticks: II', *Scribner's Monthly* 11 (January), 342–9

——, 1878a. *The House Beautiful: Essays on Beds and Tables, Stools and Candlesticks*, New York: Scribner, Armstrong and Company; copyright 1877

——, 1878b. 'Recent Church Decoration', *Scribner's Monthly* 15 (February), 569–77

——, 1883. 'Art in America in 1883', *Princeton Review* 59 (May), 311–20

Cormack, Peter, 2015. *Arts & Crafts Stained Glass*, New Haven and London: Yale University Press

Cottier, Daniel, 1866. 'Colour the Handmaid of Architecture', *Building News* 13: 2 (2 March), 142

'Cottier & Co.', 1874. *Scribner's Monthly* 8: 4 (August), 500–1

Cottier & Co. Sale, 1878. *Fine Oil Paintings and Watercolors by the Great Modern Classic Painters Imported by Cottier & Co. 144 Fifth Avenue ...*, New York

Cottier & Co. Sale, 1913. The Artistic Property of the Well-Known House of Cottier and Company, New York, New York: American Art Galleries, 19–26 November

Cottier & Co. Sale, 1915. *Paintings, Art Objects, Books, Fixtures, and Artistic Furniture comprising the entire stock of the firm of Cottier & Company To be sold without reserve by order of Walter P. Fearon, Esq., Percival Wilds, Esq. Attorney for Trustee*, New York: Metropolitan Art Association

Cottier and Co., [*c*.1876–81]. *144, Fifth Avenue, New York, 8, Pall Mall, London*, London: Chiswick Press, n.d; https://www.historicnewengland.org/explore/collections-access/gusn/242255/

Cottier Collection Sale, 1892. *Catalogue of Ancient and Modern Pictures ...*, Paris: Durand-Ruel

Crawford, Elizabeth, 2002. *Enterprising Women: The Garretts and their Circle*, London: Francis Boutle

Crawford, Robert, 2015. *The Young Eliot: From St. Louis to the Wasteland*, New York: Farrar, Straus & Giroux

Cross, Morag, 2014. 'Andrew Wells, Stained glass Artist: Some Recent Biographical Discoveries', *AHSS: The Magazine of the Architectural Heritage Society of Scotland* 35 (Spring 2014), 24–5

Dakers, Caroline, 1999. *The Holland Park Circle: Artists and Victorian Society*, New Haven and London: Yale University Press

'Daniel Cottier, Artist and Stained Glass Maker: A Manx Worthy', 1938. *Journal of the Manx Museum* 4: 56 (September), 47–9, 64

Danto, Arthur C., 2003. *The Abuse of Beauty: Aesthetics and the Concept of Art*, Paul Carus Lectures 21, Chicago: Open Court Publishing

D'Apice, Richard, 2017. 'Heraldic Record of the Commanders-in-Chief', in Jennifer Sanders, ed., *Collecting for the Nation: The Australiana Fund*, Sydney: NewSouth, 111–13

Davies, Rev. John Llewelyn, 1904. *The Working Men's College 1854–1904: Records of its History and its Work for Fifty Years, by Members of the College*, London and New York: Macmillan Co.

Day, Lewis Foreman, 1882. *Every-day Art: Short Essays on the Arts not Fine*, London: B. T. Batsford

De Libra [James Green], 1892. 'Exhibition of Academy of Arts of Australia: The Decorative Work', *Australasian Builder & Contractors' News* 30 (July), 62

Dekkers, Dieuwertje, 1996. '"Where are the Dutchmen?" Promoting the Hague School in America, 1875–1900', *Simiolus* 24: 1, 54–73

——, ed., 1999. *Jozef Israëls, 1824–1911*, exh. cat., Groningen: Groninger Museum; Amsterdam: Joods Historisch Museum

Dickie, W., 1916. 'In Praise of the House of God', in *Dowanhill United Free Church Jubilee*, 5–10

——, 1926. *History of Dowanhill Church, 1823–1923*, Glasgow: Stanley Works

Dictionary of Scottish Architects 1660–1980, 2016. http://www.scottisharchitects.org.uk

Dimmick, Lauretta, Donna J. Hassler and Thayer Tollis, 2000. *American Sculpture in the Metropolitan Museum of Art: A Catalogue of Works by Artists born before 1865*, New York: Metropolitan Museum of Art

'Discovery of a Cottier Stained-glass Window in Lezayre', 1939. *Journal of the Manx Museum* 4: 59 (June), 125

Dobson, Margaret, 1973. 'John Lamb Lyon and Francis Ernest Stowe', *Leichhardt Historical Journal* 4 (July), 6

Donnelly, Max, 1998. 'Cottier and Company (1864–1915): Establishing a Context for the Second Glasgow School', MA thesis, Sotheby's Institute, London

——, 1999. 'Daniel Cottier, Pioneer of Aestheticism', *The Journal of the Decorative Arts Society* 23: 33–51

——, 2001. 'Cottier and Company, Art Furniture Makers', *The Magazine Antiques* 159: 6 (June), 916–25

——, 2011a. '"Ideas of Their Own": Patronage and Cottier & Company's Memorial Windows', *The Journal of the Decorative Arts Society* 35: 122–33

——, 2011b. '"Such a Noble Face": Vincent van Gogh, Daniel Cottier and the Northesk Memorials', *Burlington Magazine* 153: 1302 (September), 568–71

Donnelly, Michael, 1981. *Glasgow Stained Glass: A Preliminary Study*, Glasgow: Glasgow Museums & Art Galleries

——, 1997. *Scotland's Stained Glass: Making the Colours Sing*, Edinburgh: H.M. Stationery Office

Dresser, Christopher, 1862a. *Development of Ornamental Art in the International Exhibition*, London: Day & Son

——, 1862b. *The Art of Decorative Design*, London: Day & Son

——, 1874–6. *Studies in Design*, London: Cassell, Petter & Galpin

Eastlake, Charles Locke, 1868. *Hints on Household Taste in Furniture, Upholstery, and Other Details*, London: Longmans, Green, & Co; Boston: J. R. Osgood, 1872

Eckford, Henry [Charles de Kay], 1889. 'Olin Warner, Sculptor', *Century: A Popular Quarterly* 37 (January), 392–401

——, 1890. 'A Modern Colorist: Albert Pinkham Ryder', *Century: A Popular Quarterly* 40: 2 (June), 250–9

Edwards, Clive, 2012. '"Art Furniture in the Old English Style": The Firm of Collinson and Lock, London, 1870–1900', *West 86th: A Journal of Decorative Arts, Design History, and Material Culture* 19: 2 (Fall–Winter), 255–81

——, 1993. *Victorian Furniture: Technology and Design*, Manchester and New York: Manchester University Press

Ellsmore, Donald, 1993. 'Nineteenth-Century Painted Decorations in Britain and Australia: An Approach to Conservation', PhD thesis, University of York, White Rose e-Theses online, http://etheses.whiterose.ac.uk/2525/2/DX180652_2.pdf

——, 2000. 'Interiors and Decoration: John Lyon's Ambitious Aesthetics', in Peter Proudfoot, Roslyn Maguire and Robert Freestone, eds, *Colonial City Global City: Sydney's International Exhibition*, Darlinghurst, Sydney: Crossing Press, 85–99

——, 2015. 'Who Trained Australia's Pre-Eminent Art Decorators?' in *Fabric: The Threads of Conservation*, proceedings of the ICOMOS Conference, Adelaide, 1–16

Elzea, Betty, 2001. *Frederick Sandys, 1829–1904: A Catalogue Raisonné*, Woodbridge, Suffolk: Antique Collectors' Club with Norfolk Museums & Archaeology Service

Eskilson, Stephen, 2018. *The Age of Glass: A Cultural History of Glass in Modern and Contemporary Architecture*, New York: Bloomsbury

Evans, Dorinda, 1986. 'Albert Pinkham Ryder's Use of Visual Sources', *Winterthur Portfolio* 21: 1 (Spring), 21–40

Fearon, Walter, Obituary, 1935. 'Walter P. Fearon, 59, Art Dealer is Dead', *New York Times*, 17 March, 37

Ferry, Emma, 2003. '"Decorators may be compared to Doctors": An Analysis of Rhoda and Agnes Garrett's "Suggestions for House Decoration in Painting, Woodwork and Furniture" (1876)', *Journal of Design History* 16: 1, 'Domestic Design Advice', 15–33

Fidell-Beaufort, Madeleine, Herbert L. Kleinfield and Jeanne K. Welcher, 1979. *The Diaries, 1871–1882, of Samuel P. Avery, Art Dealer*, New York: Arno Press

Fourth Annual Exhibition of the Architectural League of New York, 1888. December 1888–January 1889, New York: Fifth Avenue Galleries

Fowle, Frances, 2000. 'Vincent's Scottish Twin: The Glasgow Art Dealer Alexander Reid', *Van Gogh Museum Journal* 6: 90–9

——, 2002. 'West of Scotland Collectors in Nineteenth-Century French Art', in Vivien Hamilton, ed., *Millet to Matisse: Nineteenth- and Twentieth-Century French Painting from Kelvingrove Art Gallery*, exh. cat., Glasgow: Kelvingrove Art Gallery, 31–50

——, 2010. *Van Gogh's Twin: The Scottish Art Dealer Alexander Reid, 1854–1928*, Edinburgh: National Galleries of Scotland

——, ed., 2008. *Impressionism and Scotland*, exh. cat., Edinburgh: National Galleries of Scotland

——, and Richard Thomson, eds, 2003. *Soil and Stone: Impressionism, Urbanism, Environment*, Edinburgh: VARIE; Aldershot and Burlington, Vt: Ashgate

Fraser, Hilary, 1986. *Beauty and Belief: Aesthetics and Religion in Victorian Literature*, Cambridge: Cambridge University Press

Frelinghuysen, Alice Cooney, 2020. 'New Discoveries: Daniel Cottier, Cottier & Co., *Flowers on a Latticework Trellis*, ca. 1877–80', *Nineteenth-Century Art Worldwide* 19: 2 (Autumn 2020), http://www.19thc-artworldwide.org/

——, and Nicholas C. Vincent, 2016. 'Artistic Furniture of the Gilded Age', *Metropolitan Museum of Art Bulletin*, 73: 3 (Winter)

French Gallery, 1864. *Catalogue of the Eleventh Annual Exhibition in London of Pictures, the Contributions of Artists of the French and Flemish Schools*, London: French Gallery

Fyfe, Dorothea Hamilton, and Charles Sinclair Minto, 1970. *John Forbes White: Miller, Collector, Photographer, 1831–1904*, Edinburgh: Edinburgh Corporation, Libraries and Museums Committee

Gardner, Deborah S., and Christine G. McKay, 2009. *An Artist's Retreat: J. Alden Weir's Farm in Connecticut*, United States Department of the Interior: National Park Service

Garrett, Miranda, 2018. 'Professional Women Interior Decorators in Britain, 1871–1899', PhD thesis, University of the Arts London, https://ualresearchonline.arts.ac.uk/id/eprint/14242/1/Garrett

Georgi, Karen L., 2013. *Critical Shift: Rereading Jarves, Cook, Stillman, and the Narratives of Nineteenth-Century American Art*, College Park: Penn State Press

Gere, Charlotte, 2010. *Artistic Circles: Design and Decoration in the Aesthetic Movement*, London: V&A Publishing

——, 2017. 'The Alma-Tademas' Two Homes in London', in Elizabeth Prettejohn and Peter Trippi, eds, *Lawrence Alma-Tadema: At Home in Antiquity*, exh. cat., Leeuwarden, Netherlands: Fries Museum; Vienna: Belvedere; London: Leighton House, 74–97

Gibbs, Shallard & Co., 1882. *Illustrated Guide to Sydney and its Suburbs and to Favourite Places of Resort in New South Wales*, Sydney: Gibbs, Shallard & Co.

Gildard, Thomas, 1888. 'Greek Thomson', *Proceedings of the Royal Philosophical Society of Glasgow*, 30 January, 191–210

Girouard, Mark, 1977. *Sweetness and Light: The 'Queen Anne' Movement 1860–1900*, Oxford: Oxford University Press

Gossman, Lionel, with Ian R. Mitchell and Iain B. Galbraith, n.d. *A Stained Glass Masterpiece in Victorian Glasgow: Stephen Adam's Celebration of Industrial Labor*, http://www.princeton.edu/~lgossman/Adam.pdf

Gould, Brian, 1969. *Two Van Gogh Contacts: E. J. Van Wisselingh, Art Dealer; Daniel Cottier, Glass Painter and Decorator*, London: Naples Press

Goulding's New York City Directory, 1877. Vol. 3, 1 May 1877–1 May 1878, New York: Goulding

Gray, Christopher, 2007. 'The Best Seat in the House: A Brief History of the Green Alcove', *Society Library Newsletter*, 1 (June)

Greenshields, E. B., 1906. *Landscape Painting and Modern Dutch Artists*. New York: Baker & Taylor Co.

Grosse, Franziska, 2015. 'J. & W. Guthrie (later J. & W. Guthrie and A. Wells): Stained Glass Production 1874–1902', *The Journal of the Decorative Arts Society* 39: 58–79

Gurney, George, 1978. 'Olin Levi Warner (1844–1896): A Catalogue Raisonné of his Sculpture and Graphic Works', 2 vols, PhD dissertation, University of Delaware

Hall, Michael, 1996. '"Furniture of Artistic Character": Watts and Company as House Furnishers, 1874–1907', *Furniture History* 32: 179–204

Hamilton, William, 1882. *The Aesthetic Movement*, 3rd edn, London: Reeves & Turner

Hardie, William, 1976. *Scottish Painting 1837–1939*, London: Studio Vista

Harrison, J. F. C., 1954. *A History of the Working Men's College: 1854–1954*, London: Routledge & Kegan Paul

Harrison, Martin, 1980. *Victorian Stained Glass*, London: Barrie & Jenkins

Harrower, Ina Mary, 1918. *John Forbes White*, Edinburgh and London: T. N. Foulis

Havard, Henry, 1884. *L'Art dans la maison*, Paris: Rouveyre & Blond

Haweis, Mary Eliza [Mrs H.R.], 1881. *The Art of Decoration*, London: Chatto & Windus

——, 1882. *Beautiful Houses; Being a Description of Certain Well-Known Artistic Houses*, London: Low, Marston, Searle & Rivington; New York: Scribner & Welford

——, 1872. 'The Art of Beauty. Part II. Practical Hints and Suggestions', *Saint Pauls Magazine* 10 (February), 189–99, repr. in *Eclectic Magazine of Foreign Literature, Science, and Art*, n.s., 15 (April 1872), 472–9

Hawthorne, Mrs Julian, 1876. 'Art in London – II: An Hour with Corot, at Cottier's', *The Aldine* 8: 4, 126–8

Hay, David Ramsay, 1828. *The Laws of Harmonious Colouring adapted to House Painting*, Edinburgh: D. Lizars, London: G. B. Whittaker, Dublin: W. Curry, Jun. & Co.

——, 1836. *The Laws of Harmonious Colouring, Adapted to Interior Decorations, Manufactures, and other Useful Purposes*, Edinburgh: William & Robert Chambers

Heijbroek, J. F., and Esther L. Wouthuysen, 1999. *Portret van een kunsthandel: de firma Van Wisselingh en zijn compagnons, 1838 – heden*, Zwolle: Waanders

Hellerstedt, Karen, et al., 1988. *Clayton: The Pittsburgh Home of Henry Clay Frick: Art and Furnishings*, Pittsburgh: University of Pittsburgh Press (for the Helen Clay Frick Foundation)

Henderson, W. J., 1886. 'Some New York Theatres', *Magazine of Art* 9 (September), 401–7

Henley, William E., 1888. *Memorial Catalogue of the French and Dutch Loan Collection, Edinburgh International Exhibition*, Edinburgh: David Douglas

——, 1892. 'Daniel Cottier 1838–1891', in Cottier Collection Sale, *Catalogue of Ancient and Modern Pictures ...*, Paris: Durand-Ruel, ix–xiii

Hermens, Erma, and Suzanne Veldink, 2017. *Matthijs Maris at Work*, Amsterdam: Rijksmuseum

Hobler, Margaret H., 1987. 'In Search of Daniel Cottier, Artistic Entrepreneur', MA thesis, Hunter College, City University, New York

Holly, Henry Hudson, 1878. *Modern Dwellings in Town and Country Adapted to American Wants and Climate, with a Treatise on Furniture and Decoration*. New York: Harper & Brothers

Howe, Bea, 1967. *Arbiter of Elegance*, London: Harvill Press

Hudson, Henry, 1878. *Modern Dwellings in Town and Country Adapted to American Wants and Climate. With a Treatise on Furniture and Decoration*, New York: Harper & Brothers

Illustrated New York: The Metropolis of To-day, 1888. New York: International Publishing Co.

'Impression of America on a Dutch Impressionist', 1904. [Interview with Bernard Blommers], *New York Times*, 1 May

Inglis, James S., 1907. Obituary, 'The Late James S. Inglis', *American Art News* 6: 10 (21 December), 4

——, 1908. Obituary, *Academy Notes* 3: 9 (February), 149

——, 1909. [Sale], *The Valuable Paintings and Other Art Property to be sold to facilitate the settlement of the estate of the late James S. Inglis of Cottier and Company, New York*, New York: Mendelssohn Hall and American Art Galleries

International Exhibition, 1862. *Medals and Honorable Mentions awarded by the International Juries*, London: Eyre & Spottiswoode

Jack, Ian, 2013. *The St Andrew's Book*, Sydney: St Andrew's College

Jones, Owen, 1856. *The Grammar of Ornament*, London: Day & Son

Kaemmerer, Frederik, and Jaap Versteegh, eds, 2001. *F. H. Kaemmerer, 1839–1902: Brieven van 'oom Frits' (aan zijn vader en zuster Betje)*, Oosterbeek: Jeanette Versteegh

Kelley, Donald R., 2001. 'Eclecticism and the History of Ideas', *Journal of the History of Ideas* 62: 4 (October), 577–92

Kinchin, Juliet, Hilary Macartney and David Robertson, eds, 2011. *Cottier's in Context: Daniel Cottier, William Leiper and Dowanhill Church, Glasgow*, Edinburgh: Historic Scotland

Kirchhoff, Francis, 1867. *Reports of Artisans Selected by a Committee Appointed by the Council of the Society of Arts to Visit the Paris Universal Exhibition*, London: Bell & Daldy for the Society for the Encouragement of the Arts, Manufactures, and Commerce

Knowles, Valerie, 2004. *From Telegrapher to Titan: The Life of William C. Van Horne*, Toronto: Dundurn Press

Lane, Terence, and Jessie Serle, 1990. *Australians at Home: A Documentary History of Australian Domestic Interiors from 1788–1914*, Melbourne: Oxford University Press

Lathrop, George Parsons, 1881. 'John La Farge', *Scribner's Monthly* 21 (February), 503–16

Leeman, Fred, and Hannah Pennock, 1996. *Museum Mesdag: Catalogue of Drawings and Paintings*, Zwolle: Waanders

Lennon, Jane, 1994. 'Paradise Lost: The Garden of Sir James Martin at "Clarens"', *Australian Journal of Art* 12: 1, 113–23

Lepine, Ayla, 2012. 'On the Founding of Watts & Co., 1874', *BRANCH: Britain, Representation and Nineteenth-Century History*, ed. Dino Franco Felluga (June), http://www.branchcollective.org/?ps_articles=ayla-lepine-on-the-founding-of-watts-co-1874

Lewis, Arnold, James Turner and Steven McQuillin 1987. *The Opulent Interiors of the Gilded Age. All 203 Photographs from "Artistic Houses," with New Text*. Mineola, New York: Dover Publications

Liefde-van Brakel, Tiny de, 2001. *Tussen Katwijk en Parijs: David Adolphe Constant Artz 1837–1890*, exh. cat., Katwijk: Katwijks Museum

Lindenhovius, Willemijn, ed., 2015. *The Glasgow Boys: Schots Impressionisme*, exh. cat., Assen: Drents Museum

Loffelt, Antonie C., 1896. 'Fransche schilderkunst in Pulchri Studio – III',

Het nieuws van den dag: kleine courant, 4 December, 9

Loftie, Mrs [Martha J.], 1878. *The Dining-Room*, London: Macmillan & Co.

London International Exhibition of 1871. *Official Catalogue: Fine Arts Department, 1871*. 2nd edn, London: J. M. Johnson & Sons

Lyon, Heather, 1994. *Through All the Changing Scenes*, Kew, Victoria: School of Early Childhood Studies, University of Melbourne

Lyon, John Lamb, Obituary, 'Death of Mr. John L. Lyon', 1916. *Australasian Decorator and Painter*, 1 July, 257

Maas, Jeremy, 1975. *Gambart: Prince of the Victorian Art World*, London: Barrie & Jenkins

MacCarthy, Fiona, 1994. *William Morris: A Life for Our Time*, London: Faber & Faber

MacDonald, Sally, 1987. 'Gothic Forms Applied to Furniture: The Early Work of Bruce James Talbert', *Furniture History* 23: 39–66

McFadzean, Ronald, 1979. *The Life and Work of Alexander Thomson*, London, Boston and Henley: Routledge & Kegan Paul

Mackinnon, Lachlan, 1935. *Recollections of an Old Lawyer*, Aberdeen: D. Wyllie & Son

Madigan, Mary Jean Smith, 1975. 'The Influence of Charles Locke Eastlake on American Furniture Manufacturing, 1870–90', *Winterthur Portfolio* 10: 1–22

Madox Ford, Ford [Joseph Leopold Ford Hermann Madox Hueffer], 1896. *Ford Madox Brown: A Record of his Life and Work*, London: Longmans, Green

Mallet, Robert, and Johnson, J. Henry, 1862. *The Practical Mechanic's Journal: Record of the Great Exhibition, 1862*

Mavor, James, 1923. *My Windows on the Street of the World*, vol. 1, London and Toronto: J. M. Dent & Sons

Melville, Jennifer, 2000. 'John Forbes White and George Reid: Artists and Patrons in North-East Scotland, 1860–1920', PhD thesis, University of Edinburgh, http://hdl.handle.net/1842/8162

Memorial Catalogue of the French and Dutch Loan Collection, 1888. *Edinburgh International Exhibition 1886*, Edinburgh: David Douglas

Menz, Christopher, 1994. *Morris & Company: Pre-Raphaelites and the Arts & Crafts Movement in South Australia*, Adelaide: Art Gallery Board of South Australia

Miller, Tom, 2012. 'Daytonian in Manhattan', blogpost, http://dayton-inmanhattan.blogspot.com/2012/07/superb-cast-iron-address-plaques-at-no.html, 13 July

Millet, Josiah B., 1921. *Julian Alden Weir: An Appreciation of his Life and Works*, New York: Century Association

Mitchell, Bruce, 1988. *House on the Hill: Booloominbah, Home and University 1888–1988,* Armidale, New South Wales: University of New England

Montana, Andrew, 2000. *The Art Movement in Australia: Design, Taste and Society 1875–1900*, Carlton South, Melbourne: Melbourne University Press

——, 2018. 'W. J. Williams: Art Decorator of Ayers House, North Terrace, Adelaide', *Australiana* 40: 4 (November), 5–13

'Montezuma' [Montague Marks], 1888. 'My Notebook', *Art Amateur* 18: 5 (April), 104–5

Morrison, W. Frederic, 1888. *Aldine Centennial History of New South Wales*, 2 vols, Sydney: Aldine Publishing Company

Muthesius, Stefan, 2009. *The Poetic Home: Designing the 19th-Century Interior*, London: Thames & Hudson

Nehamas, Alexander, 2007. *Only a Promise of Happiness: The Place of Beauty in a World of Art*, Princeton, N.J.: Princeton University Press

O'Brien, Maureen C., 1986. *In Support of Liberty: European Paintings at the 1883 Pedestal Fund Art Loan Exhibition*, exh. cat., Southampton, N.Y.: Parrish Art Museum

Ochsner, Jeffrey Karl, 1984. *H. H. Richardson: Complete Architectural Works*, Boston: MIT Press

Official Catalogue of Exhibits from the Colony, 1886. *Forwarded to the Colonial and Indian Exhibition, London, 1886*, London: Thomas Richard

Orr, Lynn Federle, and Stephen Calloway, eds, 2011. *The Cult of Beauty: The Victorian Avant-Garde, 1860–1900*, exh. cat., London: V&A Publishing

Paris Universal Exhibition of 1867, 1868. *Catalogue of the British Section*, London: Her Britannic Majesty's Commissioners

Pater, Walter H., 1873. *Studies in the History of the Renaissance*, London: Macmillan & Co.

——, 1877. 'The School of Giorgione', *Fortnightly Review* 22 (June–December), 526–38

Pedestal Fund Art Loan Exhibition, 1883. *Catalogue of the [exhibition] at the National Academy of Design*, New York

Pennock, Hannah, 1996. 'Cousins and Colleagues: The Lives of Hendrik Willem Mesdag and Lawrence Alma-Tadema', *Van Gogh Museum Journal* 2: 56–75

Penot, Agnès, 2017. 'The Perils and Perks of Trading Art Overseas: Goupil's New York Branch', *Nineteenth-Century Art Worldwide* 16: 1, https://doi.org/10.29411/ncaw.2017.16.1.4

'Personal: Mr John L. Lyon', *Australasian Decorator and Painter* (August 1909), 263–4

Porter, Rev. Edward G., 1888. *Memoir of John C. Phillips with the Remarks of Hon. Robert C. Winthrop, and Other Tributes*, Cambridge: John Wilson & Son Press

Reid, George, and John Forbes White [*Veri Vindex*], 1868. *Thoughts on Art and Notes on the Exhibition of the Royal Scottish Academy of 1868*, Edinburgh

Rensselaer, M. G. van, 1881. 'The New York Art Season', *Atlantic Monthly* 48: 286 (August), 192–202

Reynolds, Peter, Lesley Muir and Joy Hughes, eds, 2002. *John Horbury Hunt: Radical Architect 1838–1904*, exh. cat., Sydney: Historic Houses Trust of New South Wales

Rimmel, Eugene, 1868. *Recollections of the Paris Exhibition of 1867*, London: Chapman & Hall; Paris: E. Dentu

Riordon, R., 1890. 'American Stained Glass', *Decorator and Furnisher* 15: 4 (January), 107–9

Robertson, Denise, 1988. 'John Lamb Lyon: His Life and Work', BArch thesis, University of New South Wales, School of Architecture, Sydney

Rogers, Dorothy, 1973. *A History of Kew*, Kilmore, Victoria: Lowden Publishing

Ruskin, John, 1859. *The Two Paths, Being Lectures on Art and its Application to Decoration and Manufacture, Delivered in 1858–9*, London: Smith, Elder & Co.

——, 1894. *Selections from the Writings of John Ruskin 1860–1888*, London: George Allen

Rutledge, Martha, 1986. 'John Lamb Lyon', entry in *Australian Dictionary of Biography*, Melbourne: Melbourne University Press

Ryder, Albert Pinkham, Obituary, 1917. *American Art News* 15: 25 (31 March), 4

S[eddon], J[ohn] Pollard], 1871. 'Stained Glass at the International Exhibition', *Building News*, 26 May, 414

Saint, Andrew, 2010. *Richard Norman Shaw*, New Haven and London: Yale University Press, 1st edn 1976

Saint-Gaudens, Homer, ed., 1913. *The Reminiscences of Augustus Saint-Gaudens*, 2 vols, London: Andrew Melrose

Sands' Sydney & New South Wales Directory, 1875. Sydney: John Sands

Sands' Sydney & New South Wales Directory, 1891. Sydney: John Sands

Sands & McDougall Melbourne Directory, 1889. Melbourne: John Sands

Sewter, A. Charles, 1974. *The Stained Glass of William Morris and his Circle*, vol. 1, New Haven and London: Yale University Press

——, 1975. *The Stained Glass of William Morris and his Circle*, vol. 2, New Haven and London: Yale University Press

Sheldon, George William, 1883–4. *Artistic Houses: Being a Series of Interior Views of a Number of the Most Beautiful and Celebrated Homes in the United States, with a Description of the Art Treasures Contained Therein*, 2 vols. New York: D. Appleton & Co.

——, 1886–7. *Artistic Country-Seats: Types of Recent American Villa and Cottage Architecture with Instances of Country Club-Houses*, 2 vols. New York: D. Appleton & Co.

Sheon, Aaron, 1979. *Monticelli: His Contemporaries, his Influence*, exh. cat., Pittsburgh: Museum of Art, Carnegie Institute

Sherman, Frederic Fairchild, 1920. *Albert Pinkham Ryder*. New York: Privately Printed

Sherry, Beverly, 1991. *Australia's Historic Stained Glass*, Sydney: Murray Child, 1991

——, 1987. 'Treasures in Stained Glass at the University of Sydney', *Heritage Australia* 6: 4, 2–5

Smith, James, ed., 1904. *Cyclopedia of Victoria*, Melbourne: Cyclopedia Company

Smith, John Moyr, 1887. *Ornamental Interiors: Ancient and Modern*, London: Crosby, Lockwood & Co.

Society of Artists Spring Exhibition, 1897. Exh. cat., Sydney: W. H. Maclardy

'Some of the Union League Decorations', 1881–2. *The Century Illustrated Monthly Magazine* 23, n.s., no. 1, 745–52

Soros, Susan Weber, 1999a. *The Secular Furniture of E. W. Godwin*, New Haven and London: Yale University Press

——, ed., 1999b. *E. W. Godwin: Aesthetic Movement Architect and Designer*, New Haven and London: Yale University Press

Stamp, Gavin, 2002. *An Architect of Promise: George Gilbert Scott Junior (1839–1897) and the Late Gothic Revival*, Donington: Shaun Tyas

——, and Sam McKinstry, eds, 1994. *'Greek' Thomson*, Edinburgh: Edinburgh University Press

Stapleton, Annamarie, 2002. *John Moyr Smith 1839–1912: A Victorian Designer*, Ilminster: Richard Dennis

——, 1996. 'John Moyr Smith 1839–1912', *The Journal of the Decorative Arts Society* 20: 18–28

Stebbins, Theodore, Jr., Kimberly Orcutt and Virginia Anderson, eds, 2008. *American Paintings at Harvard*, vol. 2, New Haven and London: Yale University Press

Sterling, Charles, and Margaretta M. Salinger, 1966. *French Paintings: A Catalogue of the Collection of the Metropolitan Museum*, vol. 2, Greenwich, Conn: New York Graphic Society

Stott, Annette, 1998. *Holland Mania: The Unknown Dutch Period in American Art and Culture*, New York: Overlook Press

Sullivan, Louis H., 1896. 'The Tall Office Building artistically considered', *Lippincott's Magazine*, 57, 403–9

Sydney International Exhibition, 1879, 1879. *Official Catalogue of the British Section*, London: Johnson & Sons

Sydney International Exhibition, 1879, 1880. *Official Catalogue of the New South Wales Court* Sydney: Thomas Richards, Government Printer

Taintor's Route and City Guides, 1877. *The City of New York: A Complete Guide*, New York: Taintor Brothers

Third Annual Exhibition of the Art Society of New South Wales, 1883. Sydney: John Sands

Thompson, James, and Barbara Wright, 1996. *Eugène Fromentin, 1820–1876: Visions d'Algérie et d'Egypte*, Courbevoie: ACR Editions

Toy, Ann, and Robert Griffin, 2011. *Government House*, Sydney: Historic Houses Trust of New South Wales

Van Heteren, Marjan, ed., 2003. *Jacob Maris (1837–1899): ik denk in mijn materie*, exh. cat., Oss: Jan Cunen Museum; Haarlem: Teylers Museum

——, 2006. *Willem Roelofs 1822–1897: De adem der natuur*, exh. cat., Oss: Jan Cunen Museum; Rotterdam: Kunsthal

Veblen, Thorstein, 1912. *The Theory of the Leisure Class*, New York: Macmillan Company

Veldink, Suzanne, 2009–10. '"Be-Marised or Bemused!": R. T. Hamilton Bruce and the International Exhibition of 1886', *Journal of the Scottish Society for Art History* 14: 51–8

——, 2015. 'De Glasgow Boys en het voorbeeld van de Haagse School', in Willemijn Lindenhovius, ed., *The Glasgow Boys: Schots Impressionisme*, exh. cat., Assen: Drents Museum, 172–9

Victorian Intercolonial Exhibition 1875, Preparatory to the Philadelphia Centennial Exhibition of 1876, 1875. *Official Record Containing Introduction, Catalogues, Official Awards*, Melbourne: McCarron, Bird & Co.

Vince, Millicent, 1925. 'Agnes Garrett: Pioneer of Women House Decorators', *The Woman's Leader*, 11 September, 259–60

Wainwright, Clive, 1989. *The Romantic Interior: The British Collector at Home, 1750–1850*, New Haven and London: Yale University Press

Waters, William, and Alastair Carew-Cox, 2017. *Damozels & Deities: Pre-Raphaelite Stained Glass, 1870–1898*, Abbots Morton: Seraphim Press

Watson, Andrew M., 2010. *James Duncan: An Enlightened Victorian*, Edinburgh: Royal Botanic Garden

Weinberg, Helene Barbara, 1974. 'John La Farge and the Decoration of Trinity Church, Boston', *Journal of the Society of Architectural Historians* 33: 4 (December), 323–53

Wells, Andrew, 1892a. 'Decoration', *Australasian Builder & Contractors' News*, 7 May, 331–5

——, 1892b. 'Growth of Ornament Art', *Building & Engineering Journal*, 13 August, 66–8

——, 1893. 'The Treatment of Stained Glass in Decoration', *Australasian Builder & Contractors' News*, 11 November, 237–9

——, 1902. 'The Late Daniel Cottier', *The Journal of Decorative Art and British Decorator* 12 (May), 145

Williams, Ichabod T., Obituary, 1899. 'Ichabod T. Williams', *New York Times*, 3 March

——, Sale, 1915 (1). *Notable Collection of Valuable Paintings Formed by the Late Ichabod T. Williams, Esq.*, New York: American Art Galleries and American Art Association, 3 and 4 February

——, Sale, 1915 (2). *Catalogue of the Artistic Property Belonging to the Estate of the Late Ichabod T. Williams Esq.*, New York: American Art Galleries and American Art Association, 25–7 February

Wolf, Albert, 1883. *Exposition de peinture: cent chefs-d'oeuvre des collections parisiennes*, Paris: Pillet & Dumoulin

Worsdall, Francis, 1966. 'A Victorian Architect: William Leiper RSA 1839–1916', *Scottish Field* (June), 30–1

Wright's Australian and American Commercial Directory and Gazetteer, 1881–2. New York: George Wright

Yarnall, James L., 1990. *John La Farge: Watercolors and Drawings*, exh. cat., Yonkers: Hudson River Museum of Westchester

Zielinski, Paul, 2006. *The Church that moved: A History of the Parish of Our Lady and St Cuthbert, Prudhoe, 1870–2005*, [England]: Paul J. Zielinski

Zimmermann, H. Russell, 1987. *Magnificent Milwaukee: Architectural Treasures 1850–1920*. Milwaukee: Milwaukee Public Museum

Zukowski, Karen, 2006. *Creating the Artful Home: The Aesthetic Movement*, Layton, Ut: Gibbs Smith

PHOTOGRAPH CREDITS

Colin McLean: image on p. i, 2, 6, 7, 13, 14, 21, 29, 36, 39, 48, 194; Courtesy of Annan Museum: image on p. ii; © CSG CIC Glasgow Museums and Libraries Collections: 1, 5, 8, 27, 64, 74, 75, 77, 78, 121; © Scottish Stained Glass Trust and Symposium: 3; © The Stained Glass Museum: 4; © Crown Copyright: HES: 9, 11, 12, 17, 18; © Iain Graham / Bridgeman Images: 10; Alastair Carew-Cox: 15, 16, 22, 26, 28, 30, 32; Courtesy of Sotheby's Picture Library: 23; Courtesy of Aberdeen City Libraries: 24; Courtesy the Fine Art Society, Edinburgh: 34; © Historic Environment Scotland: 35, 40, 41, 42, 43, endpapers; By kind permission of the Royal Highland and Agricultural Society of Scotland: 36; © Aberdeen City Council (Art Gallery & Museums Collections): 37, 38, 56, 58, 60, 63; By kind permission of the University of Edinburgh: 39; Historic England Archive: 44; Woolley & Wallis Auctioneers: 45; © Courtesy of Christie's Images 2001: 49; © Victoria and Albert Museum, London: 50; Courtesy of Sotheby's, Inc. © 2006: 51; Lyon & Turnbull Auctioneers: 52; © National Museums Scotland: 53; H. Blairman & Sons Ltd / Prudence Cummings: 54, 55; Andrew Watson: 59; Mesdag Collection, The Hague: 61, 68, 69; Rijksmuseum, Amsterdam: 62, 72, 73; Columbus Museum of Art, Ohio: 65; © The National Gallery, London: 66; Kimbell Art Museum, Fort Worth, Texas: 67; Courtesy of Historic New England: 70; Culture Perth & Kinross: 71; Ingalls Library, Cleveland Museum of Art: 79; Steven Day (American Academy of Art and Letters, NY, NY): 80; © Manx National Heritage: 81; Tom Miller: 82, 83; Petra Chu: 84, 85, 90, 130a and b; Brooklyn Museum: 86, 195; Image courtesy of Skinner, Inc.: 87; Frick Art and Historical Center, Pittsburgh: 89, 95a and b, 103; Smithsonian American Art Museum, Washington, DC: 91, 126; Metropolitan Museum of Art, New York: 92, 100, 101, 120, 129, 197; Joseph Fanvu: 94; Art and Architecture Collection, New York Public Library: 96, 125; Hudson River Museum: 97; Image Courtesy of Freeman's: 98; Boston Museum of Fine Arts: 102; Trinity Church in the City of Boston: 105; Stephen Sylvester and Yosi A. R.-Pozeilov, Digital Imaging and Photography Group Harvard College Libraries: 107, 108; Aurelia S. Watson, Salt Covenant Baptist Church: 109; © Tate: 110; Courtesy of Richard Krapf: 111; Wikimedia Commons: 112, 113; Ronald Bradford, for Church of the Incarnation: 114; Chazen Museum of Art, University of Wisconsin, Madison: 115; Courtesy of Sotheby's, Inc.: 116; Musée d'Orsay, Paris: 117; Digital Image, Whitney Museum of American Art, licensed by Scala / Art Resource, New York: 118; National Gallery of Canada: 122; Musée des Beaux-Arts, Montreal: 123; Centraal Museum, Utrecht: 124; Manuscripts and Archives Division, New York Public Library: 127; New Britain Museum of American Art: 128; Caroline Simpson Library and Research Collection, Sydney Living Museums: 132, 138, 139, 165, 180; Courtesy of John Lyon, Perth: 133; Mitchell Library, State Library of New South Wales, Sydney: 134, 137, 141, 143a and b, 144, 160, 166, 170, 179, 189, 192; Susan G. Hunt: 135a and b; Noel Mclaughlin: 136, 149, 150, 151, 152, 161a, 162, 163; Courtesy of Government House, Sydney: 140; National Library of Australia, Canberra: 142; Courtesy of Glenleigh Estate, Penrith: 145, 146, 147; Christopher Shain: 148; Courtesy of All Saints Anglican Cathedral, Bathurst: 153, 154, 167; St Thomas' Anglican Church, North Sydney: 155, 156; Courtesy of the Great Synagogue, Sydney: 157, 158, 159; Beverley Sherry: 161b; Courtesy of Kirkbride complex, Callan Park, Sydney: 164; Collection of Andrew Montana: 168, 172; Mandy Crook, Museum of Applied Arts and Sciences, Sydney: 169; Courtesy of Australian and New Zealand Banking Group Limited, Melbourne: 173, 174, 175; Courtesy of Lowy Institute, Sydney: 176; Courtesy of the Anglican Parish of Hunter's Hill: 177; St John's Anglican Church, Ashfield: 178; St Stephen's Uniting Church, Sydney (formerly St Stephen's Presbyterian Church): 181; Courtesy of the University of New England, Armidale: 182, 183, 184a and b, 185, 186, 187; Ross Schultz, Courtesy of the Council of the King's School, Parramatta: 188a and b, 190; Courtesy of the Ian Potter Museum of Art, University of Melbourne Art Collection: 191a and b; Sydney Hospital: 193a and b; © Mark Fiennes Archive / Bridgeman Images: 196; Hin Lim: 171, 198

INDEX

Page numbers in *italics* indicate illustrations and their captions